ONLINE RESOURCES

IMPORTANT:

HERE IS YOUR REGISTRATION CODE TO ACCESS YOUR PREMIUM McGRAW-HILL ONLINE RESOURCES.

For key premium online resources you need THIS CODE to gain access. Once the code is entered, you will be able to use the Web resources for the length of your course.

If your course is using **WebCT** or **Blackboard**, you'll be able to use this code to access the McGraw-Hill content within your instructor's online course.

Access is provided if you have purchased a new book. If the registration code is missing from this book, the registration screen on our Website, and within your WebCT or Blackboard course, will tell you how to obtain your new code.

Registering for McGraw-Hill Online Resources

To gain access to your McGraw-Hill web resources simply follow the steps below:

1. USE YOUR WEB BROWSER TO GO TO: **http://www.mhhe.com/gregory7**
2. CLICK ON **FIRST TIME USER**.
3. ENTER THE REGISTRATION CODE* PRINTED ON THE TEAR-OFF BOOKMARK ON THE RIGHT.
4. AFTER YOU HAVE ENTERED YOUR REGISTRATION CODE, CLICK **REGISTER**.
5. FOLLOW THE INSTRUCTIONS TO SET-UP YOUR PERSONAL UserID AND PASSWORD.
6. WRITE YOUR UserID AND PASSWORD DOWN FOR FUTURE REFERENCE. KEEP IT IN A SAFE PLACE.

TO GAIN ACCESS to the McGraw-Hill content in your instructor's **WebCT** or **Blackboard** course simply log in to the course with the UserID and Password provided by your instructor. Enter the registration code exactly as it appears in the box to the right when prompted by the system. You will only need to use the code the first time you click on McGraw-Hill content.

Thank you, and welcome to your McGraw-Hill online resources!

Mc Graw Hill Higher Education

* YOUR REGISTRATION CODE CAN BE USED ONLY ONCE TO ESTABLISH ACCESS. IT IS NOT TRANSFERABLE.

0-07-297413-3 T/A GREGORY: PUBLIC SPEAKING FOR COLLEGE AND CAREER, 7E

REGISTRATION CODE

ADUI-ZS6W-V2BZ-66W0-QGRM

Mc Graw Hill Higher Education

Public Speaking for College and Career

Hamilton Gregory
Asheville-Buncombe Technical Community College

7th Edition

Boston Burr Ridge, IL Dubuque, IA Madison, WI New York San Francisco St. Louis
Bangkok Bogotá Caracas Kuala Lumpur Lisbon London Madrid Mexico City
Milan Montreal New Delhi Santiago Seoul Singapore Sydney Taipei Toronto

The McGraw-Hill Companies

Higher Education

PUBLIC SPEAKING FOR COLLEGE AND CAREER
Published by McGraw-Hill, a business unit of The McGraw-Hill Companies, Inc., 1221 Avenue of the Americas, New York, NY, 10020.

This book is printed on acid-free paper.

1 2 3 4 5 6 7 8 9 0 DOW/DOW 0 9 8 7 6 5 4

ISBN 0-07-286285-8 (student edition)
ISBN 0-07-295859-6 (annotated instructor's edition)

Publisher: *Phillip A. Butcher*
Senior sponsoring editor: *Nanette Giles*
Director of development and media technology: *Rhona Robbin*
Senior marketing manager: *Leslie Oberhuber*
Producer, Media technology: *Jessica Bodie Richards*
Project manager: *Diane M. Folliard*
Production supervisor: *Janean A. Utley*
Design manager: *Laurie J. Entringer*
Supplement producer: *Kate Boylan*
Photo research coordinator: *Alexandra Ambrose*
Art editor: *Jennifer DeVere*
Photo researcher: *PoYee Oster*
Cover design: *Laurie J. Entringer*
Interior design: *Kiera Pohl*
Typeface: *10/12 New Baskerville*
Compositor: *GTS-Los Angeles, CA Campus*
Printer: *R. R. Donnelley/Willard*
Cover Credits: *All cover photos are © AP/Wide World Photos except the bottom left, © Getty Images.*

Library of Congress Cataloging-in-Publication Data

Gregory, Hamilton.
Public speaking for college and career / Hamilton Gregory.-- 7th ed.
p. cm.
Includes index.
ISBN 0-07-286285-8 (softcover : alk. paper)-- ISBN 0-07-295859-6 (annotated instructor's ed. softcover: alk. paper)
1. Public speaking. I. Title.
PN4121.G716 2005
808.5′1-- dc22 2003064870

www.mhhe.com

To my mother, *Rachel Smith Gregory*

Brief Contents

Contents

Part 3

Preparing Content

Part 4

Organizing the Speech

Part 5

Presenting the Speech

Part 6

Types of Public Speaking

Preface

"The first purpose of education," the American essayist Norman Cousins once said, "is to enable a person to speak clearly and confidently." [1]

The primary goal of this book is to show students how to achieve clarity and confidence during the speeches they must give in college classes, in career settings, and in their communities.

To reach this goal, I cover the basic principles of speech communication, drawn from contemporary research and from the accumulated wisdom of over 2,000 years of rhetorical theory. At the same time, I try to show students the real-life applicability of those principles by providing many examples and models from both student and professional speeches.

Key Elements

Like previous revisions, this new edition emphasizes the skills that are crucial for success in public speaking.

Focusing on Audience

Audience-centered communication is emphasized throughout the book: how to analyze listeners; how to be sensitive to their needs and interests; and how to talk *to* and *with* them, not *at* them. Students are encouraged to communicate ideas to real people, rather than merely stand up and go through the motions of "giving a speech."

Planning and Organizing

A rule of thumb in American seminaries is that ministers should spend an hour of preparation for each minute of actual delivery. Since this ratio is a good one for any speaker, I devote 11 chapters to showing students how to go through the preliminary stages of speechmaking systematically—analyzing the audience, selecting a topic and specific purpose, devising a central idea, finding verbal and visual support material, organizing the material into a coherent outline, and practicing effectively.

Building Confidence

A major concern for most beginning speakers is how they can develop and project confidence in themselves and in their ideas. Chapter 2 ("Controlling Nervousness") provides a reassuring discussion on nervousness and shows students how to turn their speech anxiety into an asset by using it as constructive energy.

Speaking in Real-World Situations

Examples, stories, and photos throughout the book depict real people in real communication settings. "Tips for Your Career" appear in all chapters to give students useful advice for their professional development. "Special Techniques" sections provide detailed explanations on such topics as "How to Use Humor."

Public Speaking PowerWeb, a new resource offered on this book's Online Learning Center website, features speeches given in business, professional, and political settings. Videos of three of these speeches can be viewed on the *SpeechMate CD-ROM.* In the text, "Using PowerWeb" exercises at the end of each chapter give students an opportunity to investigate speeches and articles in *PowerWeb.*

Developing Ethical Values

Ethical behavior and personal values are important considerations for all communicators. Rather than restrict the discussion of ethics to an isolated chapter, I discuss ethical issues throughout the book at relevant points. There are 22 "Ethical Issues" sections throughout the seventh edition. Icons in the text margins call attention to this material.

Incorporating Technology

Students receive updated information on using multimedia (for example, how to use visual presenters such as ELMO) and the Internet (for example, how to use search engines effectively). In view of the growing use of PowerPoint by student and professional speakers, a new section, "A Brief Guide to Using PowerPoint," has been added to Chapter 9 ("Visual Aids"), and a revised and expanded PowerPoint tutorial appears on the *SpeechMate* CD. Several speeches in the book and on the CD are accompanied by PowerPoint slides. At the same time, students are warned in Chapter 9 about the pitfalls of using PowerPoint ineffectively.

Conducting and Evaluating Research

Some librarians and instructors report that many students want to use the Internet—and nothing else—for research, but are unaware of how to use the Internet skillfully. To address this issue, "Building Internet Skills" exercises are located at the end of every chapter. Chapter 6 ("Finding Information") shows students how to use the Internet effectively, but also describes the limitations of the Internet and encourages students to call upon traditional library resources, too.

Building Critical-Thinking Skills

In recent surveys, many instructors and employers have lamented that students and employees often fail to apply critical-thinking skills when evaluating information, especially information from the Internet. To help students sharpen these skills, Chapter 7 ("Using Information Wisely and Ethically") provides guidelines on how to separate credible from unreliable information and how to develop a healthy skepticism. In addition, "Building Critical-Thinking Skills" exercises appear at the end of each chapter. Throughout the book, when each stage of preparation and delivery is discussed, students are encouraged to engage in critical analysis of their topic, audience, and material. Also, speech videos on the *SpeechMate* CD are accompanied by critical-thinking questions.

Exploring Diversity and Teamwork

Some employers are expressing a distinct interest in college graduates who can exhibit skillfulness in two related areas: (1) communicating with people from diverse backgrounds and (2) participating in teams. In response to these emerging opportunities, this book emphasizes understanding and valuing diversity. In addition to examples, tips, and photos throughout the book, there are "Building Teamwork Skills" exercises at the end of each chapter. Chapter 1 confronts the problem of stereotyping and scapegoating. Chapter 4 has a detailed discussion of listeners from other countries and various ethnic groups, as well as tips regarding disabilities, gender, age, educational background, occupations, religious affiliation, and economic and social status. Chapter 19 provides guidelines on how individuals can work effectively in teams.

Using Visual Imagery

Believing that visual imagery can enhance learning, I have provided over 130 graphics, including photos, drawings, tables, and sample presentation aids. Most of these visuals are new to this edition.

Highlights of the Seventh Edition

This edition offers a rich variety of examples, stories, photos, and learning aids, many of which are new or revised. Here are some of the highlights:

Enhanced SpeechMate CD-ROM

An integral part of this text is *SpeechMate 3.0,* a two-disk CD set that is packaged free with every new copy of the book. The enthusiastic reaction of instructors and students who used *SpeechMate* with the previous edition of this text has been gratifying. Thanks to feedback from many of those students and instructors, *SpeechMate* has been revised and improved. Accompanying it is a fully illustrated booklet that provides a guide to using *SpeechMate* and this book's Online Learning Center Website (www.mhhe.com/gregory7). Here are descriptions of the components of *SpeechMate*:

Speech Videos. Disk One of the *SpeechMate* CD-ROM provides a total of 11 full-length speeches and 18 speech excerpts. Except for one popular speech from the previous CD-ROM ("Indian Weddings"), all of the videos are new. They were filmed by professional videographers to ensure high-quality video, editing, and sound. To show students how a mediocre speech contrasts with a model speech, two speeches that need improvement—one informative, the other persuasive—are shown, along with their improved versions. Most of the speeches on the CD are accompanied by audio introductions, critical-thinking questions, outlines, and on-screen identification of the various elements of a speech (for example, transitions). In the book itself, icons in the text margin prompt readers to view relevant video clips.

Disk Two of the *SpeechMate* CD-ROM contains videos of three full speeches that show business and professional speakers in career settings. The speakers are Dr. Richard F. Corlin, president of the American Medical Association, who gives a commemorative speech that is a blend of informative, persuasive, and inspirational speaking; Anne M. Mulcahy, chairman and chief executive officer of Xerox Corporation, whose speech is primarily informative, with some elements of persuasive and inspirational speaking; and Robert Ingram, chief operating officer, and president of Pharmaceutical Operations, GlaxcoSmithKline, whose speech is persuasive, aimed at convincing listeners that pharmaceutical price increases are justified because of the need for research and development of life-saving drugs. The Mulcahy speech shows an entire program, inluding a master of ceremonies' welcome, the pledge of allegiance and an invocation, a speech of introduction, and a question-and-answer period. Each speech is divided into segments, with accompanying commentary. The text of these speeches can be accessed through *PowerWeb* (visit www.mhhe.com/gregory7, click on STUDENT EDITION and then POWERWEB: CONTENTS).

Outlining Aids. The CD offers students two options for organizing their material in an outline. *Outline Tutor* is an interactive program that shows the various parts of an outline and makes it easy for users to insert content into the appropriate sections of the outline. Alternatively, an outline template in Microsoft Word format may appeal to students who prefer to do their work in Word.

To improve outlining abilities, *SpeechMate* also includes Outline Exercises, which involve unscrambling the parts of an outline by "dragging and dropping" those elements into the proper sequence with a mouse.

Practice Tests. To prepare for classroom tests, students can take a practice test for each chapter, with 15 multiple-choice and 15 true-false questions. When students choose an incorrect answer, they are given an immediate explanation of their mistake. Then they are invited to try again.

Checklist for Preparing and Delivering a Speech. This practical list of steps not only helps speakers manage the preparation of their classroom speeches but also provides a valuable guide for speeches they may be asked to give in their careers and their communities.

Topic Helper. For students who have trouble coming up with a topic for a speech, *Topic Helper* lists hundreds of sample topics for their consideration.

Speech Critique. *Speech Critique* is a software program that enables both students and instructors to evaluate speeches, either on a computer or on a printed evaluation sheet. One's input is quantitative, but the result is a carefully constructed qualitative report, with full-sentence observations and recommendations. One valuable feature permits evaluators to edit the "comments" templates to suit individual preferences.

PowerPoint Tutor. Basic steps in creating and displaying a PowerPoint presentation are explained in this tutorial, which has been expanded for this edition.

Bibliography Aids. A new feature, *BiblioMaker,* is a software program that automatically formats bibliography entries, after students enter key information, according to two of the most popular style guides: Modern Language Association (MLA) and American Psychological Association (APA).

Another aid is *Bibliography Formats,* which gives examples of how to cite a wide variety of types of source material from MLA and APA.

Key Terms. Two features help students study and prepare for tests vis à vis the key terms in the book: an alphabetical *Glossary* of all terms and their definitions and *Flashcards,* a software application that manages the text glossary by chapter and allows the user to create customizable "decks" of key terms.

Chapter-Opening Features

Every chapter opens with a four-part pedagogical plan. The first thing a reader will see is a photo and explanatory caption that relate directly to the chapter. Opposite the photo is a page that presents an outline and the objectives for the chapter. When the page is turned, the reader will see an introductory vignette, illustrated by a photo or artwork. These features are designed to heighten interest in the chapter's contents, to help the reader map out the chapter's contents, and to dramatize how actual speakers implement key chapter principles in the real world.

Sample Speeches

Sample speeches, most of them new to this edition, provide models of how to effectively choose, organize, and develop materials. Many of these speeches are accompanied by outlines and commentary to help students focus on the most important elements.

Here are the key speeches:

- Chapter 1 ("Introduction to Public Speaking"): At the suggestion of reviewers, two new speeches have been added to the first chapter. They are "Here Comes the Clown," a self-introduction speech, and "Misty Morning," a speech in which a student introduces a classmate.
- Chapter 8 ("Supporting Your Ideas"): "Workplace Bullies" is a persuasive speech (problem–solution pattern) that demonstrates how to use support materials such as examples and statistics. It includes a commentary.
- Chapter 10 ("The Body of the Speech"): A speech entitled "Affinity Fraud" is divided and shown in two separate chapters. In Chapter 10, the body of the speech is given, with a commentary, to show the use of main points and supporting points.
- Chapter 11 ("Introductions and Conclusions"): This chapter includes the remainder of "Affinity Fraud," with a commentary, so that students can see the introduction and conclusion.

- Chapter 12 ("Outlining the Speech"): A new persuasive speech, "The Power of Light," uses the statement-of-reasons pattern. An outline, accompanied by a commentary, precedes a transcript of the speech as it was delivered. Two PowerPoint slides and a sample of the speaker's notes are also shown.
- Chapter 15 ("Speaking to Inform"): "How to Identify Poison Ivy" is a process speech, accompanied by a PowerPoint slide.
- Chapter 15 ("Speaking to Inform"): "Finding Your Dream Job" is a new informative speech with an outline (accompanied by commentary) and transcript. Four PowerPoint slides are shown.
- Chapter 16 ("Speaking to Persuade"): A new persuasive speech—"E-911 Will Save Lives"— uses the motivated sequence. The outline is presented with a commentary, followed by a transcript of the speech as delivered. The student's visual aid, a poster, is shown.
- Chapter 18 ("Special Types of Speeches"): Brief samples illustrate the entertaining speech, the speech of tribute, and other special-occasion speeches.
- The Appendix includes a speech of self-introduction, an informative speech, and a persuasive speech (using the motivated sequence).

Business Templates

In keeping with this book's focus on careers, a new resource offered on the Online Learning Center is a series of business document templates for creating cover letters, résumés, agendas, and memos.

Major Revisions

Innovations and refinements to the *SpeechMate* CD were presented in the preceding section of this preface. A large number of changes were also made in the text itself, with the most significant revisions described below:

- Throughout this seventh edition are many new examples, stories, and photos. The men and women who are spotlighted represent a broad range of speakers, including college students, firefighters, business executives, attorneys, physicians, and professors. Some of the speakers are famous; in Chapter 2, for example, actor Leonardo DiCaprio makes a surprising confession of his problems with extreme fear of public speaking.
- Of the sample speeches discussed above, six are completely new.
- New exercises at the end of each chapter direct students to assignments in the *PowerWeb* component of this book's Online Learning Center.
- Chapter 1 ("Introduction to Public Speaking") has a major change. The section in previous editions entitled "Self-Introduction Speech" has been expanded and given a new heading, "Speech Introducing Yourself or a Classmate." New sample speeches are included in this section –

one is a self-introduction speech, and the other is a speech in which a student introduces a classmate.

- Chapter 6 ("Finding Information") has been revised to update content related to the Internet (such as addresses of leading reference sources) and to reflect recent changes in the MLA style guidelines for bibliography formats. A new Tip for Your Career—"Take Time to Browse"—advises readers who search for information on the Internet to take time to use subject directories, rather than always using search engines, in order to find unexpected and useful material.
- Chapter 7 ("Using Information Wisely and Ethically") includes updates on new domain suffixes on the Internet (such as ".biz") and a new Tip for Your Career—"Avoid Vagueness When Citing Internet Sources."
- Chapter 9 ("Visual Aids") has been updated to include a new section, "A Brief Guide to Using PowerPoint." This complements a feature I have retained from the previous edition, which instructors throughout the United States said they were glad to have—a Tip for Your Career entitled "Beware the Perils of PowerPoint." This chapter also features a new section on how to effectively use visual presenters (such as ELMO).
- Chapter 11 ("Introductions and Conclusions") includes an important new caveat for students: In the introduction of a speech, avoid asking questions that can fizzle. The chapter also features a PowerPoint slide with an intriguing attention-getter that asks, "Who can best predict a breakup?" Is it the couple themselves? Or is it *his* friends? Or *her* friends? (See the caption for Figure 11.1 on page 255 for the answer.)
- Chapter 12 ("Outlining the Speech") includes an important new Tip for Your Career ("Decide How You Will Reveal Your Sources") that describes two options that speakers can use to relay their sources to audience members. The instructor, of course, can recommend one of the options, or a combination.
- Chapter 17 ("Persuasive Strategies") opens with a new mind-teaser designed to show students that a well-reasoned argument, by itself, is often insufficient to persuade a target audience. One must also craft an argument that deals with the listeners' motivations and preconceptions.

Resources for Instructors and Students

An extensive and integrated set of resources is available for extending the concepts and the pedagogical methods of the book.

Digital and Video Resources

SpeechMate. *SpeechMate* is a two-disk CD-ROM set that is described above.

Online Learning Center. The website for this book (www.mhhe.com/gregory7) contains an extensive variety of resources for instructors and students, including chapter quizzes, key terms, chapter overviews, learning objectives, PowerPoint slides, articles on relevant topics, and interactive exercises. In the text, icons directing students to relevant resources on the Online Learning Center appear in the margins at appropriate points.

From the Online Learning Center, students can access *Survey Tutor,* a software program that enables a speaker to prepare questionnaires to assess and analyze an audience before a speech is given. The surveys can be printed and distributed to audience members, or they can be sent via e-mail.

The Online Learning Center provides a gateway to *Public Speaking PowerWeb,* a password-protected website that is offered free with new copies of the text. It provides instructors and students with the following resources: recent speeches from *Vital Speeches of the Day;* news and journal articles on topics that are relevant to public speaking, such as speech anxiety, visual aids, and persuasion; articles on a variety of topics that students may use as source material for their speeches; and a newsworthy, annotated "speech of the week." To access PowerWeb, visit www.mhhe.com/gregory7, click on STUDENT EDITION and then POWERWEB: CONTENTS. A feature called *Weblinks* enables readers to get quick updates for Internet addresses referred to in the text and any other information that has changed since publication of the book. To access this service, visit the site, click on STUDENT EDITION, and then WEBLINKS.

A printed ancillary available in earlier editions, *Supplementary Readings and Worksheets,* is no longer being offered. However, its contents have been retained and expanded on this book's Online Learning Center, with the worksheets located in the Interactive Exercises section and the readings located in the Supplementary Readings section. The Interactive Exercises cover important tasks such as a developing the central idea, creating an outline, and using language effectively. The readings on the website include a transcript of Martin Luther King's famous "I Have a Dream" speech accompanied by a detailed commentary; brief handouts that crystallize what students need to know about job interviews, résumés, and letters of application; an article on speech phobia, which gives tips for self-therapy to those students whose fear goes far beyond the normal range discussed in Chapter 2 of the text; and articles that cover special subjects such as: "How to Prepare a Speech Without Feeling Overwhelmed," "Speaking in Front of a Camera," "Oral Interpretation of Literature," and "Public Speaking Tips for ESL Students."

The instructor's manual—minus the test bank—now appears on the Online Learning Center. A new feature in the manual is a Resource Integrator that describes textbook features, activities, and multimedia materials that are relevant to each chapter. This feature can help instructors to create syllabi and lecture outlines that incorporate the resources found on the *SpeechMate* CD-ROM and Online Learning Center. For a password to access the instructor's materials, instructors should contact their McGraw-Hill representative.

Instructor's Resource CD. The Instructor's Resource CD, or IRCD, includes the Instructor's Manual (described above), the Test Bank, PowerPoint slides comprised of chapter highlights and video clips, and *Building an Outline,* a PowerPoint-based tutorial that shows students how to organize their ideas in an outline. Two sample outlines are constructed step by step so that students can see the process applied to an informative speech and to a persuasive speech.

With this edition, the PowerPoint slides include video clips, as mentioned above, of speech excerpts from the *SpeechMate* CD, so that instructors can refer directly to these speeches during their lectures.

New to the Instructor's Resource CD is "Teaching Public Speaking Online with *Public Speaking for College and Career.*" This guide, written by Sam Zahran of Fayetteville Technical Community College, is designed to help instructors develop and implement online public speaking courses using the pedagogical resources found in the text, *SpeechMate* CD, and Online Learning Center.

The test bank is provided on the IRCD in two formats: as a Word document and as a Computerized Test Bank application with versions for Windows and MacIntosh. In addition, the IRCD contains Word files of four ready-to-reproduce tests for each chapter: Form A has true-false questions; Forms B and C have multiple-choice questions, and Form D contains short-answer questions.

Videotapes. McGraw-Hill offers a comprehensive Video Library for public speaking. For this specific edition of *Public Speaking for College and Career,* the Student Speeches Video in VHS format includes the same speeches featured on the *SpeechMate* CD-ROM.

PageOut. *PageOut* is designed for instructors just beginning to explore Web options for their courses. In less than an hour, even the novice computer user can create a unique course Website with a template provided by McGraw-Hill (no programming knowledge required). PageOut lets you offer your students instant access to your syllabus, lecture notes, and original material. And you can pull any of the McGraw-Hill content from the Gregory Online Learning Center into your Website. To find out more about PageOut, ask your McGraw-Hill representative for details, or fill out the form at www.mhhe.com/pageout. All online content for this text is compatible not only with PageOut but with WebCT, eCollege.com, and Blackboard.

Annotated Instructor's Edition

The annotated edition of this book has marginal notes that provide teaching ideas, quotations, examples, and suggestions for group activities and class discussions.

Acknowledgments

More than 140 instructors have reviewed this book in its successive editions. Their advice has not only shown me how to improve the book but also helped me improve my own classroom teaching. I am deeply grateful to the reviewers for their insights, encouragement, and willingness to help a colleague.

Though space does not permit a listing of all reviewers of previous editions, I would like to cite those who gave me helpful feedback for this edition. Their names are listed on page xxvi.

For contributing his excellent speech-evaluation software ("Speech Critique") that is a component of the *SpeechMate* CD-ROM, I am deeply indebted to Dick Stine of Johnson County Community College. Betty Dvorson of City College of San Francisco gave me valuable advice about providing sample speeches that show speakers citing their sources as they proceed through their presentation. A nationally known trailblazer in creating and teaching online courses, Sam Zahran of Fayetteville Technical Community College made a valuable contribution to this book's Instructor's Resource CD by writing a guide on how to teach public speaking online. For their encouragement and creative ideas, special thanks to Betty Farmer and Jim Manning, both of Western Carolina University; Tom W. Gregory, Trinity College in Washington, DC; Greg Cheek, St. Mary College in Kansas, and Jim McDiarmid, speech instructor on U.S. Navy ships under the PACE (Program of Afloat College Education) program.

For the third straight edition, I was fortunate to work with Rhona Robbin, a wise and perceptive editor, whose flexibility, patience, and light touch made our collaboration enjoyable. She cared about the book as much as I did—an attribute that writers love to find in an editor. Her enthusiastic support for the book was matched by Nanette Kauffman Giles, senior sponsoring editor for communication studies, who is a creative genius in planning pedagogical improvements and ancillaries, and by Jessica Bodie Richards, media producer, who tirelessly coordinated and helped develop the many components of the *SpeechMate* CD-ROM and Online Learning Center, proving that it is humanly possible to juggle 36 balls at the same time. With skill, care, and patience, project manager Diane Folliard guided the book through the daunting production stages. Despite joining the team late in the process, Leslie Oberhuber, senior marketing manager, quickly developed an excellent plan for publicizing the book.

I was fortunate to have the wholehearted backing of other key executives at McGraw-Hill: Phil Butcher, publisher, humanities and social sciences, and Steve Debow, president. The physical beauty of this book is due to the creative efforts of Laurie J. Entringer, design manager and cover illustrator, and Kiera Pohl, interior designer. I also wish to acknowledge the valuable assistance of other McGraw-Hill staff members and freelancers: Alexandra Ambrose, Jen DeVere, Kathleen Boylan, Janean Utley, Gerry Williams, Josh Hawkins, Maria Romano, Brian Pecko, PoYee Oster, Betsy Blumenthal, and Jan Nickels.

I am grateful to the following colleagues for ideas, inspiration, and support: Kenet Adamson, Jan Caldwell, Loretta Carlton, Jim Cavener, Rebecca Davis, Ren Decatur, Jill English, Lynne Gabai, Paul Good, Sandi Goodridge, Deborah L. Harmon, Tony Hodge, David Holcombe, Debra P. Holmes, Lisa Johnson, Alison Long, Deborah Lonon, Deb Maddox, Mary McClurkin, Shirley McLaughlin, Rolfe Olsen, Susan Paterson, Maretta Pinson, Judith Robinson, Lee Schleining, and Chris Tibbetts.

I am indebted to the hundreds of students in my public speaking classes over the years who have made teaching this course a pleasant and rewarding task. From them I have drawn most of the examples of classroom speeches.

And for their support and patience, special thanks to my wife Merrell and to our children, Jess, Jim, and June.

Hamilton Gregory

For updates and additional information, visit the book's Website (www.mhhe.com/gregory7).

Reviewers

Ann Baldinger, Holy Cross College
Charlene Handford Barlow, Louisiana State University–Shreveport
Carole Bennett, Oakland Community College
Doug Binsfeld, Southwest State University
Ferald J. Bryan, Northern Illinois University
Paula M. Cohen, North Central State College
Claire B. Gordon, Lincoln Land Community College
Richard Harrison, Kilgore College
Lisa Hischke-Bryant, Kingwood College
Beth Hoffmann, Lincoln Land Community College
Mary G. Jarzabek, Louisiana State University–Shreveport
Brenda Jolley, Stillman College
Mona Klinger, North Idaho College
Camille Langston, Northwest Vista College
Tracy McGrady, Ozarks Technical Community College
Amy Hull Ramos, Piedmont Technical College
Erin Rawson, Mesa Community College
Kristi Schaller, University of Hawaii at Manoa
Michael Tew, Eastern Michigan University
Christina S. Toy, Caldwell Community College and Technical Institute
Charles W. Weedin, Yakima Valley Community College

A Visual Preview of

Public Speaking *for* College & Career

SEVENTH EDITION

Public Speaking for College and Career

Public Speaking for College and Career offers a practical, accessible, and non-intimidating approach to public speaking. Combining a wealth of school-and work-oriented examples with patient step-by-step instruction, this new edition includes many fresh examples and sample speeches. Keeping current with rapidly changing technologies, the new edition also introduces "A Brief Guide to Using PowerPoint" and current information on Internet research.

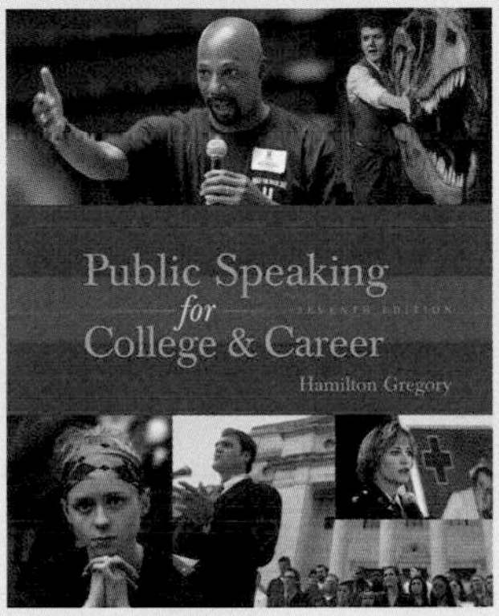

SpeechMate CD-ROM

SpeechMate CD-ROM 3.0 (now a two-disk set) is fully integrated with the text. CD icons in the text margins guide students to the CD resources (e.g. speech videos, interactive quizzes, and outlining software), which extend the pedagogical methods of the text to enhance comprehension and to help build confidence in public speaking for all types of learners.

The Gregory Online Learning Center

The Gregory Online Learning Center, also fully integrated with the text through margin icons, offers students and instructors an array of resources such as chapter quizzes, Web links, interactive exercises, and PowerPoint slides. The Online Learning Center also provides a gateway to *Public Speaking PowerWeb*, a unique site that offers the transcripts of recent speeches from *Vital Speeches of the Day*, news and journal articles on topics that are relevant to public speaking, such as speech anxiety, visual aids and persuasion, articles on topics that students may use as source material for their speeches, and a newsworthy, annotated "speech of the week."

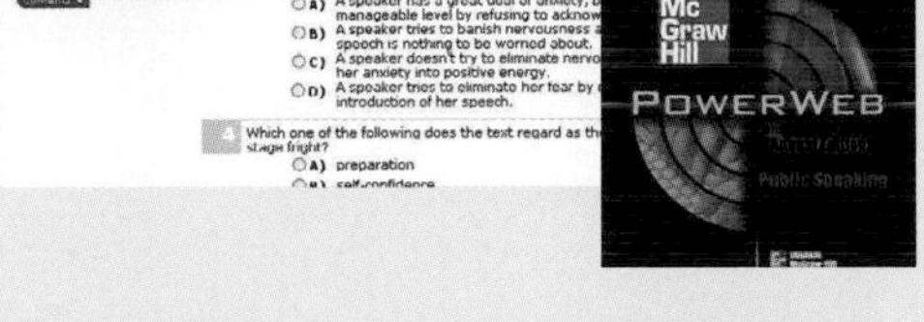

This visual preview provides a guide to the special features of the text, CD, and Website.

SpeechMate CD-ROM Makes Public Speaking Accessible to a Variety of Student Learning Styles

SpeechMate CD-ROM

SpeechMate 3.0 (a two-disk set) is a robust, yet easy-to-use CD-ROM that provides a variety of resources to help all types of learners prepare, organize, and deliver speeches. It also offers a range of engaging study tools for exam preparation. Icons in the margins of the text prompt students to use corresponding features on *SpeechMate*.

Video Clips & Full Speeches

Eighteen video excerpts and fourteen full speeches by student and professional speakers illustrate the various presentation techniques and elements of a speech. Through these examples, students will experience speechmaking in action, cultivate an understanding of different kinds of speeches, and ultimately establish the confidence to speak. All but one of the videos are new, and we now also include for pedagogical comparison two sets of "model" and "needs improvement" speeches: Speeches 1 and 2, "Animal Helpers" and Speeches 3 and 4, "Bicycle Helmets."

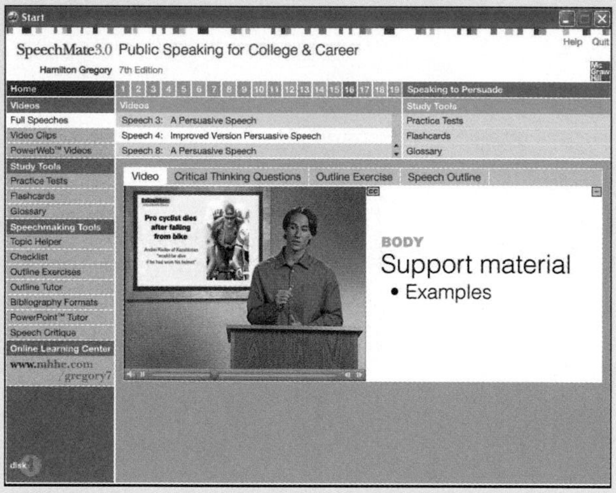

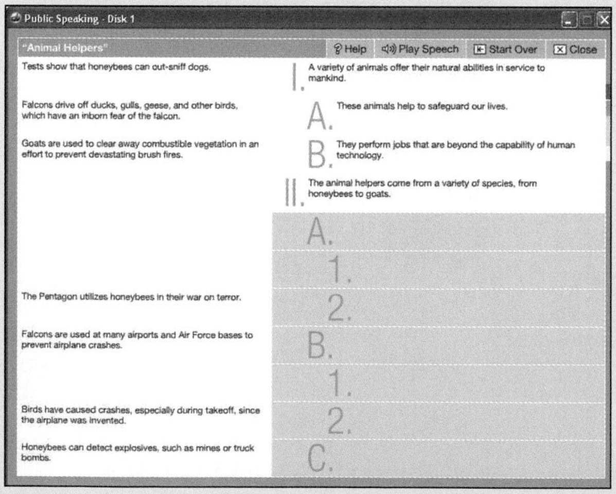

New Outline Exercises

By dragging and dropping parts of a scrambled outline into a properly sequenced outline, students can practice outlining with actual content, and become skilled at outlining five types of speeches: informative, persuasive, demonstration, speech of tribute, and self-introduction. The exercises are based on nine different speech outlines.

For Technical Support, Call Toll-Free 1-800-331-5094

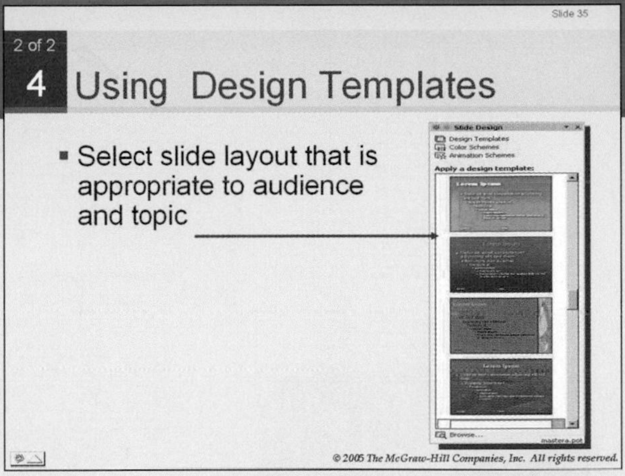

PowerPoint Tutor

Basic steps in creating and using PowerPoint in a presentation are explained in this vivid tutorial. With PowerPoint Tutor, users can now learn how to use two different methods for creating templates, how to insert and scale graphics, and how to create "builds."

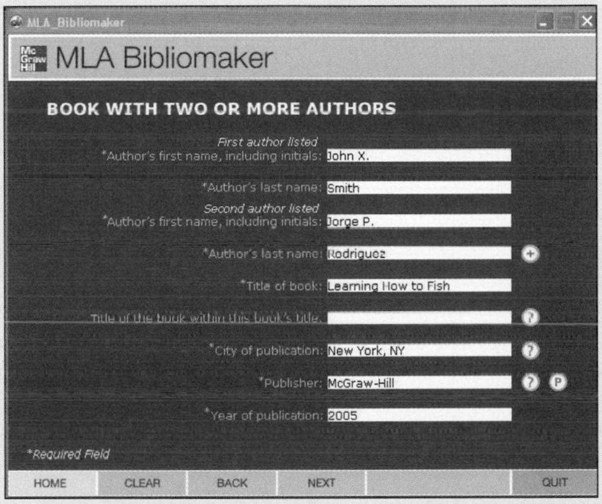

New BiblioMaker

After receiving key bibliographic information from the user, BiblioMaker automatically formats the entry according to either APA or MLA style guidelines.

Also on *SpeechMate*

Study Tools
- 19 Interactive Practice Tests with 30 questions each
- 191 Glossary Flashcards
- Glossary

Link to Online Learning Center
- www.mhhe.com/gregory7

Speechmaking Tools
- Outline Tutor
- Topic Helper
- Speech Preparation Checklist
- Bibliography Formats with guidance for fifteen types of citations
- Speech Critique (with unique templates for informative, persuasive, and commemorative speeches)

Numerous School- and Work-Related Examples Connect Public Speaking to Everyday Practice

One of the greatest heartbreaks for firefighters occurs when they fail to rescue a child from a burning building because the child—frightened by smoke and noise—hides under a bed or in a closet and is later found dead.

Saddest of all, sometimes children catch a glimpse of the masked firefighter but hide because they think they have seen a monster.

To prevent such tragedies, firefighter Eric Velez gives talks to children in his community, explaining why they should never hide during a fire. He displays firefighters' equipment, including the oxygen mask, which he encourages his listeners to play with and put on. "If you see us," Velez tells them, "don't hide. We are not monsters. We have come to rescue you."

Velez gives his presentations in English and Spanish. (Growing up in San Francisco, he learned Spanish from his immigrant parents: His mother is from Nicaragua, his father from Puerto Rico.)

Velez—and other firefighters throughout North America who give similar presentations—will never know how many lives they save through their talks, but it is a fact that informative speaking saves lives. For example, several months after his public speaking class, Pete Gentry of Swannanoa, North Carolina, rescued his

Left: When small children mistake a firefighter for a Darth Vader monster, a terrible tragedy can occur.
Below: During informative presentations, firefighter Eric Velez encourages children to play with and try on "scary" oxygen masks.

348

brother, who was choking on food, by using the Heimlich maneuver, which he had learned by listening to an informative speech delivered by student speaker Julie Parris.

In addition to saving lives, informative speakers help people learn new skills, solve problems, and acquire fascinating facts about the exciting world in which they live.

Your goals in informative speaking are to convey knowledge, create understanding, and help listeners remember important points. Your task is to be a teacher—not an advocate. To give facts—not opinions.

In this chapter we will look at four types of informative speeches and then discuss guidelines to help you create informative speeches that are clear, interesting, and memorable.

Types of Informative Speeches

SpeechMate CD-ROM
For samples, view Speech 2, 5, 6, or 7 on Disk 1 of the CD.

Informative speeches can be categorized in many different ways, but in this chapter we will concentrate on four of the most popular types: definition, description, process, and expository.

Definition Speech

Do you know what *synesthesia* is? Most people don't, so let me give you a dictionary definition: "a condition in which one type of stimulation evokes the sensation of another."

Still not sure what I'm talking about? Here are some elaborations.[1]

- Neurologist Richard Cytowic says that two people out of every million experience a mingling of senses so that they may taste a shape, hear a color, or see a sound. "Music, for example, is not just a sound and a melody, but it's like a visual fireworks that they see in front of them . . . rather than in the mind's eye."
- A woman named Kristen tastes words, and often the spelling affects the flavor. "Lori," for example, tastes like a pencil eraser, while "Laurie" tastes lemony.
- Persons who experience synesthesia, says Cytowic, are not crazy, but as children they often fear that they are, and they hide their sensitivity. Carol Steen, a New York artist, recalls, "When I was about 7, I was walking back from elementary school with a classmate, and we must have been learning how to write. I said that the letter 'A' was a wonderful shade of pink, and she was quiet, and then she looked at me and said, 'You're weird.' And I didn't say another word until I was 20."

349

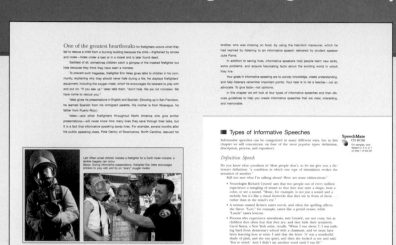

Chapter-Opening Vignettes

Each chapter opens with an intriguing example or story to dramatize key principles and show how speakers in the real world—in classrooms, communities and careers—actually use these principles.

Sample Speeches

Sample speeches, six of them new to this edition, provide models of how to effectively choose, organize, and develop speech content. Many of these speeches provide commentary to focus students on salient elements, techniques and strategies.

184 Part 3 Preparing Content

Commentary

Karen Miyamoto opens with a ***narrative*** *that is designed to capture the attention and interest of the audience.*

Workplace Bullies

Mark Montana, a 28-year-old chef at a catering service in Seattle, loved his job and made his supervisors happy—until a few years ago when a new boss made his life unbearable. The boss constantly belittled Montana in front of others, cursing him in a loud, angry voice; blaming him for any mistakes that he himself made; and threatening to ruin his reputation in the culinary field if he didn't "shape up." Montana says, "I began to feel bad about myself and I doubted my own competence. I developed severe headaches and had trouble sleeping." Finally, after a few months of this abuse, he quit.

Mark Montana was the victim of a workplace bully. I'd like to show you that bullying in the workplace is a serious problem, but we don't have to be passive victims. Let's begin by looking at the scope of the problem.

The speaker gives a ***definition*** *to make sure that the audience understands precisely what behavior she is talking about.*

Bullies are found throughout the workforce. "Workplace bullying" is defined as "deliberate, repeated, hurtful mistreatment of one person by another. It can be emotional or physical, but it's usually emotional." This definition is from Dr. Gary Namie, a California psychologist who heads the Campaign Against Workplace Bullying.

This section of the speech gives a variety of ***statistics*** *to add interest and give a clear picture of the extent of the problem.*

In Dr. Namie's research, most bullies are bosses—no surprise there, but I was surprised by some of his other findings: In 30 percent of the cases, the bullies were women. When the bully was a male, the victims were males in 72 percent of the cases. When the bully was a female, the victims were females in 68 percent of the cases. Dr. Harvey Hornstein, a psychologist at Columbia University, has completed an eight-year study that estimates that one in five U.S. workers will be the victim of workplace bullies during their careers.

Here and elsewhere in the speech, the speaker uses ***testimony*** *from experts.*

Dr. Harry Levinson, a psychologist in Waltham, Massachusetts, has studied workplace bullies for 40 years and gives this picture of what they do: They overcontrol, micromanage, and display contempt for others, usually by repeated verbal abuse and sheer exploitation. They constantly put others down with snide remarks or harsh, repetitive, and unfair criticism. They don't just differ with you, they differ with you contemptuously; they question your adequacy and your commitment. They humiliate you in front of others.

A ***vivid image*** *provides a description of what a bully in action looks like.*

Some specific ***examples*** *of health problems demonstrate the damage caused by bullies.*

Workplace bullies inflict harm on both employees and the company or agency. According to Dr. Hornstein, employees who are victimized by bullies suffer from anxiety, depression, heart problems, gastrointestinal disorders, headaches, skin rashes, insomnia, and sexual dysfunction. As employees suffer, the company or agency suffers. Productivity declines, mistakes

Tips for your CAREER

Tip 2.1 Prepare for Memory Lapses

A psychologist tells of the time when he was speaking at a convention as the presiding officer. At one point he wanted to praise an associate, who was sitting next to him at the head table, for her hard work in planning the convention. "As I began my words of tribute," he said, "my mind suddenly went blank, and I couldn't remember her name! It was awful. This was a woman I had worked with for years. She was like a sister."

Fortunately, he said, everyone was wearing name tags, so he leaned over, saw her name, and used it in his remarks—without the audience suspecting his memory lapse.

Such lapses are common, especially during ceremonies, but don't be alarmed. There is a simple solution: Prepare a card with all basic information—names, dates, phone numbers—and keep the card with your other notes for easy access.

This "card trick" is used by many ministers, politicians, and other public speakers. "When I perform weddings, even if I'm an old friend of the couple," says one minister, "I have their names printed in big letters on a card that I keep in front of me."

Also use a card for any familiar passages, such as the Lord's Prayer or the Pledge of Allegiance, that you are supposed to recite or to lead the audience in reciting. You may never need to read the card, but it's nice to have a backup in case of emergency.

Please don't misinterpret this tip to mean that you should write out an entire speech. Brief notes—a few words or phrases—are still recommended. Use the "card trick" only for names, numbers, and wordings that must be recalled with complete accuracy.

The "card trick" provides security for speakers at ceremonies such as weddings.

Don't Speak Too Fast

Because of nervous tension and a desire to "get it over with," many speakers race through their speeches. "Take it slow and easy," advises Dr. Michael T. Motley of the University of California, Davis. "People in an audience have a tremendous job of information-processing to do. They need your help. Slow down, pause, and guide the audience through your talk by delineating major and minor points carefully. Remember that your objective is to help the audience understand what you are saying, not to present your information in record time."[25]

To help yourself slow down, rehearse your speech in front of friends or relatives and ask them to raise their hands whenever you talk too rapidly. For the actual delivery of the speech, write yourself reminders in large letters on your notes (such as "SLOW DOWN"). While you are speaking, look at your listeners and talk directly to them in the same calm, patient, deliberate manner you would use if you were explaining an idea to a friend.

41

"Tips for Your Career"

These critically-acclaimed sections, a hallmark of this text, demonstrate the relevance of public speaking in the workplace, and offer guidance on subjects such as citing Internet sources, avoiding common PowerPoint pitfalls, and preparing for memory lapses.

Research-Related Content Develops Skills with an Eye on Ethics and Critical Thinking

Developing Research Strategies

Chapter 6, "Finding Information," acquaints students with a variety of research options and provides a step-by-step guide to doing research skillfully using the Internet.

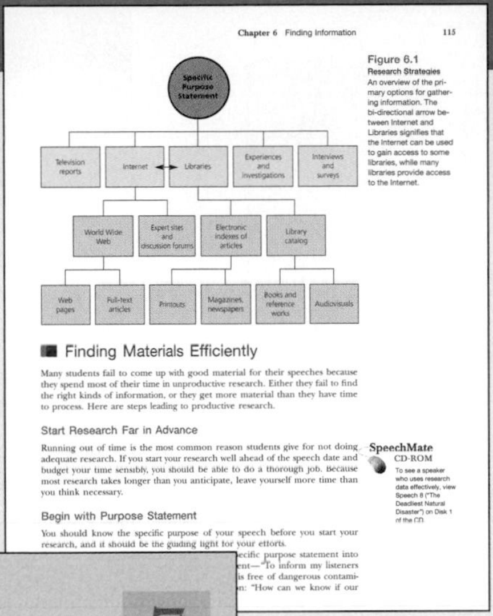
Chapter 6 Finding Information 115

Figure 6.1
Research Strategies
An overview of the primary options for gathering information. The bi-directional arrow between Internet and Libraries signifies that the Internet can be used to gain access to some libraries, while many libraries provide access to the Internet.

Finding Materials Efficiently

Many students fail to come up with good material for their speeches because they spend most of their time in unproductive research. Either they fail to find the right kinds of information, or they get more material than they have time to process. Here are steps leading to productive research.

Start Research Far in Advance

Running out of time is the most common reason students give for not doing adequate research. If you start your research well ahead of the speech date and budget your time sensibly, you should be able to do a thorough job. Because most research takes longer than you anticipate, leave yourself more time than you think necessary.

SpeechMate CD-ROM
To see a speaker who uses research data effectively, view Speech 8 ("The Deadliest Natural Disaster") on Disk 1 of the CD.

Begin with Purpose Statement

You should know the specific purpose of your speech before you start your research, and it should be the guiding light for your efforts.

...ecific purpose statement into ...ent—"To inform my listeners ...is free of dangerous contami-...n: "How can we know if our

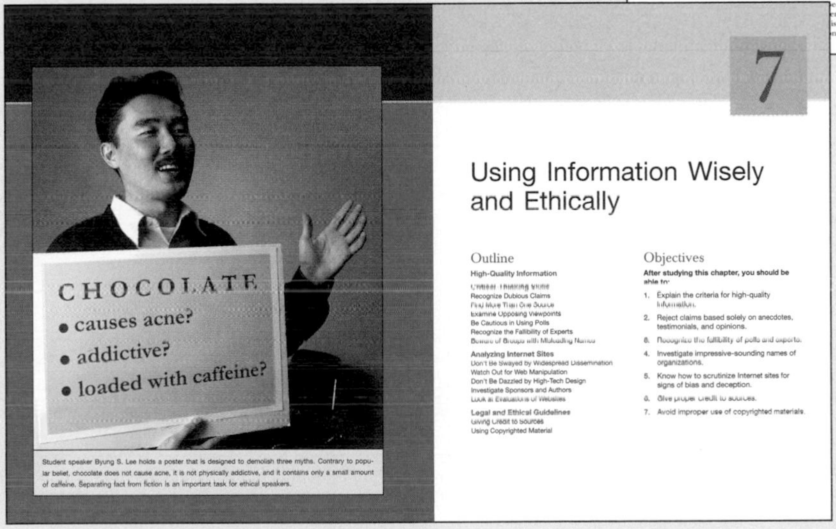

Student speaker Byung S. Lee holds a poster that is designed to demolish three myths. Contrary to popular belief, chocolate does not cause acne, it is not physically addictive, and it contains only a small amount of caffeine. Separating fact from fiction is an important task for ethical speakers.

7

Using Information Wisely and Ethically

Outline

High-Quality Information
Critical Thinking Skills
Recognize Dubious Claims
Find More Than One Source
Examine Opposing Viewpoints
Be Cautious in Using Polls
Recognize the Fallibility of Experts
Beware of Groups with Misleading Names

Analyzing Internet Sites
Don't Be Swayed by Widespread Dissemination
Watch Out for Web Manipulation
Don't Be Dazzled by High-Tech Design
Investigate Sponsors and Authors
Look at Evaluations of Websites

Legal and Ethical Guidelines
Giving Credit to Sources
Using Copyrighted Material

Objectives

After studying this chapter, you should be able to:

1. Explain the criteria for high-quality information.
2. Reject claims based solely on anecdotes, testimonials, and opinions.
3. Recognize the fallibility of polls and experts.
4. Investigate impressive-sounding names of organizations.
5. Know how to scrutinize Internet sites for signs of bias and deception.
6. Give proper credit to sources.
7. Avoid improper use of copyrighted materials.

Evaluating Websites

Chapter 7, "Using Information Wisely and Ethically," challenges students to think critically in evaluating information and judging source credibility, with a special focus on the Internet.

New "Using PowerWeb" Exercises

These end-of-chapter exercises direct students to feature articles and actual speech texts on the *Public Speaking PowerWeb*, an original McGraw-Hill website that is dedicated to the public speaking course. *Public Speaking PowerWeb* is a linked site within www.mhhe.com/gregory7.

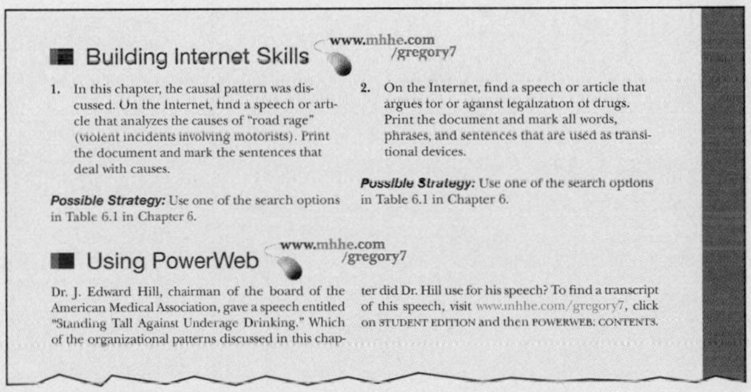

Building Internet Skills

www.mhhe.com/gregory7

1. In this chapter, the causal pattern was discussed. On the Internet, find a speech or article that analyzes the causes of "road rage" (violent incidents involving motorists). Print the document and mark the sentences that deal with causes.

Possible Strategy: Use one of the search options in Table 6.1 in Chapter 6.

2. On the Internet, find a speech or article that argues for or against legalization of drugs. Print the document and mark all words, phrases, and sentences that are used as transitional devices.

Possible Strategy: Use one of the search options in Table 6.1 in Chapter 6.

Using PowerWeb

www.mhhe.com/gregory7

Dr. J. Edward Hill, chairman of the board of the American Medical Association, gave a speech entitled "Standing Tall Against Underage Drinking." Which of the organizational patterns discussed in this chapter did Dr. Hill use for his speech? To find a transcript of this speech, visit www.mhhe.com/gregory7, click on STUDENT EDITION and then POWERWEB: CONTENTS.

Visual Aids Content Establishes Guidelines for Effective Presentation Visuals

212 **Part 3** Preparing Content

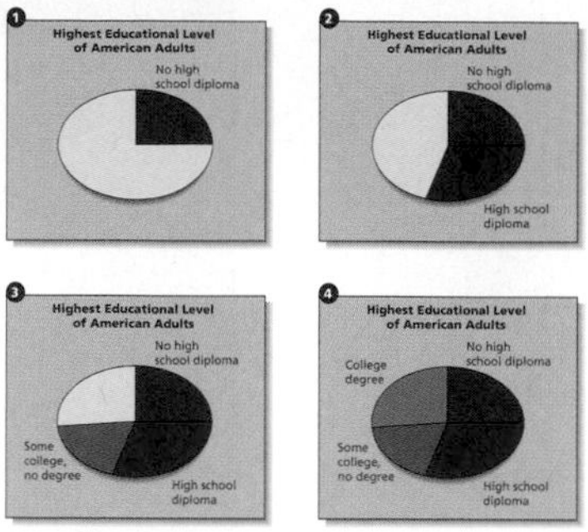

Figure 9.12
A build is an effective technique in electronic presentations. This pie chart in a PowerPoint presentation shows the educational attainment of adult Americans: less than a high school diploma, 24.8 percent; high school diploma, 30 percent; some college but no degree, 18.7 percent; and college degree, 26.5 percent. (Source: *Chronicle of Higher Education*.)

Present Your Slides

SpeechMate CD-ROM
To see a speaker who uses PowerPoint ineffectively, view Speech 3 (Persuasive Speech That Needs Improvement) on Disk 1 of the CD.

Before speech day, rehearse with all necessary equipment so that you don't fumble during the actual speech. Practice operating the computer or remote control until you become proficient.

During the speech, make yourself—not the screen or TV—the center stage of your speech. You can achieve this by (1) keeping the room partially lit so that you are not totally in shadows, (2) using slides only occasionally, and (3) focusing your eyes and your energy on the audience. Avoid the common mistake of turning away from the audience to read your slides.

Be prepared to use extra slides. For most speeches, there are marginal issues that you don't have time to cover in your speech, but if you are asked about them in the question-and-answer period, it is helpful to have relevant slides that you can display. Simply place such slides at the end of your main slide show and use them if and when you need them.

(*Continued on page 214.*)

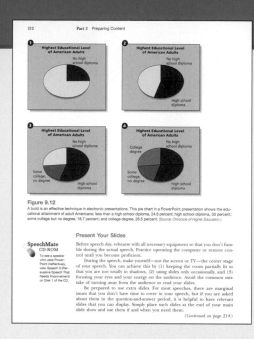

Creating Visual Aids

Chapter 9, "Visual Aids," shows students how to create and make use of a variety of visual aids in their speeches.

Chapter 9 Visual Aids 209

Table 9.2 Creating Slides in PowerPoint (*Continued*)

Step 4.	For the bulleted text items, you can add a new item by pressing the Enter button at the end of a line. (Not shown here: You can change the size and appearance of text by swiping across it with your mouse and then choosing Format, followed by Font.)	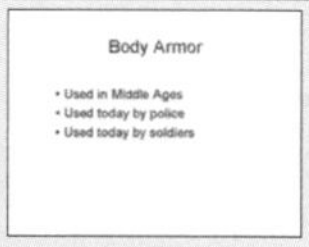
Step 5.	To add a color background, go to the Format menu, click on Background (shown here) and use the pulldown menu (indicated by the "down" button). Choose the "More Colors" option and select a color. Press OK. Finally, click on "Apply to All" so that all of your slides will have the same background color.	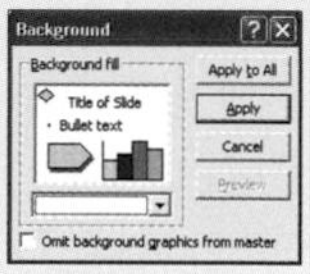
Step 6.	When you are using a background color, choose a light color (such as yellow or light blue) if your text is black. Use a dark color (such as blue or brown) if your text is white.	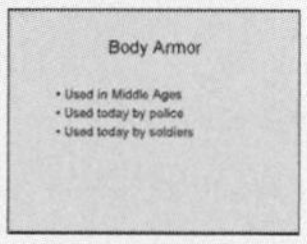

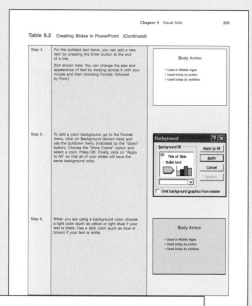

New "A Brief Guide to Using PowerPoint"

This section in Chapter 9 offers advice on creating and using PowerPoint skillfully in a speech or presentation, and on avoiding the pitfalls associated with this technology.

Finding Multimedia Resources

Table 9.1 provides information on where to find free graphics, video, and audio materials on the Internet.

198 **Part 3** Preparing Content

Table 9.1 Free Multimedia Materials on the Internet

For classroom speeches, students may download and use multimedia files from Websites without getting permission because they are engaged in a school project. But for many career and community presentations, speakers must seek and receive permission before using Web materials. (See Chapter 7 for details.)

Website	Options
Google www.google.com	Click on Images and then Advanced Image Search, which permits you to specify file size (small, large, very large) and format (JPEG, etc.).
AltaVista www.altavista.com	Choose Images, Audio, or Video. While most of the material is free, AltaVista does include some photo collections that require a fee for downloading.
Ixquick www.ixquick.com	Choose the Pictures or MP3 (audio) button before searching.
Ditto.com www.ditto.com	This service searches for photos, drawings, and cartoons.
Lycos Multimedia www.multimedia.lycos.com	Choose Pictures, Audio, or Video.
Librarians' Index to the Internet www.lii.org	In the search box, type "photos" or "graphics."
Digital Librarian www.digital-librarian.com	Click on "Images" for a comprehensive list of photos, most of them historical.

Note: Internet addresses and features sometimes change. For an update on these sites, visit this book's Website (www.mhhe.com/gregory7), click on STUDENT EDITION and then WEBLINKS, and look at notes for this page.

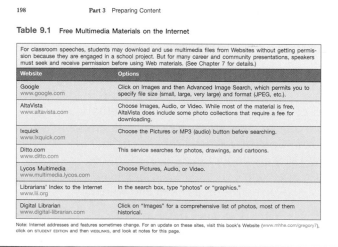

 For Technical Support, Call Toll-Free 1-800-331-5094

Diversity and Teamwork Are Valued as Critical Components of Classrooms, Communities and Careers

Nurul Izzah Anwar, an engineering major at a college in Malaysia, became a world-famous public speaker after her father, Malaysian pro-democracy leader Anwar Ibrahim, was jailed and tortured. She gives speeches throughout Asia and Europe, urging other nations to pressure the Malaysian government to make democratic reforms and release her father, and she has won the support of many world leaders. Her technique of persuasion is simple but effective: every time she makes a point, she immediately illustrates it with a true story. Using stories is a powerful tool that will be discussed in this chapter in the section on narratives.

Valuing Diversity

This book emphasizes understanding and valuing diversity. There are textual and visual representations of speakers and listeners from a variety of cultures and ethnic groups, as well as guidelines for audience analysis concerning disabilities, gender, age, and other social variables.

Chapter 1 Introduction to Public Speaking 15

Some speakers are condescending and arrogant because they are experts on their topic and they view their listeners as ignorant simpletons. Such speakers may adopt a more respectful attitude if they heed the wisdom contained in two observations by the American humorist Will Rogers: "Everybody is ignorant, only on different subjects" and "There is nothing as stupid as an educated man if you get him off the thing he was educated in."[16] When you are the expert on a subject, remember that your "ignorant" listeners, on other topics, can reverse roles with you.

Reject Stereotyping and Scapegoating

Are blondes dumb? Are redheads temperamental?

To see if hair color affects a person's chances of getting a job, researchers at California State University, San Marcos, asked 136 college students to review the résumé and photograph of a female applicant for a job as an accountant. Each student was given the same résumé, but the applicant's picture was altered so that in some photos her hair was blonde, in some red, and in some brown.

The result? With brown hair, the woman was rated more capable and she was offered a higher salary than when she had blonde or red hair.[17] Other studies have found similar results: many respondents rate blondes as less intelligent than other people, and redheads as more temperamental.[18]

Blondes and redheads are victims of the common practice of stereotyping. A **stereotype** is a simplistic or exaggerated image that humans carry in their minds about groups of people. For example, "Lawyers are shrewd and dishonest" is a popular stereotype.

stereotype
an oversimplified or exaggerated image

Stereotyping can occur in public speaking classes. When trying to choose a speech topic, some males think that women are uninterested in how to repair cars, while some females think that men are uninterested in creative hobbies such as knitting and needlepoint.

You should reject stereotypes because they are "mental cookie cutters," forcing all people in a group into the same simple pattern. They fail to account for individual differences and the wide range of characteristics among members of any group. Some lawyers are dishonest, yes, but many are not. Some women are uninterested in repairing cars, yes, but some are avid mechanics.

Even stereotypes that seem positive and harmless should be rejected. Because of the successes of many Asian Americans in science and technology, a stereotype is widespread: "All Asian Americans are gifted in math and science." Like all positive stereotypes, this one seems benign but should be avoided because it fails to consider the unique characteristics of each person. One of my students, a Japanese American, said he was teased and chided by high school math teachers because he loved poetry and hated math. Rather than expecting him to fit into an ethnic mold, they should have respected him for his individual qualities.

The best way to avoid stereotyping is to treat all listeners as individuals, not as representatives of a group whose members are all basically alike.

While avoiding stereotyping, you also should reject its close cousin, scapegoating, which is the creation of a **scapegoat**—a person or group unfairly blamed for some real or imagined wrong. Here is an example of how stereotypes interact with scapegoating: The stereotype of the dark-skinned person as criminally inclined has led some police officers to scapegoat dark-skinned

scapegoat
an individual or group that innocently bears the blame of others

Avoiding Stereotyping

Chapter 1, "Introduction to Public Speaking," confronts the problem of stereotyping and scapegoating.

Building Teamwork Skills

"Building Teamwork Skills" exercises at the end of each chapter encourage students to work in groups to find information and solve problems.

Building Teamwork Skills

1. In a group, create a list of six attributes of good delivery that are of utmost importance to group members when they are in an audience. Taking a vote, rank the attributes in order of importance. Then discuss why the top two attributes are more important than the others.
2. To practice impromptu speaking, members of a group should take turns playing the role of candidate in a job interview, while the rest of the group act as interviewers. Make the interview as realistic as possible, with serious questions and answers. After each candidate is interviewed, the group should give a brief critique of his or her verbal and nonverbal responses.

A Variety of Learning Aids Support Special Themes, Techniques, and Skills

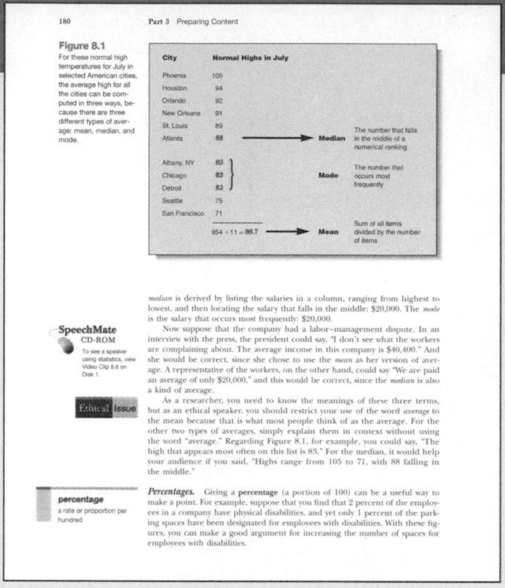

Figure 8.1
For these normal high temperatures for July in selected American cities, the average high for all the cities can be computed in three ways, because there are three different types of average: mean, median, and mode.

City	Normal Highs in July		
Phoenix	105		
Houston	94		
Orlando	92		
New Orleans	91		
St. Louis	89		
Atlanta	88	Median	The number that falls in the middle of a numerical ranking
Albany, NY	83		
Chicago	83	Mode	The number that occurs most frequently
Detroit	83		
Seattle	75		
San Francisco	71		
	954 ÷ 11 = 86.7	Mean	Sum of all items divided by the number of items

median is derived by listing the salaries in a column, ranging from highest to lowest, and then locating the salary that falls in the middle: $20,000. The *mode* is the salary that occurs most frequently: $20,000.

SpeechMate CD-ROM To see a speaker using statistics, view Video Clip 8.6 on Disk 1.

Now suppose that the company had a labor–management dispute. In an interview with the press, the president could say, "I don't see what the workers are complaining about. The average income in this company is $40,400." And she would be correct, since she chose to use the *mean* as her version of average. A representative of the workers, on the other hand, could say "We are paid an average of only $20,000," and this would be correct, since the *median* is also a kind of average.

Ethical Issue

As a researcher, you need to know the meanings of these three terms, but as an ethical speaker, you should restrict your use of the word *average* to the mean because that is what most people think of as the average. For the other two types of averages, simply explain them in context without using the word "average." Regarding Figure 8.1, for example, you could say, "The high that appears most often on this list is 83." For the median, it would help your audience if you said, "Highs range from 105 to 71, with 88 falling in the middle."

percentage a rate or proportion per hundred

Percentages. Giving a **percentage** (a portion of 100) can be a useful way to make a point. For example, suppose that you find that 2 percent of the employees in a company have physical disabilities, and yet only 1 percent of the parking spaces have been designated for employees with disabilities. With these figures, you can make a good argument for increasing the number of spaces for employees with disabilities.

Ethical Issues Icons

Twenty-two "ethical issues" icons appear throughout the book in the margin next to passages that deal with issues of honesty and fairness.

Special Techniques

How to Use Humor

"My mother," stand-up comedian Judy Tenuta says, "used to tell me, 'You won't amount to anything because you procrastinate!'"

I said, "Just wait."

Humor used effectively is a good way to keep an audience interested in your speech. It creates a bond of friendship between you and the listeners, and it puts them into a receptive, trusting mood. Here are some guidelines.

1. Use humor only when it is appropriate.
A speech about a solemn subject such as euthanasia would not lend itself to an injection of humor.

2. Tell jokes at your own risk.
A popular kind of humor is the joke—a funny story that depends on a punch line for its success. If you are an accomplished humorist, you may be able to use jokes effectively, but I don't recommend that any novice speaker use them, for these reasons: (1) jokes usually don't tie in smoothly with the rest of the speech, (2) few speakers (whether experienced or inexperienced) can tell jokes well, (3) a joke that is successful with your friends might bomb with a large audience, (4) the audience may have heard the joke already, and (5) the audience may not be in a receptive mood.

I have seen speakers tell a joke that no one laughed at—not one single soul. Maybe the audience had heard the joke before, or maybe it was too early in the morning or too late in the evening. Whatever the reason, a joke that fizzles can be devastating to the speaker's morale. "But it looks so easy on TV," some students say. It looks easy and is easy because TV joketellers have advantages that most speakers lack: They have studio audiences that are predisposed to laugh at virtually any joke the comedians tell (your audiences will probably not be poised for laughter in this way). They have a supporting cast of gag writers who test the jokes out before they are used. Most important of all, they have years of joke-telling experience before they appear on national TV.

3. Use low-key humor.
You can use other kinds of humor besides jokes. A mildly amusing story, quotation, or observation can be as effective as a side-splitting joke. The best thing about low-key humor is that it's safe. While the success of a joke depends on the audience laughing immediately after the punch line, the success of a light story or witty observation does not depend on laughter—or even smiles. Sometimes the only audience response is an inner delight. In a speech urging her listeners to invest in the stock market, student speaker Jacqueline Wallace said:

If you invest in blue chip stocks, you will have the satisfaction of getting a dividend check every three months from each of your investments. As the writer Dorothy Parker once said, "The two most beautiful words in the English language are 'check enclosed.'"

Notice that the Dorothy Parker quotation was the kind of wry humor that does not depend on belly laughs; also notice that Wallace tied the humor in with the purpose of her speech. This is an example of how you can sneak humor in, so that the audience sees it as part of your speech, not as a "joke." If they laugh or smile, fine; if they don't, no harm has been done. It's still enjoyable and relevant.

4. Humor must always relate to the subject matter.
Never tell an amusing story about a farmer unless your speech is about farming and the story ties in with the rest of the speech.

5. Never use humor that might be offensive to any person in the audience.
Avoid humor that is obscene or that ridicules members of any group in society (racial, ethnic, religious, political, gender, and so on). Even if the audience contains no members of a particular group, you are unwise to ridicule that group because you risk alienating listeners who dislike such humor.

6. Never let your face show that you expect laughter or smiles.
Let's say that you cleverly inject a delicious note of ironic humor into your introduction. After you make your humorous remark, don't stand with an expectant grin on your face. If no one smiles back or laughs, you will feel very foolish. By the way, failure to get any smiles or laughs doesn't necessarily mean that the listeners did not appreciate your humor. As I mentioned above, some kinds of humor elicit only an inner delight.

7. If listeners are spread apart, move them together.
If you have 15 people scattered about in a large hall, it will be easier to make contact with them if you first have them move to seats at the front and center. Nightclub comedians are very sensitive to seating arrangements; they make sure tables are pushed close together because they know that patrons are more likely to laugh if they are jammed together in warm coziness. Some comedians would never tell jokes to an audience widely scattered in a large room; people feel isolated, and they are afraid that if they laugh,

428

"Special Techniques" Sections

These sections provide detailed explanations of the following topics: how to avoid design mistakes in visual aids, how to use leave-behinds, and how to use humor in a speech.

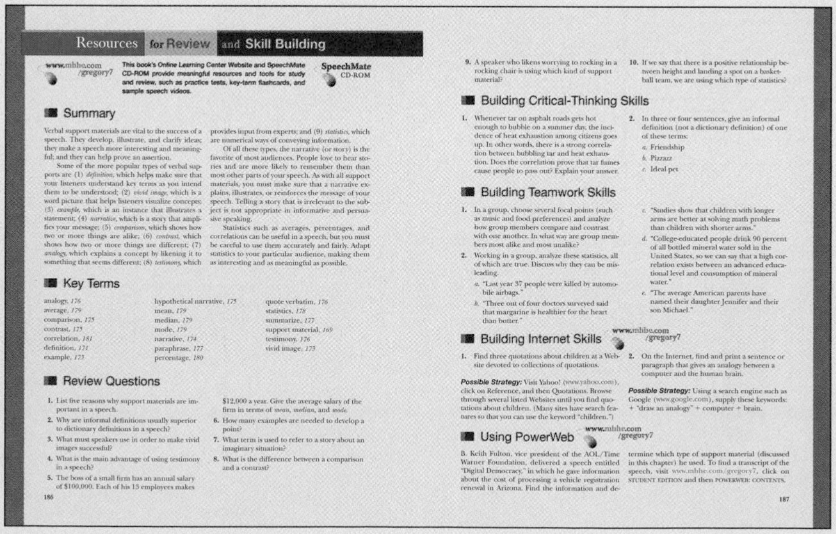

Resources for Review and Skill Building

www.mhhe.com/gregory7 This book's Online Learning Center Website and SpeechMate CD-ROM provide meaningful resources and tools for study and review, such as practice tests, key-term flashcards, and sample speech videos. SpeechMate CD-ROM

Summary

Verbal support materials are vital to the success of a speech. They develop, illustrate, and clarify ideas; they make a speech more interesting and meaningful; and they can help prove an assertion.

Some of the more popular types of verbal supports are (1) *definition*, which helps make sure that your listeners understand key terms as you intend them to be understood; (2) *vivid image*, which is a word picture that helps listeners visualize concepts; (3) *example*, which is an instance that illustrates a statement; (4) *narrative*, which is a story that amplifies your message; (5) *comparison*, which shows how two or more things are alike; (6) *contrast*, which shows how two or more things are different; (7) *analogy*, which explains a concept by likening it to something that seems different; (8) *testimony*, which provides input from experts; and (9) *statistics*, which are numerical ways of conveying information.

Of all these types, the narrative (or story) is the favorite of most audiences. People love to hear stories and are more likely to remember them than most other parts of your speech. As with all support materials, you must make sure that a narrative explains, illustrates, or reinforces the message of your speech. Telling a story that is irrelevant to the subject is not appropriate in informative and persuasive speaking.

Statistics such as averages, percentages, and correlations can be useful in a speech, but you must be careful to use them accurately and fairly. Adapt statistics to your particular audience, making them as interesting and as meaningful as possible.

Key Terms

analogy, *176*
average, *179*
comparison, *175*
contrast, *175*
correlation, *181*
definition, *171*
example, *173*
hypothetical narrative, *175*
mean, *179*
median, *179*
mode, *179*
narrative, *174*
paraphrase, *177*
percentage, *180*
quote verbatim, *176*
statistics, *178*
summarize, *177*
support material, *169*
testimony, *176*
vivid image, *173*

Review Questions

1. List five reasons why support materials are important in a speech.
2. Why are informal definitions usually superior to dictionary definitions in a speech?
3. What must speakers use in order to make vivid images successful?
4. What is the main advantage of using testimony in a speech?
5. The boss of a small firm has an annual salary of $100,000. Each of his 13 employees makes $12,000 a year. Give the average salary of the firm in terms of *mean*, *median*, and *mode*.
6. How many examples are needed to develop a point?
7. What term is used to refer to a story about an imaginary situation?
8. What is the difference between a comparison and a contrast?

186

9. A speaker who likens worrying to rocking in a rocking chair is using which kind of support material?
10. If we say that there is a positive relationship between height and landing a spot on a basketball team, we are using which type of statistics?

Building Critical-Thinking Skills

1. Whenever tar on asphalt roads gets hot enough to bubble on a summer day, the incidence of heat exhaustion among citizens goes up. In other words, there is a strong correlation between bubbling tar and heat exhaustion. Does the correlation prove that tar fumes cause people to pass out? Explain your answer.
2. In three or four sentences, give an informal definition (not a dictionary definition) of one of these terms:
   a. Friendship
   b. Pizzazz
   c. Ideal pet

Building Teamwork Skills

1. In a group, choose several focal points (such as music and food preferences) and analyze how group members compare and contrast with one another. In what way are group members most alike and most unalike?
2. Working in a group, analyze these statistics, all of which are true. Discuss why they can be misleading.
   a. "Last year 37 people were killed by automobile airbags."
   b. "Three out of four doctors surveyed said that margarine is healthier for the heart than butter."
   c. "Studies show that children with longer arms are better at solving math problems than children with shorter arms."
   d. "College-educated people drink 90 percent of all bottled mineral water sold in the United States, so we can say that a high correlation exists between an advanced educational level and consumption of mineral water."
   e. "The average American parents have named their daughter Jennifer and their son Michael."

Building Internet Skills www.mhhe.com/gregory7

1. Find three quotations about children at a Website devoted to collections of quotations.

Possible Strategy: Visit Yahoo! (www.yahoo.com), click on Reference, and then Quotations. Browse through several listed Websites until you find quotations about children. (Many sites have search features so that you can use the keyword "children.")

2. On the Internet, find and print a sentence or paragraph that gives an analogy between a computer and the human brain.

Possible Strategy: Using a search engine such as Google (www.google.com), supply these keywords: + "draw an analogy" + computer + brain.

Using PowerWeb www.mhhe.com/gregory7

B. Keith Fulton, vice president of the AOL/Time Warner Foundation, delivered a speech entitled "Digital Democracy," in which he gave information about the cost of processing a vehicle registration renewal in Arizona. Find the information and determine which type of support material (discussed in this chapter) he used. To find a transcript of the speech, visit www.mhhe.com/gregory7, click on STUDENT EDITION and then POWERWEB: CONTENTS.

187

Resources for Review and Skill Building

These end-of-chapter sections include a summary, a list of key terms, review questions, and a series of exercises that focus on "Building Critical Thinking Skills," "Building Teamwork Skills," "Building Internet Skills," and "Using PowerWeb."

Integrated Web Resources Enhance Interest and Foster Interactivity

Online Learning Center

To support and extend the content of the text, the Gregory Online Learning Center, a text-specific website, offers students and instructors an array of resources, including chapter quizzes, interactive worksheets, vocabulary-enhancing crossword puzzles, articles on relevant topics, web links and other helpful resources (www.mhhe.com/gregory7). Icons in the text margins direct students to relevant resources on the Online Learning Center.

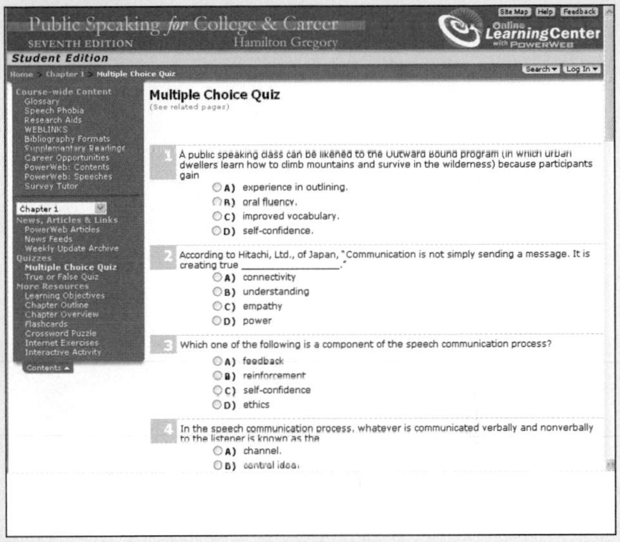

Public Speaking for College & Career
SEVENTH EDITION
Hamilton Gregory
Online Learning Center with POWERWEB
Student Edition
Multiple Choice Quiz
Course-wide Content
Glossary
Speech Phobia
Research Aids
WEBLINKS
Bibliography Formats
Supplementary Readings
Career Opportunities
PowerWeb: Contents
PowerWeb: Speeches
Survey Tutor
Chapter 1
News, Articles & Links
PowerWeb Articles
News Feeds
Weekly Update Archive
Quizzes
Multiple Choice Quiz
True or False Quiz
More Resources
Learning Objectives
Chapter Outline
Chapter Overview
Flashcards
Crossword Puzzle
Internet Exercises
Interactive Activity
1 A public speaking class can be likened to the Outward Bound program (in which urban dwellers learn how to climb mountains and survive in the wilderness) because participants gain
A) experience in outlining.
B) oral fluency.
C) improved vocabulary.
D) self-confidence.
2 According to Hitachi, Ltd., of Japan, "Communication is not simply sending a message. It is creating true ________."
A) connectivity
B) understanding
C) empathy
D) power
3 Which one of the following is a component of the speech communication process?
A) feedback
B) reinforcement
C) self-confidence
D) ethics
4 In the speech communication process, whatever is communicated verbally and nonverbally to the listener is known as the
A) channel.
B) central idea.

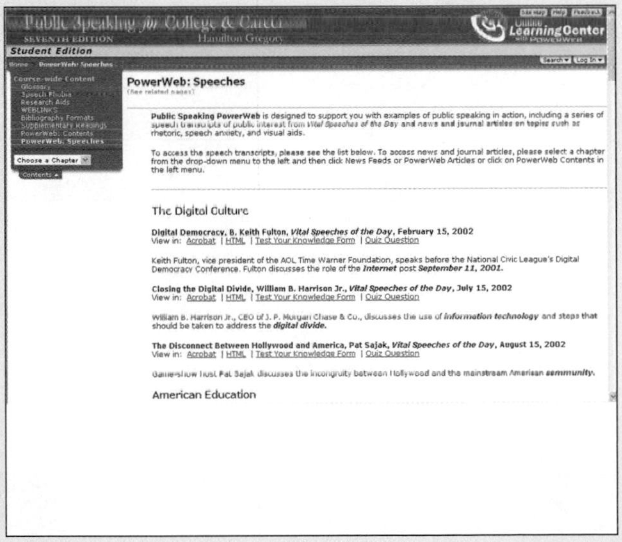

New Public Speaking PowerWeb

The Online Learning Center provides a gateway to *Public Speaking PowerWeb*, a password-protected website that is offered free with new copies of the text. It provides instructors and students with the following resources: recent speeches from *Vital Speeches of the Day*; news and journal articles on topics that are relevant to public speaking, such as speech anxiety, visual aids, and persuasion; articles on a variety of topics that students may use as source material for their speeches, and a newsworthy, annotated "speech of the week."

Public Speaking for College and Career

One of the greatest benefits of a public speaking class is being able to practice your skills, says Lt. Col. Patricia Horoho, who is shown giving a speech at a Red Cross ceremony in which she was honored for her bravery in the aftermath of the 9/11 terrorist attack on the Pentagon. Horoho raced from her desk to give first-aid treatment to more than 75 victims. She was able to act quickly and efficiently, she says, because she had carried out extensive practice sessions in nursing school. In a similar way, students in a public speaking class can develop and fine-tune their skills. "You never know when you'll have to talk to a group," she says. "The more practice you get in a public speaking class, the better off you will be in your career."

1

Introduction to Public Speaking

Outline

Benefits of a Public Speaking Course

The Speech Communication Process
Elements of the Process
Overview of the Process

The Speaker's Responsibilities
Maintain High Ethical Standards
Enrich Listeners' Lives
Take Every Speech Seriously

Speech Introducing Yourself or a Classmate
Sample Speeches

Quick Guide to Public Speaking
Preparation
Delivery

Objectives

After studying this chapter, you should be able to:

1. Explain at least three benefits of a public speaking course.
2. Identify and explain the seven elements of the speech communication process.
3. Describe the main responsibilities that speakers have toward their listeners.
4. Prepare a speech introducing yourself or a classmate.

Why do some women remain in a relationship with a man who abuses them?

To understand why, says Mary Ignatius, a student at City College of San Francisco, you must examine the "cycle of violence," which has three phases: (1) Tension Increasing (a build-up of stress and threats), (2) Violence (physical, emotional, or sexual abuse), and (3) Honeymoon (the man is loving and remorseful).[1]

It is the Honeymoon phase that keeps a woman in an abusive relationship, as she hopes for a true and lasting change. But then tensions build, and the terrible cycle continues. Once a woman understands the process, says Ignatius, she can take steps to break the cycle.

To educate both men and women about domestic abuse, Ignatius gave over 20 presentations to various classes at her college as part of the requirements of a course on violence against women. Her presentations received praise from students and faculty, and she soon found herself taking her message to the larger community beyond the campus as an advocate for San Francisco Women Against Rape.

By helping audiences understand the dynamics of violence against women, Mary Ignatius makes a contribution to her campus and her community.

Ignatius credits her success as a communicator to a public speaking course she took earlier at the University of San Francisco. That course also brought other benefits:

- "It enabled me to be more proactive in my classes—asking questions, challenging thoughts, and promoting discussions."
- "I have had to give many presentations in a variety of classes from biology to social work, and I have the confidence to articulate my thoughts."
- "I am a waitress at night to help pay for college. Believe it or not, one really has to have public speaking skills in order to sell a product—in this case, the specials of the evening. I have to make constant eye contact and describe the food in a way that makes the customer's mouth begin to water."[2]

Public speaking skills not only help you to succeed in college and career, but they also give you a chance to make a contribution to others. You can touch lives—whether you are training new employees, demonstrating a useful product, or advocating a worthwhile cause.

Benefits of a Public Speaking Course

Many college graduates look back on all the courses they took in college and say that public speaking was one of the most valuable.[3] Here are some of the reasons why this course is considered so important.

1. You learn how to speak to a public audience. Knowing how to stand up and give a talk to a group of people is a rewarding skill you can use throughout your life. Imagine yourself in these public speaking scenarios:

- For a research project in one of the courses in your major, you must explain your findings in a 30-minute presentation to faculty and students.
- To 50 colleagues at work, you give a brief speech appealing for contributions to the United Way charity drive.
- In court you explain to a jury why a traffic accident was not your fault.
- At a retirement banquet for a co-worker, you give a brief talk praising her accomplishments.
- To a gathering of neighbors, you explain your ideas for curbing crime in the neighborhood.

You will encounter many such occasions that require public speaking ability.

2. You learn skills that apply to one-on-one communication. Although the emphasis of this course is on speaking to groups, the principles that you learn also apply to communication with individuals.[4] Throughout your lifetime you will be obliged to talk in situations such as these:

- In a job interview, a human resources manager says, "We've got 50 applicants for this job. Why should we hire you?" If you know how to give a reply that is brief, interesting, and convincing, you obviously improve your chances of getting the job (assuming, of course, that your qualifications are as good as those of the other 49 applicants). In a public speaking course, you learn how to organize and present persuasive messages.
- You sit down with a bank executive to ask for a loan so that you can buy a new car. The skills of nonverbal communication (such as eye contact and facial expression) that you learn in a public speaking course should help you convey to the banker that you are a trustworthy and reliable person who will repay the loan.

After taking a public speaking course, many students report that their new skills help them as much in talking to one person as in addressing a large audience.

3. You develop the oral communication skills that are prized in the job market. When you go to a job interview, which of the following is most likely to influence the employer when he or she decides whether to hire you?

- The reputation of your school
- Your grade-point average
- Letters of reference
- Technical knowledge in your field
- Oral communication skills—speaking and listening
- Written communication skills—reading and writing

Research shows that "oral communication skills" is the correct answer—a finding that surprises many students.[5] Surely "technical knowledge in your field" is the most important factor for jobs in science and technology, isn't it? Not according to employers. "Good grades and technical skills are important, of course," says Marilyn Mackes, executive director of the National Association of Colleges and Employers, but they are not as highly prized as oral communication skills. You can be brilliant in your field, she says, but if you can't communicate successfully with co-workers and the public, your brilliance is of little value.[6]

www.mhhe.com/gregory7

See "Career Opportunities" on this book's Website.

Once you have a job, being a good communicator can help you win promotions. "If a dozen equally skilled technicians are competing for the job of manager, the winner is most likely to be the one with the best communication skills," says Cristina Silva, human resources manager of a plant in Los Angeles.[7]

4. You practice and gain experience in an ideal laboratory. Just as carpenters become experts in their trade by learning woodworking skills and then practicing them, effective speechmakers become adept by learning certain skills and then practicing them. The classroom is a good laboratory for practicing your skills because (1) it is an unthreatening setting—no one will deny you a job or a raise on the basis of your classroom speeches, and (2) your audience is friendly and sympathetic—made up of students who must go through the same experience.

Extremely valuable to you are the critiques given by your instructor (and, in some cases, by fellow students). If, for example, you say "um" or "uh" so often that it distracts your listeners, you are probably unaware of this unconscious habit. Being told of the problem is the first step toward correcting it.

5. You gain self-confidence. Giving a public speech is a challenging task, so if you learn to do it well, you gain an extraordinary amount of self-assurance. The situation is similar to the experiences of many participants in Outward Bound, the program that teaches city dwellers to climb mountains and survive in the wilderness. "After Outward Bound," one graduate of the program told me, "I can take on any challenge." Many students have the same feelings of pride and self-worth after completing a public speaking course.

6. You develop an ability that can provide pleasure and satisfaction for yourself and others. While attending a funeral service for a beloved aunt, Karen Walker heard the minister give a brief eulogy and then say, "Would anyone like to say a few words at our 'open mike'?" A few people went to the microphone and shared some reminiscences, but most audience members were silent. "I wanted to pay tribute to my aunt, but I was too scared," said Walker. "Most of my relatives had the same reaction. I felt really bad because there were a lot of important things about my aunt and her life that were never said." A few years later, Walker took a public speaking class, and a year or so afterwards, she attended another funeral—for her grandfather. "This time I vowed that I would not pass up the opportunity to honor a wonderful person. I asked to be part of the service, and I spoke about my childhood memories of my grandfather."

The eulogy, said Walker, was enjoyed and appreciated by her family. "A lot of my relatives told me that I expressed beautifully what they would have said if they had had the courage and skills to stand up and speak. It gave me a good feeling to know that I could represent the family in this way."

Being able to speak in public—offering a toast, sharing information, providing encouragement, attempting persuasion—can bring pleasure and joy to yourself and to others. Walker said that her success was possible because of what she had learned in her public speaking class.[8]

The Speech Communication Process

Some speakers mistakenly think that when they have given a speech, communication has *necessarily* taken place. It often does take place, of course, but it sometimes does not, for this reason: *Speaking and communicating are not the same thing.* You can speak to a listener, but if the listener does not understand your message in the way you meant it to be understood, you have failed to communicate it.[9] Here's an example:

> A man was attending a business convention in Arlington, Virginia, across the Potomac River from the nation's capital. On the last afternoon of the convention, some free time was available, and the man was invited to join a group of associates on a trip "to the mall."
>
> "No thanks," he said. He had no interest in going shopping—what he really wanted to do was visit the Capitol, the White House, and the Lincoln Memorial. Not wanting to travel alone, he ended up spending the afternoon in his hotel room watching TV.
>
> When his associates returned, they talked about how much they had enjoyed touring the White House and other historic sites. Saddened, the man learned that the mall they had visited was not a

shopping mall, but The Mall, which is the official name for the park and historic buildings in the heart of Washington.[10]

This incident illustrates that speaking and communicating are not synonymous. The colleagues (playing the role of speaker) gave information, but true, effective communication failed to take place because the man (the listener) interpreted the message incorrectly. According to Hitachi, Ltd., of Japan: "Communication is not simply sending a message. It is creating true understanding—swiftly, clearly, and precisely."[11]

Elements of the Process

Speech communication can be viewed as a process, with seven distinct components. Using Figure 1.1 as our guide, let's examine the components in greater detail.

Speaker

speaker
the originator of a message sent to a listener

When you are a **speaker,** you are the source, or originator, of a message that is transmitted to a listener. Whether you are speaking to a dozen people or 500, you bear a great responsibility for the success of the communication. The key question that you must constantly ask yourself is not "Am I giving out good information?" or "Am I performing well?" but rather "Am I getting through to my listeners?"

And when you get through to your listeners—when you engage their hearts and minds—make sure you give them a worthwhile message, not torrents of words that are quickly forgotten.

Listener

listener
the receiver of the speaker's message

The **listener** is the recipient of the message sent by the speaker. As we have noted, the true test of communication is not whether a message is delivered by the speaker, but whether it is accurately received by the listener. "A speech," says management consultant David W. Richardson of Westport, Connecticut, "takes place in the minds of the audience."[12] In other words, no matter how eloquent the speaker, no matter how dynamic the speaker's delivery, if the listeners don't receive and interpret the message correctly, the desired communication has failed to take place.

Who is to blame for such failure: the speaker or the listener? Depending on the situation, the blame could be placed on either, or both. While speakers share part of the responsibility for communication, listeners also must bear some of the burden. They must try hard to pay attention to the speaker, fighting off the temptation to daydream or think about personal concerns. They must listen with an open mind, avoiding the tendency to prejudge the speaker or discount a speaker's views without a fair hearing.

Message

message
whatever is communicated verbally and nonverbally to the listener

The **message** is whatever the speaker communicates to the listeners. The message is sent in the form of *symbols*—either *verbal* or *nonverbal.*

Verbal symbols are words. It's important for you to recognize that words are not things; they are *symbols* of things. If you give me an apple, you transfer a solid object from your hand to mine. But if you're making a speech and you mention

Figure 1.1 **The Speech Communication Process**
In this model of the speech communication process, a **speaker** creates a **message** and sends it via a **channel** to the **listener,** who interprets it and sends **feedback** via a channel to the speaker. **Interference** is whatever impedes accurate communication. The **situation** refers to the time and place in which communication takes place.

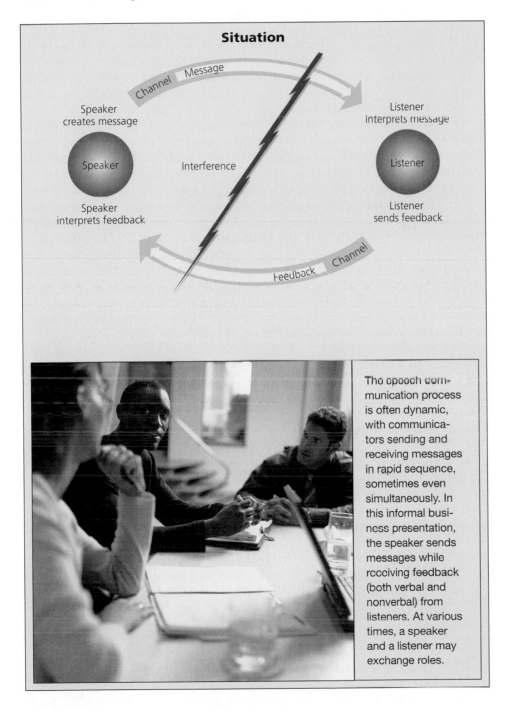

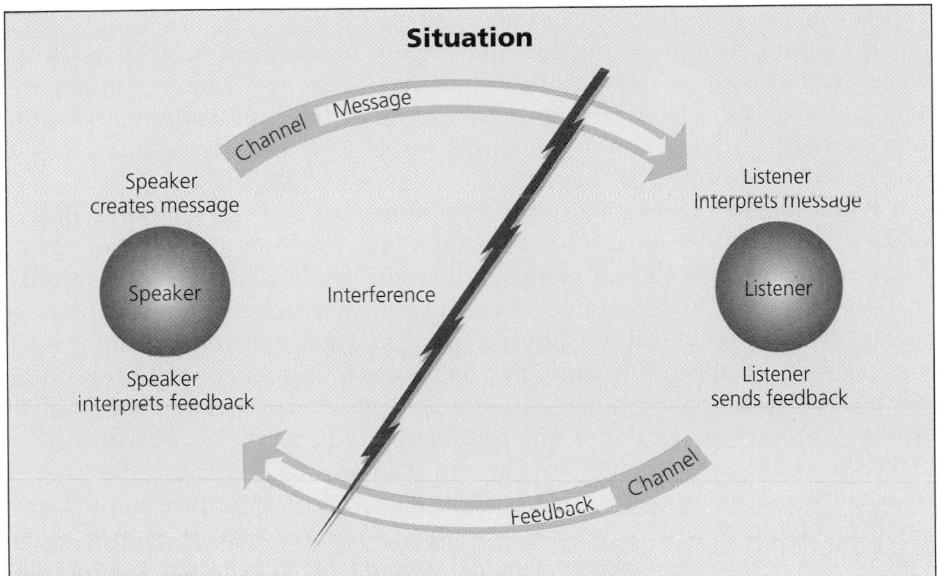

The speech communication process is often dynamic, with communicators sending and receiving messages in rapid sequence, sometimes even simultaneously. In this informal business presentation, the speaker sends messages while receiving feedback (both verbal and nonverbal) from listeners. At various times, a speaker and a listener may exchange roles.

the word "apple," you are no longer transferring a concrete thing. You are transferring a symbol, which may be interpreted by your listeners in ways that are quite different from what you had in mind. When you say "apple," one listener may think of a small green fruit, while another conjures an image of a big red fruit. One listener might think of crisp tartness, while another thinks of juicy sweetness.

Nonverbal symbols are what you convey with your tone of voice, eyes, facial expression, gestures, posture, and appearance.

Everything that you express in a message is in the form of symbols. If, for example, you want to tell me about your headache, you cannot transfer the ache and pain from your head to mine. You must transmit a symbolic description of it. The symbols you use might be verbal ("My head feels as if it's splitting apart") and nonverbal (a grimace).

When listeners receive messages, they must interpret the symbols—that is, make sense out of the speaker's verbal and nonverbal symbols. This process can cause misunderstanding and confusion because symbols are only an approximation of reality. The listener who hears of your headache might interpret the words "My head feels as if it's splitting apart" in a way that you did not intend. For example, persons who have never had a severe headache might have trouble imagining the pain. Some listeners might misinterpret the verbal symbols "splitting apart" and think that you were having a psychotic break with reality.

As a speaker, you should strive to use symbols that will cause the listener to arrive at a meaning that is as close as possible to the one in your mind. Don't say, "Smoking may cause you a lot of trouble." The vague verbal symbols at the end of the sentence—"a lot of trouble"—might be interpreted by some listeners to mean "coughing," by others to mean "stained teeth," or by still others to mean "cancer." Be specific: "Smoking may cause lung cancer."

When you use abstract words like *socialism, feminism,* and *censorship,* you must be especially careful to define precisely what you mean because listeners often have their own, widely varying interpretations. The term *censorship* might mean "stamping out filth" to some listeners and "total government control of the press" to others.

Ideally, the two types of symbols, verbal and nonverbal, are harmonious; but when they are not, the listeners receive a mixed message. Suppose you say to an audience, "I'm delighted to be here tonight," but your face has a mournful expression and your tone of voice is regretful. The listeners are getting a mixed message. Which will they believe, your words or your nonverbal behavior? In most instances of mixed messages, listeners accept the nonverbal behavior as the true message. In this case, they will believe that you are *not* delighted to be there. This is an example of how your intended message is not always the same as the actual message received by listeners.

The solution to this problem is to make sure the nonverbal part of your message reinforces, rather than contradicts, the verbal part. In other words, smile and use a friendly tone of voice when you say, "I appreciate the opportunity to speak to you tonight."

Channel

channel
the pathway used to transmit a message

The **channel** is the medium used to communicate the message. A speech can reach an audience by means of a variety of channels: radio, television, the Internet, a public-address system, or direct voice communication.

For public speaking in the classroom, your primary channel is auditory (your voice), accompanied by a visual channel (gestures, facial expressions, visual aids).

For some speeches in the workplace, you may have a public-address system. This channel can be very effective (if the system works well and the acoustics in the room are good), because it enables you to speak in an easy, conversational style without having to raise your voice.

Feedback

feedback
verbal and nonverbal responses made by a listener to a speaker

Feedback is the response that the listeners give the speaker. Sometimes it is *verbal,* as when a listener asks questions or makes comments during a lecture. In most public speeches and certainly in the ones you will give in the classroom, listeners refrain from giving verbal feedback until the question-and-answer period at the end of the speech.

Listeners also give *nonverbal* feedback. If they are smiling and nodding their heads, they are obviously in agreement with your remarks. If they are frowning and sitting with their arms folded, they more than likely disagree with what you are saying. If they are yawning and looking at you with a glazed expression, they are probably bored or weary. ("A yawn," wrote English author G. K. Chesterton, "is a silent shout.")

If you receive negative feedback, try to help your listeners. If, for example, you are explaining a concept, but some of your listeners are shaking their heads and giving you looks that seem to say, "I don't understand," try again, using different words, to make your ideas clear.

While some audience feedback, such as a bewildered look, is easy to understand, there are times when audience behavior is difficult to decipher. If a couple of listeners are dozing, it does not necessarily mean that your speech is boring. It could mean that the room is stuffy or that these listeners stayed up late the night before and are drowsy.

Interference

interference
anything that obstructs accurate communication of a message

Interference is anything that blocks or hinders the accurate communication of a message. There are three types:

- *External* interference arises outside the listener: someone coughing, a baby crying, people talking loudly in the hall, or an air-conditioning breakdown that leaves the listeners hot and sticky and preoccupied with their discomfort.
- *Internal* interference comes from within the listener. Some listeners might be daydreaming or worrying about a personal problem. Some might be too tired to expend mental energy on listening. As a speaker, you can help listeners overcome internal distractions by making your speech so lively and interesting that the audience feels compelled to listen to you.
- *Speaker-generated* interference occurs when the speaker uses words that are unfamiliar to the audience, or that are interpreted in a way that the speaker did not intend. If the speaker wears bizarre clothing, some listeners might scrutinize the attire instead of concentrating on the speech.

Tips for your CAREER

Tip 1.1 Seek Feedback*

Probably unaware of what he was doing, one college professor during his lectures would roll his tie all the way up to his collar, release it, and then roll it up again. Students in the class were distracted by this habit. One day they made bets on how many times he would roll the tie up during class.

Such distracting mannerisms and foibles can mar your speechmaking, and you may not even be aware of what you're doing. You may, for example, develop the unconscious habit of smoothing your hair or straightening your clothes as you talk. The best way to discover and discard these quirks is to get feedback (in the form of an evaluation) from your listeners.

While feedback is valuable for pinpointing delivery problems, it is even more important as a way to assess the *content* of your speech: Are your remarks enlightening or confusing to the listeners?

You don't need an evaluation of every speech in your career, but you should seek feedback occasionally. Strive to get both positive and negative input, so that you can keep the good while eliminating the bad. Here are four good methods:

1. Ask several friends or colleagues for a critique of your speech.

Don't make an imprecise request like "Tell me how I do on this" because your evaluators will probably say at the end of your speech, "You did fine—good speech," regardless of what they thought of it, to avoid hurting your feelings. Instead give them a specific assignment: "Please make a note of at least three things that you like about the speech and my delivery, and at least three things that you feel need improvement." Now your listeners know they can be frank and not worry about hurting your feelings; as a result, you are likely to get helpful feedback.

2. Pass out evaluation forms to all your listeners.

Ask them to make comments anonymously and then drop the forms in a box near the exit. The form can contain the requests mentioned above, or you can create your own items.

3. Invite a small group of listeners to sit down with you after a meeting to share their reactions.

This is especially useful in finding out whether the listeners understood and accepted your message. Try to listen and learn without becoming argumentative or defensive.

4. Have a presentation videotaped.

Invite colleagues to watch the tape with you and help you evaluate it. Because many people are *never* pleased with either themselves or their speeches on videotape, colleagues often can provide objectivity. For example, an introduction that now seems dull to you might strike your colleagues as interesting and captivating.

*The sources for Tips are cited in the Notes section at the end of the book.

Sometimes listeners will strive to overcome interference—for example, straining to hear the speaker's words over the noise of a truck roaring down the street outside. At other times, though, some listeners will fail to make the extra effort, and no communication takes place.

When you are a speaker, watch for any signs of interference and, if possible, take steps to overcome the problem. If a plane roars overhead, causing your listeners to lean forward to hear your words, you can either speak louder or pause until the plane's noise has subsided.

Situation

situation
the setting in which communication takes place

The **situation** is the context—the time and place—in which communication occurs. Different situations call for different behaviors by both speaker and listener. A speaker who delivers a eulogy in the stately hush of a cathedral would not crack jokes, but in an entertaining after-dinner speech at a convention, jokes would be appropriate. In some settings, listeners can cheer and clap, but at other times, they must remain silent.

Time of day plays a part in how receptive an audience is. Many listeners, for example, tend to be sluggish and sleepy between 3 and 5 P.M. If you give a presentation during that period, make it lively. Perhaps you could use colorful visual aids and involve listeners in a hands-on project to keep them awake and stimulated. If your speech is a long one, you might invite listeners to stand up and stretch at the halfway point to shake off their sleepiness.

When you prepare a speech, find out as much as possible about the situation: Where will the speech be given, indoors or outdoors? What is the nature of the occasion? How many people are likely to be present? By assessing these variables in advance, you can adapt your speech to make it appropriate to the situation.

Overview of the Process

Look once again at Figure 1.1 (on page 9). The diagram at the top of the page is deliberately simplified to help clarify the different components. Don't interpret the diagram as meaning that speakers and listeners ordinarily take turns at communicating. As suggested by the photo at the bottom of the page, communicators often send and receive messages at the same time. Thus, communication is not a ball tossed back and forth between speaker and listener, but two (or more) balls tossed simultaneously. For example, you go into your boss's office to ask for a raise. As you start your (verbal) message, she is giving you a friendly, accepting smile, a (nonverbal) message that seems to say that she is glad to see you. But as your message is spelled out, her smile fades and is replaced by a grim expression of regret—negative feedback. "I wish I could give you a big raise," she says, "but I can't even give you a little one." As she is saying these last words, she interprets your facial expression as displaying disbelief, so she hastily adds, "Our departmental budget just won't permit it. My hands are tied." And so on . . . a lively give-and-take of verbal and nonverbal communication.

www.mhhe.com/gregory7

For an interactive exercise on the speech communication process, visit Chapter 1 of this book's Website

The Speaker's Responsibilities

A speaker who stands before an audience has certain responsibilities that a conscientious person should accept. Here are some guidelines.

Maintain High Ethical Standards

The standards of conduct and moral judgment that are generally accepted by honest people in our society are called *ethics*. In public speaking, ethics focuses on how speakers handle their material and how they treat their listeners.[13] Speakers should be honest and straightforward with listeners, avoiding all methods and goals that are deceitful, unscrupulous, or unfair.

Because ethics is such an important concern, the icon in the margin of this page will appear throughout this book at points where ethical issues are discussed. Let's examine three important ethical responsibilities of the speaker.

Ethical Issue

Never Distort Information

As an ethical speaker, you should always be honest about facts and figures. Distorting information is not only dishonest—it's foolish. Let's say that in your career, you persuade some colleagues to take a certain course of action, but it is later discovered that you got your way by distorting facts and statistics. Henceforth your colleagues will distrust everything you propose—even if you have sound logic and impeccable evidence on your side. "A liar will not be believed," said the Greek fabulist Aesop, "even when he [or she] speaks the truth."[14]

Imagine this scenario: you are crusading for a good cause, and you believe that the only way you can win the audience to your side is to twist a few statistics to fit your argument. Furthermore, you feel certain that your listeners will never detect your deception. Is it all right to fudge the facts a bit? No. Even when a good cause is at stake, an ethical speaker will never sacrifice honesty.

Respect Your Audience

An ethical speaker treats his or her listeners in the way he or she would like to be treated if the roles were reversed—that is, with dignity, courtesy, and respect.

A few years ago, a large manufacturer had a major employee problem: all of the workers in one building reported a string of vexing medical problems while at work—skin rashes, headaches, nausea. Productivity plummeted as workers complained and often went home early, too sick to work. Investigators could find no cause, and the company suspected that the employees were victims of mass hysteria—a delusion that occurs when a group of people simultaneously complain of physical complaints that have no organic basis.

The company hired a physician to speak to the workers to try to calm them. He began by telling a few jokes, and then he urged the workers to try to relax and not allow fear and worry to undermine their health. In a condescending tone of voice, like an all-knowing adult talking to foolish children, he said, "It's possible, you know, to talk yourself into becoming sick."

The workers were furious. One of them said later, "The doctor was putting us down, not taking us seriously. He obviously thought our troubles were all in our heads."

The physician, who sincerely believed that he was dealing with mass hysteria, thought that his jokes would create a cheerful atmosphere, but they were inappropriate for the occasion and the audience. He thought his advice regarding fear and worry would be helpful, but he came across as patronizing, insensitive, and disrespectful. Angry workers took their story to the local news media, and the company was now faced with not only a health problem, but a public relations disaster as well.

A few weeks later, the company called in another speaker, a physician who used a completely different approach. During her talk, she told no jokes, and she said things like "I have talked to many of you and I know that you have legitimate, serious concerns. We need to continue to investigate this problem until we find out what is making you sick." This speaker was successful. Most of the workers felt that the company was finally listening.

Some months later, by the way, the company announced that a new, more-extensive investigation had found VOCs (volatile organic chemicals) seeping from building materials in the walls and ceilings of the building involved. The workers were vindicated.[15]

Some speakers are condescending and arrogant because they are experts on their topic and they view their listeners as ignorant simpletons. Such speakers may adopt a more respectful attitude if they heed the wisdom contained in two observations by the American humorist Will Rogers: "Everybody is ignorant, only on different subjects" and "There is nothing as stupid as an educated man if you get him off the thing he was educated in."[16] When you are the expert on a subject, remember that your "ignorant" listeners, on other topics, can reverse roles with you.

Reject Stereotyping and Scapegoating

Are blondes dumb? Are redheads temperamental?

To see if hair color affects a person's chances of getting a job, researchers at California State University, San Marcos, asked 136 college students to review the résumé and photograph of a female applicant for a job as an accountant. Each student was given the same résumé, but the applicant's picture was altered so that in some photos her hair was blonde, in some red, and in some brown.

The result? With brown hair, the woman was rated more capable and she was offered a higher salary than when she had blonde or red hair.[17] Other studies have found similar results: many respondents rate blondes as less intelligent than other people, and redheads as more temperamental.[18]

Blondes and redheads are victims of the common practice of stereotyping. A **stereotype** is a simplistic or exaggerated image that humans carry in their minds about groups of people. For example, "Lawyers are shrewd and dishonest" is a popular stereotype.

stereotype
an oversimplified or exaggerated image

Stereotyping can occur in public speaking classes. When trying to choose a speech topic, some males think that women are uninterested in how to repair cars, while some females think that men are uninterested in creative hobbies such as knitting and needlepoint.

You should reject stereotypes because they are "mental cookie cutters," forcing all people in a group into the same simple pattern. They fail to account for individual differences and the wide range of characteristics among members of any group. Some lawyers are dishonest, yes, but many are not. Some women are uninterested in repairing cars, yes, but some are avid mechanics.

Even stereotypes that seem positive and harmless should be rejected. Because of the successes of many Asian Americans in science and technology, a stereotype is widespread: "All Asian Americans are gifted in math and science." Like all positive stereotypes, this one seems benign but should be avoided because it fails to consider the unique characteristics of each person. One of my students, a Japanese American, said he was teased and chided by high school math teachers because he loved poetry and hated math. Rather than expecting him to fit into an ethnic mold, they should have respected him for his individual qualities.

The best way to avoid stereotyping is to treat all listeners as individuals, not as representatives of a group whose members are all basically alike.

While avoiding stereotyping, you also should reject its close cousin, scapegoating, which is the creation of a **scapegoat**—a person or group unfairly blamed for some real or imagined wrong. Here is an example of how stereotypes interact with scapegoating: The stereotype of the dark-skinned person as criminally inclined has led some police officers to scapegoat dark-skinned

scapegoat
an individual or group that innocently bears the blame of others

motorists, blaming them for the traffic in drugs. In recent years, tens of thousands of African American and Latino motorists have been stopped and searched by police simply because their skin color fits a "racial profile" of drug couriers. One study found that in Florida, 80 percent of those stopped were African American or Latino, while they constituted only 5 percent of all drivers.[19] Victims of these humiliating searches often say sarcastically that they have been found guilty of DWB—Driving While Black (or Brown).

In the public speaking arena today, some unethical speakers target recent immigrants to the United States and Canada as scapegoats, blaming them for every imaginable societal problem. Some politicians have even used the scapegoating of immigrants as a way to win elections.

Note: The above advice does not mean that you should disregard differences among your listeners. As we will see in Chapter 4, you should be sensitive and responsive to the needs and interests of listeners of different ages, cultures, and backgrounds. What is being condemned here is the use of unfair, exaggerated, or simplistic notions about individuals or groups.

Enrich Listeners' Lives

Before a speech, some speakers make remarks such as these to their friends:

- "I hope not many people show up."
- "When I ask for questions, I hope no one speaks up."
- "I want to hurry and get this over with."

Often these comments are made because the speaker is nervous. As you will discover in Chapter 2, I am sympathetic to speakers who experience stage fright. Nevertheless, I dislike hearing such remarks because it's obvious that the speaker is focused on his or her own emotions rather than upon the audience.

Instead of viewing a speech as an ordeal, consider it an opportunity to make a contribution to the lives of your listeners. One of my students, Mary Crosby, gave a classroom speech on poisonous spiders—what they look like, how to avoid them, what to do if bitten, and so on. It was vital information that every listener needed. She had spent 6 hours researching the topic. If the 17 of us in the audience had duplicated her research, spending 6 hours apiece, we would have labored for 102 hours. Thus, Crosby saved us a great deal of time and effort and, more importantly, enriched our lives. (Most of us, of course, probably never would have taken the time to do this research, so her speech was all the more valuable.)

To make a contribution, you don't necessarily have to present life-saving tips. You can persuade your audience to take action to solve a vexing problem; you can provide fascinating information that satisfies intellectual curiosity; you can entertain with anecdotes that divert people from their daily toils—all of these messages can be worthwhile gifts.

One of the best things you can do for listeners is avoid wasting their time. Most people are very busy, and they consider time a precious asset. If you can give them a speech that means time well spent—a speech that is meaningful and relevant to their lives—they will appreciate your efforts. But if you waste their time, they will regret having listened to you.

Take Every Speech Seriously

Consider two situations that some speakers erroneously assume are not worth taking seriously.

Classroom speeches. Contrary to what some students think, your classroom speeches are as important as any speeches that you may give in your career, and they deserve to be taken seriously. Here is why:

1. Speech class is an ideal place to practice, and, as with any endeavor in life, you get the maximum benefit from practice if you exert yourself to the fullest. High jumpers who win gold medals in the Olympics do so by trying as hard in practice as they do in Olympic competition.
2. Although the classroom is a laboratory for speechmaking, the speeches are not artificial. They deal with real human issues and they are given by real human beings. As a teacher, I look forward to classroom speeches because I learn a lot from them. In recent years, I have learned how to save the life of a person choking on food, how to garden without using pesticides, and how to set up a tax-free savings account for my children. Because of the persuasive abilities of several students, I have modified my views on gun control. One student speaker, Lisa Hannah, persuaded me to buy a carbon monoxide detector for my home.

Small audiences. Some speakers mistakenly think that if an audience is small, or a great deal smaller than they expected, they need not put forth their best effort. You should try as hard to communicate with an audience of five as you would with an audience of 500. At conventions, a number of speakers are usually scheduled at the same time in different meeting rooms. I have seen some speakers get so angry at seeing only a handful of people show up for their talk (while hundreds are crowding in to hear the speaker across the hall) that they let their disappointment color their speech. They give their speech in a peevish mood. Isn't it ironic? They are irritated at the people who did not come, but their negative "vibrations" go out to the people who honored them by attending. They impatiently hurry through their presentation, or even cut it short; their attitude seems to be: why should I take pains with just a handful of people?

For contrast, observe Nido R. Qubein, a professional speaker who was scheduled to give a talk at a convention of the Associated General Contractors of America. Because of some last-minute scheduling changes, he found that his competition was none other than the president of the United States! Instead of having an audience of hundreds, he found himself with only about 30 listeners. "It would have been easy for me to assume that . . . it was a hopeless situation," he said. "But I realized that those people who came really wanted to hear my message, and I tried twice as hard to please them. I called them up to the front of the room, seated them around a large table, and we had a group discussion. They got so involved that it was hard to break it off at the appointed time."[20]

Professional speakers have learned to take every audience seriously, even if it is an audience of only one. James "Doc" Blakely of Wharton, Texas, tells of a colleague who traveled to a small town in the Canadian province of

Saskatchewan to give a speech and found that only one person had shown up to hear him. He gave the lone listener his best efforts, and later that listener started a national movement based on the speaker's ideas.[21]

SpeechMate CD-ROM

View Christine Fowler's self-introduction speech "Scars and Bruises" on Disk 1 of the CD (Speech 11).

Speech Introducing Yourself or a Classmate

A speech introducing yourself or a classmate to the audience is often assigned early in a public speaking class. The speech gives you an opportunity to use an easy topic to gain experience. It also gives you and other members of the class a chance to learn key information about one another—so that future classroom speeches can be tailored to the needs and interests of the audience.

Strive to show your audience what makes you or your classmate interesting and unique. Unless your instructor advises otherwise, you can use the checklist below. Depending upon your time limits, you may not be able to include all items.

Background Information

- Name
- Marital status
- Hometown
- Family information
- Work experience
- Academic plans
- Post-graduation goals

Unique Features

- Special interests (hobbies, sports, clubs, etc.)
- One interesting or unusual thing about yourself or your classmate
- One interesting or unusual experience

The last three items are especially important because they give the audience a glimpse into the qualities, interests, and experiences that make you or your classmate unique.

Sample Speeches

In the first speech below, John Zachary introduces himself to a public speaking class. In the second speech, Oscar Cordero introduces classmate Misty Jones.

Here Comes the Clown

INTRODUCTION

When you were a little kid, what did you want to be when you grew up? A lot of kids—when they are asked that question—say they want to join the circus and be a clown. Well, when I was a kid, I had already achieved that status: I was a clown.

BODY

My name is John Zachary, and I was the kind of clown that all of you knew in school: I was the class clown. You remember him. Always in trouble, never sitting still, constantly disrupting the class. I was that kind of clown. I was restless and impulsive. And I was always being punished. I spent hours and hours standing in the corner or sitting in the principal's office.

Being a clown was no fun for me. Deep down I was miserable. Everyone disliked me. I had no friends. Adults hated to see me walk into a room. I dropped out of school in the ninth grade. I just couldn't learn. My mind couldn't concentrate on the important stuff. I was constantly distracted by insignificant little things. If a kid nearby dropped a pencil, my mind was focused on the pencil, and I was lost to whatever the teacher was saying. Even when I stayed in my seat, my mind was like a drunken monkey, scampering all over the place.

It wasn't until a few years ago that I truly understood why my school years were filled with failure and misery. I have a condition called ADHD. That stands for Attention Deficit/Hyperactivity Disorder. No one knows what causes ADHD, but there are medications available. A few years ago I started taking one of these medications, and it has helped me enormously. I am much less impulsive and distractible than I used to be.

Thanks in part to the medication, I am able to attend college. Even though I was a high-school dropout, I had no trouble getting in because the admissions people said I have a high IQ. The medication I take—by itself—is not enough. I also have to use a lot of self-discipline. You might have noticed that I sit on the front row and I constantly take notes. That's to help me pay attention. I also have to simplify my life. For example, last year—my first year in college—I lived in the dorm, but this caused a lot of problems. All the distractions—phones ringing, TV shows, people coming in and out—were just overwhelming. This year, I got a private apartment off-campus that is very quiet. For the first time in my life, I can really and truly study.

I have told you a lot about ADHD, but that's not my whole life. I run about five miles and lift weights on alternating days. Exercise brings down my stress level and makes me feel good. I have friends—real friends—for the first time in my life. I am majoring in education because someday I want to teach middle school kids. I think I will have a special affinity for kids with problems.

CONCLUSION

In fact, my experiences have made me more sympathetic to everyone in the world. All of us have weaknesses and imperfections. As someone once said, "The only normal people are the ones you don't know very well."

Misty Morning

INTRODUCTION

The person I am introducing to you is named Misty, and when you hear that name, you might think that her parents simply chose a beautiful name for her, but there's a story behind it.

BODY

Her full name is Misty Morning Jones. Her parents chose that name because she was born on—you guessed it—a misty morning.

Misty has lots of hobbies and special interests, but the great passion of her life right now is playing fast-pitch softball. I don't mean playing an occasional pick-up game. She was a star player in high school and now she's a star player in college.

She can play several positions, but she's usually assigned to pitch. She can throw the ball at 60 miles per hour, and has racked up three no-hitters in her brief career. If you've ever watched professional baseball on TV, you know that most pitchers are lousy at all other aspects of the game. Well, Misty is more versatile than that. She's a good hitter, with a .370 average, and a good base-runner—she is effective at laying down a bunt and stealing base.

Misty is enrolled in the emergency medical technician program—EMT. In her hometown, she is a volunteer fire and rescue worker. Her goal is to fly in medical helicopters as a paramedic.

CONCLUSION

Misty Jones was born on a misty morning, but her life is at noon now, and the sun is shining brightly on this talented young woman.

Quick Guide to Public Speaking

SpeechMate CD-ROM

To learn from speeches that need improvement, view speeches 1 and 3 on Disk 1 of the CD. For samples of effective speechmaking, view any of the other speeches on the CD.

To help you with any major speeches that you must give before you have had time to study this entire book, here is an overview of the basic principles of preparation and delivery.

Preparation

Audience. The goal of public speaking is to gain a response from your listeners—to get them to think, feel, or act in a certain way. To reach the listeners, find out as much as you can about them. What are their ages, gender, racial and ethnic backgrounds, religion, and educational level? What are their attitudes toward you and the subject? How much do they already know about the subject? When you have completed a thorough analysis of your listeners, adapt your speech to meet their needs and interests.

Topic. Choose a topic that is interesting to you and about which you know a lot (either now or after doing research). Your topic also should be interesting to the listeners—one they will consider timely and worthwhile. Narrow the topic so that you can comfortably and adequately cover it within the time allotted.

Purposes and central idea. Select a general purpose (to inform, to persuade, etc.), a specific purpose (a statement of exactly what you want to achieve with your audience), and a central idea (the message of your speech boiled down to one sentence). For example, suppose you want to inform your audience about fraud and abuse in the U.S. government's student-aid program. You could create objectives such as these:

Tips for your CAREER

Tip 1.2 Avoid the Five Biggest Mistakes Made by Speakers

In a survey by the author, 64 business and professional speakers were asked to cite the most common mistakes made by public speakers in the United States today. Here are the mistakes that were listed most often.

1. Failing to tailor one's speech to the needs and interests of the audience.

A *poor* speaker bores listeners with information that is stale or useless. A *good* speaker sizes up the listeners in advance and gives them material that is interesting and useful.

2. Being poorly prepared.

A good speech does not just happen. The speaker must spend hours researching the topic, organizing material, and rehearsing the speech before he or she rises to speak. Therese Myers, head of Quarterdeck Office Systems, says, "I've learned that slapping together a presentation during an hour on the plane the day before doesn't cut it. Now I take at least two weeks to prepare a talk."

3. Trying to cover too much in one speech.

Some speakers are so enthusiastic and knowledgeable about their topic that they try to cram a huge amount of material into a single speech. As Arnold "Nick" Carter, a corporate executive in Chicago, puts it: "They try to put ten pounds of information in a one-pound bag."

Covering too much material causes the listeners to suffer from "information overload." They simply cannot absorb huge quantities of information in one sitting.

4. Failing to maintain good eye contact.

Listeners tend to distrust speakers who don't look them in the eye. Yet some speakers spend most of their time looking at their notes or at the floor or at the back wall.

Myers offers this advice: "Instead of addressing the room, talk for a few seconds to one person, then another, then another, then another." This not only helps with eye contact, but also makes you feel more at ease "because it's like having a one-on-one conversation."

5. Being dull.

A speech can be made boring by poor content or by poor delivery. To avoid being dull, you should (a) choose a subject about which you are enthusiastic, (b) prepare interesting material, (c) have a strong desire to communicate your message to the audience, and (d) let your enthusiasm shine forth during your delivery of the speech.

General Purpose: To inform

Specific Purpose: To tell my listeners what happens when some unscrupulous schools abuse the federal student-aid program

Next, ask yourself, "What is my essential message? What big idea do I want to leave in the minds of my listeners?" Your answer is your central idea. Here is one possibility:

Central Idea: By manipulating the student-aid program, some schools cheat both taxpayers and students.

This central idea is what you want your listeners to remember if they forget everything else.

SpeechMate CD-ROM

For handy guidelines, see "Checklist for Preparing and Delivering a Speech" on the CD.

Finding materials. Gather information by reading books and periodicals (such as magazines and journals), searching for information on the Internet, interviewing knowledgeable persons, or drawing from your own personal experiences. Look for interesting items such as examples, statistics, stories, and quotations. Consider using visual aids to help the audience understand and remember key points.

Organization. Organize the body of your speech by devising two or three main points that explain or prove the central idea. To continue the example from above, ask yourself this question: "How can I get my audience to understand and accept my central idea?" Here are two main points that could be made:

I. Some schools resort to fraud and abuse of the student-aid program in order to scoop millions of dollars from the federal treasury.
II. Despite an investment of time and money, many students receive little or no useful training and end up saddled with debt.

The next step is to develop each main point with support material such as examples, statistics, and quotations from experts. Underneath the first main point, these two items could be used to illustrate the misuse of tax dollars:

- To expand student enrollment, some schools have rounded up homeless people and enrolled them for classes that they never attend, says James Thomas, the U.S. Department of Education inspector general.
- Three Texas schools received $7.4 million in student-aid payments for training security guards, but security experts testified that the training time had been inflated and that $260,000 would have been a reasonable cost, according to an investigation by *U.S. News & World Report.*

Transitions. To carry your listeners smoothly from one part of the speech to another, use transitional words or phrases, such as "Let's begin by looking at the problem," "Now for my second reason," and "Let me summarize what we've covered."

Introduction. In the first part of your introduction, grab the attention of the listeners and make them want to listen to the rest of the speech. Attention-getters include fascinating stories, intriguing questions, and interesting facts or statistics. Next, prepare listeners for the body of the speech (by stating the central idea and/or by previewing the main points). Give any background information or definitions that the audience would need in order to understand the speech. Establish credibility by stating your own expertise or by citing reliable sources.

Conclusion. Summarize your key points, and then close with a clincher (such as a quotation or a story) to drive home the central idea of the speech.

Outline. Put together all parts of the speech (introduction, body, conclusion, and transitions) in an outline. Make sure that everything in the outline serves to explain, illustrate, or prove the central idea.

Speaking notes. Prepare brief speaking notes based on your outline. These notes should be the only cues you take with you to the lectern.

Practice. Rehearse your speech several times. Don't memorize the speech, but strive to rehearse ideas (as cued by your brief speaking notes). Trim the speech if you are in danger of exceeding the time limit.

Delivery

Self-confidence. Develop a positive attitude about yourself, your speech, and your audience. Don't let fear cripple you: nervousness is normal for most speakers. Rather than trying to banish your jitters, use nervousness as a source of energy—it actually can help you to come across as a vital, enthusiastic speaker.

Approach and beginning. When you are called to speak, leave your seat without sighing or mumbling, walk confidently to the front of the room, spend a few moments standing in silence (this is a good time to arrange your notes and get your first sentences firmly in mind), and then look directly at the audience as you begin your speech.

Eye contact. Look at all parts of the audience throughout the speech, glancing down at your notes only occasionally. Avoid staring at a wall or the floor; avoid looking out a window.

Speaking rate. Speak at a rate that makes it easy for the audience to absorb your ideas—neither too slow nor too fast.

Expressiveness. Your voice should sound as animated as it does when you carry on a conversation with a friend.

Clarity and volume. Pronounce your words distinctly and speak loud enough so that all listeners can clearly hear you. Avoid verbal fillers such as *uh, ah, um, er, okay, ya know.*

Gestures and movement. If it's appropriate, use gestures to accompany your words. Make them naturally and gracefully, so that they add to, rather than distract from, your message. You may move about during your speech, as long as your movements are purposeful and confident—not random and nervous. Refrain from jingling keys or coins, riffling note cards, or doing anything that distracts the audience.

Posture and poise. Stand up straight. Try to be comfortable, yet poised and alert. Avoid leaning on the lectern or slouching on a desk.

Use of notes. Glance at your notes occasionally to pick up the next point. Don't read them or absentmindedly stare at them.

Enthusiasm. Don't simply go through the motions of "giving a speech." Your whole manner—eyes, facial expression, posture, voice—should show enthusiasm for your subject, and you should seem genuinely interested in communicating your ideas.

Ending and departure. Say your conclusion, pause a few moments, and then ask—in a tone that shows that you sincerely mean it—"Are there any questions?" Don't give the appearance of being anxious to get back to your seat (by pocketing your notes or by taking a step toward your seat).

Resources for Review and Skill Building

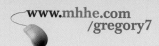

www.mhhe.com
/gregory7

This book's Online Learning Center Website and SpeechMate CD-ROM provide meaningful resources and tools for study and review, such as practice tests, key-term flashcards, and sample speech videos.

SpeechMate
CD-ROM

Summary

A public speaking course helps you develop the key oral communication skills (speaking well and listening intelligently) that are highly prized in business, technical, and professional careers. You gain both confidence and experience as you practice these skills in an ideal speechmaking laboratory—the classroom—where your audience is friendly and supportive.

The speech communication process consists of seven elements: speaker, listener, message, channel, feedback, interference, and situation. Communication does not necessarily take place just because a speaker transmits a message; the message must be accurately received by the listener. When the speaker sends a message, he or she must make sure that the two components of a message—verbal and nonverbal—don't contradict each other.

Communicators often send and receive messages at the same time, creating a lively give-and-take of verbal and nonverbal communication.

Speakers should maintain high ethical standards, never distorting information, even for a good cause. They should respect their audiences and avoid taking a condescending or contemptuous attitude. They recognize the diversity to be found in today's audiences and reject stereotypes.

Good communicators don't view a speech as an ordeal to be endured, but as an opportunity to enrich the lives of their listeners. For this reason, they take every speech seriously, even if the audience is small.

Key Terms

channel, *10*
feedback, *11*
interference, *11*
listener, *8*
message, *8*
scapegoat, *15*
situation, *12*
speaker, *8*
stereotype, *15*

Review Questions

1. Why are communication skills important to your career?
2. Name five personal benefits of a public speaking course.
3. What are the seven elements of the speech communication process?
4. Why is speaking not necessarily the same thing as communicating?
5. If there is a contradiction between the verbal and nonverbal components of a speaker's message, which component is a listener likely to accept as the true message?
6. If communication fails, who is to blame: the speaker or the listener?
7. What two channels are most frequently used for classroom speeches?
8. What are the three types of interference?
9. What are stereotypes? Give some examples.
10. According to a survey, what is the number one mistake made by public speakers?

Building Critical-Thinking Skills

1. Describe an instance of miscommunication between you and another person (friend, relative, salesperson, etc.). Discuss what caused the problem, and how the interchange could have been handled better.

2. One of the elements of the speech communication process—feedback—is important for success in business. Imagine that you work in a travel agency and you have to give presentations on crime prevention to clients who have purchased overseas tours. How would you seek and use feedback?

Building Teamwork Skills

1. Working in a group, analyze a particular room (your classroom or some other site that everyone is familiar with) as a setting for speeches (consider size of the room, seating, equipment, and potential distractions). Prepare a list of tips that speakers can follow to minimize interference and maximize communication.

2. Taking turns, each member of a group states his or her chosen (or probable) career, and then group members work together to imagine scenarios (in that career) in which oral communication skills play an important part.

Building Internet Skills*

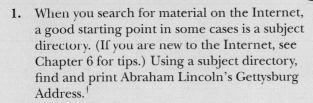

www.mhhe.com/gregory7

1. When you search for material on the Internet, a good starting point in some cases is a subject directory. (If you are new to the Internet, see Chapter 6 for tips.) Using a subject directory, find and print Abraham Lincoln's Gettysburg Address.[1]

Possible Strategy: Go to Yahoo! (www.yahoo.com) and click on the category "Arts & Humanities." You will see many subcategories. Click on "Humanities," then select "History," followed by "U.S. History," and "Archives." Investigate several of the Websites listed (such as Douglass—Archives of American Public Address) until you find the Gettysburg Address.

2. Whether you are a beginner or an experienced Internet researcher, you can profit from tutorials offered on-line. Examine at least one tutorial that has tips you can use, and print a copy for future reference.

Possible Strategy: Try one of these sites for tutorials:

- The University of California, Berkeley, Library www.lib.berkeley.edu/TeachingLib/Guides/Internet
- The Internet Public Library www.ipl.org

*Throughout the chapters, Internet exercises list Web addresses that were current when this book was printed. But because these addresses often change or disappear, please check for updates at www.mhhe.com/gregory7. Click on Student Edition and then Weblinks.

Using PowerWeb

www.mhhe.com/gregory7

In a speech entitled "Success in Management," Anne M. Mulcahy, chairman and CEO of Xerox Corporation, says, "Someone just counted up the amount of time I devoted to communicating internally the past two years. It surprised even me." What examples does she give of her on-the-job communication efforts? To find a transcript of this speech, visit www.mhhe.com/gregory7, click on STUDENT EDITION and then POWERWEB: CONTENTS. A video of Mulcahy's speech appears on Disk 2 of SpeechMate CD-ROM.

Johnny Lee, victim services coordinator for a police department, experienced stage fright when he conducted a vigil for crime victims and their families, but he controlled his nervousness by focusing on his audience rather than on himself. To worry about yourself and your image, he says, "is a kind of vanity—you are putting yourself above your audience and your message."

2

Controlling Nervousness

Outline

Reasons for Nervousness

The Value of Fear

Guidelines for Controlling Nervousness

In the Planning Stage

Immediately before the Speech

During the Speech

Objectives

After studying this chapter, you should be able to:

1. Describe the four kinds of fear that engender nervousness in speechmaking.
2. Explain why controlled nervousness is beneficial for a public speaker.
3. Apply techniques that can be used before and during a speech to control nervousness.

Movie star Leonardo DiCaprio vividly remembers his two worst bouts of stage fright. The first occurred when he was in the eighth grade and he went out on his first date. "She was a beautiful Spanish girl named Cessi," he recalls, "and when I saw her, I was petrified. I couldn't even look her in the eye or speak to her." The movie they attended was no problem, since conversation was unnecessary, but dinner afterwards was a disaster because DiCaprio was painfully shy and tongue-tied. He was "so mortified" by his behavior that he avoided her for the next year even though he was "madly in love."

The second scare happened when DiCaprio, at age 19, was attending the Academy Awards ceremony and was terrified by the realization that he might win an Oscar and have to give an acceptance speech to a live audience of 4,000 people and a TV audience of 35 million. "I was shaking in my seat," he says. "My palms were sweaty, and I had this gut-wrenching fear that if I had to speak, I would slip up and do something horrible." When another actor won the award, he was immensely relieved. During the next few years, whenever he was asked to give speeches to various organizations, he declined because he was afraid to speak to "big audiences."

By the time he was 25, however, he had become a different man. At the Earth Day 2000 rally in Washington, D.C., he confidently delivered a smooth, polished

Actor Leonardo DiCaprio gives a presentation about global warming to the National Resources Defense Council. Once terrified of public speaking, DiCaprio gives speeches to audiences of all sizes, including one that numbered 500,000 people.

speech to 500,000 people. Since then, he has given dozens of other successful speeches to large audiences throughout the world.

What happened to DiCaprio to transform him from petrified to polished? He explains: "I realized that if I make a mistake, so what? It's no big deal. There's no point in putting all that pressure on myself."[1]

If you experience nervousness as a public speaker, you are not alone. Most people—even performers like DiCaprio—suffer from stage fright when called upon to speak in public.[2] In fact, when researchers ask Americans to name their greatest fears, the fear of speaking to a group of strangers is listed more often than fear of snakes, insects, lightning, deep water, heights, or flying in airplanes.[3]

With the tips offered in this chapter, you will be able to control your nervousness and—like Leonardo DiCaprio—become a confident speaker.

Reasons for Nervousness

Is it foolish to be afraid to give a speech? Is this fear as groundless as a child's fear of the boogeyman? I used to think so, back when I first began making speeches. I was a nervous wreck, and I would often chide myself by saying, "Come on, relax, it's just a little speech. There's no good reason to be scared." But I was wrong. There *is* good reason to be scared; in fact, there are *four* good reasons:

1. **Fear of being stared at.** In the animal world, a stare is a hostile act. Dogs, baboons, and other animals sometimes defend their territory by staring. Their hostile gaze alone is enough to turn away an intruder. We human beings have similar reactions; it is part of our biological makeup to be upset by stares. Imagine that you are riding in a crowded elevator with a group of strangers. Suddenly you realize that the other people are staring directly at you. Not just glancing. *Staring.* You probably would be unnerved and frightened because a stare can be as threatening as a clenched fist—especially if it comes from people you don't know. That is why public speaking can be so frightening. You have a pack of total strangers "attacking" you with unrelenting stares, while you are obliged to stand alone, exposed and vulnerable—a goldfish in a bowl, subject to constant scrutiny.
2. **Fear of failure.** "We're all afraid of looking stupid," says Jim Seymour, a columnist for *PC* magazine. "I give about 40 speeches a year. . . . Yet every single time I get ready to walk out in front of an audience, I get that old, scary feeling: *What if I make a fool of myself?* That's as deeply embedded in our psyches as our DNA chains are embedded in our cells, I suspect; I don't know anyone who doesn't get the sweats at the prospect of looking dumb to someone else."[4]
3. **Fear of rejection.** What if we do our best, what if we deliver a polished speech, but the audience still does not like us? It would be quite a blow to

our egos because we want to be liked and, yes, even loved. We want people to admire us, to consider us wise and intelligent, and to accept our ideas and opinions. We don't want people to dislike us or reject us.

4. **Fear of the unknown.** Throughout our lives we are apprehensive about doing new things, such as going to school for the first time, riding a bus without our parents, or going out on our first date. We cannot put a finger on exactly what we are afraid of, because our fear is vague and diffused. What we really fear is the unknown; we worry that some unpredictable disaster will occur. When we stand up to give a speech, we are sometimes assailed by this same fear of the unknown because we cannot predict the outcome of our speech. Fortunately, this fear usually disappears as we become experienced in giving speeches. We develop enough confidence to know that nothing terrible will befall us, just as our childhood fear of riding in a bus by ourselves vanished after two or three trips.

All four of these fears are as understandable as the fear of lightning. There is no reason to be ashamed of having them.

The Value of Fear

In the first hour of my public speaking class, many students tell me that one of their goals is to completely eliminate all traces of nervousness. My response may surprise you as much as it surprises them: *You should not try to banish all your fear and nervousness. You need a certain amount of fear to give a good speech.*

You *need* fear? Yes. Fear energizes you; it makes you think more rapidly; it helps you speak with vitality and enthusiasm. Here is why: When you stand up to give a speech and fear hits you, your body goes on "red alert," the same biological mechanism that saved our cave-dwelling ancestors when they were faced with a hungry lion or a human foe and had to fight or flee in order to survive. Though not as crucial to us as it was to our ancestors, this system is still nice to have for emergencies: if you were walking down a deserted street one night and someone tried to attack you, your body would release a burst of **adrenaline** into your bloodstream, causing fresh blood and oxygen to rush to your muscles, and you would be able to fight ferociously or run faster than you have ever run in your life. The benefit of adrenaline can be seen in competitive sports: athletes *must* get their adrenaline flowing before a game begins. The great home-run slugger Reggie Jackson said during his heyday, "I have butterflies in my stomach almost every time I step up to the plate. When I don't have them, I get worried because it means I won't hit the ball very well."[5]

adrenaline
a hormone, triggered by stress, that stimulates heart, lungs, and muscles and prepares the body for "fright, flight, or fight"

Many public speakers have the same attitude. John Farmer, a criminal trial attorney in Norton, Virginia, who has argued high-profile murder cases before the Virginia Supreme Court as well as in local courts, was asked recently if he still gets nervous in the courtroom. "Oh, yes," he replied, "the day I stop being nervous is the day that I'll stop doing a good job for my clients."[6]

In public speaking, adrenaline infuses you with energy; it causes extra blood and oxygen to rush not only to your muscles but also to your brain, thus enabling you to think with greater clarity and quickness. It makes you come across to your audience as someone who is alive and vibrant. Elayne Snyder, a speech teacher, uses the term **positive nervousness,** which she describes in this way: "It's a zesty, enthusiastic, lively feeling with a slight edge

positive nervousness
useful energy

to it. Positive nervousness is the state you'll achieve by converting your anxiety into constructive energy. . . . It's still nervousness, but you're no longer victimized by it; instead you're vitalized by it."[7]

If you want proof that nervousness is beneficial, observe speakers who have absolutely no butterflies at all. Because they are 100 percent relaxed and cool, they give speeches that are dull and flat, with no energy, no zest. There is an old saying: "Speakers who say they are as cool as a cucumber usually give speeches about as interesting as a cucumber." Most good speakers report that if they don't have stage fright before a public appearance, their delivery is poor. One speaker, the novelist I. A. R. Wylie, said, "I rarely rise to my feet without a throat constricted with terror and a furiously thumping heart. When, for some reason, I *am* cool and self-assured, the speech is always a failure. I need fear to spur me on."[8]

Another danger in being devoid of nervousness: you might get hit with a sudden bolt of panic. A hospital official told me that she gave an orientation speech to new employees every week for several years. "It became so routine that I lost all of my stage fright," she said. Then one day, while in the middle of her talk, she was suddenly and inexplicably struck with paralyzing fear. "I got all choked up and had to take a break to pull myself together."

Many other speakers have reported similar cases of sudden panic, which always hit on occasions when they were too relaxed. I once suffered such an attack, and the experience taught me that I must get myself "psyched up" for every speech. I remind myself that I need nervous energy in order to keep my listeners awake and interested. I encourage my butterflies to flutter around inside, so that I can be poised and alert.

Guidelines for Controlling Nervousness

We have just discussed how a complete lack of nervousness is undesirable. What about the other extreme? Is *too much* nervousness bad for you? Of course it is, especially if you are so frightened that you forget what you were planning to say, or if your breathing is so labored that you cannot get your words out. Your goal is to keep your nervousness under control, so that you have just the right amount—enough to energize you, but not enough to cripple you. How can you do this? By paying heed to the following tips for the three phases of speechmaking: the planning stage, the period immediately before the speech, and during the speech.

In the Planning Stage

By giving time and energy to planning your speech, you can bypass many anxieties.

Choose a Topic about Which You Know a Great Deal

Nothing will get you more rattled than speaking on a subject about which you know little. If you are asked to talk on a topic with which you're not comfortable, decline the invitation (unless, of course, it is an assignment from an instructor or a boss who gives you no choice). Choose a topic about which you

Sach Oliver, president of student government at Arkansas State University, speaks outside the Capitol in Little Rock at a rally of student leaders who are protesting proposed cutbacks in education funding. Oliver says he controls his nervousness by being well-prepared and by practicing. "My family, my roommates, my girlfriend, and many others have heard my speech before I actually give it to the 'real' audience."

know a lot (or about which you can learn by doing extensive research). This will give you enormous self-confidence; if something terrible happens (for example, you lose your notes), you can improvise because your head will be filled with information about the subject. Also, familiarity with the topic will allow you to handle yourself well in the question-and-answer period after the speech.

Prepare Yourself Thoroughly

Here is a piece of advice given by many experienced speakers: *The very best precaution against excessive stage fright is thorough, careful preparation.* You have heard the expression, "I came unglued." In public speaking, solid preparation is the "glue" that will hold you together.[9] Joel Weldon of Scottsdale, Arizona (who quips that he used to be so frightened of audiences that he was "unable to lead a church group in silent prayer"), gives his personal formula for controlling fear: "I prepare and then prepare, and then when I think I'm ready, I prepare some more."[10] Weldon recommends five to eight hours of preparation for each hour in front of an audience.[11]

Start your preparation far in advance of the speech date, so that you have plenty of time to gather ideas, create an outline, and prepare speaking notes. Then practice, practice, practice. Don't just look over your notes—actually stand up and rehearse your talk in whatever way suits you: in front of a mirror, a camcorder, or a live audience of family or friends. Don't rehearse just once—run through your entire speech at least four times. If you "give" your speech four times at home, you will find that your fifth delivery—before a live audience—will be smoother and more self-assured than if you had not practiced at all.

Never Memorize a Speech

Giving a speech from memory courts disaster. Winston Churchill, the British prime minister during World War II who is considered one of the greatest orators of modern times, learned this lesson as a young man. In the beginning of his career, he would write out and memorize his speeches. One day, while giving a memorized talk to Parliament, he suddenly stopped. His mind went blank. He began his last sentence all over. Again his mind went blank. He sat down in embarrassment and shame. Never again did Churchill try to memorize a speech. This same thing has happened to many others who have tried to commit a speech to memory. Everything goes smoothly until they get derailed, and then they are hopelessly off the track.

Even if you avoid derailment, there is another reason for not memorizing: you will probably sound mechanical, like a robot with a tape recorder in its mouth. In addition to considering you dull and boring, your audience will sense that you are speaking from your memory and not from your heart, and they will question your sincerity.

Imagine Yourself Giving an Effective Speech

Let yourself daydream a bit: picture yourself going up to the lectern, nervous but in control of yourself, then giving a forceful talk to an appreciative audience. This visualization technique may sound silly, but it has worked for many speakers and it might work for you. Whatever you do, don't let yourself imagine the opposite—a bad speech or poor delivery. Negative daydreams will add unnecessary fear to your life in the days before your speech, and rob you of creative energy—energy that you need for preparing and practicing. Actress Ali MacGraw says, "We have only so much energy, and the more we direct toward the project itself, the less is left to pour into wondering 'Will I fail?'"[12]

Notice that the daydream I am suggesting includes nervousness. You need to have a realistic image in your mind: picture yourself as nervous, but nevertheless in command of the situation and capable of delivering a strong, effective speech.

This technique, often called **positive imagery,** has been used by athletes for years. Have you ever watched professional golf on TV? Before each stroke, golfers carefully study the distance from the ball to the hole, the rise and fall of the terrain, and so on. Many of them report that just before swinging, they imagine themselves hitting the ball with the right amount of force and watching it go straight into the cup. Then they try to execute the play just as they imagined it. The imagery, many pros say, improves their game.

positive imagery
visualization of successful actions

Positive imagery works best when you can couple it with *believing* that you will give a successful speech. Is it absurd to hold such a belief? If you fail to prepare, yes, it is absurd. But if you spend time in solid preparation and rehearsal, you are justified in believing in success.

Know That Shyness Is No Barrier

Some shy people think that their shyness blocks them from becoming good speakers, but this is erroneous. Many shy introverts have succeeded in show business: Gwyneth Paltrow, Kristin Kreuk, Halle Berry, Dana Carvey, Mariah Carey, Elizabeth Hurley, and David Letterman, to name just a few.[13] Many less-famous people also have succeeded. "I used to stammer," says Joe W. Boyd of Bellingham, Washington, "and I used to be petrified at the thought of speaking before a group of any size." Despite his shyness, Boyd joined a Toastmasters club to develop his speaking skills. Two years later, he won the

Toastmasters International Public Speaking Contest by giving a superb speech to an audience of over 2,000 listeners.[14]

Shift Focus from Self to Audience

Before a speech, some speakers cause their anxiety to mushroom because of excessive preoccupation with themselves, focusing on what listeners will think about them rather than concentrating on the audience.

"Here's how I get my jitters under control," says Carlos Jimenez, a member of a Toastmasters club in Northern California. "I try not to worry about whether I will be perceived as a brilliant, eloquent expert. Who am I to be so selfish? Who am I to think that the way I look and talk is more important than the people who are sitting in the audience? I look at public speaking as a way to help people, and I can't really help people if my mind is filled with 'me, me, me' instead of 'you, you, you.'"[15]

One good way to shift the focus from self to audience is to change your "self-talk." Whenever you have a self-centered thought like "I will make a total fool out of myself," substitute an audience-centered thought like, "I will give my listeners information that will be very useful in their lives." This approach not only will liberate you from the grip of anxiety but also will empower you to connect with your audience.

Plan Visual Aids

Research shows that using a visual aid helps reduce anxiety.[16] Visual aids can help you in two ways: (1) you shift the audience's stares from you to your illustrations and (2) you walk about and move your hands and arms, thereby siphoning off some of your excess nervous energy. Whatever illustrations you decide to use, make sure they are understandable, appropriate, and clearly visible to everyone in the room.

Make Arrangements

www.mhhe.com/gregory7
For additional tips, see "Speech Phobia" in the Supplementary Readings on this book's Website.

Long before you give your speech, inspect the place where you will speak and anticipate any problems: Is there an extension cord for the slide projector? Do the windows have curtains so that the room can be darkened for your slide presentation? Is there a chalkboard? Some talks have been ruined and some speakers turned into nervous wrecks because at the last moment they discover that there isn't an extension cord in the entire building.

Devote Extra Practice to the Introduction

Because you are likely to suffer the greatest anxiety at the beginning of your speech, you should spend a lot of time practicing your introduction.

Most speakers, actors, and musicians report that after the first minute or two, their nervousness moves to the background and the rest of the event is relatively easy. Ernestine Schumann-Heink, the German opera singer, said, "I grow so nervous before a performance, I become sick. I want to go home. But after I have been on the stage for a few minutes, I am so happy that nobody can drag me off." Perhaps happiness is too strong a word for what you will feel, but if you are a typical speaker, the rest of your speech will be smooth sailing once you have weathered the turbulent waters of the first few minutes.

Immediately before the Speech

Here are a few tips for the hours preceding your speech.

Verify Equipment and Materials

On the day of your speech, arrive early and inspect every detail of the arrangements you have made. Is the needed equipment in place and in good working order? If there is a public-address system, test your voice on it before the audience arrives so that you can feel at ease with it. Learn how to adjust the microphone.

Get Acclimated to Audience and Setting

It can be frightening to arrive at the meeting place at the last moment and confront a sea of strange faces waiting to hear you talk. If you arrive at least one hour early, you can get acclimated to the setting and chat with people as they come into the room. In this way, you will see them not as a hostile pack of strangers, but as ordinary people who wish you well.

Henry Heimlich is the creator of the famed Heimlich Maneuver for rescuing people who are choking. Even though he frequently gives lectures throughout the world, Dr. Heimlich says, "I am always a little nervous wondering how a particular audience will accept me and my thoughts. It is good to meet some of the audience socially before lecturing to them, in order to relate to their cultural and intellectual backgrounds. You are then their 'friend.'"[17]

Danielle Kennedy of Sun Valley, Idaho, says that when she began her speaking career, she was so nervous she would hide out in a bathroom until it was time for her to speak. Now, she says, she mingles with the listeners as they arrive and engages them in conversation. "This reminds me that they are just nice people who want to be informed. I also give myself pleasant thoughts. Things like: 'Can you imagine, these people drove 100 miles just to hear me. I am so lucky. These people are wonderful.' I get real warm thoughts going by the time I get up there."[18]

Use Physical Actions to Release Tension

We have seen that adrenaline is beneficial, providing athletes and public speakers with wonderful bursts of energy, but it also has a bad side. When your body goes on red alert, you get pumped up and ready for action, but you also get trembling hands and jittery knees. If you are an athlete, this is no problem because you will soon be engaged in vigorous physical activity that will drain off excess nervous energy. As a public speaker, you lack such easy outlets. Nevertheless, there are several tension releasers you can use:

- Take a few deep breaths. Be sure to inhale slowly and exhale slowly.
- Do exercises that can be performed quietly without calling attention to yourself. Here are some examples: (1) Tighten and then relax your leg muscles. (2) Push your arm or hand muscles against a hard object (such as a desktop or chair) for a few moments, then release the

pressure. (3) Press the palms of your hands against each other in the same way: tension, release . . . tension, release . . .

During the Speech

Here are some important pointers to keep in mind as you deliver a speech.

Pause a Few Moments before Starting

All good speakers pause a few moments before they begin their talk. This silence is effective because (1) it is dramatic, building up the audience's interest and curiosity; (2) it makes you look poised and in control; (3) it calms you; and (4) it gives you a chance to look at your notes and get your first two or three sentences firmly in mind.

Many tense, inexperienced speakers rush up to the lectern and begin their speech at once, thus getting off to a frenzied, flustered start. In the back of their mind they have the notion that silence is a terrible thing, a shameful void that must be filled up immediately. To the contrary, silence is a good breathing space between what went before and what comes next. It helps the audience tune in to the speaker and tune out extraneous thoughts.

Deal Rationally with Your Body's Turmoil

If you are a typical beginning speaker, you will suffer from some or all of the following symptoms as you begin your talk:

- Pounding heart
- Trembling hands
- Shaky knees
- Dry, constricted throat
- Difficulty in breathing
- Quivering voice
- Flushed face

You usually suffer the greatest discomfort during the first few minutes of a speech, but then things get better. If, however, your symptoms get worse as you go along, it might be because your mind has taken a wrong path. Examine the two paths diagrammed in Figure 2.1. If you take Route A, you are trapped in a vicious circle. Your mind tells your body that disaster is upon you, and your body responds by feeling worse. This, in turn, increases your brain's perception of disaster.

You can avoid this rocky road by choosing Route B, in which your mind helps your body stay in control. The mental trick is to remind yourself that nervousness is an ally that can help energize you. Tell yourself that your symptoms, rather than being a prelude to disaster, are evidence that you are keyed up enough to give a good speech.

Think of Communication, Not Performance

Regard your task as *communication* rather than *performance.* Dr. Michael T. Motley of the University of California, Davis, says that speakers who suffer from

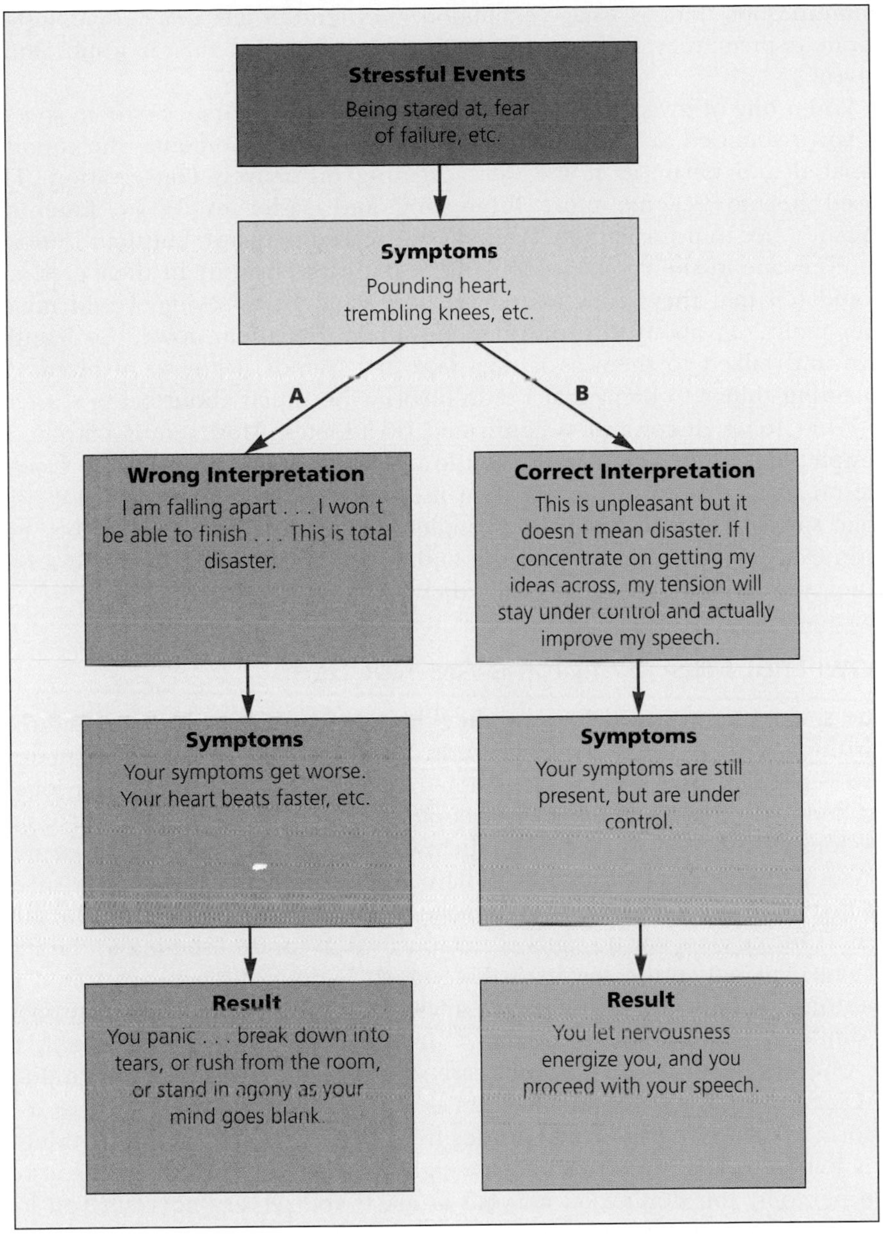

Figure 2.1
The alternative paths that a speaker feeling stressed might take.

excessive anxiety make the mistake of thinking of themselves as *performing* for listeners, whom they see as hostile evaluators. Such people say, "The audience will ridicule me if I make a mistake. I'll be embarrassed to death." But in fact, says Dr. Motley, audiences are more interested in hearing what you have to say "than in analyzing or criticizing how [you] say it." Audiences "usually ignore errors and awkwardness as long as they get something out of a speech."[19]

When speakers stop worrying about "How well am I performing?" and start thinking about "How can I share my ideas with these people?" two things usually happen: (1) their anxiety comes down to a manageable level and (2) their delivery improves dramatically. By treating speechmaking as more like one-on-one communication than as a stage exhibition, they tend to talk *with* people, instead of orate *at* them; they tend to speak conversationally rather than in a stiff, unnatural way.

When one of my students, Maxine Jones, began her first classroom speech, her voice sounded artificial and cold; but after a few moments, she sounded animated and warm, as if she were carrying on a lively conversation. This caused her to become more interesting and easier to follow. Later she explained her transformation: "At first I was scared to death, but then I noticed that everyone in the room was looking at me with curiosity in their eyes, and I could tell that they really wanted to hear what I was saying. I told myself, 'They really *care* about this information—I can't let them down.' So I settled down and talked to them as if they were my friends. I got so involved with explaining things to them that I didn't worry too much about being scared."

What Jones discovered is confirmed by athletes. Most tennis players, for example, are gripped by nervous tension before a match, but if they concentrate on hitting the ball, their tension recedes into the background. Likewise, public speakers may be filled with anxiety before a speech, but if they concentrate on communicating with the audience, their anxiety moves to a back burner, where it provides energy for the task.

Know That Most Symptoms Are Not Seen

Some speakers get rattled because they think the audience is keenly aware of their thumping heart and quaking hands. You, of course, are painfully aware of these symptoms, but—believe it or not—your audience is usually oblivious to your body's distress. Remember that people are sitting out there wanting to hear your ideas. They are not saying to themselves, "Let's see, what signs of nervousness is this person displaying?" I have had students tell me after a speech that they were embarrassed about their jittery performance, yet I and the other listeners in the class saw no signs of nervousness. We were listening to the ideas and failed to notice the speaker's discomfort. Various studies have found the same thing to be true: audiences are unaware of the symptoms that the speakers think are embarrassingly obvious.[20] In other words, you are probably the only one who knows that your knees are shaking and your heart is pounding.

Dick Cavett, who spent many years as a TV talk-show host, notes that a TV performer's level of stage fright "varies from night to night. The best thing to do is tell yourself it doesn't show one-eighth as much as you feel. If you're a little nervous, you don't look nervous at all. If you're very nervous, you look slightly nervous. And if you're totally out of control, you look troubled. It scales down on the screen." People who appear on a talk show, says Cavett, should always remind themselves that everything they are doing *looks* better than it *feels*. "Your nervous system may be giving you a thousand shocks, but the viewer can only see a few of them."[21] The same thing holds true for a speech: you look better than you feel.

Never Mention Nervousness or Apologize

Despite what I've just said, there may be times when an audience does notice your nervousness—when, for example, your breathing is audibly labored. In such a case, resist the temptation to comment or apologize. Everyone knows that most people get nervous when they talk in public, so why call attention to it or apologize for it?

Commenting about nervousness can create two big dangers. First of all, you might get yourself more rattled than you were to begin with. I remember listening to a teacher who was giving a talk to a PTA meeting one night. In the middle of her remarks she suddenly blurted out, "Oh my god, I knew I would fall apart." Up to that time, I had not been aware of any discomfort or nervousness. She tried to continue her talk, but she was too flustered. She gave up the effort and sat down with a red face. I don't know what kind of internal distress she was suffering, of course, but I am certain that if she had said nothing about her nervousness, she could have dragged herself through the speech. When she sat down, I felt irritated and disappointed because I had been keenly interested in her remarks. How selfish of her, I thought, to deprive me of the second half of her speech simply because she was nervous. I know that my reaction sounds insensitive, but it underscores an important point: your listeners don't care about your emotional distress; they only want to hear your ideas.

The second risk in mentioning symptoms: Your audience might have been unaware of your nervousness before you brought it up, but now you have distracted them from your speech and they are watching the very thing you don't want them to scrutinize: your body's behavior. If you say, "I'm sorry that my hands are shaking," what do you think the audience will pay close attention to, at least for the next few minutes? Your hands, of course, instead of your speech. Keep your audience's attention focused on your ideas, and they will pay little or no attention to your emotional and physical distress.

Is this listener displeased with the speaker's remarks? Maybe he is, but one shouldn't jump to conclusions. Perhaps what looks like a frown is really his habitual expression when he's absorbed in listening to an interesting subject. Speakers should not let such expressions upset them. Some listeners who look displeased are actually quite pleased.

Don't Let Your Audience Upset You

Some inexperienced speakers get rattled when they look out at the audience and observe that most listeners are poker-faced and unsmiling. Does this mean they are displeased with your speech? No. Their solemn faces have nothing to do with your performance. This is just one of those peculiarities of human nature: in a conversation, people will smile and nod and encourage you, but when listening to a speech in an audience, the same people will wear (most of the time) a blank mask. The way to deal with those stony faces is to remind yourself that your listeners want you to succeed; they hope that you will give them a worthwhile message. If you are lucky, you will notice two or three listeners who are obviously loving your speech; they are nodding in agreement or giving you looks of appreciation. Let your eyes go to them frequently, for they will give you courage and confidence.

If you are an inexperienced speaker, you may get upset if you see members of an audience whispering to one another. You may wonder, "Are these people making negative comments about me?" If the listeners are

www.mhhe.com/gregory7
For an interactive exercise on nervousness, visit Chapter 2 of this book's Website.

smiling, it's even worse: You ask yourself, "Did I say something foolish? Is there something wrong with my clothes?" If this happens to you, keep in mind that your rude listeners are probably talking about something other than the quality of your speech or your personal appearance. Most likely, they are just sharing some personal gossip. If by chance they *are* whispering about something you've said, it's not necessarily negative. They may be whispering that they agree with you 100 percent.

What if you see faces that look angry or displeased? Don't assume the worst. Some people get a troubled look on their face whenever they concentrate on a speaker's message. Michelle Roberts, a defense attorney in Washington, D.C., studies the facial expressions of every juror when she addresses the jury during a trial, but she has learned that sour faces do not necessarily signify disapproval. "Sometimes jurors seem like they're scowling and actually they're with you."[22]

What if a listener stands up and walks out of the room? For some inexperienced speakers, this is a stunning personal setback, a cause for alarm. Before you jump to conclusions, bear in mind that the listener's behavior is not necessarily a response to your speech: he or she may have another meeting to attend or may need to use the rest room or may have become ill suddenly. But what if the listener is indeed storming out of the room in a huff, obviously rejecting your speech? In such a case, advises veteran speaker Earl Nightingale, "don't worry about it. On controversial subjects, you're bound to have listeners who are not in agreement with you—unless you're giving them pure, unadulterated pap. Trying to win over every member of the audience is an impossible and thankless task. Remember, there were those who disagreed with wise, kind Socrates."[23]

Act Poised

To develop confidence when you face an audience, act as if you already are confident. Why? Because playing the role of the self-assured speaker can often transform you into a speaker who is genuinely confident and poised. In various wars, soldiers have reported that they were terrified before going into combat, but nevertheless they acted brave in front of their buddies. During the battle, to their surprise, what started off as a pretense became a reality. Instead of pretending to be courageous, they actually became so. The same thing often happens to public speakers.

Look Directly at the Audience

If you are frightened of your audience, it is tempting to stare at your notes or the back wall or the window, but these evasions will only add to your nervousness rather than reduce it.

Force yourself to establish eye contact, especially at the beginning of your speech. Good eye contact means more than just a quick, furtive glance at various faces in front of you; it means "locking" your eyes with a listener's for a couple of seconds. Locking eyes may sound frightening, but it actually helps to calm you. In an article about a public speaking course that she took, writer Maggie Paley said, "When you make contact with one other set of eyes, it's a connection; you can relax and concentrate. The first time I did it, I calmed down 90 percent, and spoke . . . fluently."[24]

Tips for your CAREER

Tip 2.1 Prepare for Memory Lapses

A psychologist tells of the time when he was speaking at a convention as the presiding officer. At one point he wanted to praise an associate, who was sitting next to him at the head table, for her hard work in planning the convention. "As I began my words of tribute," he said, "my mind suddenly went blank, and I couldn't remember her name! It was awful. This was a woman I had worked with for years. She was like a sister."

Fortunately, he said, everyone was wearing name tags, so he leaned over, saw her name, and used it in his remarks—without the audience suspecting his memory lapse.

Such lapses are common, especially during ceremonies, but don't be alarmed. There is a simple solution: Prepare a card with all basic information—names, dates, phone numbers—and keep the card with your other notes for easy access.

This "card trick" is used by many ministers, politicians, and other public speakers. "When I perform weddings, even if I'm an old friend of the couple," says one minister, "I have their names printed in big letters on a card that I keep in front of me."

The "card trick" provides security for speakers at ceremonies such as weddings.

Also use a card for any familiar passages, such as the Lord's Prayer or the Pledge of Allegiance, that you are supposed to recite or to lead the audience in reciting. You may never need to read the card, but it's nice to have a backup in case of emergency.

Please don't misinterpret this tip to mean that you should write out an entire speech. Brief notes—a few words or phrases—are still recommended. Use the "card trick" only for names, numbers, and wordings that must be recalled with complete accuracy.

Don't Speak Too Fast

Because of nervous tension and a desire to "get it over with," many speakers race through their speeches. "Take it slow and easy," advises Dr. Michael T. Motley of the University of California, Davis. "People in an audience have a tremendous job of information-processing to do. They need your help. Slow down, pause, and guide the audience through your talk by delineating major and minor points carefully. Remember that your objective is to help the audience understand what you are saying, not to present your information in record time."[25]

To help yourself slow down, rehearse your speech in front of friends or relatives and ask them to raise their hands whenever you talk too rapidly. For the actual delivery of the speech, write yourself reminders in large letters on your notes (such as "SLOW DOWN"). While you are speaking, look at your listeners and talk directly to them in the same calm, patient, deliberate manner you would use if you were explaining an idea to a friend.

Get Audience Action Early in the Speech

I said earlier that it's a bit unnerving to see your listeners' expressionless faces. In some speeches, you can change those faces from blank to animated by asking a question. (Tips on how to ask questions will be discussed in Chapter 11.) When the listeners respond with answers or a show of hands, they show themselves to be friendly and cooperative, and this reduces your apprehension. When they loosen up, you loosen up.

Eliminate Excess Energy

For siphoning off excess energy during the speech, you can use visual aids (as mentioned above) and these two tension releasers:

- Let your hands make gestures. You will not have any trouble making gestures if you simply allow your hands to be free. Don't clutch note cards or thrust your hands into your pockets or grip the lectern. If you let your hands hang by your side or rest on the lectern, you will find that they will make gestures naturally. You will not have to think about it.
- Walk about. Though you obviously should not pace back and forth like a caged animal, you can walk a few steps at a time. For example, you can walk a few steps to the left of the lectern to make a point, move back to the lectern to look at your notes for your next point, and then walk to the right of the lectern as you speak.

In addition to reducing tension, gestures and movement make you a more exciting and interesting speaker than someone who stands frozen in one spot.

Accept Imperfection

If you think that you must give a perfect, polished speech, you put enormous—and unnecessary—pressure on yourself. Your listeners don't care whether your delivery is perfect; they simply hope that your words will enlighten or entertain them. Think of yourself as merely a package deliverer; the audience is more interested in the package than in how skillfully you hand it over.

Making a mistake is not the end of the world. Even experienced speakers commit a fair number of blunders and bloopers. If you completely flub a sentence or mangle an idea, you might say something like, "No, wait. That's not the way I wanted to explain this. Let me try again." If you momentarily forget what you were planning to say, don't despair. Pause a few moments to regain your composure and find your place in your notes. If you can't find your place, ask the audience for help: "I've lost my train of thought—where was I?" There is no need to apologize. In conversation, you pause and correct yourself all the time; to do so in a speech makes you sound spontaneous and natural.

If you make a mistake that causes your audience to snicker or laugh, try to join in. If you can laugh at yourself, your audience will love you—they will see that you are no "stuffed shirt." Some comedians deliberately plan "mistakes" as a technique for gaining rapport with their audiences.

Welcome Experience

If you are an inexperienced speaker, please know that you will learn to control your nervousness as you get more and more practice in public speaking, both in your speech class and in your career. You should welcome this experience as a way to further your personal and professional growth.

One student told her public speaking instructor at the beginning of the course that she just *knew* she would drop out of the class right before her first speech. She stayed, though, and developed into a fine speaker. She later got a promotion in her company partly because of her speaking ability. "I never thought I'd say this," she admitted, "but the experience of giving speeches—plus learning how to handle nervousness—helped me enormously. Before I took the course, I used to panic whenever I started off a talk. I had this enormous lump in my throat, and I thought I was doing terrible. I would hurry through my talk just to get it over with." But as a result of the course, she said, "I learned to control my nervousness and use it to my advantage. Now I'm as nervous as ever when I give a speech, but I make the nervousness work *for* me instead of *against* me."

In your career, rather than shying away from speaking opportunities, seek them out. An old saying is true: experience is the best teacher.

After reading this chapter, if you feel that you need additional tips on managing your anxiety, see the article entitled "Speech Phobia" in the Supplementary Readings on this book's Website (www.mhhe.com/gregory7).

Resources for Review and Skill Building

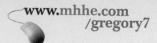

www.mhhe.com /gregory7

This book's Online Learning Center Website and SpeechMate CD-ROM provide meaningful resources and tools for study and review, such as practice tests, key-term flashcards, and sample speech videos.

SpeechMate CD-ROM

Summary

The nervousness engendered by stage fright is a normal, understandable emotion experienced by most public speakers. The major reasons for speakers' nervousness are (1) fear of being stared at, (2) fear of failure, (3) fear of rejection, and (4) fear of the unknown.

Instead of trying to eliminate nervousness, welcome it as a source of energy. Properly channeled, it can help you give a better speech than you would deliver if you were completely relaxed.

The best way to avoid excessive, crippling nervousness is to pour time and energy into preparing and practicing your speech. Then, when you stand up to speak, deal rationally with your nervous symptoms (such as trembling knees and dry throat); remind yourself that the symptoms are not a prelude to disaster, but instead are evidence that you are keyed up enough to give a good speech. Never call attention to your nervousness and never apologize for it; the listeners don't care about your emotional state—they just want to hear your message. Concentrate on getting your ideas across to the audience; this will get your mind where it belongs—on your listeners and not on yourself—and it will help you move your nervousness to a back burner, where it can still simmer and energize you without hindering your effectiveness.

Key Terms

adrenaline, *30*

positive imagery, *33*

positive nervousness, *30*

Review Questions

1. What are the four main reasons for speakers' nervousness?
2. Why are fear and nervousness beneficial to the public speaker?
3. Why is delivering a speech from memory a bad method?
4. Is shyness a liability for a speaker? Explain your answer.
5. How can a speaker reduce excessive tension before a speech?
6. Does an audience detect most of a speaker's nervous symptoms? Explain your answer.
7. Why should you never call attention to your nervousness?
8. Explain the idea, "Think of communication, not performance."
9. Why should speakers not be upset when they see the solemn faces of their listeners?
10. Why should a speaker act as if he or she is confident?

Building Critical-Thinking Skills

1. In an experiment, psychologist Rowland Miller asked college students to do something embarrassing, such as singing "The Star-Spangled Banner," while classmates watched. Those students who reported a great degree of embarrassment thought that their classmates would consider them fools and like them less, but Miller found just the opposite: The classmates

expressed greater regard for the easily embarrassed students after the performance than before. What lessons can a public speaker draw from this research?

2. Imagine that while you are speaking to an audience, you notice that (a) everyone is very quiet, (b) a man in the front is rubbing his neck, and (c) a woman is looking in her purse. Using two columns on a piece of paper, give a negative interpretation of these events in the first column, and then give a positive interpretation in the adjacent column.

Building Teamwork Skills

1. In a group, make a list of the nervous symptoms that group members have experienced before and during oral communication in public (this may include being asked for comments during a class discussion). Then discuss ways to control nervousness.
2. Worrying about future events, say mental-health therapists, can be helpful at certain times and harmful at other times. In a group, discuss the pros and cons of worrying, giving examples from everyday life. Then decide which aspects of speech preparation and delivery deserve to be worried about and which do not.

Building Internet Skills

www.mhhe.com/gregory7

1. Toastmasters International, which has clubs in towns and cities throughout the world, recognizes stage fright as a serious problem for most speakers. Find and print out a list of Toastmasters' tips for handling nervousness.

Possible Strategy: Visit www.toastmasters.org and look for public speaking tips.

2. Many musicians and other performers suffer from stage fright. Find and print out an article that discusses a performer's jitters.

Possible Strategy: Use a search engine such as Google (www.google.com) and type in the keywords "performer" and "nervous."

Using PowerWeb

www.mhhe.com/gregory7

In an article entitled "7 Steps to Fearless Speaking," speech coach Lilyan Wilder has a section on perfectionism. What is her opinion about the role of "devotion to flawlessness" in public speaking? To find this article, visit www.mhhe.com/gregory7, click on STUDENT EDITION and then POWERWEB: CONTENTS.

Heather McConnell of Haworth, New Jersey, listens intently to a speaker at the College of New Jersey. When listeners are engaged and attentive, they not only learn a lot from a speech, but they also help to energize and encourage the speaker.

3

Listening

Outline

The Problem of Poor Listening Skills

How to Listen Effectively

Prepare Yourself

Be Willing to Expend Energy

Listen Analytically

Take Notes

Resist Distractions

Avoid Fake Listening

Give Every Speaker a Fair Chance

Control Emotions

The Listener's Responsibilities

Avoid Rudeness

Provide Encouragement

Find Value in Every Speech

Speech Evaluations

When Evaluating

When Receiving Evaluations

Objectives

After studying this chapter, you should be able to:

1. Explain the difference between hearing and listening.
2. Describe eight keys to effective listening.
3. Define three major responsibilities that listeners have toward speakers.
4. Listen effectively to speeches in the classroom and in the community.
5. Know how to give and receive evaluations of speeches.

In her early days as an emergency room physician, Dr. Joanna Meyer of Atlanta treated a child whose arm and hand had suffered a second-degree burn. After the child had been treated and was being prepared for discharge, Dr. Meyer talked to the parents about how they should care for the child at home. Also listening to her were a half dozen other family members—grandparents, uncles, and aunts. A few hours later, when she came to say good-bye, the family asked her to settle an argument they had been having over exactly what advice she had given.

"As I talked to them, I was amazed," she said. "All of them had heard the simple instructions I had given just a few hours before, but they had three or four different versions. The most basic details were garbled. I was surprised because these were intelligent people."

This episode gave Dr. Meyer her first clue to "something every doctor learns sooner or later: most people just don't listen very well." Nowadays, she says, she repeats her instructions, and even conducts a reality check with some patients: she

Because of ineffective listening by most people, some physicians repeat key instructions and ask patients to state their understanding of the message.

asks them to tell her what they think they are supposed to do. She also provides take-home sheets, which are computer printouts tailored to the patient's situation.[1]

Dr. Meyer's listeners are not unusual. When new or difficult material is presented, almost all listeners are faced with a challenge because human speech lacks the stability and permanence of the printed word. Oral communication is fast-moving and impermanent—"written on the wind."

Studying the art of listening—the focus of this chapter—can help you to better understand and retain key information, and it also can enhance your speaking abilities: As you become more aware of the difficulties of the listening process, you will be able to make adjustments in your presentations—as Dr. Meyer learned to do—to ensure that everyone in your audience receives your message clearly and accurately.

The Problem of Poor Listening Skills

Listening and hearing are not synonymous. **Hearing** occurs when your ears pick up sound waves being transmitted by a speaker. **Listening** involves making sense out of what is being transmitted. As Keith Davis put it, "Hearing is with the ears, listening is with the mind."[2]

hearing
the process by which sound waves are received by the ear

listening
the act of interpreting and evaluating what is being said

In almost all jobs, people spend far more time listening than they spend reading and writing. Yet most of us never receive any focused training in how to improve listening skills. This is strange when one considers that most people are ineffective listeners. According to Dr. Lyman K. Steil of the University of Minnesota in St. Paul, "Tests have shown that immediately after listening to a 10-minute oral presentation, the average listener has heard, understood, properly evaluated, and retained approximately half of what was said. And within 48 hours, that drops off . . . to a final 25 percent level of effectiveness. In other words, we quite often comprehend and retain only one-quarter of what is said."[3]

The problems caused by ineffective listening are staggering in number: instructions misunderstood, equipment broken from improper use, productivity decreased, profits lowered, sales lost, feelings hurt, morale lowered, rumors started, and health harmed.[4] Dr. Steil estimates that listening mistakes each week in American business might cost as much as a billion dollars.[5]

How to Listen Effectively

Though mistakes abound, listeners can be taught techniques to improve their understanding and retention of spoken material, as some American businesses have discovered.[6] To boost productivity and sales, giant corporations such as 3M, AT&T, and General Electric routinely send employees to special listening-skills classes. Troubled by declining sales to 200 "problem accounts," Abbott

Laboratories conducted listening-skills classes for employees handling the accounts. Three years later, Abbott had experienced a $9 million jump in sales to those accounts.[7]

In this section we will look at some specific advice on listening effectively.

Prepare Yourself

Listening to difficult material is hard work, so prepare yourself as thoroughly as a runner prepares for a race.

Prepare yourself *physically.* Get plenty of sleep the night before. If necessary, exercise right before the speech or lecture. Let's suppose that you will be sitting in a warm room in mid-afternoon and are therefore likely to become drowsy and lethargic. You could take a brisk walk before entering the room to make yourself alert.

Prepare yourself *intellectually.* If the subject matter of the speech is new or complex, do research or background reading beforehand. In this way, the speech will be much easier to understand. The American philosopher Henry David Thoreau once said, "We hear and apprehend only what we already half know."

Be Willing to Expend Energy

When you listen to a comedian cracking jokes on TV, do you have to work hard to pay attention? Of course not. You simply sit back in a comfortable chair and enjoy the humor. It is easy, effortless, relaxing.

If you are like many listeners, you assume that when you go into a room for a lecture or a speech on a difficult subject, you should be able to sit back and absorb the content just as easily as you grasp a comedian's jokes. This is a major misconception because the two situations are quite different. Listening to light material requires only a modest amount of mental effort, while listening effectively to difficult material requires work. You must be alert and energetic, giving total concentration to the speech, with your eyes on the speaker, your ears tuned in to the speaker's words, and your mind geared to receive the message.

According to Dr. Ralph G. Nichols, who did pioneering work on listening skills at the University of Minnesota, listening "is characterized by faster heart action, quicker circulation of the blood, and a small rise in body temperature."[8]

If you tend to drift away mentally whenever a speaker begins to talk about unfamiliar or difficult material, try to break yourself of the habit. Vow to put as much energy as necessary into paying attention.

Listen Analytically

You should analyze a speech as it is being presented—not to nitpick or poke holes in it, but to help you understand and remember the speaker's message, and to determine which parts of the speech are valuable to you and which are worthless. There are two elements that you should examine analytically: the main ideas and the support materials.

Focus on main ideas. Some listeners make the mistake of treating all of a speaker's utterances as equal in importance. This causes them to "miss the forest for the trees": they look so hard at individual sentences that they fail to see the "big picture," the larger meaning.

Try to distinguish the speaker's primary ideas from the secondary material—such as facts, figures, and stories—that are used to explain, illustrate, or prove the primary ideas. If a speaker tells an interesting story, for example, ask yourself, "Why is the speaker telling me this? What main idea is the speaker trying to get across to me by telling this story?"

Main points are more important than support materials, as you can see in the sample notes in Figure 3.1.

Evaluate support materials. Effective speakers use support materials (such as stories, statistics, and quotations) to explain, illustrate, or prove their main points. As a listener, you should evaluate these supports, asking yourself these questions:

- Is each main point amplified with support materials?
- Do the support materials seem to be accurate and up to date? Are they derived from reliable sources or are they merely hearsay?
- Do they truly explain or prove a point?

Learning to listen analytically not only will help you become a better listener, it also will help you improve the quality of your own speeches. You will find yourself avoiding the mistakes you see in the speeches of others.

Take Notes

You should take notes whenever you listen to a speech—for the following reasons:

1. *Note taking gives you a record of the speaker's most important points.* Unless you have superhuman powers of memory, there is no way you can remember all of a speaker's key ideas without taking notes.

www.mhhe.com/gregory7

See "Listening Profile" and "Notes" template in Supplementary Readings on this book's Website.

2. *Note taking sharpens and strengthens your ability to listen analytically.* When you take notes, you force your mind to scan a speech like radar, looking for main points and evidence. You end up being a better listener than if you did not take any notes at all.[9]
3. *Note taking is a good way to keep your attention on the speaker and not let your mind wander.* For this reason, it's a good idea to take notes on *all* speeches—not just on important lectures at school. A colleague explains why he takes notes at every meeting he attends, even though he often throws his notes away soon afterward:

    I take notes at any talk I go to. I review the notes right after the meeting to solidify the key points in my mind. Afterwards, I may save the notes for my files or for some sort of follow-up, but I usually throw them away. This doesn't mean that I had wasted my time by taking notes. The act of writing them helped me to listen actively and analytically. It also—I must confess—kept me from daydreaming.

There are many different ways of taking notes, and you may have already developed a method that suits you. Some listeners use a variety of methods because speakers have different organizational and delivery styles, and a method that works with one speaker might not work with another.

Speaker's Words

"Many people don't pledge to become organ donors because they think there is a surplus of organs available. This is tragic because there is actually a dire shortage in all parts of the country, according to the *Los Angeles Times*. Many patients will die while waiting for a desperately needed organ. The situation is especially grim for liver and heart patients. Last year, according to the United Network for Organ Sharing, 7,467 patients were on the national waiting list for a liver; 954 of them—13 percent—died while waiting. For people needing hearts: 3,698 were on the list; 746 died while waiting—that's 20 percent. According to the *Times*, the situation is even worse than these statistics indicate: thousands of people needing organs, such as those injured in car accidents, die before their names can reach the official waiting lists."

Figure 3.1

Two methods of notetaking are shown as Option A and Option B.

Option A

The speaker's message is analyzed and sorted. (See text for details.)

Main ideas	Support material	Response
Shortage of organs	All parts of U.S.	
Many will die waiting	Liver—13% died last year	
	Heart—20% died	Why is heart stat higher?
Situation worse than it looks	1000s die before names can reach lists	

Option B

Because it is sometimes hard to distinguish between main ideas and subpoints while a speaker is talking, some listeners jot down one item per line.

Shortage of organs
All parts of U.S.
Many will die waiting
Liver—13% died last year
Heart—20% died—why higher?
Situation worse than it looks
1000s die before names can reach lists

Later, the listener can analyze the notes, using a highlighter to focus on key ideas and a red pen for follow-up items.

Shortage of organs
All parts of U.S.
Many will die waiting
Liver—13% died last year
Heart—20% died—why higher?
Situation worse than it looks
1000s die before names can reach lists

Tips for your CAREER

Tip 3.1 Take Notes in Important Conversations and Small-Group Meetings

Whenever your superiors and colleagues talk to you (either one-on-one or in a group meeting) about work-related matters, take notes. Not only does this give you a written record of important discussions, but it also is a compliment, a nonverbal way of saying, "Your ideas are important to me—so important that I want to make sure I get them down correctly." Contrary to what some may think, taking notes does *not* signify to others that you have a poor memory.

One of the most common gripes of employees is that "the boss never listens to what we say." So, if you are ever in a supervisory position, take notes whenever one of your subordinates comes to you with a suggestion or a complaint. Doing so demonstrates that you value the employee's comments and are prepared to take action if necessary. Even if you can't take action, the employee's morale is boosted because you have shown you truly listen and truly care.

Can you ever rise so high in your career that you no longer need to take notes? Not if you're Robert Stempel, former chairman of General Motors. Though he headed one of the world's largest corporations and could have hired a platoon of secretaries to take notes for him, Stempel took his own notes at management meetings.

Whatever system you use, your notes should include major points, with pertinent data or support materials that back up those points. You also may want to leave space for comments to yourself or questions that need to be asked.

Two methods are shown in Figure 3.1. In Option A, the first column is designated for main ideas and the second column for support materials. The third column is for your responses—questions and concerns that come to mind during the speech. When the question-and-answer period begins, you can scan the response column and ask questions. (If a question that you jotted down gets answered later in the speech itself, your effort hasn't been wasted; having raised the question will cause you to listen to the explanation with special interest.) The response column also can be used to plan follow-up research (for example, you might remind yourself: "Look up more info on this in library."). The response column does not require an entry for each of the speaker's points; use it only as needed.

Option B is a good choice when a speaker talks fast and does not present his or her material in an easily recognized pattern or does not clearly distinguish between main points and subpoints. Write one note per line. Later use a highlighter to mark the key ideas and a red pen to circle items that you need to follow up on.

Whatever method you use, don't try to write down every sentence that the speaker says. Summarize; put the speaker's ideas into your own words. This will help you make sure that you are understanding the speaker's message. If you try to copy all utterances, as if you were a court stenographer, you would wear your hand out, and you would fall into the habit of transcribing without evaluating.

Soon after a presentation, review your notes and, if necessary, clarify them while the speaker's words are still fresh in your mind. If any parts of your notes are vague or confusing, seek help from another listener (or the speaker, if available).

Resist Distractions

Concentrating on a speech is made difficult by four common types of distractions: (1) *auditory*—people coughing or whispering, a noisy air conditioner, loud music from an adjacent room; (2) *visual*—cryptic comments on the board

Kwon Myoung-hee, front left, and Sun Young-moon, front right, of Seoul, South Korea, listen to a speech at a banquet in Beijing, China. At banquets, listeners often have to try extra hard to concentrate on the speaker's message because of physical distractions (such as difficulty in sitting comfortably) and auditory distractions (such as clattering dishes and bustling servers).

from a previous meeting, a nearby listener who is intriguing to look at, an appealing magazine on the desk or table; (3) *physical*—a headache or stuffy nose, a seat that is too hard, a room that is too hot or too cold; (4) *mental*—daydreams, worries, and preoccupations.

Mental distractions are often caused by the fact that your mind runs faster than a speaker's words. As a listener, you can process speech at about 500 words per minute, while most speakers talk at 125 to 150 words a minute. Thus, your brain works three or four times faster than the speed needed for listening to a speech. This gap creates a lot of mental spare time. Dr. Nichols says:

> What do we do with our excess thinking time while someone is speaking? If we are poor listeners, we soon become impatient with the slow progress the speaker seems to be making. So our thoughts run to something else for a moment, then dart back to the speaker. These brief side excursions of thought continue until our mind tarries too long on some enticing but irrelevant subject. Then, when our thoughts return to the person talking, we find he's far ahead of us. Now it's harder to follow him and increasingly easy to take off on side excursions. Finally we give up; the person is still talking, but our mind is in another world.[10]

How can you resist distractions? By using rigorous self-discipline. Prepare yourself for active listening by arriving in the room a few minutes early and getting yourself situated. Find a seat that is free from such distractions as blinding sunlight or friends who might want to whisper to you. Make yourself comfortable, lay out paper and pen for taking notes, and clear your mind of personal matters. When the speech begins, concentrate all your mental energies on the speaker's message. Two other things you can do to aid your concentration—listening analytically and taking notes—will be discussed below.

Avoid Fake Listening

If you are like most people, you have indulged in fake listening many times. You go to history class, sit in the third row, and look squarely at the instructor as she speaks. But your mind is far away, floating in the clouds of a pleasant daydream. Occasionally you come back to earth: the instructor writes an important term on the board, and you dutifully copy it in your notebook. Every once in a while the instructor makes a witty remark, causing others in the class to laugh. You smile politely, pretending that you have heard the remark and found it mildly humorous. You have a vague sense of guilt that you are not paying close attention, but you tell yourself that any material that you miss can be picked up from a friend's notes. Besides, the instructor is talking about road construction in ancient Rome, and nothing could be more boring. So back you go into your private little world. Only later do you realize that you have missed important information for a test.

Faking attention presents problems outside the classroom as well. It can cause you to botch a personal or business relationship, as shown by writer Margaret Lane's account of an embarrassing instance of fakery:

> Years ago, fresh out of college and being interviewed for a job on a small-town newspaper, I learned the hard way . . . [that] the ability to listen and respond can make all the difference in any relationship. . . . My interview had been going well, and the editor, in an expansive mood, began telling me about his winter ski trip. Eager to make a big impression with a tale of my own about backpacking in the same mountains, I tuned him out and started planning my story. "Well," he asked suddenly, "what do you think of that?" Not having heard a word, I babbled foolishly, "Sounds like a marvelous holiday—great fun!" For a long moment he stared at me. "Fun?" he asked in an icy tone. "How could it be fun? I've just told you I spent most of it hospitalized with a broken leg."[11]

Fake listening is rarely exposed so painfully, but this does not mean that you can get away with deception most of the time. Many speakers are sensitive to facial cues and can tell if you are merely pretending to listen. Your blank expression, your unblinking gaze, and the faraway look in your eyes are the cues that betray your inattentiveness.

Even if you are not exposed, there is another reason to avoid fakery: it is easy for this behavior to become a habit. For some people, the habit is so deeply ingrained that they automatically start daydreaming the moment a speaker begins talking on a subject that seems complex or uninteresting. As a result, they miss a lot of valuable information.

Give Every Speaker a Fair Chance

www.mhhe.com/gregory7
For interactive exercises, visit Chapter 3 of this book's Website.

Don't reject speakers because you dislike their looks or clothes or the organization they represent. Instead, focus on their message, which might be interesting and worthwhile.

If speakers have ragged delivery, or they seem shaky and lacking in confidence, don't be too quick to discount the content of their speech.

Wyatt Rangel, a stockbroker, relates an incident:

> At a dinner meeting of my investment club, one of the speakers was a woman from Thailand who had lived in the U.S. only a year or so, and she spoke English with a heavy accent. It took a lot of concentration to understand what she was saying, and frankly I didn't think a recent immigrant could give me any worthwhile information. I was tempted to tune her out, but I made the effort, and I'm glad I did. She had some good insights into Asian corporations, and I was able to parlay her tips into financial gain a few months later.

Give every speaker a fair chance. You may be pleasantly surprised by what you learn.

Control Emotions

Some listeners don't listen well because they have a powerful emotional reaction to a topic or to some comment the speaker makes. Their strong emotions cut off intelligent listening for the rest of the speech. Instead of paying attention to the speaker's words, they "argue" with the speaker inside their heads or think of ways to retaliate in the question-and-answer period. They often jump to conclusions, convincing themselves that the speaker is saying something that he or she really is not.

During many question-and-answer periods, I have seen listeners verbally attack a speaker for espousing a position that any careful listener would know was not the speaker's true position.

When you are listening to speakers who seem to be arguing against some of your ideas or beliefs, make sure you understand exactly what they are saying. Hear them out, and *then* prepare your counterarguments.

The Listener's Responsibilities

As we discussed in Chapter 1, the speaker who is honest and fair has ethical and moral obligations to his or her listeners. The converse is also true: the honest and fair listener has ethical and moral obligations to the speaker. Let's examine three of the listener's primary responsibilities.

Avoid Rudeness

Are you a polite listener? To make sure that you are not committing acts of rudeness, consider the advice in the following two sections.

Follow the Golden Rule of Listening

If you were engaged in conversation with a friend, how would you feel if your friend yawned and fell asleep? Or started reading a book? Or talked on a cellular phone? You would be upset by your friend's rudeness, wouldn't you?

Many people would never dream of being so rude to a friend in conversation, yet when they sit in an audience, they are terribly rude to the speaker. They fall asleep or study for a test or carry on a whispered conversation with their friends. Fortunately, a public speaking class cures some people of their rudeness. As one student put it:

> I had been sitting in classrooms for 12 years and until now, I never realized how much a speaker sees. I always thought a listener is hidden and anonymous out there in a sea of faces. Now that I've been a speaker, I realize that when you look out at an audience, you are well aware of the least little thing somebody does. I am ashamed now at how I used to carry on conversations in the back of class. I was very rude, and I didn't even know it.

Ethical Issue

Follow the Golden Rule of Listening: "Listen unto others as you would have others listen unto you." When you are a speaker, you want an audience that listens attentively and courteously. So when you are a listener, you should provide the same response.

Reject Electronic Intrusion

In recent years, a new kind of rudeness has become rampant throughout society, says reporter Julie Hill. "Hardly a meeting, presentation, movie, or even church service is not interrupted by the ringing of at least one cell phone and then (even more annoying) the sound of a one-way conversation from the idiot who actually takes the call."[12]

These outrages are committed by people who should know better. "A business student in Milwaukee," writes Hill, "stumbled through an in-class presentation that was worth 20 percent of his grade, painfully aware that his professor was chatting on a cell phone through most of it."[13]

Unfortunately, it is common for some audience members to discuss materials and talk on a cell phone during a presentation. Some people claim they can simultaneously listen to a speech and carry on other activities, but such an attempt is ridiculous and rude.

A laptop computer—which is useful for taking notes—can be another source of distraction. In some classes, every student has a laptop and is connected to the Internet. Instead of listening carefully to the professor, some students send e-mails to one another and play computer games.[14] In a class at Columbia University School of Business, students were observed spending their time in class trading stocks—"occasionally interrupting the lecture with whoops of joy or sighs of pain over their trades."[15]

Because of these rude behaviors, some instructors and other public speakers ban laptops, cell phones, and pagers during presentations.

Here are some rules of courtesy that civilized listeners should heed:

- Don't use a laptop computer for taking notes unless you ascertain in advance that there are no objections from the speaker and the people sitting near you.
- If you have permission to use a laptop, confine yourself to taking notes. Save games and e-mail for later.

Tips for your CAREER

Tip 3.2 Learn How Listeners Show Respect in Different Cultures

While Gail Opp-Kemp, an American artist, was giving a speech on the art of Japanese brush painting to an audience that included visitors from Japan, she was disconcerted to see that many of her Japanese listeners had their eyes closed. Were they turned off because an American had the audacity to instruct Japanese in their own art form? Were they deliberately trying to signal their rejection of her?

Opp-Kemp later found out that her listeners were not being disrespectful. Japanese listeners sometimes close their eyes to enhance concentration. Her listeners were paying tribute to her by meditating upon her words.

Someday you may be either a speaker or a listener in a situation involving people from other countries or members of a minority group in North America. Learning how different cultures signal respect can help you avoid misunderstandings. Here are some examples:

- In the deaf culture of North America, many listeners signify applause not by clapping their hands but by waving them in the air.
- In some cultures (both overseas and in some minority groups in North America), listeners are considered disrespectful if they look directly at the speaker. Respect is shown by looking in the general direction but avoiding direct eye contact.
- In some countries, whistling by listeners is a sign of approval, while in other countries, it is a form of jeering.

For detailed information about different cultures, visit the author's website (www.mhhe.com/gregory7), select STUDENT EDITION, click on WEBLINKS, and explore links for this page.

- Don't speak on a cell phone during a presentation. Even whispers are a distraction.
- When a meeting or lecture begins, turn off any electronic equipment that is capable of beeping or ringing. Some cell phones and pagers have a vibrate option, which can be used discreetly. If you feel a vibration, you can either ignore the signal or (if you think it involves an emergency) you can leave the room before answering the call. In the latter case, don't be disruptive by standing outside the door and shouting into the phone.

Provide Encouragement

Encourage the speaker as much as possible—by giving your full attention, taking notes, leaning slightly forward instead of slouching back in your seat, looking directly at the speaker instead of at the floor, and letting your face show interest and animation. If the speaker says something you particularly like, nod in agreement or smile approvingly. (If the speaker says something that offends you or puzzles you, obviously you should not give positive feedback; I am not recommending hypocrisy.)

The more encouragement a speaker receives, the better his or her delivery is likely to be. Most entertainers and professional speakers say that if an audience is lively and enthusiastic, they do a much better job than if the audience is sullen or apathetic. From my own experience, I feel that I always do better in giving a speech if I get encouragement. Maybe just a few people are displaying lively interest, but their nods and smiles and eager eyes inspire me and energize me.

When we help a speaker to give a good speech, we are doing more than an act of kindness; we are creating a payoff for ourselves: the better the speaker, the easier it is to listen. And the easier it is to listen, the better we will understand, remember, and gain knowledge.

Tips for your CAREER

Tip 3.3 Express Appreciation to a Speaker

Whenever you listen to a speech that you find enjoyable or profitable, let the speaker know. It will provide him or her with much-needed uplift.

Even when presentations seem effective, many speakers sit down with a nagging doubt: Did it go okay? After a major speech, a speaker is often physically and emotionally exhausted. A word of thanks or a compliment from a listener is as refreshing as a cool glass of water given to a dehydrated runner. (If you can't express your appreciation in person right after the speech, write the speaker a brief note.)

Be sure to say something positive about the *content* of the speech. A corporation president told me of a commencement address he had delivered to a college several years before. "I sweated blood for a whole month putting that speech together and then rehearsing it dozens of times—it was my first commencement speech," he said. "When I delivered the speech, I tried to speak straight from my heart. I thought I did a good job, and I thought my speech had some real nuggets of wisdom. But afterwards, only two people came by to thank me. And you know what? They both paid me the same compliment: they said they were grateful that I had kept the speech short! They said not one word about the ideas in my speech. Not one word about whether they enjoyed the speech itself. It's depressing to think that the only thing noteworthy about my speech was its brevity."

Sad to say, there were probably dozens of people in the audience whose hearts and minds were touched by the eloquent wisdom of the speaker—but they never told him.

Listeners exert a tremendous power over the speaker. At one college, some psychology majors conducted an experiment to prove that professors can be as easily manipulated as laboratory rats by means of positive reinforcement. In one political science class, if the professor walked to the left side of the classroom during his lecture, the students would give him approving looks, nod their heads in agreement, and enthusiastically scribble notes in their notebooks. But when he stayed in the middle or walked to the right side of the room, they would lay down their pencils and look away from him with glum expressions on their faces. Before long the professor was spending the entire hour standing on the left side of the room. Carrying their experiment a step further, the students "rewarded" the professor with encouraging looks and nods only if he stood on the left side next to the window and absentmindedly played with the lift cord of the venetian blinds. Soon the professor was spending all his lecture time holding the lift cord, blithely unaware that he was the "guinea pig" in a behavior-modification experiment.[16]

I tell this story not to suggest that you manipulate a speaker, but to show the power that you as a listener exert. Use that power wisely. Use it to encourage and uplift the speaker.

Find Value in Every Speech

Sometimes you will be obliged to hear a speech that you feel is boring and worthless. Instead of tuning the speaker out and retreating into your private world of daydreams, try to exploit the speech for something worthwhile. Make a game of it: see how many diamonds you can pluck from the mud. Is there any new information that might be useful to you in the future? Is the speaker using techniques of delivery that are worth noting and emulating?

If a speech is so bad that you honestly cannot find anything worthwhile in it, look for a how-not-to-do-it lesson. Ask yourself, "What can I learn from this speaker's mistakes?" Here is an example of how one business executive profited from a poor speech:

> At a convention recently I found myself in an extremely boring seminar (on listening, ironically enough). After spending the first half-hour wishing I had never signed up, I decided to take advantage of the situation. I turned my thought, "This guy isn't teaching me how to run a seminar on listening," into a question: "What is he teaching me about how *not* to run a seminar?" While providing a negative example was not the presenter's goal, I got a useful lesson.[17]

"When life hands you a lemon, make lemonade," some wise person once advised. If you look for value or a how-*not*-to-do-it lesson in every poor speech, you will find that the sourest oratorical lemon can be turned into lemonade. "Know how to listen," the Greek writer Plutarch said 20 centuries ago, "and you will profit even from those who talk badly."

Speech Evaluations

Both evaluators and speakers profit from a speech evaluation. Evaluators gain insights into what works and what doesn't work in speechmaking. Speakers can use suggestions to improve their speaking skills.

When Evaluating

SpeechMate CD-ROM

See the CD for the Speech Critique software program that enables you to evaluate speeches, either on a computer or on a printed evaluation sheet.

Evaluating speeches should not be limited to a public speaking class. You also can apply these techniques to speeches that you hear in your career.

Establish criteria. Before you listen to a speech, decide upon the criteria for judging it. This will keep you from omitting important elements. For classroom speeches, your instructor may give you a checklist or tell you to analyze certain features of a speech. Otherwise, you can use the "Quick Guide to Public Speaking" in Chapter 1 for your criteria.

Listen objectively. Keep an open mind. Don't let yourself be swayed emotionally by the speaker's delivery or appearance. If, for example, a speaker sounds ill-at-ease and uncertain, this doesn't necessarily mean that her arguments are inferior. Don't let your own biases influence your criticism; for example, if you are strongly against gun control but the speaker argues in favor of it, be careful to criticize the speaker's ideas fairly and objectively.

Take notes. Jot down your observations throughout the speech. Otherwise, you will forget key items.

Concentrate on one criterion at a time. If you try to evaluate everything at once, you will find your attention scattered too widely. Focus on one item at a time: evaluate eye contact, then gestures, and so on. If time permits, you may want to use videotape to take a second or third look at the speech.

Look for both positive and negative aspects. Emphasize the positive (so that the speaker will continue doing what works well) as well as pointing out the negative (so that he or she can improve).

Give positive comments first. When it comes to public speaking, most people have fragile, easily bruised egos. If you start out a critique with negative remarks, you can damage the speaker's confidence and self-esteem. Always begin by discussing his or her strengths. Point out positive attributes that might seem obvious to you but may not be obvious to the speaker. For example, "You looked poised and confident."

Couple negative comments with positive alternatives. When you point out a flaw, immediately give a constructive alternative. For example, you can inform a speaker that he has the habit of jingling coins in his pocket, and then you can suggest an alternative: "Instead of putting your hands in your pockets, why don't you rest them on the lectern?"

In most cases, ignore nervousness. Because people cannot prevent themselves from being jittery, don't criticize nervousness—unless you can give a useful tip. In other words, saying, "You looked tense and scared" is unhelpful, but saying, "Put your notes on the lectern so that your trembling hands don't rustle the paper" is helpful advice.

Be specific. It is not useful for the speaker to hear generalized comments such as "You did great" or "Your delivery was poor." Be as specific as possible. Instead of saying, "You need to improve your eye contact," say, "You looked too much at the floor."

When Receiving Evaluations

To get maximum benefit from evaluations, follow these guidelines.

Don't be defensive. Try to understand criticism and consider its merits. Don't argue or counterattack.

Seek clarification. If an evaluator makes a comment that you don't understand, ask for an explanation.

Strive for improvement. In your next speech, try to make corrections in problem areas. But don't feel that you must eliminate all errors or bad habits at once.

Resources for Review and Skill Building

www.mhhe.com /gregory7

This book's Online Learning Center Website and SpeechMate CD-ROM provide meaningful resources and tools for study and review, such as practice tests, key-term flashcards, and sample speech videos.

SpeechMate CD-ROM

Summary

Listening effectively is often a difficult task, but it can be rewarding for the person who is willing to make the effort. The guidelines for effective listening include the following:

1. Prepare yourself for the act of listening. Do whatever background reading or research that is necessary for gaining maximum understanding of the speech.
2. Be willing to put forth energy. Since listening is hard work, especially if the material is new or difficult, you must have a strong desire to listen actively and intelligently.
3. Listen analytically, focusing on main ideas and evaluating support materials.
4. Take notes, not only for a record of key points but as a way of keeping your mind from wandering.
5. Resist distractions, both external and internal. Use rigorous self-discipline to keep your mind concentrated on the speaker's remarks.
6. Avoid fakery. Don't pretend to be listening when in fact your mind is wandering; this kind of behavior can settle into a hard-to-break habit.
7. Give every speaker a fair chance. Don't discount a speaker because of personal appearance or the organization he or she represents.
8. Control your emotions. Don't mentally argue with a speaker: you might misunderstand what he or she is really saying.

As a listener you have three important obligations to a speaker: to avoid all forms of rudeness, to provide encouragement, and to find value in every speech. The more support you give a speaker, the better the speech will be, and the more you will profit from it.

Evaluating speeches can help you improve your own speechmaking skills. Look for both positive and negative aspects of a speech, and give specific, constructive suggestions. When you are on the receiving end of evaluations, don't be defensive. Try to understand the criticism and then make improvements.

Key Terms

hearing, *49*

listening, *49*

Review Questions

1. What is the difference between *hearing* and *listening*?
2. Name at least four problems caused by ineffective listening in business.
3. Why should a listener avoid faking attention?
4. What is the difference between listening to easy material and listening to complex material?
5. List at least two ways in which you can prepare yourself physically and intellectually to listen to a speech.
6. The text lists four types of distractions: auditory, visual, physical, and mental. Give two examples of each type.
7. What two speech elements should a listener examine analytically?

8. List three advantages of taking notes during a speech.
9. When you are a listener, how can you encourage a speaker?
10. When you evaluate a speech, how should you handle both the positive and the negative aspects that you observe?

Building Critical-Thinking Skills

1. Some psychologists characterize listening as "an act of love." To illustrate what this statement means, describe a real or imaginary conversation between two people (spouses, close friends, doctor/patient, etc.) who are truly listening to each other.
2. Science writer Judith Stone wrote, "There are two ways to approach a subject that frightens you and makes you feel stupid: you can embrace it with humility and an open mind, or you can ridicule it mercilessly." Translate this idea into advice for listeners of speeches.

Building Teamwork Skills

1. In a group, conduct this role play: one student gives an impromptu speech describing his or her classes this term, while all of the other group members exhibit rude behaviors (chatting, reading a magazine, putting head on desk, solving math problems with a calculator, etc.). Then the speaker discusses how he or she felt about the rudeness. (If time permits, other group members can play the speaker's role.)
2. Working in a group, compile a list of the attributes that would describe "the ideal listener" for a speech. Then do likewise for a conversation. In what ways are the lists similar and different?

Building Internet Skills

www.mhhe.com/gregory7

1. On the Internet, find quotations on the subject of listening and print two that you especially like.

Possible Strategy: Visit the quotations page at the Website of the International Listening Association (www.listen.org/quotations/quotes.html).

2. The Internet contains audio and video clips of famous speeches. What is the date of the earliest audio recording of a speech by an American president? (Exclude silent films and readings or re-enactments by actors.)

Possible Strategy: Visit the PBS archives of Great American Speeches (www.pbs.org/greatspeeches) and investigate dates of audio clips.

Using PowerWeb

www.mhhe.com/gregory7

In an article entitled "Good Listeners Are Better Communicators," Bob Lamons discusses a study on the amount of oral information a student can retain. What difference was found between first graders and high school students? If the study is accurate, what conclusions can be drawn? To find this article, visit www.mhhe.com/gregory7, click on STUDENT EDITION and then POWERWEB: CONTENTS.

Students listen intently to a speech at the University of Pennsylvania. Audiences hope that speakers will feed their minds and hearts—and not waste their time.

4

Reaching the Audience

Outline

The Audience-Centered Speaker

Analyzing and Adapting

Getting Information about the Audience
Interviews
Surveys

Audience Diversity
International Listeners
America's Diverse Cultures
Listeners with Disabilities
Gender
Age
Educational Background
Occupation
Religious Affiliation
Economic and Social Status

Audience Knowledge
Analyzing Audience Knowledge
Adapting to Different Levels of Knowledge

Audience Psychology
Interest Level
Attitudes
Needs and Desires

The Occasion
Time Limit
Purpose of the Occasion
Other Events on the Program
Audience Size

Adapting during the Speech

Objectives

After studying this chapter, you should be able to:

1. Describe the difference between a speaker who is audience-centered and one who is not.
2. Define audience analysis and audience adaptation and state why they are important.
3. Use interviews and surveys to gain information about an audience in advance.
4. Explain how speakers can be responsive to diverse audiences.
5. Describe how speakers can adapt to varying levels of audience knowledge, attitudes, interest, and needs and desires.
6. Explain how speakers should adapt to the occasion (time limit, purpose, and size of audience).
7. Describe how a speaker can adapt to the audience during a speech.

When U.S. astronaut Joan Higginbotham is not flying and working in space, she might be found somewhere on earth giving a speech.

Higginbotham, who grew up in Chicago and became an engineer before joining NASA, gives about a dozen speeches a year. Each speech is different because she tailors her remarks to each audience. Through interviews and e-mails, she finds out in advance her listeners' educational levels and what information they want to know. On the subject of space walks, for example, audiences vary in their interests and how much complexity they can comprehend:

- To a group of elementary school children, Higginbotham may discuss a problem that many kids want to know about: "How do astronauts in a spacesuit eat, drink, and go to the bathroom?" Answer: The spacesuit is really a small spacecraft, with room for food and water containers and a waste-collection system.
- To a high school audience, she might satisfy a curiosity that often arises in her pre-speech interviews with students who obviously have seen a lot of science-fiction movies: "Do astronauts carry weapons in case they encounter enemies in space?" Answer: No.
- To a group of scientists, she might provide technical details on such topics as the spacesuit's elaborate insulation layers that are designed to protect the astronaut from the lethal temperature extremes of space—the side of the suit

Do astronauts carry weapons in case they encounter enemies in space? This is one of the issues discussed by U.S. astronaut Joan Higginbotham of Chicago when she gives speeches about flying and working in space.

facing the sun may reach 250° Fahrenheit, while the other side may get as cold as −250° Fahrenheit.

Just as rigorous preparation is required for success in space, Higginbotham says that it is important for speakers to learn as much as possible about their listeners before a speech because "every audience is different."[1]

The Audience-Centered Speaker

Higginbotham does more than just learn about her listeners in advance. When she speaks, she looks directly at them and talks with enthusiasm. She *connects* with her listeners.[2]

To dramatize the importance of connecting, let's contrast Higginbotham with two speakers who fail to connect:

- Speaker A is a smart student—a computer networking major—but he makes a poor choice when deciding on a topic for his first major speech in his public speaking class. He speaks on "client/server enterprise solutions"—a topic he chooses because he recently has written a report on the subject for a computer class and he figures he can save time by using the same material—without modifying it for nontechnical people. He doesn't stop to think—or perhaps he doesn't really care—that most of the students in the public speaking class are not computer-science majors and will consider his speech boring, incomprehensible, and a waste of time. To make matters worse, he doesn't speak conversationally from notes, but *reads* his report in a monotone voice, scarcely glancing at his listeners, who are soon half asleep.
- Speaker B starts out admirably: She chooses a topic that interests the audience—breakthroughs in genetic medicine—and she is enthusiastic and well-informed about her subject. Unfortunately, when she speaks, she overwhelms her audience. She is a fountain of knowledge, pouring out a huge amount of information rapidly, unaware that listeners need help in processing the material—a patient, unhurried delivery with plenty of explanations and examples. Ironically, this type of speaker causes listeners to drown in information while thirsting for knowledge.[3]

www.mhhe.com/gregory7
For career and community speeches, see "Checklist for Audience and Occasion" in Supplementary Readings on this book's Website.

What these two speakers have in common is a low sensitivity to their audience—a failure to understand and reach the people sitting in front of them.

When you stand before an audience, is your goal merely to deliver a good speech and then sit down? If your focus is yourself or your speech, you will never be an effective speaker. Your goal should be to reach your listeners and change them, so that they walk away with new information or new beliefs or a warm feeling in their hearts.

Tips for your CAREER

Tip 4.1 Develop a Positive Attitude Toward Each Audience

Have you ever seen this old comedy routine on TV? A nervous young man is waiting for his blind date to appear at a prearranged spot. As he waits, he fantasizes how she will react to him. The TV camera captures the fantasies: about when she approaches him, she looks at him with disappointment bordering on disgust. When he introduces himself, she laughs at his name and says it is stupid. When he suggests that they go to a particular restaurant for dinner, she ridicules his idea of good food. When he tries to make small talk, she laughs at his accent. The fantasy goes on and on, from one humiliation to another. Finally, the fantasies fade away as the real, live date appears on the scene. By now, however, the young man is so enraged that he screams at her, "Well, I didn't want to go out with you, either!" and storms away, as the startled woman stands alone, blinking her eyes in confusion.

In like fashion, some speakers indulge in fantasies of audience rejection. When they actually stand up to speak, they act defensive, as if they *know* that everyone in the audience is going to reject them and their ideas. Their "body language"—tone of voice, facial expression, posture—is defensive, sometimes even angry and sullen. I saw one such speaker argue in favor of hunting animals for sport. He knew that some members of the audience were opposed to hunting. From start to finish, he acted as if the audience had just insulted him. "We are not sadistic people who enjoy watching animals suffer," he said angrily. Who said he was sadistic? Who said he enjoyed watching animals suffer? Like the young man waiting for his blind date, this speaker had unnecessarily worked himself into a rage.

Don't prejudge your audience. Most listeners are kind and sympathetic to speakers. Even if they reject your ideas, they usually respect you, as long as you respect them.

Instead of nurturing gloomy fantasies, try to develop a positive attitude toward every audience.

audience-centered speaker
one who tries to establish a meaningful connection with listeners

All good speakers are **audience-centered.** They truly want to make contact with their listeners—to inform, persuade, entertain, or inspire them. Carol Conrad, a student in one of my classes, typified this kind of speaker. In evaluating one of her speeches, another student said, "I had the feeling she was talking to me personally." How did Conrad achieve this success? She composed her speeches carefully, selecting examples, statistics, quotations, and visual aids that would capture the interest of her audience. And when she delivered a speech, she displayed a strong desire to communicate with her audience: she would look her listeners in the eye and speak directly to them. Her tone of voice and facial expression carried a clear message to the listeners: "I care about you, and I want you to understand and accept my message."

Analyzing and Adapting

When Maria Silveira of Boston heard that over 20 million children and adults throughout the world need a wheelchair but cannot afford one, she decided to become a volunteer fundraiser for the Wheelchair Foundation, a nonprofit group that provides wheelchairs for people in poor nations. She gave speeches to business groups in New England, asking wealthy executives to donate $500 apiece.

Silveira was disappointed, however, when few listeners responded to her plea. So she telephoned some of the people who had been in her audiences and tried to find out what was wrong. She learned that her listeners were dubious about the durability of wheelchairs in rough, backward countries. "In primitive conditions," said one listener, "won't the chairs be hard to move around and won't they break down quickly? Isn't this a waste of money?"

Bingo! Silveira had discovered a misconception that she could easily dispel. In subsequent speeches, she pointed out that the foundation's wheelchairs were specially designed for rough conditions, with extra-heavy wheels, robust tires, and additional welding on the frame. Thanks to this new information, she saw a big increase in donations.[4]

Silveira had learned to tackle the two tasks that all audience-centered speakers should perform: (1) **analyze** the listeners to find out exactly who they are and what they know and (2) **adapt** the speech to the listeners' knowledge level and to their needs and interests.

audience analysis
collecting information about audience characteristics

adaptation
adjusting one's material and delivery to meet listeners' needs

customize
to make or alter to a customer's specifications

Some students gain a better understanding of analysis and adaptation when they learn that the process has a synonym—**customizing,** a popular strategy in the business world. If you sell customized vans, you find out what features each customer needs and then outfit the van accordingly. For a person with paralyzed legs, you provide brake controls that are operated by hand; for a carpenter, you furnish special compartments for lumber and tools; and for a rock band, you provide storage space for drums and guitars. Customizing in public speaking means tailoring a speech to listeners' knowledge level, needs, and interests.

Here are some guidelines for customizing speeches.

Prepare a separate analysis of each audience. It is a mistake to think that if a speech works well with one group, it will surely succeed with another. Sometimes it will, but sometimes it won't.

I once delivered a speech that was received with much laughter and applause. So sweet was the success that I delivered the same speech a month later to another group. It was a dud. If I had not been so giddy with success, I would have seen that the second audience had a different educational background and a different set of attitudes. They needed a different speech.

Customize for different segments of the same audience. Many audiences contain subgroups, with the people in each subgroup sharing the same needs and level of understanding. Try to reach all the subgroups. For example, in a speech on traveling abroad, one subgroup—young parents—may want information on recreation options for children, while another subgroup—older travelers—may want information on discounts for seniors.

Ethical Issue

Never sacrifice ethical principles. Customizing does not mean telling an audience whatever it wants to hear. Many politicians—of all persuasions—tell voters that a certain program can be implemented without raising taxes, even though they know this to be untrue. An ethical speaker never lies or distorts information.

Getting Information about the Audience

A speaker's worst nightmare—being laughed at by listeners—came true for Lawrence B. Gibbs.

Speaking to an audience of 1,000 tax preparers at a convention in Las Vegas, Gibbs, who was at the time Internal Revenue Commissioner, said, "What about the gloomy predictions that this tax-filing season would drive taxpayers crazy, confuse them unmercifully, or break them financially?" *[Dramatic pause]* "It just hasn't happened, folks!"[5]

The convention hall exploded with howls of laughter. The tax preparers had just finished a tax season in which the scenario that Gibbs dismissed as nonexistent had (from their perspective) actually occurred. Regardless of whose viewpoint was accurate, Gibbs had revealed that he knew nothing about what his audience felt and believed. If he had interviewed just a few of his listeners beforehand, he could have escaped public ridicule.[6]

You can avoid this kind of blunder by knowing who your listeners are. For some speeches, you already know your audience, such as classmates at school or colleagues at work. But if you're not familiar with your listeners, collect information about them by means of interviews and/or surveys.

Interviews

Start with the program director (or whoever invited you to speak). Find out all that you can about listeners' knowledge level, attitudes, needs, interests, and backgrounds. Also, get details about the occasion—purpose of the event, other speakers on the program, time limit, and size of audience.

Next, ask for the names and phone numbers of a few prospective listeners and interview them—either in person or by telephone—to find out what they already know about your subject, what ideas and information they are hoping to receive from your speech, and whether any particular approach (such as visual aids) works well with this group. When you start your speech, you can thank—by name—the people you interviewed. Doing so will add to your credibility because it shows your desire to meet the needs and interests of your listeners.

Surveys

A good way to get information is to conduct a survey, using a questionnaire to poll listeners' knowledge, interests, and attitudes. A questionnaire can be handed out (in a classroom or elsewhere) or sent via e-mail or postal service.

Let's suppose you are planning a speech on food poisoning, and you want to ascertain whether your listeners know and apply good hygiene. The questionnaire in Table 4.1 shows the types of questions that can be asked:

Question 1: A simple yes/no question tells you the listeners' personal experiences. Probably all have suffered food poisoning, but if a sizable minority has not, you need to describe the pain and danger of the affliction to show that your speech is not about a trivial issue.

Question 2: A scale can probe for the *degree* of knowledge or ignorance on a subject. Do your listeners know about the upsurge of food-poisoning cases in recent years? If the scale indicates they are unaware, you should explain that cases have increased by 30 percent in the last five years—to 325,000 hospitalizations and 5,000 deaths annually.

SpeechMate CD-ROM

To see a speaker who uses a questionnaire effectively, view Speech 4 ("Bicycle Helmets") on Disk 1 of the CD.

Question 3: A multiple-choice question—a type familiar to all students—can gauge whether the listeners know basic food-safety facts. The second item is correct; all the others are commonly held myths. The listeners' answers can help you determine which myths need to be attacked in your speech. (There is no need, of course, to attack a myth if all your listeners know it is erroneous.)

Question 4: People should wash their hands in all of the situations listed in this checklist. Knowing how your audience behaves can tell you which of

Table 4.1
Types of Survey Questions

Yes/No	1. Have you ever suffered from food poisoning? yes ☐ no ☐
Scale	2. Please mark an X on the scale to show how you rate the risk of food poisoning in the United States today as compared with five years ago. ← Much worse — A bit worse — About the same — A bit better — Much better →
Multiple choice	3. Which one of the following statements about food safety is correct? ☐ Freezing destroys bacteria. ☐ Frozen foods that are thawed can be refrozen. ☐ Contaminated food always smells bad. ☐ Raw meat and poultry must be rinsed thoroughly before cooking.
Checklist	4. In which of the following situations do you regularly wash your hands? (Check all that apply.) ☐ Before preparing food ☐ Before eating a meal ☐ After using the bathroom ☐ After handling raw meat ☐ Other (Please specify):
Open-ended	5. Describe how you wash your hands:
Ranking	6. Where do you eat your meals? Rank these places in the order of frequency, from 1 (most often) to 5 (least often). ☐ School cafeteria ☐ Restaurant ☐ Home, prepared by yourself ☐ Home, prepared by someone else ☐ Snack bar (vending machines)
Fill in the blank	7. Food should be placed ____________________ ____________________ while it is marinating.

these matters to emphasize. Note the final "Other" category. This option is often included in questionnaires to cover unforeseen responses, and it sometimes yields surprising and useful answers.

Question 5: An open-ended question—in which a person writes out a sentence or paragraph—is useful when you need a detailed response. In this case, finding out how your listeners wash their hands will tell you whether you need

www.mhhe.com/gregory7
You can use Survey Tutor to create a questionnaire.

to inform them of basics (removing rings, using warm water and soap, and scrubbing for a minimum of 20 seconds).

Question 6: Ranking is a handy way for listeners to show relative importance or frequency. In our food-poisoning scenario, you can find out where most of your listeners eat their food, and then concentrate on food-safety tips for those places.

Question 7: A fill-in-the-blank question is similar to the open-ended question above except that it is designed to elicit only a word or two. If most of your listeners fail to record the correct answer—refrigerator—you know that you must cover the point in your speech.

Here are some guidelines for surveys:

- Keep a questionnaire short. Most people don't have time for a long document.
- Devise questions that yield precise answers. Let's say you want to find out if your audience knows that food should never be allowed to sit at room temperature for more than two hours. A question like "Do you ever leave food out at room temperature for long periods of time?" will give a yes or no answer but fail to determine whether the listener knows about the two-hour limit. Instead ask, "For how many minutes or hours can you safely permit food to sit at room temperature?"
- Before submitting a questionnaire to listeners, test it with a few friends or colleagues, who can point out any confusing questions.

Sometimes the results of a survey can be included in a speech as a point of interest. In your speech on food poisoning, for example, you can say, "According to my survey, half of you wash your hands just by quickly rinsing them. Are you aware that this method is unsafe and can lead to sickness?"

Audience Diversity

In presentations today, you are likely to see a wide diversity of listeners: men and women of different ages, races, nationalities, ethnic groups, religions, economic levels, educational backgrounds, and physical abilities. To be a successful communicator, you should welcome the opportunity to meet the needs of *all* listeners, not just those who resemble you.

International Listeners

The world today is a "global village" of interlocking interests and economies. No matter what field you are in, you must know how to interact with clients and colleagues in many different countries. You may travel overseas for meetings and presentations, or you may give speeches in the United States to visitors from abroad or immigrants to the United States and their families. In classroom speeches, your listeners may include some international students. In these situations, many of your listeners may speak English, of course, but often their command of the language is imperfect.

To meet the challenge of reaching international listeners, consider the following:

Respect taboos. Every culture has its own set of **taboos,** and violating a prohibition can seriously undermine a speaker's credibility. By learning the taboos of a culture, you can avoid committing a blunder like this:

taboo
an act, word, or object that is forbidden on grounds of morality or taste

> Kay Ainsley of Detroit, representing Domino's pizza chain, traveled to Saudi Arabia to negotiate the opening of pizza shops. When she entered a room to give a presentation, all her listeners fled! They refused to return until she had covered herself with an abaya, or traditional long black robe. She had made the cultural mistake of wearing a typical American businesswoman's dress, which is considered indecent in Saudi Arabia.[7]

How do you learn what is taboo in a culture? By consulting an expert, as discussed below.

Learn nonverbal signals. Nonverbal communication cues, such as eye contact and facial expression, vary from country to country. American business executives assume a person who won't look them in the eye is evasive and dishonest, but in many parts of Latin America, Asia, and Africa, keeping your eyes lowered is a sign of respect.[8] A few years ago, some Americans who were trying to negotiate a contract with Japanese executives were happy to see nods of assent throughout the meeting, but were later stunned when the Japanese rejected their proposal. The Americans were unaware that in Japan a nod of assent doesn't mean agreement; it signifies only that the listener understands what is being said.[9]

www.mhhe.com/gregory7
For an interactive exercise on nonverbal signals, visit Chapter 4 of this book's Website.

Are there any nonverbal cues that are recognized by everyone in the world? Not many, say anthropologists. Even the widespread act of nodding the head for yes and shaking the head for no is reversed in some countries, where nodding means no and shaking means yes. The only universals are a few innate facial expressions (such as surprise and sadness) and a few hand movements, such as making a circular motion over the stomach as a signal for "I am hungry." Of all the cues, the most understood and most useful form of communication in both business and personal transactions is the smile, says Roger Axtell, an international-behavior expert.[10] As a Mexican-American proverb puts it: *Todos en el mundo sonreimos en la misma lengua*—"Everyone in the world smiles in the same language." (The smile discussed here is the involuntary expression that all people make when they are happy—not variations such as the embarrassed smile of someone caught in a misdeed.)

Consult experts. Even though you probably don't have time to become well-versed in all the cultures in the world, you can find out what you need to know about a particular culture by consulting an expert—a business traveler or professor who knows the culture well, or a person from the culture, such as an immigrant or an international student. In the early stages of your preparation, interview him or her for facts and insights. After you prepare your speech, conduct a trial run and ask the expert to critique your words, visual aids, and delivery. Emphasize that you want to eliminate any element that could be confusing or offensive.

You also can get tips from the Internet—by browsing at Websites specializing in international cultures and by soliciting comments from people who live or travel in a particular country. For help in connecting to these sources, visit the author's Website (www.mhhe.com/gregory7), click on STUDENT EDITION, and then WEBLINKS, and explore links for this page. Books and articles also can

Tips for your CAREER

Tip 4.2 Work Closely with Interpreters

To ensure that no one is excluded, use a sign-language interpreter for deaf listeners and a foreign-language interpreter for non-English-speaking listeners. Here are ways to enhance the quality of the transmission of your message:

- Even an experienced interpreter can't be expected to smoothly and accurately render all of your terms and phrases on the spur of the moment. Therefore, you should provide a copy of your outline in advance to help him or her prepare.
- If possible, ask him or her to rehearse with you several times, and to alert you if any elements in your speech are likely to be misunderstood.
- In your opening remarks, introduce the interpreter to the audience and express your appreciation for his or her assistance.
- When using a foreign-language interpreter, you will probably employ the popular *consecutive interpretation* method, in which you and the interpreter take turns. Say only a few sentences at a time, so that neither language group gets weary of waiting its turn. (A less-frequent method is *simultaneous interpretation,* in which your words are rendered into a separate microphone a few seconds later for listeners wearing headphones. At large international meetings, a speech may be rendered into many languages simultaneously.)
- To demonstrate your desire to connect with all listeners, learn a few words and phrases from sign language and/or a foreign language to sprinkle into your presentation.
- Even if all listeners are using the services of a sign-language interpreter, you should still talk directly to the listeners, not to the interpreter.

Instructor Caryl Emrys-Peron, left, uses gestures and words to communicate with her English class at Santa Rosa Junior College in California, while Jennifer Jacobs uses sign language and facial expressions to interpret the words for deaf students. Interpreters for the deaf say that their effectiveness improves when they know the speaker's message in advance.

be good sources, but make sure they are recent because cultural information can become outdated.

Be careful with jargon and slang. Avoid using idiomatic expressions such as "cramming for an exam," "bite the bullet," and "the ball is in your court." If you must use jargon, such as "interface" or "virtual reality," explain or illustrate each term.

Maintain a serious, formal tone. Americans are accustomed to speakers using a humorous and informal approach to public speaking, but American presenters who adopt this tone with international audiences are often viewed as frivolous and disrespectful. "Most foreign audiences," says Richard Crum, senior editor for Berlitz Translation Services in Woodland Hills, California, "expect seriousness. An important presentation can be undermined by a presenter who is joking or boastful."[11]

If possible, provide handouts covering some of your main points a day or two before a presentation. (But don't give out lengthy material immediately before or during a meeting—for reasons to be discussed in Chapter 9.) Most nonnative speakers of English have greater comprehension when reading than when listening.[12] If they read the material beforehand, they can find out the meaning of any terms they don't understand, and when they come to the actual presentation, they will have a knowledge base that will maximize their understanding of your remarks.

Provide visual and tactile learning. Can you use visual aids or demonstrations to illuminate your ideas? Can you provide any hands-on experiences?

America's Diverse Cultures

The same sensitivity you show toward international listeners should be extended to ethnic, racial, religious, and other groups in the United States.

Here are some suggestions.

Avoid ethnocentrism. The belief that one's own cultural group is superior to other groups is known as **ethnocentrism.** People who are ethnocentric view the customs and standards of other groups as inferior or wrong.

ethnocentrism
judging other cultures as inferior to one's own culture

In most cases, different customs are not a matter of right and wrong, but of choice and tradition. In some African-American churches, listeners shout affirmative responses during a sermon, while in some other churches, listeners remain silent. One custom is not superior to the other; they are simply different.

Learn the expectations and viewpoints of different cultures and groups. Let's say you are a manager giving an informal training talk to a group of employees and you try to encourage them to ask questions as you go along. Some of the Asian-American employees, however, never ask questions. Before you conclude that these employees are uninvolved and uninterested, keep in mind that for some Asian Americans, asking questions is considered a disrespectful challenge to the speaker's authority.

If you don't know much about the attitudes and viewpoints of an American ethnic group, interview a few representative audience members beforehand to learn about their backgrounds and needs. Also, ask for advice from associates who have had experience communicating with the kinds of listeners to whom you will be speaking.

Focus on individuality. While becoming informed about group differences is a worthwhile goal, treat your knowledge as possible clues, not as absolute certainties. In the example above, notice that I spoke of *some* Asian Americans—not all. If you have Asian Americans in your audience, be sensitive to possible cultural differences, but you should treat these listeners primarily as individuals who may have characteristics that do not coincide with those of other Asian Americans. In dealing with diverse groups, be sensitive to possible differences and special needs, but as much as possible, focus on the individuality of each listener.

Never ridicule any group. Some people think that if no members of a particular group (such as women, gays and lesbians, or minorities) are present, it is all right to make insulting jokes. It is *never* all right. Such slurs are offensive and unfunny to many men and women who don't belong to the group being ridiculed, and they will automatically lose respect for the speaker.

Listeners with Disabilities

Because of laws protecting their rights, and a growing awareness of the contributions they can make to our society, persons with disabilities are increasingly active in the workplace and in their communities. To meet the special needs of these listeners, how can speakers know what accommodations to make? Scott H. Lewis, who describes himself as "a blind Toastmaster" (he's a member of a Toastmasters club in Port Angeles, Washington), has a simple answer: "Ask the disabled participant." Fearful of making a social blunder, some speakers shy away from the best source of information. Lewis says, "Persons of disability know what they need . . . and are the best and most qualified resources to consult when making reasonable accommodations."[13]

Here are some general tips for being sensitive to listeners with disabilities:

- If you ask your audience to gather around you for a demonstration, or if you involve them in an activity, be sure to encourage listeners with disabilities to participate to the greatest extent possible.
- Never treat adults with disabilities as if they were children. Don't use first names unless you are using first names with all others present. Don't speak in an exaggerated, condescending manner.
- Don't equate physical limitations with mental limitations. The fact that a listener is in a wheelchair doesn't mean that he or she has mental disabilities.
- The Easter Seals campaign gives this advice: "It's okay to offer help to a person with a disability if it seems needed, but don't overdo it or insist on helping. Always ask first."[14]
- Never grab the arm of a person with a mobility or visual impairment. Instead, offer your arm.

Now let's look at tips for specific types of disabilities:

Listeners with Mobility Impairments

- Try to remove barriers that would limit wheelchair access. Whenever there is a choice, ask the listener where he or she would like to sit—don't assume that he or she would prefer to be in the back of the room.
- Never patronize people in wheelchairs by patting them on the head or shoulder.
- Don't lean against or hang on someone's wheelchair, which is viewed by the person as part of his or her personal space.[15]

Listeners Who Are Deaf or Hearing-Impaired

- If hearing-impaired listeners must see your mouth to understand your words, try to avoid turning away. At the same time, don't put them in a spotlight by standing directly in front of them and looking at only them.
- "It is not necessary to exaggerate your words," says Deborah L. Harmon, a college counselor for students with disabilities, "although it may be appropriate to slow your rate of speech slightly when talking with people who are hearing-impaired."[16]
- Whenever possible, speakers should augment their remarks with visual aids, says Harmon. "Write technical terms on a board when first introduced," so that deaf audience members can see how the terms are spelled and thus can figure out their pronunciation.[17]
- Be aware that "people in the deaf community and culture," writes social worker Helen Sloss Luey, "tend to perceive deafness not as a disability, but as an alternate lifestyle and culture."[18]

Listeners Who Are Blind or Visually Impaired

- Talk in a normal voice. Just because a person has limited vision, don't assume that he or she has a hearing impairment, too.
- Don't pet or call a seeing-eye dog, says Harmon. Trying to play with it interferes with the performance of its duties. These animals are highly trained work dogs that will not disrupt a speech and thus don't need to be soothed or distracted by you.[19]
- Don't assume that listeners who are blind or visually impaired will not want copies of your handouts. "Even if they can't read them at the meeting," says Sharon Lynn Campbell of St. Louis, Missouri, "they may want to have them read aloud later."[20]
- If you say to a listener who is blind, "Do you see what I mean?" or a similar phrase, there is no need to become flustered or apologetic. The listener realizes that you are using a common phrase out of habit and that you intend no insult.

Gender

The gender of your listeners may give you some clues about their social and economic situation. For example, despite the advances made by women in the workplace in recent decades, many females still receive a lower wage than male co-workers who perform the same job. A speaker trying to persuade workers to join a labor union could stress such inequities if some of the listeners are women.

While gender can sometimes give clues, you should avoid making assumptions based on gender stereotypes. Men may become irritated by a speaker who assumes that only females are interested in issues concerning the health of babies. And women may be annoyed by a speaker who says, "For the benefit of the men in the audience, let me give some tips about buying tools for household repairs"—as if women never buy and use such tools.

sexist language
words based on gender stereotypes

Listeners can lose respect for a speaker who uses **sexist language**—that is, words that convey stereotypes about men or women. Instead of saying "the girl at the front desk," say "Ms. Martinez" or "Maria Martinez." Instead of "the best man for the job," say "the best person for the job." (Sexist language will be discussed further in Chapter 13.)

Abstain from making generalizations about what constitutes manhood and womanhood. For example, Kitty O. Locker, who teaches business communication at the Ohio State University, advises speakers to "avoid terms that assume that everyone is married or is heterosexual." Instead of announcing to employees, "You and your husband or wife are cordially invited to the company picnic," say, "You and your guest are cordially invited to the company picnic."[21]

Age

If you have a variety of ages represented in your audience, be sensitive to the interests, attitudes, and knowledge of all your listeners, giving explanations or background whenever necessary. If, for example, you are talking about a musician who is popular only with young people, you may need to give some information about her music and lifestyle for the benefit of older members of the audience.

Here is an example of insensitivity to the ages of listeners:

> At the graduation exercises of a state university, the commencement speaker told the graduates, "Your parents are proud of you . . . You are now gaining full status as adults . . . You will soon enter the work force . . . You will settle down and raise a family . . ." The speaker was treating all the graduates as if they were in their early 20s—a big mistake, because one-fourth of the graduates in front of him were over 30 and had been in the work force for years. Many of them had already raised a family. One middle-aged graduate said later, "I lost all respect for the speaker. Couldn't he just look at us and see that many of us were mature adults?"

This story illustrates that you need to find out the age range of your listeners ahead of time, and then adapt your remarks accordingly.

Be careful about making generalizations concerning any age group. If an audience is comprised of elderly people, for example, you are wise to consider the fact that many people suffer hearing loss as they age, but you shouldn't jump to the conclusion that you must shout during your speech. Not all elderly persons are hard of hearing, and those who do have problems might be wearing hearing aids. Investigate the needs of your particular listeners instead of relying on generalizations.

Educational Background

Always consider the educational background of your listeners. Avoid talking over their heads, using concepts or language that they cannot understand. Likewise, avoid the other extreme: don't talk down to your listeners. Find the happy medium.

Define terms whenever there's a chance that someone in the audience does not know what you are talking about. Fred Ebel, past president of a Toastmasters club in Orlando, Florida, says that to one audience, "I told a joke which referred to an insect called a praying mantis. I thought everyone knew what a praying mantis was. But I was greeted by silence that would have made the dropping of a pin sound like a thunderclap. Several listeners came up to me and asked, 'What is a praying mantis?' It came as a shock to me until I realized that not everyone had taken a course in biology."[22]

Occupation

Where appropriate, adapt your speeches to the occupational backgrounds of your listeners. The best examples of this kind of adaptation can be found near election time when politicians size up the needs and interests of each audience they face. With steelworkers, for example, the typical politician may discuss competition from Japanese industries; with farmers, soil erosion; with truck drivers, highway speed limits; and with bankers, credit regulations. This approach is not necessarily manipulative or unethical; it is simply good audience analysis and adaptation: steelworkers don't want to hear about soil erosion, and farmers don't want to hear about imports of Japanese steel.

Religious Affiliation

Knowing the religious affiliations of your audience will give you some good clues about their beliefs and attitudes. Most Seventh-Day Adventists, for example, are very knowledgeable about nutrition because of the strong emphasis the denomination places on health; many Adventists are vegetarians and nondrinkers. If you are asked to speak to an Adventist group on a health-related issue, you can assume that the audience has a higher level of background knowledge on the subject than the average audience. You can therefore avoid going over basic information they already know.

While religious background can give you clues about your audience, be cautious. You cannot assume that all members of a religious group subscribe to official doctrines and pronouncements. A denomination's hierarchy, for example, may call for a stop to the production of nuclear weapons, while the majority of the members of that denomination may not agree with their leaders' views.

Economic and Social Status

Be sensitive to the economic and social status of your listeners so that you can adapt your speech accordingly. Suppose you are going to speak in favor of food stamps for the poor. If your listeners have low incomes, most of them will probably be favorably disposed to your ideas before you even begin. You therefore might want to aim your speech at encouraging them to support political candidates who will protect the food-stamp program. If your listeners are upper-middle-class, however, many of them may be opposed to your ideas and you will have to aim your speech at winning them over to your way of thinking.

Audience Knowledge

Thomas Leech, a business consultant in San Diego, California, tells of a manager at an electronics firm who was asked to explain a new electronics program to a group of visiting Explorer Scouts. "He pulled two dozen visuals used for working meetings, went into great detail about technical aspects, and spoke of FLMs and MOKFLTPAC," says Leech. "He was enthusiastic, knowledgeable, and totally ineffective, since his audience was lost for about 44 of his 45 minutes."[23]

This man made a common mistake: failing to speak at the knowledge level of his listeners. To avoid this mistake, find out what your listeners know and don't know about your subject, and then adapt your remarks to their level—as we saw astronaut Higginbotham do in the beginning of this chapter.

Analyzing Audience Knowledge

For most subjects, knowledge is like a ladder, ranging from simple to complex. To move your listeners up the ladder, start where *they* are, not where you are. If you want to teach concepts on the seventh rung of the ladder, but your listeners are at the third rung, it is foolish to think that they can leap over the rungs in between.

To analyze which rungs you need to explain, gather as much information as you can about your audience (using interviews and surveys, discussed above), and then ask yourself four key questions:

1. Regarding my subject, how are the listeners unlike me?
2. What terms and concepts will they probably not understand?
3. What do I need to tell them so that they understand my meaning?
4. What misconceptions might they have?

Let's apply these questions to a real-life incident:

> In a speech on preserving one's valuable possessions, a speaker said, "If you want your most precious color photos to be preserved for your lifetime and passed on to future generations, you need to store all of your prints, negatives, and slides in archival albums."

Do you know what archival albums are? Most of the people in the audience didn't understand the term. A few listeners thought the speaker meant expensive, leather-bound albums, but they were wrong.

The speaker had failed to analyze the listeners' level of knowledge on his subject. Long before the speech, he should have asked and answered each of the four questions—like this:

1. *Regarding my subject, how are the listeners unlike me?* "They are not camera buffs like me. They haven't read dozens of photography magazines and books."
2. *What terms and concepts will they probably not understand?* "They won't understand *archival.* Once upon a time I was as ignorant on this subject as most of my listeners are today, and I didn't know what *archival* meant until I read a number of articles on preserving photographic materials."
3. *What do I need to tell them so that they understand my meaning?* "I'll explain that some plastic photo protectors and pockets contain acids that will discolor and disfigure color prints, negatives, and slides in 15 to 20 years. Archival albums are those whose pages are made of 'good' plastic that will cause no harm."
4. *What misconceptions might they have?* "They might think that any expensive photo album is archival. I'll have to alert them that some expensive albums are time bombs. What one must do is find out what kind of plastic is used. If the plastic is made of polyvinyl chloride (PVC), it is unsafe, but if it is made from mylar, polypropylene, or polyethylene, it is safe—it is archival."

These four questions help you step into the shoes of your listeners. By seeing the world from their vantage point, you enhance your chances of giving a useful speech.

Adapting to Different Levels of Knowledge

What do your listeners already know about the topic? A lot? A moderate amount? Nothing at all? Here are some tips on handling audiences at three different levels of knowledge.

Audiences that know a lot about the topic. Your listeners will be bored and resentful if you waste their time on information that everyone already knows. Instead, give them new ideas and concepts. Early in your speech, reassure them that you will cover new ground. For example, if you are speaking to an audience of advanced skiers, tell them in your introduction that you are not going to spend much time on the well-known, nearby ski resort. Instead, you will give them tips on some good out-of-the-way ski resorts that many skiers don't know about.

Audiences that know little or nothing about the topic.

- Carefully limit the number of new ideas you discuss. People cannot absorb large amounts of new information in a short period of time. If you overwhelm them with too many concepts, they will lose interest and tune you out.
- Whenever possible, use visual aids to help the listeners grasp the more complicated concepts.
- Use down-to-earth language; avoid technical jargon. If you feel that you must use a specialized word, be sure to explain it.
- Repeat key ideas, using different language each time.
- Give vivid examples.

Mixed audiences. What should you do if some listeners know a lot about your subject and others know nothing? Whenever possible, the solution is to start off at a simple level and add complexity as you go along. Suppose you are speaking on computers; you ascertain that some listeners know very little and some know a great deal. You can say something like this: "I hope the computer buffs here will bear with me, but I know that some people in the audience will be confused unless I take a few moments to explain what a disk drive is." The computer buffs will not be upset, because you have acknowledged their presence and their expertise, and they will not mind a little review session (they might even pick up something new). The computer novices, meanwhile, will be grateful for your sensitivity to their inexperience.

Audience Psychology

Your listeners do not see the world the same way you do because they have lived a different life, with different experiences, different mistakes, and different successes.

To understand your listeners psychologically, assess their level of interest, attitudes, and needs and desires.

Interest Level

All speakers want to avoid boring their audiences, but how can you tell if listeners will find your material interesting? Here are some guidelines.

Assess interest in your topic. Ask your listeners—via interviews or surveys—whether they are interested in your topic. You can have a scale, such as, "How does a speech on hunting for dinosaur fossils sound to you? _______ very interesting, _______ moderately interesting, _______ boring."

Maintain interest throughout a speech. Once you have an interesting topic, make sure that you develop it in interesting ways—with examples, stories, and visual aids. Avoid getting bogged down in technical material that will bore the audience.

SpeechMate CD-ROM

To see a speaker who fails to offer her audience new and interesting material, view Speech 1 ("Informative Speech that Needs Improvement") on Disk 1 of the CD.

If necessary, create interest. In some cases, if your audience is not very interested in a topic before you speak, you can generate interest. One student prepared a speech on handwriting analysis, a topic that she knew—from prespeech interviews with audience member—was considered boring. So she began her speech by saying, "Did you know that when you fill out papers for a job interview, some employers send the papers to handwriting experts who claim that they can determine whether you are honest and reliable?" Now the audience found the topic interesting because it obviously had a potential impact on their lives.

One of the best ways to generate interest is to relate your topic to the listeners' needs and desires (as will be discussed later in this chapter).

Attitudes

attitude
a predisposition to respond favorably or unfavorably toward a person or idea

Attitudes are the emotional inclinations—the favorable or unfavorable predispositions—that listeners bring to a speech. Each listener's attitudes are derived from a complex inner web of values, beliefs, experiences, and biases.

Before your speech, try to determine your listeners' attitudes—negative, neutral, or positive—toward your goal, yourself as speaker, and the occasion.

Attitudes Toward the Goal

Unfavorable. If listeners are negative toward your goal or objective, you should design your speech either to win them over to your views or—if that is unrealistic—to move them closer to your position.

A good strategy is to show common ground with the audience. I once saw a woman campaigning for the right of children infected with AIDS to attend a public school in her community. Appearing before an audience of parents who were demanding the expulsion of AIDS children, she began by saying that as the parent of a school-age child, she shared the fears and concerns of her audience. "You and I want the same thing—a safe and healthy environment for our children," she said. Then she explained that she had researched the issue and had found no cases of AIDS children infecting other children at school. She probably failed to win over a majority of the listeners, but she was credited by a local newspaper with lessening the anxieties and anger of parents—no small feat.

Neutral. If your listeners are apathetic or neutral, try to involve them in the issue, and then win them over to your side. For example, if an audience seems unconcerned about the extinction of hundreds of species of plants every year, you can tell them of the many medicines that are derived from plants. For example, digitalis, which is derived from the leaves of the foxglove plant, is used to treat heart disease. "Who knows," you can say, "if one of the many plants that will disappear from earth this year contains an ingredient that could have saved your life someday?" What you are trying to do, of course, is show that the issue is not a faraway abstraction but a real concern that could affect listeners' own lives.

Favorable. If your audience is favorably disposed toward your ideas, your task is to reinforce their positive views and perhaps even motivate them to take action. For example, you might give a pep talk to members of a political party in your community, urging them to campaign on behalf of the party's candidate in an upcoming election.

Attitudes Toward the Speaker

Listeners will have a negative attitude toward a speaker if they suspect that he or she is unqualified to speak on a particular subject. This skepticism can be overcome if the person introducing you states your credentials and expertise. Otherwise, you can establish your credibility yourself at the beginning of your speech. Angie Chen, a student speaker, gave a classroom speech on acupuncture. During her introduction, she revealed that she had grown up in China and had undergone acupuncture treatment herself and had watched it performed on friends and relatives. Though Chen did not claim to be a medical expert, her summary of her experiences showed that she knew a great deal about the subject.

You also can enhance your credibility by explaining how you got your information. Let's say you give a report on recovery programs for drug addicts in your community. In your introduction, it is appropriate to mention that you have read two books on the subject and interviewed a local expert on chemical dependency. This is not bragging; it is simply a way to let the audience know that your information is based on solid research.

Attitudes Toward the Occasion

Sometimes listeners are grumpy because they have been ordered to attend—they are a "captive audience"—and because they think the meeting is unnecessary. With such audiences, give a lively presentation geared to their precise needs. If possible, show an awareness of their situation and your desire to help. Here's an example:

> Computer specialist Don Hansen had to give a four-hour training session one afternoon to a group of employees who thought the training was unnecessary—a waste of time. Hansen began by telling the audience that he knew they were unhappy about the session, "but since you and I have to spend this time together, let's make it as productive as possible." Then he distributed sheets of paper divided into two columns. "In the first column, I'd like you to write down every idea I suggest that you already know. In the second column, I'd like you to write down any new ideas that I present. Afterwards, I will give your lists to management so they can see that your time is being wasted." Pleased that their discontent was being acknowledged, the employees made notes—and most of them were surprised by the end of the afternoon to discover that the new ideas outnumbered the old.

Hansen's sympathetic approach at the beginning dispelled a cloud of negativity that hovered over the occasion, and he made listeners more receptive to his presentation.

Needs and Desires

People want to be healthy, feel secure, have friends, make money, solve problems, enjoy life, and learn interesting things—to name just a few of the many human motivations. If you can offer ways for people to satisfy their needs and desires, they will listen to you with great interest. Here is an example of how one speaker related his topic to the needs and desires of his audience.

> Jamal Young, a community-development specialist, tried to persuade an audience of low-income apartment dwellers to use small-claims court to resolve a complaint against their landlord, whom they accused of refusing to repair an unsanitary sewage system. Here are some of his comments, followed in brackets by the needs he addressed.
>
> - "You don't need an attorney in small-claims court—you speak for yourself. The only cost is a $25 filing fee, and you get that back if you win the case." *[the need to be able to sue without spending a lot of money]*
> - "Many tenants in this city have gone to small-claims court and won. The court has the power to order your landlord to make repairs." *[the desire to avoid wasting time in a fruitless effort]*
> - "Small-claims court is fast. Within a couple of weeks of filing a claim, you'll be in court." *[the need for quick action to protect themselves and their families from unsanitary conditions]*

The more needs and desires you can help listeners satisfy, the stronger your speech.

The Occasion

Find out as much as you can about the occasion and the setting of your speech, especially when you are giving a speech in your community or at a career-related meeting. Here are some issues to ask about; pay special attention to the first one.

Time Limit

Many public occasions are marred by long-winded speakers who drone on and on, oblivious to the lateness of the hour and the restlessness of the audience. Always find out how much time has been allotted for your speech, and *never* exceed the limit. This rule applies when you are the sole speaker and especially when you are one of several speakers. If four speakers on a program are supposed to speak for only 10 minutes apiece, imagine what happens when each speaks for 30 minutes. The audience becomes fatigued and inattentive.

Some speakers have absolutely no concept of time. For a five-minute speech, some of my students talk for 20 minutes and then swear later that they could not have talked for more than five—something must have been wrong with my stopwatch. As we will see later, practicing your speech at home and clocking yourself will help you keep within time limits. If you tend to be a talkative speaker, follow the wise speechmaking formula of President Franklin D. Roosevelt:

- Be sincere.
- Be brief.
- Be seated.

Purpose of the Occasion

A popular columnist for a large metropolitan newspaper was asked to speak at a writing workshop for college journalists. She spent over an hour talking about the celebrities she had interviewed over the years. The gossip was fascinating, but the journalists were disappointed because the stated purpose of the workshop was to provide tips on how to write lively, interesting nonfiction. The speaker gave no tips.

Find out in advance the purpose of a meeting and then make sure you give listeners what they are expecting.

Other Events on the Program

Find out all that you can about other events on a program. Are there other speakers on the agenda? If so, on what topic will they speak? It would be disconcerting to prepare a speech on the life of Martin Luther King and then discover during the ceremony that the speaker ahead of you is talking on the same subject.

Tips for your CAREER

Tip 4.3 Be Prepared to Trim Your Remarks

One of the most exasperating situations you can face is this: because of circumstances beyond your control, your speech comes at the end of a long, tedious meeting when listeners are weary and yearning to leave. Often the best response is to trim your speech. As the following incident shows, the audience will be grateful:

> An all-day professional conference was supposed to end at 3:30 P.M. so that participants would have plenty of daylight for driving back to their hometowns. Unfortunately, most of the speakers on the program exceeded their time limit, and the final speaker found himself starting at 3:18. Without commenting on the insensitivity of the other speakers, he started out by saying, "How many of you would like to leave at 3:30?" Every hand went up. "I will end at 3:30," he promised. Though it meant omitting most of his prepared remarks, the speaker kept his promise. One of the participants said later: "We appreciated his sensitivity to us and his awareness of the time. And he showed class in not lambasting the earlier speakers who stole most of his time. He showed no anger or resentment."

Here's a technique to consider: When I am invited to speak at meetings where there are several speakers, I prepare two versions of my speech—a full-length one to use if the other speakers respect their time limits and a shorter version if events dictate that I trim my remarks.

Even more alarming is to come to a meeting and find out that you are not just giving a speech but are debating someone on your topic. Obviously you need to know such information in advance so that you can anticipate the other speaker's argument and prepare your rebuttal.

Audience Size

It can be unsettling to walk into a room expecting an audience of 20 but instead finding 200. Knowing the size of your audience ahead of time will help you not only to prepare yourself psychologically, but also to plan your presentation. Will you need extra-large visual aids? Will you need a microphone?

It's easier to connect with your listeners if they are close to you physically. If you have relatively few listeners, and they are scattered throughout a big room or they are all clumped together in the back rows, ask them to move to the front and center. Because some listeners dislike having to move, you may have to appeal for their cooperation by saying something like, "I hate to bother you, but it will save my throat if I don't have to shout."

Adapting during the Speech

Adapting your speech to your audience, so important during the preparation stages, must also take place during the actual delivery of the speech. Be sensitive to your listeners' moods and reactions, and then make any appropriate adjustments that you can. Here is an example.

> Using a portable chef's stove, Lester Petchenik, a student speaker, was demonstrating how to cook green beans *amandine.* At one point he sprinkled a large amount of salt into his pan—an action that caused several members of the audience to exchange glances of surprise. Noticing this reaction, Petchenik ad-libbed, "I know it looks like I put too much salt in, but remember that I've got three pounds of green beans in

this pan. In just a moment, when you taste this, you'll see that it's not too salty." (He was right.)

Try to overcome any barriers to communication. John Naber of Pasadena, California, an Olympic gold medalist in swimming, says that he once gave a speech in a room with poor acoustics. Realizing the audience would have trouble understanding him if he stayed at the lectern, he said, "I moved into the middle of the group and walked among them as I spoke."[24]

When you look at the "body language" of this speaker, you know she is an audience-centered speaker who adapts to her listeners during a presentation. She has moved from behind the lectern to get close to her audience and listen to a question. This speaker, who is shown at New Bedford (MA) High School, is Bernice King, a lawyer and minister and daughter of Martin Luther King.

Be sensitive to the mood of the audience. Are listeners bored, drowsy, or restless? Sometimes they are listless not because your speech is boring but because of circumstances beyond your control. It is eight o'clock in the morning, for example, and you have to explain a technical process to a group of conventioneers who have stayed up partying half the night.

Try to "wake up" a listless audience. For droopy listeners, here are some techniques you can use: (1) Invite audience participation (by asking for examples of what you are talking about or by asking for a show of hands of those who agree with you). (2) Rev up your delivery (by moving about, by speaking slightly louder at certain points, or by speaking occasionally in a more dramatic tone).

Don't jump to conclusions. Sometimes it is easy to read audience behavior. If some members of the audience are frowning when you mention a technical term, you know that you need to add a definition. In other cases, however, it is hard to interpret listeners' faces. That man in the third row with a sour face—is he displeased with your speech? Before you jump to conclusions, remember what we discussed in Chapter 2: Some listeners wear grimaces when they are concentrating. In fact, some listeners whose facial expressions seem disapproving often come up to the speaker afterward to express praise and gratitude.

Ethical Issue

Don't compromise principles to win approval. What if, contrary to our example above, listeners' frowns do mean disapproval? Should you alter your speech to make everyone happy? No, of course not. While you should try to be sensitive to the mood of the audience, never compromise your principles or violate your personal integrity simply to win approval. Your goal in public speaking is not to make the audience like you, but to communicate your ideas to them clearly and effectively.

Resources for Review and Skill Building

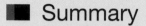

www.mhhe.com
/gregory7

This book's Online Learning Center Website and SpeechMate CD-ROM provide meaningful resources and tools for study and review, such as practice tests, key-term flashcards, and sample speech videos.

SpeechMate
CD-ROM

Summary

To be an effective speaker, concentrate your attention and energies on your audience, and have a strong desire to communicate your message to them. Analyze the listeners beforehand and adapt your materials and presentation to their needs and interests.

To get information about an audience, you can interview the program director or whoever invited you to speak, you can interview a few future listeners, or you can conduct a survey of your listeners.

A wide diversity of listeners—men and women of different ages, races, nationalities, ethnic groups, religions, economic levels, and physical abilities—are likely to be in your audiences.

When speaking to international audiences, learn as much as you can about the culture of the listeners. One of the best ways to learn is to consult an expert. Learn nonverbal signals, be careful with jargon and slang, and maintain a serious, formal tone. If possible, provide handouts covering some of your main points a day or two before a presentation.

Extend the same sensitivity to America's diverse cultures. Avoid ethnocentrism, the belief that one's own cultural group is superior to other groups. Learn the expectations and viewpoints of different cultures, but treat your knowledge as possible clues, not absolute certainties. As much as possible, treat listeners primarily as individuals who may have characteristics that do not coincide with those of others in their cultural group.

Try to accommodate the needs of listeners with disabilities. If you are in doubt about what they need, simply ask them. Never treat adults with disabilities as if they were children, and don't equate physical limitations with mental limitations.

Analyze and adapt your presentations to such factors as age, gender, educational levels, occupations, religious affiliations, and economic and social status.

Consider your listeners' level of knowledge about your material, their level of interest in your subject matter, their needs and desires, and their attitudes toward the goal, the speaker, and the occasion.

Analyze the occasion in order to gather details about the time limit, the purpose of the meeting, other events on the program, and the number of people who will attend.

Be prepared to adapt to the needs of the listeners during the speech itself. Be sensitive to the cues that indicate boredom, restlessness, or lack of understanding.

Key Terms

adaptation, *69*
attitude, *82*
audience analysis, *69*
audience-centered speaker, *68*
customize, *69*
ethnocentrism, *75*
sexist language, *78*
taboo, *73*

Review Questions

1. What is an *audience-centered* speaker?
2. What is meant by audience analysis and adaptation?
3. How can a speaker get advance information about an audience?
4. What are taboos, and why are they an important concern for a speaker?
5. Do international audiences usually prefer a presentation that is humorous and informal or one that is serious and formal? Explain your answer.
6. What is ethnocentrism?
7. Who is the best source of information about the needs of listeners with disabilities, and why?

8. What are the three elements of audience psychology that should be analyzed?
9. What guidelines should be followed for a speech to an audience that knows little or nothing about your topic?
10. What aspects of the speech occasion should you examine before giving your talk?

Building Critical-Thinking Skills

1. Several books provide ready-made speeches that readers are welcome to use as their own. Aside from the dishonesty involved, why would using such speeches be a mistake?
2. At what time of day are you normally least alert? What conditions in a room (such as temperature and noise) cause you to be inattentive? Now imagine that you are a listener in these circumstances. What would a speaker need to do to keep you awake and engaged?

Building Teamwork Skills

1. Work with a group to create a questionnaire aimed at finding out where an audience stands concerning one of these issues: (a) Should "vicious" breeds of dogs such as pit bulls be outlawed? (b) Should the legal drinking age be changed? (c) Should pain sufferers seek relief by means of acupuncture? Use all of the types of questions shown in Table 4.1.
2. In a group, create a list of 10 examples of American slang or jargon that might be misunderstood by visiting physicians from Hong Kong who speak British English.

Building Internet Skills

www.mhhe.com/gregory7

1. Visit three different Websites devoted to cultures, and print out at least one page from each site.

Possible Strategy: Go to Yahoo! (www.yahoo.com). Click on "Society and Culture," then on "Cultures and Groups," and then on "Cultures." You will see a large number of subdirectories for various cultures. Click on any of these to go to Web pages. For example, choosing "Polish" can lead to additional subdirectories about Polish Americans.

2. This chapter describes customizing. Search the Internet for examples of individuals or companies that customize for their audiences. Analyze one of the examples that you find, and explain how it illustrates the concept of customizing.

Possible Strategy: Use a search engine such as AltaVista (www.altavista.com) and enter the keywords "customize" and "audience."

Using PowerWeb

www.mhhe.com/gregory7

In "Globalization and Issues of Intercultural Communications," a speech by Susumu Yoshida, managing director of Sumitomo Chemical Asia, Yoshida relates a story about a cultural misperception that occurred when several U.S. senators met with Japanese government officials in Tokyo. What caused the misperception? To find a transcript of this speech, visit www.mhhe.com/gregory7, click on STUDENT EDITION and then POWERWEB: CONTENTS.

College student Fatima Kassam speaks at Emory University on the culture of southern India, a topic about which she is knowledgeable and enthusiastic. Speakers should always choose subjects that they find exciting and worth sharing with an audience.

5

Selecting Topic, Purpose, and Central Idea

Outline

Selecting a Topic
Select a Topic You Care About
Select a Topic You Can Master
Choose a Topic That Will Interest the Audience
Narrow the Topic

The General Purpose
To Inform
To Persuade
To Entertain

The Specific Purpose

The Central Idea
Devising the Central Idea
Guidelines for the Central Idea

Overview of Speech Design

Objectives

After studying this chapter, you should be able to:

1. Select appropriate and interesting speech topics.
2. Specify the general purpose of a speech.
3. Develop a clear, concise specific purpose statement for every speech you prepare.
4. Develop a clear, coherent central idea for every speech you prepare.
5. Understand how the specific purpose and the central idea fit into the overall design of a speech.

When Charles Long was a student in my public speaking class, I was impressed by his accomplishments (during his first year in college, he had launched a successful computer and 3D animation business), and I encouraged him to speak on the subject he loved passionately—computers.

And yet I worried that Long would give the kind of speech that so many enthusiastic "techies" give: tedious, rambling, too technical, and too long. Fortunately, he avoided these pitfalls—by choosing and developing his topics wisely. For an informative speech, for example, he showed how a computer novice can create simple 3D animations. Using effective multimedia aids, he gave a speech that was interesting and understandable, and devoid of bewildering complexities.

To many listeners, Long's presentation might have seemed easy to prepare—a piece of cake—because he knew the subject so well. But knowing a great deal creates a tough challenge: you must condense a wealth of information into a brief speech without losing clarity and fascination. In Long's case, he had to work many hours to narrow and shape his material.

For your speeches, you can narrow and shape your material if you plan carefully. This chapter will show you how to plan the vital beginning steps—selecting a topic, a general purpose, a specific purpose, and a central idea.

Charles Long, who launched a successful computer and 3D animation company while still in college, took a public speaking course and avoided a mistake often made by computer whizzes.

Selecting a Topic

For many of the speeches that you will give during your lifetime, your topic will be chosen by someone else. Your boss, for example, tells you to give a talk to your fellow employees on a new product. Or you are asked to speak to the Rotary Club on safe driving skills because you are known in the community as an expert on the subject.

SpeechMate CD-ROM

For hundreds of sample topics, see Topic Helper on Disk 1 of the CD.

In most public speaking classes, in contrast, students are permitted to choose their own topics. Given such freedom, some students spend days walking around with a dark cloud over their heads, moaning to friends, "I have to give a speech next week and I can't think of a *thing* to speak on." Don't let yourself get stuck at this stage. Choose your topic as far ahead of your speech date as possible because you will need to spend a great deal of time and energy on other important tasks, such as researching, outlining, and practicing. If you delay choosing a topic, you may find yourself without enough time to prepare the speech adequately.

As you read this chapter, keep a note pad handy and jot down ideas for topics as they come to you so that you will have a stockpile from which to draw throughout the course. In the weeks ahead, you can add to your list as you come up with more ideas.

Here are some important points to bear in mind as you look for a topic.

Select a Topic You Care About

Has anything ever happened to you that was so exciting or interesting or infuriating you could hardly wait to tell your friends about it? That's the way you should feel about your speech topic. It should be something you care about, something you are eager to communicate to others. Are you thrilled by the sport of water skiing? Speak on how to water ski. Are you fascinated by the effectiveness of using a camcorder to record the reminiscences of elderly family members? Speak on making video histories. Are you angry over the rising number of car thefts in your community? Speak on how to foil car thieves.

Enthusiasm is contagious; if you are excited, some of your excitement will spread to your listeners. If you are not excited about your topic, you are likely to do a lackluster job of preparing the speech, and when you deliver it, you will probably come across as dull and unconvincing.

Here are two examples that illustrate how enthusiasm, or the lack of it, can make the difference between a good speech and a poor one:

> In a speech on the death penalty, a student demonstrated that she had done a great deal of research—she gave statistics, examples, and quotations—but she seemed bored by the subject. Showing no emotion on her face and speaking in a monotone, she plowed through a tedious recital of facts and figures. At the end of the speech, she asked for questions or comments, but there were none. Her listeners seemed as listless as she was. After class, her instructor asked her privately if she had any strong feelings about the death penalty.
>
> No, she replied.
>
> Why, then, did she choose that topic?
>
> "Because I thought you would consider it an important topic," the student said. In other words, she chose her topic primarily to impress the instructor.

Now let's turn to the second speaker:

> Kimberly O'Connor gave a speech aimed at persuading her classmates to walk every day for exercise. Her instructor feared that the speech would be boring—after all, everyone knows that walking is good exercise—but O'Connor went beyond the obvious. She showed important features to look for when buying a pair of walking shoes. She demonstrated how walkers can check their pulse rate to determine if they are walking fast enough to receive cardiovascular benefits. She gave helpful tips: When you go to a shopping mall, she advised, park your car at the far end of the parking lot away from the mall. This not only gives you a brisk walk but spares you the stress of jockeying for the best parking places. Throughout her speech, O'Connor's face and voice conveyed a zestful, passionate interest in her subject, especially toward the end, when she related how walking had enabled her to lose 12 pounds in four months and feel much less stressed-out at school. Despite the instructor's fears, the listeners were not bored. On their speech evaluation sheets, their comments included "You've convinced me to walk across campus instead of driving my car" and "Thanks for the tips—I'm going to start today!"

Notice the stark difference between these two speakers. The death penalty is a highly emotional topic, usually a sure bet to capture an audience's interest, but the first speaker succeeded in making it dull because she had a ho-hum-I-don't-really-care attitude. Kimberly O'Connor, on the other hand, took a subject unlikely (at first glance) to have much appeal and made it into a fascinating speech, primarily because she was imbued with a contagious enthusiasm. She *cared* about her subject.

Select a Topic You Can Master

Make things easy for yourself. Speak on something with which you are already thoroughly familiar—or about which you can learn through research. If your listeners realize they know more about the subject than you do, they will lose confidence in you. This reaction can be especially painful if your speech is followed by a question-and-answer period. When I was in college, I was asked to give an oral report on a particular issue in a sociology class; I had no interest in the subject and did little research. After I gave my report, another student, who knew a great deal about the subject, ridiculed my omissions and errors. I felt like an absolute fool. But I learned an important lesson: a person should *never* give a speech unless he or she knows the subject matter extremely well.

Here are several ways to probe for topics about which you know a lot (or can learn).

Personal Experiences

If you are permitted to choose your own topic, start your search with the subject on which you are the world's foremost expert—your own life.

"But my life isn't very interesting or exciting," you might say. Not so. Maybe you are not an international celebrity, but there are dozens of aspects of your life that could make interesting speeches. Here are some examples, all involving students:

- Encountering difficulty in getting a loan for a new car, Carolyn Polonsky learned by trial and error how to go about establishing a credit rating. What she learned she passed on to her classmates in a helpful speech.
- Kirk Dockery worked as a cook in an upscale, high-volume restaurant. With the help of a videotape he had made at work, he showed his audience how orders are coordinated in the kitchen so that all customers at a table receive their dinners, hot and fresh, at the same time.
- Lauren Jones demonstrated how her favorite pastime, climbing mountains, can be carried out safely if one uses proper safety gear.
- Hans Bergenthal had the pleasant experience of adopting a cat from an animal shelter. He told his listeners of the wide variety of animals available for adoption, how much it costs to adopt, what shots the pet will need, and how to make sure the pet is healthy.

SpeechMate CD-ROM

To see a speaker who relates her own personal experiences, view Speech 7 ("Indian Weddings") on Disk 1 of the CD.

These students were *ordinary* people who chose to speak on *ordinary* aspects of their lives, but their speeches turned out the way all good speeches should turn out—interesting. When you are searching for a topic, start by looking for interesting experiences in your own life. Figure 5.1 is a personal inventory that you can fill in to help you identify topics.

After you have filled in the inventory, go back and analyze the list for possible speech topics. If you are not sure which items would make good speeches, ask your friends for advice or consult your instructor. Figure 5.2 is an example of how one student, Lisa Lorenzo, filled in the inventory.

All of the items in Lorenzo's inventory are potentially good speech topics. The best one would be whichever she is most eager to share with the audience.

Exploring Interests

Can you identify a topic that intrigues you—a topic that you have always wanted to know more about? If you choose such a topic, you not only get a subject

When he took a public-speaking class as a freshman in college, Dr. Jonathan Castro chose a speech topic that changed the course of his life. Today he is a volcano expert, shown here holding a volcanic rock. See next page for details.

Figure 5.1
This personal inventory can help you pinpoint speech topics from your own life.

Name: ____________________

Personal Inventory

Jot down as much information about yourself as you can in the categories below.

Work experience (past and present)

Special skills or knowledge

Pastimes (hobbies, sports, recreation)

Travel

Unusual experiences

School interests (academic and extracurricular)

Concerns or beliefs (politics, society, family, etc.)

that is fun to research, but you also gain a stockpile of new and interesting information. Your topic might even influence the direction of your life, as this example shows:

> In a freshman public-speaking class at Humboldt State University in California, Jonathan Castro chose a topic that he had always wanted to investigate—volcanoes. Preparing and delivering the speech ignited a passionate interest that caused Castro to choose volcanology as his life's work. After graduating from Humboldt, he earned a Ph.D. in geology at the University of Oregon, and today he is a volcano specialist at Oberlin College.[1]

Even if it doesn't change the course of your life, an intriguing topic can yield benefits. One student had always wanted to know the safest options for invest-

Name: Lisa Lorenzo

Personal Inventory

Jot down as much information about yourself as you can in the categories below.

Work experience (past and present)
- Crime lab technician
- Free-lance photographer

Special skills or knowledge
- 35mm photography
- Fingerprinting
- Crime evidence analysis

Pastimes (hobbies, sports, recreation)
- Photographing sports events
- Softball
- Volleyball
- Bicycle riding

Travel
- Spain
- Portugal
- Italy

Unusual experiences
- Took pictures at Super Bowl
- Bicycled over 300 miles in Europe

School interests (academic and extracurricular)
- Law enforcement
- Photography for school paper

Concerns or beliefs (politics, society, family, etc.)
- Gangs are outgunning police.
- Spouse abuse must be stopped.
- More bike lanes should be established on highways.

Figure 5.2
The personal inventory from Figure 5.1 as filled in by one student.

ing in the stock market. She researched and gave a speech on the subject, and a year later, she used the information to make her own investments.

Brainstorming

If the suggestions already discussed don't yield a topic, try **brainstorming** (so called because it is supposed to create intellectual thunder and lightning). In brainstorming, you write down whatever pops into your mind. For example, if you start off with the word *helicopter,* the next word that floats into your mind might be *rescue* and then the next word might be *emergencies,* and so on. Don't censor any words. Don't apply any critical evaluation. Simply write whatever comes into your mind. Nothing is too silly or bizarre to put down.

brainstorming
generating many ideas quickly and uncritically

Figure 5.3
A brainstorming guide can be helpful in finding topics.

Brainstorming Guide

People	Music
Places	Sports
Things	Current Events
Health	Social Problems

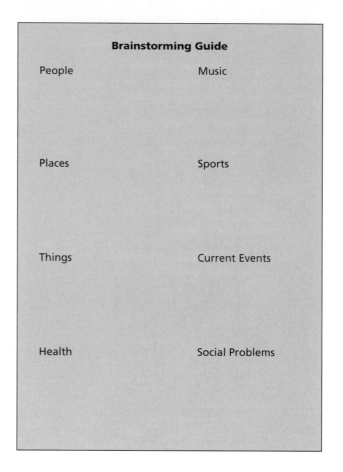

Using a sheet of paper (with categories like those in Figure 5.3), jot down words as they come to your mind. When you finish brainstorming, analyze your list for possible topics. Don't discard any possibility until you have chosen a topic.

Figure 5.4 is a sample of one student's brainstorming notes. Under most categories the student's brainstorming was fairly straightforward. It is easy to see his train of thought. But under "Social Problems," he made some interesting jumps (which is okay; writing down whatever comes to mind is the way brainstorming works). He started with aggressive drivers, a serious problem today. This led him to jot down "highway safety," perhaps because aggressive drivers sometimes cause accidents. This idea led to "air bags," and then his mind jumped to alternatives to automobile transportation—"commuter trains" and "bicycle lanes." His final entry is "pedestrian deaths," a growing problem on urban streets. Any of the ideas in this list could be developed into a strong speech.

www.mhhe.com/gregory7
For printable copies of both the Personal Inventory and Brainstorming Guide, see the Supplementary Readings on the Website.

You may be wondering why you should put all this down on paper. Why not just let all your ideas float around in your mind? The advantage of writing your thoughts down is that you end up with a document that can be analyzed. Seeing words on a page helps you focus your thinking.

Exploring the Internet

A quick and enjoyable way to find topics is to search on the Internet. Here are some good sites:

Brainstorming Guide

People	Music
Tiger Woods	rock bands
Chi Chi Rodriguez	drums
Gabriela Sabatini	synthesizers
Anna Kournikova	Korg
Venus Williams	Kurzweil
Places	**Sports**
Caribbean	snowboarding
Bahamas	skiing
Barbados	ski patrol
Virgin Islands	Alpine skiing
Cuba	ice flying
Things	**Current Events**
wedding ring	immigration
diamond	deportation
pearl	farm workers
ruby	migrant children
sapphire	abuse of immigrants
Health	**Social Problems**
HIV	aggressive drivers
AIDS	highway safety
cure	air bags
AIDS vaccine	commuter trains
mandatory testing	bicycle lanes
stigma	pedestrian deaths

Figure 5.4
One student's entries on a brainstorming guide.

- Pathfinders (ipl.si.umich.edu/div/pf)
- Yahoo! News (dailynews.yahoo.com/fc)
- Librarians' Index to the Internet (lii.org)

For updates and other links, visit the author's Website (www.mhhe.com/gregory7), click on STUDENT EDITION and then WEBLINKS, and explore links for this page.

Choose a Topic That Will Interest the Audience

To engage your audience, choose a topic that is timely, worthwhile, and interesting. A talk on why people need to take vacations would be dull and obvious—everyone already knows why. Instead, give a lively presentation on scuba diving in the Caribbean or backpacking in the Rockies.

Don't try to convince listeners of what they already believe (as the old saying goes, "Don't preach to the converted"). Advocating the value of a college education to a college class is wasted effort. If everyone in the audience didn't already agree, they wouldn't be where they are today.

"I'm excited about my topic," some students say, "but I'm afraid the audience will be bored. How can I know?" Most listeners are bored by speeches that give them no personal enrichment. Their attitude is "What's in it for me?" To see things from their perspective, imagine a typical listener approaching you five minutes before your presentation and saying, "I'm trying to decide whether to stay for your talk. What do I stand to gain by listening to you?" If you realize that you couldn't make a compelling case, change your topic.

This doesn't mean that you must show listeners a dollar-and-cents gain, such as how to make money on the stock market. Perhaps their payoff is purely intellectual—a glimpse into a fascinating subject, such as how filmmakers use computers to "morph" (gradually transform) a human face into that of a werewolf. A speech like this would satisfy the human desire to understand behind-the-scenes tricks—a rewarding payoff. But if the only thing that listeners are offered is a dry and obvious explanation of why computers are popular, they will be bored.

Two other ways to determine whether a topic is boring or interesting: (1) Consult your instructor for his or her suggestions. (2) Several weeks before your talk, distribute a questionnaire to members of the audience to find out how interested they would be in several potential speech topics. For each topic, provide a scale for them to check, ranging from "very interesting" to "moderately interesting" to "not very interesting."

Narrow the Topic

SpeechMate CD-ROM

For handy guidelines, see "Checklist for Preparing and Delivering a Speech" on Disk 1 of the CD.

Once you find a topic, you often need to narrow it. Suppose that you want to give a speech on crime in the United States; 5 minutes—or 20—is not enough time to adequately cover such a broad topic. How about limiting yourself to just crimes of violence? Again, five minutes would be too short to do justice to the topic. How about one type of violent crime—rape? This subject perhaps could be handled in a five-minute speech, but it would be advisable to narrow the topic down even more—to one aspect of the subject: "how to fight off a rapist" or "why some men rape."

Narrowing a topic helps you control your material. It prevents you from wandering in a huge territory: you are able to focus on one small piece of ground. Instead of talking on the vast subject of Native Americans before Columbus, you might limit yourself to describing life in Acoma, a town atop a mesa in New Mexico that has been inhabited by Pueblos since about A.D. 1100.

Ask yourself this question: Is my topic one that can be adequately and comfortably discussed in five minutes (or whatever your time limit is)? If the honest answer is no, you can keep the topic, but you must narrow the focus.

Here are some examples of broad topics that can be narrowed:

Too broad: Native Americans
Narrowed: Shapes, colors, and legends in Pueblo pottery

Too broad: Prisons
Narrowed: Gangs in federal and state prisons

Too broad: Birds
Narrowed: How migrating birds navigate

An important way to narrow your topic is to formulate a specific purpose, which will be discussed later in this chapter. First, let's take a look at your general purpose.

The General Purpose

Establishing a **general purpose** for your speech will help you bring your topic under control. Most speeches have one of the following purposes:

general purpose
the broad objective of a speech

- To inform
- To persuade
- To entertain

Speeches may have other purposes—to inspire, to stimulate, to introduce, to create goodwill, and so on—but these three are the most common.

To Inform

In an informative speech, you are concerned about giving new information to your listeners. You can define a concept (such as hate crimes); explain a situation (how overdosages of vitamin pills cause health problems); demonstrate a process (the correct way to cross-country ski); or describe a person, place, object, or event (a volcanic eruption).

SpeechMate CD-ROM
To see an informative speech, view Speech 6 ("Food Poisoning") on Disk 1 of the CD.

Your main concern in this kind of speech is to have your audience understand and remember new information. You are in effect a teacher—not a preacher, salesperson, or debater. Here is a sampling of topics for informative speeches:

- Protecting oneself in the event of a biochemical attack
- How to make a home or apartment burglar-proof
- Traditional West African drumming and dancing
- Combining studies and vacation in other countries
- Growing vegetables in an organic garden

To Persuade

Your aim in a persuasive speech is to convince the listeners to come over to your side, to adopt your point of view. You want to *change* them in one or both of these ways:

1. *Change their minds.* You try, for example, to persuade them that television cameras should be barred from courtrooms.
2. *Change their behavior.* You try to bring about a transformation in either a positive or negative direction; that is, you try to get your listeners to either *start* doing something they normally don't do (such as using seat belts) or to *stop* doing something they normally do (such as sprinkling salt on their food).

SpeechMate CD-ROM
To see a persuasive speech, view Speech 9 ("Native American Crafts") on Disk 1 of the CD.

Here are some examples of topics for persuasive speeches.

- The dumping of garbage and toxic chemicals into the world's oceans should be stopped.
- A parent who reneges on child-support payments should be forced to pay or be sent to prison.

- The medical profession should make a greater effort to pressure states to deny licenses to physicians who are demonstrably incompetent or impaired.
- State and local governments should increase the number of bicycle pathways built along abandoned railroad rights-of-way.
- Couples should not go into debt for any purchase except a home.

To Entertain

An entertaining speech is aimed at amusing or diverting your audience. It is light, fun, relaxing.

Some students mistakenly think that an entertaining speech is a series of jokes. While jokes are an obvious component of many entertaining speeches, you can amuse or divert your audience just as easily with other types of material: stories, anecdotes, quotations, examples, and descriptions. (For more details, see Chapter 18.)

Here are some examples of topics for entertaining speeches:

- Rehabilitating an injured owl
- Mountain biking and hiking on the Route of the Hiawatha trail on the Idaho–Montana border
- "Jumbo shrimp," "plastic silverware," "freezer burn," "war games," and other oxymorons
- A frequent flyer's nominations for worst airline food
- The Hawaiian folktale of Ru and Hina, explorers of the Pacific
- Being an "extra" in a Hollywood movie was sometimes fun, but involved many boring hours of waiting

The Specific Purpose

After you have chosen a topic and determined your general purpose, your next step is to formulate a **specific purpose,** stating exactly what you want to accomplish in your speech. Here is an example:

specific purpose
the precise goal that a speaker wants to achieve

Topic: Foodborne illnesses

General Purpose: To inform

Specific Purpose: To tell my listeners how to protect themselves from foodborne illnesses

Later, when you create a speech outline, the statement of your specific purpose will occupy a key position at the top of the outline, but it is not a statement that you actually say in your speech. Rather, it is a tool used for planning.

Devising a specific purpose forces you to put your ideas into sharp focus, so that you don't wander aimlessly in your speech and lose your audience.

If you were to choose a topic such as protection of the environment, and then did nothing to bring it into sharp focus, you might make the mistake of cramming too many different issues into one speech. How about protecting national parks? This is more manageable, especially if you emphasized just one specific park:

Topic: Preserving Yosemite National Park
General Purpose: To persuade
Specific Purpose: To persuade my audience to support steps to reverse overcrowding and neglect in Yosemite National Park

Now you have a sharp focus for your speech. You have limited yourself to a topic that can be covered adequately in a short speech.

Here are some guidelines for formulating a specific purpose statement.

Begin the Statement with an Infinitive

An **infinitive** is a verb preceded by *to*—for example, *to write, to read.* By beginning your purpose statement with an infinitive, you clearly state your intent.

infinitive
a verb form beginning with "to"

Poor: Pyramids in Egypt
Better: To explain to my audience how the pyramids in Egypt were constructed

For informative speeches, your purpose statement can start with such infinitives as "to explain," "to show," and "to demonstrate." For persuasive speeches, your purpose statement can start with infinitives such as "to convince," "to prove," and "to get the audience to believe."

Include a Reference to Your Audience

Your specific purpose statement should refer to your audience. For instance, "To convince my listeners that . . ." This may seem like a minor matter, but it serves to remind you that your goal is not just to stand up and talk, but to communicate your ideas to real flesh-and-blood human beings.

Poor: To explain how some employers are using psychological tests to determine whether prospective employees are honest
Better: To explain to my listeners how some employers are using psychological tests to determine whether prospective employees are honest

Limit the Statement to One Major Idea

Resist the temptation to cover several big ideas in a single speech. Limit your specific purpose statement to only one idea.

Poor: To convince the audience to support efforts to halt the destruction of rain forests in Central and South America, and to demand higher standards of water purity in the United States
Better: To convince the audience to support efforts to halt the destruction of rain forests in Central and South America

www.mhhe.com/gregory7

For interactive exercises on purpose statements and the central idea, visit Chapter 5 on the Website.

In the first example, the speaker tries to cover two major ideas in one speech. While it is true that both themes pertain to the environment, they are not closely related and should be handled in separate speeches.

Make Your Statement as Precise as Possible

Strive to formulate a statement that is clear and precise.

Poor: To help my audience brighten their relationships

Better: To explain to my listeners three techniques people can use to communicate more effectively with loved ones

The first statement is fuzzy and unfocused. What is meant by "to help"? What is meant by "brighten"? And what kind of relationships are to be discussed: marital, social, business? The second statement is one possible improvement.

Make Sure You Can Achieve Your Objective in the Time Allotted

Don't try to cover too much in one speech. It is better to choose a small area of knowledge that can be developed adequately than to select a huge area that can be covered only sketchily.

Poor: To tell my audience about endangered species

Better: To convince my audience that international action should be taken to prevent poachers from slaughtering elephants

The first statement is much too broad for a speech; you would need several hours to cover the subject. The second statement narrows the topic so that it can be covered easily in a short speech.

Don't Be Too Technical

You have probably sat through a speech or lecture that was too technical or complicated for you to understand. Don't repeat this mistake when you stand at the lectern.

Poor: To explain to my listeners the chemical composition of vegetable oils

Better: To explain to my audience how to choose the right vegetable oil for cooking different kinds of food

The first statement is too technical for the average audience. Many listeners would find the explanation tedious and over their heads. The second statement focuses on useful information that people can use in their own kitchens.

The Central Idea

In a college class, a counselor from an alcohol rehabilitation center spoke on alcoholism, giving many statistics, anecdotes, and research findings. I did not hear the speech, but afterward, I overheard some of the listeners arguing about

Tips for your CAREER

Tip 5.1 Examine Your Hidden Purposes

In an essay in *Harper's* magazine, Professor Jane Tompkins confesses that earlier in her career, while teaching at Columbia University, she was more concerned about making a good impression than meeting students' needs. "I was . . . focused on: (a) showing the students how smart I was; (b) showing them how knowledgeable I was; and (c) showing them how well prepared I was for class. I had been putting on a performance whose true goal was not to help the students learn but to act in such a way that they would have a good opinion of me."

If other speakers were as candid as Professor Tompkins, they would admit that they, too, often have hidden, unstated objectives that are far afield from listener-focused purposes such as "to inform" or "to persuade." If their purposes were written out, they might look like this:

- To dazzle my boss with my presentation skills.
- To demonstrate that I am smarter and more eloquent than my colleagues.
- To get listeners to like me and consider me a wise and humorous person.

Hidden objectives are not necessarily bad. All of us have unstated goals such as looking our best and delivering a polished speech. But we should eliminate ulterior purposes that make us self-centered and insensitive to our listeners' needs.

We also should eliminate purposes that sabotage our avowed purpose. An architect told me that when he started out in his profession, he was determined to prove that he knew as much about designing houses as his older competitors, so he focused on impressing potential customers with his vast knowledge. "I would give people a long spiel instead of talking about what they wanted to know. Most of them, of course, took their business elsewhere." Once he realized that his hidden purpose (to impress potential clients) was thwarting his avowed purpose (to persuade people to use his services), he began focusing on his listeners' needs and was able to win customers.

it. Several contended that the speaker's message was "Drink moderately—don't abuse alcohol," while others thought the speaker was saying, "Abstain from alcohol completely." Still others said they were confused—they didn't know what the speaker was driving at.

If this happens to you—if you give a speech and people later wonder or debate exactly what point you were trying to make—you have failed to accomplish your most important task: to communicate your **central idea.**

central idea
the key concept of a speech

The central idea is the core message of your speech expressed in one sentence. It is the same as the *thesis sentence, controlling statement,* or *core idea*—terms you may have encountered in English composition courses. If you were forced to boil your entire speech down to one sentence, what would you say? *That* is your central idea. If, one month after you have given your speech, the audience remembers only one thing, what should it be? *That* is your central idea.

As we will see in later chapters, the central idea is a vital ingredient in your outline for a speech. In fact, it *controls* your entire speech: everything you say in your speech should develop, explain, illustrate, or prove the central idea. Everything? Yes, everything—all of your facts, anecdotes, statistics, and quotations.

If you are unclear in your own mind about your central idea, you will be like the counselor who caused such confusion: Listeners will leave your speech wondering, "What in the world was that speaker driving at?"

Devising the Central Idea

Let's imagine that you decide to give a speech on why governments should spend money to send powerful radio signals into outer space. The specific purpose statement of your speech might look like this:

> *Specific Purpose:* To persuade my listeners to support government funding of radio transmissions into outer space

How are you going to persuade your audience? Can you simply say, "Folks, please support radio transmissions into outer space"? No, because merely stating your position isn't likely to sway your listeners. They might say to themselves, "I don't want my tax dollars being spent on some harebrained scheme to beam radio signals into the sky." To convince them, you need to sell the audience on a central idea that, if believed, might cause them to support your position:

> *Central Idea:* Most scientists agree that radio transmissions are the best means for making contact with extraterrestrial civilizations (if any exist).

If you can sell this idea, you will probably succeed in your specific purpose: To persuade the listeners to support public funding of radio transmissions. They will be persuaded because the central idea is so intriguing: Most people like the notion of communication with aliens from faraway planets, and if most scientists back the idea, it cannot be considered far-out and impractical. "Yes," the listeners will say, "let's spend some of our tax dollars to explore the universe."

After you decide upon a central idea, your task in preparing the rest of the speech is to find materials—such as examples, statistics, and quotations—to explain and prove the central idea. In this case, you would need to explain the technology and cite the testimony of eminent scientists who support radio transmissions into space.

SpeechMate CD-ROM

To see a speaker who effectively conveys a central idea, view Video Clip 5.1 on Disk 1 of the CD.

Some students have trouble distinguishing between the specific purpose and the central idea. Is there any significant difference? Yes. The specific purpose is written from your point of view—it is what *you* set out to accomplish. The central idea is written entirely from the listeners' point of view—it is the message *they* go away with.

To learn to distinguish between the specific purpose and the central idea, study the examples in Table 5.1.

In planning your speech, the specific purpose statement should be written first—before you start gathering material. In many cases, you will be able to write the central idea immediately afterward. Sometimes, however, you may need to postpone formulating the central idea until you have completed your research. Imagine that you are preparing a speech on the use of steroids by athletes and bodybuilders. From watching news on television, you know that coaches and health experts are warning people not to use steroids, and you feel certain that your investigation will confirm this view. So you start off with a specific purpose statement like this:

> *Specific Purpose:* To inform my audience of the health risks of using steroids for developing muscles

Table 5.1 How Topics Can Be Developed

Topic	General Purpose	Specific Purpose	Central Idea
Space junk	To inform	To inform my audience about the dangers of "space junk" (dead satellites and bits of expended rocket stages) that orbits the earth	The 9,000+ pieces of debris that orbit the earth threaten commercial and scientific satellites.
Hypnosis	To inform	To explain to my listeners how hypnosis is being used in modern medicine	Hypnosis is being used to relieve pain in cancer patients, burn victims, and backache sufferers.
Buying a car	To persuade	To persuade my audience to avoid high-pressure sales tactics when buying a car	By comparing prices and using reputable car guides, consumers can avoid being "taken for a ride" by car salespeople.
Security guards	To persuade	To convince my listeners that better screening and training are needed for private security guards	Poorly screened and poorly trained, some security guards victimize the people they are hired to protect.
Driving tests	To entertain	To amuse my audience with the true story of my abysmal failure to pass my driving test	Taking the test for a driver's license is a scary and sometimes disastrous event.
Roberto Clemente	To inspire	To uplift my listeners by relating the achievements of Roberto Clemente, the first Puerto Rican player to make baseball's Hall of Fame	Baseball star Roberto Clemente, who died in a plane crash while on a Nicaraguan earthquake relief mission, was an inspiration to millions.

You haven't done any research yet, so you can't really write a central idea. But after you spend a few days in the library, studying articles on steroids, you become able to create your central idea:

Central Idea: Persons who chronically use steroids risk kidney and liver damage, as well as serious mental disorders.

Now that you have a clear statement of the key idea of your speech, your task will be to show the audience that what you say about steroids is true by citing statistics, case studies, and the testimony of experts.

Guidelines for the Central Idea

1. **Every speech should have only one central idea.** Why not two? Or three? Because you are doing well if you can fully illuminate one big idea in a speech. If you try to handle more than one, you run the risk of overwhelming the listeners with more information than they can absorb.
2. **Put the central idea on paper.** It is important that you actually write down your central idea rather than have some vague notion floating around in your mind. Writing it down gives you a clear sense of the direction your speech will take.

3. Limit the central idea to a single sentence. Whenever theatrical producer David Belasco was approached by people with an idea for a play, he would hand them his business card and ask them to write their concept on the back. If they protested that they needed more space, he would say, "Then you don't have a clear idea."[2]

4. Make an assertion rather than an announcement or a statement of fact. A common mistake is to formulate the central idea as a mere announcement:

Ineffective: I will discuss robots as surgeons. *(This is a good topic, but what idea does the speaker want to communicate?)*

Another mistake is to put forth nothing more than a statement of fact:

Ineffective: Several operations at Johns Hopkins Medical Center have been performed by surgeons using robots. *(This is interesting, but it is just a fact—a piece of information that can be included in the speech but does not stand alone as an overarching theme.)*

Now let's turn to a better version—one that makes an assertion:

Effective: Robots are valuable assistants in surgery because they can perform repetitive actions with great precision and no fatigue. *(This is a good central idea because it asserts a worthwhile point that can be developed in a speech.)*

5. Let the central idea determine the content of the entire speech. As you prepare your outline, evaluate every potential item in light of the central idea. Does Fact A help explain the central idea? If yes, keep it. If no, throw it out. Does Statistic B help prove the central idea? If yes, keep it. If no, throw it out.

Let's assume that you want to give a talk on the following:

Topic: Daytime use of headlights

General Purpose: To persuade

Next you write down what you want to accomplish with your audience:

Specific Purpose: To persuade my audience to turn on their low-beam headlights while driving during the day

To carry out your specific purpose, you need to plant one key idea in the minds of your listeners:

Central Idea: Driving with low-beam headlights on during the day is a simple way for American drivers to reduce the risk of traffic accidents.

Now you have your speech in a nutshell. As you decide what to put in the speech, let the central idea control the process. Let's say, for example, that you find an interesting story about how headlights became a standard feature on cars. Fascinating, but does it relate to the central idea? No, so discard it. Next, you discover some research showing a 20 percent drop in car accidents in two foreign countries after low-beam lights during the day were required by law. Does this support your central idea? Yes, so include it.

Overview of Speech Design

How do the items discussed in this chapter fit into the overall design of a speech? If you look at Figure 5.5, which is an overview of a typical plan for a speech, you will see this chapter's items listed in the top ellipse, labeled "Objectives." These items—general purpose, specific purpose, and central idea—are planning tools to help you create a coherent speech. They are *not* the opening words of your speech. The items in the bottom ellipse, "Documentation," are also planning tools and do not represent the final words of a speech. The actual speech that you deliver is shown in the rectangles.

Don't make the mistake of assuming that a speaker should create the rectangles from top to bottom, in the order in which they appear. For reasons that will be obvious later, it makes sense to work on the body first, and then tackle the introduction and the conclusion.

Here is a preview of the next seven chapters, as we learn how to build a speech that is as solid as a brick building. First we will look at how to find raw materials and produce strong bricks (Chapters 6–9). Next we will examine how to sort and organize the bricks—in the body of the speech (Chapter 10) and the introduction and conclusion (Chapter 11). Finally, we will discuss how to put our best bricks together to create a coherent structure (Chapter 12).

All of this work may seem wasteful of your time and energy, but in the long run, they pay rich dividends. They channel your thinking and prevent you from scattering your efforts across too wide a field. They help you fashion an orderly, understandable speech, increasing the chances that you will enlighten, rather than confuse, your listeners.

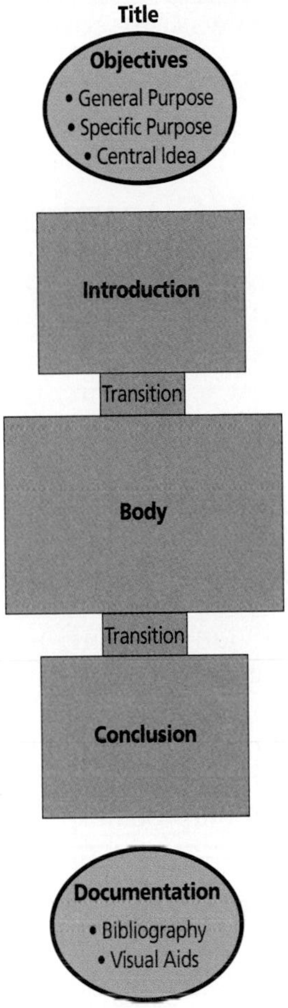

Figure 5.5
An overview of a typical plan for a speech. "Objectives" are explained in this chapter. The other terms will be covered in Chapters 6–12.

Resources for Review and Skill Building

www.mhhe.com/gregory7

This book's Online Learning Center Website and SpeechMate CD-ROM provide meaningful resources and tools for study and review, such as practice tests, key-term flashcards, and sample speech videos.

SpeechMate CD-ROM

Summary

In choosing a topic for your speech, think of subjects (1) about which you care a great deal, (2) about which you know a lot (either now or after you complete your research), and (3) that your audience will find interesting.

In looking for topics, start with yourself. What personal experiences might yield an interesting speech? If you want to go outside your own life, explore topics that intrigue you—subjects about which you have always wanted to know more.

Other methods for finding a topic include brainstorming (writing down ideas that come to your mind) and exploring Internet sites that list subjects for college papers and speeches.

After you choose a topic, decide upon your general purpose in speaking (such as to inform, to persuade, or to entertain) and then formulate your specific purpose—exactly what you hope to accomplish in the speech. Follow these guidelines: (1) Begin the statement with an infinitive. (2) Include a reference to your audience. (3) Limit the statement to one major idea. (4) Make your statement as precise as possible. (5) Make sure you can achieve your objective in the time allotted. (6) Don't be too technical.

Next, write out your central idea: the one key idea that you want your audience to remember even if they forget everything else in the speech. Make sure the central idea is phrased as an assertion rather than an announcement or a statement of fact.

In the long run, these preliminary steps will help you organize your ideas in a coherent, understandable form.

Key Terms

brainstorming, *97*
central idea, *105*
general purpose, *101*
infinitive, *103*
specific purpose, *102*

Review Questions

1. When a speaker is enthusiastic about his or her ideas, how do listeners usually react?
2. How does brainstorming work?
3. What are the characteristics of speeches that listeners find boring?
4. List three *general* purposes for speeches.
5. Are jokes required for an entertaining speech? Explain your answer.
6. List the six criteria discussed in this chapter for writing a specific purpose statement.
7. What is the central idea of a speech?
8. What is the difference between the specific purpose and the central idea?
9. Give an example of an infinitive.
10. What are hidden purposes, and how should you handle them?

Building Critical-Thinking Skills

1. Narrow down the following broad subjects to specific, manageable topics:
   a. Outdoor recreation
   b. Musical groups
   c. Illegal drugs
   d. Saving money
   e. Cloning

2. All but one of these specific purpose statements are either inappropriate for a brief classroom speech or incorrectly written.
3. Name the good one, and rewrite the bad ones so that they conform to the guidelines in this chapter:
   a. To inform my audience of the basics of quantum inelastic scattering and photodissociation code
   b. To inform my listeners about creativity on the job, getting raises, and being an effective manager
   c. To explain to my audience how to perform basic yoga exercises
   d. How persons with disabilities can fight back against job discrimination
   e. Immigration since 1800
   f. To persuade my audience to be careful

Building Teamwork Skills

1. Beforehand, each group member should list five potential speech topics. In your group, evaluate each topic: Is it interesting and appropriate for a classroom speech?
2. In a group, brainstorm topics that would be boring or inappropriate for speeches in your class. Choose one person to write down the topics. Remember that no one should criticize or analyze during the brainstorming session. Afterwards, the group (or the class) can discuss each choice (Does everyone agree? Why is the topic inappropriate?).
3. Follow the instructions for the above item, except brainstorm topics that would be interesting and appropriate for speeches in your class.

Building Internet Skills

www.mhhe.com/gregory7

1. Use the Internet to take the broad topic "American justice" and narrow it to one famous trial. Write a short paragraph describing the trial.

Possible Strategy: Visit Librarians' Index to the Internet (lii.org) and click on "Government and Law" and then "Trials."

2. Find and print a list of topics that would be suitable for a classroom speech. Circle five of the topics and rank them from most interesting (rated "1") to least interesting (rated "5").

Possible Strategy: Go to www.yahoo.com, click on "Society and Culture," and then "Issues and Causes." Select one or more of the categories to see a list of topics.

Using PowerWeb

www.mhhe.com/gregory7

Richard A. Abdoo, president and CEO of Wisconsin Energy Corporation, states his central idea at the beginning of a speech entitled "Coal Is Not a Four-Letter Word." What is the central idea? To find a transcript of this speech, visit www.mhhe.com/gregory7, click on STUDENT EDITION and then POWERWEB: CONTENTS.

If you were buying this diamond ring, says student speaker Ryan Maney, would you prefer to pay $7,000 at a jewelry chain store in a mall or $5,000 at an independent jewelry store? Maney discovered the price difference during his research for a speech on jewelry. He relied on books, Internet searches, and personal interviews with local merchants.

6

Finding Information

Outline

Objectives

After studying this chapter, you should be able to:

1. Use the Internet effectively to find information.
2. Understand why the Internet is sometimes a less desirable source than traditional library materials.
3. Recognize the value of drawing upon personal experiences and investigations in preparing a speech.
4. Find reference works, books, and articles in the library in preparation of your speeches.
5. Conduct interviews with knowledgeable persons effectively and courteously.
6. Develop research strategies for finding materials quickly and efficiently.
7. Take notes with precision, care, and thoroughness.

"The air we breathe," said Dr. Lindsay Bridges, a family physician, "is hurting us." This statement—made during a speech in which Dr. Bridges argued for greater controls over pollution—was provocative and sweeping. Could she back it up?

In the rest of her speech, Dr. Bridges gave an impressive array of facts and figures showing that the quality of air has deteriorated at an alarming rate in the United States in recent years, causing an increase in respiratory problems and a rise in the number of deaths caused by asthma. Her speech was persuasive because she derived her material from rigorous medical studies (reported in medical journals, reference books, and Internet documents) and from interviews with experts and her own asthmatic patients. In other words, she was not spouting mere opinion, but giving credible information based on solid research.[1]

Doing research not only gives you good information, but it also bolsters your confidence. You fortify yourself against the fear of making a fool of yourself—both in a speech and in the question-and-answer period.

Figure 6.1 shows an overview of the options available for gathering information. In this chapter we will discuss all of these options except surveys (which were covered in Chapter 4). In Chapter 7, we will discuss how to *evaluate* the information that you find, paying particular attention to material found on the Internet.

Dr. Lindsay Bridges, a family physician, uses solid research when she speaks out against air pollution.

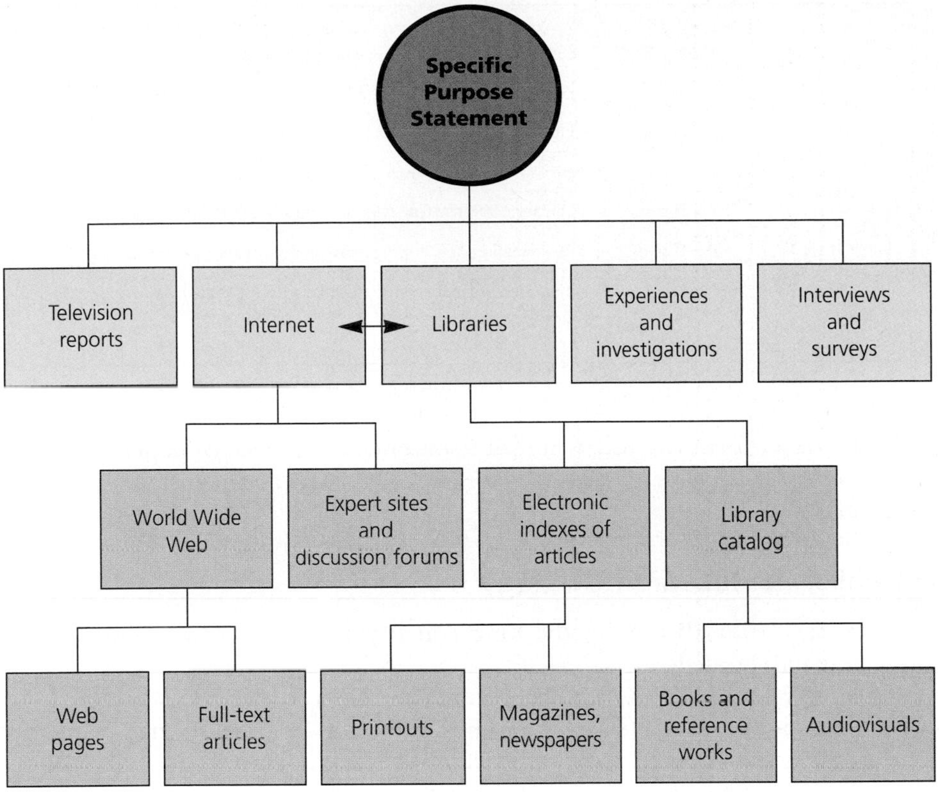

Figure 6.1

Research Strategies

An overview of the primary options for gathering information. The bi-directional arrow between Internet and Libraries signifies that the Internet can be used to gain access to some libraries, while many libraries provide access to the Internet.

Finding Materials Efficiently

Many students fail to come up with good material for their speeches because they spend most of their time in unproductive research. Either they fail to find the right kinds of information, or they get more material than they have time to process. Here are steps leading to productive research.

Start Research Far in Advance

Running out of time is the most common reason students give for not doing adequate research. If you start your research well ahead of the speech date and budget your time sensibly, you should be able to do a thorough job. Because most research takes longer than you anticipate, leave yourself more time than you think necessary.

SpeechMate CD-ROM

To see a speaker who uses research data effectively, view Speech 8 ("The Deadliest Natural Disaster") on Disk 1 of the CD.

Begin with Purpose Statement

You should know the specific purpose of your speech before you start your research, and it should be the guiding light for your efforts.

Some students find it helpful to turn the specific purpose statement into a question. For example, if you had this statement—"To inform my listeners how they can determine if their drinking water is free of dangerous contamination"—you could easily turn it into a question: "How can we know if our water is safe to drink?"

Figure 6.2
Research Schedule
A schedule can help you organize your time. Check off items as they are completed.

☑	Feb. 4	11 a.m.	Call to reserve Internet workstation in library for Feb. 8
☑	Feb. 4	2 p.m.	See reference librarian; explain my topic and get advice
☑	Feb. 5	3 – 5 p.m.	Library: look for info in books and encyclopedias
☐	Feb. 8	7 – 9 p.m.	Surf Internet for info; start with Google
☐	Feb. 9	7 – 9 p.m.	Library: look for full-text articles in CD-ROM databases
☐	Feb. 11	4 – 5 p.m.	Review all notes in preparation for interview tomorrow
☐	Feb. 12	10 a.m.	Interview with Suzanne Ludtke at Pure Water Analysis office, 836 Broadway

Whichever form you use, write your sentence on a piece of paper and keep it in front of you at each step of your research. It will be a constant reminder of precisely what you are searching for.

Establish a Research Strategy

You can save yourself time in the long run if you spend a few minutes devising a research strategy.

Decide whom you will consult, such as librarians and interviewees, and call to make appointments. Decide which library resources you will investigate.

Devise a schedule, such as the sample shown in Figure 6.2. Post the schedule in a conspicuous place in your room, or carry it with you. Try to abide by it.

Using Research Sources Wisely

Researchers can choose from a vast array of powerful resources. In this section we will focus on the ones that are most useful.

Getting Help

Librarians

A library is a wonderful treasury of resources for your speeches. Your campus library is the best place to begin; a public library is a good second choice; and your community also may have specialized libraries maintained by historical societies, museums, professional associations, law firms, medical societies, and large businesses.

Rather than wandering inside a library hoping to stumble upon good information, seek help from library staff members. An important part of their job is helping patrons find materials, so don't be shy about asking for help.

When you start your research, introduce yourself to a member of the library staff and explain the nature of your project. In large libraries, there is usually at least one reference librarian whose sole job is to help people track down information. Many reference librarians are experts on searching the Internet.

Most libraries offer handouts on what services are provided, and they frequently provide guided tours or videotaped presentations on library offerings. Look for information near the library entrance or checkout desk.

InterLibrary Loan

If your college or public library lacks a book or magazine article that you need, don't despair—use **interlibrary loan.** For a book, librarians can perform a search (often very quick and computerized) of other libraries in your state or region until they find it and borrow it for you. It often takes less than two weeks to get the book, and usually there is no charge. For a magazine article, the librarians will find a library that carries the publication and request a photocopy of the article. A photocopying fee (typically 10 cents per page) is sometimes charged. (Some libraries are members of regional consortia and offer free services between cooperating libraries.)

interlibrary loan
sharing of materials and services among libraries

While inter-library loan is a good resource, you cannot count on a quick response to your request; some books and periodicals are hard to locate, and mail delivery can be slow. Ask your librarian for details.

A Guide to the Internet

The **Internet** is a global supernetwork linking thousands of computer networks in order to share information. It has become a popular avenue for research in colleges and in professional life.

Internet
a vast network of networks, linking computers throughout the world

Common Misconceptions

The success of the Internet has given rise to some misconceptions about its role in research:

Misconception: The Internet has everything a researcher needs, so traditional library resources are superfluous.

Reality: Printed materials in libraries are superior to the Internet in many ways. Take books, for example. The Internet has a relatively small number of books, most of them literary classics whose copyrights have expired: the novels of Jane Austen, the plays of William Shakespeare, the speeches of Frederick Douglass. Libraries, in contrast, have thousands of books, including expensive reference works, that aren't on the Internet. Books offer greater depth and elaboration than you can find on the Internet. If you are studying the travels of migratory birds, for example, you can find dozens of books with rich, detailed information, while the Internet material merely skims the surface.

Misconception: If you have a personal computer and Internet access, you don't need a library's electronic services.

Reality: Although you can find a lot of material on your own by using the Internet, your college library can provide access to high-quality information that is not available to the general Internet user. Libraries purchase databases (via Internet licensing or CD-ROMs) that contain thousands of full-text articles from newspapers, magazines, and scholarly journals on a wide range of topics. Under terms of contract, only a library's patrons are permitted access. You have to go to the library itself and use its computers, or, in some cases, you can use an access code to enter the databases from a personal computer at a remote location. (Ask your librarians for details.)

Websites

Imagine an immense multimedia encyclopedia containing over 200 million items—text pages, color pictures, video clips, and audio programs. Now imagine that those 200 million items are scattered here and there throughout the world.

What you are picturing is the **World Wide Web,** the part of the Internet that you, as a researcher, are most likely to use. The Web is a linkage of thousands of farflung **sites,** or locations. Each site contains **Web pages,** or documents. Some sites have only a few pages, while others have hundreds. (Though pages, technically, are the different parts of a site, most people use the terms "Website" and "Web page" interchangeably.) When you browse the Web, you usually see only one Web page at a time.

World Wide Web
a global Internet system for delivering and displaying documents that may contain images, sound, and video as well as text

Website
any location on the World Wide Web

Web page
the file you see on the screen when you are visiting a Website

hyperlink
a highlighted word or picture that when clicked transports you to another place within a document or to another Website

Hyperlinks. What makes the Web a powerful research instrument is **hyperlinks,** a way of transporting you from one Web page to a different, but related, page. Let's say you are looking at a Web page on pop music and you see an underlined, highlighted reference to a Web page on famous singers. You click on this hyperlink with your mouse, and your computer takes you to a new Web page that lists the five top-selling singers. You click on the name Céline Dion and then listen to a performance by the French-Canadian chanteuse. While at this page, you see a hyperlink for a biography of Dion, so you click on this link and read the story of her life, including her childhood in a poor but musical family in a Quebec village. As you proceed, you visit dozens of different pages, gathering a rich variety of information.

Basic Procedures. To access and use Websites, follow these steps:

1. Connect to the Internet.
2. Type in an address (also known as **URL,** or Uniform Resource Locator). Don't add spaces. Don't use capital letters unless they are part of the address. For example, the address for the president of the United States is www.whitehouse.gov.
3. If you don't know an address, use a **search engine.** In the opening screen of a search engine, type in **keywords,** and the search engine will try to find Websites that mention your keywords. If it is successful, it will display a list of results—called "hits." Click on a site that looks promising, and you will be transported to it.
4. If you want to visit sites of related interest, look for hyperlinks, which are always underlined and sometimes printed in a color that is different from surrounding text. When you click on a hyperlink, you will be transferred to its site.
5. If you want to return to Web pages that you have just visited, you can click on the "Back" button at the top of your screen. There is also a "Forward" button. This procedure lets you move backwards and forwards a few steps, and then head off in a different direction.

URL (rhymes with "hurl")
Uniform Resource Locator; the address of a Website

search engine
a service that lets you search for keywords on Web pages throughout the world

keyword
a word looked for in a search command

6. If you are using your own computer, save time in the long run by creating a permanent list of sites that you like and may want to visit again. These indexed sites are called **bookmarks,** or **favorites.** To index the site that you are currently visiting, go to the Bookmarks (or Favorites) menu at the top of your screen and click on Add Bookmark (or Add to Favorites).
7. Print any pages you want for later reference. An alternative is to download pages onto a hard drive, CD-R, or a diskette for later use; choose "Print to file" under the Print menu. (If you want to download a graphic, you must click on it and choose "Save as . . ." from the File menu.)
8. In order to document your sources (discussed later in this chapter), make note of the Internet address of any Web page from which you draw information. (Having the address will also come in handy if you want to return to a site later.) The address appears at the top of the page and looks like the Web addresses in this chapter except that it might be preceded by "http," which stands for HyperText Transport Protocol. This is technically part of the address but is no longer needed when accessing Web pages.

bookmark (or favorite)
link to a Website that you want to revisit in the future

Expert Sites and Discussion Forums

Suppose that you want to find out the best books to read to small children. Or maybe you want to discover whether extremely loud music can damage one's hearing. To find answers to such questions, you can often go to the Internet and find people who are eager and willing to share their expertise and knowledge.

For public speakers, two types of Websites are especially useful:

Expert sites are question-and-answer services that sometimes provide information that you cannot get anywhere else on the Internet. But beware: the quality varies. Some sites have top people in a given field, while other sites have self-chosen experts whose expertise may be dubious. Therefore, you should be cautious, using some of the evaluation techniques discussed in Chapter 7. For addresses of expert sites, see Table 6.1.

expert site
a Website offering expertise on requested topics

Discussion forums (sometimes called newsgroups) are message centers where people who have similar interests can share ideas and observations. Forums are devoted to a wide variety of topics, such as how to prepare delicious meals, where to find a job, and how to repair a computer. For a researcher, the vital part of a forum is its archives. Messages are organized by "threads"—that is, all the messages that deal with an original query can be viewed, one after another. For example, one person asked for comments about a company that was offering her a college scholarship. In response, over a dozen people from different geographic regions posted messages warning that they had been defrauded by the company's scholarship scam. All of these messages, organized by thread, can be viewed sequentially in the archives.

discussion forum
a message center for people with a common interest

Note of caution: While it is acceptable to ask a discussion forum for help with small, specific items, don't ask the group to prepare a speech for you. Such a query is not only unethical, but unwise. People in forums are friendly and generous, but they get irritated when a lazy student writes, "I've got to give a speech next week on the death penalty, and I'd appreciate all the help I can get."

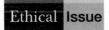

Ethical Issue

To access discussion forums, visit the sites listed in Table 6.1.

Internet Search Tools

There's a vast amount of information on the Internet, but finding what you need is sometimes difficult. It's like searching for tiny nuggets of gold in huge piles of dirt. To find the gold, use subject directories and search engines.

Subject Directories

Subject directory
a list of Websites categorized by subject

A good place to begin an Internet search is a **subject directory,** a catalog that starts off with broad subject areas, which are then subdivided into smaller categories. This structure helps you drill down from broad to narrow topics.

Table 6.1 Internet Search Tools

Internet addresses and features sometimes change. For an update on these search options, visit this book's Website (www.mhhe.com/gregory7), click on STUDENT EDITION and then WEBLINKS, and look at notes for this page.	
Search Engines	
Google www.google.com	A fast and comprehensive search engine, Google is the first option that many searchers try. Its "Advanced Search" feature is worth learning and using.
AltaVista www.altavista.com	Select AltaVista's "Advanced Search" for highly sophisticated features such as "NEAR."
Ixquick www.ixquick.com **MetaCrawler** www.metacrawler.com	Ixquick and MetaCrawler are meta-search engines that collect results from over a dozen search engines at once. This prowess sounds impressive—and sometimes meta-search engines do find what you want—but for difficult-to-find material, a single search engine is superior.
Subject Directories	
Yahoo www.yahoo.com	Although Yahoo has a search feature, its strength is its directory. Select a broad category and "drill down" to narrower and narrower subcategories. For example, to find documents on cloning, select these headings in succession: Science > Biology > Genetics > Cloning.
About www.about.com	Use this site as a subject directory first, and then—if you still haven't found what you're looking for—try its search feature. Each category on the Website is hosted by a man or woman who is identified as a guide, or expert.
Gateways to Specialized Resources	
Librarians' Index to the Internet www.lii.org	Librarians at the University of California, Berkeley, created this site for their campus and then made it available to students throughout the world.
Internet Public Library www.ipl.org/	Operated by the University of Michigan, Internet Public Library provides links to quality sources—hand-picked by librarians.
WWW Virtual Library www.vlib.org	Virtual Library is a catalog run by volunteers who compile pages of key links for particular areas in which they are expert.
Collections of Full-Text Articles	
Yahoo Full Coverage dailynews.yahoo.com/fc	For current events, Yahoo News provides well-chosen packets of news paper and magazine articles.
FindArticles.com www.findarticles.com	This free online service searches for the complete text of articles in more than 300 magazines and journals.

Table 6.1 Internet Search Tools, continued

Magazine Portal www.magportal.com/	This portal leads to thousands of magazine articles on a wide variety of subjects.
LibrarySpot www.libraryspot.com	Under Shortcuts, click on "Search full-text articles." Follow the links to the websites of many different publications.
Books and Book Pages	
Amazon.com www.amazon.com	Use keywords or phrases to search over 120,000 books. For some books, you can see the actual page, or pages, where your key words appear.
The Online Books Page digital.library.upenn.edu/books/index.html	The University of Pennsylvania provides links to over 20,000 books that are available on the Internet.
Expert Sites	
Abuzz www.abuzz.com	Abuzz is a network for asking questions and sharing knowledge. When you pose a question, you may get dozens of answers—or none. The archives are helpful in showing what has been written on your subject in the past.
Yahoo www.yahoo.com	For links to sites that feature advice and opinions of experts, visit Yahoo, select "Reference" and then "Ask an Expert."
Google Answers answers.google.com	You can pay a fee for expert advice, although sometimes you can find the answer at no charge by searching through the site's archived comments.
Discussion Forums	
Google Groups groups.google.com	On hundreds of different topics, people throughout the world everyday post messages on discussion forums. To find out what has been written on a given topic, use keywords to search the archives.
Yahoo! Groups groups.yahoo.com	These discussion forums are similar to the groups accessed by Google. You can search the archives of any group.

Here is the opening menu of categories in Yahoo!, the most popular subject directory on the Internet:

- Business & Economy
- Computers & Internet
- News & Media
- Entertainment
- Recreation & Sports
- Health
- Government
- Regional
- Society & Culture
- Education
- Arts & Humanities
- Science
- Social Science
- Reference

Here is an example of how to use a subject directory to drill down from general to specific: Let's say you want to find information about business opportunities in Vietnam. Click on "Regional," and you find subcategories. Click on "Countries," and you see a huge list of nations. Click on "Vietnam," and you are offered dozens of options about Vietnam. Two worth exploring are "Business and Economy" and "Society and Culture." Click on "Business and Economy" and you find links to many Websites about commercial activities in Vietnam.

To visit some of the best subject directories, see addresses in Table 6.1.

Search Engines

Search engines find documents on the Internet that match the keywords you have provided. Most search engines return results in order of relevance—the most relevant at the top, the least relevant at the bottom.

Some of the best search engines are listed in Table 6.1. The most popular is Google, which is fast and comprehensive and has a special feature that is quite useful in handling a common problem. While searching on the Internet, you are likely to click on a link but find nothing. You have encountered a **dead link**—a frustrating experience whenever a link looks promising. If you're in Google when you encounter a dead link, you have the option of clicking on a label called "Cached." This will give you the document as it looked on the day that Google found it. It may be somewhat dated, of course, but a dated document is better than none at all.

dead link
a URL that leads to no existing document

meta-search engine
a service providing results from many different search engines

Some search engines in Table 6.1 are called **meta-search engines.** These combine results from many different search engines. Using them is sometimes more effective than using a single engine, but sometimes less effective.

In recent years, most search engines have added subject directories, making themselves hybrids. However, their subject directories are inferior to true subject directories. Your best strategy is to observe the distinction made in Table 6.1 between the two formats. Use search engines when you have specific keywords and want a quick hit. Use subject directories when you want to browse a general topic and narrow it down to subtopics.

The Invisible Web

There is a vast area of the Internet that search engines never visit. Known as the **invisible Web,** this area includes specialized resources—information on narrow, specific topics, such as immigration law—and collections of full-text articles from magazines, newspapers, and other sources. To access these hidden treasures, use the addresses in Table 6.1 under the headings "Gateways to Specialized Resources" and "Collections of Full-Text Articles."

invisible Web
the part of the Internet unreached by search engines

Search Tips

Some Internet researchers become upset because either they find nothing for which they are looking or they are buried by an avalanche of mostly worthless material. In most cases, these two extremes can be avoided if you use good search techniques, as shown in Table 6.2 and in the tips below.

Use keywords. On the Internet, keywords are like magic keys that unlock the right doors. Before you start a search, compile a list based on this question: What words are likely to appear in the documents I'm seeking?

An effective search usually requires more than one keyword. Imagine that you wanted information about "bootlegging"—illegally making recordings of bands in concert and then selling them on CDs (compact disks). If you entered just the keyword "bootlegging," you would get lots of unwanted information about other forms of bootlegging—involving alcohol, satellite dishes, and football plays. Instead, you need to use such words as "music" and "bands."

To illustrate the value of multiple keywords, here is a sequence of queries in a search engine, starting with one word and ending with five. (For an explanation of the plus signs, see Table 6.2.)

Keywords	Documents Found
+music	1,668,530
+music +bands	979,596
+music +bands +concerts	7,934
+music +bands +concerts +CDs	1,312
+music +bands +concerts +CDs +bootlegging	39

Table 6.2 Search Options

Research Question: "Why do some women stay in relationships in which they are physically abused?"		
Option	**Example**	**Discussion**
Keywords unmarked	women abuse physical	This option flags all pages that contain any of the key words—a strategy that sometimes yields too many documents. In this example, the researcher would get thousands of irrelevant hits on such issues as child abuse and physical fitness. If this option is unsatisfactory, the strategies below can be tried to make a search more manageable.
Plus sign	+women +abuse +physical	A plus sign in front of a word means that all documents retrieved *must* contain that word—a good way to trim the number of hits. In this example, a document must contain all three words.
Minus sign	+women +abuse +physical war prison work	Minus signs exclude pages that contain these words. In this case, the researcher doesn't want information about violence against women in war, prison, and the workplace.
Phrase	"domestic violence against women"	Using double-quotation marks creates a searchable phrase. Although often highly fruitful, this option will omit relevant pages that don't use the exact phrase.
Wild card	+abus* +women +physical	A wild card (represented by a symbol such as an asterisk) finds words that start the same but end differently. In this example, abus* will yield documents that contain "abuse," "abusive," "abused," and "abuser."
AND, OR	violence AND (women OR wives) AND (spouse OR husband OR partner)	These options, like the two below, are called Boolean operators, and they permit fine-tuning. Note that parentheses allow the use of synonyms.
NOT	women AND violence NOT workplace NOT office	This query would be useful if one wanted to focus just on the home and exclude violence at work.
NEAR	women NEAR violence	NEAR finds words that appear within 5 to 30 words of one another (each search engine that carries this feature has a different range). This powerful option avoids a common situation: an article that mentions women on one page and violence on another, but doesn't discuss violence against women.

Note: Most search engines offer some, but not all, of these options. Only a few–such as AltaVista (www.altavista.com)—offer all of them. In some cases, the options are available only if you click on "Advanced Search." Each search engine has a Help service that will tell you what features are available and how to use them.

By having five keywords, you narrow your search and end up with a manageable number of documents—39 are easier to handle than over a million! More importantly, those 39 are pure gold. They give you the precise information for which you are looking.

Sometimes, if you use plus symbols with a large number of keywords, a search engine will provide no results. In this case, lop off the last word or two and try again.

Place your most important keywords at the front of your list because search engines give more weight to the first one or two keywords than to the later ones.

Use more than one search tool. A piece of information that you can't find with your first search engine might be retrieved with a second engine. Why? Because search engines—contrary to a common misconception—do not comb the entire Internet at the moment of your search. What they really are doing is sifting through a huge database—an index of keywords that have been gleaned previously from various Websites. In other words, search engines have already done their roaming "homework" before you request a search. Because search engines have different methods of gathering keywords, each engine has a different database.

Use the "Find" feature. Once you arrive at a Web page, you might discover that it is very lengthy and contains much extraneous material. To save time, you can go straight to what you are looking for by using the Find command (Control Key + F). If you are looking for the term "pediatric," this command will zip to it quickly, even if it's on page 38 of a long document.

Consult the Help menu. Because a search engine sometimes adds or revises strategies, click on Help for an explanation of current features.

Strive for expertise. To save yourself time in the long run, become an expert on at least one search engine. Study its Help guidelines and practice using advanced features.

When all else fails, look for information inside Websites. When search engines and the specialized resources listed in Table 6.1 fail to find what you are looking for, go to Websites that are likely to have the material and explore inside them. For example, let's say you need information about a murder trial in San Francisco. You fail to find any information using search tools. Your solution is to go to SF Gate, a Website for the *San Francisco Chronicle,* and search from within the Website. (Search engines cannot explore the articles in the SF Gate Website. You have to do this yourself.) Using the SF Gate archives, you should be able to find articles about the trial.

Take advantage of the difference between subject directories and search engines. Subject directories are superior for general information, while search engines are better for specific items. If, for example, you want general information about the creation of special effects in movies, you can go to the Yahoo subject directory and drill down in this order: Entertainment > Movies > Filmmaking > Special Effects. As you explore the Special Effects listings, you gain a

Tips for your CAREER

Tip 6.1 Take Time to Browse

Imagine that your boss asks you to prepare a presentation that requires some research. If you are like many speakers, you go straight to the Internet and exploit the blazing speed of search engines like Google. You don't even think of using a subject directory because browsing through the subdirectories seems slow and unproductive.

But ignoring subject directories can cause you to miss some unexpected treasures. Let's say you are searching for information on the origin of the names of bands like Pennywise (named after a clown in a Stephen King novel). Using a search engine to hunt for bands you already know can give you quick hits, but let's see what happens when you browse in a subject directory—in this case, Yahoo. You select, in succession, Entertainment > Music > Band Naming. You are given a list of top Websites devoted to band names. As you browse a few of these Websites, you glean some new information—for example, N*E*R*D stands for "No one Ever Really Dies," Dimmu Borgir is Icelandic for "Black Castle," and Portishead was named after a small town next to Bristol, England.

lot of background knowledge. If, however, you want a specific fact—such as how many professional stunt women are in Hollywood—a search engine would be the more effective option.

Books

To find books on your speech subject, the quickest method is to consult your library's *catalog*, a compilation of all books owned by the library. (A sample entry is shown in Figure 6.3.)

The catalog permits you to make a quick, computerized search in at least three categories: (1) author's name, (2) title, and (3) subject. Which category you should use depends on your situation. If you don't know much about your

Call Number	E184.A1 F474
Author	Femandes, Ronald
Title	America's Banquet of Cultures
Publisher	Westport, Conn.: Praeger, 2000
Subjects	1. Minorities–United States–Social Conditions. 2. Immigrants–United States–Social Conditions. 3. United States–Ethnic relations.
Notes	258 pages; includes illustrations, bibliographical references, and index.
Status	Not checked out

Figure 6.3
Sample Library Catalog Entry

Call number tells where to find the book on the shelves.

Knowing the date helps you determine if information is timely.

Subject headings will help you find books on the same topic.

It is helpful to know that the book has an index, references, and illustrations.

Status tells whether book is available.

www.mhhe.com /gregory7
For an interactive exercise on choosing good research strategies, visit Chapter 6 of this book's Website.

topic, the subject category is helpful. For example, if you want to do research on marine life but don't know the titles of any relevant books, begin by searching for books under the subject heading "marine biology." If you know the name of an author in the field, you can go directly to that name in the author category and see a list of his or her books. For example, if you know that Alice Jane Lippson is an expert on marine biology, search for the author's last name, "Lippson." Finally, if you know of a book called *Secrets of the Deep,* but you cannot recall the author's name, search for the title in the title category.

Many library catalogs can display on the computer screen a list of all books in the library that contain keywords such as "ocean" in the title. Some catalogs will indicate on screen whether a book is already checked out (saving you the time of hunting for it) and will permit you to place a "hold" on a checked-out book so that as soon as it is returned to the library, it will be reserved for you.

An important item is the call number, for this tells you where to find the book in the library's stacks. The call number is based on either the Library of Congress Classification System or the Dewey Decimal Classification System. Most libraries have a chart or map showing how to use call numbers to locate books in the stacks. If you have any problems, ask a librarian for help.

Articles

Sometimes articles in magazines, journals, newspapers, and Web pages are more up-to-date than books and may even contain information that will never appear in book form.

The best way to find articles on a given topic is not to leaf through a stack of magazines, but to use search tools in libraries and on the Internet. Articles exist in two formats:

1. *Print.* Libraries carry current printed editions of a wide variety of publications and keep past issues for at least one year.
2. *Electronic.* Most libraries have databases of articles on CD-ROM or online via the Internet. Online databases can be accessed from either library computers or your personal computer.

If you need a copy of a printed article, most libraries provide coin operated copiers. For computer-generated material, some libraries let you make printouts at no cost, while others charge a small fee. Most libraries permit you to e-mail an article to your own computer, or to download onto a diskette or CD-R for viewing or printing elsewhere.

Indexes of Articles

index to periodicals
a list of articles published in magazines, journals, and newspapers
citation
basic facts about a source

An **index to periodicals** gives you a list of articles on a topic. Many libraries have electronic indexes that can show a list of articles very quickly. Electronic databases provide information in three forms (some databases offer only one of these types; some offer all three):

1. *Citation.* A **citation** is a basic bibliographical reference that includes the title of the article, the name(s) of the author(s), the name of the magazine, date, and page numbers.

Tips for your CAREER

Tip 6.2 Develop a Filing System for Important Ideas

Do you have a stockpile of key ideas in your field? If not, start building one today. Knowledge is power, and to succeed in any career, you must have information available on short notice.

Extensive files come in handy when it's time to write a report or prepare a presentation. And managers and colleagues will be impressed by the wealth of relevant information at your fingertips. They will view you as an indispensable employee on whom they can rely to know the latest developments in the field.

Even if you are not yet employed in your chosen field, you should start developing files now because they can provide information for your college classes, and when you do enter your field, you will have a good stockpile on hand.

I recommend a two-part system:

1. *Computer files.* Keep computer files of Internet and other digitized documents, photos, and illustrations. If you use diskettes or CDs, label them with a few descriptive words that will clearly indicate contents. If you use the hard drive of your computer, create a subdirectory for each broad category and give each file an obvious name (for example, TAXLAW for a file on tax laws in your field).
2. *File folders.* For each folder, use a stick-on slip as a label (this makes it easier for you to consolidate overlapping topics or to discard a topic that is no longer of interest). Start with broad categories; later, when a folder starts overflowing, you can create subcategories. In the beginning, you can put your folders in a cardboard box; later, when they become bulky, you can store them in a filing cabinet.

Here are some guidelines for your filing system:

- Clip or photocopy articles from professional journals and newsletters. Download promising Internet information.
- Keep a legal pad, index cards, or stick-on slips handy so that you can jot down notes of important ideas that you encounter in articles, books, TV programs, speeches, workshops, and interviews.
- Since many of your instructors are experts in their fields, you may want to file lecture notes from some of your college classes.
- When you take notes during presentations and interviews, record the name of the speaker, date, place, and occasion. When you clip or photocopy an article, record the name of the publication, date, and page numbers.

Don't worry about accumulating too many notes. You can go through your files once or twice a year and discard any deadwood.

2. *Abstract.* An **abstract,** or brief summary, of an article is designed to give you enough information to decide whether you want to see the complete text of that article. Sometimes, however, the abstract itself gives you all the information you need.
3. *Full text.* Some databases offer complete or **full texts** of articles. You can read the text on the screen, making notes on paper as necessary, or you can print out the text on a computer-linked printer and keep the printout for later analysis.

abstract
summary of key information

full text
every word of a document

If you need to see an entire article but the index does not provide full text, your next step is to find out whether your library subscribes to the publication. Some electronic indexes are programmed to tell you whether your library subscribes to the publication being cited, thus saving you the time it would take to hunt down this information yourself. Otherwise, you can consult your library's list of its periodicals. If the publication is in the library, it will be available to you either as an original copy or printed on microfilm. If it is not in the library, you can order a photocopy or fax of the article via interlibrary loan.

Table 6.3 Where to Find Materials

Question	Likely Sources
Where can I find books on a particular subject?	Your library's electronic catalog lists the books it has on your topic. If it doesn't have a book that you want, it can probably borrow it from another library for you. If you want to buy a book, you can visit a bookstore or order on the Internet via on-line stores like Amazon.com (www.amazon.com).
Where can I find the complete text of magazine, journal, and newspaper articles?	The best selection of articles is likely to be found on the electronic data bases licensed by your college library and available only to its patrons. A lesser, but sometimes adequate, source is Internet collections of articles (see Table 6.1 for addresses).
Where can I get information about recent news events?	Your library carries daily newspapers and weekly newsmagazines. On the Internet, visit sites such as *The New York Times* (www.nytimes.com), *The Washington Post* (www.washingtonpost.com), and Yahoo! News (dailynews.yahoo.com). Links for other publications can be found at Refdesk.com (www.refdesk.com).
Where can I find background information on a subject?	Consult encyclopedias. For a list of Internet encyclopedias, consult Internet Public Library (www.ipl.org/div/subject/browse/ref32.00.00). For narrow subjects, your library should have specialized works such as *The Harvard Guide to Women's Health* and *Encyclopedia of the American Military.*
Where can I find on-line books, magazines, poems, and speeches?	Visit Internet Public Library (www.ipl.org), click on Reading Room, and select the type of publication that you want (book, magazine, etc.). To view copies of pages in books, go to Amazon.com (www.amazon.com) and use keywords and phrases to search for relevant pages.
Where can I get transcripts or summaries of television reports?	Visit PBS (www.pbs.org), ABC (www.abc.go.com), CBS (www.cbs.com), and NBC (www.nbc.com). If a report is not listed, you may find it in the site's archives.
Where can I find government information such as laws and statistics?	Go to LibrarySpot (www.libraryspot.com). Under "Reference Desk," choose "Government." For activities and laws of the U. S. Congress, visit THOMAS (thomas.loc.gov).
Where can I find pictures and video clips?	Visit Google (www.google.com), choose Images, and then Advanced Image Search in order to specify size and format. AltaVista (www.altavista.com/image/default) links to images (photos and illustrations), audio clips, and video clips. Ixquick (www.ixquick.com/) offers similar options.
If Internet search engines and subject directories don't find what I'm looking for, is there any other option on the Internet?	Before you give up on the Internet, try the sites listed in Table 6.1 under "Gateways to Specialized Resources." Also try AllSearchEngines.com (www.allsearchengines.com), Profusion (www.profusion.com) and Infomine (infomine.ucr.edu).
How can I contact organizations dedicated to causes and issues?	Go to Yahoo! (www.yahoo.com). Select "Society & Culture," and then "Issues and Causes." Choose a category, and you will find lists of organizations. Another approach is to use keywords on a search engine (see Table 6.1).
Where can I find information about cultures and ethnic groups?	Your library has reference works such as *Africana* and *The Encyclopedia of the Irish in America.* On the Internet, visit Yahoo! (www.yahoo.com) and select, in succession, "Society & Culture," "Cultures and Groups," "Cultures," and then a particular group.

Table 6.3 Where to Find Materials, continued

How can I contact experts for information?	On your campus and in your community, interview local experts. On the Internet, some Web pages cite experts and give their e-mail address; for example. The Asia Society (www.asiasource.org) has a database of scholars to whom you can send letters or e-mail. You also can pose questions to experts on expert Websites (see Table 6.1).
How can I find out what issues and concerns are being discussed on other college campuses?	To enhance a speech with the experiences and observations of students on other campuses, browse on-line campus newspapers. For listings, visit directory.google.com and follow this sequence: News > Colleges and Universities > Newspapers > United States.
Where can I find statistics, maps, and technical data?	Libraries have technical reference books, almanacs of statistical data, and atlases and gazetteers containing maps and geographical information. On the Internet, visit LibrarySpot (www.libraryspot.com) and choose an appropriate heading under "Reference Desk."
Where can I find word definitions, pronunciation, synonyms, and history?	In the library, consult general dictionaries such as *Oxford English Dictionary* or specialized dictionaries such as *Random House American Sign Language Dictionary.* On the Internet, Bartleby.com (www.bartleby.com) offers the *American Heritage Dictionary* and *Roget's Thesaurus* (for synonyms). Some sites, such as Encarta World English Dictionary (dictionary.msn.com) offer audio clips of the correct pronunciation.
Where can I find biographies of famous people?	Your library has biographical dictionaries such as *Distinguished Asian Ameri cans* and *Women in World History.* On the Internet, visit LibrarySpot (www.libraryspot.com) and select "Biographies" for several good links.
Where can I find quotations?	Your library should have collections such as *The Beacon Book of Quotations by Women.* On the Internet, Bartleby.com (www.bartleby.com) lets you search two excellent anthologies of quotations (*Simpson's* and *Bartlett's*), the King James Bible, and the entire works of Shakespeare. For quotations Websites, visit Yahoo! (www.yahoo.com) and select "Reference" and then "Quotations."

Note: Internet addresses and features sometimes change. For an update on these search options, go to this book's Website (www.mhhe.com/gregory7), click on STUDENT EDITION and then WEBLINKS, and look at notes for this page.

Databases of Full-Text Articles

Full-text articles on every topic imaginable are available from electronic databases. While some of these databases can be accessed by anyone using the Internet (see Table 6.1), the best collections are available only to library patrons, as discussed earlier.

Your college library probably has at least one general-interest database such as Lexis/Nexis, EBSCO, Academic Search, and ProQuest, and it also may have some special-interest collections such as PsychLit (psychology), CINAHL (nursing), and ERIC (education). Check with your librarians for details.

For more information on articles and other sources, see Table 6.3.

Reference Materials

For depth, detail, and reliability, reference materials in your library are unsurpassed. Most of these works—such as encyclopedias, dictionaries, and maps—are carefully researched and painstakingly doublechecked for accuracy.

Reference materials are available in three formats: print, CD-ROM, and the Internet. All three formats are offered by most libraries and are housed in a library's reference section. See Table 6.3 for more information on reference materials and other sources.

Often-Overlooked Resources

Concentrating on books and articles, some students overlook some valuable resources.

Multimedia

Most libraries have audiovisual materials, such as videos on DVD or VHS, which can be checked out. These media resources not only make good research material, but sometimes they can be incorporated in your speech. For example, a *National Geographic* video on space exploration might provide valuable background information, as well as dramatic footage to illustrate weightlessness in space.

Television programs—especially documentaries and investigative reports—are a good source of material. You can take notes during a show, or you can make a videotape for later analysis. If you need data from a TV report but are unable to videotape the show, you often can order a transcript. See Table 6.3 for details.

Experiences and Investigations

In gathering materials for a speech, some speakers overlook their personal experiences, which can be a gold mine of good material. If it is relevant, a story from your own life can be the most interesting part of a speech. Your personal experiences can be especially useful when they are used to amplify information you have gleaned from books or magazine articles. For example, if you escaped serious injury in a car accident because you were wearing a seatbelt, you can use the story to supplement national statistics on the value of seatbelts.

In some cases you can undertake personal investigations to gather material for a speech. For a speech on littering, for example, you can visit a trash-filled stream or shore, observing and perhaps making color slides or videotape. For a speech on prison conditions, you can visit a county jail or state prison and then tell your audience what you have seen. For a speech on animal overpopulation, you can tour a local animal shelter and interview the director.

If you need more than one investigator, enlist friends to help you. At the University of Connecticut, Marcel Dufresne got help from 12 students in his investigation of abuses of disabled-parking spaces. The students recorded the license and permit numbers of cars parked in reserved spaces, and then searched a state database of disability permits (Figure 6.4). They found some outrageous abuses of the system, including:

- One student would bring his wife's 81-year-old grandmother to campus with him, so that he could park in a space for the disabled. While he went to class, she waited in the library.
- Another student used a parking permit that he apparently had stolen from an amputee two years earlier.
- Six students without disabilities, who frequently parked in disability-reserved spaces, used permits that belonged to other people.[2]

Figure 6.4
Students at the University of Connecticut investigated and uncovered abuses of the disabled-parking system on campus.

Community and Out-of-Town Resources

You often can get literature and visual aids from companies and agencies in your community. One student, Rhonda Murchison, visited an office of the American Red Cross and told them she wanted to give a talk on CPR (cardiopulmonary resuscitation); they lent her a portable dummy to use in her demonstration speech.

A vast amount of literature on a wide variety of subjects can be ordered at no charge (or for a very small fee) from thousands of corporations and associations. To find out how to contact national groups, go to Yahoo (www.yahoo.com) and type "organizations" in the search box. Often you can send a request via a computer.

Note of caution: If you request that materials be mailed to you, don't rely too heavily on these items because they may not arrive in time for your speech; even if they do, they may turn out to be of little value.

Interviews

Interviews with people who are knowledgeable about your subject can yield valuable facts and insights. Often these individuals can provide up-to-date information not yet available in magazines or books. In the world of computers, for example, change occurs so rapidly that a magazine article published three months ago on a particular kind of software may be hopelessly outdated today.

Let's look at two avenues for interviews: e-mail and face-to-face.

E-Mail

Electronic mail—sending messages from one computer to another—has become a popular way to communicate short, simple letters. The widespread use of the Web has made **e-mail** a good tool for interviewing experts.

e-mail
short for electronic mail; transmission of messages from one computer to another

How do you find experts on the Internet? First, look at Websites and note that most of them have a spot to click for e-mail. Even if you don't know the name of an expert, you can post a query and hope for a reply. Second, post queries on discussion forums, as discussed earlier in this chapter.

Personal

For face-to-face interviews, where can you find experts? Start with your own college; some faculty members may be well-versed on your speech topic. Then look at the larger community beyond the campus; are any businesses, industries, or agencies involved in your subject? If so, telephone them and ask for the person who is most knowledgeable on the topic. If you are speaking on snakebites, for example, call the nearest zoo and ask to speak to the chief herpetologist. In some cases, you may want to interview fellow students. For a speech on communication problems between males and females, for instance, you could collect the ideas, experiences, and observations of other students.

If you are lucky, there can sometimes be a wonderful bonus from an interview: you might develop a professional contact or personal friendship that will prove rewarding to you in the future. Consuela Martinez, an accounting major in one of my classes several years ago, interviewed an official at a local bank to get information for a speech. The official was so impressed with Martinez that when she graduated and returned to the bank seeking a job, he hired her. Another student, Skyler MacPherson, interviewed a well-known poet in his community; after the interview, the poet asked MacPherson to come to his house for dinner; and a long-term friendship began, with the poet helping MacPherson to get some of his own poems published.

Don't let fear of rejection deter you from asking for an interview. Some students have the idea that the knowledgeable persons they want to interview are so important and so busy they will certainly have no time for questions from a "lowly" student. On the contrary, my students have found that everyone they approach loves to be interviewed. If this surprises you, think about yourself for a moment: when a friend asks you for advice (on a matter such as how to repair a computer or how to solve an algebra problem), don't you enjoy holding forth as an "expert"? The same is true of knowledgeable people in your community: they are flattered to be interviewed by a student.

Here are some guidelines for planning and conducting interviews.

Preparing for an Interview

Before an interview, there are a few things you should do.

Telephone for an appointment. To arrange a time that is convenient for the person you want to interview, telephone beforehand. Don't just drop by and expect the person to agree to an interview on the spot; you may catch him or her off guard or during a hectic time of day. When you call to line up the appointment, explain briefly what you are trying to find out and why you think he or she can help you. Such an explanation gives the person time to get his or her thoughts together before talking to you.

Conduct research before the interview. Read up on your subject *before* you go to an interview. Why? First of all, you need to know enough about the subject to ask intelligent questions. Suppose you are planning to interview a psychiatrist about schizophrenia. If you read articles and books on the mental disorder beforehand, you will know enough about the subject to ask an important question, such as, "Do researchers feel that they are close to discovering a cure?" In addition to helping you ask intelligent questions, research will help you avoid asking embarrassing questions like, "How does the split in personality occur?" Such a question would be embarrassing because it would reveal your ignorance of what the term *schizophrenia* means. (It means a psychotic break with reality, not a Jekyll-and-Hyde split in personality.)

Second, if you find something in your reading that you don't understand, the interviewee may be able to explain it. Suppose that while you are doing your library research on schizophrenia, you come across the term *folie à deux*. You look up the term in a dictionary but cannot make sense out of the formal definition. In your interview with a psychiatrist, you ask for a plain-English explanation of what the term means (it refers to a psychotic delusion that one person persuades another person to share).

Finally, if you fail to find vital information in your library research, you often can get it from the interviewee. Suppose that you are investigating the effectiveness of automobile air bags in traffic accidents. You want to know, "Will air bags save a motorist's life if he or she is driving at 55 miles per hour and has a head-on collision with a car traveling at the same speed?" Your weekend spent in the library sifting through government studies failed to turn up the answer, but five minutes with a traffic-safety expert may give you the information.

Prepare questions. Decide ahead of time exactly what questions you want to ask, and write them down on a piece of paper: Be sure to put the most important ones first—in case you run out of time.

If possible, send the most important questions ahead of time via letter or e-mail to help the interviewee prepare for the interview.

Decide how to record the interview. It is a mistake to think that you can conduct an interview without a pencil or a tape recorder and then remember all the key information later when you are organizing your speech. Since human memory is highly fallible, you need a system for recording the interview. Most interviewers use either or both of the following methods:

1. *Writing down key ideas.* Jot down key ideas only; if you try to write down every word the person is saying, you will be completely absorbed in transcribing sentences instead of making sense out of what is being said, which is far more important.
2. *Using video- or audiotape.* A videocassette camcorder (on a tripod) or an audiotape recorder can be ideal when it is important to get a word-for-word record of the interview. Taping means that you need not worry about forgetting key points or misquoting your source. Some interviewees, knowing they are being recorded, may try extra hard to be precise and accurate in giving information. In some cases, you can use some of your videotape in your actual speech (as did one speaker, who interviewed an engineer at the construction site of a bridge).

Ethical Issue

If you want to use a recorder, seek permission from the interviewee beforehand. Most people will permit recording, but a few will refuse (because it makes them feel uncomfortable or intimidated). You should, of course, respect their wishes. Using a hidden tape recorder is unethical.

Important note: Even if you use a recorder, you should still take notes for two reasons: (1) A mechanical foul-up might cause you to lose your entire tape; having notes would give you a backup record of the interview. (2) The act of making notes forces you to concentrate on the key ideas of your interviewee, thereby making you more alert in your questioning.

If you plan to take notes and make a recording simultaneously, you may want to have a friend accompany you to help with the recording. This frees you of all worry about operating the equipment.

Conducting an Interview

Here are some tips on how to conduct an interview.

Start in a friendly, relaxed manner. Before you begin your questions, you need to establish rapport. You can express appreciation ("Thanks for letting me come by to talk to you today") and engage in small talk on obvious topics (the weather, the beautiful painting on the wall, and so on). Small talk is an important lubricant in conversation, especially at the beginning of a dialogue, so you need not feel that it is a waste of time. You should also repeat the purpose of the interview; the person may have forgotten exactly what you are seeking. While these preliminary remarks are being made, you can set up your recorder (if you have previously received permission to use one).

Get biographical information. Since the person you are interviewing is one of your sources, you need to be able to tell your audience later why he or she is an authority on your subject. If you have not been able to get background information in advance, the early part of the interview is a good time to get it because it continues the building of rapport. You could say, for example, "Where did you get your doctorate?" or "How long have you been working on this problem?"

Ask both prepared and spontaneous questions. Earlier we noted that you should decide ahead of time exactly what questions you want to ask. Make these questions as specific as possible. It would be ludicrous to walk into the office of an expert on robots and say, "Tell me what you know about robots." Such a question would probably draw a laugh and a comment like, "Have you got two months to listen?" A better, more specific question would be something like this: "Will robots someday replace all automobile assembly-line workers?"

There are two types of questions that can be prepared in advance.

closed question
a question requiring only a short, specific response
open question
a question that permits a broad range of responses

Closed questions require only yes or no responses or short, factual answers. Examples: "Do Democrats outnumber Republicans in this state?" "What percentage of registered voters actually voted in the last presidential election?" Closed questions are effective in getting specific data.

Open questions give the interviewee a wide latitude for responding. For example, "How do you feel about negative political ads?" The advantage of such a broad question is that the interviewee can choose the points he or she wishes to emphasize—points about which it may not have occurred to you to ask. The disadvantage is that such questions may allow an interviewee to wander off the subject into irrelevant side issues.

There are two other types of questions, which cannot be prepared in advance but may need to be asked spontaneously during the interview.

Clarifying questions are used when you are confused about what the person means. Ask a question like this: "Could you explain that a little more?" Or: "Correct me if I'm wrong, but I understand you to say that . . ." Don't shy away from asking clarifying questions because you are afraid of showing your ignorance. Remember that you are there to interview the person precisely because you are "ignorant" in his or her area of expertise. So ask about any point that you don't understand. If you cannot make sense of it during the interview, there is not much chance you will succeed later.

clarifying question
a question designed to clear up confusion

Follow-up questions are designed to encourage the interviewee to elaborate on what he or she has been saying—to continue a story or to add to a comment. Here are some examples: "What happened next?" "Were you upset about what happened?" "Could you give me some examples of what you're talking about?"

follow-up question
a question designed to stimulate elaboration

Make the interview more like a relaxed chat than an interrogation. Be natural and spontaneous, and follow the flow of conversation. In other words, don't act as if you must plow through your list of questions item by item. The flow of conversation might lead to questions being answered "out of order." Simply check off the questions as they are answered. Toward the end of the interview, ask those questions that still have not been answered. Also, the person may bring up surprising aspects of your topic that you have not thought about; this should inspire you to ask spontaneous follow-up questions.

When the interviewee mentions things that are not on your checklist, write them down, even if they seem inconsequential at the time, because you may find a use for them later. This advice would not apply if the person goes off on a tangent, telling you things that are totally unrelated to the subject. In such a case, tactfully steer the conversation back toward the pertinent topic.

Maintain eye contact. Show with your eyes that you are listening attentively and comprehending what is being said. You can do this even if you use a notepad (just jot down key ideas, keeping your eyes on the interviewee most of the time).

Ask about other sources and visual aids. Interviewees may know of other persons you can interview or library resources that you are unaware of. They may have a pamphlet or a book that they are willing to lend you. In some cases, they may even lend you a map or chart or some other kind of visual aid that you can use in your speech.

Ask if you've omitted any questions. When you have gone through all the prepared questions, ask the interviewee if there are any items that you have failed to ask about. You may find that you have inadvertently overlooked some important matters.

End the interview on time. Respect the amount of time that was granted when you set up your appointment; if you were allotted 20 minutes, stay no more than 20 minutes—unless, of course, the interviewee invites you to stay longer. If you still have questions when the time is up, you can ask for a second interview (perhaps a few extra questions can even be handled over the telephone).

Following Up

After you leave the interview, you have three important tasks.

Promptly expand your notes. Immediately after the interview, go through your notes and expand them (by turning words and phrases into complete sentences) while the conversation is fresh in your mind. If you wait two weeks to go over your notes, they will be stale and you may have to puzzle over your scribbling or you may forget what a particular phrase means.

Evaluate your information. Evaluate your notes to see if you got exactly what you were looking for. If you are confused on any points, or if you find that you need more information on a particular item, telephone or e-mail the interviewee and ask for help. This should not be a source of embarrassment for you—it shows that you care enough about the subject and the interviewee to get the information exactly right.

Write a thank-you note. A brief note thanking the interviewee is a classy finale. If possible, mention some of the interviewee's points that you will probably use in your speech.

Recording Information Effectively

You should systematically record the key information that you find. There are many different ways to accomplish this, and you may have already developed a system that works well for you. If not, consider this method, which many business and professional speakers use:

1. **Use multicolored file folders for subtopics.** Break your topic down into small segments and designate one folder for each subtopic. Don't write the subtopic name on the folder; instead, write it on a stick-on slip, which can be placed on the folder tab. Thus you can easily reorganize your folders from time to time, throwing away labels for subtopics that fail to materialize, adding new labels, combining folders, and so on.
2. **Use stick-on slips for research notes.** The slips can be attached to the insides of a folder.
3. **Insert photocopies and printouts.** In the same folder as your stick-on slips, place printed documents.

Some researchers prefer index cards to stick-on slips, while others prefer to feed their material into a computer.

Printouts and Photocopies

If you make printouts of Internet pages and photocopies of articles and book pages, analyze them carefully to extract the most important details and to plan any necessary follow-ups.

Use a color highlighter to spotlight certain items. Be careful to use highlighting judiciously; marking almost all of the text would be self-defeating.

On all printouts and photocopies, be sure to identify author, publication or Website, date, and page numbers.

If time permits, it's a good idea to make notes from your printouts and photocopies, using the techniques discussed below.

Notes

There are two types of notations you should make: bibliography citations and notes of key ideas.

Bibliography Citations

As you gather materials, jot down the names of books and articles that seem promising. These citations will help you locate materials, and will come in handy later when you put together the bibliography for your speech. In addition, if you need to consult a book or article again for clarification or amplification of facts, the data on your citation should help you find it quickly. Figure 6.5 shows two sample bibliography citations.

www.mhhe.com/gregory7

Insert key information into BiblioMaker software, and it will create a bibliography in the correct form.

Make a bibliography notation for every book or article that you think might be helpful. You may end up with more sources than you have time to consult,

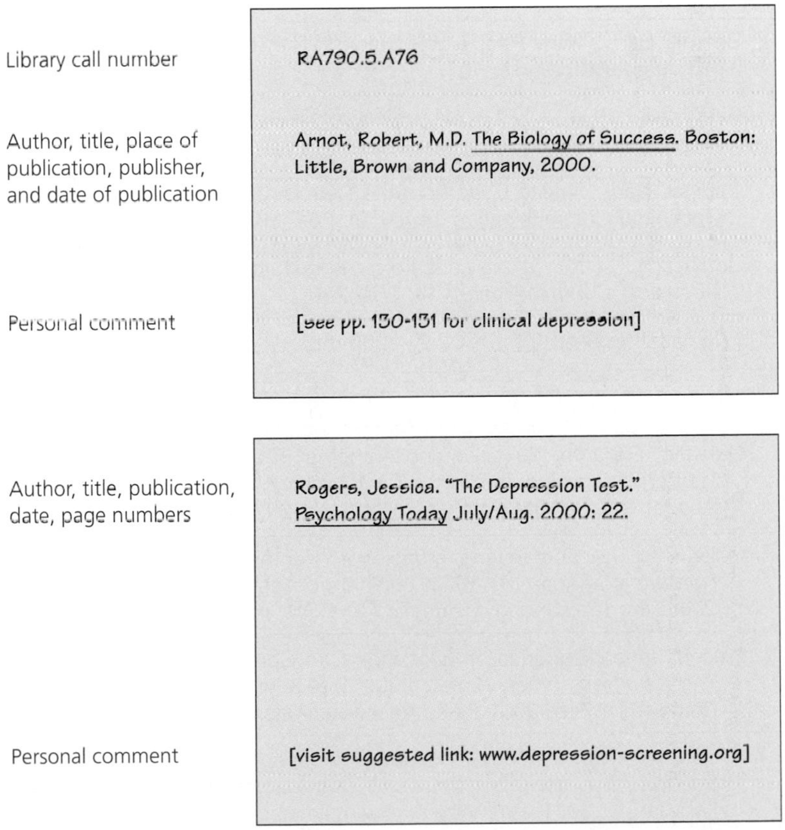
Library call number
RA790.5.A76
Author, title, place of publication, publisher, and date of publication
Arnot, Robert, M.D. The Biology of Success. Boston: Little, Brown and Company, 2000.
Personal comment
[see pp. 130-131 for clinical depression]
Author, title, publication, date, page numbers
Rogers, Jessica. "The Depression Test." Psychology Today July/Aug. 2000: 22.
Personal comment
[visit suggested link: www.depression-screening.org]

Figure 6.5
Sample Bibliography Citations for a Book and a Magazine Article

www.mhhe.com/gregory7
Bibliography samples (Table 6.4) are updated if MLA or APA makes a change in style.

but it is better to have too many sources than not enough. Leave space on each citation for personal comments, which can help you evaluate which sources are most likely to yield good information.

Table 6.4 shows how to format citations, using the style guidelines of either the Modern Language Association (MLA) or the American Psychological Association (APA). Find out if your instructor has a preference.

Table 6.4 How to Cite Sources

Book with one author	MLA	Harris, Phyllis. From the Soul: Stories of Great Black Parents and the Lives They Gave Us. New York: Berkley Publishing Group, 2003.
	APA	Harris, P. (2003). *From the soul: Stories of great black parents and the lives they gave us.* New York: Berkley Publishing Group.
Book with two or three authors	MLA	McMillon, Bill, Doug Cutchins, and Anne Geissinger. Volunteer Vacations: Short-Term Adventures That Will Benefit You and Others. 8th ed. Chicago: Chicago Review Press, 2003.
	APA	McMillon, B., Cutchins, D., & Geissinger, A. (2003). *Volunteer vacations: Short-term adventures that will benefit you and others* (8th ed.). Chicago: Chicago Review Press.
Book with more than three authors	MLA	Brand-Miller, Jennie, et al. The New Glucose Revolution. New York: Marlowe & Company, 2003.
	APA	Brand-Miller, J., Wolever, T., Colagiuri, S., & Foster-Powell, K. (2003). *The new glucose revolution.* New York: Marlowe & Company.
Magazine article	MLA	Bearak, Barry. "Why People Still Starve." The New York Times Magazine 13 July 2003: 32–37.
	APA	Bearak, B. (2003, July 13). Why people still starve. *The New York Times Magazine,* 32–37.
Scholarly journal article	MLA	Carliner, Saul. "Taking Cues from the Culture." Journal of Business & Technical Communication 14 (2000): 264–289.
	APA	Carliner, S. (2000). Taking cues from the culture. *Journal of Business & Technical Communication, 14,* 264–289.
Article with no author listed	MLA	"Wireless Worries." Time 31 July 2000: 68.
	APA	Wireless worries. (2000, July 31). *Time,* 68.
Article reproduced in CD-ROM database	MLA	Galeano, Eduardo. "Miracles and Anthems: The Alchemy of Soccer." Harper's Magazine Jan. 2003 (63–67 in original publication). Expanded Academic CD-ROM database. Retrieved 20 Jan. 2004.
	APA	Galeano, E. (2003, January). Miracles and anthems: The alchemy of soccer. *Harper's Magazine* (63–67 in original publication). Retrieved January 20, 2004, from Expanded Academic CD-ROM database.
Article reproduced on Internet	MLA	Fritsch, Jane. "Evidence of Innocence Can Come Too Late for Freedom." The New York Times 30 July 2000 (WK-3 in original publication). Retrieved 4 Feb. 2001 <http://www.nytimes.com>.
	APA	Fritsch, J. (2000, July 30). Evidence of innocence can come too late for freedom. *The New York Times* (WK-3 in original publication). Retrieved February 4, 2001, from http://www.nytimes.com

Table 6.4 How to Cite Sources, continued

Web document with author listed	MLA	Clark, Jessica. "Access to Usable Water: A Growing Global Concern." Britannica. 15 June 2001. Retrieved 14 Feb. 2003 <http://www.britannica.com>.
	APA	Clark, J. (2001). Access to usable water: A growing global concern. *Britannica.* Retrieved February 14, 2003, from http://www.britannica.com
Web document with author listed	MLA	"Workplace Wellness." Women Connect. 2001. Retrieved 14 Jan. 2003 <http://www.womenconnect.com>.
	APA	Workplace wellness. (2001). *Women Connect.* Retrieved January 14, 2003, from http://www.womenconnect.com
Discussion forum posting	MLA	Westerfield, Mike. "Request for Smallpox Information." Online posting. 1 Jan. 2003. <sci.med.immunology>. Retrieved 13 Feb. 2003 on Google Groups <http://groups.google.com>.
	APA	Westerfield, M. (2003, January 1). Request for smallpox information. Message posted to sci.med.immunology. Retrieved Feb. 13, 2003, from http://groups.google.com
E-mail	MLA	Gomez, Maria, curator, Brookridge Museum of Art. "Pre-Columbian Art." E-mail to Natalie Pellegrino. 14 Aug. 2003.
	APA	Gomez, M., curator, Brookridge Museum of Art. (2003, August 14). Pre-Columbian art. E-mail to Natalie Pellegrino.
Interview	MLA	Ahmed, Helen, M.D., pediatrician. Personal interview. 3 Aug. 2003.
	APA	Ahmed, H., M.D., pediatrician. (2003, August 3). Personal interview.
TV program	MLA	Diaz, Arnold, narrator. "Safe Shopping Online." 20/20. ABC News. 2 Aug. 2000.
	APA	Diaz, A., narrator. (2000, August 2). Safe shopping online. *20/20.* ABC News.
DVD or Videocassette	MLA	National Geographic. Into the Great Pyramid. DVD. Washington, D.C.: National Geographic Video, 2003.
	APA	National Geographic (2003). *Into the great pyramid* [DVD]. Washington, D.C.: National Geographic Video.

For situations not covered here, see MLA and APA style guides on the Internet: Go to this book's website (www.mhhe.com/gregory7), click on STUDENT EDITION and then WEBLINKS, and explore links for this page.

Notes of Key Ideas

As you read through books and articles, make notes of key ideas. Put a subject heading at the top of each note, as shown in Figure 6.6. These headings will be valuable when you finish making your notes because they will help you to group the notes into related batches. Identify each note with the author's name. There is no need to write down full bibliographical information because those details are already on your bibliography citations.

In making notes, follow these steps:

- Quickly read through the material to see if there is anything worth noting.
- If there is, reread the material, this time very carefully.

Figure 6.6
Sample Note for an Article Summary

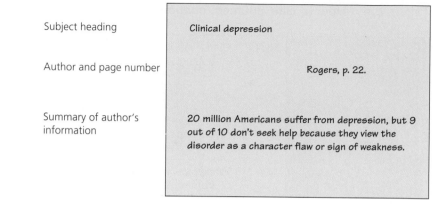

Subject heading	Clinical depression
Author and page number	Rogers, p. 22.
Summary of author's information	20 million Americans suffer from depression, but 9 out of 10 don't seek help because they view the disorder as a character flaw or sign of weakness.

- Try to summarize the key points in a few simple sentences. Resist the temptation to copy huge chunks of undigested information. Your task is to interpret, evaluate, and boil down ideas, not convey a text verbatim.
- While striving for brevity, make sure that you put summarized information in a coherent form. If you jot down a phrase like "anorexia—Cheerios," and then wait five days before organizing your notes, you may forget the meaning of that note. Write out a coherent sentence such as this: "One anorexic woman bragged about eating nothing but Cheerios—one Cheerio a day."
- Occasionally, you will find an arresting phrase or a short, vivid sentence that you want to convey to your listeners in the form of a direct quotation. Be sure to put quotation marks around such passages in your notes. Don't use too many direct quotations in your notes, however, because you may fall into the trap discussed above—copying large blocks of text without proper evaluation and condensation.
- Take more notes than you probably will need. It is better to have too much raw material than not enough.
- You can add personal comments at the end of a note to provide ideas on how to use the note or how to connect it to other notes. You also can express a personal reaction, such as, "This sounds implausible—check other sources." Use square brackets or some other device to distinguish your own comments from the text that you are summarizing.
- Use a separate note for each idea. This will make it easy to sort your notes by subject headings.

In the next chapter, we will turn our attention to how to evaluate the information that you have gathered.

For updates and additional research opportunities, visit the author's website (www.mhhe.com/gregory7), click on STUDENT EDITION and then WEBLINKS, and explore links for the pages of this chapter.

Resources for Review and Skill Building

www.mhhe.com/gregory7

This book's Online Learning Center Website and SpeechMate CD-ROM provide meaningful resources and tools for study and review, such as practice tests, key-term flashcards, and sample speech videos.

SpeechMate CD-ROM

Summary

Devising a research strategy can help you find materials efficiently. Start early and follow your plan systematically. Use your specific purpose statement as a guide. If necessary, get help from librarians and use interlibrary loan.

Use the Internet to find information quickly. The parts of the Internet that are especially useful are Websites, expert sites, and discussion forums. To find data, use subject directories for a broad view and search engines for specific queries. When using a search engine, employ plus signs in front of several keywords so that you get a manageable, high-quality list of results.

Don't overlook traditional library resources, such as books and articles. Most libraries have computerized indexes to more articles than can be accessed on the Internet. Libraries are also superior to the Internet in the area of reference materials, which are unsurpassed for depth, detail, and reliability.

There are some other valuable resources that are often overlooked: graphics and audiovisuals, television reports, personal experiences and observations, and community and out-of-town resources.

Interviewing knowledgeable people on your campus or in your community can yield up-to-date information in many fields. To prepare for an interview, do extensive research on the topic and then draw up a list of questions to be asked. Conduct the interview in a relaxed, conversational manner. You also can conduct interviews via e-mail on a computer.

To record information effectively, use stick-on slips, index cards, or a computer. On all notes of key ideas, put a subject heading at the top, and have only one idea per note. These notes can later be arranged systematically as you organize and outline your material.

Key Terms

abstract, *127*
bookmark, *119*
citation, *126*
clarifying question, *135*
closed question, *134*
dead link, *122*
discussion forum, *119*
e-mail, *131*
expert site, *119*
follow-up question, *135*
full text, *127*
hyperlink, *118*
index to periodicals, *126*
inter-library loan, *117*
Internet, *117*
invisible Web, *122*
keyword, *118*
meta-search engine, *122*
open question, *134*
search engine, *118*
subject directory, *121*
URL, *118*
Web page, *118*
Website, *118*
World Wide Web, *118*

Review Questions

1. What role should your specific purpose statement play in the research stage of preparation?
2. What is inter-library loan and how can it help you?
3. In what ways are traditional library resources superior to the Internet?

4. What is a hyperlink?
5. When using a search engine, why are multiple keywords usually better than a single keyword?
6. What is "the invisible Web"?
7. Why should most of your research be done *before* you call someone for an interview?
8. What are the advantages and disadvantages of using a video- or audiotape recorder in an interview?
9. What steps should you take after an interview is completed?
10. In your research, why should you take more notes than you probably will need?

Building Critical-Thinking Skills

1. Any person of any age can host a Website on any subject and include anything he or she desires. From the viewpoint of a researcher, what are the advantages and disadvantages of this wide-open system?
2. If you use a search engine to find information on the Internet about a breed of dogs and you enter the keyword *bulldogs,* what kind of irrelevant Websites are you likely to find in your list of results?

Building Teamwork Skills

1. In a group, choose a topic about which everyone would like to know more. Then brainstorm at least 15 questions that could be asked in an interview with an expert to elicit the most important information about the subject.
2. Working in a group, discuss which approach—Internet or traditional library resources (books, magazines, etc.)—would be superior for finding answers to these research questions: (a) What are the causes of Arab–Israeli antagonism? (b) How many people were killed in house fires last year? (c) How effective are flu shots? (d) What was the impact of the Black Death on European civilization? (e) What are the title and cost of the latest Amy Tan novel?

Building Internet Skills

www.mhhe.com/gregory7

1. On a search engine that uses plus and minus signs, enter these unmarked keywords for a search related to prisoners: *crime prison.* Note how many documents are listed. Next, add +*juveniles,* search again, and note the number of hits. Finally, change the plus sign to a minus: −*juveniles.* Search and write down the number of hits. Which of the three options yielded the most hits and which gave the least?

Possible Strategy: Use Alta Vista (www.altavista.com), and click on "Advanced Search."

2. Find and write down the names of three Filipino dishes.

Possible Strategy: Go to Yahoo! (www.yahoo.com), choose "Regional," and then "Countries." Click on "Philippines," and then "Society and Culture." Next, select "Food and Drink" and then visit at least one of the Websites listed.

Using PowerWeb

www.mhhe.com/gregory7

An article entitled "Basic Library Research" shows how Boolean operators (discussed in Table 6.2) can be used to narrow one's search for information. Following the example shown in the article, draw three overlapping circles, and use cross-hatching, to show the interaction of these keywords: "American AND hot air AND ballooning." To find this article, visit www.mhhe.com/gregory7, click on STUDENT EDITION and POWERWEB: CONTENTS, and choose STUDY TIPS (under STUDENT RESOURCES). Click on BASIC LIBRARY RESEARCH.

Student speaker Byung S. Lee holds a poster that is designed to demolish three myths. Contrary to popular belief, chocolate does not cause acne, it is not physically addictive, and it contains only a small amount of caffeine. Separating fact from fiction is an important task for ethical speakers.

7

Using Information Wisely and Ethically

Outline

High-Quality Information

Critical-Thinking Skills
Recognize Dubious Claims
Find More Than One Source
Examine Opposing Viewpoints
Be Cautious in Using Polls
Recognize the Fallibility of Experts
Beware of Groups with Misleading Names

Analyzing Internet Sites
Don't Be Swayed by Widespread Dissemination
Watch Out for Web Manipulation
Don't Be Dazzled by High-Tech Design
Investigate Sponsors and Authors
Look at Evaluations of Websites

Legal and Ethical Guidelines
Giving Credit to Sources
Using Copyrighted Material

Objectives

After studying this chapter, you should be able to:

1. Explain the criteria for high-quality information.
2. Reject claims based solely on anecdotes, testimonials, and opinions.
3. Recognize the fallibility of polls and experts.
4. Investigate impressive-sounding names of organizations.
5. Know how to scrutinize Internet sites for signs of bias and deception.
6. Give proper credit to sources.
7. Avoid improper use of copyrighted materials.

Vegans (pronounced "vee-guns") are vegetarians who avoid all foods of animal origin, including meat, eggs, milk, butter, cheese—even honey. The *New England Journal of Medicine* recently reported a case in which a 33-year-old man in France became blind after 13 years on the vegan diet. Doctors said his loss of vision was caused by deficiencies of vitamins B_{12} and B_1.[1]

Excitedly displaying a magazine article about the case, one of my students, Raven Sanders, told me that she planned to devote her next speech to blasting the vegan diet. Not only did she want to alert classmates to the dangers of the diet, but she also confessed an ulterior motive: "I know some vegans, and they think they're morally superior. I'd like to take them down a notch or two."

In this spread, a person following the vegan diet would be permitted to eat nuts, fruits, and vegetables, but not meat, fish, eggs, and cheese. Can the vegan diet cause blindness? One student investigated.

Then Sanders went off to do her research. She returned a week later with several books and a stack of Internet printouts. "Guess what?" she said. "I've got to change my topic." Because of her research, she was now convinced that the French patient became blind not because he had followed the vegan diet, but because he had failed to follow it correctly. "All the vegan experts and Websites say the same thing: you *must* take vitamin supplements or you will ruin your health. This guy in France never took any supplements." Her research not only led her away from attacking the vegan diet, but caused her to have respect for it. "It's actually a healthy system, if you do it right."

Sanders decided to change the focus of her speech to show that everyone—vegetarians and nonvegetarians—should eat a balanced diet and take special care to include sufficient vitamins. "That's the real lesson from the French patient," she said.[2]

Not everyone would have acted like Sanders. Some speakers would have done no research beyond the first article—the one that seemed to have damning evidence against the vegan diet. Other speakers might have probed further and found the additional information that Sanders unearthed, but they would have ignored the pro-vegan findings, choosing to plow ahead with an anti-vegan message. Such speakers seem to have the attitude, "I'm on a crusade, and I don't care what the other side says." Note that Sanders did not let emotions overrule her sense of fair play. Even though—on an emotional level—she had originally wanted to "take [vegans] down a notch or two," she was willing to change her mind and admit that they followed a healthful system.

Conscientious, ethical speakers like Sanders share two characteristics:

1. *They are willing to work hard.* Avoiding intellectual laziness, they dig for all relevant facts and refuse to rely on opinions, hearsay, and first impressions.
2. *They are honest.* Once the facts are unearthed, they analyze them objectively and draw reasonable conclusions—even if (as in Sanders' case) they have to admit that their original idea is erroneous. They are more interested in finding and sharing truth than in espousing a cherished cause or winning an argument.

In the preceding chapter, we looked at many different sources of information. In most cases, these sources yield reliable information, but sometimes they do not. In this chapter, we will examine how to evaluate materials and use them in an ethical manner.

High-Quality Information

As you examine information you have collected for a speech, your task is to determine which items are worthless and which are valuable. But how do you separate the good from the bad? To be considered high-quality, information should meet the following criteria:

1. *Factual.* Is the information based on facts—not on hearsay, distortions, or oversimplifications?
2. *Reliable.* Does the information come from sources that are trustworthy and authoritative?
3. *Well supported.* Do the sources provide strong evidence to prove a case?
4. *Current.* Is the information up-to-date?
5. *Verifiable.* Can the information be cross-checked against a large number of reliable sources?
6. *Fair.* Does the information come from unbiased and evenhanded sources, and is it presented in a spirit of fair play?
7. *Comprehensive.* Does the information include all relevant data?

To help you use these criteria in evaluating information, let's turn to a valuable set of skills.

Critical-Thinking Skills

www.mhhe.com/gregory7

For an interactive exercise on evaluating dubious evidence, see Chapter 7 on this book's Website.

To be a savvy consumer of information, you need to develop critical-thinking skills—the ability to evaluate evidence with fairness and intellectual rigor. You need *healthy* skepticism, which is not sour negativity that rejects everything, but open-minded inquiry that asks probing questions: "What is the source of this information?" "How do you know this is true?" "Why did this happen?"

Critical thinkers go beyond the obvious. Not content with placid surface appearances, they dive deep for underlying truth.

Here are some critical thinking techniques:

Recognize Dubious Claims

At first glance, some claims are compelling because they seem to coincide with common sense. But look more closely and you will see major flaws.

Reject claims based solely on anecdotes. Do you think that crimes are more likely to be committed during a full moon than at other times? If so, you are among a majority, according to polls. Most people also believe that births are more frequent during a full moon.[3]

Both of these notions, however, are false. For decades, researchers have studied crime and birth statistics, trying to see if there are upswings on the dates of a full moon. They have found no significant correlation with a full moon or any other phase of the moon. (Seasons and weekends do influence crime and births, but the moon does not[4]).

Here is how the misconception arose: Sometimes there is indeed an increase of crime and/or births during a full moon (just as sometimes there is an increase during other lunar phases). Doctors and nurses delivering babies and law enforcement officers investigating crimes would notice the upsurge on those occasions and say, "Yes, no wonder. It's a full moon tonight." They would then tell their friends and families about what happened. Their accounts—or **anecdotes**—became widely believed as proof of the influence of a full moon. But researchers pointed out that the professionals failed to make a special mental note when there was an upsurge of crime and births on days when the moon was *not* full, and they also failed to notice when a full moon coincided with a dip in crimes and births. Thus, they failed to see that their "full moon" cause-and-effect theory was wrong.[5]

anecdote
a short account of an incident

This case illustrates the mistake of relying upon anecdotes—by themselves—for proof. You would need more information, such as statistical verification, before you could prove the "full moon" theory. This doesn't mean, however, that anecdotes are necessarily bad. You can collect them in your research for possible use in a speech. Rightly used, they can add interest to your ideas. Just make sure that you don't accept an assertion that is based exclusively on "anecdotal evidence."

Reject claims based solely on testimonials. Like anecdotes, **testimonials** can be collected for possible use in a speech, but beware of claims based on nothing but personal recommendations.

testimonial
a statement supporting a benefit received

Let's imagine a con artist who wants to make a lot of money fast by concocting and selling a cure for warts. In his basement lab, he mixes skin moisturizer, honey, and lemon juice, and then bottles the stuff with an attractive label, "Guaranteed Miracle Wart Remover." He sets up a Website and sells the salve by mail. Before long, he is getting testimonials from people who are delighted and amazed. "This salve really is miraculous," says one enthusiastic user. "All my warts are gone."

Believe it or not, this scenario is not far-fetched because his concoction really will remove warts. So will peanut butter or shoe polish or anything else lying around your home. In fact, anything under the sun will remove warts—or at least get credit for doing so. Here's why: Scientists have found that if warts are left untreated, 85 percent of them will disappear on their own.[6] This explains the popularity, for centuries, of such unlikely wart removers as pork fat and cow dung. No matter how weird, each cure "worked" for a large percentage of patients, and those grateful people gave enthusiastic testimonials to their friends and neighbors.

When you examine claims, don't let testimonials sway you, especially in the area of medicine. Many human maladies are like warts: they disappear on their own. Dr. Lewis Thomas, physician and essayist, once said, "The great secret, known to internists . . . but still hidden from the general public, is that most things get better by themselves. Most things, in fact, are better by morning."[7] But people are impatient to get well, and they rush to procure the remedies of both conventional and unconventional medicine. When their health returns (not because of the remedy but because of the passage of time), they gratefully give testimonials to the wonderful power of the remedy.

Testimonials can give us an indication of what might work, but they do not constitute proof. Be suspicious of claims that have no other substantiation.

opinion
a conclusion or judgment that remains open to dispute, but seems true to one's own mind

Reject claims based solely on opinions. Avoid being swayed by the strongly held **opinions** of your sources. Advocates who believe passionately in their ideas are often highly persuasive and charismatic, winning people over with their sincerity and burning conviction. But unless your sources' opinions are supported by solid evidence, they are worthless. Everyone is entitled to his or her opinion, but opinions are not facts.

Find More Than One Source

When my wife and I started lifting weights, we had a disagreement about the correct way to breathe. Based on a weightlifting book I had checked out of the library, I said that one should inhale when lifting; she argued that one should exhale.

To settle the argument, we searched the Internet for articles on the subject. The first article we found agreed with her: exhale. "It's a toss-up," I said. But then we looked at eight more articles. They all said the same thing: exhale.

I lost the argument but avoided an exercise mistake—thanks to our persistence in checking more than one source. (The book turned out to be 10 years old, advocating a method that fitness experts now agree is inferior.)

Never settle for just one source because it might turn out to be wrong.

Examine Opposing Viewpoints

Some researchers stockpile a mass of information from many sources, thereby avoiding the mistake just mentioned, but they fall into a different trap: All their sources represent just one side of an issue. A better strategy is to find out what a wide variety of people, including opponents, have to say. Here's why:

Ethical Issue

1. Ethical researchers want to find truth, even if it means they have to revise their arguments or—in some cases—admit error and change their position.
2. From a practical point of view, knowing the opposition's case helps a speaker anticipate the objections that might come from listeners. It's better to know counterarguments before a speech than get blindsided by them during the question-and-answer period.

Be Cautious in Using Polls

Take care in interpreting data from polls and surveys because of two frequent shortcomings.

Some people do not respond honestly. After a recent election, pollsters for *Time* magazine found that 56 percent of eligible American voters said they had cast ballots, but actual election returns revealed that only 39 percent had done so.[8] In another poll, the Gallup Organization reported that in the United States, 45 percent of Protestants and 51 percent of Roman Catholics said that they attend church services weekly, but a team of sociologists analyzing actual church records discovered that only 20 percent of Protestants and 28 percent of Catholics show up on Sundays.[9]

What's going on? Professor Mark Chaves of Notre Dame University explains: "Most people believe voting or going to church is a good thing to do and, when surveyed, often say they did vote or go to church even when they didn't."[10]

In another form of lying, some people will offer an opinion on an issue about which they know nothing. The American Jewish Committee once sponsored a survey of American attitudes toward various ethnic groups, and they included a nonexistent group called Wisians to see if some Americans tend to dislike all ethnic groups. Most of the people surveyed responded with "no opinion" concerning Wisians, but 40 percent expressed a view—a dim view. They gave the Wisians a low favorability rating—4.12 on a scale of 0 to 9.0.[11]

Results often depend upon how a question is asked. If asked, "Do you favor the United States giving foreign aid to other nations?" most people say no. But if the question is put into different words—"Do you favor the United States sharing at least a small portion of its wealth with those in the world who are in great need?"—almost everyone says yes. Thus, opponents of foreign aid would ask the first question, and then use the results to show that the public rejects foreign aid, while advocates of foreign aid would ask the second question, and then use the results to show that the public favors foreign aid.[12]

As you can see, polls can be slippery. Before using polling data in a speech, investigate these issues: What survey questions were asked? Were they free of bias? Did the respondents have any reason to answer untruthfully? Do the pollsters have a hidden agenda?

Recognize the Fallibility of Experts

Experts can be a valuable source of information on any subject, but don't assume that they are infallible. Every year experts in science and medicine are proven wrong in one theory or another. Until recently, most medical experts believed that stomach ulcers were caused by an excess of stomach acid that was induced by stress. We now know the ulcers are caused by a bacterium, and that 90 percent of ulcers can be cured within a few weeks.

The medical experts were not only wrong—they were stubbornly and persistently wrong. When an unknown Australian physician, Barry Marshall, introduced the bacterium theory in 1983, he was ridiculed. Doesn't everyone know that bacteria cannot survive in the acids of the human stomach? Because his theory was brushed aside, Marshall took the unusual step of dramatically infecting himself by drinking a bacteria-laden cocktail. His experiment worked: He demonstrated that bacteria can indeed live in the stomach. Nevertheless, for the next dozen or so years, most experts resisted the bacterium theory until slowly accumulating research created a mountain of convincing evidence. Finally, the experts had to capitulate and admit that Marshall was right.[13]

Some students think that if sources have a Ph.D. or an M.D. and are affiliated with a university or medical facility, they must be trustworthy. Unfortunately, there are crackpots and con artists in every field. Dr. Arthur Butz, professor of engineering at Northwestern University, is the author of *The Hoax of the Twentieth Century*, which asserts that the Holocaust (the Nazi killing of millions of Jews, Poles, gypsies, and others) never happened.[14] On the Internet there are many M.D.s who sponsor Websites that advertise various potions, lotions, and pills—many of which are worthless, and some harmful. For example, the Food and Drug Administration has found over 800 cases in which a widely advertised herb called ephedra (or ma huang) caused adverse reactions, including strokes, seizures, and heart attacks. Three dozen people died after using dietary supplements that contained ephedra.[15]

Tips for your CAREER

Tip 7.1 Be Willing to Challenge Reports in the Media

Here is a math problem for you to solve:

> How much change should you get back after putting down $3 to pay for a 60-cent cup of soup and a $1.95 sandwich? (Do not figure tax or tip.)

Please do the problem before looking at the answer (which is given at the end of this article).

The math problem was featured in a column by John Leo of *U.S. News and World Report* magazine. Citing a Department of Education study, he said that 56 percent of American college graduates were unable to give the correct answer—an example, Leo said, of the "new stupidity" of Americans.

One of my students showed me the article and said, "I'm not good in math, but even I can answer this correctly. I just can't believe that most college graduates would give a wrong answer."

I, too, was skeptical so I did an experiment. I tested a class of first-year college students: Everyone answered correctly. Next, I went to a local high school and tested a class of juniors: Everyone answered correctly. Then I tested the 9th grade remedial math class (the poorest math students in the entire school): About 70 percent answered correctly (and some of those who gave the wrong answer may have done so because they were immigrants with a poor grasp of English).

When I wrote to John Leo about my findings, he defended his column by saying that he was just quoting a government study.

What Leo should have done was what my student did: raise an eyebrow over "facts" that defy common sense. After all, if most college graduates in America can't solve a simple math problem, the nation is in dire trouble.

Some people, while being willing to question claims on Websites, are reluctant to challenge what they hear in the mainstream news media (newspapers, magazines, TV) because of the attitude, "Who am I to question those bright writers and TV producers?" If this is your attitude, you need to trust your common sense, the inner voice that says, "Nonsense!" when you encounter information that seems distorted or untrue. And you need to realize that talented writers and producers can sometimes give information that is ridiculous and wrong. For example, an NBC news program recently televised a report extolling the virtues of "ear candling," in which a lighted hollow candle is placed in the ear to draw out earwax, ear mites, and accumulated debris. If you had watched this report and said, "Nonsense!" you would have been right. It turns out that candling (according to medical experts) is worthless in extracting gunk, and even worse, hot dripping candle wax can cause severe injuries to the ear canal and eardrum.

(Answer to the above problem: 45 cents.)

What should be your attitude toward experts? Examine what they say because they often have valuable insights, but don't suspend your skepticism. Evaluate the comments of both their defenders and their critics.

Beware of Groups with Misleading Names

Research studies from worthy organizations can be valuable sources of information, but use caution if you are not thoroughly familiar with a group. Sometimes organizations use impressive names to suggest that they are unbiased, neutral, and fair-minded when in reality they have hidden backers with an agenda that is different from what the public expects. Consider these cases:

- A few years ago *The Princeton Dental Resource Center* sounded like a reliable research institute when it announced a surprising discovery: Contrary to what most parents think, chocolate candy does *not* cause dental cavities in children; even more amazing, chocolate *prevents* cavities. Before a stampede to candy stores could occur, however, the group's chief financial backer was exposed. It was none other than the maker of M&M's chocolate candy![16]

- *The National Wetlands Coalition* sounds like an environment-protection group, but *The Wall Street Journal* reports that it is financed by oil companies and real-estate developers whose goal is to reduce the amount of wetlands protected by federal law.[17]
- *Mothers Opposing Pollution,* a group in Australia, claimed to have thousands of supporters in a battle against plastic milk containers. The group argued that plastic containers clogged landfills, and that the interaction of milk and plastic caused cancer. Investigative reporters discovered that the "group" had only one member—a public relations executive who was being paid by the makers of *paper* milk cartons.[18]

Hundreds of groups like these—simply on the strength of their impressive names—arrange to have their spokespersons appear in TV interviews, and their press releases are often reprinted by unsuspecting newspapers and magazines. Their views and findings may have some merit, but they undermine their credibility when they use a misleading name and hide their backers.

To find out whether a group has hidden backers and undisclosed goals, use search engines to conduct keyword searches and evaluate what is being said by both friends and foes of the group.

Analyzing Internet Sites

Because information on the Internet ranges from extremely useful to totally useless, how can you sort out the good from the bad? Here are some suggestions.

Don't Be Swayed by Widespread Dissemination

When some people make preposterous claims and their "facts" are challenged, they defend themselves by saying, "It must be true—it's all over the Internet." But widespread appearance on the Internet is no proof of accuracy. Unfortunately, misinformation can be spread to all parts of the planet in the twinkling of an eye.

Millions of people have received the following e-mail:

> *Urgent Alert!*
>
> If you are driving after dark and see an oncoming car with no headlights on, DO NOT flash your lights at them! This is a common gang member "initiation game." Here is how the game works: The new gang member under initiation drives along with no headlights, and the first car to flash their headlights at him is now his "target." He is now required to turn around and chase that car, and shoot at or into the car in order to complete his initiation requirements. Make sure you share this information with all the drivers in your family![19]

This alert is a hoax, but it has been widely distributed on the Internet in articles as well as in e-mails. Newspaper reporters and police investigators have discovered that it is considered to be true by many people, who say they will no longer engage in headlight flashing. There is no evidence that any gang ever used such an initiation, but the hoax did apparently inspire one "copycat" incident—a drive-by shooting in Wichita, Kansas. A 38-year-old woman was shot at after flashing her lights at a pickup that had its lights off, Wichita police said. Neither the woman nor her car was hit.[20]

Some widespread information on the Internet can be deadly. Many cancer patients, avoiding medical treatment that might save their lives, try (unsuccessfully) to cure themselves by using miracle cures that various Internet sites tout as guaranteed to eliminate cancer.[21]

Watch Out for Web Manipulation

When you watch TV, you can easily spot an infomercial—a show that tries to look like an informational report but really is a scripted commercial. For example, you see five people chatting about how the Fabulous Flat-Tummy Machine chiseled their torsos and made them live happily every after.

The Internet equivalent of infomercials is harder to detect. Let's say you are searching for information on how to take care of an automobile, and you come across a Web page with 12 tips on maintaining a car's exterior. The suggestions look like objective, reliable material. One of the tips ("Use high-quality wax") has a link that, when clicked, takes you to a page that is openly commercial—it sells exterior wax. Unknown to you, the original page and the wax page are both operated by the same source—a company that sells wax. The company has done nothing illegal, but it has acted unethically in leaving you with the impression that the tips page was written by impartial researchers who are honestly recommending the best product. You have been manipulated.

To avoid being manipulated, weigh Web advice carefully and verify that the information is corroborated by sources that you know you can trust.

Don't Be Dazzled by High-Tech Design

News reports periodically tell the sad story of Internet users—including highly intelligent, college-educated men and women—who are lured into buying worthless merchandise or nonexistent services. How can con artists fool so many bright people? One of their techniques is to create a Website that has beautiful graphic design. The high-tech sparkle gives the Website an aura of professionalism, wealth, and respectability.

Look at the advertisement in Figure 7.1. Does it look legitimate to you? Some of my students—when shown this ad among a stack of both honest and dishonest Web ads—rate it as probably reliable. In fact, it is a fraud. I created it on my home computer to demonstrate how easy it is for Internet crooks to create impressive-looking graphics.

If you apply a bit of skepticism, you can tell the cruise is a rip-off because of the ridiculously low price. A ship that charged so little would quickly go out of business.

But what about the photo of the ship? Some students say that they were fooled because the photo makes the ad look authentic. Don't be dazzled by photos. In this case, the vessel shown is a real cruise ship, but I did not have to fly in a helicopter over the ocean to photograph it. I simply located the photo on a Corel 100-photo royalty-free CD costing $19.95, imported it into my computer, added text, and then printed the final copy. Total time: 20 minutes.

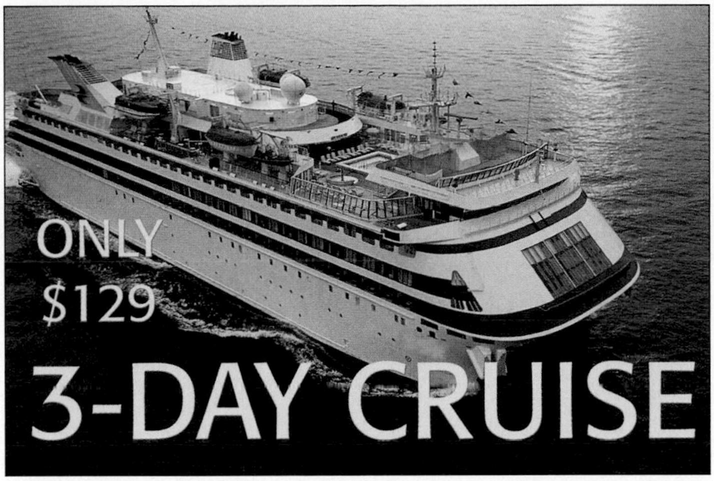

Figure 7.1
If you saw this advertisement on a Website, would you find anything questionable about it?

Quickly and inexpensively, a crackpot or a con artist can create a gorgeous Website.

Whether you are looking for information or wealth, remember that high tech does not necessarily equal high value.

Investigate Sponsors and Authors

Who is behind a Website? Are the owners and writers honest and unbiased? To help you evaluate a site, use these strategies:

Look for Author Credentials

Is the author of a Web page qualified to write authoritatively on the subject at hand? Look for some mention of his or her credentials or achievements. If none are listed, look for an e-mail link and send a message like this: "I am gathering materials for a speech, and I need to evaluate the credibility of your Web page. Could you please tell me about your qualifications and experience on this subject?"

Get Background Information on Sponsors

Who is funding or sponsoring a Website? If the site does not display this information on the opening screen, sometimes you can get details by clicking on a button (such as "About Us"). Or, if there is an e-mail link, you can send a message requesting background information.

Try investigating the Website by feeding the keywords of its name into a search engine like Google. Evaluate what supporters and opponents of the Website are saying about it.

Examine Internet Domain Names

An Internet address is known as a **domain** name. The suffix at the end of the name signifies the "top-level domain," indicating whether the address belongs to a business, an educational institution, or one of the other broad categories shown in Table 7.1. For example, the address www.npr.org is the domain name

domain
a group of computers on a network that operate under common rules

Table 7.1
Top Level Domains

Original	
.com	commercial (business)
.org	nonprofit organization
.net	networks
.gov	government nonmilitary organization
.mil	U.S. military branches
.edu	educational and research institutions
Additional	
.biz	businesses
.info	informational
.name	individuals

Note: For updates on new suffixes, visit the author's Website (www.mhhe.com/gregory7), click on STUDENT EDITION and then WEBLINKS, and explore links for this page.

for National Public Radio. The suffix ".org" (pronounced dot-org) denotes a nonprofit organization.

The top-level domains (in Table 7.1) are worth noting because they give you an important clue about a source's objectivity and motivations.

Commercial Web pages (.com) tend to be the least objective of all the domains. Let's say that you search for information on pain relievers and you come across an Internet page extolling the virtues of aspirin. If you note that the page is produced by bayer.com, you would be wise to consider that Bayer is in the business of selling aspirin and can't be expected to objectively view the efficacy of aspirin. If, however, you find a pro-aspirin site with an educational address (.edu)—for example, the Johns Hopkins Medical School—the chances are higher that the research is objective and accurate.

But don't jump to the conclusion that all ".com" addresses are untrustworthy. Many businesses offer excellent information, not only about their products and services, but also about the general topic. The Healthy Choice line of foods, for example, has a Web page (www.healthychoice.com) that does far more than advertise; it provides dozens of recipes and tips (that do not require buying Healthy Choice products).

Some ".com" sites are operated by magazine and newspaper publishers who provide objective, reliable reporting. For example, the on-line *Christian Science Monitor* (www.csmonitor.com) is a business enterprise, but it has a reputation for honest, careful journalism.

Though ".edu" sites tend to be more objective and accurate than ".com" sites, this is not always the case. Some university research projects are funded by corporations that have a vested interest in a certain outcome. A professor at the University of Wisconsin recently announced on an ".edu" site that he had discovered that purple grape juice can help prevent heart attacks. A few days later, Reuters news agency revealed that the professor's study was funded by a juice manufacturer.[22] The professor's findings may prove accurate, but until they are confirmed by researchers who are not paid by juice companies, we should remain skeptical.

We also should retain skepticism when considering other noncommercial domains. For example, nonprofit organizations (.org) are often reliable sources, but they, too, have biases. The United Nations (www.un.org) can provide trustworthy international statistics, but it obviously has a bias in reporting U.N. peacekeeping operations.

The vast majority of sites on the Web are ".com," and they can create a lot of clutter when you are trying to find purely educational material. To overcome this problem, several search engines, such as Google's Advanced Search (www.google.com and click on "Advanced Search"), allow you to search by domain. In other words, you can specify that you want returns only from ".edu" sites.

www.mhhe.com /gregory7

Since Internet addresses may change or disappear, look for updates on this book's Website. Click on STUDENT EDITION and then WEBLINKS.

Look for Country of Origin

Gathering information from throughout the world can be rewarding. If you are researching ways to combat soil erosion and you find a Web page on an innovative program in Costa Rica, you have broadened your knowledge base.

Beware, however, of using such material incorrectly. Suppose you come across an appealing Web page that lists major prescription drugs and the ailments they treat. If you notice that the page originates in another country, you would be wise to use the information carefully, if at all. Other countries have different trade names and different rules on which drugs are permissible. A prescription drug that is available in England may not be FDA-approved for the United States.

Most Websites display an address or give some indication of the place of origin. For those that do not, you will have to look for clues:

1. **Investigate place names that do not sound familiar.** If you are looking for articles on criminal law and you find a Web page about legal cases in New South Wales, you should find out just where New South Wales is located. When you discover that it is a state in Australia, you should explore whether the information applies to the United States.
2. **Look for abbreviations in the Internet address.** Websites in various countries may use the same identifiers used by American sites—.org, .net, and so on. But sometimes their addresses include two-letter international abbreviations. For example, "www.cite-sciences.fr" is the address for a French science site.

You can find a list of international abbreviations at one of these sites:

- www.wap.org/info/techstuff/domains.html
- www.ics.uci.edu/pub/websoft/wwwstat/country-codes.txt

A few abbreviations that are sometimes misinterpeted:

- **ca** stands for Canada, not California (which is **ca.us**).
- **ch** stands for Confederation Helvetica (Switzerland), not China (which is **cn**).
- **co** stands for Colombia, not Colorado (which is **co.us**).
- **de** stands for Deutschland (Germany), not Denmark (which is **dn**).

Examine Date

Most Web pages will give the date on which the information was created or updated. If the page is old, you may need to find another, more recent source.

Table 7.2 Evaluations of Websites

Directories with Rated Sites These directories provide links to Websites that are ranked according to quality.	• Librarians' Index to the Internet (www.lii.org) selects only reliable sites and often appends an evaluation, which you can reach by clicking on the "Comments" box. • Infomine (infomine.ucr.edu/) features Websites that have been evaluated by librarians at several top U.S. colleges. Look for "Browse Options."
Selective Directories These directories don't assign a rank, but all their links are to sites that are considered worth visiting.	• New York Times Cyber Times Navigator (www.nytimes.com/ref/technology/cybertimes-navigator.html) lists the top reference sites used by *Times* reporters. See "Collections for Journalists" and "Reference Desk." • WWW Virtual Libary (www.vlib.org) lists high-quality academic sites.
Misinformation Alerts These services try to expose scams, quackery, and phony news—not only in Websites, but in society at large.	• Quackwatch (www.quackwatch.com) is edited by Stephen Barrett, M.D., former professor of health education at Pennsylvania State University. • The Skeptic's Dictionary (www.skepdic.com) is edited by Robert T. Carroll, professor of philosophy at Sacramento City College. • About (www.about.com) has many articles that can be retrieved by searching for "Net hoaxes" and/or "Scams."

Note: Internet addresses and features sometimes change. For an update on these sites, visit the book's Website (www.mhhe.com/gregory7), click on STUDENT EDITION and then WEBLINKS, and look at notes for this page.

Look at Evaluations of Websites

If you are investigating the reliability of a Website, the best strategy is what we've already suggested: Look for other sources, especially opposing views. Another good strategy is to see how other people rate a particular Website. Table 7.2 provides links to services that evaluate Websites for reliability.

Bear in mind that these services do not pretend to rate all Websites. Also, don't accept the reviews as indisputable. Just as a movie reviewer's good rating does not guarantee you a movie that you will enjoy, a Web reviewer's good rating does not guarantee you a reliable source.

Ethical Issue

Legal and Ethical Guidelines

When using material created by others, avoid the ethical and legal pitfalls of plagiarism and copyright infringement. Here are some guidelines.

Giving Credit to Sources

plagiarism
stealing the ideas or words of another and passing them off as one's own

oral footnote
a spoken citation of the source of one's material

Plagiarism—passing off someone else's words or ideas as your own—is unethical and in some cases illegal. To avoid plagiarism, you must give credit to the sources of your information.

Giving credit in a speech is achieved by using an **oral footnote** (which is the equivalent of a footnote in a written document); for example, "According to the *CBS Evening News* of March 15th of this year . . . " and "In the words of Thomas Jefferson . . . "

Oral footnotes do more than just give credit: They also bolster your credibility. You are saying, in effect, "I didn't pull this information out of thin air; I derived it from someone who is an authority on the subject."

Tips for your CAREER

Tip 7.2 Avoid Vagueness When Citing Internet Sources

"I got my information from the Internet."

This is a common statement by many speakers in business and professional settings. It is vague and worthless—sort of like saying, "I got my information from people."

Be specific. Say something like this: "My information about military aircraft comes from an article by General John Jumper, chief of staff of the United States Air Force. The article was posted on the official Website of the Air Force."

If citing the Internet is too vague, is it acceptable to cite a search engine like Google? Linda King, a wildlife biologist at the Corbett Wildlife Management Area near West Palm Beach, Florida, attended PowerPoint presentations by a group of college seniors majoring in environmental science. "I was astonished," she said, "when at least 10 of the students cited Google as their source."

Google is *not* a source—it's a delivery system. Giving credit to Google is like citing the U.S. Postal Service as the source of medical information mailed to you by the American Medical Association. Don't even mention Google. Instead say, "My information about cancer medications comes from Dr. Nancy H. Nielson, who provided a detailed report on the Website of the American Medical Association."

If you got information from an interview, you could say something like this: "According to Elizabeth Smith, director of advertising for our city's largest retail store . . . "

For material from books or magazines, you could say, "In an article in this month's issue of *Scientific American,* Dr. Paul Rhodes says that . . . " Or: "The graph on this slide is based on data I found in this year's issue of the *World Almanac.*"

When you are quoting verbatim, use "oral" quotation marks, such as "To quote Abraham Lincoln . . . " or "In the words of Plato . . . " Using expressions like these is smoother than saying "Quote" at the beginning of a statement and "Unquote" at the end. A slight pause at the end of the quotation should be an adequate signal that you have finished quoting. Another approach: Hold up the card or page containing the quotation so that listeners can see that you are reading word-for-word; when you put the paper down, it is clear that you have finished quoting.[23]

Using Copyrighted Material

Some people find themselves in court because they have improperly used audiovisual, printed, or Internet material created by others. A person can be charged under criminal law for **copyright infringement,** which is a felony (with a maximum penalty of $100,000 in fines—for each infringement and one year in jail), and can be sued under civil law (with financial damages determined by judge and/or jury).[24]

copyright infringement
unauthorized use of legally protected material

Under U.S. and international copyright laws, all printed, electronic, and audiovisual creations—including books, magazines, artwork, cartoons, movies, TV shows, photographs, Web pages, computer software, and music—are considered copyrighted and owned by the creators *even if there is no copyright notice attached to them.* Before you can use these materials in a presentation or in handouts, you must get prior permission (and in some cases, pay a fee)—unless an item falls under one of these three exceptions: materials in the public domain, fair use of copyrighted material, and royalty-free material.

Public Domain

public domain
what is owned by the community at large; unprotected by patent or copyright

Anything published or created before 1923 is no longer protected by copyright and is said to be "in the **public domain,**" which means you are free to use it however you please.[25] If, for example, you find a drawing of Niagara Falls in a 1920 encyclopedia, you can use it in a speech or publication without violating the law.

Any publication of the *federal* (not state) government is not copyrighted and can be used freely. Thus, a U.S. Department of Agriculture booklet on avoiding food poisoning can be reproduced and distributed without your needing to get permission or pay a fee.

Note of caution: In the realm of copyright, the U.S. Postal Service is not considered a part of the federal government; it is an incorporated business and therefore can copyright its postage stamp designs. You cannot copy stamp designs without getting permission.

Fair Use

fair use
allowable and reasonable exceptions to copyright rules

A loophole in copyright laws—called the **fair use** doctrine—was created to enable scholars, writers, and public speakers to disseminate information without having to spend enormous amounts of time getting permission for every item used. The fair use doctrine allows you "to quote from [printed works] or to reproduce small amounts of graphic or pictorial material for purposes of review or criticism or to illustrate or buttress [your] own points," according to *The Chicago Manual of Style,* a reference work widely consulted by editors and publishers.[26]

Legal interpretations of the fair use doctrine are complex, but you can be sure that you are on firm legal ground if you are careful to meet *all three* of the following tests.[27]

1. You use only a small and relatively insignificant portion of a copyrighted work.
2. Your purpose is primarily educational, rather than commercial.
3. You do not cause economic harm to the copyrighted work.

Let's apply these tests to several scenarios.

Case #1. In a talk on suicide, you quote four lines from a long poem by the American poet Anne Sexton to illustrate loneliness and despair. Must you get permission (and possibly pay a fee)? No, because you easily meet *all three* tests for fair use.

Case #2. Part of your job at a hospital is giving presentations to patients who have just undergone heart surgery. To provide your audience with some material to study at home, you hand each patient a photocopy of a six-page pamphlet (produced by a health-communications firm) on dietary and exercise suggestions for post-operative patients. You have not asked permission or paid a fee. Are you violating the law? Yes. You violate test #1 by photocopying an entire publication, and you violate test #3 by depriving the publisher of revenues. If you were sued for copyright infringement, the courts most likely would rule that you made the photocopies to avoid paying for the pamphlets. (You would not win the case by pleading that you were in a hurry and didn't have time to buy copies.)[28]

Case #3. To illustrate a talk on immigration into the United States, you show an overhead transparency that is an enlargement of a world map you downloaded from an on-line magazine on the Internet. Illegal? No, because your purpose is educational.

Case #4. Same situation as #3, but this time your listeners must pay admission to hear your presentation and the proceeds go into your pocket. Can you still use the map? Not unless you get written permission from the magazine publisher. This time you are clearly in a commercial realm, and using the map without permission would be copyright infringement. In the eyes of the law, the magazine spent time and money creating the map and must be compensated for your commercial use of it. (*Important note:* It is a mistake to think that because copying material from the Internet is easy, it is always legal to do so.)

Case #5. In a college presentation on the unreliability of eyewitness testimony, you perform an experiment with your listeners. You show a 15-second clip from a commercial movie about an armed robbery, then ask the audience to write down a description of the robber. When you read aloud their widely differing descriptions, the audience gets the point: Eyewitnesses often cannot remember basic facts correctly. If you use the movie excerpt without getting permission, are you violating the law? No. As long as your purpose is educational, you are abiding by the fair-use guidelines.

Case #6. You conduct a free workshop for the public on how to prepare federal income tax forms, and you distribute photocopies of worksheets from *J. K. Lasser's Your Income Tax*, a national bestseller, without seeking the publisher's permission. An important part of your presentation is leading the audience through the worksheets. Illegal? Yes. While you meet the second test (educational), you violate the first test because those worksheets—even though they are a small percentage of the total book—are not relatively insignificant. They are major features of the book. You also fail the third test because you are hurting the publisher economically. If you were sued, the courts probably would rule that your listeners might have bought the Lasser book had you not given them free excerpts. Thus, you deprived the publisher, Prentice Hall, of revenues to which it was entitled. You should have bought copies of the book—or had your listeners buy copies—and then led the audience through the worksheets.

What's the difference between the last two cases? In case #5, the use of the movie is incidental to the speech—a minor part. But in case #6, the worksheets play a central role. One of the best ways to determine legality is to step into the shoes of the copyright holder and ask, "Would I feel ripped off?" In case #5, if you were the owner of the movie, I don't think you would feel cheated, but in case #6, if you were the publisher, you probably would feel that you had been deprived of revenues.

Two notes of caution: (1) Fair use does not remove the need to cite your sources. You still should give credit. (2) A common mistake is to think that if you take a copyrighted work and make some changes here and there, it is no longer protected by copyright law and becomes your property. This is wrong. If you take the transcript of a speech, change some words, rewrite some sentences, and modify the visual aids, the speech is still not yours. If you find a magazine photo of a movie star, scan it into your computer, and change the color of her hair and dress, the photo still does not belong to you. To think that manipulating a work makes it your property, says Steven Blaize, president of a multimedia production company, "is like saying as long as you paint flames on a stolen car before you display it in your collection, it's yours."[29]

Royalty-Free Material

royalty-free
devoid of restrictions or fees

To avoid fees and legal uncertainties, many speakers, writers, and editors are buying artwork (such as drawings and photos) and multimedia works (such as music, sound effects, and videos) that are **royalty-free**—that is, free of restrictions and fees. In other words, when you pay for a royalty-free product, you are buying the right to use it in a publication, speech, or video production without having to ask permission or pay anything extra. If, for example, you produce a training videotape for your company, you can use a royalty-free rendition of a Beethoven symphony as background music.

Resources for Review and Skill Building

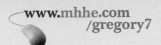

www.mhhe.com/gregory7

This book's Online Learning Center Website and SpeechMate CD-ROM provide meaningful resources and tools for study and review, such as practice tests, key-term flashcards, and sample speech videos.

SpeechMate CD-ROM

Summary

When you evaluate material, look for high-quality information that is factual, reliable, well supported, current, verifiable, fair, and comprehensive.

Apply healthy skepticism, probing for erroneous or unreliable data. Reject claims that are based solely on anecdotes, testimonials, or opinions. Don't use just one source, because it might turn out to be wrong. Examine opposing viewpoints in an effort to find truth and to anticipate possible listener objections.

Be cautious in using polls because some people don't respond honestly, and results often depend upon how a question is asked.

Recognize the fallibility of experts. Don't assume that a Ph.D or M.D. is always trustworthy. Don't assume that affiliation with a prestigious university is assurance of credibility.

Watch out for groups with names that can mislead the public into thinking they are unbiased. Find out who is financially backing the group.

In analyzing Internet sites, watch out for subtle manipulation on Web pages. Examine domain names for clues on a source's objectivity and motivation. See if the material comes from a foreign country. If a Website has a beautiful, sophisticated design, don't assume that it is reliable and highly professional. Investigate its sponsors and authors to see if they are legitimate authorities on their subject matter.

Legally and ethically, it's important to give credit for material you derive from sources. Don't use copyrighted material unless you get permission from the copyright holder or unless the material falls into one of three categories: public domain, fair use, and royalty-free.

Key Terms

anecdote, *149*
copyright infringement, *159*
domain, *155*
fair use, *160*
opinion, *150*
oral footnote, *158*
plagiarism, *158*
public domain, *160*
royalty-free, *162*
testimonial, *149*

Review Questions

1. What are the characteristics of high-quality information?
2. What is anecdotal evidence, and why does it fail to constitute proof of an assertion?
3. How do opinions differ from facts?
4. Why should more than one source be consulted?
5. Why are polls often unreliable?
6. What are the domain names for commercial, nonprofit, and educational Websites?
7. What is meant by *public domain*?
8. Define *fair use*.
9. What use can be made of a product that is *royalty-free*?
10. What is an *oral footnote*?

Building Critical-Thinking Skills

1. Imagine a Website called www.clearskin.com that touts a miracle drug that banishes facial blemishes. The drug is praised on the Website by a man identified as Roger Taschereau, M.D. You are trying to decide whether to recommend the medicine in a speech you are preparing. What is your evaluation of the Website up to this point? What additional steps should you take before recommending the drug?
2. Project Gutenberg (promo.net/pg) is a Website with links to hundreds of books, poems, and plays that are in the public domain. If you want to copy a poem or book chapter for distribution to listeners at a business presentation, must you get permission? Explain your answer.

Building Teamwork Skills

1. Can a person find relief from pain by attaching tiny magnets to an injured area? In a group, discuss how to find reliable information on "biomagnetic therapy," which has grown in popularity in recent years. Rank the sources below from (probably) most reliable to (probably) least reliable. Discuss why some of these sources are likely to be more reliable than others.
   a. A Website devoted to debunking the claims of alternative medicine.
   b. A Website that sells magnets and is operated by a self-styled "alternative healer," who claims that a magnetic mask placed on one's face can cure head colds.
   c. A brochure by Bioflex, a corporation that sells over $1.5 billion worth of magnetic materials each year.
   d. A recently published scholarly book, with reference notes, by a biology professor at the University of Washington.
   e. An endorsement of magnets by the Montreal Expos' star pitcher, Hideki Irabu, who places them on his pitching arm.
   f. An e-mail interview this week with Edward McFarland, M.D., head of sports medicine at Johns Hopkins University, who has studied biomagnetics.
2. Working in a group, compile a list of current information sources used by you and other group members (for example, ABC News, *USA Today, The Tonight Show with Jay Leno,* e-mail from friends). Next, place these sources into three categories: very reliable, fairly reliable, and not reliable. Justify your evaluation.

Building Internet Skills

www.mhhe.com/gregory7

1. Choose one of the issues below and search the Internet for both "pro" and "con" arguments. Print at least one document from each side of the issue that you select.
   a. Should states permit medical use of marijuana?
   b. Should the World Wide Web be censored?
   c. Should immigration to the United States be limited?
   d. Should states privatize prisons?
   e. Should companies use polygraphs (lie detectors) to screen job applicants?

   Possible Strategy: Use archives of newspapers and magazines (see Chapter 6 for addresses).

2. Using the Internet improperly at work can get you into trouble—and even cause you to be fired. Find and print an article that gives at least three examples of misuse of the Internet in the workplace.

   Possible Strategy: Go to a search engine, such as Google (www.google.com), and use these keywords: "Internet workplace misuse."

Using PowerWeb

www.mhhe.com/gregory7

An article entitled "The CARS Checklist" has five "Indicators of a Lack of Accuracy" regarding Websites. List all five indicators. To find the article, visit www.mhhe.com/gregory7, click on STUDENT EDITION and then POWERWEB: CONTENTS, and choose WEB RESEARCH (under STUDENT RESOURCES). Click on ACCURACY ONLINE—THE CARS CHECKLIST.

Nurul Izzah Anwar, an engineering major at a college in Malaysia, became a world-famous public speaker after her father, Malaysian pro-democracy leader Anwar Ibrahim, was jailed and tortured. She gives speeches throughout Asia and Europe, urging other nations to pressure the Malaysian government to make democratic reforms and release her father, and she has won the support of many world leaders. Her technique of persuasion is simple but effective: every time she makes a point, she immediately illustrates it with a true story. Using stories is a powerful tool that will be discussed in this chapter in the section on narratives.

8

Supporting Your Ideas

Outline

Reasons for Using Support Materials

Types of Support Materials

Definition
Vivid Image
Example
Narrative
Comparison and Contrast
Analogy
Testimony
Statistics

Sample Speech with Commentary

Objectives

After studying this chapter, you should be able to:

1. Explain why support materials are needed in a speech.
2. Describe nine types of support materials: definitions, vivid images, examples, narratives, comparison, contrast, analogies, testimony, and statistics.
3. Discuss the use and abuse of statistics in speeches.

Imagine that you are sitting in the audience when student speaker Rob Russo makes this statement:

> The most exciting and promising trend in medicine today is—believe it or not—the use of poison. Already, toxic substances produced by plants and animals are being used as medicines to relieve pain and save lives. And the future holds great hope for the discovery of more and more poisons.

What is your reaction? If you are like many listeners, you are probably skeptical. You are probably wondering, "Is this really true? Are these claims legitimate, or are they farfetched or exaggerated?" You need evidence. You need elaboration. Fortunately, Russo provides some *examples:*

- John Daley, a scientist at the National Institutes of Health, has discovered that a toxin from the skin of the tiny Ecuadorian poison-dart frog can provide morphine-like pain relief to humans without morphine's addiction risk.
- In large amounts, botulinum toxin, a poisonous bacterium also known as Botox, can cause botulism, a deadly form of food poisoning, but in small doses, it can erase wrinkles from the skin, eliminate migraine headaches, and help cerebral palsy patients to gain muscle control.
- Researchers have found that a chemical derived from the vampire bat can save the lives of stroke patients, poison from the puffer fish can ease the pain of cancer patients, and a substance derived from the Gila monster lizard can regulate insulin production in diabetes patients.

The skin of the tiny Ecuadorian poison-dart frog contains a toxin that wards off predators. The toxin is also effective as a pain reliever for humans.

After hearing these examples, you may still be a bit skeptical. Can the speaker relate a story of a person who has actually benefited from poison? Yes; here is a *narrative* that he provides:

> Duane Rualo, a 24-year-old accounting major at California State University at Long Beach, was diagnosed with glioma (a type of cancer) in 2001, and he was told he probably would not live long enough to attend his graduation in 2003. Then he was treated with seven injections of a newly discovered poison that has the ability to travel straight to tumors and kill them without damaging nearby healthy cells. The poison is the venom of the giant yellow Israeli scorpion. Since the injections, Rualo has graduated from college, and his brain scans have shown no signs of cancer. Today, he enjoys visiting a zoo near his home and viewing a scorpion exhibit to see the scary animal that saved his life.

At this point, you are probably much less skeptical, but you may wonder if Rualo's experience signifies a promising new trend or is merely an isolated case. What do scientists have to say about toxins? Russo provides *testimony* from an expert:

> Peter H. Raven, professor of botany at Washington University, predicts that in the near future, we will have an abundance of medicine derived from toxins. He says we have barely scratched the surface of nature's therapeutic potential. "There are 10 million organisms out there waging chemical warfare against each other," he says. "The abundance of possible drugs cannot even be imagined."[1]

By now, you are probably convinced that Russo has a valid point, thanks to the strong **support materials** that he uses to provide evidence. When you are a speaker, you must do more than make assertions and trust the audience to believe you. You must back up your statements with solid, credible support.

support material
elements that illustrate or substantiate a point

Reasons for Using Support Materials

Support materials enable you to move from general and abstract concepts, which are often hard for audiences to understand and remember, to specific and concrete details, which are easily grasped. Support materials add spice and flavor to a speech, but they are more than just seasonings; they are basic nourishment that is essential to the success of a speech. Let's look at five reasons why support materials are so important.

To Develop and Illustrate Ideas

In a speech on sharks, student speaker Austin Fitzgerald pointed out that, unlike most creatures of the sea, sharks behave unpredictably. To develop and illustrate his point, he said:

> In his book on sharks, Jacques-Yves Cousteau, the famous oceanographer, says that he has seen sharks flee from an almost naked, completely unarmed diver, but soon afterward hurl themselves against a steel diving cage and bite furiously at the bars. Sometimes a diver can

> scare off a shark by waving his or her flippers at it, while at other times sharks are so determined to attack that they are not deterred by the sight of five divers with spears. The terrifying thing, Cousteau says, is that sharks never give clues as to what kind of behavior they will exhibit.

Without these examples, Fitzgerald's contention that sharks behave unpredictably would have been weak. With the examples, the listeners got a clear picture of sharks' volatile nature. Notice, too, that Fitzgerald enhanced the credibility of his remarks by attributing his information to a well-known authority.

To Clarify Ideas

www.mhhe.com/gregory7
For an interactive exercise on support materials, visit Chapter 8 in this book's Website.

Helping the listener make sense out of your ideas is one of the main reasons for using support material. Student speaker Maria Burton gave a speech on pit-and-fissure sealants, which are used to cover the rough surfaces of teeth and prevent cavities.

"Sealants," Burton explained, "are thin, clear plastic coatings that are painted on the teeth, much like nail polish on fingernails."

With this analogy, the audience had a clear picture of what sealants are.

To Make a Speech More Interesting

In a speech on how explorers from earth would experience life on Mars, student speaker Diane Weber said,

> Most of the time Mars is much colder than the coldest regions of earth, with summer temperatures dipping down as low as 126 degrees below zero and winter temperatures twice that cold. Sometimes, however, at the equator of Mars, the temperature does warm up to an earthly level of comfort. For a few minutes, the temperature can climb to a high of 68 degrees—sort of like a pleasant October afternoon in New England.

Instead of merely reciting statistics, which would have been boring, Weber made her subject interesting by comparing and contrasting the climate of the two planets, using images (such as the October afternoon in New England) that her listeners could appreciate.

To Help Listeners Remember Key Ideas

Jeffrey Scott, a high school English teacher, says that his students are more likely to remember the meaning of a word in a vocabulary lesson if they are told the story of the word's origin. For example, he tells his students that we get the word *tantalize* from a king called Tantalus in Greek mythology: "As punishment for betraying Zeus, Tantalus was sentenced to hang from the branch of a fruit tree that spread out over a pool of water. Whenever he got hungry and reached for fruit, the wind would blow it out of his reach. Whenever he got thirsty and leaned over to drink from the pool, the water would recede." This story, Scott says, helps his students to remember that when we tantalize people, we torment them by showing them something that is desirable but unattainable.

To Help Prove an Assertion

When you want to prove a point, you must have evidence. If, for example, you wanted to prove that more counterfeiters are being caught today than ever before, you could quote a Secret Service official who states that the number of counterfeiting convictions this year is 10 times that of any previous year. Such a statistic from a reliable source is solid proof of your statement.

Note of caution: Support materials do not necessarily constitute proof. Suppose a speaker argues that drinking a glass of carrot juice daily can protect a person from heart disease. To prove his claim, he tells of a 93-year-old man who has consumed carrot juice every day for the past 60 years and has a healthy heart. This is an interesting example, but it proves nothing. There are probably many 93-year-old men who have healthy hearts but have never tasted carrot juice. To prove his point, the speaker would need indisputable findings by reputable medical authorities, based upon long-term studies of thousands of people.

Types of Support Materials

In this chapter we will look at *verbal* support materials, reserving *visual* supports for the next chapter. The cardinal rule in using verbal supports is that they must be relevant; they must develop, explain, illustrate, or reinforce your message. They should not be thrown in simply to enliven a speech.

Let's examine eight categories of verbal supports.

Definition

One of the biggest obstacles to successful communication is the assumption that your listeners define words and phrases the same way you do. If you are speaking on gun control, it is not enough to say, "I'm in favor of gun control." Exactly what does "gun control" mean? To some members of your audience, it may mean that citizens must surrender all of their firearms. To some, it may mean that citizens must give up only their handguns. To others, it may mean that citizens can keep their guns if they register them with the authorities. If you say that you are in favor of gun control without giving your **definition** of the term, some listeners may misunderstand your position and angrily reject everything that you say on the subject. So define your terms at the outset; for example: "When I talk about gun control, I'm not talking about confiscation of all guns; I'm talking about citizens registering the serial numbers of their guns with the authorities." Now you and your audience have a common basis for an evaluation of your views.

definition
a statement of the meaning of a word or phrase

Do you know what a "boss button" is? It's an icon supplied with many computer games that can be clicked if you are playing an unauthorized game on your computer at work and the boss walks into your office. Instantly, the game disappears and is replaced by a spreadsheet so that your boss thinks that you are doing your work. One speaker mentioned "boss button" in a speech, but many in the audience didn't know the meaning of the term. You can avoid this speaker's mistake if you always define terms that are not universally known. If you are experienced with digital imagery, for example, you must be careful to

A Native American leader who spoke to the United Nations at age 18, Winona LaDuke of the Ojibwe tribe of Northern Minnesota goes beyond a formal dictionary definition to define a term: "Quality of life does not have to do with income. Quality of life has to do with having clean air, feeling safe in your house, feeling that your children are safe on the streets, feeling that you are valued as a human being, that you have good relationships with other people, and that what you do feeds your soul and your day."

define terms like JPEG and TIFF (abbreviations for two types of digital files) that are well-known to you but not to the general public.

Avoid using formal dictionary definitions, if possible. They tend to be tedious and hard to grasp. Instead, use informal definitions that can be easily understood by the audience. Here is an instructive case: *chutzpah,* a slang word that the English language has borrowed from Yiddish, is defined by the *Random House College Dictionary* as "unmitigated effrontery or impudence." I once heard a speaker give a humorous, informal definition of the word: "Chutzpah is the kind of audacity and gall that a youngster would show if he killed both of his parents and then demanded that the court be lenient to him because he was an orphan." This informal definition drives home the point that chutzpah is more than ordinary gall; it is the *ultimate* form of gall. Such a definition does more than help the listeners understand the term—it also helps them remember it.

Vivid Image

Student speaker Nancy Li described a fascinating form of slavery in the animal world:

> Polyergus ants in Arizona have completely lost the ability to care for themselves, according to Dr. Howard Topoff of the American Museum of Natural History. They can't hunt for food for themselves, they can't feed the young, they can't feed and guard the queen, and they can't clean their own nest. The only thing they can do is fight. In order to survive, they capture slaves to do their work for them. Periodically

> about 1,500 Polyergus warriors will travel up to 500 feet and invade the nest of a different type of ant, the Formica. They expel the Formica queen and workers, and capture the pupae—the developing young—which they take back to their own nest. When the Formica ants are hatched, they assume the role of slaves. They forage for food to sustain their Polyergus masters, they remove wastes, and they excavate new chambers. A typical colony has 2,000 Polyergus masters and 3,000 Formica slaves. Without their slaves, the Polyergus would perish.[2]

SpeechMate CD-ROM

To see a speaker using a vivid image, view Video Clip 8.1 on Disk 1.

This passage is an example of **vivid images**—word pictures that are created by describing objects, animals, people, places, or situations. To make your description come alive in the minds of your listeners, you must use *specific details,* for they are the brush strokes that provide richness, color, and vividness. Instead of merely saying, "The dessert tasted good," say "The crunchy pretzels were coated with a soft, white yogurt icing, giving a delicious blend of sweetness and salt in each bite."

vivid image
a description that evokes a lifelike picture within the mind of the listener

Example

An **example** is an instance or fact that illustrates a statement or backs up a generalization. In a speech on illiteracy, student speaker Pat Ferguson made the following point:

example
an instance that serves to illustrate a point

> Illiterate adults cannot read the important things that the rest of us take for granted in our everyday lives.

If Ferguson had said no more on the subject, she would have forced her listeners to guess for themselves just what kind of reading material she was referring to. Fortunately for the audience, she gave examples:

SpeechMate CD-ROM

To see a speaker using an example, view Video Clip 8.2 on Disk 1.

> These adults cannot read the poison warnings on a can of pesticide, a highway directional sign, the front page of a newspaper, or a letter from their child's teacher.

While these examples are short, you may want to give longer examples in some cases. In a speech on drug smuggling, student speaker William Murphy gave examples of the clever ways that smugglers use to move cocaine into the United States:[3]

- Agents along the Mexican border discovered the "cone scam," in which an ice cream cone contained cocaine covered by a layer of ice cream. The cone was licked very slowly as the smuggler strolled across the border.
- A shipment of sneakers from Colombia to New York had false compartments in the soles stuffed with 12,000 pounds of cocaine worth $30 billion.
- In Miami, customs officials found 1,000 pounds of cocaine worth $3.4 million packed into hollow plaster shells that were shaped and painted to look like yams.
- A few years ago it became popular to conceal kilo bricks of cocaine beneath false bottoms of containers that held poisonous snakes. When

> drug agents discovered this ruse, smugglers began placing the drugs *inside* the snakes. "You've got cobras that are 12 feet long," says one customs official. "Who's going to pull it out and feel it?"

How many examples do you need to develop a point? In some cases, one example is sufficient, while other situations might require a series of examples. Ask yourself, "If I were those people sitting out there, how many examples would I need in order to understand, remember, or be convinced?"

Narrative

narrative
a story that illustrates a point

A **narrative** is a story that explains or illustrates your message. Narratives are audience favorites, lingering in the mind long after a speech has ended. People *love* stories, and even a sleepy or distracted member of the audience finds it hard to resist listening. As with all support materials, narratives must be relevant to your message. Never tell a story, no matter how spellbinding, if it fails to develop, explain, illustrate, or reinforce your key ideas.

Dr. Mark Johnson of the University of North Carolina Hospital in Chapel Hill performs kidney transplants. In a speech aimed at showing how easy it is to be a donor, Johnson told the heartwarming story of events leading to one of his operations. Here is a summary of the story:

> When Michael Carter was in the 8th grade in Fayetteville, North Carolina, he needed a kidney transplant. He had lost one kidney to disease, and the other was weakening. Despite 22 operations and thrice-weekly dialysis treatments, his condition was desperate, but no matching donor could be found, even though a dozen relatives had been tested.
>
> One day his science teacher, Jane Smith, noticed that he had trouble running on the playground. "I assumed he couldn't run because his pants were baggy." When she asked why he wore them, he said, "They're more comfortable. I'm on dialysis, Ms. Smith. I need a kidney."
>
> Her reply was instantaneous. "Well, I've got two. Want one?"
>
> Smith was soon tested, and it was discovered that she and Carter had compatible blood group and tissue

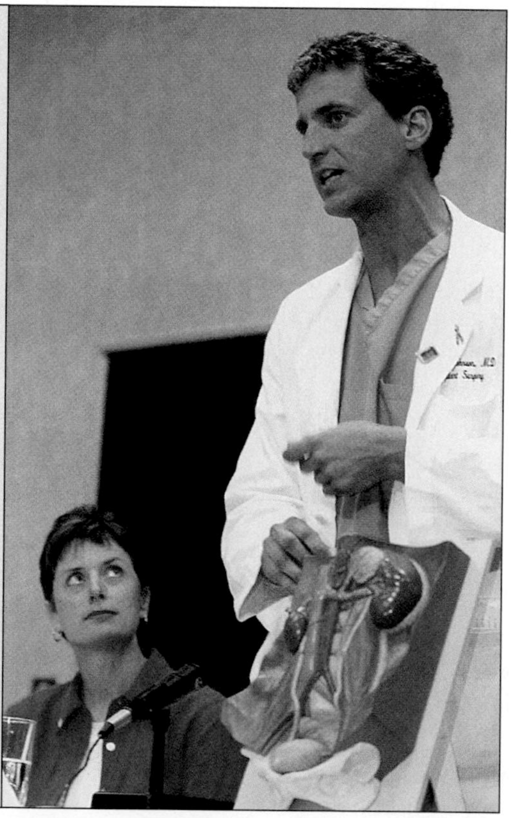

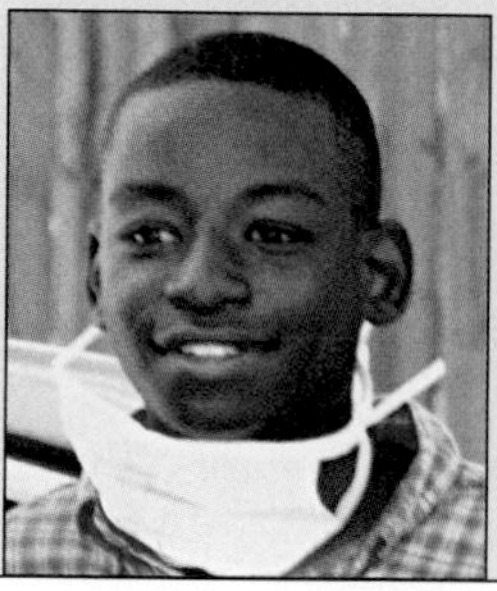

Looking on as Dr. Mark Johnson of Chapel Hill, North Carolina, discusses kidney transplants is science teacher Jane Smith, who donated one of her kidneys to her student Michael Carter (shown in photo below).

type. A few months later, she checked into Dr. Johnson's hospital and donated a kidney, which was transplanted into Carter's body 35 minutes later.

In the months that followed, neither the donor nor the recipient showed any ill effects, and today Michael Carter lives a normal life as a high-spirited, basketball-playing teenager.[4]

While the above story is factual, there are occasions when you may want to use a narrative that is **hypothetical,** that is, about an imaginary situation. Katrina Benjamin, a private investigator, wanted to explain how computers have invaded the average person's privacy:

hypothetical narrative
imaginary story related to help listeners visualize a potential situation

A company is trying to decide whether to hire you, and they ask me to investigate you. All I have is your name and address. I sit down in front of my computer and within five hours, I know a great deal about you: I know what jobs you have held and how much you got paid. I know the names of your parents, siblings, spouse, and children. I know what kind of car you drive and how much you paid for it. I know if you have ever been arrested or charged with a crime—even if it's just a ticket for speeding. I know the amount of the monthly payment on your home mortgage. I know what kinds of medical problems you have, and I know the names of all the prescribed medications you have taken in the past and are taking right now.[5]

This hypothetical scenario dramatically demonstrates the intrusiveness of computers.

Comparison and Contrast

Sometimes the best way to explain a thing or a concept is to make a **comparison**—that is, show how it resembles something else. In a lecture on the development of the English language, a speaker noted the following similarities:

comparison
showing how two or more items are alike

The Frisian language, spoken by 300,000 Frisians in the marshy headlands of northern Holland, is more closely related to English than any other language. Our *glass of milk* is their *glass milk,* our *butter* is their *butter,* our *dream* is their *dream,* our *boat* is their *boat,* our *green* is their *grien,* our *house* is their *hus,* our *cow* is their *ko,* our *goose* is their *goes,* our *sunshine* is their *sinneskine* . . .

By giving many points of comparison, the speaker strongly illustrated how similar the two languages are.

While a comparison shows how things are similar, a **contrast** shows how they are different. To show why many corporations are transferring thousands of technology jobs from the United States to other countries, Stephanie Moore, vice president for outsourcing at Forrester Research, describes a dramatic contrast:

contrast
showing how two or more items are different

SpeechMate CD-ROM
To see a speaker who makes a contrast, view Video Clip 8.3.

You can get crackerjack Java programmers in India right out of college for $5,000 a year versus $60,000 here [in the United States]. The technology is such, why be in New York City when you can be 9,000 miles away with far less expense?[6]

Sometimes it is helpful to use both comparison and contrast. For example, comparing and contrasting Japanese and American cars could help the listener understand more fully the features of each.

Analogy

analogy
resemblance in some respects between things that are otherwise dissimilar

A special type of comparison is the **analogy,** which explains a concept or object by likening it to something that is—at first glance—quite different. For example, computer-security expert William Cheswick explained how easily criminals can breach security walls at Internet sites. "The Internet is like a vault with a screen door on the back. I don't need jackhammers and atom bombs to get in when I can walk in through the door."[7]

SpeechMate CD-ROM
To see a speaker using an analogy, view Video Clip 8.4 on Disk 1.

How do analogies differ from ordinary comparisons? While ordinary comparisons show similarities between two things of the same category (two cars), analogies show similarities between two things of different categories (punctuation marks work like road signs and traffic signals). Student speaker Cheryl Williams used an analogy to show the futility of worry:

> Worrying is like sitting in a rocking chair and rocking furiously. There is a great deal of movement and agitation, but you don't go anywhere.

An analogy tries to show that what is true in one case is true in another. Student speaker Lisa Rathbone used this analogy:

> Cramming for a test the night before is like baking a cake faster by raising the oven temperature from 350 to 550 degrees. It just won't work.

Testimony

SpeechMate CD-ROM
To see a speaker citing testimony, view Video Clip 8.5 on Disk 1.

Suppose that one of your classmates gives a speech on the jury system in the United States, and she tells you that the method of selecting and using jurors in most communities is inefficient, overly expensive, and demoralizing to the jurors. Would you believe her? Probably not, if all she gave was her personal opinion—after all, she is not a lawyer or a judge. But what if she quoted the Chief Justice of the U.S. Supreme Court saying the exact same thing? Now would you believe her? You probably would, because the Chief Justice is one of the nation's experts on what happens in our courts.

testimony
statement by a knowledgeable person, used by a speaker to explain or bolster a point

When you use what knowledgeable people have to say on your subject, you are using **testimony** to back up your assertions. The main advantage of using testimony is that it gives you instant credibility; quoting an expert is a way of saying, "I'm not the only one who has this idea; it has the backing of a leading authority on the subject."

How to Use Testimony

There are three ways of using testimony:

quote verbatim
to cite the exact words used by a source

1. Quote verbatim. Sometimes it is effective to quote a source word for word. For example, Lorraine Vallejo made the following point in a speech on dreams:

Tips for your CAREER

Tip 8.1 Cite Experts Whom Your Audience Will Trust

If you were trying to sell computer products to an audience of executives, would you strengthen your appeal by including a quotation from Bill Gates, founder of Microsoft and the world's richest individual?

Not necessarily. Some executives admire Gates and respect his computer savvy, but others consider him an unethical manipulator whose company has impeded progress and unfairly destroyed superior competing products. While a quotaton by Gates might be received favorably by some listeners, it could cause other listeners to react with anger—an emotional response that could weaken their trust in you.

Even if an expert is admired, he or she might have low credibility on the topic under discussion. If, for example, you are speaking on foreign policy and you have a colorful quotation from a football star, would your audience consider the player's views on foreign policy as relevant and trustworthy? If not, quoting the player could weaken, rather than strengthen, your case.

People with advanced training and technical experience—such as scientists, medical researchers, and engineers—are good possibilities for testimony because they are usually rated high in credibility. This doesn't mean, however, that you can't use nontechnical people. A classmate who has sampled and rated low-fat entrees at many different restaurants in your area is an expert on the best places for low-fat dining. A celebrity who leads a national campaign to combat diabetes because she herself has diabetes is not a medical authority, but she has first-hand experience that an audience would value.

As much as possible, find out in advance whether your audience is likely to respect and believe the experts whom you are planning to cite. You can gain this knowledge by interviewing several of your future listeners or distributing a questionnaire to all members of the audience (see Chapter 4 for details).

> For all of us, dreams are weird, chaotic, and crazy. An expert on dreams, Dr. William Dement, says: "Dreaming permits each and every one of us to be quietly and safely insane every night of our lives."

Quoting the expert verbatim was very effective because the statement was phrased in a colorful way that would have been weakened if it had been paraphrased.

2. **Summarize.** When a statement is lengthy, quoting it verbatim can bore the audience, so it is best to summarize any quotation that is more than one or two sentences. In another part of Vallejo's speech, she took a long quotation and boiled it down into one brief sentence:

summarize
to give the substance of a statement in condensed form

> Sigmund Freud believed that dreams reflect unconscious wishes and urges that we are afraid to think about during our daytime waking hours.

3. **Paraphrase.** If a quotation has archaic or technical language or is laced with jargon, you should paraphrase it. If, for example, you want to quote a skin-care expert who says, "Don't use photoallergenic cosmetics if you will be outdoors," you can paraphrase this jargon into plain English by saying, "Don't go outdoors wearing any moisturizer, perfume, or cologne that is photoallergenic because sunlight will activate certain chemicals that irritate the skin."

paraphrase
to restate material, using different words

Ethical Considerations

Ethical Issue

Here are some guidelines for using testimony in an ethical and responsible manner:

Make sure quotations are accurate. If you are not careful with a quotation, you can unwittingly change its meaning. For example, Ralph Waldo Emerson is often quoted as saying, "Consistency is the hobgoblin of little minds." That is an unfortunate misquotation. What he really said is quite different in meaning: "A foolish consistency is the hobgoblin of little minds." With the misquotation, consistency itself is condemned, but with the correct quotation, only a foolish consistency is deemed stupid.

Use testimony from unbiased sources. Ethical speakers avoid using sources that are biased. Suppose you are researching the question of whether polygraphs (lie detectors) are accurate, and you come across glowing pro-polygraph statements by two "experts" who are on the payroll of a firm that manufactures polygraph machines. Could you expect such sources to be unbiased? Of course not. They would probably lose their jobs if they said anything negative about the machines. Reject such "evidence" and look instead for statements by people who have no vested interest in the issue.

State the credentials of your source. If you quote a famous person like Abraham Lincoln, you don't need to give any background information about the person. But for authorities who are not well known, be sure to give some biographical data to establish their credibility. For example, "Jack Smithson, who spent 25 years as a research scientist for NASA, says that . . ."

Statistics

For a speech explaining the immense distances of space, Paula Schiller began with some mind-boggling facts:

> Proxima Centauri, the star that is closest to our solar system, is only 4.28 light years away. That doesn't sound like a very great distance, does it? Is there any chance that we can reach that star—or one of its planets—in our lifetime? Before you start fantasizing about being the first human to travel to our nearest star, consider this fact: if you traveled to Proxima Centauri in the fastest spacecraft now in existence, it would take you *40,000 years* to make the trip.

statistics
numerical facts assembled to present significant information about a subject

Schiller was using **statistics,** which are numerical ways of expressing information. As this example illustrates, statistics don't have to be dry and boring. They can be made interesting and even exciting.

Statistics can be especially effective in persuading an audience to accept a particular point. In our society, people put a lot of trust in statistics. If a television commercial says that 78 percent of physicians prefer Cure-All pain reliever over all competing brands, many consumers will rush out to buy Cure-All.

In a speech in which she tried to persuade her audience to drive their cars less and walk more, Carol Morris wanted to prove that Americans are less fit than they once were, in part, because of all the time they spend driving in their cars, when they could be walking instead. She could have made a vague statement such as, "Because of the automobile, we Americans are getting soft and flabby." Instead, she gave a fascinating statistic to prove her point: "Since the advent of the auto, the average waistline of American adults has increased one inch every generation." That single statistic, short and surprising, was one of the most persuasive parts of her speech.

Puerto Rican singer Ricky Martin was an outspoken foe of the U.S. Navy's policy of using the Puerto Rican island of Vieques for bombing practice. He used statistics in his campaign to halt the bombings: "More than 9,300 people live in Vieques. Because of 60 years of bombing, the island has been contaminated by toxic smoke, napalm, and uranium residue. According to a study by the Puerto Rico Department of Health, the cancer rate in Vieques is 27 percent higher than in the rest of Puerto Rico." In 2003, the persuasion campaign ended in victory, as the U.S. Navy announced it would no longer use the island for bombing exercises.

Understanding Statistics

While statistics can provide powerful support for ideas, they also can be easily misused, either willfully or through carelessness or ignorance. Unfortunately, there is much truth in the old statement, "You can prove anything with statistics." To understand how statistics are used (and abused), let's look at several of the more popular varieties.

Averages. The most popular kind of statistic is the **average.** It can provide interesting views of a subject, as when one speaker pointed out, "On an average day, 24 mail carriers in the United States receive animal bites." Giving the average in a case like this is much more interesting than simply stating the annual total.

Though averages seem like straightforward pieces of statistical data, there are pitfalls: most people are unaware that there are actually three different kinds of averages: the mean, the median, and the mode. To understand these terms, consider Figure 8.1, which shows three ways for figuring the average of normal high temperatures in July in selected American cities.

The **mean,** which is what most people use when they are asked to compute an average, is derived by adding all the temperatures (for a total of 954) and dividing by the number of cities (11). This gives us 86.7 as the mean.

The **median** is derived by listing the numerals, ranging from highest to lowest (or lowest to highest), and then locating the numeral that falls in the middle. (*Memory aid:* Just as the median is the strip in the *middle* of a highway, the median is the *middle* number.) In this case 88 is precisely in the middle, so it is our median. Our example has an *odd* number of figures—this makes it easy to find the median; when you have an *even* number of figures, the median is defined as the number halfway between the median pair.

The **mode** is simply the number that occurs most frequently: in this case, 83.

Since all three of these terms can be called the average, problems arise in communicating information. Suppose a company is made up of a president with an annual salary of $290,000, a vice president with a salary of $170,000, three managers with salaries of $50,000 each, and 20 workers with wages of $20,000 each. What is the average income of the people who work at this company? If one uses the *mean* as the average, the answer is derived by totaling the salaries and dividing by 25 (the total number of employees): $40,400. The

average
a single value that represents the general significance of a set of unequal values

mean
in a set of numbers, the sum of all figures divided by the number of figures

median
the number that falls in the middle of a numerical ranking

mode
the figure that appears most frequently in a set of figures

Figure 8.1
For these normal high temperatures for July in selected American cities, the average high for all the cities can be computed in three ways, because there are three different types of average: mean, median, and mode.

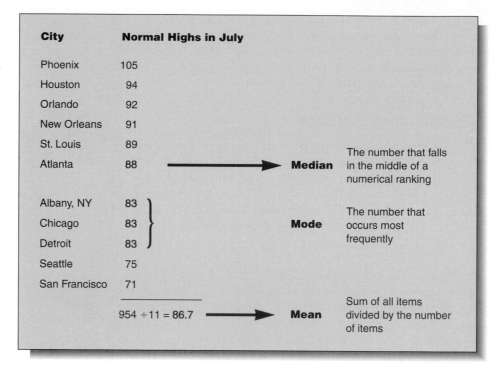

City	Normal Highs in July		
Phoenix	105		
Houston	94		
Orlando	92		
New Orleans	91		
St. Louis	89		
Atlanta	88	→ **Median**	The number that falls in the middle of a numerical ranking
Albany, NY	83	}	
Chicago	83	} **Mode**	The number that occurs most frequently
Detroit	83	}	
Seattle	75		
San Francisco	71		
	954 ÷ 11 = 86.7	→ **Mean**	Sum of all items divided by the number of items

median is derived by listing the salaries in a column, ranging from highest to lowest, and then locating the salary that falls in the middle: $20,000. The *mode* is the salary that occurs most frequently: $20,000.

SpeechMate CD-ROM
To see a speaker using statistics, view Video Clip 8.6 on Disk 1.

Now suppose that the company had a labor–management dispute. In an interview with the press, the president could say, "I don't see what the workers are complaining about. The average income in this company is $40,400." And she would be correct, since she chose to use the *mean* as her version of average. A representative of the workers, on the other hand, could say "We are paid an average of only $20,000," and this would be correct, since the *median* is also a kind of average.

Ethical Issue

As a researcher, you need to know the meanings of these three terms, but as an ethical speaker, you should restrict your use of the word *average* to the mean because that is what most people think of as the average. For the other two types of averages, simply explain them in context without using the word "average." Regarding Figure 8.1, for example, you could say, "The high that appears most often on this list is 83." For the median, it would help your audience if you said, "Highs range from 105 to 71, with 88 falling in the middle."

percentage
a rate or proportion per hundred

Percentages. Giving a **percentage** (a portion of 100) can be a useful way to make a point. For example, suppose that you find that 2 percent of the employees in a company have physical disabilities, and yet only 1 percent of the parking spaces have been designated for employees with disabilities. With these figures, you can make a good argument for increasing the number of spaces for employees with disabilities.

Unfortunately, percentages can be misleading. A television commercial might say, "Eighty percent of the doctors interviewed said they recommend Feel Good medicated tablets for their patients." How many doctors were involved? If only ten doctors were interviewed, and eight of them gave the endorsement, the commercial is accurate (8 out of 10 amounts to 80 percent) but misleading.

The following statement is true: In one recent year Switzerland experienced a 50 percent jump in unemployment, causing that nation to rank number one in the world in the percentage increase of unemployed over the previous year. Sounds terrible, doesn't it? Is the prosperous little country sliding toward economic catastrophe? But here is another way of reporting the facts: In the year cited, there were 51 jobless persons in Switzerland as compared to 34 in the previous year. This represents a 50 percent increase, but when you look at the actual number of people involved, you find no reason for the Swiss to be alarmed.

Correlations. The term **correlation** refers to the degree of relationship between two sets of data. Let's say that I have two sets of data concerning you and 20 of your friends: I have the scores (or IQs) from an intelligence test that all of you took, and I also have your grade-point averages. When I compare the two sets of data, I find that for most of you, the higher the IQ, the higher the grade point average. I can now state that there is a high correlation between the two sets of data. This should be no surprise: For most people in our society, the higher the IQ, the greater the level of academic achievement. Statisticians would say that IQ scores and grade-point averages are highly correlated.

correlation
the degree of relative correspondence between two sets of data

Now let's suppose that I compare the IQ scores with the shoe sizes of you and your friends. Will I find that the larger the foot, the higher the IQ? No, of course not. Will I find that the smaller the foot, the higher the IQ? Again, no. There is absolutely no pattern to observe—no correspondence between foot size and intelligence. In the language of statisticians, there is no correlation at all.

Correlation is a handy statistical device because it can help us predict probable outcomes for individuals. For example, because a high correlation is known to exist between exercising regularly and living a long time, medical experts can predict that a person who jogs regularly is likely to live longer than someone who doesn't exercise.

Correlation, however, is often misunderstood and misused because some people think that it proves a cause-and-effect relationship. Just because two sets of data are correlated, we cannot conclude that one causes the other. For example, some medical researchers once thought that drinking milk might cause cancer because they found a high correlation between milk consumption and the incidence of cancer in some European countries, while finding a rarity of that disease in underdeveloped nations where milk consumption is low. When the researchers analyzed their data, however, they found that a third factor was involved: cancer most often strikes people who are over 40; most of the people studied in the underdeveloped nations did not live long enough to get the disease. So a correlation between milk consumption and cancer does exist (people who drink a lot of milk have high cancer rates), but there is no cause-and-effect relationship (the milk is not what causes cancer).

Guidelines for Using Statistics

Here are some guidelines to consider when you are evaluating statistics for possible use in a speech:

Use statistics fairly and honestly. In one recent year, newspapers and TV stations reported some alarming news: Four of America's largest cities—Los Angeles, San Diego, Dallas, and Phoenix—had experienced a record number of murders during the previous year. The story was true, but misleading. All four of those cities had also reached new highs in population, with the per-capita murder rates staying the same. In other words, there were more murders because there were more people.[8]

Ethical Issue

This case illustrates that even a true statistic can sometimes leave a false impression. An unethical speaker could cite the study and let the audience draw the wrong conclusion—that murder was becoming rampant in four big cities. An ethical speaker, in contrast, would analyze the statistics for their true significance and explain to the audience that the murder rate—the only fair yardstick—had not increased.

Make sure that your sources for statistics are unbiased. If a pharmaceutical company comes out with a new drug it claims is 100 percent effective in eliminating migraine headaches, you would be wise to treat the claim with skepticism. Look for an evaluation by a source that has no vested interest in the product—such as a university medical school.

Use statistics sparingly. A long recital of statistics is hard for the audience to absorb:

Poor: According to the U.S. Census Bureau, 222,600,798 Americans speak English at home; 38,844,979 speak a different language at home. Of the latter number, 19,339,172 speak Spanish; 2,189,253 speak Chinese; 2,102,176 speak French; 1,947,099 speak German; and 1,908,648 speak Italian. All other languages have under one million users.

Better: According to the U.S. Census Bureau, 85 percent of Americans speak English at home. Of the 15 percent speaking other languages, one-half speak Spanish. Four languages—Chinese, French, German, and Italian—are each spoken by roughly 5 percent of the non-English group.

The statistics in the first version would be fine in a written essay, but in a speech they would be hard for the audience to follow. The second version, streamlined and simple, would be easier for the audience to digest.

Round off long numbers. In print, a long number is no problem, but in a speech, it is hard for the listener to absorb the information. A rounded-off number is easy to say and easy for the audience to grasp.

Poor: In the last presidential election, 96,274,564 Americans voted.

Better: In the last presidential election, over 96 million Americans voted.

Translate your statistics into vivid, meaningful language. If you have a statistic that would be meaningless to most listeners or difficult for them to visualize, translate it into simple, down-to-earth language. To help her audience understand the dangers of pieces of debris in space, student speaker Melissa Pollard said:

> Right at this moment, there are about 2,000 tons of garbage sailing around earth. Most of this is leftovers from previous space missions—fragments of spacecraft, rocket launchers, and dead satellites. To give you an idea of the danger that is caused by all this junk, consider this: If a fragment less than an inch wide were to hit a spaceship, the impact would be like being struck by a bowling ball that is traveling at 65 miles per hour.

If Pollard had given statistics about velocity and size ratios, the audience might have been unable to visualize the point she was making. By translating the statistics into the image of the bowling ball, she gave a clear, meaningful picture of the problem.

Adapt statistics to your particular audience. Whenever possible, adapt your statistics to the needs and interests of your particular audience. Imagine that you are planning a speech on Alaska and you want to give your audience an idea of that state's immense size. All you need to do is take a pocket calculator with you to the library, look up the areas of states in a reference work like the *World Almanac,* and make a few simple calculations. If you live in California, for example, you could give your audience a sense of Alaska's size by saying, "You could put three Californias inside Alaska's borders and still have room left over for Oregon."

Relate statistics to familiar objects. One way to make statistics dramatic is to relate them to something familiar. In a speech on bats, student speaker Sally Ingle wanted to give the audience an idea of the incredibly small size of one variety of bat. Instead of giving its weight in grams, which would have meant little to most of the audience, she said, "One variety of bat is so tiny than when it is full-grown, it weighs less than a penny." Knowing the lightness of a penny, the audience could easily get a notion of the smallness of the bat.

Since every American has a clear visual image of the width and length of a football field, you can use the field as a point of reference for size and distance. To show that a baseball diamond uses more space than one would suspect from its appearance, you could say, "The distance that a home run hitter travels around the bases is 60 feet more than the length of a football field." To show how relatively small a basketball court is, you could say, "A regulation court, if placed on a football field, will extend from the goal line to the thirty-one yard line; its width will cover less than a third of the width of the field."

Sample Speech with Commentary

To see how support materials can be used, let's look at a speech by student speaker Karen Miyamoto on bullies in the workplace.[9] A commentary alongside the speech points out the types of support materials that are used.

Workplace Bullies

Commentary

*Karen Miyamoto opens with a **narrative** that is designed to capture the attention and interest of the audience.*

Mark Montana, a 28-year-old chef at a catering service in Seattle, loved his job and made his supervisors happy—until a few years ago when a new boss made his life unbearable. The boss constantly belittled Montana in front of others, cursing him in a loud, angry voice; blaming him for any mistakes that he himself made; and threatening to ruin his reputation in the culinary field if he didn't "shape up." Montana says, "I began to feel bad about myself and I doubted my own competence. I developed severe headaches and had trouble sleeping." Finally, after a few months of this abuse, he quit.

Mark Montana was the victim of a workplace bully. I'd like to show you that bullying in the workplace is a serious problem, but we don't have to be passive victims. Let's begin by looking at the scope of the problem.

*The speaker gives a **definition** to make sure that the audience understands precisely what behavior she is talking about.*

Bullies are found throughout the workforce. "Workplace bullying" is defined as "deliberate, repeated, hurtful mistreatment of one person by another. It can be emotional or physical, but it's usually emotional." This definition is from Dr. Gary Namie, a California psychologist who heads the Campaign Against Workplace Bullying.

*This section of the speech gives a variety of **statistics** to add interest and give a clear picture of the extent of the problem.*

In Dr. Namie's research, most bullies are bosses—no surprise there, but I was surprised by some of his other findings: In 30 percent of the cases, the bullies were women. When the bully was a male, the victims were males in 72 percent of the cases. When the bully was a female, the victims were females in 68 percent of the cases. Dr. Harvey Hornstein, a psychologist at Columbia University, has completed an eight-year study that estimates that one in five U.S. workers will be the victim of workplace bullies during their careers.

*Here and elsewhere in the speech, the speaker uses **testimony** from experts.*

*A **vivid image** provides a description of what a bully in action looks like.*

Dr. Harry Levinson, a psychologist in Waltham, Massachusetts, has studied workplace bullies for 40 years and gives this picture of what they do: They overcontrol, micromanage, and display contempt for others, usually by repeated verbal abuse and sheer exploitation. They constantly put others down with snide remarks or harsh, repetitive, and unfair criticism. They don't just differ with you, they differ with you contemptuously; they question your adequacy and your commitment. They humiliate you in front of others.

*Some specific **examples** of health problems demonstrate the damage caused by bullies.*

Workplace bullies inflict harm on both employees and the company or agency. According to Dr. Hornstein, employees who are victimized by bullies suffer from anxiety, depression, heart problems, gastrointestinal disorders, headaches, skin rashes, insomnia, and sexual dysfunction. As employees suffer, the company or agency suffers. Productivity declines, mistakes proliferate, and good employees quit to find employment elsewhere.

Now that we have seen the nature and extent of the problem, let's see what we can do about it. If you are ever the victim of bullying, you should defintely take action. The first step—recommended by all the experts I read about—is to talk to the bully privately and tell him or her that you will not tolerate being abused. If this is not effective, keep a daily log to document the pattern of behavior. After 20 incidents, take your log to a higher administrator and demand that the bullying be stopped.

*A **hypothetical narrative** imagines a situation in which the listener is bullied and then takes action. This technique helps listeners to see the relevance of the speaker's ideas.*

At this point, the company should take action, as spelled out in the company's code of conduct. If the company has no such code, urge them to create one. Firms such as American Express, Burger King, and J.C. Penney have banned offensive behavior. Any employee who bullies another is dismissed.

*Specific **examples** of companies illustrate that the problem is being taken seriously by some employers.*

Rather than firing the offender, some companies provide counseling with a mental health professional. Counseling can sometimes help bullies to get insights into what motivates their behavior. Dr. Hornstein says that bullies feel insecure and inadequate in their personal lives, and they compensate by becoming aggressive on the job. They feel small, so they belittle others in the futile hope that it will make them appear big. It's sad when the only way some people can build themselves up is by tearing others down.

*The speaker uses **contrast** to show the difference between the bullies' inner reality and their outer behavior.*

When some abusive managers are asked to change, they think they are being advised to become weak. They need to be taught that a manager can avoid the two extremes—weakness at one end and aggression at the other—by being in the middle: firm and fair. Tommy Lasorda, the former manager of the Los Angeles Dodgers, once said, "Managing is like holding a dove. Squeeze too tight, and you'll kill it. Open your hand too much, and you'll let it fly away."

*An **analogy** that draws a parallel between holding a dove and managing people helps the audience to see the need for middle ground.*

What should you do if your employer takes no action? You can consider filing a lawsuit; or you can quit and seek a job elsewhere. One thing is certain: You should never stay in an abusive situation. No person should tolerate being bullied.

To summarize, there are many bullies in the workplace, and if you are ever their victim, you should take action to stop them. Talk to them privately, and if that doesn't stop their behavior, document their actions and report them to top management. If necessary, seek another job.

We wouldn't tolerate a schoolyard bully who beats up little kids, and we must not tolerate workplace bullies who beat up people emotionally.

*In her closing statement, Miyamoto gives a **comparison** between two varieties of bullies.*

Resources for Review and Skill Building

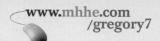

www.mhhe.com/gregory7

This book's Online Learning Center Website and SpeechMate CD-ROM provide meaningful resources and tools for study and review, such as practice tests, key-term flashcards, and sample speech videos.

SpeechMate CD-ROM

Summary

Verbal support materials are vital to the success of a speech. They develop, illustrate, and clarify ideas; they make a speech more interesting and meaningful; and they can help prove an assertion.

Some of the more popular types of verbal supports are (1) *definition,* which helps make sure that your listeners understand key terms as you intend them to be understood; (2) *vivid image,* which is a word picture that helps listeners visualize concepts; (3) *example,* which is an instance that illustrates a statement; (4) *narrative,* which is a story that amplifies your message; (5) *comparison,* which shows how two or more things are alike; (6) *contrast,* which shows how two or more things are different; (7) *analogy,* which explains a concept by likening it to something that seems different; (8) *testimony,* which provides input from experts; and (9) *statistics,* which are numerical ways of conveying information.

Of all these types, the narrative (or story) is the favorite of most audiences. People love to hear stories and are more likely to remember them than most other parts of your speech. As with all support materials, you must make sure that a narrative explains, illustrates, or reinforces the message of your speech. Telling a story that is irrelevant to the subject is not appropriate in informative and persuasive speaking.

Statistics such as averages, percentages, and correlations can be useful in a speech, but you must be careful to use them accurately and fairly. Adapt statistics to your particular audience, making them as interesting and as meaningful as possible.

Key Terms

analogy, *176*
average, *179*
comparison, *175*
contrast, *175*
correlation, *181*
definition, *171*
example, *173*
hypothetical narrative, *175*
mean, *179*
median, *179*
mode, *179*
narrative, *174*
paraphrase, *177*
percentage, *180*
quote verbatim, *176*
statistics, *178*
summarize, *177*
support material, *169*
testimony, *176*
vivid image, *173*

Review Questions

1. List five reasons why support materials are important in a speech.
2. Why are informal definitions usually superior to dictionary definitions in a speech?
3. What must speakers use in order to make vivid images successful?
4. What is the main advantage of using testimony in a speech?
5. The boss of a small firm has an annual salary of $100,000. Each of his 13 employees makes $12,000 a year. Give the average salary of the firm in terms of *mean, median,* and *mode.*
6. How many examples are needed to develop a point?
7. What term is used to refer to a story about an imaginary situation?
8. What is the difference between a comparison and a contrast?

9. A speaker who likens worrying to rocking in a rocking chair is using which kind of support material?

10. If we say that there is a positive relationship between height and landing a spot on a basketball team, we are using which type of statistics?

Building Critical-Thinking Skills

1. Whenever tar on asphalt roads gets hot enough to bubble on a summer day, the incidence of heat exhaustion among citizens goes up. In other words, there is a strong correlation between bubbling tar and heat exhaustion. Does the correlation prove that tar fumes cause people to pass out? Explain your answer.

2. In three or four sentences, give an informal definition (not a dictionary definition) of one of these terms:
   a. Friendship
   b. Pizzazz
   c. Ideal pet

Building Teamwork Skills

1. In a group, choose several focal points (such as music and food preferences) and analyze how group members compare and contrast with one another. In what way are group members most alike and most unalike?

2. Working in a group, analyze these statistics, all of which are true. Discuss why they can be misleading.
   a. "Last year 37 people were killed by automobile airbags."
   b. "Three out of four doctors surveyed said that margarine is healthier for the heart than butter."
   c. "Studies show that children with longer arms are better at solving math problems than children with shorter arms."
   d. "College-educated people drink 90 percent of all bottled mineral water sold in the United States, so we can say that a high correlation exists between an advanced educational level and consumption of mineral water."
   e. "The average American parents have named their daughter Jennifer and their son Michael."

Building Internet Skills

www.mhhe.com/gregory7

1. Find three quotations about children at a Website devoted to collections of quotations.

Possible Strategy: Visit Yahoo! (www.yahoo.com), click on Reference, and then Quotations. Browse through several listed Websites until you find quotations about children. (Many sites have search features so that you can use the keyword "children.")

2. On the Internet, find and print a sentence or paragraph that gives an analogy between a computer and the human brain.

Possible Strategy: Using a search engine such as Google (www.google.com), supply these keywords: + "draw an analogy" + computer + brain.

Using PowerWeb

www.mhhe.com/gregory7

B. Keith Fulton, vice president of the AOL/Time Warner Foundation, delivered a speech entitled "Digital Democracy," in which he gave information about the cost of processing a vehicle registration renewal in Arizona. Find the information and determine which type of support material (discussed in this chapter) he used. To find a transcript of the speech, visit www.mhhe.com/gregory7, click on STUDENT EDITION and then POWERWEB: CONTENTS.

Using a PowerPoint slide, Brianne Berkson of New York City describes the actions of seizure-alert dogs, who can sense when a person with epilepsy is about to have a seizure. A golden retriever named Max barks 15 minutes before his owner Kathy Benton has a seizure, giving Benton time to reach safety. This warning makes it possible for Benton to drive a car without worrying about losing control.

9

Visual Aids

Outline

Objectives

After studying this chapter, you should be able to:

1. Explain at least seven advantages of using visual aids in a speech.
2. Describe the types of visual aids.
3. Describe the media for visual aids.
4. Create and use PowerPoint presentations effectively.
5. Use visual aids effectively, with maximum comprehension and clarity.

The Tietê River in Brazil is an open sewer that causes health problems for thousands of residents in and near South America's largest city, São Paulo. At times, the river is covered with thick mounds of toxic foam, the result of a mixture of chemical detergents, sewage, and industrial pollutants.

"The foam often spills over into adjacent communities, and sometimes the wind blows it all over a village," says Kelly M. O'Donnell, a biologist who is campaigning to raise funds to clean up the river. "The foam emits a harmful acidic gas, which has caused thousands of cases of respiratory ailments." The contaminated water in the river has killed all vegetation on its banks and has caused many outbreaks of hepatitis among humans.

When O'Donnell speaks to audiences throughout the United States and Latin America, she relies heavily on visual aids (such as Figure 9.1). "Without the visuals," she says, "people would have trouble comprehending the true significance of this environmental disaster. They might even think I'm exaggerating." But with the visuals, she says, listeners see the enormity of the problem with their own eyes.[1]

Visuals are powerful tools for informing and persuading. Because most people have grown up with television and therefore are conditioned to learn via imagery, visual aids are considered a vital part of most business, technical, and professional presentations today. The attitude throughout society is: "Don't just tell me; show me."

Figure 9.1
Sanitary workers cross a bridge over the Tietê River in Brazil. The bridge has a water spray to try to reduce the size of the toxic foam that blankets the river.

Advantages of Visual Aids

SpeechMate CD-ROM

To see a speaker who uses visual aids effectively, view Speech 5 ("How to Hide Valuables") on Disk 1 of the CD.

While *verbal* supports (discussed in the preceding chapter) are important for explaining and illustrating your ideas, you also should look for *visual* support. Let's examine some reasons for using visual aids.

1. **Visual aids can make ideas clear and understandable.** Your listeners can quickly grasp how to jump-start a car if you display a drawing that shows where to connect battery cables.
2. **Visual aids can make a speech more interesting.** In a speech on pollution, a chemist showed color slides of gargoyles and statues in Europe that had been eaten away by acid rain. The slides added a lively, provocative element to a technical subject.
3. **Visual aids can help an audience remember facts and details.** Research shows that oral information alone is not as effective as oral information coupled with visual aids.[2] In one experiment, two groups of college students were given a speech on drunk driving. The first group was shown a large drawing of a clock face with 10 P.M. to 2 A.M. marked as a big, red pie wedge—to emphasize the hours when most alcohol-related accidents occur. Students in the second group were told the same information but were not shown the clock. Two weeks later, a test was given. Asked to specify the most dangerous hours, 80 percent of the students in the first group answered correctly, while only 15 percent of the students in the second group could recall the exact hours.[3]
4. **Visual aids can make long, complicated explanations unnecessary.** In medical schools, professors use close-up slides and videotapes to teach surgical procedures. The visuals show exactly where and how to make an incision, sparing the professor from having to give a tedious verbal explanation.
5. **Visual aids can help prove a point.** In Philadelphia, a man who claimed he had been permanently disabled when his car collided with a bus sued the city of Philadelphia, which owned the bus, for compensation. The city refused payment, claiming that he was faking his disability. At a hearing, the man entered in a wheelchair and told the court that he was no longer able to earn a living. In rebuttal, the city's attorney played a videotape (surreptitiously taken by a detective) of the man skiing vigorously down the slopes of a New England mountain a few weeks earlier. The city won the case.[4]
6. **Visual aids can add to your credibility.** When you display good visuals during a speech, the audience is impressed, for it is obvious you have spent time and energy in order to make the speech interesting and understandable. Researchers at the University of Pennsylvania found that presenters who used visual aids were rated by listeners as "better prepared, more professional, more persuasive, more credible, and more interesting" than presenters who used no visuals.[5] But other research also needs to be mentioned as a warning: If listeners think that visual aids are poor, their confidence in the speaker declines.[6] In other words, you are better off using no visual aids at all than poor ones.
7. **Visual aids enhance communication with people who speak English as a second language.** As more and more audiences include professionals and businesspeople from other countries, international students, immigrants, and others whose command of English is imperfect, visual aids have become a crucial way to overcome language limitations.

Types of Visual Aids

In this section, we will look at nine types of visual aids—graphs, charts, drawings, photographs, videotape, computer graphics, objects, models, and yourself—and then in the next section, we will discuss how to present them, using a variety of media.

Important note: Don't make the mistake of thinking that some of these types, such as charts and graphs, are suitable only for low-tech media such as posters and handouts. To the contrary, most of the types can be conveyed effectively in high-tech media such as PowerPoint presentations.

Graphs

line graph
a visual consisting of lines (charted on a grid) that show trends

bar graph
a visual that contrasts two or more sets of data by means of parallel rectangles of varying lengths

pie graph
a circle showing a given whole that is divided into component wedges

Graphs help audiences understand and retain statistical data. The **line graph,** which is widely used in textbooks, uses a horizontal and a vertical scale to show trends and the relationship between two variables, such as "death rate" and "years" in Figure 9.2.

A **bar graph** consists of horizontal or vertical bars that contrast two or more variables, as in Figure 9.3. A bar graph can effectively display a great deal of data in a clear, easily comprehended manner.

A **pie graph** is a circle representing 100 percent and divided into segments of various sizes. A pie graph in a speech should have no more than seven or eight wedges. A common mistake occurs when students see a 20-piece pie graph in a book and copy it as a visual for a speech. Although such a graph is acceptable in a book because readers can scrutinize it as long as they wish, it could come across to listeners as cluttered, distracting, and confusing. Figure 9.4 shows a pie graph.

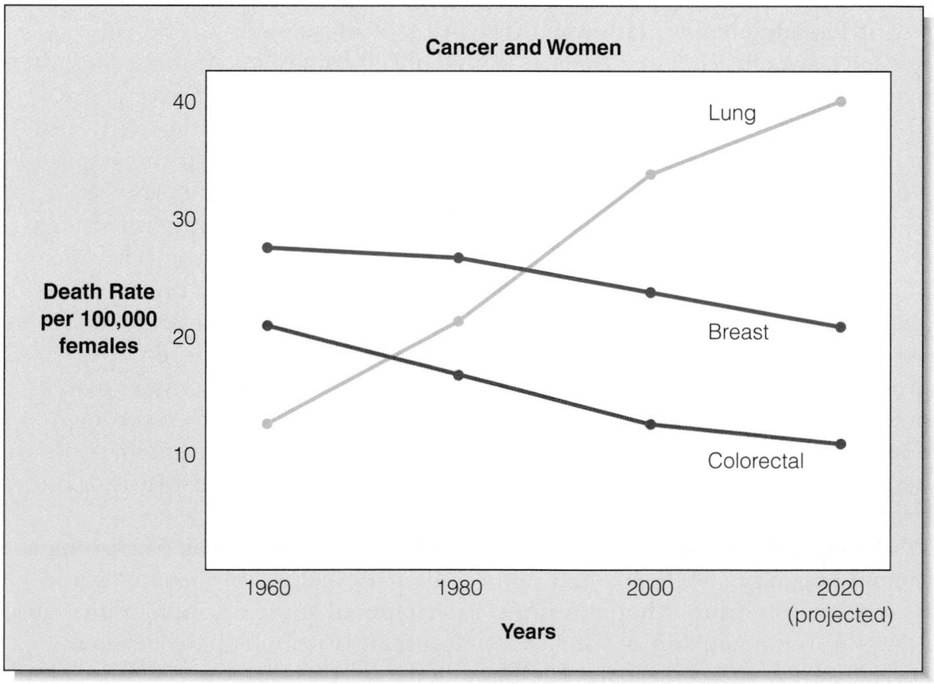

Figure 9.2
Sample Line Graph
This PowerPoint slide shows that for American women, the death rate has declined for all cancers except lung cancer. (The three most common cancers are shown here.) The rise in lung cancer deaths is due to the increase since the 1960s in smoking among women, and the trend is expected to increase because more than 25 percent of adolescent girls in the United States smoke.

(*Source:* American Cancer Society.)

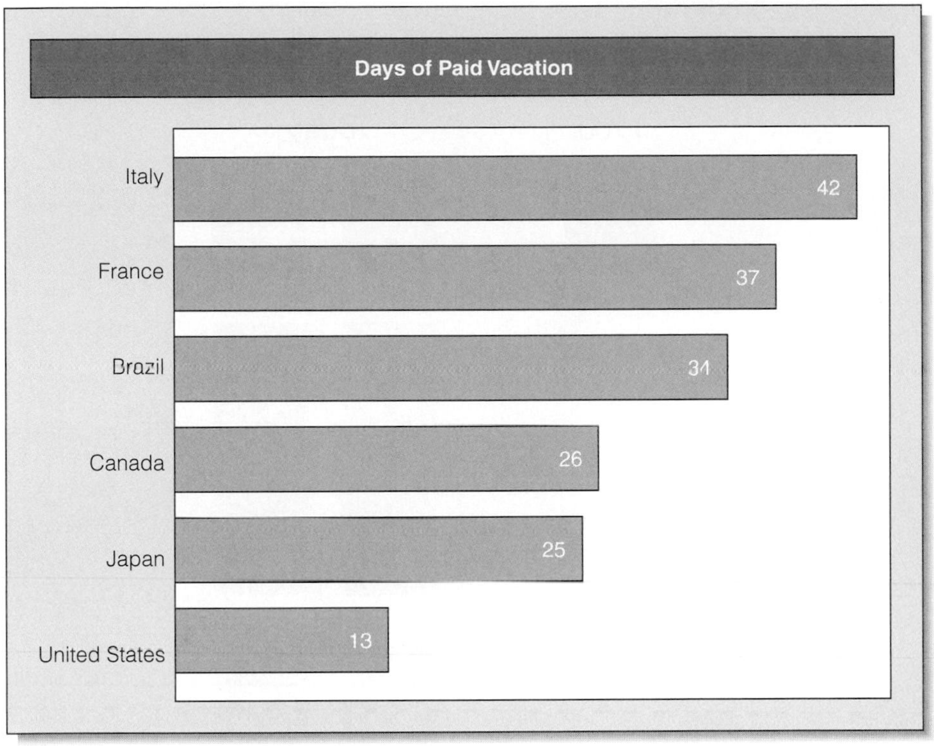

Figure 9.3
Sample Bar Graph
Displayed in a speech arguing for more vacation time for Americans, this bar graph shows the average number of days of paid vacation per year for the workforce in six countries. A graph like this can be placed in a PowerPoint program, mounted on a poster, or reproduced on an overhead transparency.
(*Source:* World Tourism Organization.)

Of all graphs, a **pictorial graph** is perhaps the easiest to read, because it visually translates information into a picture that can be grasped instantly. Figure 9.5 is an example of a pictorial graph.

pictorial graph
a visual that dramatizes statistical data by means of pictorial forms

organization chart
a diagram showing the hierarchical structure of personnel

flowchart
a diagram that shows step-by-step progression through a procedure or system

information chart
text material arranged as a series of key points

Charts

Charts provide information in a compact, easily digested form. An **organization chart** can be used to show the hierarchy of a business or agency, with the chief executive at the top and lines of authority going downward. A **flowchart** illustrates the flow, or sequence, of related events. Figure 9.6 shows a flowchart.

An **information chart,** also called a *list of key ideas,* is a convenient way of presenting main points or steps in a process. Figure 9.7 shows a good format for presenting a list.

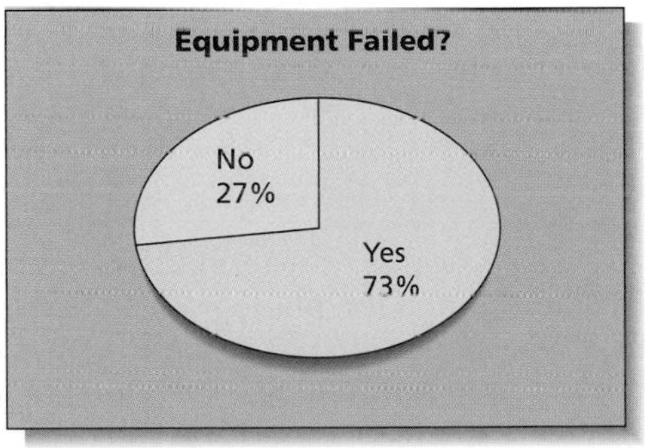

Figure 9.4
Sample Pie Graph
In a poll, presenters were asked, "Has your laptop computer, projector, or other electronic presentation equipment ever failed you during a presentation?" The pie graph shows why presenters should plan for emergencies.

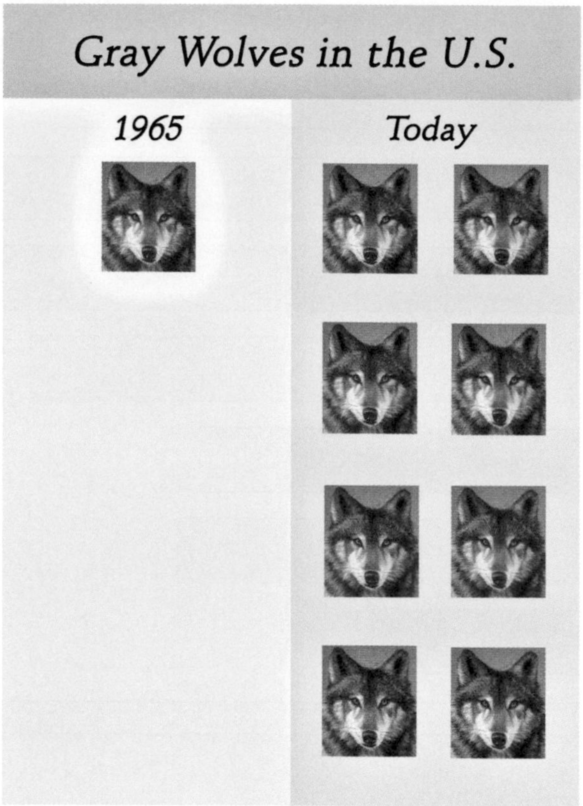

Figure 9.5
Sample Pictorial Graph
When the speaker explains that each image represents 400 wolves, the audience can quickly visualize the comeback of the gray wolf, an endangered species that had an estimated 400 survivors in 1965. Thanks to protection mandated by federal law, the gray wolf population has climbed to 3,200.

table
numbers or words arranged systematically in rows and columns

An information chart can sometimes take the form of a **table,** in which information is presented in rows and columns. Figure 9.8 shows how easy it can be to understand a table.

Note of caution: Most instructors dislike a speech that is nothing more than a recitation of a lengthy list. One student's entire speech was a list of 42 lucrative careers—a lazy way of doing a speech.

Drawings

Drawings make good visual aids because they can illustrate points that would be hard to explain in words. One kind of drawing that is highly effective is a map. By sketching a map yourself, you can include only those features that are pertinent to your speech. If you were speaking about the major rivers of America, for example, you could outline the boundaries of the United States and then draw heavy blue lines for the rivers, leaving out extraneous details, such as cities. Figure 9.9 shows a map.

Photographs

Because photographs have a high degree of realism, they are excellent for proving points. Lawyers, for example, often use photographs of the scene of an accident to argue a case. In a speech, you should not use a photograph unless it can be enlarged so that everyone can see it clearly. (Options for enlargement will be discussed later in this chapter.)

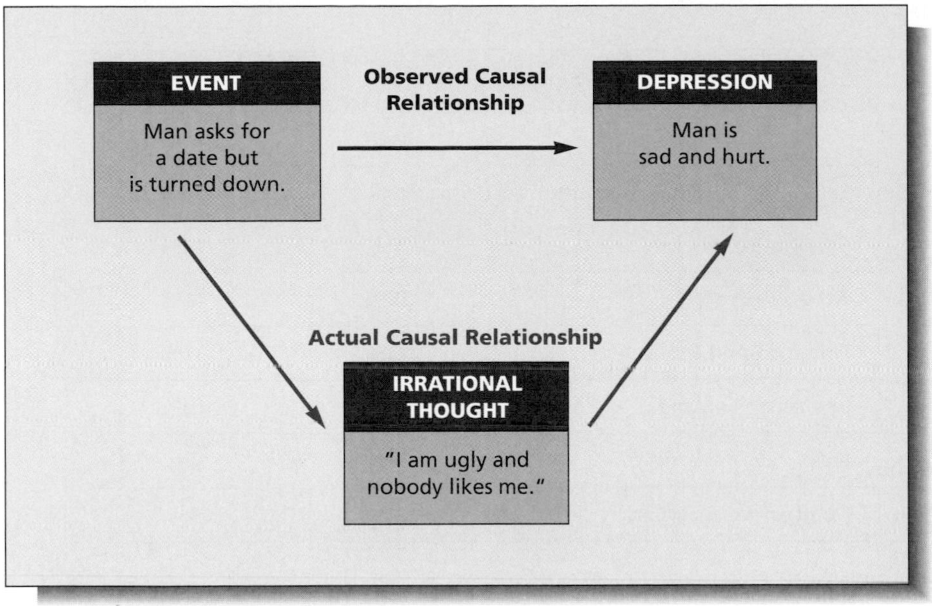

Figure 9.6
Sample Flowchart
Cognitive psychologists believe that depression is not caused by an event, such as being turned down when asking for a date, but by a person's thoughts (often irrational) about the event.

With the growing popularity of multimedia programs like PowerPoint, more and more presenters are using digitized photos. A digitized photo can be taken with a digital camera and then imported directly into a computer for use in a multimedia program, or it can be obtained by a digital scan of traditional camera film or a print. If you need help, consult your campus media department.

Videotape and DVD

With videotape or DVD, you can transport your audience to any corner of the world. To give listeners a glimpse of the rich spectacle of Mexican weddings,

Figure 9.7
Sample Information Chart
An information chart, or list of key ideas, can be written on transparencies, slides, or posters. If possible, display only one item at a time so that listeners stay with you and don't read ahead.

Figure 9.8

Sample Table

A table is an effective type of information chart. This table, which is based on a survey of 3,000 single Americans who were asked to describe themselves, would be most effective if the speaker used progressive revelation, showing only one horizontal row at a time.

(*Source: Health* magazine.)

How Single Americans Describe Themselves

	Men	Women
Extremely Handsome/Beautiful	5%	3%
Very Attractive	9%	12%
Attractive/Pretty	28%	13%
Average Good Looks	33%	47%
Interesting Looking	11%	12%
Plain	6%	4%
Don't Know/Uncertain	8%	9%

student speaker Victor Treviño showed a videotape of ritual, music, and dance at the wedding celebration of his sister in Guadalajara.

If you videotape an interview as part of your research, you may be able to use some excerpts in your speech. Student speaker Adrienne Shields interviewed a bank official on how crooks steal from ATMs (automated teller machines). In her speech, Shields played video segments of the official as he

Figure 9.9

Sample Map

This map illustrates that half of all Americans live in the nine most populous states.

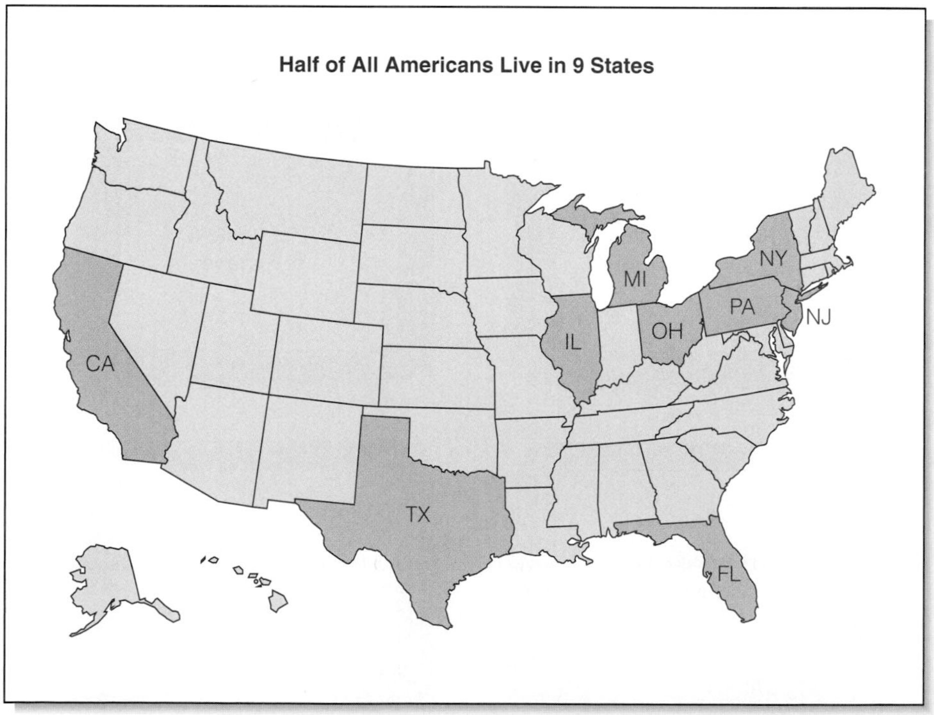

Tips for your CAREER

Tip 9.1 Never Let Visuals Substitute for a Speech

Because visual aids are so powerful, some speakers let them dominate a speech. The visuals become the real show, with the speaker acting as a mere technician. It is easy for this to happen, especially if you have some dazzling slides or a spectacular video. The punch and glitz of the visuals make you feel inadequate, and you think you ought to step aside and let the graphics take command. This attitude is misguided, as shown by the experience of Preston Bradley, vice president of Graystone Corporation:

> Several years ago I made a presentation in which I used a commercially produced videotape. Thinking that the audience would prefer animated, full-color images to my words, I let the videotape take up most of the time; I merely added a few comments at the end and fielded a few questions. Later, several listeners told me that the videotape had been far less helpful than my remarks, and they recommended that in the future I talk more and use videotape less. The reason: during my informal talk I was able to explain tough concepts and interact with the audience. The videotape, on the other hand, zipped along, incapable of sensing whether the audience was absorbing the information.

People can see jazzy video productions on TV at any hour of the day, but a speech has a dimension that TV lacks—a living, breathing human engaged in the stimulating act of direct communication. Don't let visuals rob your speech of aliveness and rapport.

demonstrated the machine's vulnerabilities. The videotape was much more effective than a verbal description alone would have been.

If you have access to a video camcorder, you can make your own videotape, as Adrienne Shields did, or you can show segments from a commercially produced videotape. Because of the ease in rewinding and advancing a videotape, you can show key segments of a tape, eliminating irrelevant or redundant parts.

Don't use your entire allotted time to play a videotape or DVD. Instead, use video only at carefully selected moments—especially whenever listeners are likely to need visual help in understanding technical material. Sometimes a brief segment at the beginning can serve as an appetizer to whet the taste buds for the main course, the body of your speech. In some speeches you can use a video segment at the end if you think it will motivate the audience to take action on your proposals.

Computer and Internet Multimedia

With a computer, you can access these kinds of multimedia aids for a speech:

- *Photos* are available in such categories as news events, historical persons, wildlife, travel scenes, and space exploration.
- *Drawings* include maps, charts, cartoons, and reproductions of art masterpieces.
- *Video clips* are available for TV news reports, public events, speeches, health tips, and animated cartoons.
- *Audio clips* can be found for music, speeches, interviews, and sound effects.

The easiest way to gather these materials is to take them from the Internet—if your computer has sufficient power and space. Most computers can handle

SpeechMate CD-ROM

To see a speaker who uses Internet graphics, view Video Clip 9.1 on Disk 1.

Table 9.1 Free Multimedia Materials on the Internet

For classroom speeches, students may download and use multimedia files from Websites without getting permission because they are engaged in a school project. But for many career and community presentations, speakers must seek and receive permission before using Web materials. (See Chapter 7 for details.)

Website	Options
Google www.google.com	Click on Images and then Advanced Image Search, which permits you to specify file size (small, large, very large) and format (JPEG, etc.).
AltaVista www.altavista.com	Choose Images, Audio, or Video. While most of the material is free, AltaVista does include some photo collections that require a fee for downloading.
Ixquick www.lxquick.com	Choose the Pictures or MP3 (audio) button before searching.
Ditto.com www.ditto.com	This service searches for photos, drawings, and cartoons.
Lycos Multimedia www.multimedia.lycos.com	Choose Pictures, Audio, or Video.
Librarians' Index to the Internet www.lii.org	In the search box, type "photos" or "graphics."
Digital Librarian www.digital-librarian.com	Click on "Images" for a comprehensive list of photos, most of them historical.

Note: Internet addresses and features sometimes change. For an update on these sites, visit this book's Website (www.mhhe.com/gregory7), click on STUDENT EDITION and then WEBLINKS, and look at notes for this page.

photos, drawings, and audio clips, but a powerful system is needed to download video clips.

Is it legal to download without getting permission? For classroom speeches, yes. Copyright restrictions do not apply because you are engaged in noncommercial, educational, one-time use of materials. For many business and professional presentations, however, you need to seek permission. (See Chapter 7 for details.) To find multimedia materials on the Internet, use the search options for free materials shown in Table 9.1.

To download an image from a Website, follow these steps:

1. On most computers, position the mouse pointer over the image, click the right-hand mouse button, and choose "Save Image As" from the menu. (If these instructions don't work for your computer, find the correct steps by going to a search engine such as MetaCrawler, www.metacrawler.com, and searching by phrase, "how to download an image.")
2. As you save the image, designate a location for storage, such as your computer's hard drive, a diskette, or a CD.

low resolution
lacking fine detail

Now for a complication: Most of the free, downloadable images on Websites have **low resolution,** which means they are sharp and clear only at small sizes. This may not be a problem if you are using the images for PowerPoint or for a small illustration in a handout. But you can't use "low-res" for anything that requires enlargment, such as posters or overhead transparencies, because they would be fuzzy and indistinct. Instead you would need **high-resolution** images, which are sharp and clear at both small and large sizes.

high resolution
possessing great detail

(If you are not sure whether an image has high or low resolution, import it into a word-processing program, enlarge it to 8 × 10 inches, and print it. If it comes out muddy and distorted, it's low resolution; if it's crisp and clear, it's high resolution.)

Some images on Websites are **thumbnails**—tiny images with very low resolution. Often you can click on a thumbnail to display a bigger version, which is a better choice for reproduction. Although the bigger version may not have high resolution, at least it will have more resolution than the thumbnail.

thumbnail
reduced image

Though not as plentiful as low-resolution images, high-resolution images are available via the Internet; some of them can be downloaded at no cost, as described above, but most of them require a fee to download. Some sites offer them on CDs. To find high-resolution images, go to Yahoo! (www.yahoo.com) and follow this sequence: Business and Economy > Shopping and Services > Photography > Stock Photography.

When considering high-resolution images, one of the best options is to choose **royalty-free images.** Once you purchase an image, you don't have to seek permission or pay an additional fee each time you use it. Here's an example: Let's say you frequently give talks on weather patterns. You can buy a royalty-free CD of 100 maps showing the entire world and various continents and countries. You can use the maps in your presentations again and again—and, if you wish, you can modify them on your computer to create your own customized versions. To find royalty-free images, go to Yahoo! and follow the steps listed in the paragraph above, except when you get to "Stock Photography," go one step further by clicking on "Royalty-free."

royalty-free images
ready-made images that do not require one to seek permission or pay a fee

Objects

Three dimensional objects make good visual aids, provided they are large enough for everyone in the audience to see. You could display such things as a blood-pressure gauge, a hibachi, handmade pottery, mountain-climbing equipment, and musical instruments.

Models

A model is a representation of an object. One speaker used a model of the great pyramids to discuss how the ancient Egyptians probably built them. Another speaker used a homemade "lung," the interior of which consisted of clean cotton. When cigarette smoke was sucked through a tube, the lung turned from white to a sickening yellow-brown. One advantage of a model is that you can move it around. If you had a model airplane, for example, you could show principles of aerodynamics more easily than if you had only a drawing of a plane.

Yourself and Volunteers

Using yourself as a visual aid, you can demonstrate yoga positions, judo holds, karate chops, stretching exercises, relaxation techniques, ballet steps, and tennis strokes. You can don native attire, historical costumes, or scuba-diving equipment. One student came to class dressed and made up as a clown to give a speech on her part-time job as a clown for children's birthday parties.

Volunteers can enhance some speeches. You could use a friend, for example, to illustrate self-defense methods against an attacker. (For a classroom speech, be sure to get permission from your instructor before using a volunteer.)

Make sure you line up volunteers well in advance of speech day and, if necessary, practice with them to make sure they perform smoothly. Have substitutes lined up in case the scheduled volunteers fail to appear. Give instructions in advance so that volunteers know when to stand, when to sit, and so on. You don't want your volunteers to become a distraction by standing around when they are not needed.

Media for Visual Aids

The types of visual aids we have just discussed—charts, graphs, and so on—can be conveyed to the audience via a variety of different media.

Electronic Presentations

electronic presentation
computerized program capable of conveying text, drawings, photos, video, and audio

An **electronic presentation** involves visual aids that are powered by a computer. As a speaker talks, he or she can display text slides, photos, drawings, animation, and video clips. Voice and music also can be played.

Electronic presentations are often called PowerPoint presentations because of the popularity of one program, Microsoft PowerPoint. Later in this chapter, a section will be devoted to using PowerPoint.

The method for displaying an electronic presentation should be determined by the size of the audience. For small groups of five or six people, an average-sized computer monitor may be large enough. For larger groups, you can use a large TV or a screen; in addition to a computer, you may need a computer-linked multimedia projector.

Boards

marker board
rectangular surface, usually white, upon which dry-erase markers can be used for text and graphics

The two most widely used types of presentation boards today are chalkboards and **marker boards.** The latter type (also called dry-erase or "white" board) has a white surface on which the presenter writes with a special pen available in many different colors. The pen writes as a liquid, but the writing can be erased as if it were chalk. You must be sure to use the special pen: If you use an ordinary marking or highlighting pen, the writing may not come off.

Either type of board makes a good tool for visual aids if you have a few technical words that you need to write for your audience. If you use a big word like *transmogrification* (which means a change into a different, sometimes bizarre, form), you can step over to the board and write it down in big letters. A board is also effective if you have complex drawings that require constant insertions and erasures—for example, if you are diagramming plays for a soccer team.

Boards have some disadvantages. If you put your visual—a graph, say—on a board during your speech, you have to turn your back on the audience; while you're drawing, their attention drifts away from you, and you may find it hard to regain it. Would it be a good idea to put your graph on the board before the speech begins? No, because the audience would be distracted by it; they would scrutinize it before you are ready to talk about it. (It would do no good to say, "Don't pay any attention to this until I get to it." Such a request would make the graph all the more interesting—and therefore distracting.) There is one possible solution: cover the part of the board on which you have written, but this can be awkward. You would have to find something large enough to do the job without being distracting. Another problem is that speakers preceding you might also be planning to use the board, and they might have to erase your visual aid.

Because of the limitations of boards, some instructors forbid their use in a classroom speech, so be sure to find out your instructor's policy.

Posters

You can put many kinds of visual aids—such as graphs, drawings, and charts—on posters. They do the same work as boards, but they are usually neater and more visually appealing.

The size of the poster should depend upon the size of the audience. Ask yourself: Will the person in the back row be able to see the words or artwork clearly? For huge audiences, posters are obviously unsuitable.

Make sure there is a reliable place to put your posters. If you prop them against a chalkboard or tape them on a wall, they may fall to the floor during the middle of the speech. Using thumbtacks might work if a corkboard or other suitable place for tacking is available. One technique is to pile your posters on a desk and hold them up one at a time, being sure to hold them steady. Another method is to put your poster on an easel (which your school's audiovisual department may be able to provide). Even with an easel, however, some posters tend to curl and resist standing up straight. To prevent this, tape a second poster or a piece of cardboard to the back of your poster. (*Tip:* An even better solution to the problem of curling is to buy poster stocks that are sturdier than the standard stock sold at drugstores. Office-supply and craft stores have *foamboards.* Though more expensive than standard poster stock, these materials will not sag or curl.)

Flip Charts

A **flip chart** is a giant writing pad whose pages are glued or wired together at the top. It can be mounted on an easel. When you are through with each page, you can tear it off or flip it over the back of the easel.

flip chart
a large book consisting of blank sheets (hinged at the top) that can be flipped over to present information sequentially

You can prepare the visuals on each page in advance, or you can "halfway" prepare them—that is, lightly pencil in your sheets at home; then during the speech, with a heavy marker, trace over the lines. With some flip charts, the paper may be so thin that ink will seep to the next page, so you may need to leave a blank page between each drawn-on sheet.

Be aware that some instructors disapprove of student speakers writing on a flip chart during a speech.

Handouts

Despite the availability of high-tech tools, one of the most popular formats used in business and professional presentations is the paper **handout.** It is easy to explain the enduring popularity of handouts: they are easy to prepare, can be

handout
material distributed to an audience as part of a speaker's presentation

updated quickly at the last moment, and provide a permanent document that listeners can take with them when they leave a presentation.

Though handouts are popular, they are often misused. I have witnessed the following fiasco dozens of times: A presenter distributes stacks of handouts at the beginning of a talk. While he or she discusses each handout, the room is filled with the sound of rustling papers, as the listeners race ahead, reading material the presenter has not yet reached, ignoring or only half-listening to what he or she is saying. (Some speakers try to solve this problem by imploring the audience to stay with them and not read ahead, but this is futile; humans are naturally curious, and their eyes cannot resist reading.)

Because listeners study the pages instead of paying attention to the speaker, handouts are banned in some public speaking classes. Even if your instructor permits them, they are usually unsuitable during a classroom speech because distributing them eats up time and creates a distraction.

The best use of handouts—especially lengthy, complex documents—is to give them *after* the question-and-answer period so that listeners can take them to office or home for further study and review. (For classroom speeches, check with your instructor; he or she may prefer that you wait until the end of the class period; if you give out material at the end of your speech, students might read it instead of listening to the next speaker.)

One exception to the above advice: for informal presentations in career and community settings, it is permissible to distribute a handout during a presentation if it is short and simple—a one-page document with an easy-to-understand graphic or a *small* amount of text. In such situations, follow these guidelines: (1) Never distribute a handout until you are ready to talk about it—a premature handout grows stale. (2) Avoid talking about a handout while you are distributing copies. Wait until every listener has a copy before you start your explanation.

Visual Presenters

visual presenter
a device capable of producing images of both two- and three-dimensional objects

A **visual presenter,** also known as a document camera or ELMO (the name of a leading manufacturer), is a camera mounted on a stand and pointed at a platform below (see Figure 9.10). What the camera sees is shown on a TV or video monitor, or projected onto a screen via a digital projector. Visual presenters can show two-dimensional items such as photos and diagrams, and they also can show three-dimensional objects such as jewelry. A zoom feature permits very small items, such as a coin, to be enlarged for easy viewing.

Visual presenters are popular because they are easy to use, and a speaker can make last-minute changes. Unfortunately, they are often used in a clumsy fashion that makes the speaker look like a fumbler who has lost eye contact with the audience. Here is what can happen:

> Some speakers bring a book or magazine that contains an illustration, but when they try to use the visual presenter, they have trouble holding the material in place, they spend a lot of time positioning the illustration correctly, and they waste time zooming in and out. When they finally get the illustration in position, two more problems may emerge: (1) the illustration may be bordered by extraneous material that is distracting, and (2) if it is printed on glossy paper, it may be obscured by glare.

Figure 9.10
A visual presenter can convert a photo to a digital image that can be displayed in a large size on a screen or a TV.

To use a visual presenter skillfully, follow these guidelines:

1. Discard an illustration if it not crisp and clear. If you have a dark, blurry snapshot, using a visual presenter will not improve its appearance. It will show up on the screen as a dark, blurry picture, and the audience will be displeased. Find a replacement or do without.
2. If possible, use an assistant to handle the presentation of material. This frees you to look at your audience and not waste time in positioning items.
3. Several days beforehand, rehearse the speech in the actual room where the speech will be given. If you are using an assistant, have him or her practice using the equipment and displaying the visuals at the appropriate times.
4. When using books and magazines, frame your illustrations by using stick-on slips to mask all extraneous material.
5. Minimize glare by making sure that a page lies flat. If necessary, you or your assistant can press down on the area surrounding the illustration to ensure flatness.
6. Immediately before your speech, adjust the camera's zoom feature so that you have the correct setting. Remember that a preceding speaker might have used a setting that is wrong for your needs.

Overhead Transparencies

Overhead projectors are illuminated boxes that project images from **transparencies** (clear sheets of acetate) onto a screen. Once the most popular of all presentation tools, overhead projectors have declined in popularity in recent years, but they are still widely used.

transparency
clear sheets on which visuals are drawn or printed, and then viewed by light shining from an overhead projector

Advantages. There are five advantages in using overhead transparencies: (1) The transparencies are simple to produce. (2) You can easily make last-minute changes in artwork or statistics. (3) You don't need another person to operate the machine for you. (4) The room usually doesn't need to be darkened, so you and the audience can see each other at all times (and have enough light for you to read your notes and for listeners to take notes). (5) When you want to point to an item on your visual, you don't have to turn your back to the audience by going to the screen; you can simply point to the proper place on the transparency with a pencil or pen.

Creating overheads. To create a transparency, you can write directly on the acetate sheet with a variety of color pens, or you can make a master copy on plain white paper and use an office copier to make the transparency. (Most copiers today can print on transparencies, but you need a special kind of acetate that won't melt inside the copier.) Your college's audiovisual department may be able to help you produce transparencies for a small fee, or a quick-print shop in your community can make the transparencies from your master copy.

During a speech, you can use your pen to circle key words, draw arrows, or insert updated statistics. But don't try to create an entire visual aid from scratch during the speech because you might lose your audience's attention while you write or draw.

When you create transparencies in advance, use a marking pen especially designed for overheads. If you use an ordinary marker to prepare a transparency the night before your speech, the graphics may look fine at the time, but by the next day, ink may evaporate, leaving you with only thin traces. Avoid storing transparencies directly against one another because the ink might transfer. Put them in file folders or store them with a sheet of paper between each one.

While it is true that you don't have to darken a room for overhead transparencies, you may want to do so for transparencies that are copies of color photographs. A dark room will make the photo more vivid.

35mm Slides

When people speak of slides today, they often refer to electronic, or PowerPoint, slides. However, for most of the 20th century, slides referred to 35mm transparency film, which was unsurpassed for its sharpness and vivid colors.

35mm slide
transparent film used in a camera

In recent years, film has lost ground to new digital cameras. Nevertheless, the **35mm slide** continues to be used widely in education, science, and publishing.

The 35mm slide allows a great deal of flexibility: you can insert and delete slides quickly and easily, thus adapting a slide show to meet the needs of different kinds of audiences.

Although a 35mm slide can be digitized and shown by a multimedia projector, the old-fashioned slide projector still gives the most vivid results. Projectors are easy to operate. You can set your own pace, lingering over a slide that requires long explanation, while hurrying through slides that need little or no commentary. If you have a remote-control device on a long cord, you can stand next to the screen and point out items without having to walk back to the projector to change slides.

To be seen clearly, slides must be shown in a completely darkened room. This situation is both good and bad: Good, because your listeners' eyes cannot wander and become distracted—they are concentrated on the screen; bad, because you and your listeners lose eye communication with each other, and you have to rely solely on your voice to make contact. To solve this problem, some speakers show slides in a semidark room, but even dim light makes the slides appear washed out and hard to see.

Once you have finished discussing a slide, don't leave it on the screen to distract your audience. If you are not yet ready to go to the next slide, project a light-colored blank slide on the screen while you talk, or turn off the projector and turn on the lights until you are ready for the next slide.

Television and Video Projectors

For a small audience (under 35 people), a standard television set is usually suitable for showing a televised program, videotape, or DVD. For larger audiences, you need either a mammoth-screen TV or several monitors positioned throughout the room.

In the case of videotapes and DVD, a third option is available for large audiences: a **video projector,** which is connected to a VCR, DVD player, or camcorder; it can project images onto a large, theater-style screen with only a small loss of video quality.

video projector
machine that projects videotaped images onto a large screen

A common problem with video is setting the correct volume. Here's the solution: Before listeners arrive, play the video and find a sound level that seems right for the people in the back row. Then increase the level slightly. (The absorption of sound waves by the audience's clothing makes this necessary.)

A Brief Guide to Using PowerPoint

A speech can be enhanced by using PowerPoint for slides, animations, sound, and video clips. In this section, we will offer a brief guide to creating PowerPoint slides and using them effectively in a speech. For more detailed technical information on how to create slides using PowerPoint, you have two options: the Help menu in the PowerPoint program or the PowerPoint Tutor on the SpeechMate CD-ROM that accompanies this textbook.

SpeechMate CD-ROM
For guidance in creating and displaying PowerPoint presentations, see the PowerPoint Tutor on Disk 1 of the CD.

If new versions of PowerPoint are released, you can get updated information by visiting this book's Website (www.mhhe.com/gregory7). Click on STUDENT EDITION and then WEBLINKS, and look at notes for this page.

Prepare Your Speech First

When one student speaker prepared a speech on immigration to the United States, he began by finding photos on the Internet, including a beautiful picture of the Statue of Liberty. When he gave his speech, he devoted a lot of time to the Statue and its history, and this forced him (because of his time limit) to eliminate some of his important points about immigration. While the Statue by itself would have made a good speech topic, it had only marginal value in a speech on immigration. He had let the dazzling photo skew his priorities.

To avoid the mistake of letting PowerPoint graphics overly influence your planning, use this approach:

1. Finish the outline of your speech before you even think about creating PowerPoint slides.
2. Ask yourself: "How can I use visuals to highlight or clarify key ideas in my speech?" You may be able to come up with ideas for photos, drawings, graphs, charts, and lists of key points.
3. Choose slides that are aids or helpers—not a replacement—for a speech. Ask yourself this crucial question: "If I stand up to speak and the equipment fails to work, will I be able to present my ideas?" You should be able to say yes. If you say no, you are relying too much on the slides to carry the burden of communication.

Create Slides

To create slides, follow the steps in Table 9.2. Note that the table shows the "Blank Presentation" approach, which is recommended for beginners because of its simplicity. Another choice is "From Design Template," but you are advised to use it with extreme caution. It contains some ready-made templates that are tempting to use because a lot of design work has been done for you. But many of the templates have glitzy artwork that is gaudy and distracting. Worst of all, text printed on top of such artwork is hard to read.

Avoid Overwhelming Your Audience

Some presenters think that using PowerPoint means—almost by definition—that they must have slides for every part of their speech. So they create a large number of slides, with a lot of information on each slide. When they speak, they spend their entire time plowing through one slide after another. The result is a numb and weary audience.

The best approach is to have as few slides as possible. Create a slide only when it will help the audience understand and remember a point or when it will make a part of your speech more interesting.

Make Your Slides Simple and Attractive

Create slides that are inviting and uncluttered. When you use text, display just a few words. If you look at the slides in Figure 9.11, you will see that the first slide is a snoozer, especially if there are 30 more just like it. The second slide is superior because it crisply emphasizes the key points without fatiguing the audience. The speaker can elaborate on each point in a conversational way.

If possible, use short, to-the-point phrases instead of complete sentences. Sometimes it is effective to separate the phrases by using a bullet in front of each phrase.

Make text large enough for comfortable reading. How large is large enough? One guideline is to use 44-point size (or larger) for titles, and 28-point size (or larger) for text. Some self-styled PowerPoint experts stipulate that text should have the same point size on every slide in a presentation, but this rule is too rigid. Sometimes you have to make the font size smaller to accommodate a graphic; at other times, you may need to enlarge text size to emphasize the importance of your material. As we discuss elsewhere in this chapter, the best way to assess the readability of a visual aid is to go beforehand to the room where the speech will be given, display the visual, sit in the back row, and determine whether a listener sitting in that spot could easily and clearly see all parts of the visual.

Figure 9.11

Wrong Way
This PowerPoint slide has too many words. If listeners have to read slide after slide of text material, they become weary and dissatisfied.

Right Way
This slide has just a few words to help the audience follow and remember key points. Not many words are needed on the slide because the speaker elaborates on each item. The bullet points should be displayed as a "build"—one at a time.

Use Graphics Judiciously

Graphics such as photos and drawings are more interesting and appealing than text, so try to use good artwork whenever you can. In some cases, the artwork can stand by itself without needing any text. If you are describing a tornado, for example, a drawing of a twister might be all that you need as you explain details to your audience.

In other cases, a graphic accompanied by a few words is an effective approach. To see a good example, look at Figure B in this chapter's Special Techniques feature entitled "How to Avoid Eight Design Mistakes." (Also look at the bad example in Figure A.)

But a warning: Don't use artwork just because using artwork is a recommended practice. Irrelevant or inappropriate artwork is worse than none at all. For instance, using a photo of a camel when you are discussing Middle Eastern oil is a "stretch." Drop the camel and insert an oil well. If you can't find a picture of an oil well, use no artwork.

(*Continued on page 210.*)

Table 9.2 Creating Slides in PowerPoint

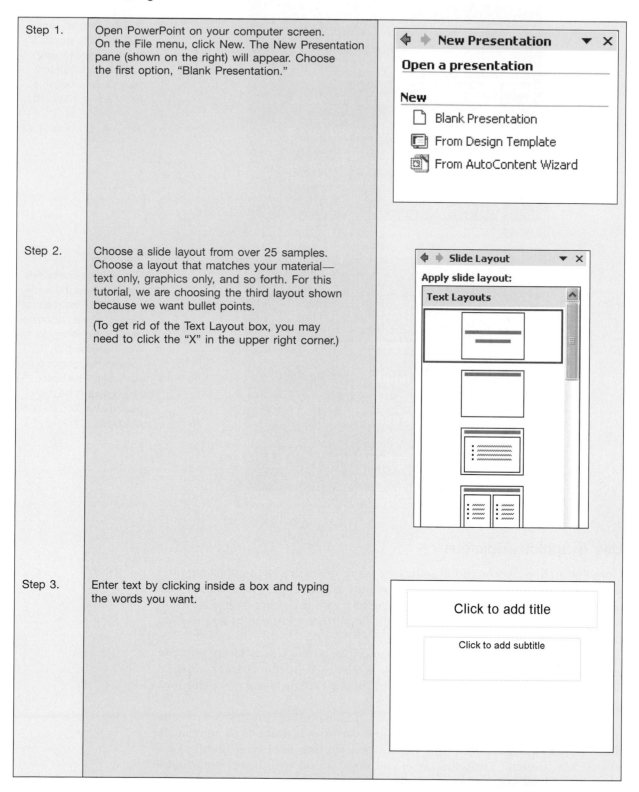

<table>
<tr><td>Step 1.</td><td>Open PowerPoint on your computer screen. On the File menu, click New. The New Presentation pane (shown on the right) will appear. Choose the first option, “Blank Presentation.”</td><td>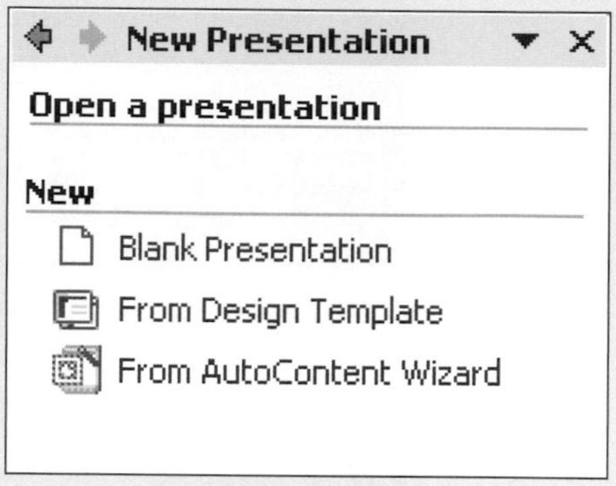
</td></tr>
<tr><td>Step 2.</td><td>Choose a slide layout from over 25 samples. Choose a layout that matches your material—text only, graphics only, and so forth. For this tutorial, we are choosing the third layout shown because we want bullet points.

(To get rid of the Text Layout box, you may need to click the “X” in the upper right corner.)</td><td>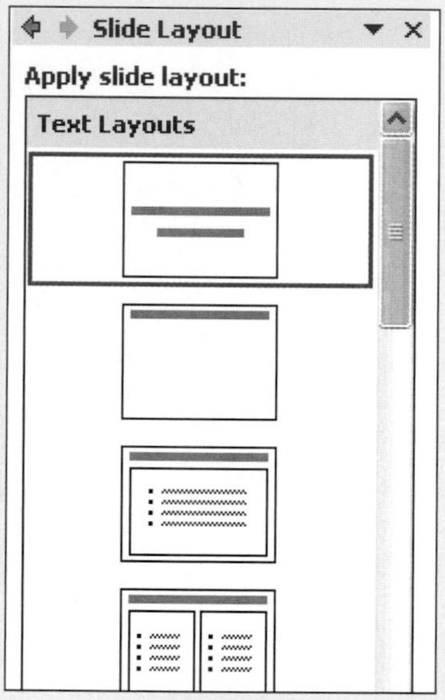
</td></tr>
<tr><td>Step 3.</td><td>Enter text by clicking inside a box and typing the words you want.</td><td>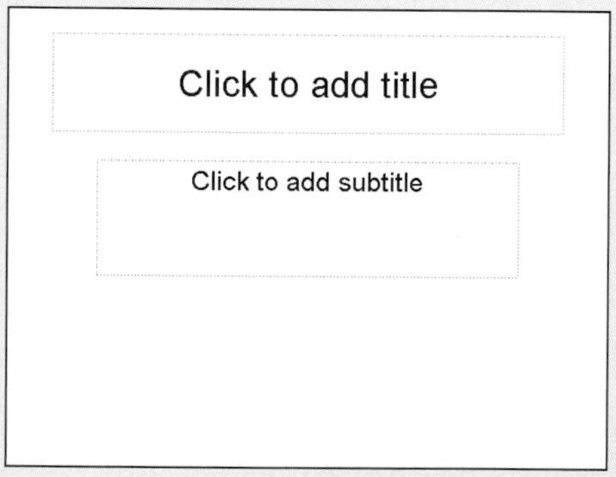
</td></tr>
</table>

Table 9.2 Creating Slides in PowerPoint (*Continued*)

Step 4.	For the bulleted text items, you can add a new item by pressing the Enter button at the end of a line. (Not shown here: You can change the size and appearance of text by swiping across it with your mouse and then choosing Format, followed by Font.)	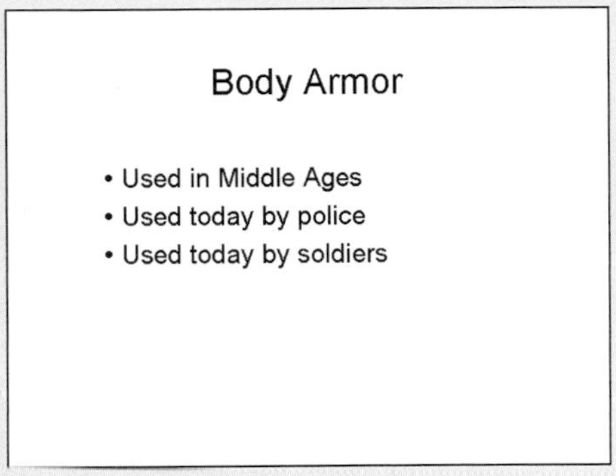
Step 5.	To add a color background, go to the Format menu, click on Background (shown here) and use the pulldown menu (indicated by the "down" button). Choose the "More Colors" option and select a color. Press OK. Finally, click on "Apply to All" so that all of your slides will have the same background color.	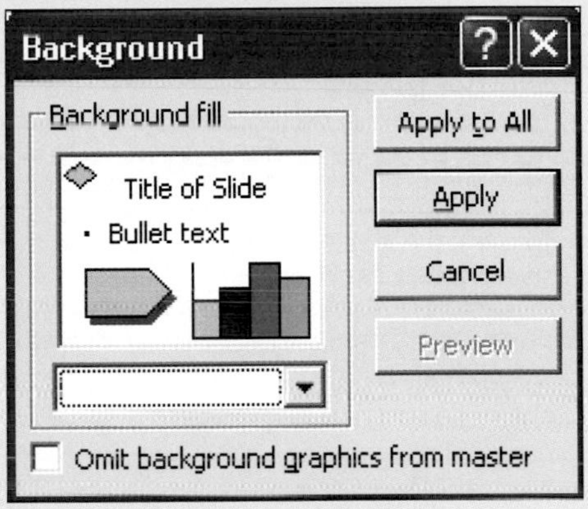
Step 6.	When you are using a background color, choose a light color (such as yellow or light blue) if your text is black. Use a dark color (such as blue or brown) if your text is white.	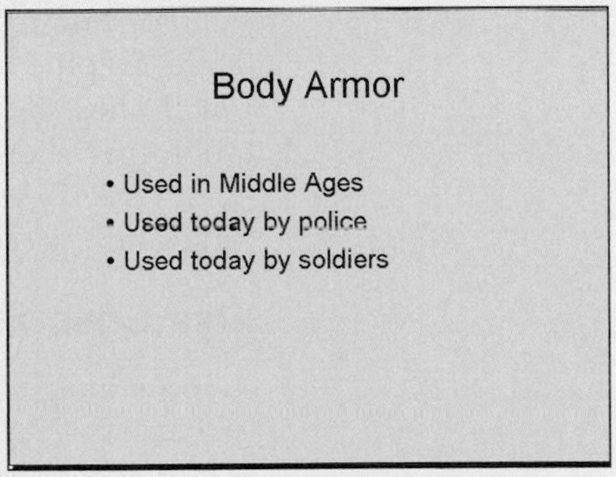

Table 9.2 Creating Slides in PowerPoint *(Continued)*

Step 7.	To place graphics, click at the point where you want an image. Pull down the Insert menu and choose Picture and then From File. Specify the file name of your image. To change the size of an image, click on it, place the mouse pointer over any of the corner "handles," hold down the mouse button while pressing on the Shift key, and move the mouse inward or outward. When you have the desired size, release the mouse button and Shift key. To re-position the image, place the mouse pointer in the center, hold down on the mouse button, and drag the image to the desired place.	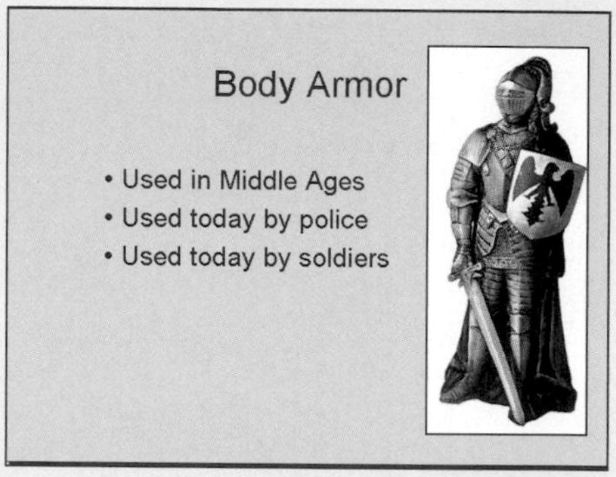
Additional Options • To add a new slide, choose the Insert menu and then New Slide.		
• To move from slide to slide, choose View and select Slide Sorter. Double-click a slide to enlarge it to full screen.		
• To view the entire slide show, choose View and select Slide Show. To go to a new slide, press Enter. To exit the show, press Escape.		
• Save your show onto a CD-R or diskette for use on a computer linked to a digital projector or a TV.		

Be careful with cute cartoons and amateurish clip art. While silliness designed to inject a light note may be appropriate in some situations, many PowerPoint presenters include drawings simply because they are available. Unfortunately, the drawings look foolish, and they distract from the message.

For PowerPoint, a rule of thumb is to use only one graphic per slide. One large graphic is easier for the audience to see and understand than several small ones. If you have four photos, for example, create four slides with one photo per slide instead of one slide with four photos. (This is one case where it is a good idea to ignore the rule that one should minimize the number of slides in a presentation.)

Use Crisp Illustrations

Choose images that are sharp, clear, and well-exposed. When enlarged on a big screen or a TV, a photo does not improve. In fact, any defects such as blur and darkness will be magnified.

Many of the images you find on the Internet have resolution sizes that are too small for projection as a PowerPoint slide. They might look fine on your computer, but when enlarged on a screen, they are blurry.

How can you know whether an Internet image has high enough resolution for PowerPoint? Follow these steps:

1. When you are considering an image, find out its resolution by placing your cursor over the image and right-clicking. Select "Properties" and you should see how many pixels are in the image (for example, 240 × 320).
2. Reject images that have a resolution below 200 × 200. This is a rough "rule," but it usually works. For example, a 65 × 110 image and a 145 × 165 image are unacceptable, while 250 × 375 and 200 × 240 are fine.

Rescue Dark Images

Let's say you have a photo on your computer. Maybe you got it from the Internet or maybe somebody e-mailed it to you. Or maybe it's a print that has been scanned and turned into a digital file. What do you do if the photo is too dark? How can you lighten it?

Many word-processing programs, such as Microsoft Word, have rudimentary photo-editing tools (see the Help menu on your program) that will enable you to improve a dark photo. Otherwise, use PowerPoint's tools:

1. Import an image (using Insert > Picture > From File).
2. Click on the image, choose Format, and click on Picture.
3. Under Image Control, slide the Brightness and/or Contrast sliders to the left or right. To see your results, click on Preview. Adjust the sliders until you get a satisfactory result.

Animate Text and Objects

PowerPoint permits animation of objects, meaning that you can show movement over time (for example, an animation of a car accident would show cars entering an intersection, followed by a collision) or you can make portions of a slide appear independently in a prearranged sequence.

One type of animation is called a **build,** in which a visual is displayed in stages from a small piece to the finished graphic. See Figure 9.12 for an illustration. To create a build, follow these steps:

build
a dramatic process in which words or graphics are added one part at a time

1. Click on the Slide Show menu.
2. Choose Animation Schemes. (An animation scheme applies a predefined special effect to slide objects. The best one is called Appear. There are fancier ones, but the wise presenter will avoid them in most cases because they are too gimmicky and distracting.)
3. In the Slide Design task pane, under Apply to Selected Slides, click on Appear.
4. If you want to apply the scheme to all slides, click the Apply to All Slides button.

SpeechMate CD-ROM
To see a PowerPoint "build" in action, view Video Clip 9.2 on Disk 1 of the CD.

A build is a good technique to use when you have several bullet items in a list. Let's say you have five bullet phrases. Display just bullet 1 and talk about it; then add bullet 2 and discuss it, and so on, until all five bullets appear.

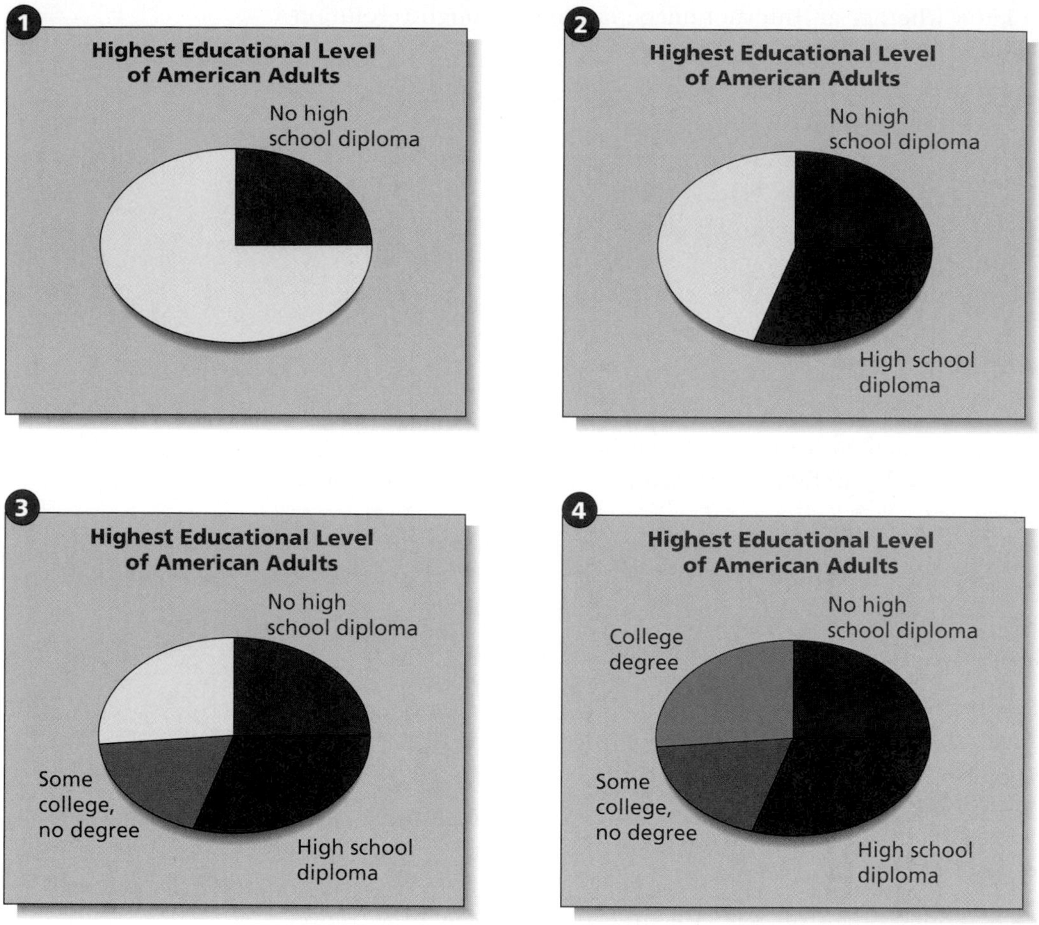

Figure 9.12

A build is an effective technique in electronic presentations. This pie chart in a PowerPoint presentation shows the educational attainment of adult Americans: less than a high school diploma, 24.8 percent; high school diploma, 30 percent; some college but no degree, 18.7 percent; and college degree, 26.5 percent. (Source: *Chronicle of Higher Education.*)

Present Your Slides

SpeechMate CD-ROM

To see a speaker who uses PowerPoint ineffectively, view Speech 3 (Persuasive Speech That Needs Improvement) on Disk 1 of the CD.

Before speech day, rehearse with all necessary equipment so that you don't fumble during the actual speech. Practice operating the computer or remote control until you become proficient.

During the speech, make yourself—not the screen or TV—the center stage of your speech. You can achieve this by (1) keeping the room partially lit so that you are not totally in shadows, (2) using slides only occasionally, and (3) focusing your eyes and your energy on the audience. Avoid the common mistake of turning away from the audience to read your slides.

Be prepared to use extra slides. For most speeches, there are marginal issues that you don't have time to cover in your speech, but if you are asked about them in the question-and-answer period, it is helpful to have relevant slides that you can display. Simply place such slides at the end of your main slide show and use them if and when you need them.

(*Continued on page 214.*)

Tip 9.2 Beware the Perils of PowerPoint

While PowerPoint has been praised and illustrated in this book, it is true that PowerPoint presentations are widely hated for being boring and tedious. "PowerPoint," says *Sales & Marketing Management* magazine, "has become synonymous with a bad presentation." And *Industry Week* says, "PowerPoint presentations have drugged more people than all the sleeping pills in history."

Some corporations have discouraged their employees from using PowerPoint. One such corporation is Willowbrook Enterprises, whose CEO, Carl Zucker, recalls one bad experience: "There was a well-meaning guy from the legal department who was briefing top management, and he had his entire speech printed out on about 50 slides. He read one slide after another. By the time he got to slide 7 or 8, I looked around the room and realized that everyone was either asleep or had a glazed, stupefied look. I decided then and there that PowerPoint was counterproductive."

The problem is not the software itself, but the widespread abuse of the program. Here are the major mistakes made by PowerPoint presenters:

Wordy Text Slides

If you want to make listeners sleepy and unhappy, display sentence after sentence on the screen and read them to your audience. Do this from the beginning of your speech to the bitter end.

The ideal approach is to use images instead of words, but this is not always possible, so when you must use text, use it sparingly. See Figure 9.11.

Overuse of Special Effects

Audio and video gimmicks are incorporated into PowerPoint and can sometimes be used effectively, but Bill Howard, senior executive editor of *PC Magazine,* advises: "Go easy on the fly-in, swivel, wipe, zoom, laser text, and similar PowerPoint special effects. They get old in a hurry." For example, one presenter used the audio "gunshot" effect as each word was flashed in sequence on the screen. One irritated listener said later, "I felt like I was on a firing range."

The best use of special effects is to help clarify points. For example, a lawyer using animated drawings to recreate an automobile accident can help the jury understand what happened.

Letting PowerPoint Distort Priorities

In preparing a PowerPoint presentation, some people pour most of their energy into creating their visuals (choosing colors, filling in templates, finding artwork), and they lose sight of their true task: to get a message across to the audience. This misguided concentration on mechanics often causes them to fill the presentation with junk (such as unnecessary text slides and irrelevant artwork), and they succumb to the temptation to show more visuals than the audience can absorb. When they actually give the presentation, they let PowerPoint become the main event, as they stand off to one side in the shadows—meek servants of a powerful master.

When you start preparing a multimedia speech, don't focus on PowerPoint. Instead, concentrate on creating a message that will meet the needs and interests of your audience. Then, after your message is nailed down, look for ways to use multimedia here and there—only if truly needed to explain complicated points or make information more interesting and memorable. If a multimedia item fails to enhance your message, don't use it.

When it's time to stand and deliver your speech, make sure that you—not the electronics—are the "star of the show," the center of everyone's attention. Talk directly and enthusiastically to the audience, giving the key points and elaborations yourself, using PowerPoint only for reinforcement or clarification.

Using PowerPoint When It Is Not Needed

Some business and professional speakers fear that if they don't use PowerPoint slides, they will be perceived as lazy or old-fashioned. Nonsense. As you can surmise from the negative comments quoted above, many listeners would be grateful for visuals other than PowerPoint. In some situations, PowerPoint slides are far less effective than a few simple props or posters. For example, some courtroom lawyers have access to PowerPoint, but they prefer to use posters on easels because the posters can be kept on display for long periods, enabling jury members to glance at them whenever they need to refresh their memories. (Normally you shouldn't keep posters on display after you've discussed them, but this situation is an exception to the rule.)

Guidelines for Using Visual Aids

Here are some guidelines for using visual aids effectively in your speeches.

Choose Visuals That Truly Support Your Speech

Before using a visual, ask yourself: Will it help clarify or illustrate an important idea in my speech? If the honest answer is no, discard it. Your job is not to dazzle people with pretty colors on a screen or to impress them with your creative artwork. A beautiful drawing of an airplane in flight, for example, would not contribute much to a speech on touring the castles of Europe.

Appeal to as Many Senses as Possible

While the visual channel is powerful, don't overlook the other senses.

Sense of hearing. To accompany a slide presentation on dolphins, marine biologist Jennifer Novak played an audiotape of the clicks, whistles, and other sounds that dolphins use to communicate with each other.

Sense of taste. In a speech on Korean cuisine, chef Chong Man Park cooked and served rice and vegetable dishes while explaining Korean culinary techniques to listeners.

Sense of smell. Floral designer Charlene Worley gave a speech on how flowers provide not only messages of love and consolation but also medicine and food. At the end of her talk, she invited the audience to sniff a bouquet she had created. She also appealed to the sense of taste by serving crackers on which she had spread jam made from violets.

Sense of touch. Wishing to disprove the notion that snakes have slimy skin, herpetologist Jeanne Goldberg invited listeners to come forward and stroke the nonpoisonous king snake she was holding. Many listeners were surprised to find the skin dry and firm, with a texture like glass beads tightly strung together.

One speaker who appeals to all five senses is Miyuki Sugimori of Tokyo, the only woman among Japan's 15 rice-candy sculptors, who carry on a 250-year tradition (Figure 9.13). When she demonstrates her art in Japan, Europe, and the United States, Sugimori asks listeners to name their favorite animal, and then she creates and paints candy sculptures of dragons, horses, monkeys, and other creatures. The listeners use all five senses: watching the process, listening to her explanation of the history of the art, and then touching, smelling, and tasting the finished product.[7]

Prepare and Practice Far in Advance

Don't create your visuals while you are actually giving your speech: Few people can write or draw effectively while speaking to an audience. Make them far in advance so that they are not sloppy and unpolished.

Practice using your visuals as you rehearse your speech. If you will be using unfamiliar equipment, such as overhead projectors or videotape players, rehearsals will help prevent fumbling or faltering during your speech.

Figure 9.13

Five senses are involved in a demonstration by Tokyo artist Miyuki Sugimori of the Japanese art of making candy sculpture. After hearing and watching, listeners can touch, smell, and taste the finished product.

Don't Use Too Many Visuals

Some speakers believe that the more graphics they display while talking, the better the speech. This notion is untrue: If there are too many visuals, the listeners could suffer "sensory overload" and become blinded to the speaker's true message.

Speakers who use too many visuals usually do so because they are attempting to cover too many points. Audiences cannot absorb a huge quantity of new information. Limit a speech to only a few key points, and limit visuals to those that are necessary to clarify or illustrate those points.

Make Visual Aids Simple and Clear

If you want to see good examples of visual aids, look at outdoor advertisements, such as the one in Figure 9.14. To be successful, these ads must grab attention and convey a message quickly and simply. A motorist traveling past a billboard has only two or three seconds to look. A typical student strolling past an outdoor campus bulletin board casts only a quick glance.

A speech is different, of course. A visual aid in a speech can be displayed for more than just a few seconds, so it can contain a greater amount of information than an outdoor ad can provide. Even so, a speaker should try to imitate the simplicity and clarity of outdoor ads. For example, if you were giving a speech, you could use the outdoor ad in Figure 9.14 without making any changes. But, you might say, what about all the details that the ad leaves out?

(*Continued on page 218.*)

How to Avoid Eight Design Mistakes

In designing visuals, there are eight common mistakes you should avoid. All eight blunders are shown in Figure A, while a corrected version is shown in Figure B.

Mistake 1: Too Much Text.

Some speakers put several sentences on a visual, and then read the material to the audience. In effect, the visual is a giant cue card—good for the speaker, bad for the audience. Too much text is ugly and boring. Place only a few words on each visual, and if any elaboration is needed, provide it orally.

Mistake 2: Too Many Words per Line.

A rule of thumb is to have no more than seven words per line.

Mistake 3: Overuse of All-Capital Letters.

Researchers have found that a large number of words printed in all-capital letters can cause readers to become fatigued and even give up reading. Words that use both upper- and lowercase are easier on the eye. This doesn't mean you should never use all-caps; just limit them to titles or headlines.

Mistake 4: Too-Tight Spacing.

Avoid jamming words and lines too close together. A handy guideline: leave the space of the letter "n" between words and two "n's" (one on top of the other) between lines:

Leave**n**plenty
n
n
of space

Mistake 5: Excessive Artwork.

As shown in Figure A, too many graphics create unpleasant visual "noise," which distracts listeners from paying attention to the speaker. Notice that the speaker prints text on top of a photo. This is a technique that is often seen in magazines, but many graphics experts frown on it because they say it mars the legibility of the words and creates clutter.

Some presenters create excessive artwork because they think white space should be filled up, but this is a mistaken notion. Empty space around text and pictures is desirable—it spotlights the key material. Figure B gains much of its power from the wise use of just one picture. (If the speaker wants to show photos of swimmers and runners, additional slides can be created, each one utilizing the elegant simplicity of Figure B.)

Mistake 6: Too Many Colors.

Color adds pizzazz, but don't be like an exuberant artist in kindergarten who uses every crayon in a 64-crayon box. Color works best when it is used to draw attention to an important feature: If you wanted to put a spotlight on just 3 of the 50 states in the United States, you could display a black-and-white map of the United States with the three states—say, New Jersey, Kansas, and Washington—colored in bright red. If you wanted to pinpoint three states that are contiguous—for example, Maine, New Hampshire, and Vermont—you could use three different colors to help listeners distinguish them.

How many different colors are acceptable? For text, select one main color (black is fine) and use a second, contrasting color only if you want to emphasize a word or number. For graphics, use a wide variety of colors only when the situation warrants: In pie charts, for example, a different color for each slice helps the audience separate one piece from another.

Avoid neon colors. They are distracting and hard to see.

Mistake 7: Too Many Different Typefaces.

Stick with one or two styles of lettering. If you are using a computer, your word-processing software probably lets you use a wide variety of typefaces; resist the temptation to print a gaudy mélange.

Choose readable typefaces. The simple, dignified typeface in Figure B is easier to read than the fancy, jazzy typefaces included in Figure A.

Mistake 8: Use of Italics and Underlining for Emphasis.

To stress certain words or phrases, *italics* are used in printed material and underlining is used in handwritten documents, but neither style is effective in large visuals. Instead, use **bold** print or a **contrasting color**.

ONE OF THE MOST GRUELING EVENTS IN THE WORLD OF SPORTS IS THE TRIATHLON. SOME CALL IT THE IRONMAN TRIATHLON. iT FEATURES A 2.4-MILE SWIM, A 112-MILE BIKE RACE, AND A COMPLETE MARATHON, WHICH EVERYONE KNOWS IS 26.2 MILES. THEY ARE DONE ONE RIGHT AFTER THE OTHER! UNBELIEVABLE! THE ATHLETES HAVE 17 HOURS TO COMPLETE THE TRIATHLON, FROM 7 IN THE MORNING TILL MIDNIGHT.

Figure A

Eight Design Mistakes

This visual commits the eight design mistakes discussed in this feature. Can you identify all eight?

Triathlon
• Swim 2.4 miles
• Bike 112 miles
• Run 26.2 miles

Figure B

Corrected Version

Avoiding all eight mistakes, this visual does not distract the audience from listening to the speaker. It omits many details, but these can be supplied orally or covered in a series of concise visuals.

Figure 9.14
This outdoor ad grabs attention and gives key information quickly. A well-designed outdoor ad is a good model for a visual aid in a speech—simple, concise, easily grasped.

No problem. You can give background information while the audience enjoys the sight of a crisp, appealing, and uncluttered graphic.

Two rules of billboard design are worth heeding: (1) Use graphics instead of words whenever possible. (2) If you must use words, use only a few.

Make each visual aid so simple that your listeners can quickly grasp its meaning—either at a glance or after minimal explanation by you. Avoid complexity. Too much information can confuse or overwhelm the listeners.

Does a wonderful graphic in a book translate into a wonderful graphic in a speech? Not necessarily. Some visual aids in books are jampacked with fascinating details; they are suitable in a book because the reader has ample time to analyze them, but they're too complex for a speech.

In visuals such as graphs, make all labels horizontal. (In a textbook, many labels are vertical because readers of a book can turn the visual sideways, but listeners should not be forced to twist their necks to read vertical lettering.) You need not label every part of your visual, as you are there to explain the aid.

If you are displaying a multidimensional object, be sure to turn it during your talk so that everyone can see all sides of it.

Aim for Back-Row Comprehension

I once saw the head of a large corporation show an overhead transparency to an audience of over 1,000 people, but only 300 or 400 of them were close enough to be able to read the words and decipher the charts on the screen.

Ridiculous? Yes, but this mistake is made in countless meeting rooms throughout the world every day. Business and professional people I have interviewed are unanimous in saying that the most frequent audiovisual mistake made by presenters is using graphics that are difficult or impossible for everyone in the audience to see.

The best way to achieve comprehension by everyone is to design every visual aid for the back row. *If all lettering and details cannot be seen easily and comfortably by a person in the rear of the room, don't use the visual.*

To help you meet the needs of the people in the back row, here are some guidelines.

If you prepare a visual from scratch, make letters, numbers, and graphics much larger than you think necessary. I've never heard anyone complain about visuals being too large. For guidelines on scaling the size of letters and numbers to the size of your audience, see Table 9.3, but remember that these are minimum sizes. To be safe, you can make letters and numbers even larger.

Use thick, bold strokes. Whether you are creating by hand or using a computer, you need big, bold, thick strokes for lettering and graphics. Thin strokes tend to be weak and hard to see:

Thin strokes **Thick strokes**

Make enlargements. You can magnify a too-small visual by using videotape, visual presenters, overhead transparencies, electronic presentations, slides, or posters. Here are three of the easiest options:

- A camcorder with a zoom lens can be used to make a close-up videotape of a snapshot, a drawing, or a small object such as jewelry. A blank videotape costs less than $5 and can be erased and used later for other purposes.
- To turn a photo or drawing into a PowerPoint slide, you can have the item scanned and converted into a digital file. Try the media center on your campus or visit a photo store in your community.
- If you have access to a visual presenter (discussed earlier in this chapter), you can easily enlarge both two- and three-dimensional items. For example, a speaker can demonstrate the chemical changes taking place in a small test tube, while the enlargement on a TV or

Table 9.3 Minimum Size of Letters & Numbers

	Posters, Boards, Flip Charts	Overhead Transparencies
Conference room (10–15 listeners)	At least $1\frac{1}{2}''$ high	At least $\frac{1}{3}''$ high (33-point type)
College classroom (15–35 listeners)	At least $2\frac{1}{2}''$ high	At least $\frac{1}{2}''$ high (48-point type)
Lecture hall (35–100 listeners)	At least 4″ high	At least $\frac{3}{4}''$ high (72-point type)
Auditorium	Use slides or multimedia projected onto a giant screen.	

a wall screen ensures that everyone in the audience can see the results clearly.

Test the visibility of your visuals. Before the day of your speech, go to the room where you will be speaking, display your visual aid in the front of the room, and sit in the back row to determine whether you can see it clearly. (Even better, have a friend sit in the back row to pass judgment.) If your visual cannot be seen with crystal clearness from the back row, discard it and create another (or simply don't use one).

Never Circulate Visual Aids among the Audience

Some people try to solve the problem of a too-small visual aid (such as a piece of jewelry) by passing it around the room, but this is a mistake. People will look at the visual instead of listening to the speaker. And there's likely to be distraction, perhaps even whispered comments, as it is being passed from one person to another. Some speakers walk from listener to listener to give each person a close-up view of the visual aid. This is also a poor technique; the listeners who are not seeing the visual may get bored or distracted, and they may start whispering comments to their friends. Moreover, the listeners who are looking at the aid may ask questions that mean nothing to the rest of the audience. In a case like this, the speaker can easily lose the audience's attention and interest.

One way to solve the problem of a too-small object is to leave it in the front of the room and invite the audience to see it *after* the speech. This strategy is acceptable unless listeners need to see the aid during your speech in order to understand what you are talking about. In this case, the best solution is to create an enlarged image of the object (discussed above), which you display during the speech, and then permit listeners to take a look at the real object after the speech.

When they need to show steps in a process, some speakers invite the audience to come to the front of the room and gather around a table. One speaker did this so that everyone could see him making garnishes out of vegetables (a tomato was transformed into a "rose"). If you are considering this approach, here are three guidelines: (1) Use the technique only with small audiences. (2) Make sure no disabled listeners are excluded from participating. (3) Get your instructor's permission before trying this in a classroom speech.

Remove Physical Barriers

Right before a speech, move any objects or furniture that might block the view of some listeners. If you're using equipment such as an overhead projector, make sure it doesn't obstruct anyone's vision. If, despite your best efforts, some listeners will be blocked from seeing your visuals, ask them (before you start your introduction) to shift their chairs or move to a different part of the room.

Explain Your Visual Aids

No matter how simple your visual aid is, you should explain it to your audience. Some speakers slap a transparency of a graph onto an overhead projector, talk about it for a moment, and then whisk it off. To such speakers, the graph is simple and obvious; they don't stop to think that the listeners have

Tips for your CAREER

Tip 9.3 With International Audiences, Avoid Informality

During a presentation to American audiences, you can write on boards, posters, flip charts, and overhead transparencies because spontaneity is considered appropriate. In some cultures, however, such informality is interpreted as a sign of unpreparedness and disrespect. Listeners may feel that the speaker did not value them highly enough to prepare proper visuals.

For an international audience, therefore, always use visuals that are created in advance.

never seen it before and need time to analyze and absorb the information it presents.

As you discuss a part of your visual aid, don't wave your hand in the general direction of the aid and assume that the audience will know which feature you are pointing out. Be precise. Point to the specific part that you are discussing. For pointing, use a finger, ruler, pen, or extendable pointer. To avoid twisting your body, use the hand nearer the aid.

Choose the Best Time to Show Visuals

Many speakers undermine their speech's effectiveness by showing visual aids at inappropriate times. Here are several guidelines.

Don't display a visual before your speech begins. If visual aids are in plain sight before you start, you deprive your speech of an element of drama and freshness. There are exceptions, of course, as when you must set up items for a demonstration on a table in front of the room.

Show a visual in the introduction if it will spark interest. One speaker gave a talk on how to restore old, broken porcelain dolls but didn't show any samples until the end, when she displayed three beautiful restored dolls. Her listeners probably would have had greater interest in the talk if she had shown the dolls at the beginning. They would have realized why restoration was a worthwhile goal.

Don't withhold a visual if it would help listeners understand the body of the speech. One speaker gave a talk on underground rock formations in caves but waited until the end to show slides illustrating his points. During the body of the speech, listeners were mystified and frustrated: What do these rock formations look like? Though he ultimately showed slides, his listeners would have experienced a much greater understanding and appreciation of the subject matter if he had displayed the pictures as he went along.

If listener comprehension is unharmed, it is acceptable to delay. In some cases you may want to withhold a visual or a demonstration in order to build suspense. As long as you are not depriving listeners of material needed for understanding the body of the speech, you may wait until the end. In a speech on how to use Tae kwon do karate techniques to break objects, Lee Wentz stood in front of a cement block as he spoke, waiting until the end to demonstrate the actual breaking of the block with one hand. This built suspense—the audience wondered whether he would succeed. (He did, and the listeners applauded.)

Don't Let Visuals Distract from Your Message

The cardinal rule for visual aids, says business writer Kristen Schabacker, "is that they should complement your presentation, not distract the audience from what you're saying."[8] The following are tips on how to avoid distracting your audience.

Show one visual at a time. If you display five posters, neatly lined up on a chalk tray, your listeners will scrutinize the fourth poster while you are talking about the first. To keep the eyes and minds of your listeners focused on your remarks, show a visual, discuss it fully, put it away, and then display your next visual.

There is one exception to this rule: If you have a visual aid that can provide a simple, undistracting backdrop or evoke a mood, you may leave it on display during the entire speech. One speaker kept a bouquet of flowers on the front table throughout her speech on gardening; the flowers provided a pleasing complement to her remarks.

Beware of using animals or children as visuals. Exotic pets and cute kids can easily draw the attention of your listeners away from your ideas, so use them carefully, if at all. One speaker brought in a ferret to demonstrate what great pets they make. The only trouble was that the ferret acted up during the speech, causing the audience to laugh at its antics rather than listen to the speech. Some instructors disapprove of using animals in speeches, so be sure to get permission before bringing an animal into the classroom.

Watch for misspelled words. On an overhead transparency, one speaker wrote *Frist* for *First.* Another speaker showed a poster listing types of emotional abuse, including *Treats,* instead of *Threats.* Double-check the spelling of all words in time to correct any mistakes.

Don't Talk to Your Visual Aid

Many speakers are so intent on explaining a visual aid that they spend most of their time talking to it instead of to the audience. You should stand next to your aid and face the audience during most of your discussion. Look at the aid only in two situations: (1) When you introduce it, look at it for several seconds—this is long enough to draw the listeners' attention toward it. (2) Whenever you want to direct the audience's attention to a particular segment, look at the aid for one or two seconds as you point out the special feature.

Use Progressive Revelation

progressive revelation
piece-by-piece unveiling of a visual

Whenever possible, use **progressive revelation**—that is, reveal only one part or item at a time. If, for example, you are presenting a bar graph on an overhead transparency, use opaque strips (heavy paper or letter-size envelopes) to mask everything except the top bar; discuss it; then reveal the

Tips for your CAREER

Tip 9.4 Ask a Friend to Assist You

For speeches that you give on the job or in the community, you may want to ask a friend to assist you. Here are some of the ways in which an assistant can be useful:

1. An assistant can help you set up and operate audio-visual equipment, turn lights off and on, or search for a missing extension cord. Such assistance will free you to concentrate on getting your message across to the audience.
2. If you are speaking to strangers, the presence of your friend can give you a psychological boost—you have an "ally" in the room.
3. An assistant might be able to handle any distractions or emergencies that arise. If, for example, a group of people start a loud conversation right outside the room in which you are speaking, the assistant can open the door and whisper a request for silence.
4. Your assistant can stand or sit in the back of the room while you are speaking and give you advice via hand signals on which the two of you have agreed in advance. For example:
   - "Slow down—you're talking too fast."
   - "Speak louder—I can barely hear you."
   - "You're looking at your notes too much."
   - "You've reached the time limit—wrap things up and sit down."
5. An assistant can give you a critique of your speech afterward, so that you can learn from any mistakes you have made. Sometimes the assistant can mingle with the audience in the hall after your speech and find out how listeners responded to the presentation, so that you can learn about your strengths and weaknesses.

second bar, and so on. Likewise, if you have five steps in a process, reveal one step at a time.

A variation of this technique was shown earlier in this chapter (Figure 9.12) when we discussed "builds."

Progressive revelation creates suspense, making the listeners curious about what comes next, and it prevents them from reading or studying ahead of you. Another bonus: When you walk over and reveal a new item, you create movement and action, thus keeping listeners alert and breaking up the monotony of a speech.

Plan How You Will Handle Emergencies

With visual aids, there is always a chance of a foul-up, so you should plan carefully how you will handle any problems that might arise. Before you use any electronic media, talk with your instructor or the program chairperson to make arrangements (for darkening the room, getting an extension cord, and so on). Always check out the location of your speech in advance. Is there an electrical outlet nearby? If not, can you get an extension cord? Can the room be darkened for slides? Is there a place to put your posters? Is there a chalkboard or white board?

Be prepared for the unexpected—the multimedia projector malfunctioning, the bulb in the overhead projector burning out, videotape breaking in the middle of the program. Some of these disasters can be mitigated by advance planning. For example, carry a spare bulb for the overhead projector; if the videotape breaks, be ready to fill in the missing information. If equipment breaks down and cannot be fixed quickly, continue with your speech as best you can. Try to keep your poise and sense of humor.

Resources for Review and Skill Building

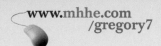

www.mhhe.com/gregory7

This book's Online Learning Center Website and SpeechMate CD-ROM provide meaningful resources and tools for study and review, such as practice tests, key-term flashcards, and sample speech videos.

SpeechMate CD-ROM

Summary

Visual aids can enrich and enliven your speech in many ways: They can make your ideas clear and understandable; make your speech more interesting and memorable; help an audience remember facts and details; make long, complicated explanations unnecessary; help prove a point; add to your credibility; and enhance communication with people who speak English as a second language.

The major types of visual aids include graphs, charts, drawings, photographs, videotape and DVD, computer and Internet multimedia, objects, models, yourself, and volunteers. They can be conveyed to the audience via various media: electronic presentations, boards, posters, flip charts, handouts, visual presenters, overhead transparencies, slides, television, and video projectors.

Presenters using PowerPoint should make their visuals crisp and appealing, and they should avoid overwhelming their audience with a torrent of slides. Using advanced features such as text animation can be effective.

Guidelines for using visual aids: (1) Choose visual aids that truly support your speech. (2) Appeal to as many senses as possible. (3) Prepare and practice far in advance. (4) Don't use too many visuals. (5) Make your aids as simple and clear as possible. (6) Aim for comprehension by everyone, including the people in the back row. (7) Never circulate a visual aid among the audience. (8) Remove physical barriers so that everyone has an unimpeded view. (9) Explain each aid, regardless of how simple it is. (10) Decide on the best time to show visuals. (11) Make sure the aids don't distract from your message: Show just one visual at a time, beware of using animals or children, and watch for misspelled words. (12) Don't talk to your aids. (13) Use progressive revelation. (14) Plan how you would handle equipment failure and other emergencies.

Key Terms

bar graph, *192*
build, *211*
electronic presentation, *200*
flip chart, *201*
flowchart, *193*
handout, *201*
high resolution, *199*
information chart, *193*
line graph, *192*
low resolution, *198*
marker board, *200*
organization chart, *193*
pictorial graph, *193*
pie graph, *192*
progressive revelation, *222*
royalty-free images, *199*
35mm slide, *204*
table, *194*
thumbnail, *199*
transparency, *203*
video projector, *205*
visual presenter, *202*

Review Questions

1. List at least six types of visual aids.
2. List at least five media for presenting visual aids.
3. What is progressive revelation?
4. A *list of key ideas* is another name for which kind of chart?
5. Is it legal to use graphics from the Internet in a student speech in the classroom? Explain your answer.
6. The text recommends that you "aim for back-row comprehension." What does this mean and why is the advice necessary?

7. How can speakers test the visibility of their visuals?
8. Is it always a mistake for a speaker to wait until the conclusion of a presentation to show a visual or perform a demonstration? Explain your answer.
9. Why would it be a mistake to circulate a small photograph during your speech?
10. Explain three options that a speaker can take to magnify a too-small visual.

Building Critical-Thinking Skills

1. "Some pictures may be worth a thousand words, but a picture of a thousand words isn't worth much," says corporate executive Don Keough. Explain what this means in terms of oral presentations.
2. At one Website devoted to communication, public speakers are advised to distribute thought-provoking handouts at the beginning of a speech so that "if members of the audience get bored during the speech, they will have something interesting to read." Do you agree with this advice? Defend your position.

Building Teamwork Skills

1. Working in a group, review the guideline "Appeal to as Many Senses as Possible." Create a scenario in which a sales representative gives a presentation that appeals to all five senses.
2. In a group, review the Special Techniques feature, "How to Avoid Eight Design Mistakes," in this chapter. Create an ugly graphic that makes at least five of the eight mistakes. Then create a new graphic that corrects all the mistakes of the ugly one.

Building Internet Skills

www.mhhe.com/gregory7

1. Find and print a Web page that includes a photo of earth taken by astronauts.

Possible Strategy: Go to Yahoo! (www.yahoo.com) and follow this sequence: Science > Astronomy > Solar System > Planets > Earth > Pictures. Explore various options until you find a photo of earth.

2. Find and list the names of the "Paris paintings" of French impressionistic painter Claude Monet.

Possible Strategy: Visit WebMuseum, Paris (http://www.ibiblio.org/wm/) and click on "Famous Artworks." Choose "Impressionism" and then "Monet, Claude." Click on "Paris" to view Monet's works about Paris. (To see an enlargement of each painting, click on the miniature version.)

Using PowerWeb

www.mhhe.com/gregory7

In an article by Mark McMaster entitled "Performance Anxiety," speaker Joe Carino tries and fails to get Internet access for an important presentation to Loews Hotels. How does he handle the potential disaster? To find this article, visit www.mhhe.com/gregory7, click on STUDENT EDITION and then POWERWEB: CONTENTS.

Dr. Micah McCreary, a psychology professor at Virginia Commonwealth University, speaks to families and survivors of the 9/11 World Trade Center attacks. His presentation was part of a daylong event aimed at helping the audience to deal with their loss and "still achieve their dreams." In planning his speeches, Dr. McCreary often uses the problem–solution pattern, one of the organizational patterns discussed in this chapter.

10

The Body of the Speech

Outline

The Importance of Organization

Creating the Body
Overview of the Process
How to Develop Material

Devising Main Points
Limit the Number of Main Points
Restrict Each Main Point to a Single Idea
Avoid Announcements
Customize Points for Each Audience
Use Parallel Language Whenever Possible

Organizing Main Points
Chronological Pattern
Spatial Pattern
Causal Pattern
Problem–Solution Pattern
Topical Pattern

Selecting Support Materials

Supplying Transitions
Bridges
Internal Summaries
Signposts
Spotlights

Simplifying the Process

Objectives

After studying this chapter, you should be able to:

1. Explain the importance of skillfully organizing the body of the speech.
2. Formulate main points to develop the central idea of a speech.
3. Organize main points according to a logical scheme.
4. Identify and use five patterns of organization: chronological, spatial, causal, problem–solution, and topical.
5. Identify and use four types of transitional devices: bridges, internal summaries, signposts, and spotlights.

Have you ever heard of tobacco toothpaste? That's just one of many tobacco products that are popular in India, the world's second most populous nation. Cigarettes are the most widely used form of tobacco, of course, but Indians also are fond of a wide selection of smokeless, chewable varieties—despite the fact that India has the world's highest rate of tobacco-related diseases such as cancer and emphysema. Because many children and adolescents chew tobacco from morning till night, the incidence of mouth cancer has skyrocketed.[1]

Leading a campaign to warn India's youth of the dangers of tobacco is Ruby Bhatia, who gives many speeches and television interviews. Bhatia was born in Alabama, grew up in Canada, and majored in philosophy at the University of Toronto. She moved to India a few years ago, already fluent in Hindi and English (two of India's major languages), and quickly became one of India's most popular TV talk-show hosts.

Bhatia says that her TV experience helps her create anti-tobacco speeches that are short and persuasive. "If you give a hodgepodge of ideas that are only loosely tied together, you won't win your case. Your ideas must have a logical sequence." TV reports—which she says are a good model for public speakers to follow—often use a chronological, story-telling pattern (beginning–middle–end) or a problem–solution pattern (explanation of a problem, followed by an analysis of its solution).[2] These two patterns are among those discussed in this chapter.

Before we plunge into this chapter, let's look at where we stand in the speech-preparation process. In the last four chapters, we discussed finding and using materials such as statistics, examples, and visual aids. Our next task is to use these materials to build a coherent structure. This chapter will focus on organizing the body of the speech, Chapter 11 on creating introductions and conclusions, and Chapter 12 on putting all the parts together in an outline.

Ruby Bhatia, who gives speeches to warn India's youth of the dangers of tobacco, says that to be effective, a speech must have a logical sequence.

List A

Indian python
Cheetah
Great white shark
Gorilla
Hawksbill turtle
Hawaiian crow
Gray wolf
California condor
Common sturgeon
Polar bear
Whooping crane
Giant catfish
Shore plover
Painted terrapin
Cutthroat trout
American crocodile

List B

Mammals

Polar bear	Gorilla
Cheetah	Gray wolf

Birds

California condor	Hawaiian crow
Shore plover	Whooping crane

Reptiles

American crocodile	Indian python
Hawksbill turtle	Painted terrapin

Fish

Giant catfish	Cutthroat trout
Great white shark	Common sturgeon

Figure 10.1
A list of endangered species is shown in two formats. Because it is organized in logical clusters, list B is easier to memorize and retain than list A.

The Importance of Organization

A well-organized speech has vast advantages over a poorly organized one:

1. **A well-organized speech is easier to understand.** Los Angeles Municipal Court Judge Wesley J. Smith, who once presided over a small-claims court similar to *The People's Court* on TV, says, "The most effective cases I heard involved people who presented their side of the issue as if they were telling a story. Their cases were organized logically, with a beginning, a middle, and an end. That not only kept my interest but helped me quickly understand the issues."[3]
2. **A well-organized speech is easier for the audience to remember.** In an experiment with a list of endangered species, one group of students memorized list A in Figure 10.1 and another group memorized list B. When tested two weeks later, the students who had learned list A recalled 56 percent of the terms, while the students who had learned list B recalled 81 percent.[4]

List B is easier to remember because items are grouped in meaningful clusters. In a good speech, you should apply the same principle: Group your ideas in meaningful clusters that are easy to comprehend and recall.

3. **A well-organized speech is more likely to be believed.** Studies show that if you present a poorly organized speech, your listeners will find you less believable at the end than they did at the beginning of the speech.[5] If your speech is well-organized, however, you will come across as someone who is in full command of the facts, and therefore believable.

Creating the Body

Before we scrutinize the different parts of the body of a speech, let's look at the overall picture.

Overview of the Process

To create the body of a speech, start with your *specific purpose,* which is the goal of your speech, and your *central idea,* which is the key concept that you want to get across to your audience. (If you are unsure about these terms, please review Chapter 5 before proceeding in this chapter.)

Suppose you have been reading about the effect of chronic quarreling on a person's health, and you want to share with your audience some of the findings of medical researchers. You come up with the following purpose statement:

Specific Purpose: To explain to my audience the impact that hostility has on the health of couples and roommates.

Next, ask yourself, "What is my essential message? What big idea do I want to leave in the minds of my listeners?" The answer is your central idea. Here is one possibility:

Central Idea: Couples and roommates who frequently quarrel tend to have more illnesses than do people in amicable relationships.

This central idea is your speech boiled down to one sentence. It is what you want your listeners to remember if they forget everything else.

The next step is to ask yourself this question: "How can I get my audience to understand and accept my central idea?"

The best way to get the central idea across to your audience is to implant in their minds a few **main points** that are based on the central idea. In our health example, here are two main points that could be made:

main points
key assertions made by a speaker to develop his or her central idea

I. Studies show that couples and roommates who have constant fights suffer a weakening of their immune systems.
II. Studies show that people who interact amicably with friends and family are generally healthier than people who interact angrily.

The main points provide a contrast between hostile relationships and friendly interactions.

Next, ask yourself, "How can I support these main points so that listeners understand and remember them?" The answer is to back up each main point with support materials such as narratives, examples, and statistics. For example, here is how you could develop main point I:

I. Studies show that couples and roommates who have constant fights suffer a weakening of their immune systems.
   A. Researchers at Ohio State University Medical Center brought 90 couples into a lab and asked them to resolve an issue of disagreement; continuous blood monitoring for 24 hours revealed that couples who had high levels of hostility displayed significant deterioration on eight measures of the immune system.[6]
   B. "The more hostile you are during a marital argument, the harder it is on your immune system," said Dr. Janice Kiecolt-Glaser, the physician in charge of the Ohio State study.
   C. Researchers at Cambridge University in England found that couples who had constant quarrels were 13 times as likely to develop a serious illness as couples who rarely fought.

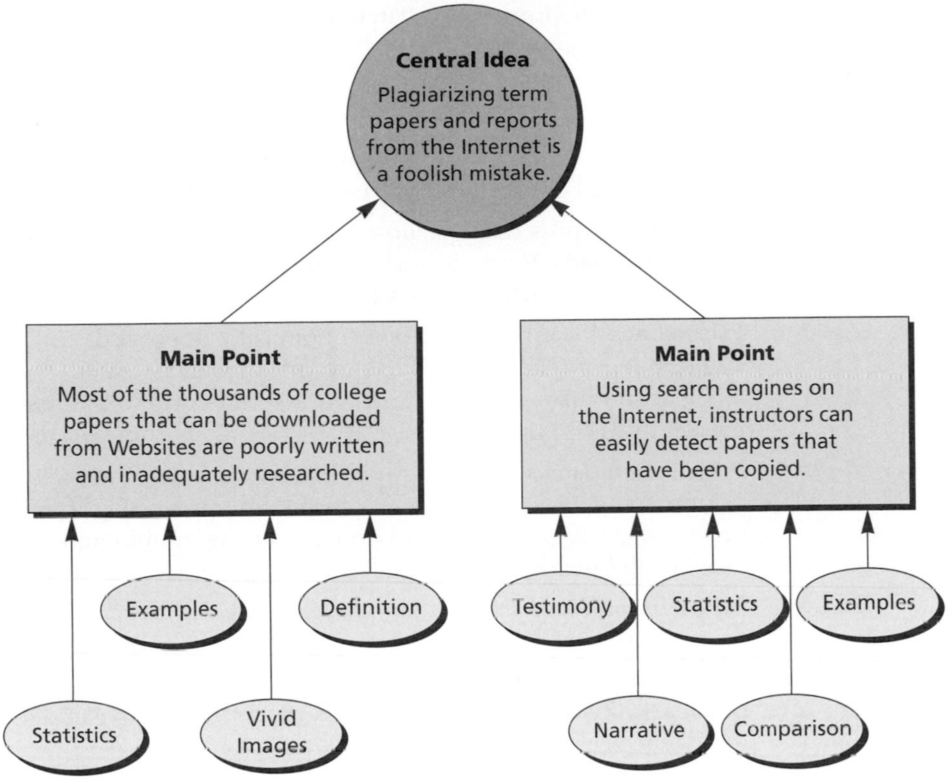

Figure 10.2
Every speech should have a central idea that is developed by two or three (or occasionally four) main points. The main points are strengthened by a variety of support materials, such as examples and statistics.

D. A study of students at Yale University discovered that roommates who disliked each other had far more colds and flus and visits to physicians than did roommates who liked each other—and the greater the dislike, the higher the number of illnesses.

The second main point could be developed in the same way—with statistics and quotations from research studies.

If you arrange a speech in this way, you will have an effective method for getting your message across.

Figure 10.2 shows how the body of a typical speech is constructed. The central idea is sustained by main points, which in turn are buttressed by support material (examples, statistics, and so on). All three levels are necessary: Your listeners will not believe your central idea unless you have strong main points, and they will not believe your main points unless your support material is convincing.

How to Develop Material

I've heard people say something like this, "When I'm putting together a speech, I get lost in my notes. How do I know which are main points and which are subpoints? How do I know what to put in and what to leave out?"

To develop your material, take these important steps:

Cluster Your Research Notes

Your first step is to cluster your research notes into logical categories. Let's say you conduct research on a new trend: some communities in the United States are campaigning to have new prisons constructed in their locales (in contrast to earlier times, when most communities fought against having a prison in their backyards). When you finish your research, you have a large accumulation of notes. Imagine grouping them into clusters like these:

Cluster 1: **Communities** (Sample note: Like many economically depressed communities, Fort Dodge, Iowa, competed to win a state prison.)

Cluster 2: **Construction Jobs** (Sample note: A new women's prison near Zion Crossroads, Virginia, cost $53 million and provided hundreds of construction jobs.)

Cluster 3: **Prison Jobs** (Sample note: For economically depressed communities in West Texas, 28 new prisons have created 8,000 prison jobs—guards, clerks, and so on—with an annual payroll of $176 million.)

Cluster 4: **Private Companies** (Sample note: In Ohio and California, private companies hire prisoners to do data processing inside prison; the executives of these companies buy homes and pay taxes in the nearby communities.)

Cluster 5: **Prisoners on Road Crews** (Sample note: Snyder, Texas, relies on convicts to clear vegetation and trash from roadsides.)

Cluster 6: **Prisoners as Recyclers** (Sample note: Folsom, California, uses prisoners at Folsom State Prison to sort out the city's garbage in a waste recycling plant inside the prison.)

Grouping your research notes into clusters is an important way to gain control of your material. Otherwise, you might have a mishmash of unconnected information.

Create Main Points and Support Them

SpeechMate CD-ROM

For handy guidelines, see "Checklist for Preparing and Delivering a Speech" on Disk 1 of the CD.

Your next step is to create main points and then back them up with support materials. You can do this by systematically answering the following questions (we will continue our prison construction scenario to illustrate each question).

1. What is the specific purpose of my speech? The goal of your speech can be expressed in this way:

Specific Purpose: To explain to my listeners why some communities are competing for new prisons

Note that you have narrowed your topic to something that can be managed in a short speech. You don't have time to cover the broad subject of prisons in American society.

2. What is my central idea, the key concept that I want my listeners to understand, believe, and remember? The essence of your speech can be expressed very simply:

Central Idea: Once unwanted, prisons are eagerly welcomed in some economically depressed communities in the United States.

3. What main points can I present to drive home the central idea? Put yourself in the place of the listeners. What would they say in response to your central idea? They would probably say, "Why would any town want a prison?" Based on your notes, you create these main points:

I. Prisons are regarded as a rich source of jobs for communities.
II. Prisons are viewed as a provider of free labor for public projects.

Both of your points are drawn from your clusters: The first four clusters coalesce into main point I; the last two clusters form the basis for main point II. That's the advantage of clustering: It helps you shape your points.

Why these particular points? If you examine the central idea again, you will see that these points (or ones very similar) are the ones that explain why some communities are welcoming prisons.

4. **What support material (narratives, statistics, quotations, etc.) will I need under each main point to explain or prove it?** By themselves, your main points are bland. They need the spice and nourishment of stories, examples, and statistics. The rich variety you have accumulated in your clusters will nicely illustrate each main point.

Discard Irrelevant Material

Be selective, choosing only those items that directly relate to the central idea. If you include irrelevant information, you risk confusing your listeners or overloading them with too much information.

Let's say you come across some fascinating stories about prison labor in China. For a short speech on communities' bids for prisons in the United States, these stories would be irrelevant. Discard them.

Devising Main Points

"Do I need more than one main point?" some students ask. Yes. If you have only one main point to develop your central idea, you have a weak structure, like a bridge that has only one pillar to hold it up. If you provide only one main point, your listeners have only *one* reason to believe your central idea. If you give them two or three main points, you multiply your chances of convincing them.

"How many main points should I have?" you may be asking. To answer this and other questions, let's examine some guidelines for refining main points.

Limit the Number of Main Points

A common mistake of public speakers is to cram too many points into a speech. They do this because they are approaching the speech from their own viewpoint and not from the viewpoint of the listeners. If you ask yourself, "How much information can I squeeze into the five minutes allotted?" you are approaching the speech from your own viewpoint. To approach from the audience's viewpoint, you should ask, "How much information can the audience comfortably pay attention to, understand, and remember?" Audiences simply cannot absorb too much new information. You should know this from your own experience; you can probably recall many speakers (including some teachers) who overwhelmed you with a barrage of ideas, facts, and figures. Don't be reluctant to cut and trim your material.

Exactly how many main points should you have? In a short speech (5 to 10 minutes), you should limit yourself to two or three (or occasionally four) main points. That is as much as an audience can absorb. In a longer speech, you could have as many as five main points, but most experienced speakers cover only two or three, regardless of the length of their speech. It is a rare—and usually ineffective—veteran speaker who attempts six or more.

Restrict Each Main Point to a Single Idea

Each main point should focus on just one idea. Consider the following:

Poor: I. Some employees who are diagnosed with cancer lose their jobs, and some of them lose their health-insurance coverage.

Better: I. Some employees who are diagnosed with cancer lose their jobs.

II. Some lose their health-insurance coverage.

The first set makes the mistake of covering two issues; the second set splits the material into two distinct points.

Avoid Announcements

Rather than simply announce a topic, each main point should make an assertion, a forthright declaration of the idea that you want to convey. Imagine that you create the following:

Poor: I'll talk about hot-dog headaches.

What about it? What's your point? You have done nothing but announce your topic.

Better: Sodium nitrites contained in hot dogs cause many people to suffer headaches.

Now you have made a point—a clear assertion of what you are driving at.

Customize Points for Each Audience

As you play with ideas in your search for main points, ask yourself, "What main points would work best with this particular audience?" If you tailor your speech to each audience's needs and desires, you may end up using different main points with different audiences.

Let's say you plan to give speeches in your community aimed at persuading people to take up nature photography as a hobby. If you talk to a group of college students, you can anticipate that they will raise an objection: Photography is too expensive. So you create a main point—"Photography is not out of reach for people with modest incomes"—and devote a good portion of your speech to giving specific examples and prices. If, however, you speak to an audience of wealthy individuals who could easily afford any kind of camera, this point might be unnecessary.

Another potential main point is that nature photography teaches a person to see the world with fresh eyes—to find "splendor in the grass," the visual glories that abound in nature for those who develop keen perception. This would be a good point to make with an audience of urban dwellers who rarely explore the outdoors. But if your audience is a birdwatchers' society, this point is probably unnecessary; these people have already trained their eyes to detect nature's nuances.

Use Parallel Language Whenever Possible

Parallel language means that you use the same grammatical forms throughout a sentence or paragraph. Read the following sentence aloud: "Joe enjoys hunting, fishing, and to camp." There is nothing wrong with the sentence grammatically, but it doesn't sound as pleasant to the ear as this version: "Joe enjoys hunting, fishing, and camping." Rather than the discord of *-ing, -ing,* plus *to,* our ears prefer the rhythm of *-ing, -ing, -ing,* as in the second sentence.

parallel language
equivalent grammatical forms to express equivalent ideas

Suppose that you started with the following:

Specific Purpose: To persuade my audience to swim for exercise

Central Idea: Swimming is an ideal exercise because it dissipates nervous tension, avoids injuries, and builds endurance.

Now decide which of the following sets of main points would be more effective:

First set:
I. You can work off a lot of nervous tension while swimming.
II. Muscle and bone injuries, common with other sports, are not a problem with swimming.
III. Swimming builds endurance.

Second set:
I. Swimming dissipates nervous tension.
II. Swimming avoids muscle and bone injuries.
III. Swimming builds endurance.

The second set is preferable because it follows a parallel grammatical form throughout (the noun *swimming* followed by a verb). This consistent arrangement may not be practical in every speech, but you should strive for parallelism whenever possible.

Organizing Main Points

Main points should be organized in a logical, easy-to-follow pattern. Five of the most popular patterns used by speakers are chronological, spatial, causal, problem–solution, and topical.

Chronological Pattern

In the **chronological pattern,** you arrange your main points in a *time* sequence—what occurs first, what occurs second, and so on. If, for example, you are describing a process, you can use the chronological pattern to show the step-by-step progression. For an illustration, see Figure 10.3.

chronological pattern
an arrangement of information in a time sequence

How to Treat a Bee Sting

Step 1	Get the stinger out quickly.
Step 2	Wash sting area with soap and water.
Step 3	Apply ice pack for 15 minutes.

Figure 10.3
Chronological Pattern
The process of treating a bee sting is a chronological pattern (or time sequence)—what to do first, second, and third.

The chronological pattern is a logical choice for a speech dealing with periods of time in history. If, for example, you were speaking on the history of immigration in the United States, you could divide your subject into centuries, from the seventeenth to the twentieth.

If you were speaking on the life of a person, you might divide your speech according to the stages of life, as in the following example:

Specific Purpose: To inform my listeners of the heroism of Harriet Tubman, a leading 19th century abolitionist

Central Idea: Harriet Tubman was a courageous woman who escaped from slavery and then returned to the South to rescue others.

Main Points:

(Childhood) I. Born a slave on a plantation in Maryland, Tubman suffered many whippings while growing up.

(Youth) II. She escaped to freedom by using the Underground Railroad.

(Adulthood) III. Wearing various disguises, Tubman smuggled over 300 slaves to safe havens from 1850 to 1860.

Spatial Pattern

spatial pattern
an arrangement of information in terms of physical space, such as top to bottom

In the **spatial pattern,** you organize items according to the way in which they relate to each other in *physical space*—top to bottom, left to right, north to south, inside to outside, and so on. If you were speaking on the solar system, for example, you could discuss the sun first, then move outward in space to Mercury, Venus, Earth, Mars, and so on. Here is an example in which the speaker divides a car into space-related sections:

Specific Purpose: To tell my audience how to inspect a used car before deciding whether to buy it

Central Idea: If you examine a used car carefully and critically, you can avoid buying a "lemon."

Main Points:
I. Inspect the condition of the body of the car.
II. Inspect the condition of the motor.
III. Inspect the condition of the interior.

Figure 10.4
Spatial Pattern
For a discussion of "The Jester" by 17th century Dutch artist Judith Leyster, a speaker could use the spatial (physical space) pattern, progressing from top to bottom.

For an example of the spatial pattern as used from top to bottom, see Figure 10.4.

Causal Pattern

In some speeches, you are concerned with why something happens or happened—a cause-and-effect relationship. For example, some people refuse to ride in elevators because they have an inordinate fear of closed spaces. Their claustrophobia is the *cause* and their refusal to ride in elevators is the *effect*. For an illustration of a **causal pattern** in a speech, see Figure 10.5.

causal pattern
a scheme that links outcomes (effects) and the reasons for them (causes)

Sometimes it is more effective to start with the effects and then analyze the causes, as in this case:

Specific Purpose: To explain to my listeners why many people are unable to get bank loans for a new car or house

Central Idea: If you are denied a loan for a new car or house, it could be because you have been incorrectly branded as a poor credit risk by credit-rating companies.

Main Points:
(Effect) I. Many people are barred from getting loans for a new car or house without ever knowing the reason.
(Cause) II. The credit-rating companies that keep computerized files on 90% of Americans frequently make mistakes without the consumer ever knowing.

In this case, putting the effect first is good strategy because it makes the listeners receptive to the rest of the speech—they are curious to know what caused the situation.

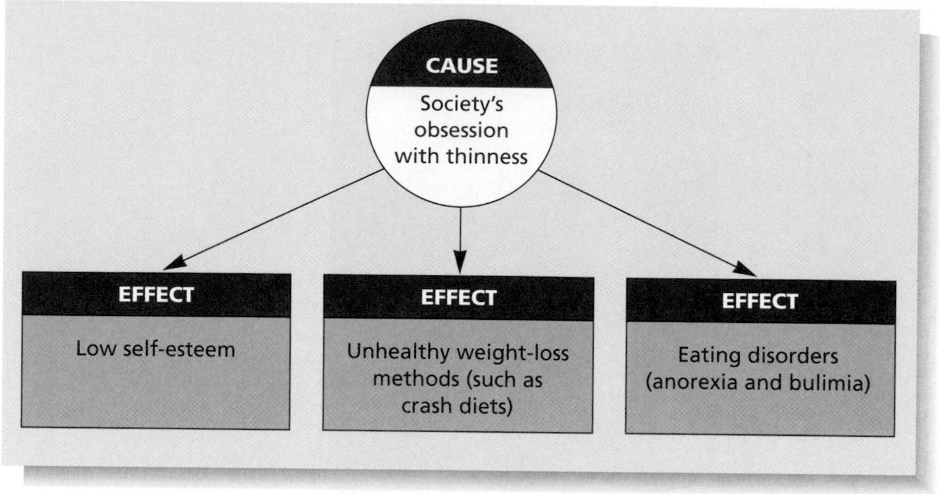

Figure 10.5
Causal Pattern
For a speech about society's emphasis on thinness, a speaker could show a cause-and-effect relationship.

Problem–Solution Pattern

problem–solution pattern
an arrangement of information that explores a problem and then offers a solution

A much-used device for persuasive speeches is the **problem–solution pattern,** which divides a speech into two main sections: a problem and its solution. Here is an example:

Specific Purpose: To persuade my audience to support "pet therapy" for lonely elderly people in nursing homes.

Central Idea: Contact with a pet can decrease the loneliness and improve the physical and emotional health of elderly people in nursing homes.

Main Points:

(Problem) I. Many elderly people in nursing homes are lonely and depressed—emotional states that harm their physical health.

(Solution) II. Researchers have discovered that contact with a pet improves the elderly person's physical and emotional health.

This pattern has the advantage of simplicity. You convince the listeners that a particular problem exists, and then you tell them how it can be solved. See Figure 10.6.

Topical Pattern

topical pattern
a division of a topic into components, types, or reasons

In the **topical pattern,** you divide your central idea into components or categories, using logic and common sense as your guides.

Thus, a speech on the symphonic orchestra could be divided into three sections: string instruments, wind instruments, and percussion instruments. A speech on job interviews could be divided into three types of interviews: personal, video, and computer. See Figure 10.7 for another example.

Here is a portion of an outline that illustrates the topical pattern:

Specific Purpose: To inform my audience of the two kinds of sleep that all persons experience

Figure 10.6
Problem–Solution Pattern
A speech on the correct way to lift heavy items could explain the problem (back pain from lifting incorrectly) and the solution (lifting with one's legs, keeping the back straight).

Central Idea: The two kinds of sleep that all persons experience at alternating times during the night are NREM (non-rapid-eye-movement) sleep and REM (rapid eye-movement) sleep.

Main Points:
I. NREM (non-rapid-eye-movement) sleep is the period in which a person does very little dreaming.
II. REM (rapid eye-movement) sleep is the period in which a person usually dreams.

A variation of the topical pattern is sometimes called the **statement-of-reasons pattern.** The speaker subdivides an idea by showing reasons for it, as in the following example:

statement-of-reasons pattern
a variation of the topical pattern in which a speaker gives reasons for an idea

Specific Purpose: To persuade my listeners that telephone companies should use alternatives to cellular phone towers

Central Idea: Telephone companies should be required to place their cellular antennas on buildings and trees rather than on freestanding towers.

Figure 10.7
Topical Pattern
A speech on typefaces could be divided into an explanation of three major styles. Serif letters have lines or curves projecting from the end of a letterform, while sans-serif letters do not have finishing strokes. Script letters simulate fancy handwriting.

www.mhhe.com/gregory7
To review organizational patterns, do the interactive exercise in Chapter 10 on this book's Website.

Main Points:		
(First reason)	I.	Cellular phone towers are huge and ugly.
(Second reason)	II.	Cellular telephone antennas work as effectively on church steeples, tall trees, and high buildings as they do on freestanding towers.
(Third reason)	III.	Steeples, trees, and buildings are easily available because many churches, landowners, and businesses desire the fees that telephone companies pay for antenna placement.

Note of caution: Some students make the mistake of thinking that the topical pattern is a formless bag into which anything can be dumped. Though you have a great deal of liberty to organize your points in whatever order you choose, you still must apply logic—by, for example, arranging your points from least important to most important, or separating your material into three major subdivisions.

Selecting Support Materials

In the preceding sections, we concentrated on main points, but main points by themselves are not enough for the body of a speech. You also need support materials—such as examples, narratives, testimony, and statistics—to develop and amplify your main points. As discussed in Chapter 8, support materials help your audience to understand and remember main points.

To see how support materials can be developed for main points, let's take a look at an outline of the body of a speech by student speaker Amber Wright, who uses the problem–solution pattern.[7] The introduction and conclusion for this speech are printed in Chapter 11.

General Purpose: To persuade

Specific Purpose: To persuade my audience to beware of scam artists who practice affinity fraud

Central Idea: Affinity fraud is a clever scam, but it can be defeated.

Commentary	Body
The body has two main points, the first devoted to the problem and the second to the solution.	**I.** Affinity fraud is a widespread scam that uses religious, ethnic, or professional affiliations to gain the trust of victims.
*Wright gives a **definition** of affinity fraud that goes beyond a mere dictionary definition. She explains the term.*	A. We like and trust people who are similar to us. B. The scam artist pretends to be a group member who is devoted to helping other members of the group.
*To show the gravity of the problem, the speaker uses **statistics** from a trustworthy source.*	C. According to *The Wall Street Journal,* investors have lost more than $2 billion in affinity scams over the last three years.

D. The scam is ingenious, as described by the *Washington Post.*

*An **example** helps the audience to understand how affinity fraud works.*

1. The scam artist joins a church and sells—or even gives—shares to several prominent members, who quickly realize a profit.
2. The scammer goes to other church members, who trust him because of the success of the prominent members.
3. The scammer gets a lot of money and then disappears.

E. The same approach has been used with doctors, lawyers, accountants, and other professionals.

F. Scammers often target ethnic groups, especially immigrants.

*A **narrative** (or story) is effective to show the human suffering caused by affinity fraud.*

1. According to *Newsday,* a New York area newspaper, Ha Im and his wife Jung Im had spent five years operating a dry-cleaning shop in Flushing, New York, and they dreamed of buying a house.
2. They were approached by a stockbroker who shared their heritage as Korean-Americans.
3. The stockbroker persuaded them to put their life savings—$170,000—into his hands.
4. A few years later, all of the money had evaporated.
5. Although this happened two years ago, the couple is still devastated.
6. Today, Jung Im says, "I can't eat; I can't digest anything. I'm like a vegetable. I feel like I've died."

(*Transition:* Now that we have looked at the problem, let's examine the solution.)

II. You can avoid becoming a victim of affinity fraud.

The second main point, like the first, is developed by good support materials.

A. Even if a person promoting a scheme seems to have a lot in common with you, don't let your guard down.

B. Melanie Lubin, securities commissioner for the state of Maryland, says, "If there's someone who an investor can look at and say, 'Well, they're like me; they're not going to do anything wrong,' the con artist has already crossed the hurdle of credibility."

__Testimony__ from an expert is effective.

C. Beware of testimonials from other group members.

*Another **example** is given.*

1. A few years ago, thousands of doctors lost $50 million in an investment scheme because

a few of their fellow doctors had reported financial success.

2. Remember what we said earlier: A scammer lets a few realize a handsome profit so that he or she can fleece a larger number of members of a particular group.

D. Don't succumb to pressure.

1. The promoter will say that if you don't act quickly, you will lose an opportunity to make a lot of money.

*"Big red flag" is a **vivid image.***

2. This is a big red flag that should warn you that the promoter may be phony.

E. Check out the promoter and the investment.

1. Seek professional advice from a neutral outside expert not in your group—a financial planner, for example.

2. Call your local Better Business Bureau and ask for information about the promoter.

If possible, distribute your supporting materials evenly. In other words, don't put all your support under point I and leave nothing to bolster point II. This does not mean, however, that you should mechanically place the same number of supporting points under every main point. You have to consider *quality* as well as *quantity*. A single powerful anecdote may be all that is required to illustrate one point, whereas five minor supports might be needed for another point.

When you are trying to decide how many supporting points to place underneath a main point, use this rule of thumb: Have enough supporting points to adequately explain or bolster the main point, but not so many that you become tedious and repetitious.

Supplying Transitions

transition
an expression that links ideas and shows the relationship between them

Words, phrases, or sentences that show logical connections between ideas or thoughts are called **transitions.** They help the listeners stay with you as you move from one part of your speech to the next. To get an idea of how transitions work, take a look at two paragraphs, the first of which has no transitions:

Poor: Olive oil is used extensively in Mediterranean cooking. It never became popular in Latin America. Olive trees can grow in Mexico and coastal regions of South America. The colonial rulers in Spain did not want anyone competing against Spain's farmers. They banned the production of olive oil in Latin America. The oil had to be imported. It was very expensive.

Now let's add transitions (shown in bold print):

Better: Olive oil is used extensively in Mediterranean cooking. **However,** it never became popular in Latin America. Olive trees can grow

> in Mexico and coastal regions of South America, **but** the colonial rulers in Spain did not want anyone competing against Spain's farmers, **so** they banned the production of olive oil in Latin America. The oil had to be imported **and therefore** was very expensive.

The transitions obviously make the second paragraph superior.

In a speech, transitions clarify the relationship between your ideas, thereby making them easy to comprehend. They serve as signals to help the listeners follow your train of thought. Here is a sampling of the many transitional words or phrases in the English language:

- To signal addition: *and, also, furthermore, moreover, in addition*
- To signal time: *soon, then, later, afterward, meanwhile*
- To signal contrast: *however, but, yet, nevertheless, instead, meanwhile, although*
- To signal examples: *for example, to illustrate, for instance*
- To signal conclusions: *in summary, therefore, consequently, as a result*
- To signal concession: *although it is true that, of course, granted*

In public speaking, special types of transitions can be employed to help your listener follow your remarks. Let us look at four of them: bridges, internal summaries, signposts, and spotlights.

Bridges

In crossing a bridge, a person goes from one piece of land to another. In giving a speech, the speaker can build **bridges** to tell the listeners of the terrain they are leaving behind and the terrain they are about to enter: It is a way of saying, "I've finished Thought A; now I'm going to Thought B."

bridge
a transitional device that links what went before with the next part of a speech

Imagine that you had the following as your first main point in a speech on workplace violence:

I. Violence in the workplace has increased in recent years.

You give examples and statistics to back up this point, and now you are ready for your second main point:

II. Workplace violence can be reduced if managers and employees are trained in conflict resolution.

How can you go from point I to point II? You could simply finish with point I and begin point II, but that would be too abrupt. It would fail to give the listeners time to change mental gears. A smoother way is to refer back to the first main point at the same time you are pointing forward to the second:

> Although workplace violence has increased dramatically, the situation is not hopeless. There is a way to reduce the number of incidents—a way that has proven successful in many companies throughout the world.

This is a successful bridge because it smoothly and gracefully takes your listeners from point I to point II. It also has the virtue of stimulating their curiosity about the next part of the speech.

Tips for your CAREER

Tip 10.1 Test Your Material

Will your audience find your speech understandable, accurate, and believable? You can test the strength of your material in advance by using these techniques:

- In regard to each main point, think of the typical people who will be in your audience and ask yourself, "How will they react to this?" Then shape your material accordingly. If your imaginary listeners say, "How do you know this is true?" give the name and credentials of the expert from whom you derived your material. If they ask, "What do you mean by that?" give them an explanation. If they say, "Who cares?" show them the importance of your subject.
- Try out your material on friends or relatives. Victoria Vance, a hospital nutritionist who gives talks in her community on diet and nutrition, tests her ideas with her husband and teenage children at the dinner table. "I tell them, 'I'm going to give a speech at a high school next week. Here's what I plan to say.' Then I casually tell them the main points of my speech. Occasionally one of the kids will break in with something like, 'But, Mom, are you saying that *all* fast food is bad for you?' That tells me the places in the speech where I need to add some more explanations or examples."
- Do an "expert check"—that is, discuss your key ideas with someone who is knowledgeable about your subject, so that he or she can point out any errors or omissions.

Internal Summaries

At the end of a baseball game, announcers always give a summary of the game. But during the game itself, they occasionally give a summary of what has taken place up to the present moment ("We're in the middle of the fifth inning; Detroit is leading Milwaukee 4 to 3 on a grand-slam homer by . . . "). Though this summary is primarily designed for the viewers who have tuned in late, it is also appreciated by the fans who have been watching the entire game because it gives them a feeling of security and confidence—a sense of knowing the "main facts." You can achieve the same effect in a speech. During the body of a speech, when you finish an important section, you may want to spend a few moments summarizing your ideas so that they are clear and understandable. This device, called an **internal summary,** is especially helpful if you have been discussing ideas that are complicated or abstract. An internal summary can be combined with a bridge to make an excellent transition, as follows:

internal summary
a concise review of material covered during the body of a speech

> [*Internal summary*] By now I hope I've convinced you that all animal bites should be reported to a doctor or health official immediately because of the possibility of rabies. [*bridge*] While you're waiting for an ambulance or for an examination by a doctor, there is one other important thing you should do.

Signposts

signpost
an explicit statement of the place that a speaker has reached

Just as signposts on a road tell motorists their location, **signposts** in a speech tell listeners where they are or where they are headed. If you gave a speech on how to treat a cold, you could say, "Here are three things you should do the next time you catch a cold." Then the audience would find it easy to follow your points if you said, "First, you should . . . Second, you should . . . Third, you should . . ." Using these signposts is much more effective than linking your points by saying, "Also . . ." or "Another point is . . ."

Spotlights

Spotlights are transitional devices that alert the listeners that something important will soon appear. Here are some examples:

spotlight
a device that alerts listeners to important points

- Now we come to the most important thing I have to tell you.
- What I'm going to explain now will help you understand the rest of the speech.
- If you take with you only one idea from this speech . . .

Spotlights can build up anticipation: "And now I come to an idea that can mean extra money in your pocket . . ." Or: "If you want to feel healthier and happier, listen to the advice of Dr. Julia Brunswick . . ."

When you choose transitional devices, remember that your listeners are totally unfamiliar with your speech, so try to put yourself in their shoes at each juncture. Ask yourself, "How can I lead the listener from one point to another in a way that is logical and smooth?"

Simplifying the Process

Organizing bits and pieces of material into a coherent, logical speech can be a difficult task, but it can be simplified if you use the following method:

1. **Survey all your material.** Bring together and examine your personal observations, interview notes, research notes, and visual aids.
2. **Choose an organizational method.** Three options are recommended:

   - **Computers.** Most word processing programs permit split screens, so that you can have notes in one window and an outline in another, making it easy to look over your notes and transform them into items for your outline.
   - **Stick-on slips.** This method uses file folders of different colors, with a different-colored folder for each major part of the speech. Stick-on slips (such as the 3M Post-it™ slips) are placed inside the folders.
   - **Cards.** This method is similar to the stick-on slips, except that index cards are used. The cards can be kept together by a rubber band or stored in a file folder.

   All three options give you flexibility. You can easily move items around, add extra material, and delete unimportant points. Items can be spread out—stick-on slips in file folders, computer entries on a screen, and cards on a tabletop. This procedure lets you see the "big picture"—the overall architecture of your speech.
3. **Identify each item that you may want to include in your speech.** Jot down or type each potential point, example, narrative, statistic, and quotation.

4. Limit each note to just one idea. To make the method work effectively, *you must use a separate slip, card, or computer entry for each point.* This will make it easy to move items around.

5. Focus on three major parts. A speech works best if it is divided into three well-developed sections: introduction, body, and conclusion.

6. Create the body first. Many experienced speakers find it easier to prepare the body of the speech first and then prepare the introduction. If you stop to think about it, this makes sense: How can you introduce the body until you know its full nature?

7. Experiment with different sequences. Try several ways of arranging your material until you find a good sequence, a smooth flow that will be easy for the audience to follow. Marcia Yudkin, a business trainer from Boston, uses the card system, but her advice can be applied to stick-on slips and computer screens as well:

> Sit in a comfortable chair and shuffle those ideas, asking yourself questions like, "What if I start with this, and move on to this, then this . . .?" You're looking for a smooth, natural flow from each point to the next. Some sort of sequence will eventually emerge from this exercise. Don't get perturbed if you end up with extra cards that refuse to fit in; any leftover material might be perfect for the question-and-answer period after your speech, or for another presentation.[8]

8. Transfer your material to a formal outline. Once you have your information arranged, it's a good idea to transfer it to a formal outline—as a way to gain control over it and to test its strength and continuity. Your instructor may have a required format for the outline. If not, I suggest you use the format shown in Chapter 12.

Resources for Review and Skill Building

www.mhhe.com/gregory7

This book's Online Learning Center Website and SpeechMate CD-ROM provide meaningful resources and tools for study and review, such as practice tests, key-term flashcards, and sample speech videos.

SpeechMate CD-ROM

Summary

A well-organized speech is more understandable, credible, and memorable than a poorly organized one.

The body of the speech should be organized with two or three (occasionally four) main points that develop the central idea of the speech. Some guidelines for main points: (1) Restrict each main point to a single idea. (2) Avoid announcements. (3) Customize points for each audience. (4) Use parallel language whenever possible.

Arrange the main points in a logical pattern, such as *chronological,* in which main points are placed in a time sequence; *spatial,* in which items are arranged in terms of physical space; *causal,* in which causes and effects are juxtaposed; *problem–solution,* in which a problem is explained and a solution offered; or *topical,* in which a central idea is divided into components.

Next, select support materials to back up the main points, and then supply transitions to help the listeners stay with you as you move from one part of your speech to the next. Common types of transitions are bridges, internal summaries, signposts, and spotlights.

To simplify the task of organizing material, use one of these three options: stick-on slips, computers, and cards. Put one item on each slip, computer entry, or card so that you can easily add, delete, and rearrange your material.

Key Terms

bridge, *243*
causal pattern, *237*
chronological pattern, *235*
internal summary, *244*
main points, *230*
parallel language, *235*
problem–solution pattern, *238*
signpost, *244*
spatial pattern, *236*
spotlight, *245*
statement-of-reasons pattern, *239*
topical pattern, *238*
transition, *242*

Review Questions

1. How many main points should you have in a speech?
2. How many ideas should be represented in each main point?
3. What is meant by the advice to "customize points for each audience"?
4. Which pattern of organization would be best suited for a speech on the solar system?
5. Which pattern of organization would be ideal for a speech on food contamination and how the problem can be corrected?
6. Which pattern of organization would be best suited for a speech on the three major reasons why businesses declare bankruptcy?
7. Why are transitions important in a speech?
8. In terms of speech organization, what is an internal summary?
9. Describe the transitional device called *bridge.*
10. Describe the transitional device called *spotlight.*

Building Critical-Thinking Skills

1. Which organizational pattern is used in the following:

Specific Purpose: To inform my listeners how to soundproof a room

Central Idea: A room can be insulated so that sounds do not penetrate.

Main Points:

(*Top*) I. The ceiling can be covered by acoustic tile and a tapestry to block sounds from above.

(*Middle*) II. The walls can be covered with ceiling-to-floor tapestries (and heavy, lined drapes for windows) to block noise from outside.

(*Bottom*) III. The floor can be covered with acoustic padding and wall-to-wall carpet to block sounds from below.

2. Which organizational pattern is used in the following:

Specific Purpose: To tell my listeners how to revive a person who is in danger of drowning

Central Idea: To revive a person who is in danger of drowning, you should follow three simple procedures.

Main Points:

(*First*) I. With the victim on his or her back, tilt the head back so that the chin juts upward.

(*Second*) II. Give mouth-to-mouth resuscitation until the victim breathes regularly again.

(*Third*) III. Place the victim on his or her stomach with the head facing sideways.

Building Teamwork Skills

1. Working in a group, examine the following scrambled statements and decide which is the central idea and which are the main points. (One item below is a central idea and the other two are main points to develop the central idea.) Discuss what kinds of support materials would be needed under each main point.

a. Many U.S. companies that have instituted the 30-hour workweek report higher job satisfaction and performance with no loss of profits.

b. A 6-hour day/30-hour workweek should be the standard for full-time employees in the United States.

c. All Western European countries have fewer working hours than the United States.

2. In a group, discuss which organizational pattern would be most effective for the following speech topics.

a. Why most fatal car accidents occur

b. Three types of working dogs

c. How to giftwrap a present

d. Stalking—and what can be done to stop it

e. The Amazon River

Building Internet Skills

www.mhhe.com/gregory7

1. In this chapter, the causal pattern was discussed. On the Internet, find a speech or article that analyzes the causes of "road rage" (violent incidents involving motorists). Print the document and mark the sentences that deal with causes.

Possible Strategy: Use one of the search options in Table 6.1 in Chapter 6.

2. On the Internet, find a speech or article that argues for or against legalization of drugs. Print the document and mark all words, phrases, and sentences that are used as transitional devices.

Possible Strategy: Use one of the search options in Table 6.1 in Chapter 6.

Using PowerWeb

www.mhhe.com/gregory7

Dr. J. Edward Hill, chairman of the board of the American Medical Association, gave a speech entitled "Standing Tall Against Underage Drinking." Which of the organizational patterns discussed in this chapter did Dr. Hill use for his speech? To find a transcript of this speech, visit www.mhhe.com/gregory7, click on STUDENT EDITION and then POWERWEB: CONTENTS.

University of Chicago paleontologist Paul Sereno begins a lecture by displaying a model of the dinosaur skull that he discovered in the Sahara Desert. Sereno likes to grab audience attention and interest at the beginning of a speech by showing a dramatic visual aid.

11

Introductions and Conclusions

Outline

Introductions
Gain Attention and Interest
Orient the Audience
Guidelines for Introductions

Conclusions
Signal the End
Summarize Key Ideas
Reinforce the Central Idea with a Clincher
Guidelines for Conclusions

Sample Introduction and Conclusion with Commentary

Objectives

After studying this chapter, you should be able to:

1. Formulate effective attention material for the introductions of your speeches.
2. Formulate effective orienting material for the introductions of your speeches.
3. Create effective conclusions for your speeches.

Courtroom battles are like dramas, with three distinct parts:

- Beginning (opening statement)
- Middle (examination of evidence)
- End (closing argument)

While all three parts are important, most attorneys say that their opening and closing statements to the jury usually determine whether they win or lose a case.[1] "When you first talk to the jury, you've got to make a favorable impression and win their empathy immediately," says Michelle Roberts, a defense attorney in Washington, D.C. Later, near the end of the trial, "your closing argument must be powerful and persuasive."[2]

In speeches outside the courtroom, the stakes are rarely so high: No one will be forced to go to prison or pay a million dollars in damages if the introduction and conclusion are weak. Nevertheless, these two parts have great importance. If you don't have a lively introduction, you can lose your audience. "People have remote controls in their heads today," says Myrna Marofsky, an Eden Prairie, Minnesota, business executive. "If you don't catch their interest, they just click you off."[3] And a conclusion that is weak or clumsy can mar the effectiveness of what otherwise might have been a good speech.

Prosecuting attorney Debra Riva presents her closing arguments in a murder trial in Sarasota, Florida. She was successful in persuading the jury to find the defendant guilty of killing his ex-wife. For Riva and other attorneys, their opening and closing remarks to a jury often determine whether they win or lose a case.

Introductions

The introduction to your speech has two main goals: first, to capture and hold your audience's attention and interest, and second, to prepare your audience intellectually and psychologically for the body of the speech. Let's examine each goal in greater detail.

Gain Attention and Interest

If you were sitting in an audience, would you want to listen to a speech that begins with: "I'd like to tell you about what I do in my spare time—writing paragraphs"?

Writing paragraphs sounds pretty dull. You might say to yourself, "Who cares?" and let your attention drift to something more interesting, such as the party you are planning to attend next weekend.

Now imagine that you were sitting in the audience when Jeanne-Marie Bellamy began a speech by holding up a $100 bill and saying, "How would you like to earn one hundred dollars by writing just one paragraph?" She went on to explain that magazines pay $100 to $400 for the little paragraphs used to fill up space at the end of a big article. "These 'fillers' are usually anecdotes about interesting or humorous things that have happened in a person's life," she said, adding that she earned an average of $700 per month in her spare time by writing paragraphs about "the amusing little things that happen to me and my family."

When Bellamy held up the $100 bill and asked her intriguing question, the listeners were hooked. How could they possibly turn their attention away? Bellamy's technique was to use attention material as a lure, just as a fisher dangles bait in front of a fish.

A lure needs to be dangled in front of listeners because of an unfortunate fact: Audiences don't automatically give every speaker their full, undivided, respectful attention. As you begin a speech, you may find that some listeners are engaged in whispered conversations with their neighbors (and they don't necessarily stop in midsentence when you start speaking); some are looking at you but their minds are far away, floating in a daydream or enmeshed in a personal problem; some are shifting in their seats to get comfortable; others are thinking about what the preceding speaker said or looking around the room for people they know. So your task is clear: Grab their attention when you start talking.

But grabbing their attention is not enough: Your introduction also must *keep* their attention, so that they want to hear your entire speech. Your introduction must deprive the listeners of any possible excuse to sink back into their private thoughts and daydreams. If you simply say, "I'm going to talk about writing paragraphs," you leave it up to the listeners to decide whether they want to listen to the rest of the speech. Don't give them a choice! Devise an attention-getter that is so interesting that it is impossible for anyone *not* to listen to the entire speech.

In this book, these "grabbers" are called **attention material,** which should always be the first part of your introduction. In the section below we will examine some of the more common varieties. Sometimes two or more grabbers can be combined.

attention material
the part of the introduction designed to capture audience interest

SpeechMate CD-ROM

To see a speaker who tells an interesting story, view Video Clip 11.1 on Disk 1.

Relate a Story

Telling a story is one of the most effective ways to begin a speech because people love to listen to narrative accounts. Cynthia Wray of Western Carolina University began a speech with this story:

> A few years ago, over 100 third-graders were on a field trip at Chicago's O'Hare International Airport. Suddenly, an 87-year-old man lost control of his car and slammed into the group. One child was killed, and 67 children and 10 adults were injured.[4]

Wray went on to argue that older drivers should be tested frequently and denied a license if found to be impaired. As Wray demonstrates, a story should always provide an easy and natural entry into the rest of the speech.

hypothetical illustration
imaginary scenario that illuminates a point

Besides the real-life story, you can use a **hypothetical illustration,** as demonstrated by Jerome David Smith, an attorney, who used the following hypothetical illustration in a speech:

> One day you become angry over the nasty pollution of a river near your home, so you sit down and write a letter to the editor of your local newspaper. The letter is a scathing attack on a corporation that you believe is responsible for ruining the river. Two weeks later, you get a letter from the corporation's attorney informing you that you are being sued for $100,000 for "harming the reputation, prestige, and credibility of the corporation." Does this sound incredible? Can this happen in a country that celebrates freedom of speech? Yes, it can happen . . .

In the rest of his speech, he explained how lawsuits have become a way for companies and public officials to retaliate against criticism.

Ask a Question

Asking a question can be an effective way to intrigue your listeners and encourage them to think about your subject matter as you discuss it. There are two kinds of questions that you can use as attention material: the rhetorical question and the overt-response question.

rhetorical question
a question asked solely to stimulate interest and not to elicit a reply

With a **rhetorical question,** you don't want or expect the listeners to answer overtly by raising their hands or responding out loud. Instead, you want to trigger their curiosity by challenging them to think about your topic. For example:

> With powerful radio signals being beamed into outer space at this very moment, is there any realistic chance that during our lifetime we human beings will establish radio contact with other civilizations in the universe?

Not only does such a question catch the attention of the listeners, but it also makes them want to hear more. It entices them into listening to your speech for the answer to the question.

overt-response question
a question asked to elicit a direct, immediate reply

With an **overt-response question,** you want the audience to reply by raising their hands or answering out loud. For example, student speaker Meredith Bollinger began a speech by asking:

> There is only one Olympic sport in which men and women compete against each other head to head in direct confrontation. Which sport am I talking about?

Who can best predict
a breakup?
a. the couple
b. his friends
c. her friends

Figure 11.1
If you want to know whether a couple in a romantic relationship will stay together or break up, the most accurate predictions come from "c." Researchers at Purdue University have found that *her* friends are better at predicting the outcome than the couple themselves. One student speaker intrigued his audience with this attention-grabbing question on a PowerPoint slide.

One listener guessed water polo—wrong. Another guessed softball—wrong. Another guessed synchronized swimming—wrong. Finally, Bollinger gave the correct answer: equestrian (horseback) competition. Figure 11.1 shows another example of an attention-getting question.

Here are some pitfalls to avoid when asking questions:

Avoid questions that can fizzle. One college student began a speech by asking, "How many of you are familiar with Future Farmers of America?" Everyone raised a hand, so the speaker looked foolish as he continued, "Today I'd like to inform you about what FFA is." Before you choose a question, imagine the answers you might get from the audience. Could they cause embarrassment or awkwardness?

When you ask questions, don't drag out the suspense. If listeners are forced to guess and guess until the right answer is found, they may become exasperated, wishing that the speaker would get to the point.

Never ask embarrassing or personal questions. Avoid such questions as, "How many of you have ever tried cocaine?" or "How many of you use an underarm deodorant every day?" An audience would rightfully resent such questions as intrusions into their private lives.

Never divide your audience into opposing camps by asking "loaded" questions. An example of a loaded question: "How many of you are smart enough to realize that capital punishment is an absolute necessity in a society based on law and order?" By phrasing your question in this way, you insult those who disagree with you.

When asking overt-response questions, don't expect universal participation. With some overt-response questions, you can try to get every member of the audience to participate, but this can be very risky, especially if you poll the audience in this way: "How many of you favor the death penalty? Raise your hands. Okay . . . Now, how many of you are opposed to the death penalty? Okay, thanks . . . How many of you are undecided or unsure?" What if three people raised their hands for the first question, five for the second question, ten for the third—but the remaining 67 people never raised their hands? When this happens, and it often does, it is a major embarrassment for the speaker. Sometimes audiences are in a passive or even grumpy mood; this is especially true with "captive" audiences—that is, audiences that are required (at work or at school) to listen to a speech. In such a case, refrain from asking questions that require the participation of the entire audience.

Make sure the audience understands whether you are asking a rhetorical question or an overt-response question. If you ask, "How long will Americans continue to tolerate shoddy products?" the audience knows you are not expecting someone to answer, "Five years." It is clearly a rhetorical question. But suppose you ask a question like this: "How many of you have ever gone swimming in the ocean?" The listeners may be confused about whether you want them to raise their hands. Make it clear. If you want a show of hands, say so at the beginning: "I'd like to see a show of hands, please: How many of you have ever gone swimming in the ocean?" Alerting them in advance not only helps them know what you want but also makes them pay special attention to the question since they know that you are expecting them to respond.

Make a Provocative Statement

An opening remark that shocks, surprises, or intrigues your listeners can certainly grab attention. (Just make sure the statement is not one that would offend or alienate the audience.) Student speaker Vanessa Sullivan began a speech on human cloning with this statement:

> I have seen a human clone with my own eyes. And so have you.

Then she explained:

> Richard Lewontin, professor of biology at Harvard University, says that about 30 human genetic clones appear every day in the United States. You and I know them as identical twins. Dr. Lewontin says that "identical twins are genetically more identical than a cloned organism is to its donor."[5]

Sullivan went on to argue that despite important ethical problems, cloning is not as far from human experience as many people think.

Some speakers transform statistics into a provocative statement. For example, you could take the fact that 25 percent of all Americans will be afflicted by cancer, and restate it in terms that can shock an audience:

> There are 40 of you sitting out there in the audience. According to medical statistics, 10 of you will someday be afflicted by one of the most dreaded of all diseases—cancer.

Such an opener is certain to draw your listeners in.

Cite a Quotation

A quotation can provide a lively beginning for a speech. In a speech on how to avoid being a bore in conversation, student speaker Mandy Wilder began by saying:

> The writer Elsa Maxwell says, "Under pressure, people admit to murder, setting fire to the village church, or robbing a bank, but never to being bores." Would you like to learn how to carry on a conversation without being a bore?

SpeechMate
CD-ROM
To see a speaker who cites a quotation, view Video Clip 11.2 on Disk 1.

Quotations usually work best when they are short. Don't use a quotation that is so long that the listeners lose track of where the quotation ends and your remarks begin. The best way to indicate that you have finished quoting is to pause at the end of the quotation. The pause acts as an oral punctuation device, signaling the end of one thought and the beginning of another.

I don't recommend using the quotation as the first sentence of your opener. Consider the following:

Poor: "The creative conquest of space will serve as a wonderful substitute for war." These words, by James S. McDonnell, builder of the Mercury and Gemini space capsules, offer a powerful reason for space exploration.

Better: The builder of the Mercury and Gemini space capsules, James S. McDonnell, offers a powerful reason for space exploration. He says, "The creative conquest of space will serve as a wonderful substitute for war."

While the first version is better for a written composition, the second is better for a speech. The listeners need time to tune out distracting thoughts and tune in to you, and if some of them don't catch the name of the expert you are quoting, no harm has been done; what you want them to absorb is the quotation.

If a quotation is too concise, it may go by so fast that the audience cannot retain it. Therefore, you should repeat it, as in this example:

> The great English ballerina Margot Fonteyn once said, "The one important thing I have learned over the years is the difference between taking one's work seriously and taking one's self seriously. The first is imperative and the second is disastrous." Think about that for a moment: . . . "taking one's work seriously and taking one's self seriously. The first is imperative and the second is disastrous."

In print, the repetition looks silly, but in a speech the audience is grateful for the instant replay. It allows time for the idea to sink in.

Arouse Curiosity

An effective attention getter is one that piques the curiosity of the audience. Brenda Johnson, a chef, began a speech by saying:

> I am addicted to a drug. I have been addicted to it for many years now. I feel like I need it to make it through the day. If I don't get this

SpeechMate
CD-ROM
To see a speaker who provokes audience curiosity, view Video Clip 11.3 on Disk 1.

> drug, my head aches. I'm nervous, irritable, and I begin to tremble. It's true—I am addicted.

Having aroused the curiosity of her listeners, Johnson continued:

> I am addicted to caffeine. Most people don't realize that caffeine is a drug—and that it is very addictive. It is present not only in coffee and tea and soft drinks but also in many legal drugs such as weight-control pills and pain relievers.

Johnson spent the rest of the speech giving details about caffeine and how listeners could reduce their intake.

Provide a Visual Aid or Demonstration

Any of the visual aids we discussed in Chapter 9 could be used to introduce a speech, but you must be sure that while the aids get the audience's attention, they also are relevant to the main points of your speech. One student showed slides of sunbathers on a beach to begin a talk on sharks. Though there was a logical link (sometimes sunbathers who go into the water must worry about sharks), the connection was too weak to justify using these particular slides. In a case like this, it would be better to show a slide of a ferocious shark while describing a shark attack.

A demonstration can make an effective opener. Working with a friend, one student gave a demonstration of how to fight off an attacker, and then talked on martial arts. If you want to give a demonstration, get permission from your instructor beforehand. *One note of caution:* Never do anything that might upset the listeners. Holding a revolver and firing a blank to start off a speech on gun control or suicide would upset some people and put them out of a receptive mood.

Give an Incentive to Listen

SpeechMate CD-ROM

To see a speaker who gives his audience an incentive to listen, view Speech 5 ("How to Hide Valuables") on Disk 1.

At the beginning of a speech, many listeners have an attitude that can be summed up in these two questions: "What's in it for me? Why should I pay attention to this speech?" Such people need to be given an incentive to listen to the entire speech. So, whenever possible, state explicitly why the listeners will benefit by hearing you out. It is not enough to simply say, "My speech is very important." You must *show* them how your topic relates to their personal lives and their own best interests. If, for example, you were giving a talk on cardiopulmonary resuscitation (CPR), you could say, "All of you may someday have a friend or loved one collapse from a heart attack right in front of your eyes. If you know CPR, you might be able to save that person's life." Now each person in the audience sees clearly that your speech is important to his or her personal life.

It is a mistake to assume that listeners will be able to detect the connection between your speech and their lives. You must spell it out. Here is how entrepreneur Don Aslett started a speech at a business convention on how to find a job:

> [Imagine that] everyone in here is fired as of right now. You have no job. You are unemployed.

Knowing that some listeners would think that the fantasy did not apply to them, Aslett continued:

> Some of you are smiling comfortably and saying to yourself, "It can't happen to me." Did you know that last month 28,000 people, secure in their jobs and positions for 16 years or more, were told to go with not much more than "thanks" and a good record?[6]

After this, all the listeners should have realized that they could indeed lose their job someday, and that they ought to listen closely to Aslett's tips.

If you know some listeners have probably heard most of your speech material before, you can use incentives especially designed for them. Joel Weldon of Scottsdale, Arizona, gave a talk to over 700 business and industrial trainers at a national convention of the American Society for Training and Development. His speech consisted of tips on how to train people. In his introduction, he said:

> I know some of you are pros who have been involved in training for 20 years. When you hear some of these ideas, you're going to say, "I've heard all this before." I'm sure you have. But as you say that to yourself, ask yourself these two questions: Am I using this idea? And how can I improve it?[7]

Weldon's technique was effective because he acknowledged the presence and the experiences of the "pros," and then he challenged them to give his "old" ideas a fresh look.

Orient the Audience

Once you have snared the interest of your listeners by means of the attention material, you should go into the second part of your introduction, the **orienting material,** which gives an orientation—a clear sense of what your speech is about, and any other information that the audience might need in order to understand and absorb your ideas. The orienting material is a road map that makes it easy for the listeners to stay with you on the journey of your speech and not get lost and confused.

orienting material
the part of the introduction that gives listeners the information they need to fully understand and believe the rest of the speech

The orienting material does more than prepare the listeners intellectually for your speech; it also prepares them psychologically. It reassures them that you are well-prepared, purposeful, and considerate of their needs and interests. It shows them you are someone they can trust.

The three most common ways to orient the audience are (1) give background information, (2) establish your credibility, and (3) preview the body of the speech. They are listed in this order because number 3 is usually delivered last, as a prelude to the body.

Do you need all three options in every speech? For classroom speeches, follow your instructor's guidelines. For some career speeches, you may not need the first two. The best advice is to use an option if it will promote audience understanding and acceptance.

Give Background Information

Part of your orienting material can be devoted to giving background information—definitions, explanations, and so on—to help your listeners understand your speech. In a speech on the Boston-to-Washington megalopolis, Vandana Shastri used her orienting material to define the term:

> A megalopolis is a region made up of several cities and their suburbs which sprawl into each other. The biggest megalopolis in the United States is a densely populated, 500-mile-long corridor that starts in Boston and goes southward through Connecticut, New York City, northern New Jersey, Philadelphia, Wilmington (Delaware), Baltimore, and then ends in the Washington, D.C., suburbs of northern Virginia.

Sometimes it helps the audience if you explain the boundaries of your speech. For example, assume that you are giving a speech on the notion that criminals should make restitution to their victims. If you are not careful, many people in your audience will reject your argument immediately by saying to themselves, "Restitution, baloney! How can a murderer make restitution to his victim?" So in your orienting material, you head off such objections by saying, "In this speech I will talk about criminals making restitution to their victims, but I'm only talking about nonviolent criminals such as swindlers, embezzlers, and bad-check writers. I'm not talking about rapists and murderers." By showing the boundaries of your subject, you increase the chances that the audience will listen with open minds.

Establish Your Credibility

No one expects you to be the world's authority on your subject, but you can increase your audience's chances of accepting your ideas if you establish your **credibility**—that is, give some credentials or reasons why you are qualified to speak on the subject. When student speaker Randy Stepp talked on how to escape a burning building, he enhanced his credibility by mentioning that he was a volunteer firefighter in a rural community and had fought many fires.

credibility
audience perception of a speaker as believable, trustworthy, and competent

Some people shy away from giving their credentials or background because they think that doing so would make them seem boastful and arrogant. This concern is unfounded if you provide facts about yourself in a modest, tactful manner. In other words, if you are speaking on air pollution, say something like "I'm a chemist and I've analyzed in my lab the content of the air that we breathe in this community" instead of "I'm a professional chemist, so I know more about air pollution than anybody else in this room."

For information that does not come from your personal experience, you could cite your sources in the orienting material. For example, one speaker said, "The information I am giving you today comes from a book by David E. Hoffman entitled *The Oligarchs: Wealth & Power in the New Russia.*"

Note: Mentioning your sources in the orienting material is just one of two options for citing sources. See Tip 12.2 in the next chapter. Before choosing an option, find out your instructor's preference.

In some speeches, you should tell the audience your connection to the topic—why you are speaking on that particular subject. For example, "I am speaking on defective automobile tires because my sister was seriously hurt in an accident that was caused by bad tires."

Confess any conflict of interest or bias. For example, "I am urging you to use Ask-an-Expert.com for Internet searches because I think it's the best expert site, but I should tell you that I get paid for being one of their experts."

Sometimes you can enhance your credibility by explaining how you arrived at your central idea. Student speaker Colleen Allen said:

> Have you ever seen TV investigations about people who suffer a minor injury while using a product and then sue for millions and millions of dollars? I sure have, and I decided to prepare a speech on how we can eliminate this nonsense. But as I did research, I found a different picture. It is true that a few ridiculous cases capture public attention, but a more typical case is that of Jim Hoscheit, a student in Caledonia, Minnesota, who lost both arms in a farm accident that could have been prevented by a safety guard costing two dollars. In court, the design engineer admitted that he knew that the safety guard would have made the product 100 percent safer, but he did not use it. In my research, I found that the vast majority of product-liability lawsuits are justifiable.

By relating her change of mind, the speaker enhanced her credibility. She showed herself to be honest and open-minded, a person who could be trusted.

Preview the Body of the Speech

Have you ever had trouble listening to a speech or lecture because the information seemed jumbled and disconnected and you couldn't grasp the significance of example A and statistic B? An important way to avoid this problem is for the speaker to give the listeners a **preview** of the body of the speech.

preview
a preliminary look at the highlights of a speech

To help you see the value of a preview, consider this analogy: Suppose I give you a sack containing the 400 pieces of a jigsaw puzzle and ask you to complete the puzzle. You will have a hard time because you lack a sense of how the puzzle is supposed to look when finished. Now imagine that I hand you a full-color picture of what the puzzle looks like when it is completely assembled—a panoramic view. Will your task be easier now? Yes, because the pieces "make sense"—you instantly recognize that a light blue piece belongs to the sky in the upper part of the picture, a dark brown piece is part of a tree on the left side, and so on.

A speech is just like the puzzle. If you fail to give a preview, you are giving out bits of information—pieces of the puzzle—without providing listeners with any clues as to how they all fit together. If you do give a preview, you are providing your listeners with a panoramic view of the speech. Then, as you progress through the body, you give details—the pieces of the puzzle—and the listeners are able to fit them into a logical, coherent picture in their minds.

SpeechMate CD-ROM
To see an effective preview, view Speech 6 ("Food Poisoning") on Disk 1.

Your instructor may have specific requirements for what you must put in your preview. In general, and unless he or she advises you otherwise, I recommend that you include your central idea or your main points or both.

1. State the central idea. Your audience can listen intelligently to your speech if you stress your central idea in the orienting material. For example, "Acid rain is killing all the trees on our highest peaks in the East. To prove this, I will give you evidence from leading scientists." (Occasionally, in special situations, it is best to withhold divulging your central idea until late in the speech; we will discuss this technique in Chapter 17.)

In a speech on losing weight, Mary E. McNair, a nurse, stated her central idea in this way:

> Fad and crash diets can actually backfire, causing a person in the long run to gain more weight than was originally lost.

This helped the audience listen with "the right set of ears." They knew to pay attention to what she had to say about the counterproductive effects of fad and crash diets.

2. State the main points. In most speeches listeners appreciate being given a brief preview of your main points. For example, Barbara LeBlanc said,

> I believe that passive-solar heating should be used in every home—for two reasons: First, it's easy to adapt your house to passive solar. Second, the energy from passive solar is absolutely free. Let me explain what I'm talking about.

By stating the main points, LeBlanc not only helped the audience listen intelligently but also gave them an incentive to listen: She mentioned the possibility of saving money.

Giving a preview by stating the central idea and the main points reassures the listeners that you are not going to ramble. In other words, you give the audience a message that says, loud and clear, "I'm well-prepared; I know exactly what I'm going to say; I'm not going to waste your time."

Guidelines for Introductions

Here are some points to keep in mind for introductions.

www.mhhe.com/gregory7

For an interactive exercise on introductions, see Chapter 10 on this book's Website.

1. Don't prepare your introduction first. When you prepare a speech, what usually works best is to complete the body of the speech and *then* work on your introduction. Once you have developed your main points, you are in a stronger position to decide how to introduce them.

2. Make your introduction simple and easy to follow, but avoid making it too brief. Your audience needs time to get into the groove of your speech. If the introduction is too short, it may go by too fast for the listeners to absorb. That is why effective joke tellers stretch out their introduction to give the listeners time to get "into" the joke.

If the idea of stretching out an introduction sounds wrong to you, it is probably because you have been taught in English classes to write concisely. While it is a sin in English composition to stretch out essays, it is a virtue to do so with a speech's introduction that might otherwise be too abrupt for an audience.

A note of caution: Don't let this tip cause you to go to the opposite extreme—being tedious and long-winded. Be brief, but not too brief. If you are unsure about whether you have achieved a happy medium, deliver your speech to relatives or friends and then ask them if they thought your introduction was too long or too short.

3. Make sure that your introduction has a direct and obvious tie-in with the body of the speech. A common mistake is for speakers to give an introduction that has a weak or dubious link with the rest of the speech. This kind of introduction can be annoying and confusing to the listeners.

4. Never apologize. You weaken your speech and hurt your credibility if you say things like "I didn't have much time to prepare" or "This may be too technical for you" or "I'm sorry I didn't draw a diagram."

Tips for your CAREER

Tip 11.1 Use an "Icebreaker" to Start Off a Community Speech

You have probably noticed that many speakers at business and professional meetings start off by saying something like this: "I'm glad to have a chance to speak to you today." They are giving an *icebreaker*—a polite little prologue to "break the ice" before getting into their speech.

In outline form, here is how an introduction with an icebreaker would look:

I. Icebreaker

II. Attention Material

III. Orienting Material

When you give speeches in the community, an icebreaker is helpful because it eases your nervous tension and it lets the audience get accustomed to your voice. You don't need an icebreaker for classroom speeches because your audience has already settled down and is ready to listen (besides, most instructors would disapprove of using one).

I don't like "Hello, how are you?" as an icebreaker. It sounds too breezy and flip. It leaves a question as to whether the speaker wants the audience to roar a response like "Fine, thank you!" It is much better to say, "I appreciate the opportunity to speak to you tonight." But, you might object, phrases like this have been used so often, they are meaningless. Yes, they are. They are clichés. Nevertheless, they are valuable aids to smooth social relationships. When you engage in small talk with your friends, you use sentences like, "Hi, how are you?" Such expressions are trite but they are necessary because they lubricate the wheels of human discourse.

In addition to expressing appreciation for the invitation to speak, you can include a thank-you to the person who introduced you or a reference to the occasion ("I'm delighted to take part in the celebration of Martin Luther King's birthday"). Some speakers also use the icebreaker to formally greet the audience. This custom, however, has fallen out of fashion. In the old days, orators would begin speeches like this: "Madame President, Distinguished Members of the Paradox Society, Honored Guests, Ladies and Gentlemen, Greetings!" Such introductions are used today only in formal, traditional settings, such as a college commencement. In most of the speeches you will give in your life, a flowery greeting would sound pompous.

A note of caution: An icebreaker should be very brief—just a sentence or two. If you are too slow getting into the attention material of your introduction, you may cause some listeners to tune you out.

Conclusions

SpeechMate CD-ROM

To see pre-speech events and a speaker giving an icebreaker, view Anne M. Mulcahy's speech on Disk 2.

When movies are made, the producers spend a lot of time and energy on getting a "perfect" ending because they know that if the ending is unsatisfying, the viewers will tend to downgrade the film as a whole. As with the movies, the ending of a speech can either add to or subtract from the audience's opinion of the entire speech. So it is worthwhile to spend a lot of time working on your conclusion.

In your conclusion, you should do three important things: (1) signal the end of the speech to satisfy the audience's psychological need for a sense of completion, (2) summarize the key ideas of the speech, and (3) reinforce the central idea with a clincher. Let us discuss these points in greater detail.

Signal the End

Imagine that you are listening to your favorite song on the radio and letting your mind float freely with the music. Then suddenly, before the song is finished, the disc jockey cuts in with a commercial or a news bulletin. You missed only the last 10 seconds of the song, but you feel annoyed. Why? Because most people need to experience a sense of completion.

In listening to a speech, we have the same need for a sense of finality. We don't like an abrupt halt—we like to hear a conclusion that is psychologically satisfying.

To give listeners a satisfying finale, provide signals that the end is approaching. These signals can be verbal or nonverbal or both.

Verbal signals. You can openly announce that you are coming to your conclusion by saying, "So, in conclusion, I'd like to say . . .," or "Let me end by saying . . . ," or "Let me remind you of the three major points I've been trying to explain today."

Nonverbal signals. Two nonverbal cues are subtle but important: (1) say your conclusion with a tone of dramatic finality and (2) subtly intensify your facial expression and gestures. These cues should come naturally to you, since you have seen numerous speakers use them in your lifetime. If you feel unsure of yourself, practice your conclusion in front of a mirror or, better yet, in front of a friend (who can give you feedback). You also can say it into a tape recorder and play it back to check whether you have the appropriate tone of finality in your voice.

Summarize Key Ideas

SpeechMate CD-ROM

To see an effective summary, view Speech 2 ("Animal Helpers") on Disk 1.

Because listening is often a difficult mental task, some people in the audience might get drowsy or inattentive toward the end of your speech. But when you signal that you are about to finish, listeners usually perk up. If they know they can rest soon, they are better able to stay alert for a few more minutes. Like runners near the finish line, they can bring forth an extra burst of energy.

This mental alertness of your listeners gives you a good opportunity to drive home your message one more time. One of the best ways to do this is to summarize your key ideas. There is a formula for giving a speech that has been around for over 100 years. Sometimes it is attributed to a spellbinding country preacher, sometimes to a savvy Irish politician. The true originator will probably never be known, but the formula is worth heeding:

> Tell 'em what you're going to tell 'em.
> Tell 'em.
> Then tell 'em what you told 'em.

The first sentence refers to the introduction, the second to the body, and the third to a summary in the conclusion. The summary gives you a chance to restate the central idea or the main points or both.

If you are like a lot of people, you may say, "Why do I need to repeat my message? After all, in the body of my speech, I give the audience five minutes' worth of beautifully organized, forcefully delivered information. If I hit this stuff again in the conclusion, won't I be guilty of overkill?" No, research shows that restating your main points increases the likelihood that the listeners will remember them.[8]

A summary should be brief. Don't get bogged down in explaining each point a second time; do all your explaining in the body of the speech. The following summary, for example, succinctly boils down the body of a speech about preventing car theft:

So remember, you can prevent your car from being stolen if you follow these guidelines: Always park in a well-lighted area. Always remove your key from the ignition. Always close all windows and lock all doors.

Listeners don't mind hearing this kind of information again; it helps them retain it.

Reinforce the Central Idea with a Clincher

In addition to providing a summary, close your speech with a **clincher** that reinforces the central idea—a finale that drives home the main theme of your entire speech.

clincher
a final statement in a speech that drives home the key concept of the speech

Public speakers are like carpenters driving a nail into a floor, says Edward L. Friedman. They begin with a few preliminary taps in the introduction to get the speech started right. As they get into the body of the speech, they deliver one hammer blow after another to drive the nail into its proper place with carefully executed strokes. Then in conclusion they execute a powerful, clinching blow.[9]

Use a clincher that is memorable, that leaves a lasting impression with the listener. You can find clinchers by using some of the techniques mentioned earlier in this chapter for the introduction (such as a rhetorical question or a visual aid), or by using some of the following techniques.

Cite a Quotation

A good quotation can dramatize and reinforce a speaker's central idea. After urging her audience always to buckle their seat belts, one speaker said,

I would like to close with a quotation from Laura Valdez, an emergency medicine technician in California, who said, "I have driven my ambulance to hundreds of traffic accidents. I have found many people already dead, but I have yet to unbuckle the seat belt of a dead person."

At the end of a speech on why citizens should fight social ills rather than succumb to despair, Richard Kern said:

Let me leave you with the words of Eleanor Roosevelt: "It is better to light one candle than to curse the darkness."

Eye contact is important at the end of your speech, so if you use a quotation, practice it so that you can say it while looking at the audience, with only occasional glances at your notes.

SpeechMate CD-ROM
To see a speaker citing a quotation, view Video Clip 11.4 on Disk 1.

Issue an Appeal or Challenge

In a persuasive speech, you can end by making an appeal or issuing a challenge to the audience. If you are trying to persuade the listeners to donate blood, you can end by saying:

Next week the bloodmobile will be on campus. I call upon each of you to spend a few minutes donating your blood so that others may live.

One speaker tried to convince her audience to make out a will, and in her conclusion she issued a challenge:

> The simple task of writing a will can protect your family and give you peace of mind. It is a sad fact that three out of four Americans will die without a will. Are you going to be one of them? I hope not. Why don't you write your will before you go to bed tonight?[10]

Give an Illustration

An illustration is a popular way to reinforce the central idea of a speech. In a speech urging classmates to avoid Internet gambling, one student speaker concluded with a true story:

SpeechMate CD-ROM

To see a speaker giving an illustration, view Video Clip 11.5 on Disk 1.

> In his entire life, college senior Mark Scott had never gambled until one night, when he got an e-mail that said, "Congratulations, Mark, you won $100." Scott was intrigued, and he clicked on the gambling site and began playing blackjack. After an hour, $175 of his money was gone. Three months later, he had run up a $9,000 gambling debt on his credit card.

Refer to the Introduction

Using the conclusion to hearken back to something said in the introduction is an effective way to wrap up your speech. One way to do this is to answer a question asked at the beginning of a speech. Student speaker Daniel Hirata asked in his introduction, "Should we permit job discrimination on the basis of a person's weight?" In his conclusion, Hirata repeated the question and answered it:

> Should we allow job discrimination against overweight people? From what I've said today, I hope you'll agree that the answer is no. To deny a person a job simply because he or she is overweight is as wrong as to deny a person a job because of skin color or ethnic background.

Guidelines for Conclusions

There are four pitfalls to avoid in conclusions.

1. **Don't drag out the ending.** Some speakers fail to prepare a conclusion in advance. When they reach what should be the end of their remarks, they cannot think of a graceful way to wrap things up, so they keep on talking. Other speakers signal the end of their speech (by saying something like, "So, in closing, let me say . . ."), but then they drone on and on. This gives false hope to the listeners. When they see that the speaker is not keeping the promise, they feel deceived and become restless.
2. **Don't end weakly.** If you close with a statement such as, "I guess that's about all I've got to say," and your voice is nonchalant and unenthusiastic, you encourage your listeners to downgrade your entire speech. End with confidence.
3. **Don't end apologetically.** There is no need to say: "That just about does it. I'm sorry I didn't have more time to prepare . . . ," or: "That's it, folks. I guess I should have looked up more facts on . . ." Apologies make you look incompetent. Besides, some people may not have noticed anything wrong with your speech or your delivery; you may have done better than you realized, so why apologize?

4. Never bring in new main points. It is okay to use fresh material in your conclusion; in fact, it is a good idea to do so, as long as the material does not constitute a new main point. For an illustration, look at the following conclusions, which are based on a speech about the advantages of swimming.

Poor: So if you're looking for a good sport to take up for fun and health, remember that swimming dissipates your accumulated tension, it builds up your endurance, and it gives you a good workout without putting a strain on your muscles and joints. And, oh yes, another good reason for swimming: it can prevent you from developing back problems in old age.

Better: So if you're looking for a good sport to take up for fun and health, remember that swimming dissipates your accumulated tension, it builds up your endurance, and it gives you a good workout without putting a strain on your muscles and joints. I go over to the Y for a 20-minute swim three days a week, and I always come out feeling healthy and invigorated. I wouldn't trade swimming for any other sport in the world.

The first conclusion is faulty because it lets a whole new point—the issue of back problems—slip in. Since this is the first the listeners have heard about back trouble, it could confuse them. "Huh?" they may say to themselves. "Did I miss something that was said earlier?" Some listeners would expect you to elaborate on this new main point, but if you did, you would drag out your conclusion and spoil the sense of finality. The second conclusion has fresh material, but it is not a new main point. It is merely a personal testimonial that underlines the message of the speech.

Sample Introduction and Conclusion with Commentary

In the previous chapter, we looked at the body of a speech on affinity fraud. Now let's see how Amber Wright developed an introduction and conclusion for her speech.[11]

Affinity Fraud

General Purpose: To persuade

Specific Purpose: To persuade my audience to beware of scam artists who practice affinity fraud

Central Idea: Affinity fraud is a clever scam, but it can be defeated.

Introduction

I. Attention Material

A. Imagine that a stranger calls you on the phone and offers to sell you shares in a gold mine in Nevada that will make you a very rich person.

Wright begins with a hypothetical illustration that gains the listeners' attention and interest.

B. Most of you would say, "No thanks."

C. But what if the person who calls you is not a stranger, but an acquaintance who is a member of a community or religious group to which you belong?

D. In this case, you might be tempted to invest some money in the gold mine.

II. Orienting Material

A. Unfortunately, in many cases like this, the gold mine is nonexistent, and you become a victim of fraud—a special kind of fraud known as "affinity fraud."

She states her central idea.

B. Affinity fraud is a clever scam, but you can defeat it.

A preview of the body of the speech helps listeners to follow her remarks.

C. I want to explain what affinity fraud is, and then tell you how you can avoid becoming a victim.

[The body of the speech, which appears in Chapter 10, uses the problem–solution pattern.]

Conclusion

I. Summary

The speaker gives a brief summary of the key information of the speech.

A. We like and trust people who are similar to us—who share the same religion, culture, or profession.

B. Unfortunately, some con artists take advantage of this trust and engage in affinity fraud.

C. To avoid becoming victims, we should remain skeptical and investigate the validity of any "get rich quick" scheme.

II. Clincher

A. I would like to close with some advice from Deborah R. Bortner, president of the North American Securities Administrators Association.

Wright closes with a quotation that is helpful and relevant.

B. "When choosing an investment, *always* take your time and investigate."

Resources for Review and Skill Building

www.mhhe.com/gregory7

This book's Online Learning Center Website and SpeechMate CD-ROM provide meaningful resources and tools for study and review, such as practice tests, key-term flashcards, and sample speech videos.

SpeechMate CD-ROM

Summary

Much of the success of a speech depends on how well the speaker handles the introduction and conclusion. The introduction consists of two parts: attention material, which gains listeners' attention and interest, and orienting material, which gives the audience the information they need to listen intelligently to the rest of the speech.

For attention material, you can use one or more of the following techniques: tell a story, ask a question, make a provocative statement, cite a quotation, arouse curiosity, provide a visual aid or demonstration, and provide the audience with an incentive to listen.

For orienting material, you have three options: Give background information, such as definitions; establish your credibility on your topic; and preview the body of the speech (by stating the central idea, the main points, or both).

The introduction should have a direct and obvious tie-in with the body of the speech. Avoid apologies and a too-brief introduction.

The conclusion of your speech should signal the end, summarize your key ideas, and reinforce the central idea with a clincher. A clincher may be an appeal or challenge, an illustration, a reference to the introduction, or any of the techniques mentioned for attention material (such as a rhetorical question).

Avoid conclusions that are weak, apologetic, or drawn-out. While fresh material may be used, never bring in new main points.

Key Terms

attention material, *253*
clincher, *265*
credibility, *260*
hypothetical illustration, *254*
orienting material, *259*
overt-response question, *254*
preview, *261*
rhetorical question, *254*

Review Questions

1. Why is it necessary to have attention material at the beginning of a speech?
2. What is the purpose of the orienting material in the speech introduction?
3. What is a rhetorical question?
4. What is an overt-response question?
5. How can you give listeners an incentive to listen to a speech?
6. What is credibility?
7. Why is it a mistake to use a quotation as the first sentence of your speech?
8. Why is it a mistake to end a speech abruptly?
9. What is a clincher?
10. Why should you restate your main points in the conclusion?

Building Critical-Thinking Skills

1. What advice would you give a speaker who says, in the introduction, "This speech may be too technical for you."
2. Create a rhetorical question concerning the destruction of the Central American rain forest.

Building Teamwork Skills

1. In a group, brainstorm possible attention-getters to introduce speeches on
   a. world famine
   b. burglar alarm systems
   c. vacationing in France
   d. overcoming fatigue
   e. finding an honest car repair shop
2. Working in a group, discuss how listeners react when they hear speakers make these apologies:
   a. "I didn't have much time to prepare."
   b. "I'm not much of a speaker."
   c. "I know this is a boring topic."
   d. "I had wanted to show you some color slides."
   e. "That last speech is a tough act to follow."
   f. "I hate public speaking."
   g. "I'm really nervous."

Building Internet Skills

www.mhhe.com
/gregory7

1. Mythology and folklore provide a rich trove of stories. Search the Internet for a legend or story and print it out.

Possible Strategy: Go to Yahoo! (www.yahoo.com), click on "Society & Culture," choose "Mythology and Folklore," and explore several sites.

2. The techniques discussed in this chapter for opening and closing a speech are often used by writers in magazines. On the Internet, find and print an article that begins or ends with a story, rhetorical question, or any of the other techniques.

Possible Strategy: To find magazines that are interesting to you, go to the American Journalism Review NewsLink (www.newslink.org/mag.html) and browse through several magazines.

Using PowerWeb

www.mhhe.com
/gregory7

Which type of attention-getter is used by Blouke Carus, chairman of Carus Corporation, in a speech entitled "Developing a World Class Education System"? And is the attention-getter used in accordance with the guidelines of this chapter? Explain your answer. To find a transcript of this speech, visit www.mhhe.com/gregory7, click on STUDENT EDITION and then POWERWEB: CONTENTS.

A speaker at Thai New Year in Los Angeles uses notes to refer to as she discusses her key points. Audiences prefer a presenter who speaks from a plan rather than one who rambles. This chapter will show you how to create a plan—using an outline—and then how to make brief speaking notes based on the outline.

12

Outlining the Speech

Outline

Objectives

After studying this chapter, you should be able to:

1. Understand the importance of developing an outline for a speech.
2. Create a coherent outline for a speech.
3. Create effective speaking notes based on your outline.

The most important and time-consuming part of moviemaking is creating a good outline, says Hong Kong film director John Woo. "A thoroughly developed outline," he says, "lets you see the film in its entirety. It lets you see which parts aren't working. If you don't have a good outline, you won't have a good movie."[1]

Most successful speechmakers use an outline as a planning tool, in the same way that a movie director refers to a scriptwriter's outline or a builder uses an architect's blueprint to construct a building. An outline helps speakers to organize their thoughts into a logical sequence and to see which points are irrelevant, improperly placed, or poorly developed. It prevents them from rambling.[2]

Outlining is the culmination of the process we began describing many chapters ago—the process of gaining control of our subject matter. Up to this point, we have talked about formulating objectives (Chapter 5), gathering and developing materials (Chapters 6, 7, 8, and 9), and then organizing them in the body (Chapter 10) and the introduction and conclusion (Chapter 11). Now we will discuss how to put all these elements together in outline form.

Because some students have trouble understanding how an outline fits into the overall process of speechmaking, I created Figure 12.1. This flowchart shows your next three steps: First, create an outline; second, use the outline to prepare speaking

Hong Kong film director John Woo speaks about his film *Windtalkers,* which shows how U.S. troops in World War II utilized Navajo Indians for Navajo language communications that could not be understood by enemy forces.

notes; and third, use the speaking notes to deliver the speech. The first two steps will be covered in this chapter; the third step, delivering the speech, will be discussed in Chapter 14. (For your classroom speeches, your instructor may have guidelines that differ in some degree from this sequence; you should, of course, follow his or her rules.)

Guidelines for Outlining

Instead of using an outline, why not just write out the entire speech? For one thing, a word-for-word script would create a sea of material that might overwhelm you. Even worse, you might be tempted to read the script, a method that could put the audience to sleep.

An outline is better than a script because it shows the basic structure of your ideas in a streamlined form. It also helps you to see the relationship between ideas.

In essence, outlining is a commonsense way of arranging information in a logical pattern. The Federal Bureau of Investigation's Crime Index, for example, can be broken down into two broad categories:

FBI Crime Index

I. Violent crimes
II. Property crimes

We could then break down each category into specific types of crimes:

I. Violent crimes
   A. Murder
   B. Rape
   C. Robbery
   D. Aggravated assault
II. Property crimes
   A. Burglary
   B. Larceny-theft
   C. Motor vehicle theft
   D. Arson

SpeechMate CD-ROM

For help in outlining your material, use the Outline Tutor or the Outline Template (in Microsoft Word Format) on Disk 1.

If we wanted to, we could divide items A, B, C, and D into subcategories. For example, we could break murder down into categories of weapons used, with one category for guns, one for knives, and so on.

The next section offers instructions for formatting your outlines.

Choose an Outline Format

The two most popular formats for outlines are the *topic outline* and the *complete-sentence outline.* Find out if your instructor prefers or requires one or the other. Some instructors and professional speakers recommend using both methods—

Figure 12.1

These are the three steps in the outline-to-speech process. (For classroom speeches, find out if your instructor wants you to use this system or some other plan.)

Step 1 Create an Outline

This is an excerpt from a student's outline for a speech on overcoming insomnia. An outline is the basic structure of a speaker's ideas in streamlined form; it is not a word-for-word script. A detailed outline (like this one) is used only for preparation—it is ***not*** taken to the lectern for the actual speech.

Outline

I. To induce sleep, count your breaths.

A. Count an inhale as one, an exhale as two, and so on.

B. After ten, repeat the process.

C. Instead of straining, think of gratitude.

Step 2 Prepare Speaking Notes

The speaker prepares brief notes—derived from her outline—to be used in practicing and delivering the speech. These notes contain only a few key phrases—just enough to jog her memory. By using brief notes instead of her outline, she avoids the mistake of reading a speech.

Speaker's notes

I. Count breaths

A. Inhale, 1—exhale, 2 . . .

B. 10—start over

C. No strain—gratitude

Step 3 Deliver the Speech

These are the speaker's actual words. Using her speaking notes to jog her memory, she presents the information in a natural, conversational manner.

Speaker's actual words

"Here is one of the best ways to fight insomnia and get some sleep: calm yourself down by counting your breaths. Count your inhale as one, your exhale as two, and so on—until you reach ten. Then go back to one and start over. As you breathe, don't strain. Relax and feel gratitude that you can now rest after a day filled with many activities."

the topic format in the early stages of preparation (when you are struggling to impose order on your material) and the complete-sentence format in the later stages (when you are refining and polishing your ideas).

topic outline
a systematic arrangement of ideas, using words and phrases for headings and subheadings

complete-sentence outline
a systematic arrangement of ideas, using complete sentences for headings and subheadings

Topic Outline

In a **topic outline,** you express your ideas in key words or phrases. The advantage of this format is that it is quicker and easier to prepare than a complete-sentence outline. The FBI Crime Index outline above is a topic outline. Also see the topic outline in Figure 12.2.

Complete-Sentence Outline

In the **complete-sentence outline,** all your main points and subpoints are expressed in complete sentences (see Figure 12.2). Unless your instructor tells

Topic Outline	Complete-Sentence Outline
Pre-employment Screening	Pre-employment Screening
I. Presenting self	I. Presenting yourself to a potential employer gives you a chance to highlight your qualifications for a job.
A. Job interview	A. A job interview can show your enthusiasm and commitment.
B. Résumé	B. A resumé summarizes your experience, education, and skills.
II. Testing	II. Testing is used by employers to eliminate unqualified or high-risk applicants.
A. Skills tests	A. Skills tests determine if you have the aptitudes and abilities needed for the job.
B. Physical exams	B. Physical exams determine whether your health will allow you to fulfill the duties of the job.
C. Drug tests	C. Drug tests screen for illegal substances such as cocaine and marijuana.

Figure 12.2
Some speakers use both forms of outlines: the topic outline for early drafts, the complete-sentence outline for refinements.

you otherwise, I recommend that you use complete sentences for your final outline. Here is why: (1) Writing complete sentences forces you to clarify and sharpen your thinking. You are able to go beyond fuzzy, generalized notions and create whole, fully developed ideas. (2) If another person (such as an instructor) helps you with your outline, complete sentences will be easier for him or her to understand than mere phrases, thus enabling that person to give you the best possible critique.

All the sample outlines in the rest of this book, including the one featured later in this chapter, use the complete-sentence format.

SpeechMate CD-ROM
To practice outlining, do the Outline Exercises that accompany full speeches 2 and 4–11 on Disk 1.

Note of caution: The complete-sentence outline is not your speech written out exactly as you will present it. Rather, it is a representation of your key ideas; the actual speech should elaborate on these ideas. This means that your actual speech will contain many more words than the outline. See Figure 12.1 for an example.

Use Standard Subdivisions

In the standard system of subdividing, you mark your main points with roman numerals (I, II, III, etc.); indent the next level of supporting materials underneath and mark with capital letters (A, B, C, etc.); then go to arabic numerals (1, 2, 3); then to small letters (a, b, c); and if you need to go further, use parentheses with numbers and letters. Here is the standard form:

Tips for your CAREER

Tip 12.1 When No Time Limit Is Set, Speak Briefly

We have discussed why you should never exceed your time limit, but what should you do when no time limit is set—that is, when you are invited to speak for as long as you like? The best advice is this: Be brief. Keep it short. In the words of Owen Feltham, a seventeenth-century English author, every person "should study conciseness in speaking; it is a sign of ignorance not to know that long speeches, though they may please the speaker, are the torture of the hearer."

How brief should you be?

- For a short presentation, aim for 5 to 7 minutes—a popular length, especially when several speakers are sharing the podium. *Videomaker,* a magazine for producers of commercial videotapes, says that the best length for a training videotape is about 7 minutes. If it's any longer, "people begin to squirm, perhaps because 7 minutes is the length of time between commercials on TV."
- For longer speeches, such as after-dinner addresses, I recommend no more than 20 minutes.

Audiences today prefer—and are getting—shorter and shorter speeches, possibly because television has conditioned people to assimilate only short bursts of material. The demand for brevity is even being voiced in America's churches, which once featured sermons lasting well over an hour. Most ministers today preach for no more than 30 minutes. Donald Macleod, who teaches sermon preparation at Princeton Theological Seminary, tells his seminarians that 18 minutes is the maximum time for an effective sermon.

Whenever you are in doubt about length, remember that if one must err, it is better to err on the side of brevity. If, when you finish a speech, the listeners are still hungering for more wisdom from your mouth, no harm is done. They will probably invite you to come back and speak again. But if you speak so long that they become bored, weary, and sleepy, they will resent you for wasting their time.

I. Major division
II. Major division
  A. First-level subdivision
  B. First-level subdivision
    1. Second-level subdivision
    2. Second-level subdivision
      a. Third-level subdivision
      b. Third-level subdivision
        (1) Fourth-level subdivision
        (2) Fourth-level subdivision
  C. First-level subdivision

Notice that each time you subdivide a point, you indent. For most speeches you will not need to use as many subdivisions as illustrated here.

Avoid Single Subdivisions

Each heading should have at least two subdivisions or none at all. In other words, for every heading marked "A," there should be at least a "B." For every "1" there should be a "2." The reason is obvious: how can you divide something and end up with only one part? If you divide an orange, you must end up with at least two pieces. If you end up with only one, you have not really divided the orange. One problem that arises is how to show on an outline a single example for a particular point. Below is the *wrong* way to handle the problem:

A. Many counterfeiters are turning to items other than paper money.
   1. Counterfeit credit cards now outnumber counterfeit bills.

B. . . .

This is wrong because item "A" cannot logically be divided into just one piece. There are two ways to correct the problem. One way is simply to eliminate the single item and combine it with the heading above:

A. Many counterfeiters are turning to items other than paper money: Counterfeit credit cards now outnumber counterfeit bills.

B. . . .

Another way to handle the problem is not to number the item but simply to identify it in the outline as "example":

A. Many counterfeiters are turning to items other than paper money.
   Example: Counterfeit credit cards now outnumber counterfeit bills.

B. . . .

Parts of the Outline

The parts of the outline discussed below are keyed to the sample outline presented in the next section. Your instructor may have requirements for your outline that deviate somewhat from the description in these pages. (See Figure 12.3 for a schematic overview of a typical outline.)

1. Title. Your outline should have a title, but you *do not actually say it in your speech.* In other words, don't begin your speech by saying, "How to Lose Weight Permanently" or "The title of my speech is 'How to Lose Weight Permanently.'"

If you should not say the title, why have one? For classroom speeches, your instructor may want you to write one simply to give you experience in devising titles. For some out-of-class speeches, a title may be requested so that your speech can be publicized in advance. A catchy title might entice people to come to hear you.

Your title should be brief and descriptive; that is, it should give a clear idea of what your speech is about. For example, "Why State Lotteries Should Be Abolished" is a short and helpful guide. If you want an attractive, catchy title, you can use a colorful phrase coupled with a descriptive subtitle—"A Lousy Bet: Why State Lotteries Should Be Abolished." Here are some other examples:

- Czech It Out! Why You Should Visit Prague
- Are You Being Ripped Off? How to Find an Honest Mechanic
- Ouch! What to Do When a Bee Stings You

2. Purposes and central idea. Having your general purpose, specific purpose, and central idea listed on your outline will help you bring into sharp focus the main points and supporting materials.

3. Introduction and conclusion. The introduction and conclusion are so vitally important in a speech that they deserve special attention and care. Both sections should have their own numbering sequence, independent of the body of the speech.

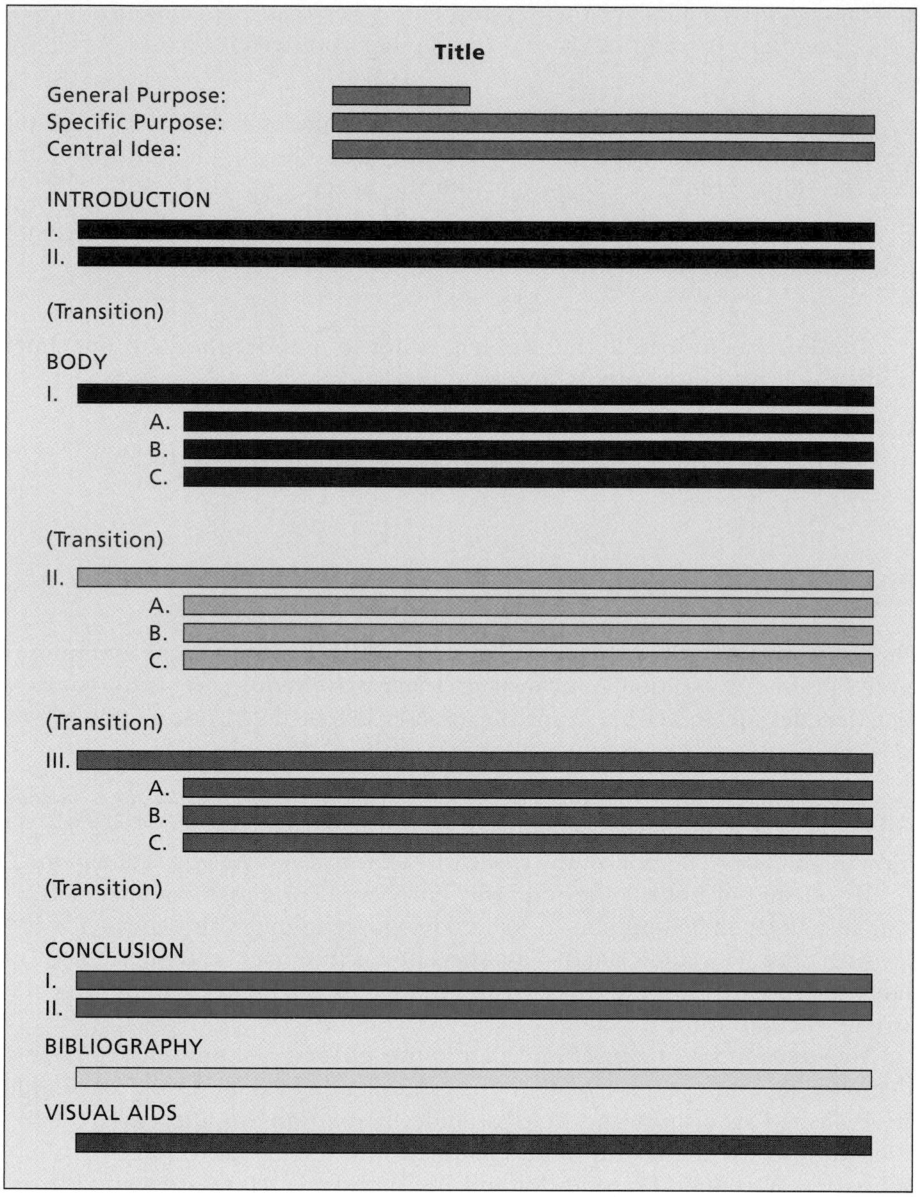

Figure 12.3
This is an overview of a typical outline. Although this outline shows three main points, a speech may have two or, occasionally, four.

www.mhhe.com/gregory7
To test your knowledge of outline parts, do the interactive exercise in Chapter 11 on this book's Website.

4. Body. In the body of the outline, each main point should be identified by roman numerals. The body has its own numbering sequence, independent of the introduction and conclusion. In other words, the first main point of the body is given roman numeral I.

5. Transitions. The transitional devices we discussed in Chapter 10 should be inserted in the outline at appropriate places. They are labeled and placed in parentheses, but they are not included in the numbering system of the outline.

While transitional devices should be placed wherever they are needed to help the listener, make sure you have them in at least three crucial places: (1) between the introduction and the body of the speech, (2) between

Tips for your CAREER

Tip 12.2 Decide How You Will Reveal Your Sources

You strengthen your credibility with your listeners if you tell them where you got your information. But it would be boring if you read aloud your bibliography. How, then, can you cite sources without bogging down the speech?

Here are two options, which can be used singly or in combination. (For classroom speeches, seek your instructor's guidance on which option to use.)

1. **Reveal the key data about your sources as you proceed through the body of your speech.** You could preface new points by saying something like, "According to an article in the latest issue of *Communication Education* . . ." or "Writing in *American Heritage* magazine, historian Christine Gibson says . . ."
2. **Cite sources in the orienting material of the introduction.** For example, one speaker said, "The information I am giving you today comes from an article by Margaret Zackowitz entitled "Royal City of the Maya" in *National Geographic* magazine, and from the website of the Mexico Tourism Board."

In some situations, you may want to add an extra element: At the end of a speech, you can give listeners a copy of your bibliography. During her speech, one speaker said, "I have a list of the books, articles, and interviews that I used to prepare this speech. You can pick up a list from the table by the door on your way out." This approach has two advantages: (1) you can list all the data (dates, page numbers, etc.) in your bibliography and (2) listeners can easily locate your source material if they want to verify information or delve further into your topic.

each of the main points, and (3) between the body of the speech and the conclusion.

6. **Bibliography.** At the end of the outline, place a list of the sources—such as books, magazines, and interviews—that you used in preparing the speech. Give standard bibliographical data in alphabetical order. Check with your instructor to see if he or she wants you to use a special format. Otherwise, see Table 6.4 in Chapter 6 for guidelines. If you used your own personal experiences, you should cite yourself as a source.

The bibliography is useful not only as a list of sources for your instructor, but also as a record if you ever give the speech again and need to return to your sources to refresh your memory or to find additional information.

7. **Visual aids.** If you plan to use visual aids, give a brief description of them. This will enable the instructor to advise you on whether the visual aids are effective.

SpeechMate CD-ROM

For sample outlines, see the outlines that accompany full speeches 2 and 4–11 on Disk 1.

Sample Outline with Commentary

Your outline should *not* include every word in your speech. It is merely the skeleton. Your actual speech will be longer.

Below is an outline by Anthony Silva, a student speaker.[3] Silva uses the statement-of-reasons pattern, a variation of the topical pattern we discussed in Chapter 10. As you study the outline, note the comments in the left-hand column.

The transcript of Silva's speech, as delivered, appears at the end of this chapter.

Commentary

The Power of Light

General Purpose: To persuade

Specific Purpose: To persuade my audience to campaign for greater use of natural light in businesses and schools

Central Idea: Natural light is superior to artificial light in the workplace and in the classroom.

Purposes and central idea should appear at the top of the outline to help the speaker stay on target.

INTRODUCTION

The introduction has its own label and numbering sequence.

I. Attention Material

Silva uses an intriguing story to grab the attention and interest of his listeners.

A. Lockheed Martin, an aerospace corporation, moved into a new building in Sunnyvale, California, a few years ago.

1. Immediately the company observed a big change in its employees.
2. A 15 percent drop in absenteeism occurred because employees had fewer illnesses.
3. A 20 percent increase in productivity occurred because employees finished their work faster and made fewer mistakes.
4. Lockheed Martin said the huge increase in productivity helped it win a $1.5 billion defense contract.

B. What caused the surprising improvement?

Silva's photos are effective in showing a dramatic contrast.

1. In the old building, employees worked in cubicles under fluorescent light. (Show photo.) [Figure 12.4]
2. In the new building, they worked in an environment that was flooded with daylight. (Show photo.) [Figure 12.5]

II. Orienting Material

A preview of the central idea and main points helps the audience to listen intelligently.

A. Natural light is better than artificial light.

B. I will explain why we should work to maximize natural light in the workplace and in the classroom.

Definitions are especially important for listeners who speak English as their second language.

C. Definitions: natural light comes from the sun, while artificial light comes from other sources, such as electric light bulbs and fluorescent tubes.

Listeners like to know a speaker's sources. In addition to his list, Silva mentions key sources in the body of the speech.

D. Afterwards, I will provide everyone with a list of my sources in case you want to do further investigation.

Transitions are placed in parentheses and are not part of the outline's number system. In the body, main points are marked by Roman numerals.

(*Transition:* Let's start with the workplace.)

BODY

I. Natural light makes employees healthier and more productive.

Figure 12.4
Does working under artificial light in a cubicle cause illness and lower productivity?

Figure 12.5
Can working in natural light make an employee more productive?

Under each main point, subpoints are marked with capital letters.

A. Scientists found out decades ago that human beings have fewer illnesses and more energy when they work in natural light instead of in artificial light. (New York Times)

B. This knowledge is being put to use by some companies when they construct new buildings.

Sub-subpoints are marked with Arabic numerals (1, 2, 3).

The speaker enhances his credibility by giving lots of specific details, such as company name, state, number of employees, and statistical data.

   1. In Wisconsin a few years ago, West Bend Mutual Insurance Company moved its 500 employees to a new building.
   2. In the old building, only 30 percent of employees worked at or near a window.
   3. In the new building, 96 percent have such access.
   4. Employees showed a 16 percent increase in the number of claims they could process each week.
   5. The rise in productivity translated into a $360,000 increase in annual profits.
   6. A survey was taken after one year.
      a. Employees said their overall health was improved, with fewer headaches and fewer sick days.
      b. Employees said their degree of job satisfaction increased after moving from the old building.

In the outline and in the speech as delivered, the speaker cites his sources.

C. Retail businesses have discovered that natural light not only makes employees healthier and happier, but it also increases sales. (The National Renewable Energy Laboratory of the U.S. Department of Energy)

Giving examples like Target is a powerful way for Silva to show the audience that he is not talking about vague generalities. He is talking about real companies in the real world.

   1. Target retail chain conducted an experiment in some of its buildings that have skylights.
   2. For a six-month period, the skylights were covered up and the only lighting was artificial.
   3. For another six-month period, the skylights were uncovered and most of the interior lighting was from daylight.
   4. Results: When natural light was used, sales were 15 to 20 percent higher than when artificial light was used.
   5. Now Target designs all of its new stores to have maximum daylighting.

D. All of us should encourage companies to improve lighting in the workplace.

   1. If a building is old, companies can remove cubicles and move employees closer to windows.

a. Not everyone can be next to a window, of course.

b. For spaces far away from windows, light reflectors and other simple devices can "pipe" light into interior space.

Silva wisely anticipates audience reaction, such as the obvious question, "What can be done to help workers who can't sit next to windows?"

2. If a company is planning to build a new building, we should encourage it to use daylighting as much as possible.

a. We already possess the technology.

b. A company could learn how to maximize daylight just by observing what other companies have done.

Each level of subordination is shown by indentation.

(*Transition:* Now let's examine another work area—the classroom.)

Transitions are needed between main points.

II. Natural light helps students to concentrate and study more effectively.

Silva uses the statement-of-reasons pattern in this speech. His two main points are in effect two reasons why natural light is superior to artificial light.

A. Researchers did a study on 20,000 students in California, Colorado, and Massachusetts. (The Heschong Mahone Group of Sacramento, California)

1. The students were comparable in age and intelligence level.

2. The only difference: 50 percent attended classes that had mainly natural light and the other 50 percent had mainly artificial light.

3. On standardized tests, the natural light students scored 26 percent higher than the artificial light students.

The speaker uses contrast effectively to make his point.

B. David Peterson, Director of Operations at Mesa Public Schools in Arizona, draws a contrast between students in classrooms without windows and students in daylit classes.

1. Students without windows are more likely to act out and be sick.

2. They are more likely to have trouble concentrating and studying.

C. We should contact school administrators to let them know that we want the children of our community to have as much natural light as possible.

While much of this speech involves information-giving, Silva makes it clear here and elsewhere that his primary purpose is to persuade.

D. One misconception must be dispelled.

1. Some schools have been designed without windows in order to eliminate distractions.

2. What school officials need to know is that architects can make designs that maximize daylight while minimizing opportunities for distractions.

3. For example, shrubbery and trees can be planted in such a way that students do not see distractions like people walking by.

The final transition prepares the audience for the conclusion.

(*Transition:* Let's summarize.)

CONCLUSION

The conclusion has its own label and numbering sequence.

Silva summarizes the main point and appeals to the audience for action.

I. Summary

A. Natural light makes employees healthier and more productive, and it helps students to concentrate and study more effectively.

B. All of us need to work together to persuade employers and school officials to maximize natural light in existing buildings and in new buildings.

II. Clincher

A. Howard Wertheimer, an architect in Atlanta, Georgia, who tries to maximize natural light in his buildings, has an observation.

The speaker closes with an apt quotation.

B. "People are like flowers—they need natural light to flourish."

BIBLIOGRAPHY

The bibliography lists all sources used to prepare the speech.

Sources are listed alphabetically.

The MLA format shown here is explained in Chapter 6, along with another format, APA.

Ander, Gregg D. Daylighting Performance and Design. New York: John Wiley & Sons, 2003.

Libby, Brian. "Beyond the Bulbs: In Praise of Natural Light." New York Times 17 June 2003: D5.

National Renewable Energy Laboratory. A Literature Review of the Effects of Natural Light on Building Occupants. Golden, CO: U.S. Department of Energy, 2002.

Peterson, David, Director of Operations, Mesa (AZ) Public Schools. E-mail to Anthony Silva. 3 June 2003.

Stigliani, Bill, Ph.D., Director of the University of Northern Iowa's Center for Energy and Environmental Education. Telephone interview. 3 June 2003.

Wertheimer, Howard, architect with Lord, Aeck & Sargent Inc., Atlanta, GA. E-mail to Anthony Silva. 9 June 2003.

VISUAL AIDS

Visual aids are described so that the instructor can give guidance.

Photo of employees in artificial light

Photo of worker in natural light

Speaking Notes

After you have devised an outline, what do you do with it? Do you use it to practice your speech? No. Do you take it with you to the lectern to assist you in the delivery of your speech? No. You use the outline only for *organizing* your ideas. When it comes to *practicing* and then *delivering* the speech, you should use brief **speaking notes** that are based on the outline.

speaking notes
brief reminders of the points a speaker plans to cover during a speech

Speaking from brief notes is a good technique because it enables you to look at your audience most of the time, occasionally glancing down to pick up your next point. It encourages you to speak naturally and conversationally.

How about using no notes at all? Would that be even better? No, without notes, you might forget important points, and you might fail to present your ideas in a logical, easy-to-follow sequence.

Notes bolster your sense of security. Even if you are in full command of the content of your speech, you feel more confident and self-assured knowing that you have notes as a safety net to rescue you if your mind goes blank and you fail to recall your next point.

By the way, some people have the idea that using notes is a sign of mental weakness or a lack of self-confidence, but this belief is unfounded. Most good speakers use them without losing the respect of an audience. After all, your notes represent a kind of compliment to your listeners. They show that you care enough about the occasion to spend time getting your best thoughts together in a coherent form. The kind of speaker that audiences *do* look down on is the windbag who stands up without notes and rambles on and on without tying things together.

Guidelines for Preparing Notes

As you read these guidelines, you may want to refer to the sample speaking notes in Figure 12.6.

SpeechMate CD-ROM
For handy guidelines see "Checklist for Preparing and Delivering a Speech" on the CD.

- Make indentations in your speaking notes that correspond to those in your outline. This will reinforce the structure of the speech in your mind. You also may want to repeat the numbering system; some speakers use only the roman numerals from their outline, while others use all the numbers and letters.
- Use only one side of a sheet of paper or note card because you might forget to turn the paper or card over.
- Write down only the minimum number of words or phrases necessary to trigger your memory. If you have too many words written down, you may overlook some key ideas, or you may spend too much time looking at the notes instead of at the audience. Exceptions to this rule are long quotations or statistics that you need to write out in full for the sake of accuracy.
- Write words in large letters that are neat and legible so that you have no trouble seeing them when you glance down during a speech.
- Include cues for effective delivery, such as "SHOW POSTER" and "PAUSE" (see the sample notes in Figure 12.6). Write them in a bright color, so that they stand out. (By the way, some speakers find it helpful

Figure 12.6
Here are samples of note cards that could be created for the speech about natural light. Only the first two cards are shown.

Cues remind the speaker to look at the audience and speak slowly during the introduction.

The speaker reminds himself to pause after a dramatic opener to let the impact sink in.

Each card is numbered so that if the speaker accidentally drops or scrambles the cards, they can be put back into order very easily.

The speaker uses only a few key words to jog his memory.

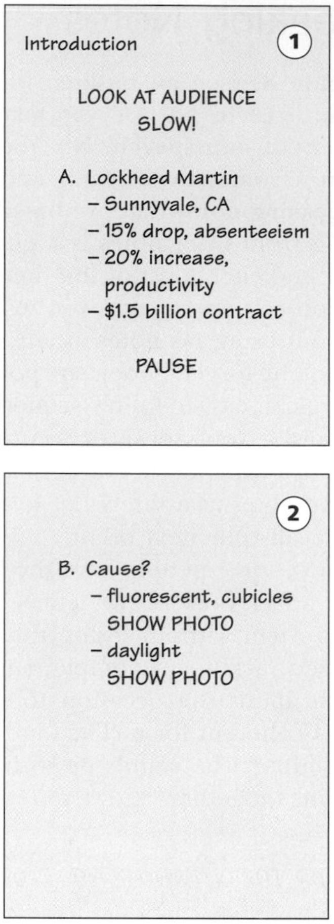

to use a variety of coded colors on their notes—for example, black for main points, green for support materials, blue for transitions, and red for delivery cues.)

- For speaking, use the same set of notes you used while rehearsing, so that you will be thoroughly familiar with the location of items on your prompts. I once practiced with a set of notes on which I penciled in so many editing marks that I made a fresh set of notes right before I delivered the speech. This turned out to be a mistake because the notes were so new that some of the key words failed to trigger my memory quickly, causing me to falter at several points. I should have stayed with the original notes. Even though they were filled with arrows and insertions and deletions, I knew them intimately; I had a strong mental picture of where each point was located. The new notes, in contrast, had not yet "burned" their image in my brain.
- Don't put your notes on the lectern in advance of your speech. A janitor might think they are trash and toss them out, or a previous speaker might accidentally scoop them up and walk off with them.

Options for Notes

Your instructor may require you to use one particular kind of note system, but if you have a choice, consider using one of these three popular methods:

Option 1: Use Note Cards

Your speaking notes can be put on note cards, as shown in Figure 12.6.

Note cards (especially the 3″ × 5″ size) are compact and rather inconspicuous, and they are easy to hold (especially if there is no lectern on which to place notes). The small size of the card forces you to write just a few key words rather than long sentences that you might be tempted to read aloud verbatim. If you use cards, be sure to number each one in case you drop or scramble them and need to reassemble them quickly.

Option 2: Use a Full Sheet of Paper

If you use a full sheet of paper, you can have the notes for your entire speech spread out in front of you. There are, however, several disadvantages: (1) Because a whole sheet of paper is a large writing surface, many speakers succumb to the temptation to put down copious notes. This hurts them in speechmaking because they end up spending too much time looking at their notes and too little time making eye contact with the audience. (2) A full sheet of paper can cause a speaker's eyes to glide over key points because the "map" is so large. (3) If a sheet is brought to the room rolled up, it can curl up on the lectern, much to the speaker's dismay. (4) If a sheet is hand-held because no lectern is available, it tends to shake and rustle, distracting listeners. (5) It is harder to make corrections on paper than on note cards. With paper, you may have to rewrite all your notes, whereas with note cards, you can simply delete the card containing the undesired section and write your corrected version on a fresh card.

If you have access to a lectern, you can use several 8.5″ × 11″ sheets in a clever way: Put notes only on the top one-third of a sheet, leaving the bottom two-thirds blank. This will help your eye contact because you can glance at your notes without having to bow your head to see notes at the bottom of the page.

A final tip: To avoid the distraction of turning a page over when you have finished with it, simply slide it to the other side of the lectern.

Option 3: Use Visual Aids as Prompts

A popular technique in business and professional speeches is to use one's visual aids (such as PowerPoint slides, transparencies, and posters) as prompts. This not only provides the audience with a visual presentation of the key points, but it also helps the speaker stay on track (without having to look down at notes on a lectern). One speaker, for example, put all her key ideas on a series of overhead transparencies. One graphic looked like this:

Longer School Year	
Yes	62%
No	26%
Unsure	12%

As she showed this transparency to the audience, she said, "In a recent poll, when parents were asked if they favored a longer school year for their children, 62 percent said yes, 26 percent said no, and 12 percent were undecided or unsure. I think this is a very strong mandate for extending the school year."

The speaker proceeded from graphic to graphic in the same manner. She had no note cards because the transparencies served as her cues.

This system "allows you to walk around the room, projecting greater confidence than you would if you remained riveted, eyes-to-paper, behind a lectern," according to media consultants Mike Edelhart and Carol Ellison.[4]

If you use this strategy, here are some suggestions: (1) Avoid using a visual aid that is primarily a cue for yourself and has no value for the audience. In other words, a visual aid should always be designed for audience enlightenment, not for speaker convenience. The notes in Figure 12.6 are fine on note cards, but if they were displayed on a transparency, they would be cryptic to the audience. (2) Avoid creating a deluge of text. Some speakers write a script and use virtually every sentence as a visual aid. This produces a tedious stream of words, causing the audience to become weary and irritated. Display only a few key words or numbers.

The options discussed above do not have to be used exclusively. They can be combined. For example, you could use note cards for part of a speech and visuals as prompts for another part.

Controlling Your Material

While preparing your outline, don't let your material become like an octopus whose tentacles ensnare you and tie you up. You must control your material, rather than letting your material control you. Here are four things you can do to make sure that you stay in control.

1. Revise your outline and speaking notes whenever they need alterations. Some students mistakenly view an outline as a device that plants their feet in concrete; once they have written an outline, they think that they are stuck with it—even if they yearn to make changes. An outline should be treated as a flexible aid that can be altered as you see fit.

2. Test your outline. One of the reasons for creating an outline is to *test* your material to see if it is well-organized, logical, and sufficient. Here are some questions that you should ask yourself as you analyze your outline (in your career, you can ask colleagues to critique your outline, using the same questions):

- Does the introduction provoke interest and give sufficient orienting material?
- Do I preview the central idea and/or main points?
- Do the main points explain or prove my central idea?
- Are the main points organized logically?
- Is there enough support material for each main point? Is there too much?
- Do I have smooth transitions between introduction and body, between main points, and between body and conclusion?
- Have I eliminated extraneous material that doesn't truly relate to my central idea?

- Does my conclusion summarize the main points and reinforce the central idea?
- Is my conclusion strong and effective?

3. Revise for continuity. Often an outline looks good on paper, but when you make your speaking notes and start practicing, you find that some parts are disharmonious, clumsy, or illogical. A speech needs a graceful flow, carrying the audience smoothly from one point to another. If your speech lacks this smooth flow, alter the outline and speaking notes until you achieve a continuity with which you are comfortable. (If you practice in front of friends, ask them to point out parts that are awkward or confusing.)

4. Make deletions if you are in danger of exceeding your time limit. After you make your speaking notes, practice delivering your speech while timing yourself. If the speech exceeds the time limit (set by your instructor or by the people who invited you to speak), go back to your outline and speaking notes and trim them. Deleting material can be painful, especially if you have worked hard to get a particular example or statistic. But it *must* be done, even if you exceed the limit by only five minutes.

Sample Speech as Presented

Earlier in this chapter, we examined the outline and sample notes for Anthony Silva's classroom speech about natural versus artificial lighting. Below is a transcript of the speech as it was delivered. Notice that the wording of the actual speech is not identical to that of the outline. The reason is that Silva delivered the speech extemporaneously, guided by brief speaking notes. If he had read from his outline or from a complete text, he might have sounded stilted and artificial. By choosing his words as he went along, he made his speech vigorous, forthright, and easy to follow. If he gave this speech 10 different times, the wording would be somewhat different each time, although the basic ideas would remain the same.

The Power of Light

A few years ago Lockheed Martin, a giant aerospace corporation, moved into a new building in Sunnyvale, California. Almost overnight, the company noticed a huge change in the behavior of the employees. There was a 15 percent decrease in absenteeism, as employees reported fewer illnesses. At the same time, there was a 20 percent increase in productivity, as employees finished their work faster and with fewer mistakes. Lockheed Martin officials said that the big jump in productivity helped them win a defense contract worth 1.5 *billion* dollars.

What happened to bring about this dramatic improvement? The answer is very simple. In the old building, employees worked under fluorescent lights, and they were bunched into cubicles. *[Speaker shows photo in Figure 12.4.]* The new building, by contrast, was designed to bring in as much daylight as possible. *[Speaker shows photo in Figure 12.5.]*

I believe that natural light is superior to artificial light. Today I want to show you why we should all work to maximize natural light in two important areas of our society—the workplace and the classroom. Just to make sure we agree on terms: natural light is the beautiful free illumination that comes from the sun, while artificial light is illumination that comes from sources that try to imitate the sun—for example, electric light bulbs and fluorescent tubes. At the end of class, I have a handout for you. It's a list of my sources that you can take with you in case you want to investigate this in greater detail.

Let's begin by looking at people on the job. Natural light makes employees healthier and more productive. According to the *New York Times,* scientists have known for decades that humans have fewer illnesses and have more energy and alertness when they work in natural light, as opposed to artificial light.

Some companies are incorporating this knowledge into their building plans. A few years ago, the 500 employees of West Bend Mutual Insurance Company in Wisconsin moved to a new building. In the old building, only 30 percent of employees had a workstation with a window view. In the new building, the number jumped to 96 percent. And that's not the only thing that jumped. Employees showed a 16 percent increase in the number of claims they were able to process per week. This meant that the company was able to increase its profits by 360,000 dollars per year.

In a survey taken after one year, employees reported that they had fewer headaches, fewer sick days, and that their overall health was better. They also said that they liked their jobs better than they did when they worked in the old building.

According to the National Renewable Energy Laboratory of the U.S. Department of Energy, retail establishments are finding that natural light not only makes employees healthier and happier, but it also increases sales. The Target chain of stores did an experiment in several stores that have skylights. For six months, the skylights were covered and only artificial light was used; then for six months, the skylights were uncovered, letting daylight pour in. Target found that when natural light illuminated the stores, sales were 15 to 20 percent higher than they were when artificial light was used. Needless to say, Target is now a believer. All of their new stores are built to let daylight flood in.

We need to encourage companies to improve the lighting options in their buildings. For existing buildings, cubicles can be removed and employees moved closer to windows. Now, I know that you can't move everybody to a place next to a window. But you can pipe light into interior spaces by using light reflectors and other devices. For new buildings, we need to encourage companies to incorporate daylighting. The technology is available. All that employers have to do is go look at buildings that are already maximized for daylight.

Now let's turn out attention to another work area—the classroom. Natural light makes it possible for students to be more effective in concentrating and in studying. The Heschong Mahone Group of Sacramento, California, did a study involving 20,000 students in California, Colorado, and Massachusetts. The students were pretty much the same in terms of age and intelligence. The only difference was that half the students attended classes that were illuminated primarily by natural light, while the other half relied mainly on artificial light. Standardized tests were given, and the results showed that the students who had natural light scored 26 percent higher than the students who had artificial light.

In Arizona, the director of operations at Mesa Public Schools, David Peterson, says there is a big difference between students in classrooms without windows and students in classrooms with natural light coming through windows. He says that students without windows are more likely to have behavior problems and illness, and they are more likely to have a difficult time concentrating and studying. All of us need to campaign with school administrators to let them know the situation. We need to tell them that we want our children to work and study in an environment that has lots of natural light.

Unfortunately, there is a big misconception that needs to be dispelled. In some schools, the designers deliberately create rooms without windows because they think they have to take away any possible distraction to the students. Here is where we—you and I—must educate the educators. We have to let them know that architects can easily design classrooms that maximize daylight while at the same time minimizing distractions. Here's an example: You can plant shrubbery and trees near windows so that students don't have distractions like people walking by.

Let's sum up what we've covered. We have seen that natural light makes employees healthier and more productive. Natural light also helps students to be more effective in their studies. I urge all of you to join with me in working to spread the word, to persuade employers and school officials that we need to maximize natural light—in both existing buildings and new buildings.

I would like to close with an observation made by Howard Wertheimer, an architect in Atlanta, Georgia, who tries to bring natural light into every nook and cranny of the buildings he designs. He says, "People are like flowers. They need natural light to flourish."

For two other complete outlines and transcripts of speeches, see the samples at the end of Chapters 15 (informative) and 16 (persuasive).

Resources for Review and Skill Building

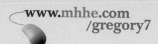

www.mhhe.com/gregory7

This book's Online Learning Center Website and SpeechMate CD-ROM provide meaningful resources and tools for study and review, such as practice tests, key-term flashcards, and sample speech videos.

SpeechMate CD-ROM

Summary

An outline is as important to a speechmaker as a blueprint is to a builder: The outline provides a detailed plan to help the speaker organize thoughts into a logical sequence and to make sure nothing important is left out.

Two popular types are the topic outline, which uses words and phrases for headings, and the complete-sentence outline, which uses entirely written-out headings. Some speakers use both forms: the topic outline for early drafts and the complete-sentence outline for refinements.

The parts of the outline include title, purposes, central idea, introduction, body, conclusion, transitions, bibliography, and visual aids.

After you complete your outline, prepare speaking notes based on it. You have three options: note cards, a full sheet of paper, or speaking notes displayed as a visual aid. Whichever you choose, avoid writing too many words because when you use notes in a speech, you want to be able to glance down quickly and retrieve just enough words to jog your memory.

Through all these stages, control your material by revising your outline and speaking notes whenever they need alterations. Test the strength of your outline, and revise for continuity—a smooth, logical flow from one part to another. Finally, make deletions if you are in danger of exceeding your time limit.

Key Terms

complete-sentence outline, *276*
speaking notes, *286*
topic outline, *276*

Review Questions

1. Why is an outline recommended for all speeches?
2. What is a topic outline?
3. What are the advantages of using complete sentences in an outline?
4. What are the parts of an outline?
5. The text says that the title of an outline should not be spoken in the speech. Why, then, should you have one?
6. Why should each subdivision of an outline have at least two parts?
7. What are the advantages of using cards for speaking notes?
8. What are the disadvantages of using a full sheet of paper for speaking notes?
9. In using visual aids as prompts, the text warns against "creating a deluge of text." Why is this a problem?
10. Give at least five questions that speakers should ask as they test the strength of their outlines.

Building Critical-Thinking Skills

1. Sort out the items below and place them into a coherent topic outline. In addition to a title, the scrambled list includes four major headings, with three subheadings under each.

   Scrabble, Cameras, Recipes, Ornamentals, Photography, Paintball, Gardening, Digital Imagery, Kitchenware, Annuals, Stoves, Hobbies & Interests, Cooking, Darkroom, Bingo, Perennials, Games

2. Transform the topic outline in the next column into a complete-sentence outline. Create a central idea for the outline.

Research

I. Library
   A. Printed material
   B. Electronic databases
   C. Audiovisuals
II. Personal
   A. Experiences
   B. Interviews
   C. Surveys

Building Teamwork Skills

1. Working in a group, create a central idea and a topic outline on one of the topics below. Put each item on a separate index card or slip of paper so that the group can experiment with different sequences. Your outline should have at least three major headings, each of which has at least three subheadings.
   a. automobile drivers
   b. fast food
   c. leisure-time activities
   d. good health
2. In a group, create a *complete-sentence* outline on how to study effectively. Include a central idea, at least three major headings, and at least four tips under each heading.

Building Internet Skills

www.mhhe.com/gregory7

1. To demonstrate an understanding of the correct way to create an outline and speaker's notes, find a brief article on the Internet on the subject of fairness and accuracy in the news media. Reduce the article to an outline, and then reduce the outline to brief speaker's notes.

   Possible Strategy: To find articles, use keywords in Yahoo! News Full Coverage (fullcoverage.yahoo.com/fc/).

2. Create a topic outline on "weather topics," with major headings and subheadings.

   Possible Strategy: To find raw material, go the Librarians' Index to the Internet (lii.org/). Click on "Science, Technology & Computers" and then "Weather."

Using PowerWeb

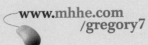

www.mhhe.com/gregory7

In "Winning Over the Boss," Rae Cook, president of a public relations firm, discusses strategies that can be used by speakers who tend to ramble. List all five strategies. To find this article, visit www.mhhe.com/gregory7, click on STUDENT EDITION and then POWERWEB: CONTENTS.

Ty Votaw, commissioner of the LPGA (Ladies Professional Golf Association), appeals to all-male, private golf clubs to stop excluding women from membership. Votaw, an Ohio attorney, uses language effectively in his speeches. For example, in regard to Augusta National Golf Club's exclusion of women, he says, "It is Augusta's right as a private organization not to admit women, but it is not the right thing to do." This play on the double meaning of the word "right" makes his point memorable.

13

Wording the Speech

Outline

The Power of Words

Finding the Right Words

Using Appropriate Words
Avoid Stereotypical Words
Avoid Sexist Pronoun Usage

Using Words Accurately
Use Precise Denotations
Control Connotations
Use Correct Grammar

Achieving Clarity
Use Simple Words
Use Concrete Words
Use Precise Words

Using Vivid Language
Create Imagery
Use Rhythm

Oral versus Written Language

Objectives

After studying this chapter, you should be able to:

1. Explain the importance of choosing words that are appropriate for the audience and the occasion.
2. Define two types of doublespeak (euphemisms and inflated language).
3. Describe the two significant differences between oral and written language.
4. Explain the value of using correct grammar.
5. Explain the importance of using words that are clear, accurate, and vivid.

"The best speaker," according to an Arab proverb, "is one who can turn the ear into an eye."

How can one perform such magic? By using words that are clear, accurate, and vivid. One speaker who performs such magic is TV talk show host Montel Williams, who says:

> I have a disease with no known cause, no cure, and no way to control the pain. Eventually it will take away my vision, my strength, my balance, my speech, and even my memory. I have a disease called MS—multiple sclerosis.

Williams uses words effectively to help us see and feel the horrors of the disease:

> For about 70 days, my feet felt like they were on fire 24 hours a day. I'm not talking about just a little bit on fire. It was as if somebody took a steel rod, stuck it into red-hot coals, and then just shoved it right through the end of my foot, through my toes and up my shinbones.[1]

By describing the ravages of MS in clear and vivid language, Williams enables his listeners to see and understand just how devastating the disease can be.

In this chapter, we will examine the magic and power of language.

TV talk show host Montel Williams speaks at a news conference in Washington, D.C., as he fights against proposed cutbacks in funding for research on multiple sclerosis, Alzheimer's disease, and cancer. With him are Nancy Davis of Los Angeles (left), who has been diagnosed with MS, and Leeza Gibbons, a TV personality whose mother has been diagnosed with Alzheimer's.

The Power of Words

If you witnessed a car crash, could you appear in court and give an accurate report of what you saw? Before you answer, consider this:

SpeechMate
CD-ROM
To see a speaker who uses language effectively, view Speech 10 ("Three Celebrity Heroes") on Disk 1.

Courtroom lawyers have discovered that they can influence eyewitness testimony simply by choosing certain words when they ask questions. To demonstrate how this technique works, psychologist Elizabeth Loftus showed a group of people a videotape depicting a two-car accident. After the video, some of the viewers were asked, "About how fast were the cars going when they *smashed* into each other?" Other viewers were asked the same question except that the word *smashed* was replaced by the word *hit*. Viewers who were asked the *smashed* question, in contrast to the *hit* viewers, gave a much higher estimate of speed, and a week later, they were more likely to state that there was broken glass at the accident scene, even though no broken glass was shown in the videotape. Why? Because "smash" suggests higher speed and greater destruction than "hit." Thus, a single word can distort our memory of what we have seen with our own eyes.[2]

The power of words also is used by advertisers and retailers, as these research items show:

- Advertising agencies have learned that sales of a product can be increased if ads contain any of these words: *new, quick, easy, improved, now, suddenly, amazing,* and *introducing*.[3]
- At the grocery store, shoppers are more apt to buy beef if it is labeled "75% lean" than if it is labeled "25% fat." Why? Because the word *lean* sounds more desirable than the word *fat*.[4]

Ethical Issue

Can mere words have such power? Yes, but we shouldn't call words "mere." As writer C. J. Ducasse says, "To speak of 'mere words' is much like speaking of 'mere dynamite.'"[5] The comparison is apt. If dynamite is used responsibly, it can clear a rockslide on a highway; if used irresponsibly, it can maim and kill. In public speaking, if powerful "dynamite" words are used responsibly, they can keep listeners awake and interested, but if used irresponsibly, they can deceive audiences, distort facts, and dynamite the truth. Ethical speakers use words responsibly—not as clever devices of deception, but as vivid portraits of truth.

To illustrate ethical versus unethical, let's contrast two fund-raising efforts:

> Fund-raisers for the nonprofit Children's Service Bureau in San Antonio, Texas, were told by United Way that they could probably increase donations if they changed the organization's name to the Emergency Shelter for Abused and Homeless Children—a name that more accurately described the organization's mission. Sure enough, after the name change, fund-raisers reported a 40 percent increase in donations.[6]

The change was a success because the old name sounded like a stuffy bureaucracy, while the new name suggested the urgent saving of lives. Was it ethical? Yes, because there was no deception.

Our second case is much different:

> In a fund-raising letter, a state representative in Illinois claimed that he had won "special recognition" by *Chicago Magazine,* but he omitted an explanation: the magazine had called him one of the state's ten worst legislators.[7]

Although this politician may amuse us with his shameless audacity, his choice of words was unethical, designed to deceive rather than enlighten.

Finding the Right Words

The difference between the right word and the almost right word, Mark Twain once observed, is the difference between lightning . . . and the lightning bug. The truth of Twain's remark can be seen in the following historical vignette: One of President Franklin D. Roosevelt's most famous speeches was his address to Congress asking for a declaration of war against Japan in the aftermath of the Japanese attack on the American fleet at Pearl Harbor. As written by an assistant, the speech began this way:

> December 7, 1941: A date which will live in world history.

Before speaking, Roosevelt crossed out the words *world history* and substituted the word *infamy*. Here is what he ended up saying:

> December 7, 1941: A date which will live in infamy.

This has become one of the most famous sentences in American history, along with such memorable statements as "Give me liberty or give me death!" And yet, if Roosevelt had used the original sentence, it never would have become celebrated. Why? Because *infamy*—a pungent word tinged with evil and anger—was the right description for the occasion; *world history*—dull and unemotional—was merely "almost right." Lightning . . . and the lightning bug.

In choosing words for your speeches, your goal should not be to select the most beautiful or the most sophisticated, but to use the *right* words for the *right* audience. As you analyze your audience before a speech, ask yourself, "How can I best express my ideas so that the audience will understand and accept them?" A word that might be ideal for one audience might be unsuitable for another.

Dr. Martin Luther King Jr., the brilliant leader of the civil rights movement of the 1960s, was a master at choosing the right words to use with the right group. To a highly educated audience, for example, he would employ sophisticated language and abstract concepts, such as this sentence from his Nobel Peace Prize acceptance speech:

> Civilization and violence are antithetical concepts.

www.mhhe.com/gregory7
For a transcript of Dr. King's "I Have a Dream" speech, plus a commentary, see Supplementary Readings on this book's Website.

Such a sentence, appropriate for an erudite audience, would have been incomprehensible to most listeners if used in his speeches to uneducated sharecroppers in Mississippi. For them, he used simple words and down-to-earth illustrations. For example, in urging African Americans to struggle for their rights despite the fear of violence, Dr. King used a simple image that could be grasped by the least educated of his listeners:

> We must constantly build dikes of courage to hold back the flood of fear.

With either kind of audience, Dr. King was highly persuasive; but what did he do when he spoke to a group made up of both educated and uneducated people? He used inspirational messages designed to appeal to every listener. In his famous "I Have a Dream" speech, delivered to 200,000 people who had marched on Washington to demand equal rights for African Americans, Dr. King used stirring words that appealed to everyone:

> I have a dream that my four little children will one day live in a nation where they will not be judged by the color of their skin but by the content of their character.

There was nothing phony about Dr. King's adaptation to his audiences. All good speakers choose the right words for each particular audience.

While considering your audience, you also should use words that are suitable for the *occasion*. If you speak at a fund-raiser, your words should be uplifting and encouraging; at a funeral, solemn and respectful; at a pep rally, rousing and emotional.

Using Appropriate Words

Never make political, religious, racial, ethnic, or sexual references that might alienate anyone in your audience. Ask yourself, "Is there any chance at all that what I'm planning to say might offend someone in the audience?" If you cannot decide whether a word is appropriate, don't use it.

Avoid Stereotypical Words

Stay away from language that reflects **sex-related stereotypes,** such as *little old lady, broad, chick,* and *typical male brutality.* Try to eliminate sexism from sex-linked occupational terms. Here are some examples:

sex-related stereotype
generalization that assigns roles or characteristics to people on the basis of gender

Ethical Issue

Original	Preferred Form
workman	worker
stewardess	flight attendant
fireman	firefighter
policeman	police officer
mailman	mail carrier
man-made	artificial
cleaning lady	housekeeper
foreman	supervisor

Janet Elliott of Los Angeles writes, "I recently attended a meeting in which nearly 80 percent of the audience was composed of young college women. The speaker was addressing the subject of career options for communications majors in business. Throughout his speech he used the term 'businessman' when referring to a business executive in general. Many members of his audience were offended by the exclusion."[8]

Tips for your CAREER

Tip 13.1 Omit Crude Language

To many listeners, a speaker who uses profane, obscene, or explicit language comes across as insensitive, unprofessional, and uneducated. And yet some presenters use crude language because (they say) it adds spice and "most people don't mind." While it may be true that most people aren't upset, it is a mistake to ignore the feelings of those who are genuinely offended. (By the way, coarse language isn't an age-related issue, with the young unbothered and the old bothered. There are people of *all* ages who feel slapped in the face when they hear such words.) Consider this:

Advertising executive Ron Hoff tells of a business presentation in which the speaker was trying to sell his company's services to a public utility firm. The speaker liberally sprinkled his talk with four-letter words, plus some five-letter varieties not often heard in public.

There were 17 people in the audience, including one man "whose body actually convulsed a little every time he heard one of those words," says Hoff. "I watched him carefully. It was like somebody grazed him every few minutes with an electric prod. His body language attempted to cover these jolts he was receiving (he'd cross his legs, cover his face, slouch in his chair—nothing worked). He physically recoiled from the language he was hearing."

That man, it turned out, was the highest-ranking representative of the firm, so it came as no surprise when the firm declined to buy the services of the speaker's company.

Hoff later asked the speaker why he had used so much crude language.

"Oh, they love it," he said. "They talk just like that all the time."

"Yeah," Hoff said to himself. "All of them *except one.*"

Avoid Sexist Pronoun Usage

For centuries the masculine pronouns *he, his,* and *him* were used in the English language to designate an individual when gender was immaterial. In a sentence such as "Every driver should buckle *his* seat belt before *he* starts the engine," the pronouns *his* and *he* were understood to refer to drivers in general, both male and female. Today, however, according to Frederick Crews, a professor of English at the University of California, Berkeley, "many [people] find those words an offensive reminder of second-class citizenship for women."[9]

To avoid offending anyone in your audience, you can handle this pronoun issue in one of three ways.

1. **Use masculine and feminine pronouns in tandem.** In other words, use *he or she* (or *she or he*) when referring to an indefinite person. For example, "Every driver should buckle *his or her* seat belt before *he or she* starts the engine." A problem arises, however, in sentences like this: "Each participant should ask *himself or herself* whether *he or she* really needs *his or her* umbrella." If you continued in this way, the pronouns could become cumbersome, perhaps even distracting the listeners from your ideas. This problem has caused many people to prefer either of the two remaining alternatives.
2. **Use plural pronouns.** Say simply, "All drivers should buckle *their* seat belts before *they* start the engine." This alternative has the advantage of being simple, while offending no one.
3. **Use the pronoun "you."** For example, "Whenever you get behind the wheel, *you* should buckle *your* seat belt before starting *your* engine." For speeches, this is often the best of the alternatives—it's not only simple and inoffensive, but also direct and personal.

Using Words Accurately

To use words accurately, you need to be sensitive to two types of meanings—denotations and connotations—as well as to the use of correct grammar.

Use Precise Denotations

The **denotation** of a word is the thing or idea to which it refers—in other words, its dictionary definition. The denotation of *chair* is a piece of furniture on which one person may sit.

denotation
the thing or idea to which a word refers

Try to use denotations precisely, bearing in mind the following cautions.

Be aware that some words have more than one denotation. The word *verbal,* for example, means "in words, either spoken or written." If I asked you to give a verbal report, you would not know whether I wanted your words spoken or written. I would have to come up with a more precise word; *oral,* for example, would be clear and unambiguous because it denotes only spoken words.

Take care with words that have different denotations to different people. What does "middle age" mean? A Louis Harris poll found that people who are 30 to 34 say that middle age starts at 40, but those who are 40 to 44 say it starts at 45.[10] If middle age is an important concept in a speech, define exactly what age span you mean by the term.

Shun fancy words unless you are certain of their denotations. Dennis Kessinger, a public speaker in Redding, California, once attended a retirement ceremony for a diligent worker whom one speaker fondly remembered as being a "superfluous" employee. Unfortunately, that word is an insult: It means nonessential, unneeded. Probably the speaker meant "superlative."[11]

Control Connotations

The **connotation** of a word is the emotional meaning that is associated with it. The words *slender, thin,* and *skinny* are synonyms; they have the same denotation, but the connotations are different: *slender* has a positive connotation, *thin* is neutral, and *skinny* has negative overtones.

As a listener and as a speaker, you should be aware of how connotations express the attitude of the person using the words. Let's say that some filmmakers produce a documentary on a Senator Dolores Perez. If they want to show that they are objective about the senator, they can describe her with a word that has a neutral connotation—*legislator.* If they want to convey approval, they can choose a term that has positive connotations—*national leader.* If they want to express disapproval, they can use a word that has negative connotations—*politician.* If they describe one of her campaign events, they could call it a *gathering* (neutral), a *rally* (positive), or a *mob* (negative). When she travels to Central America, the *trip* (neutral) could be called a *fact-finding mission* (positive) or a *junket* (negative).

connotation
the emotional overtones of a word that go beyond a dictionary definition

Connotations can make a difference in persuasive campaigns. For years environmentalists tried to save swamps from being filled in and built on; they were often unsuccessful until they began to use the synonym *wetlands.*[12] *Swamp* evokes the image of a worthless quagmire filled with creepy, crawly creatures, while *wetland* suggests a watery wilderness of exotic birds and plants.

In exploring connotations, you don't have to rely solely on your own judgment. Many dictionaries have synonym notes, which are usually located after a word's definitions. On the Internet, you can use search engines to hunt for examples of how words and phrases are used by people throughout the English-speaking world. For example, if you want to explore the connotations of the word *spunk,* you can use it as a keyword in FindArticles.com (www.findarticles.com) and then scan articles for indications of how the word is currently used.

Use Correct Grammar

People who use incorrect grammar usually do so because they are unconsciously imitating the speech habits of their relatives and friends. For this reason, I don't look down on those who make grammatical mistakes. But you must understand that in business and professional life, many people will downgrade you if you use "improper" English, which they find as offensive as body odor or food stains on the front of a shirt. For example:

- In North Carolina a corporation executive said, "I just can't stand to be around people who use bad English. I would never hire a person who said things like 'I done it.'"
- In California a man was passed over for a promotion (even though he was better qualified than the person who got the position) simply because he had the habit of saying "he don't" instead of "he doesn't."
- In New Jersey the head of a company wanted to promote a deserving part-time worker to full-time secretary, "but I can't get her to stop saying 'youse' [as the plural of 'you']," he said. "My customers just won't accept that because they're used to dealing with educated people. They might think that the sloppiness in language carries over to the way we handle their accounts."[13]

Poor grammar hurts you because to some people you sound as if you are not very intelligent. These people will seldom come right out and tell you that your grammar offends them. A boss, for example, may feel awkward about telling an employee his or her grammar is unacceptable; it is as embarrassing as telling friends that they have bad breath. So the employee is never told the real reason why he or she is being denied a promotion. Speaking at Dillard University, columnist William Raspberry told students, "Good English, well spoken and well written, will open more doors for you than a college degree. . . . Bad English, poorly spoken and poorly written, will slam doors that you don't even know exist."[14]

As for public speaking, grammatical errors cause you to lose credibility with your audience, according to business writers Courtland L. Bovée and John V. Thill, who add: "Even if an audience is broad-minded enough to withhold judgment of the speaker, a grammatical error is distracting."[15]

From my observations, the mistakes in Table 13.1 seem to be the ones that are most likely to cause some people to downgrade you. If you commit any of these errors, I urge you to learn how to correct your grammar and usage. Your school may have a tutoring service that can help you identify your grammatical

Table 13.1
Common Grammar Mistakes

Incorrect	Correct
He (or she) don't	He (or she) doesn't
You was	You were
I done it.	I did it.
Between you and I	Between you and me
I had went.	I had gone.
She's (he's) already went.	She's (he's) already gone.
I been thinking.	I've been thinking.
I've already took algebra.	I've already taken algebra.
hisself	himself
theirself	themselves
We seen it.	We saw it.
Her (him) and me went.	She (he) and I went.
I come to see you yesterday.	I came to see you yesterday.
She ain't here.	She isn't here.
She don't love me no more.	She doesn't love me anymore.
He be late.	He is late.
I had wrote it.	I had written it.
Give me them apples.	Give me those apples.

mistakes and then correct them. You also can find books on correct English in the library, or you can visit Internet sites such as Librarians' Index to the Internet (lii.org). Type in "grammar," and you will find many useful sites.

Achieving Clarity

To be clear in the words you use, you must first be clear in your thinking. Think about a word before you use it. Ask yourself, will it be clear to someone who is new to my subject? In this section we will examine how you can achieve clarity by using words that are simple, concrete, and precise.

Use Simple Words

A speechwriter for President Franklin D. Roosevelt once wrote, "We are endeavoring to construct a more inclusive society." President Roosevelt changed the wording to, "We're going to make a country in which no one is left out."[16] Roosevelt knew that although big words are sometimes needed to convey a precise meaning, a good communicator will choose simple words whenever possible.

But what if you want to convey a complex idea? Don't you need complex language—big words and weighty phrases? No. If you examine great works of literature, you will see that profound thoughts can be expressed easily and beautifully by simple words. Some of the greatest pieces of literature in the English language—the King James Bible and Shakespeare's works—use simple words to convey big ideas. For example, in Hamlet's famous soliloquy ("To be or not to be . . .") 205 of the 261 words are of one syllable. Citing an American literary classic, Abraham Lincoln's Second Inaugural Address ("With malice toward none . . ."), William Zinsser writes, "Of the 701 words in [the address], 505 are words of one syllable and 122 are words of two syllables."[17]

Big words are often used by pretentious speakers, who want to impress the audience with their intelligence, while simple words are preferred by audience-centered speakers, who want to make sure their ideas are clear. Here is an example of the contrasting styles:

Pretentious speaker:	People who are experiencing intense negative emotions directed at a significant other would be well advised to disclose their condition to that individual.
Audience-centered speaker:	If you're extremely angry at a loved one, don't keep your feelings bottled up—tell the person how you feel.

Use Concrete Words

concrete words
words that name persons and things that we can know by our five senses

abstract words
words that name qualities, concepts, relationships, acts, conditions, and ideas

Concrete words name or describe things that the listeners can see, smell, hear, taste, and touch—for example, *balloon, rose, gunblast, pizza,* and *chair.* They differ from **abstract words,** which refer to intangible ideas, qualities, or classes of things—for example, *democracy, mercy,* and *science.* While a certain amount of abstract language is necessary in a speech, you should try to keep it to a minimum. Whenever possible, choose concrete language because it is more specific and vivid, and therefore more likely to be remembered by your audience. Concrete words help you create the mental images that you want to convey to your listeners. Here are some examples:

Abstract	Concrete
She is wealthy.	She makes $400,000 a year, has a winter home in San Diego and a summer home in Switzerland, and owns four sports cars.
It was a stormy day.	The sky was gray and gloomy, and the cold, moist wind stung my face.
Rattlesnakes are scary.	Its beady eyes staring at you without ever blinking, a rattlesnake can slither through the brush without making a sound—until it suddenly coils and makes its terrible buzzing rattle.

Use Precise Words

The most commonly quoted authority in America is "they," as in the following sentences:

> They say that too much salt is bad for you.
>
> They say that loud sound is not dangerous, as long as you don't feel any pain in your ears.

Instead of a vague "they," provide a precise source. For the first sentence above, find reliable sources: "Researchers at Johns Hopkins University have found that too much salt in one's diet can cause . . ." For the second sentence, if you try to find who "they" are, you may discover, as did one student speaker, that loud sound can cause permanent damage to one's hearing even if the noise is at a level that is not painful. The mysterious "they" can be wrong.

Two kinds of words—doublespeak and misused jargon—rob a speech of precision. Let us examine each.

Each year the Academy Awards are presented to top Hollywood actors who are chosen from a list of nominees. This means, of course, that there are winners (like 2002 Best Actor Denzel Washington, shown here) and losers. But the Academy cannot bear to use the word "loser," so presenters are told to use a euphemism—"nonawardees." Do you think this is an acceptable euphemism, or do you find it unacceptable?

Ethical Issue

Beware of Doublespeak

When some federal and state legislators raise taxes, they don't refer to their action as "raising taxes." To do so might anger taxpayers. No, timidly and sneakily they say they voted for "revenue enhancement."

"Revenue enhancement" is an example of **doublespeak,** language that is deliberately misleading, evasive, meaningless, or inflated.[18] The term *doublespeak* has been made popular by the Committee on Public Doublespeak of the National Council of Teachers of English, which each year makes tongue-in-cheek "awards" for blatant examples of language abuse. Chairing the committee is Professor William Lutz of Rutgers University, who founded the journal *Quarterly Review of Doublespeak* and is author of the book *Doublespeak.*[19] Two of the most popular types of doublespeak, says Lutz, are euphemisms and inflated language.[20]

doublespeak
language that is designed to confuse or to be misunderstood

Euphemisms. These are pleasant, mild, or inoffensive terms that are used to avoid expressing a harsh or unpleasant reality. If a public official talks about *regulated organic nutrients* and says that the stuff *exceeds the odor threshold,* would you know that he is talking about sewage sludge and admitting that it stinks?[21]

euphemism
a mild, indirect, or vague word used in place of one that is harsh, blunt, or offensive

www.mhhe.com/gregory7
For interactive exercises on language, see Chapter 13 on this book's Website.

Euphemisms are not always undesirable. Lutz says:

> When you use a euphemism because of your sensitivity for someone's feelings or out of concern for a recognized social or cultural taboo, it is not doublespeak. For example, you express your condolences that someone has "passed away" because you do not want to say to a grieving person, "I'm sorry your father is dead." When you use the euphemism "passed away," no one is misled. Moreover, the euphemism functions here not just to protect the feelings of another person, but to communicate also your concern for that person's feelings during a period of mourning.[22]

When a euphemism is used to deceive, it becomes doublespeak. Here are some examples:

- After one of its planes crashed, National Airlines described the event—in its annual report to stockholders—as an "involuntary conversion of a 727," a legal term designed to conceal the truth.[23]
- Pit bulls have a reputation for ferocity. In New York City, they represent only 4 percent of the licensed dogs, but they are responsible for a third of all reported dog bites. To improve their image, a dog-training school in San Francisco says that pit bulls that pass a behavior-improvement course will henceforth be known as "Saint Francis terriers"—apparently in honor of the gentle, peace-loving Italian saint.[24]
- During the war involving ethnic groups in the Balkans, combatants who engaged in mass murder of civilians referred to their actions as "ethnic cleansing."[25]

While some euphemisms can be deciphered, others are confusing. If you heard that Chrysler Corporation had *initiated a career alternative enhancement program,* would you know that what had really happened was the firing of 5,000 workers? If a physician spoke of a *negative patient care outcome,* would you know that the term means death?[26] If a general mentioned a *ballistically induced aperture in the subcutaneous environment,* would you picture a bullet hole in a human being?[27]

Euphemisms become harmful when they mask a problem that should be dealt with. When homeless people are called "urban nomads," does this romantic euphemism cause the public to turn its eyes away from a problem that needs attention?

The best advice is this: Use euphemisms if tact and kindness require them; avoid them if they serve to deceive or confuse.

inflated language
words designed to puff up the importance of the person or thing being described

Inflated language. This kind of doublespeak, says Lutz, "is designed to make the ordinary seem extraordinary; to make everyday things seem impressive; to give an air of importance to people, situations, or things that would not normally be considered important."[28] For example:

- A used car is advertised as a *pre-owned car* or *pre-enjoyed automobile.*
- A clothing store calls its salespeople *wardrobe consultants.*
- A magazine refers to elderly people as *the chronologically gifted.*[29]
- A national pizza delivery chain announces that its drivers will henceforth be known as *delivery ambassadors.*[30]

Some inflated language seems harmless. If garbage collectors prefer to be called *sanitation engineers,* I may wince at the misuse of language but I cannot criticize too strenuously. If they believe that the term dignifies their valuable but unglamorous work, why should I object to it? But the problem is that inflated language is spreading rapidly into all areas of life, causing misunderstanding and confusion. If you saw an advertisement for a *grief therapist,* wouldn't you envision a counselor for a mourning individual whose loved one has just died? If so, you'd be wrong, because *grief therapist* is an inflated term for an undertaker. How are we to know that an *excavation technician* is a ditch digger? That a *communications monitor* is a switchboard operator? That an *architect of time* is a watchmaker? That a *traffic expediter* is a shipping clerk? That a *customer engineer* is a salesperson? That a *corrosion control specialist* is the person who sends your car through a car wash?[31]

One of my students once worked in a pet store as a cashier, but she was required to wear a badge that identified her as "Pet Counselor"—an inflated title that she resented because "it misled customers into thinking I was qualified to advise them on how to take care of their pets. All day long they would ask me questions that I couldn't answer. It was humiliating."

An inflated term may begin in kindness, but it often ends in confusion. Avoid it unless you know that it is clearly understood and preferred by your audience. In other words, call a spade a spade—unless your audience is military personnel who prefer the official name: *entrenching tool.*

Don't Misuse Jargon

Can you understand the following observation made by a biologist?

> Although solitary under normal prevailing circumstances, raccoons may congregate simultaneously in certain situations of artificially enhanced nutrient resource availability.[32]

Here's a translation into plain English:

> Raccoons live alone, but if you put some food out, they will gather around it in a group.[33]

The biologist was speaking in **jargon,** the specialized language of a group or profession. If your listeners share your specialty, you may use jargon, but if the audience includes people outside your field, avoid jargon or—if you must use a specialized term—define it.

jargon
the technical language of a group or profession

Unfortunately some speakers use jargon "not to communicate but to impress their audiences with their importance or the importance or complexity of their subject matter," says Dr. Lutz. As a result, "communication suffers and the jargon can quickly degenerate into something close to the twittering of birds."[34] Oliver Wendell Holmes Sr., a 19th century American physician, stuck a needle into the show-offs of his day: "I know there are [medical] professors in this country who 'ligate' arteries. Other surgeons only tie them, and it stops the bleeding just as well."[35]

Some speakers use jargon unthinkingly: They get so accustomed to using certain words at work that they fail to realize that people outside their field may be unaware of the words' meanings. One student speaker, who worked part-time in a hospital, gave a speech on a medical situation over which she had agonized—dealing with "no code" patients. Much to the frustration of the audience, she failed to define the term until she was asked about it during the question-and-answer period; she had wrongly assumed that everyone knew what it meant. It turns out that *no code* is the term written on a patient's chart to indicate that no artificial life-support measures should be used if he or she becomes comatose and irreversibly brain-damaged.

Be careful about using sports terms that the general public may not know. For example, if you argued for "a *full-court press* against organized crime," only people familiar with basketball would know that the term means an attempt to keep opponents from advancing.

Because many people in North America speak English as a second language, be vigilant for possible misunderstandings, such as this:

> When physicians prescribe some medications, they advise a patient to apply the medicine "locally"—that is, to a specific part of the body, such as the arm. But it turns out that some patients interpret the directions to mean, "Don't take this medicine when you go out of town."[36]

When speaking to nonnative speakers of English, you can avoid such problems either by omitting jargon or by adding synonyms and a bit of elaboration.

Using Vivid Language

Vivid words have the magical ability to paint clear, memorable pictures in your listeners' minds. Let us examine two techniques—imagery and rhythm—that can help you create such pictures.

Create Imagery

imagery
words that evoke mental pictures or images

You can bring an abstract idea to life by using **imagery**—precise, descriptive words that create images. For example, David Fields, a criminal-justice major who had visited several prisons, painted a chilling picture of prison life:

> Prison is a jungle. When you're inside, you're as vulnerable as a lion tamer who steps inside a cage with snarling lions. At any moment the prisoners might erupt in violence. You can find yourself with a dozen knife wounds as a result of an argument over something insignificant. For example, you get a box of chocolate-chip cookies from home, and another prisoner wants those cookies and will stab you with a crude, homemade shank if you don't hand them over. There is always noise in prison—even in the dead middle of night; you never have peace and quiet. Glaring lights are on all the time; you're never allowed the luxury of sleeping in the dark. And the place stinks with the odor of fear.

Field's picture conveys the reality of prison life better than a long recital of dry statistics could ever convey.

metaphor
a comparison implying similarity between two things

Two devices that are especially effective for creating mental pictures are metaphors and similes. A **metaphor** is a figure of speech in which a word or phrase that ordinarily describes one thing is used to describe another in order to suggest a resemblance. For example, "Enemy submarines were sharks that prowled the sea for prey."[37] Comparing submarines and sharks creates a metaphor that is vivid and powerful. "The virtue of metaphor," according to language scholars Bergen and Cornelia Evans, "is that it permits us to say a great deal in a few words."[38]

A **simile** is the same as a metaphor, except that the comparison between two things is made with the words "like" or "as." For example, "Langston Hughes says that a deferred dream dries up like a raisin in the sun."[39]

simile
a comparison, using like or as, of otherwise dissimilar things

If fresh images are involved, similes and metaphors can be quite vivid. Here are some examples of the effective use of these devices:

> Marriage is a cozy, calm harbor where you are protected from the storms of the outside world. *(Pamela Smith, student speaker)*
>
> The snow covered up all the brown humps and furrows of the field, like white frosting on a chocolate cake. *(Joshua Burns, student speaker)*
>
> Manic-depressives are like passengers on an emotional roller-coaster that goes up, up, up to a high of exhilaration and then down, down, down to a low of despair—without ever stopping to let them off. *(Sarah Gentry, student speaker)*

Beware of **mixed metaphors,** which occur when a speaker combines two metaphors that don't logically go together. Mixed metaphors either confuse the listeners or leave them smiling in amusement. President Dwight Eisenhower once said that "the Japanese have a tough row to hoe to keep their economic heads above water," painting an incongruous picture of farmers scratching at the soil while struggling to keep from drowning. To correct the problem, one would have to say something like this: "The Japanese will have to swim vigorously to keep their economic heads above water."

mixed metaphor
incongruously combined metaphors

Ernest Bevin, former foreign minister of Great Britain, once used this mixed metaphor: "If you let that sort of thing go on, your bread and butter will be cut out from under your feet." This ridiculous picture of people standing on their own food could be altered in the following way: "Your bread and butter will be snatched from your table."

Avoid **clichés,** which are trite, worn-out words or phrases that have lost their freshness and vividness. Here are some examples: *better late than never, last but not least, raining cats and dogs, at the crack of dawn,* and *throw caution to the winds.* To eliminate clichés, try to find fresh, lively alternatives. Instead of saying, "His tie stuck out like a sore thumb," say something like "His tie was as garish as a clown at a funeral."

cliché
an overused word or phrase

Use Rhythm

You can make your language vivid by taking advantage of rhythmic patterns. One such pattern is **parallel structure,** wherein series of words, phrases, or clauses are arranged in the same form. Here are some examples, placed in poetic form to emphasize the parallels:

parallel structure
equivalent grammatical forms used to express ideas of equal importance

We want a government . . . . . of the people,
by the people,
for the people.

We need parents who will . . . praise honest efforts,
punish bad behavior, and
ignore inconsequential acts.

Parallel structure can intensify the speaker's expression of emotions, as in this example by student speaker Georgia Adams:

> When I see fish dying in our streams because of acid rain, I am enraged. When I see trees dying on our highest peaks because of acid rain, I am enraged. When I see animal habitats destroyed because of acid rain, I am enraged.

repetition
repeating words or phrases for emotional effect

In addition to using parallel structure, Adams used another effective rhythmic technique—**repetition.** Notice that by repeating "I am enraged," she conveyed the full measure of her anger. In the next section of this chapter we will discuss repetition of key ideas to help the audience remember; here we are talking about repetition for its emotional, rhythmic effect. It is called "artful repetition" by Ivette Rodriguez, a former presidential speech-writer who became head of public relations for the giant aerospace company Boeing in Huntington Beach, California. Here is a sample from one of her speeches:

> Back in the first century A.D., a Greek philosopher expressed this time-honored truth: "Only the educated are free." Yes, only the educated are free. Free to leave the welfare lines and find gainful employment. Free to choose meaningful careers. Free to reap the benefits of our economic and political system.[40]

If you go back and read the passage aloud, you will *feel* the rhythm of artful repetition.

Oral versus Written Language

One of the biggest mistakes some speakers make is to treat oral language in a speech as being no different from written language. While the two forms of communication are similar, oral language is different in two significant respects.

1. Oral language requires more elaboration than written language. If you are watching a football game on TV and you fail to see a key block that makes a touchdown possible, you have the luxury of watching an instant replay in slow motion. If you are reading a complicated passage in your chemistry text and you find yourself hopelessly confused, you can go back a few paragraphs and study the material again. Unfortunately, these opportunities are not available when you listen to a speech. If you fail to understand what a speaker is saying, you are out of luck. There is no instant replay. There is no way to look back a few paragraphs.

Because of this handicap, oral language requires more elaboration than is necessary in written language. If a statement is too terse, the audience has trouble absorbing it. Consider the following example, which is the opening sentence of an article about immigrants:

> The first generation tries to retain as much as possible; the second to forget, the third to remember.[41]

That terse sentence is excellent in an essay. The reader can study it at leisure if the meaning does not pop up immediately. But can you imagine hearing it said aloud and immediately understanding it? It is too compact for easy comprehension. It would have to be spoken in an expanded form, such as this:

> When immigrants come to America, how do they treat their cultural heritage from the old country? The first generation of immigrants tries to retain as much as possible of the customs, cuisine, and language of the old country. But the second generation wants to forget all of that; these children of immigrants want to become "100 percent American," with no reminders of their foreign roots. Then along comes the third generation; these grandchildren want to celebrate the past, to find out all they can about their old-country heritage.

With this expanded version, the audience would be able to absorb the information.

One of the best ways to elaborate an idea is to develop it with support materials such as examples, narratives, and statistics. In general, oral communication requires more support materials than written communication. Suppose you wanted to make the following point:

> Alaska is our largest state in land area, but it's the lowest in population density.

Everyone knows the first part of this statement, but do people really grasp just how sparsely settled Alaska is? To show them, you can elaborate with statistics and contrasts:

> Alaska is so enormous that the 21 smallest states in the United States could fit inside its borders. Yet it has a tiny population—only about 620,000. More people live in metropolitan Pittsburgh, Pennsylvania, than in the entire state of Alaska. To get an idea of just how sparsely populated Alaska is, consider this: If New York City had the same ratio of residents per square mile, only 255 people would be living in all five boroughs of the city.[42]

If you limit yourself to one sentence, your point might fail to stick in your listeners' minds. If you elaborate by giving some interesting support materials, you increase your chances of driving home the point.

Note of caution: Just because it is a good idea to amplify your spoken message, don't conclude that you should pad your oral language with meaningless or windy phrases. In spoken as well as in written communication, you should omit needless words. Don't say, "In terms of the future, the military expects to meet its recruiting goals." Leave off the unnecessary five words at the beginning and say, "The military expects to meet its recruiting goals." Don't say, "in the area of statistics." Say simply, "statistics."

2. Oral language requires more repetition of key ideas than written language. "If you have an important point to make," British Prime Minister Winston Churchill advised the young Prince of Wales, "don't try to be subtle or clever. Use a pile driver. Hit the point once. Then come back and hit it again. Then hit it a third time—a tremendous whack."[43]

One of the reasons Churchill is considered one of the greatest orators of the 20th century is that he followed his own advice. For example, on the subject of determination, he said:

> Never give in! Never, never, never, never, never, never. In nothing great or small, large or petty—never give in except to convictions of honor and good sense.[44]

Too much repetition? For an essay, yes. For a speech, no.

Have you ever wondered why TV viewers are bombarded with the same commercial over and over again for weeks and months? Partly to make sure that as many people as possible see the commercial, but mainly because marketing research shows that a message must be received 3 to 12 times to be unforgettable.[45] How many times must a public speaker state an idea to ensure that listeners retain it? It is hard to say exactly because there are many variables, such as how much knowledge the listeners already possess on the subject and how interesting the speech is. Churchill's recommendation—three times—is a good rule of thumb (though some complex messages may need even more repetition).

When you repeat an idea, you may want to use the exact same wording (as when you reiterate a central idea). But sometimes it's effective to change your wording—not only to provide variety but also to enhance your chances of reaching different segments of the audience. One set of words might work well for some listeners, while another set might be needed for other listeners. Dr. Rachel Marsella, an obstetrician who gives lectures to expectant parents going through Lamaze childbirth training, says of her talks:

> I try to use some medical language to reassure the better educated men and women that I'm a health professional and to show that I'm not talking down to them. But I have to keep in mind the less-well-educated people, too, so right after I use medical language, I'll say, "In other words . . ." For example, I might say, "About half of all mothers experience post-partum depression. In other words, they feel sad and blue and 'down in the dumps' after the child is born."

Dr. Marsella's technique permits her to repeat an idea, but with a fresh set of words.

In his plays William Shakespeare used this technique to reach both the educated playgoers seated in the galleries and the "groundlings," the poor, uneducated folks who stood on the ground around the stage. After committing murder, Macbeth asks, "Will all great Neptune's ocean wash this blood clean from my hand?" His own answer: "No, this my hand will rather the multitudinous seas incarnadine, making the green one red." Shakespeare wanted to convey the idea that Macbeth has so much blood on his hand that it will change the color of the sea from green to red. The phrase *multitudinous seas incarnadine* was designed for the educated spectators, who understood Latin-derived phrases. To reach the uneducated groundlings, he immediately repeated his idea in plain Anglo-Saxon terms—*making the green one red.*[46] By repeating an idea but doing so with variety and grace, Shakespeare ensured that all listeners would understand his meaning.

Resources for Review and Skill Building

www.mhhe.com/gregory7

This book's Online Learning Center Website and SpeechMate CD-ROM provide meaningful resources and tools for study and review, such as practice tests, key-term flashcards, and sample speech videos.

SpeechMate CD-ROM

Summary

Because language has great power, the words that you use in a speech should be chosen with care and sensitivity. Always use language that is appropriate for your particular audience and occasion, avoiding words that might be over the heads of the listeners or that might offend any member of the audience.

To use words accurately, you must be sensitive to both denotation, which is a word's dictionary definition, and connotation, which is the emotional significance of the word.

Be careful to use correct grammar. In business and professional life today, "bad" English causes many listeners to lower their estimate of a speaker's intelligence and credibility.

You can achieve clarity in your language by choosing words that are simple, concrete, and precise. Beware of two types of doublespeak: euphemisms, which try to sugarcoat the unpleasant taste of reality, and inflated language, which exaggerates the importance of a person or thing. Don't use jargon, the specialized language of a group or profession, unless all listeners are certain to know the meanings of the words used.

You can achieve vividness by creating word images, such as metaphors and similes, and by using rhythmic techniques, such as parallel structure and repetition.

Oral language and written language are similar in many ways, but there are two significant differences: (1) Oral language requires more elaboration than written language and (2) oral language requires more repetition of key ideas than written language.

Key Terms

abstract words, *306*
cliché, *311*
concrete words, *306*
connotation, *303*
denotation, *303*
doublespeak, *307*
euphemism, *307*
imagery, *310*
inflated language, *308*
jargon, *309*
metaphor, *310*
mixed metaphor, *311*
parallel structure, *311*
repetition, *312*
sex-related stereotype, *301*
simile, *311*

Review Questions

1. Why did Dr. Martin Luther King Jr. use different words with different audiences?
2. What is the difference between the denotation and the connotation of a word?
3. Where can one find explanations of the synonyms of words?
4. Why is incorrect grammar a handicap for a speaker?
5. What is a euphemism? Give an example.
6. What is inflated language? Give an example.
7. "Her life was a whirlwind of meetings, deadlines, and last minute decisions." Change this metaphor to a simile.
8. "My love," said poet Robert Burns, "is like a red, red rose." Change this simile to a metaphor.

9. This sentence commits a mistake: "Learning is a spark in a person's mind that must be watered constantly." What is the term used for this error?

10. What are the two major differences between oral and written language?

Building Critical-Thinking Skills

1. Some sports teams are named after birds—in football, Philadelphia Eagles, Atlanta Falcons, Seattle Seahawks, and Phoenix Cardinals; in baseball, Toronto Blue Jays, St. Louis Cardinals, and Baltimore Orioles. Why are teams named after these birds, and yet no teams are named after vultures, crows, or pigeons?

2. A book on automobile repair was once advertised under the headline "How to Repair Cars." When the advertising agency changed the headline to read, "How to Fix Cars," sales jumped by 20 percent. Why do you think sales increased?

Building Teamwork Skills

1. In restaurants, diners are more likely to select a dish if the menu describes it in appetizing terms, such as "topped with *zesty* garlic butter." In a group, create a list of at least 10 items for a menu. Pretending that you are managers of a restaurant, make the descriptions as tempting as possible.

2. Many years ago, a poll asked people to cite what they considered the most beautiful words in the English language. Among the words mentioned were *lullaby, violet,* and *Chattanooga.* Working in a group, create a list of at least 10 words that group members think are especially beautiful. Discuss why the words are considered beautiful—is it the sounds of the words or the images the words evoke? If time permits, have group members who speak or have studied other languages contribute beautiful words from those languages.

Building Internet Skills

www.mhhe.com/gregory7

1. If you want to find out whether certain words are commonly used, you can launch a word search. To describe one group of Americans, some people prefer the word Hispanic, while others prefer Latino. To find which is more popular today, use a search engine to examine frequency of use. Write down the number of "hits" for each word. Which is more frequently used?

Possible Strategy: Go to Google (www.google.com) and enter "Hispanic" for one search, "Latino" for the other.

2. If you retrieve a document that contains a word for which you are searching, it is time-consuming to scan the pages with your eyes, looking for the word. A quicker method is to use the Find command (Control + F), which will take you immediately to the word. To examine how the word *invidious* is being used in contemporary English, find and print a document containing the word.

Possible Strategy: Go to any search engine, such as AltaVista (www.altavista.com), and search for "invidious." Select a document from the results list. When you arrive at the document, press the Control key and F simultaneously, and execute a search for "invidious." You should zip straight to it.

Using PowerWeb

www.mhhe.com/gregory7

In "Use Large Words Sparingly," writing coach Paula LaRocque quotes this sentence: "The CEO said that financial exigencies made it necessary for the company to implement budgetary measures to minimize expenditures." Find and write down her translation into plain English. To find this article, visit www.mhhe.com/gregory7, click on STUDENT EDITION and then POWERWEB: CONTENTS.

Baseball star Alex Rodriguez of the Texas Rangers illustrates some of the key techniques of effective delivery as he speaks at the dedication of a children's education center in Miami. He looks at his audience instead of reading a script, and he uses open, natural gestures. Note also that he has dressed up—to show his respect for the audience and the occasion.

14

Delivering the Speech

Outline

Methods of Speaking
Memorization
Manuscript
Impromptu
Extemporaneous

Voice
Volume
Clarity
Expressiveness

Nonverbal Communication
Personal Appearance
Eye Contact
Facial Expressions
Posture
Movement
Using Notes
Gestures
Beginning and Ending

The Question-and-Answer Period

Practice

Objectives

After studying this chapter, you should be able to:

1. Practice and deliver an extemporaneous speech.
2. Conduct a question-and-answer period.
3. Explain the four methods of delivery.
4. Describe the attributes of effective vocal delivery.
5. Describe the attributes of effective nonverbal communication in a speech.

Patricia Pena of Perkasie, Pennsylvania, never wanted to be a national public figure, giving speeches to state legislatures and appearing on CNN, NBC News, and the *Oprah Winfrey Show.* Her goal was to enjoy her family to the fullest.

But her life was turned upside down when a motorist, distracted by his cell phone, ran a stop sign and broadsided her car. The impact killed her two-year-old daughter Morgan Lee.

Four months later, in early 2000, Pena reluctantly but courageously decided to try to educate the public and to fight for laws to ban drivers from using cell phones while a car is moving. "I want to save other children from what happened to Morgan Lee," she says.

In her first speech, Pena got off to a shaky start. She was visibly trembling, her voice was soft and tentative, and her eyes were downcast. But as she got into her speech, a dramatic transformation took place: She stopped shaking, she spoke with a strong voice, and she maintained steady eye contact with her listeners. For the rest of her talk, she was a vibrant, compelling speaker. Many in the audience were moved to tears—and to action. "The next time I need to talk on my phone," one listener said, "I will pull over to the side of the road."

Later, Pena was asked what had caused her speech delivery to change from weak to powerful. Her answer: "I wanted everyone in the audience to know what I know without having to learn it from a personal tragedy."

In subsequent presentations, Pena gained a reputation as a highly effective speaker. Her appearance with Oprah Winfrey was broadcast three times, transmitting her message to over 40 million people. Her campaign increased public awareness of the problem—undoubtedly saving many lives—and prompted over 300 cities and three states to pass laws restricting the use of hand-held cell phones.[1]

As you read this chapter, I hope you will keep Patricia Pena in mind because she exemplifies an important point: *The key to good delivery is a strong desire to communicate with the audience.* Though Pena started out shakily in her first speech, she had a burning desire to communicate with the audience, and before long she was unconsciously using good delivery techniques. I have observed this phenomenon time and time again: Speakers who lack professional polish and training but who care deeply about conveying their ideas to the audience almost always do an adequate job with their delivery. A General Motors executive, R. T. Kingman, expressed it this way: "If a speaker knows what he wants to say, really wants to say it, and wants everybody in the room to understand what it is he wants to say, all the other things like looking people in the eye and using good gestures will just come naturally."[2]

I am emphasizing the speaker's desire to communicate so that you can put the ideas of this chapter into proper perspective. The dozens of tips about delivery in the pages that follow are important; you should study them carefully. But bear in mind that a strong desire to communicate with your audience is the dynamo of power that makes it possible for you to deliver a speech with strength and effectiveness.

After the death of her two-year-old daughter, Patricia Pena reluctantly became a nationally famous speaker because she wanted to save other children from what happened to her child.

Methods of Speaking

Four basic speaking methods are used by public speakers today: memorization, manuscript, impromptu, and extemporaneous.

Memorization

A few speakers memorize an entire speech and then deliver it without a script or notes. Memorizing is a bad idea for most speakers, however, because of the following liabilities:

- You are forced to spend an enormous amount of time in committing the speech to memory.
- At some point in your speech, you might suddenly forget what comes next. This could cause you to become acutely embarrassed or even panic-stricken. Once derailed from your speech, you might be unable to get back on track.

- Even if you remembered your entire speech, you would be speaking from your memory, not from your heart. This could cause you to sound remote, lifeless, unenergetic—more like a robot than a human being.

Memorizing does have one virtue: it lets you figure out your *exact* wording ahead of time. But this gain in precision fails to outweigh the disadvantages. I don't recommend this method.

Manuscript

manuscript method
delivery of a speech by reading a script

Some speakers put their entire speech word-for-word on a **manuscript.** This method, says Elayne Snyder, a speech consultant, is best used "if you are to testify at a congressional committee hearing or other official hearing where every word will appear in permanent form in an official record, or if you have been asked to deliver a paper at a scientific or educational conference and every word will appear in a conference journal."[3]

SpeechMate CD-ROM
To see the manuscript method, view Robert Ingram's speech on Disk 2 of the CD.

There are two ways to deliver such a speech. The first is simply to read the manuscript, but this approach, says Snyder, "destroys spontaneity and enthusiasm." The speaker fails to look at the audience, fails to speak with adequate expression, and often reads too quickly.[4]

The second way is to use the manuscript as a crutch, but not actually read it. Here is how this technique works: On the manuscript, underline or highlight key phrases and transitions. Then practice the speech over and over until you are thoroughly familiar with the material and the sequence of ideas. (This technique differs from the memorized method in that you thoroughly familiarize yourself with the speech but stop short of committing it to memory.) When you actually give the speech, glance at the key words to refresh your memory of which idea to cover next, but most of the time, look at the listeners and speak to them in a natural, conversational style. Your words are similar to those in the manuscript, of course, but not exactly the same.

Some speakers use this technique as an insurance policy. If their mind goes blank for a moment, they can read the script verbatim until they recover. In most cases, they never have to use the insurance policy, but merely knowing that it exists gives them a sense of security.

Although the manuscript method can be effective, it is difficult for most people to use a script and still sound lively and conversational. The great temptation is to read word-for-word in a droning, artificial voice. Unless you have had extensive theatrical or oratorical experience, I don't recommend using a manuscript.

Impromptu

impromptu method
speaking with little or no preparation

Speaking **impromptu** means speaking on the spur of the moment—with no opportunity for extensive preparation. For example, without warning you are asked to give a talk to your fellow employees about your recent convention trip to New Orleans. Or during a meeting, you are asked to give your view of a situation. Here are some guidelines for impromptu speaking:

Organize your speech. Because you usually don't have much time before standing to speak, you should quickly develop three items (on paper or in your mind)—*point, support,* and *conclusion.* Ask yourself:

- What *point* do I want to make? In a short speech, make only one assertion. Don't bring in points that you lack the time or knowledge to handle.
- How can I *support* my point? Explain or prove your point by using specific details, examples, anecdotes, and other support materials.
- What is my *conclusion?* This may be a restatement of the point and/or an appeal to the audience to take action. Formulate your closing sentence in your mind *before* you start speaking; it will prevent you from rambling and being unable to make a graceful ending.

Never apologize. Asking your listeners to forgive you for lack of preparation is unnecessary—they know you had no chance to prepare, and besides, they are not expecting a polished masterpiece. Apologizing makes you appear insecure and unconfident.

www.mhhe.com/gregory7

For articles on one kind of impromptu speaking—Job interview—see Supplementary Readings on this book's Website.

Don't rush. Try not to gallop through your remarks. Speak at a steady, calm rate. At the beginning, and at various intervals, pause for a few seconds to collect your thoughts. If you can employ pauses without a look of panic on your face, you actually enhance your credibility—you come across as thoughtful and careful.

Whenever possible, link your remarks to those of other speakers. Listening intently to what other people say in a meeting can pay dividends. When you are asked to comment or to give a talk, you often can take a statement made by a previous speaker and build upon it or try to refute it. (By the way, failing to listen carefully can hurt you. For example, if you are daydreaming during a meeting, and someone suddenly turns to you and asks, "What do you think about this proposal?" you can look very foolish if you are unable to respond, or if you respond in a way that reveals that you had not been paying attention.)

Don't feign knowledge. During a meeting or during a question-and-answer period, you may be asked to comment on a matter about which you know nothing. Simply say, "I don't know." Don't feign knowledge by "winging it"—by rambling on and on as a way of pretending that you know the answer. Some speakers think that admitting ignorance will hurt their credibility, but the opposite is often true: If you fail to admit your ignorance and try to hide it behind a smokescreen of verbal ramblings, you can make yourself look insincere and foolish. In some situations you can say, "I don't know the answer to that, but I'll look into it and get back to you as soon as I can."

Be brief. Some impromptu speakers talk too long, repeating the same ideas over and over, because they are afraid that they are doing a poor job and therefore must redeem themselves, or because they lack a graceful way of closing the speech. Whatever the case, you can never help yourself by rambling on and on. Speak briefly and then sit down.

Try to foresee situations where you are likely to be called upon to speak impromptu. Plan what you will say. For example, when you return from a convention and you are driving to work, rehearse in your mind what you will say if the boss asks you to make a little speech to your colleagues about your trip.

Extemporaneous

extemporaneous method
delivery of a speech from notes, following extensive preparation and rehearsal

The **extemporaneous** method is the most popular style of speaking in the United States today. The idea is to sound as if you are speaking spontaneously, but instead of giving the clumsy, faltering speech that many off-the-cuff speakers give, you present a beautifully organized, well-developed speech that you have spent many hours preparing and practicing.

In extemporaneous speaking, you speak from notes, but these notes don't contain your speech written out word for word. Instead they contain only your basic ideas, expressed in a few key words. When you speak, therefore, you make up the exact words as you go along. You glance at your notes occasionally to remind yourself of your next point, but most of the time you look at the listeners, speaking to them in a natural, conversational tone of voice.

This conversational tone is valued in a speech because it is the easiest kind for an audience to listen to, understand, and remember. When you speak conversationally, you are speaking directly, warmly, sincerely. Your manner is as close as possible to the way you talk to your best friends: Your voice is full of life and color; your words are fresh and vital.

SpeechMate CD-ROM
To contrast effective and ineffective delivery, view the first four speeches on the CD.

Though the extemporaneous method is popular, it provides no guarantee of success. In fact, if you are not careful, it can cause you to stumble. For example, if you fail to prepare a well-organized outline, you might find that your ideas don't hang together and your words are fuzzy and imprecise. If you fail to practice, you might find that your delivery is ragged, with awkward silences and many "uhs." For this method to work, *you must spend a lot of time preparing and rehearsing your speech.*

Speaking extemporaneously permits more flexibility than reading from a written speech because it is easier to adjust to meet the needs of an audience. If, for example, you see that some of your listeners don't understand a point, you can restate your message in different words or you can insert additional explanations. If you are the last speaker of the evening at a banquet and you sense that your audience is about to go to sleep because of the long-winded speakers who preceded you, you can shorten your speech by cutting out some of your minor points.

Voice

Some people think that to be an excellent speaker, you must have a golden voice, rich and resonant, that enthralls listeners. This is not true. Some of the greatest orators in history had imperfect voices. Abraham Lincoln's voice was described by his contemporaries as "thin, high-pitched, shrill, not musical, and . . . disagreeable"[5] and Winston Churchill "stammered and even had a slight lisp."[6] In our own day, I have observed a popular evangelist whose voice is thin and weak, a successful TV commentator who talks in an irritatingly abrasive manner, and a leading politician who speaks with an unpleasant nasal whine. Yet all three are in demand as public speakers. It is nice to have a rich, resonant voice, but other characteristics of the human voice are of greater importance for effective speechmaking: Your voice should have proper volume; it should be clear and understandable; and it should be expressive. Let's examine these characteristics in more detail.

Volume

The larger the room, the louder you have to speak. You can tell if your volume is loud enough by observing the people in the back row. Are they leaning forward with quizzical expressions as they strain to hear your words? Then obviously you need to speak louder. In some cases you may want to ask directly, "Can the people in the back row hear me all right?" In some circumstances you may have to raise your voice to overcome unavoidable noises, such as the hum of air conditioners, the chatter of people in a hallway, the clatter of dishes and silverware during a banquet, or even the sound of a band blaring in the next room.

Speaking loudly enough for all to hear does not mean shouting. It means *projecting* your voice a bit beyond its normal range. If you have never spoken to a large group or if your instructor tells you that you have problems in projecting your voice, practice with a friend. Find an empty classroom, have your friend sit in the back row, and practice speaking with extra force—not shouting—so that your friend can hear you easily. (Or set up a tape recorder in the back of the room and practice projecting your voice toward it.)

If a speech requires the use of a microphone, go to the meeting site early and spend a few minutes testing the mike before the listeners arrive. Adjust it to your height; if someone readjusts it during the ceremonies, spend a few moments getting it just right for yourself. Your audience will not mind the slight delay. When you speak into a mike, it is not necessary to have your lips almost touching it; in fact, your voice will sound better if your mouth is 6 to 12 inches away. Position the mike so that you can forget that it is there. This frees you to speak naturally, without having to bend over or lean forward. At large meetings, you don't need to raise your voice while talking into a microphone. In fact, says professional speaker Arnold "Nick" Carter, "the invention of the microphone made it possible for me to speak to 18,000 people with a whisper."[7]

Clarity

Spoken English is sometimes radically different from written English, as this news item demonstrates:

> One group of English-speaking Japanese who moved to the United States as employees of Toyota had to enroll in a special course to learn that "Jeat yet?" means "Did you eat yet?" and that "Cannahepya?" means "Can I help you?" Their English classes in Japan had failed to prepare them for "Waddayathink?" (What do you think?), "Watchadoin?" (What are you doing?), and "Dunno" (I don't know).[8]

For many speakers of English, **articulation**—the production of speech sounds by our vocal organs—is lazy and weak, especially in daily conversations. We slur sounds, drop syllables, and mumble words. While poor articulation may not hurt us in conversation as long as our friends understand what we are saying, it can hinder communication in a speech, especially if English is a second language for some of our listeners. We need to enunciate our words crisply and precisely to make sure that everything we say is intelligible.

articulation
the act of producing vocal sounds

If you tend to slur words, you can improve your speech by reading poems or essays aloud 15 minutes a day for three weeks. Say the words with exaggerated emphasis, and move your mouth and tongue vigorously. Enunciate consonants firmly and make vowel sounds last longer than normal. In real situations you should not exaggerate in this way, but the practice will help you avoid the pitfalls of slurring and mumbling.

pronunciation
correct way of speaking a word

While poor articulation stems from sloppy habits, poor **pronunciation** is a matter of not knowing the correct way to say a word. Examine the common pronunciation mistakes listed in Table 14.1.[9]

If you are like most people, you use some words that you have picked up from books but have never heard pronounced. If you rely on your own guess, you can sometimes be embarrassed. One student had read about the Sioux Indians, but apparently had never heard the tribal name pronounced; he called them the *sigh-ox.* Another common slip is to confuse words that sound alike. For example, one of my students said that a man and woman contemplating marriage should make sure they are compatible before they say their *vowels.* (One of the listeners couldn't resist the temptation to ask, at the end of the speech, whether consonants were also important for marriage.) These kinds of mistakes can be avoided by looking up a word's meaning and pronunciation in a dictionary.

Table 14.1
Common Pronunciation Mistakes

	Incorrect	Correct
across	uh-crost	uh-cross
athlete	ath-uh-lete	ath-lete
burglar	burg-you-lur	burg-lur
chef	tchef	shef
chic	chick	sheek
drowned	drown-did	drownd
electoral	e-lec-tor-ee-al	e-lec-tur-al
environment	en-vire-uh-ment	en-vi-run-ment
et cetera	ek-cetera	et-cetera
evening	eve-uh-ning	eve-ning
grievous	greev-ee-us	greev-us
height	hithe	hite
hundred	hun-derd	hun-dred
library	li-berry	li-brar-y
mischievous	miss-chee-vee-us	miss-chuh-vus
nuclear	nu-cu-lar	nu-cle-ar
perspiration	press-pi-ra-tion	per-spi-ra-tion
picture	pitch-er	pick-shur
pretty	pur-tee	prit-ee
professor	pur-fess-ur	pruh-fess-ur
quiet	quite	kwy-it
realtor	reel-uh-tor	re-ul-tor
recognize	reck-uh-nize	rec-og-nize
relevant	rev-uh-lant	rel-uh-vant
strength	strenth	strength

Expressiveness

A dynamic speaker has a voice that is warm and expressive, producing a rich variety of sounds. Let's examine five basic elements of expressiveness.

Pitch and Intonation

pitch
the highness or lowness of a sound
intonation
the use of changing pitch to convey meaning

The highness or lowness of your voice is called **pitch.** The ups and downs of pitch—called **intonation** patterns—give our language its distinctive melody. Consider the following sentence: "I believe in love." Say it in a variety of ways—with sincerity, with sarcasm, with humor, with puzzlement. Each time you say it, you are using a different intonation pattern.

In conversation, almost everyone uses a variety of intonation patterns and emphasizes particular words, but in public speaking, some speakers fail to use any variety at all. Instead, they speak in a monotone—a dull, flat drone that will put many listeners to sleep. Even worse, they run the risk of appearing insincere. They may say something dramatic like "This crime is a terrible tragedy for America," but say it in such a casual, offhand way that the audience thinks they don't really mean it.

An absence of intonation also means that some words fail to receive the emphasis they deserve. For example, take a sentence like this: "Mr. Smith made $600,000 last year, while Mr. Jones made $6,000." A speaker who talks in a monotone will say the two figures as if there were no difference between $600,000 and $6,000. But to give listeners the help they need in *hearing* the disparity, the speaker should let his or her voice place heavy emphasis on the $600,000.

Loudness and Softness

Besides using the proper volume so that everyone in the audience can hear you, you can raise or lower your voice for dramatic effect or to emphasize a point. Try saying the following out loud:

> *(Soft:)* "Should we give in to the kidnappers' demands? *(Switch to loud:)* NEVER!"

Did you notice that raising your voice for the last word conveys that you truly mean what you say? Now try another selection out loud:

> *(Start softly and make your voice grow louder as you near the end of this sentence:)* Edwin Arlington Robinson's character Richard Cory had everything that a man could want—good looks, lots of money, popularity. *(Now make your voice switch to soft:)* But he went home one night and put a bullet through his head.

Changing from loud to soft helps the listeners *feel* the tragic discrepancy between Richard Cory's outward appearance and his inner reality.

Rate of Speaking

How quickly or slowly should you speak? The ideal speed for giving a speech is like the ideal speed for driving a car—it all depends on conditions. Driving a car at 55 mph is fine for a highway but too fast for a school zone. Similarly, a rapid rate of speaking is appropriate in certain conditions—if, for example, you are describing a thrilling high-speed police chase—but a slow pace is preferred if you are introducing a technical, hard-to-understand concept.

One of the biggest mistakes inexperienced speakers make is speaking too rapidly. It is especially important that you speak at a slow, deliberate rate during your introduction (except in special situations, as when you lead off with an adventure story). Have you ever noticed how TV dramas start out very slowly? They don't divulge important details of the story until you are three or four minutes into the show. One obvious reason for this is to have mercy on the viewers who have gone to the kitchen to get a snack and are slow in returning to the TV. But the main reason is to give the viewers a chance to "tune in" to the story, to get adjusted to what is happening on the screen, to get accustomed to the characters. If too much action or dialogue takes place in the first minute, viewers are unable to absorb the story. In like fashion, you need to give your audience a chance to "tune in" to you, to get accustomed to your voice and subject matter. If you race through your introduction, they may become lost and confused, and they may decide to spend the time daydreaming rather than struggling to follow your galloping delivery.

Speaking slowly—and using pauses, especially at the beginning—will make you come across to the audience as someone who is confident and in control, as someone who cares about whether the listeners understand.

You can avoid speaking too rapidly by practicing your speech at home. Use a tape recorder and listen to yourself. Have friends or relatives listen to your speech; ask them to tell you if you are speaking too fast for easy comprehension.

Some people speak too rapidly because they write out all or most of their speech on notecards or a sheet of paper; when they rise to speak, they succumb to the temptation of reading rapidly from their script. The solution is to have brief notes, not a written script, in hand when you stand up to speak.

Pauses

When you read printed material, you have punctuation marks to help you make sense out of your reading: commas tell you when to pause, periods when to stop, and so on. In a speech, there are no punctuation marks; listeners must rely on your oral cues to guide them. One of these cues is the pause, which lets your listeners know when you have finished one thought and are ready to go to the next. Audiences appreciate a pause; it gives them time to digest what you have said. As a bonus, it gives you a moment to think of what you are going to say next.

A pause before an important idea or the climax of a story can be effective in creating suspense. For example, student speaker Stephanie Johnson told of an adventure she had while camping:

> It was late at night when I finally crawled into my sleeping bag. The fire had died down, but the moon cast a faint, spooky light on our campsite. I must have been asleep a couple of hours when I suddenly woke up. Something was brushing up against my sleeping bag. My heart started pounding like crazy. I peeked out of the slit I had left for air. Do you know what I saw? *[pause]*

By pausing at this point, Johnson had the audience on the edge of their chairs. What was it? A bear? A human intruder? After a few moments of dramatic tension, she ended the suspense: "By the light of the moon, I could see a dark little animal with a distinctive white stripe. *[pause]* It was a skunk."

A pause also can be used to emphasize an important statement. It is a way of saying, "Let this sink in." Notice how Yvette Ortiz, a political science professor, used pauses in a speech on community service:

> When I am tempted to reject those ignorant fools who disagree with me, I remind myself of the words of novelist Peter De Vries: "We are not primarily put on this earth to see through one another, *[pause]* but to see one another through." *[pause]*[10]

The strategically placed pauses gave the listeners time to reflect on the wisdom in the quotation.

In some speeches, you might find yourself pausing not because you want to, but because you have forgotten what you were planning to say next and you need to look at your notes. Or you might pause while searching your mind for the right word. Such a pause seems like an eternity, so you are tempted to fill in the silence with **verbal fillers** such as "uh," "er," or "um." If used excessively, these fillers make you sound—to some listeners—as someone who is uninformed and unprepared.

verbal fillers
vocalized pauses in which a speaker inserts sounds such as "uh"

When you grope for a word, use silence instead of "uh" and "um." There is nothing wrong with silence; there is no need to be embarrassed by it. The audience does not mind. In fact, a few such pauses can enhance your credibility, making you seem more conversational and natural. You look as if you are concerned about giving the audience the most precise words possible.

Conversational Quality

Many inexperienced speakers give their speeches in a dull, plodding, colorless voice. Yet five minutes afterward, chatting with their friends in the hall, they speak with animation and warmth.

What they need to do is bring that same conversational quality into their speeches. How can this be done? How can a person sound as lively and as "real" when talking to 30 people as when chatting with a friend? If this problem applies to you, here are two suggestions:

1. **Treat your audience not as an impersonal mass, not as a blur of faces, but as a collection of individuals.** To capture the feeling of a one-to-one conversation, here's a mental ploy you can use: At the beginning of a speech, look at one or two or three individuals in different parts of the room and act as if you are talking to them personally. You should avoid staring, of course, but looking at each face briefly will help you develop a conversational attitude. As the speech goes on, you can add other faces to your "conversation."

SpeechMate CD-ROM
To see a speaker who uses a conversational style, view Speech 8 ("The Deadliest Natural Disaster") on Disk 1.

2. **Be yourself—but somewhat intensified.** To speak to an audience with the same natural, conversational tone you use with your friends, you must speak with greater energy and forcefulness. We are not talking now about projecting your voice so that the people in the back of the room can hear you, but rather about *intensifying* the psychological dimensions of your voice—the emotional tones and the vibrancy. How can you do this? Here are two ways:

First, let your natural enthusiasm come forth. If you have chosen a topic wisely, you are speaking on something about which you care a great deal and want very much to communicate to the audience. When you stand in front of your audience, don't hold yourself back; let your voice convey all the enthusiasm that you feel inside. Many speakers are afraid they will look or sound ridiculous if they get involved with their subject. "I'll come on too strong," they say. But the truth is that your audience will not react this way; they will be impressed by your energy and zest. Think back to the speakers you have heard: Didn't you respond favorably to those who were alive and enthusiastic?

Second, practice loosening up. Some novice speakers sound and look stiff because they simply have had no practice in loosening up. Here is something you can try: Find a private location (such as a room at home or a clearing in the woods or an empty classroom late in the afternoon when no one else is around). For subject matter, you can practice a speech on which you are working, recite poetry, read from the morning newspaper, or simply ad-lib. Whatever words you use, say them dramatically. Ham it up. Be theatrical. Act as if you are running for president and you are trying to persuade an audience of 10,000 people to vote for you. Or act as if you are giving a poetry reading to 500 of your most enthusiastic fans. You will not speak so dramatically to a real audience, of course, but the practice in "letting go" will help you break out of your normal reserve. It will help you learn to be yourself, to convey your natural enthusiasm.

Nonverbal Communication

nonverbal communication
transmission of messages without words

Nonverbal communication consists of the messages that you send without words—what you convey with your eyes, facial expression, posture, body movement, and the characteristics of your voice (as discussed in the preceding section).

The words of a speech "are meaningless unless the rest of you is in synchronization," says Roger Ailes, a communications consultant who has advised various presidential candidates.[11] Corporate executives, he says, "often get up and send all sorts of weird signals to their audience. My favorite is, 'Ladies and gentlemen, I'm very happy to be here.' But they're looking at their shoes as they say it. They have no enthusiasm whatsoever. They look either angry, frightened, or depressed about being there."[12]

When there is a discrepancy between words and nonverbal behavior, the audience "will always go with the visual signals over the verbal ones," says Ailes. "They'll say to themselves unconsciously, 'He's telling me he's happy to be here, but he's really not. Therefore, he's either uncomfortable or a liar, or both.'"[13]

SpeechMate CD-ROM

See the CD for the Speech Critique software program that enables you to evaluate speeches, either on a computer or on a printed evaluation sheet.

To get your nonverbal signals synchronized with your words, you need to show enthusiasm (with your eyes, facial expression, posture, and tone of voice) as you speak to your audience. Let your body confirm that you believe in what you are saying and that you want your audience to accept your ideas.

If you are truly enthusiastic about your speech and eager to share it with your audience, much of your body language will take care of itself, as we discussed at the beginning of this chapter. But you may be asking, "What if I don't really feel happy and confident? I can't lie with my body, can I?" This is a good question, because there are times when you resent having to give a speech, as when the boss orders you to give a presentation to the board of directors or an instructor assigns you to give an oral report to the class. Sometimes you simply don't feel like standing up in front of a group. Maybe you didn't get much sleep the night before, and you have no zip, no spark. At times like these, what should you do?

Pretend. Yes, pretend to be confident in yourself and in your ideas. Pretend to be glad to appear before your audience. Pretend to be enthusiastic. But, you may ask, isn't this phony? Isn't this forcing the body to tell a lie? Yes, but we often must simulate cheerfulness and animation in life's myriad tasks: a crucial job interview, a conference with the boss, an important date with someone we love. By *acting* as if we are confident, poised, and enthusiastic, we often find that after a few minutes, the pretense gives way to reality. We truly become confident, poised, and enthusiastic.

Consider the comedians and talk-show hosts who appear night after night on TV. Do you think they are always "up"? No. Like you and me, they have their bad days, their sluggish days, their down-in-the-dumps days, their head-cold and stomach-ache days. Nevertheless, they force themselves to perform; they pretend to be enthusiastic. After about 60 seconds, most of them report, the pretense gives way to reality, and they truly *are* enthusiastic. (*A word of advice:* If this transformation fails to happen to you—if you don't feel enthusiastic after a few minutes—you should continue to pretend.)

How do you carry out this pretense? How can you make your body "lie" for you? By knowing and using the signals that the body sends out to show confidence and energy. The following discussion of the major nonverbal aspects of public speaking will help you become aware of these signals.

Personal Appearance

Your audience will size up your personal appearance and start forming opinions about you even before you open your mouth to begin your speech. You should be clean, well-groomed, and attractively dressed.

It Is important that Dr. Heinz Feldmann be well-dressed as he advises the people of Hong Kong on how to avoid SARS, an infectious disease that killed over 100 Hong Kong residents. Most people in the world, especially Asians, find speakers more trustworthy if they dress up than if they dress casually. Dr. Feldmann, a German virologist based in Winnipeg, Canada, represents the World Health Organization.

Janet Stone and Jane Bachner, who conduct workshops for women executives, have some good advice for both men and women:

> As a general rule of thumb, find out what the audience will be wearing and then wear something yourself that is just a trifle dressier than their clothes. The idea is to establish yourself as "The Speaker," to set yourself slightly apart from the crowd. . .[14]

Dressing up is not merely a way to show off. It is a compliment to the audience, sending a nonverbal message: You people are important to me—so important that I dressed up a bit to show my respect for you.

Don't wear apparel that diminishes communication. Baseball caps tend to hinder eye contact, and to some listeners, they suggest disrespect and not taking the occasion seriously enough.

Your attire should always be appropriate. In other words, don't wear anything that would distract or offend the audience. A T-shirt with a ribald or controversial slogan printed on the front, for example, might direct attention away from the speech itself, and it might offend some members of the audience.

Some students have trouble accepting the idea of dressing up. Isn't it true, they say, that people should be judged by their character and not by their clothes? Yes, but in the real world, you *are* judged by clothes. As unfair as it seems, your clothes are sometimes perceived as a clue to your character and your competence. One magazine article on dressing up has this title: "What You Wear Is Almost as Important as What You Say."[15] This is an exaggeration, of course, but the point is important: Clothes do make a difference.

Eye Contact

Look at your audience 95 percent of the time, with the other 5 percent devoted to occasional glances at your notes. Having good eye contact with your listeners is important for three reasons: (1) It creates an important bond of communication and rapport between you and them. It is, in the words of Jack Valenti, president of the Motion Picture Association of America, a "figurative handshake."[16] (2) It shows your sincerity. There's an old saying: "Don't buy a used car from a dealer who won't look you in the eye." We distrust people who won't look at us openly and candidly. If you want your listeners to have confidence in what you are saying, look at *them,* not at a spot on the back wall. (3) It enables you to get audience feedback. Looking directly at your listeners makes you instantly aware of any lapses in communication. For example, did a number of listeners look puzzled when you made your last statement? Then you obviously confused them; you need to explain your point in a different way.

The biggest spoiler of good eye contact is looking at your notes too much—a mistake that is usually made for these two reasons: (1) You are unprepared. This can be corrected by rehearsing your speech so many times that you need only glance at your notes to remind yourself of what comes next. (2) You are nervous. Some speakers are well-prepared and don't really need to look at their notes very often, but they are so nervous that they scrutinize their notes to gain security and avoid the audience. One way to correct this is to put reminders, in giant red letters, on your notes—LOOK AT AUDIENCE—to nudge you out of this habit.

Tips for your CAREER

Tip 14.1 Decide Whether and How to Use a Lectern

Experienced speakers disagree about whether a lectern should be used for career and community speeches. Some say that a lectern gives the speaker dignity and is a convenient stand for notes, especially on formal occasions such as an awards ceremony or a funeral. Others object that a lectern creates a physical barrier. "I don't want anything coming between me and my audience," a politician told me. British speech consultant Cristina Stuart says, "I am 5′2″ and some lecterns are 4′0″ high, so how can I be a powerful speaker if my listeners can only see my head peeping over the edge?" Her advice: "Even if you are over six feet tall, try to stand to one side of the lectern so that you can refer to your notes and your listeners can see all of your body."

Here is a technique that has become popular: Using the lectern as "home base," walk a few paces to the left or right of it each time you make a point. In other words, glance at the notes on the lectern to remind yourself of the point you want to make, move away from the lectern a few paces, make the point, then walk back to the lectern to pick up your next point.

If a lectern is movable, some speakers remove it and simply hold their note cards in one hand (leaving the other hand free for gesturing). For a large audience, if the lectern is unmoveable and has a stationary microphone, says Stuart, "you have no choice but to stand behind it. Stand on a box if you are short so that your upper body can be seen."

With some audiences, you can arrange for a remote or mobile microphone so that you can move away from the lectern.

Another killer of eye contact is handouts. As we discussed in Chapter 9, you should never distribute a handout during a speech unless it is simple and short. If you give listeners an eight-page packet during your speech, you will lose eye communication.

Eye contact is more than darting furtive glances at the audience from time to time. It is more than mechanically moving your head from side to side like an oscillating fan. You must have meaningful contact similar to the eye-to-eye communication you engage in with your friends. For a large audience, the best technique is to have a "conversation" with three or four people in different parts of the room (so that you seem to be giving your attention to the entire audience). For a small audience, look at *every* listener. Professional speaker Danny Cox uses a technique called "locking" whenever he speaks to a small gathering:

> I learned something once from a piano player. I couldn't believe how she held an audience in a cocktail bar. It was so quiet in there you couldn't believe it. I realized one night what she was doing. She was looking at each person and as soon as she made eye contact with them, she smiled at them. And then moved on to the next one, and smiled. She was "locking" everybody in. This is a good technique in public speaking—very simple, too.[17]

Facial Expressions

Let your face express whatever emotion is appropriate at any given moment in a speech. A student told me he was planning to speak on how to perform under pressure; his primary example was the thrilling moment in high school when he kicked the winning field goal in the final seconds of a championship football game. When he described that triumphant feat to me, his face was suffused with excitement, but when he got up in front of the class and told the same story in his speech, his face was blank. Gone was the joy; gone was the exhilaration. By having a facial expression that was incongruous with the event he was describing, he weakened the impact of the story.

If you are speaking about sad or somber topics, your face should not be grinning; if you are speaking about happy items, your face should not be grimacing. And whatever you are talking about, your face should never be devoid of emotion—it should be animated. "Animation," says speech consultant Dorothy Sarnoff, "is the greatest cosmetic you can use, and it doesn't cost a cent. Animation is energy in the face. . . . It's action that comes not only through the eyes, but around the mouth and the whole face. It tells the listener you're glad to be right where you are—at the lectern, around a conference table or across a desk."[18] How can you make your face become animated? By choosing a subject about which you care a great deal, by having a strong desire to communicate your message to your listeners, and by delivering your speech with energy and enthusiasm.

Posture

posture
the position of your body as you sit or stand

Good **posture** conveys assurance and hopefulness. Stand in front of your audience poised, with your weight equally distributed on your feet. Your body language should convey the message, "I am confident; I am in command of this situation." This does not mean that you should be cocky and arrogant, but simply that you should convey an appearance of relaxed alertness.

If you are speaking at a lectern, here are some things *not* to do: Don't lean on it. Don't slouch to one side of it. Don't prop your feet on its base. Don't rock back and forth with it.

Some speakers like to sit on the edge of a desk to deliver a speech. This posture is fine for one-hour classroom lectures because the speaker gets a chance to relax, and his or her body language bespeaks openness and informality. But for short speeches, especially the kind you are expected to deliver in a public speaking class, stand up straight. It is easier to be alert and enthusiastic if you are standing up than if your body is in a relaxed sitting position.

Movement

You don't have to stand in one place throughout your speech as if you were glued to the spot. Feel free to move about. You can walk to the board and write a key word, or walk to your visual aid. Occasionally you can move left or right from the lectern to a new position in front of the audience.

Movement gives your body a chance to dissipate nervous energy. It also can be used to recapture your listeners' attention if they are getting bored or tired; an animated speaker is easier to follow than an unanimated speaker who stays frozen in one spot.

You can use movement to emphasize a transition from one point to the next. For example, walking three steps to the left of the lectern while giving the audience a verbal "bridge" to your next point is a good way to emphasize that you are moving from one idea to another.

Movement also can be used to drive home an important point. At a crucial juncture in your speech, when you want strong audience involvement, you can take a few steps toward the listeners as you state a key idea. Moving toward them signals nonverbally that you are keenly interested in having them understand and accept what you are saying.

All of your movements should be purposeful and confident—not random and nervous. If you roam back and forth across the front of the room like a tiger in a cage, your audience will be distracted and even annoyed. Don't sway back and forth; don't rock on your heels. In short, make your movements add to your speech, rather than subtract from it.

Using Notes

For classroom speeches, your instructor will tell you whether you may use notes. For speeches in your career, the note system that was explained in Chapter 12 is highly recommended. It is a system that most professional speakers use. (Even speakers who talk without looking at notes often have notes with them as insurance—in case they lose their train of thought.)

If you do take cards or sheets of paper to a lectern, arrange them in whatever way works best for you. Some speakers place them in a stack on the lectern and consult one at a time. Other speakers spread them out, so that several are visible at a time.

www.mhhe.com/gregory7

For an alternate system for using notes, see "How to Use Check-off Notes" in Supplementary Readings on this book's Website.

Whatever note system is used, remember our earlier warning: *Use notes sparingly.* Look at your audience 95 percent of the time.

Gestures

What should you do with your hands during a speech? First of all, make sure they do nothing to distract the audience: Don't let them jingle keys or coins, riffle notecards, fiddle with a watch or jewelry, adjust clothing, smooth your hair, rub your chin, or scratch any part of your body. The best thing you can do with your hands is to let them be free to make gestures whenever you feel like making them. This, after all, is how you make gestures in conversation—naturally and without thinking. To make sure that your hands are free for gesturing, you can either let them hang by your side or allow them to rest on the lectern. Beware of doing things that prevent your hands from being free to gesture: (1) Don't grip the lectern with your hands. (2) Don't clutch your notes with both hands. (3) Don't stuff both hands into your pockets.

If you use a lectern, don't let it hide your gestures. Some speakers rest their hands on the lectern and make tiny, flickering gestures that cannot be seen by the audience. This makes the speaker look tentative and unsure. Better no gestures at all than hidden ones.

When you make gestures, use all of your arm, advises British speech consultant Cristina Stuart:

> Don't tuck in your elbows to your waist or make jerky, half-hearted, meaningless gestures. I remember a tall woman in one of my courses who, through shyness, stood hunched up, making tiny movements with her hands. We advised her to stand tall, make eye contact, and use her arms to express her enthusiasm. The result was startling—she became regal and was very impressive. Without even opening her mouth, she looked like a self-confident, interesting speaker.[19]

Poet Brod Bagert of New Orleans, Louisiana, uses expansive gestures that are appropriate for his passionate renditions of poetry for kindergarten students.

Some speeches call for lots of gestures; some call for little or none. If you were describing your battle to catch a huge fish, you would find your hands and arms constantly in motion; if you were giving a funeral eulogy, you might not make any gestures at all.

SpeechMate CD-ROM

To see a speaker who uses gestures well, view Speech 5 ("How to Hide Valuables") on Disk 1.

Most gestures should occur naturally and not be planned, but there are a few occasions when it is appropriate to plan and rehearse them. If you have three major points to make, you can practice holding up the correct number of fingers to assist the audience in following your points. If you are discussing two contrasting ideas, you can hold up your left hand when you say, "On the one hand . . ." and then hold up your right hand when you say, "On the other hand . . ."

The larger the audience, the more sweeping your gestures should be. Evangelists and political leaders who use broad, expansive arm movements in addressing multitudes in giant stadiums are doing so for a good reason: They are able to establish a bond with people who are hundreds of yards away. Small gestures would be lost in the vastness of the arena.

One last comment about gestures: If you are the kind of person who simply does not gesture much, don't worry about it. You have got enough on your mind without having to add this item to your list of worries. Just be sure to keep your hands free (not clutching notes or the lectern), so that if a gesture wells up inside you and cries out for expression, you will be able to make it naturally and forcefully.

Beginning and Ending

First impressions are important in many human events. The first impression we make on a person at a party, for example, often determines whether that person will want to spend much time chatting with us. In a speech, as one IBM executive told me, "You have only one chance to make a first impression." You make this first impression as you walk to the front and as you say your first few sentences.

Tips for your CAREER

Tip 14.2 Deal with Distractions in a Direct but Good-Humored Manner

In classroom speeches you will have an attentive, courteous audience, but at some point in your career, you may encounter an audience that contains a few rude listeners who chat among themselves while you are trying to speak, thus causing a distraction for other listeners.

Professional speakers stress that you should *not* ignore the disturbance that the rude listeners are creating. Confront these listeners, but do so in a calm, friendly, good-humored manner.

One technique is to simply stop your speech and look directly at the rude listeners (try to look friendly and not irritated). This nonverbal nudge is often all it takes to cause the persons to stop talking. Sometimes people sitting near the offenders will pick up on your cue and help you out by turning and saying, "shh."

Professional speaker Rosita Perez of Brandon, Florida, says that you may lose the respect of your entire audience if you ignore the talkative few. "Confront them *kindly,*" she advises. "Say, 'It seems to me you must have a lot of catching up to do with your friends. I wonder if you would visit outside so I can continue?'" In most such cases, the listeners will stay in the room and give the speaker respectful silence for the rest of the speech.

Speech consultant Sandy Linver says that with a large audience,

> I take the trouble to gently zero in on . . . the chatterers and pull them back in. I say something like, "Are you with me?" . . . If it's a small group, side conversations often are important to the subject at hand, so it is important not to ignore them. If I were speaking at a business meeting of 15 people or so, I might say to the 3 people talking among themselves, "That looks as if it might be important. Would you like to share it with the group?" Often they are discussing something I have said that needs clarification or elaboration, and the whole group benefits when they are encouraged to speak up.

Some speeches are marred by the incessant crying of a baby. Even though members of the audience turn and give annoyed, disapproving looks, the parents of the baby sometimes refuse to take the infant out of the room. Actor and orator Steve Allen once handled this situation by saying, "As the father of four sons I've more than once been in the position of the parents of that child. Personally I could go on even if there were several children crying at the same time, but I know that most people are too distracted by that sort of thing to concentrate on what is being said. So if you wouldn't mind taking the child out—at least until he stops crying—I'm sure the rest of our audience would appreciate it." This remark, says Allen, prompted applause from the audience and "gracious cooperation from the parents."

Katie Aldrich cradles her six-month-old son Eric as she takes part in commencement exercises at Duke University. Babies are often brought to speeches. What should a speaker do if a baby starts crying?

When you rise from your seat, avoid sighing, groaning, or mumbling words of regret. Walk forward with an air of confidence—don't shamble like a condemned prisoner en route to the guillotine.

Avoid the mistake of rushing forward and starting to speak even before you get to the front. Listeners need time to get settled, so that they can clear their minds of other things and tune in to you.

When you face your audience, pause a few seconds before speaking. Don't say a word—just stand in silence. Some inexperienced speakers are terrified by this silence; they view it as a horrible event that makes the audience think they are too frozen with fear to speak. If you have this concern, relax. A brief period of silence is a very effective technique that all good speakers use. It is a punctuation device, separating what went before from what is to come—your speech. It creates drama, giving the audience a sense of expectancy. It is a dignified quietness that establishes your confidence and authority. In some cases, you may need to wait longer than a few seconds. If you are speaking to a civic club, for example, and a large number of people are arriving late, it is best to wait until the noise created by the latecomers has settled down. Or if many members of the audience are still whispering comments related to the previous speaker, simply stand and wait until you have their attention.

During these opening moments of silence, you have a chance to make sure your notes are in order and to review once again what you will say in your introduction. The next step is very important. Before you say a word, give your audience a friendly, confident look (if possible and appropriate, smile) and then, continuing to look at your listeners instead of at your notes, say your first few sentences. You should have practiced your introduction thoroughly, so that you can say it without looking down at your notes. It is important to establish eye contact at this point. By looking at the listeners directly, your body language is saying, "I'm talking to you—I'm not up here just going through the motions of making a speech. I want to communicate. I want to reach out to you."

While first impressions are vital, final impressions are also important. Your conclusion should be well rehearsed (though not memorized), so that you can say it without looking at your notes. At the end of your speech, pause a few moments, look at your audience, and say, "I wonder what questions you have" or "I'll be happy to answer your questions now." Avoid gathering up your papers and leaning toward your seat—this sends a nonverbal message: "Please don't ask me any questions."

The Question-and-Answer Period

SpeechMate CD-ROM

To see a speaker conducting a question-and-answer period, view Anne M. Mulcahy's speech on Disk 2.

The question-and-answer period is an important way for listeners to get clarification and further information. In classroom speeches, it usually represents a small percentage of the total time spent in front of the audience, but in some presentations in business, professional, and technical fields, it is *the* most important part.[20] Your speech is just a prelude—in effect, a little warm-up to get the audience ready to ask their questions. In some sales presentations, for example, the speaker will talk for, say, 10 minutes and then the question-and-answer period will go on for over an hour, with the listeners getting down to the nitty-gritty ("Okay, you say this machine will never wear out, but what happens if . . .").

Many listeners are so accustomed to listener–speaker interaction that they will interrupt during a speech to ask questions. In some technical presentations or classroom lectures, such interruptions might be appropriate and acceptable, but in other speeches, they are a nuisance. The continuity of the speaker's remarks is broken because listeners are prematurely asking questions that will be answered later in the speech. If you feel that your speech would be marred by interruptions, you should announce (in the orienting material of your introduction), "I know many of you will have questions. I'd like to ask you to hold them until I finish my presentation and then I'll be happy to try to answer them."

Don't feel defeated if you are not asked any questions. It could mean that you have covered everything so well that the listeners truly have nothing to ask.

Here are some guidelines:

Planning

- Find out ahead of time if the person planning the program will want or permit a question-and-answer period, and, if so, how much time will be allotted.
- Decide in advance if you want to invite comments as well as questions. If you do, you can say, "I would like to hear your questions or comments." (In some situations, you may not want comments because they could mushroom into long-winded rebuttals that detract from your message and leave no time for short, clarifying questions.)
- Plan for the question-and-answer period as carefully as you plan for the speech itself. Jot down all the questions that might come from the audience, and then decide exactly how you will answer them if they are asked. Tom Kirby, a St. Petersburg, Florida, executive, recommends that you ask an associate to prepare a list of questions based on your talk, thus giving you a realistic preview of the questions you may be asked by your listeners.[21]
- Try to regard the question-and-answer period as a blessing, not a curse. It gives you valuable feedback—it helps ensure that the message you intended the listeners to receive is indeed the one they end up with. If a misunderstanding has occurred, you have an excellent opportunity to clear it up.

Fielding Questions

- Give the audience time to think of questions. Some speakers wind up their conclusion, hastily ask if there are any questions, impatiently wait three seconds, and then dash back to their seats. They don't really give the audience a fair chance. When you ask for questions, pause for as long as 10 seconds. If you get the feeling that no questions at all will be asked, you can say, "Thank you," and then sit down. But if you sense that the audience is simply shy (some listeners want to ask questions but are afraid that their question will be considered "dumb"), you may want to give them some encouragement. One way is to say, "While you're thinking of questions, let me answer one that a lot of people ask me . . ." In some community and career contexts, you may even want to involve the listeners by asking *them* a question; for example, "What do *you* think of my proposal?"

- While a person is asking a question, look directly at him or her, but as you give your answer, look at the entire audience, so that no one feels left out.
- In a large room, when a question is asked, repeat it for the benefit of listeners who may not have been able to hear it. Repeating it also gives you time to frame your answer. If a question is unclear to you, ask the listener to clarify it.
- Don't reward some questions with "That's a good question" or "I'm glad you asked that," because the questioners who receive no praise from you will feel as if their questions have been judged inferior.
- If you don't know the answer to a question, say so. Your listeners will not think less of you for an honest admission of ignorance on a particular point; they *will* think less of you if you try to fake expertise. In some situations, you may want to ask the audience for help: "I don't know the answer; can anyone help us out?"

Handling Problems

- If a listener points out a flaw in the logic of your argument or casts doubt on some of your facts and figures, try to avoid being defensive. If the listener's point seems to have merit, say so. You can say something like, "You've got a good point. I'm going to have to think about this some more." Or: "You may be right—that statistic could be outdated. I'll have to check it. Thanks for mentioning it." Not only is such a conciliatory approach honest, but it is also a good way to gain respect from the listeners. No one expects you to be perfect; if a listener finds an error in your speech, it does not mean that your whole effort has been discredited.
- Don't let one listener hog the question-and-answer period, especially if a number of other people have questions. If a person persists in asking one question after another or launches into a long monologue, don't hesitate to interrupt, saying, "Let's give others a chance to ask questions; if we have time later, I'll get back to you" or "Why don't you and I talk about this in greater detail after the meeting?"
- Decline to answer questions that are not appropriate for a discussion in front of the entire audience—for example, questions that are too personal or that require a long, technical explanation that most of the listeners would find boring and tedious. You can deflect such questions by politely explaining your reasons; for example, "That's a little too personal—I'd rather not go into that," or "I'm afraid it would take up too much time to go into the details right now." In some cases, you might tell the questioner to see you afterward for a one-on-one discussion.
- Don't let the question-and-answer period drag on interminably. If you have been allotted an hour, say, for both your speech and the Q & A period, end the session promptly at the end of an hour—even if some listeners still have questions. You should make a brief wrap-up

statement (such as "Thank you for letting me talk to you today about the need to have side air bags in all cars") and then sit down. If your speech is the last item on the program and you sense that some listeners would like to continue the question-and-answer period, you could say, "I'm going to end the formal part of my presentation now because I promised I would take up only one hour of your time and I know that some of you have other business to take care of. However, if any of you would like to stay, you can move to the seats here at the front and we'll continue with an informal question-and-answer period."

Practice

After you have written your outline and made notes based on it (as discussed in Chapter 12), you should spend a great deal of time rehearsing your speech. Practice, practice, practice—it's a crucial step that some inexperienced speakers leave out. Practice makes you look and sound fluent, smooth, and spontaneous. Practice bolsters your confidence, giving you a sense of mastery and competence.

Here are some tips:

- Start early. If you wait until the eve of your speech, you will not have enough time to develop and polish your delivery. Allow yourself at least four days of practice before your speech date.
- Practice going through your entire speech at least four times—or more, if necessary. Space your practice sessions; in other words, avoid doing most of your practicing on a single day. You will make greater progress if you have time intervals between practice sessions.
- "Practice ideas, not words" is a maxim worth heeding; in other words, learn your speech point by point, not word for word.[22] Remember that your goal in extemporaneous speaking is not to memorize or read a speech. Every time you say your speech (whether in practice or in delivery to an audience), the wording should be different. The ideas will be the same, but not the exact words.
- Time yourself during practice sessions. If your speech exceeds the time limit set by your instructor or by the group that invited you, go back to your outline and notes and trim them down.
- During most of your practice sessions, go all the way through the speech. Don't stop if you hit a problem; you can work it out later. Going all the way through helps you see whether your ideas fit together snugly, and whether your transitions from point to point are smooth.
- Some speakers find it helpful to practice in front of a mirror or to use a video camcorder or audiotape recorder. Whether or not you use one of these techniques, you should practice at least once in front of a *live* audience—friends or relatives who can give you a candid appraisal. As we discussed in Chapter 1, don't say, "Tell me how I do on this," because your evaluators will probably say, "Good job—I liked the speech," to avoid hurting your feelings. Instead give them a specific assignment: "Please note at least three positive things and at least three

www.mhhe.com/gregory7
Read the article "Can You Practice Too Much?" in the Supplementary Readings on this book's Website.

things that need improvement." Now your listeners have an assignment that they know will not hurt your feelings, and you are likely to get some helpful feedback.

- Some speakers find it helpful to make a trial run in the very room in which they will give the speech. This would be an especially good idea if you have visual aids and equipment; you can practice the mechanics, for example, of showing overhead transparencies.
- In addition to practicing the entire speech, devote special practice time to your beginning and ending—two parts that should be smooth and effective.
- Be sure that you don't put too many words on your notes. Have just the bare minimum necessary to jog your memory. Practice from the actual notes that you will use in the speech. Don't make a clean set right before the speech; the old, marked-up notes are more reliable because you're familiar with them from your practice sessions.

Resources for Review and Skill Building

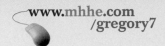

www.mhhe.com/gregory7

This book's Online Learning Center Website and SpeechMate CD-ROM provide meaningful resources and tools for study and review, such as practice tests, key-term flashcards, and sample speech videos.

SpeechMate CD-ROM

Summary

The key to good delivery is a strong desire to communicate with the audience. Speakers who concentrate on getting their ideas across to their listeners usually find themselves using good delivery techniques.

There are four methods of delivering a speech: memorization, manuscript, impromptu, and extemporaneous. Of the four, extemporaneous is the most popular and usually the most effective because the speaker delivers a well-prepared, well-rehearsed speech in a lively, conversational manner.

In delivering a speech, your voice should be loud enough for everyone to hear, your words should be spoken clearly so that they are easily understood, and your voice should be expressive so that you sound interesting and lively.

Nonverbal communication is the message you give with your body by means of personal appearance, eye contact, facial expressions, posture, movement, and gestures. All these elements should convey confidence and a positive regard for the audience. Of special importance is eye contact. You should look at your listeners during 95 percent of your speech to maintain a bond of communication and rapport with them and to monitor their feedback.

The question-and-answer period enables listeners to get clarification and further information. Anticipate what questions might be asked and prepare your answers accordingly. Try not to be defensive if you are challenged by a listener, and be prepared to say "I don't know" if you don't have an answer—in other words, don't try to fake expertise.

Practice is a vital part in the success of your speech. You should practice the entire speech over and over again—until you can deliver it with power and confidence.

Key Terms

articulation, *325*
extemporaneous method, *324*
impromptu method, *322*
intonation, *327*
manuscript method, *322*
nonverbal communication, *330*
pitch, *327*
posture, *334*
pronunciation, *326*
verbal fillers, *329*

Review Questions

1. What are the disadvantages of impromptu, manuscript, and memorized speeches?
2. What ingredient is essential for the success of an extemporaneous speech?
3. Why is it a serious mistake to speak too rapidly at the beginning of a speech?
4. What are the characteristics of good eye contact?
5. What can speakers do with their hands to make sure that they are free for gesturing?
6. Why should a speech be learned and practiced point by point, instead of word for word?
7. What form of visual aids can cause you to lose eye contact with your audience?
8. How many times should a speaker practice going through the entire speech?
9. How should you handle a listener who casts doubt on some of your facts and figures?
10. If there is a discrepancy between your words and your nonverbal behavior, which will the audience believe?

Building Critical-Thinking Skills

1. "If a man takes off his sunglasses, I can hear him better," says writer Hugh Prather. Explain the meaning of this statement in terms of public speaking.
2. Tennis coaches observe a phenomenon called "analysis equals paralysis." Players become so fixated on holding the racket correctly and swinging properly that they miss the ball. What lessons could public speakers draw from this phenomenon?

Building Teamwork Skills

1. In a group, create a list of six attributes of good delivery that are of utmost importance to group members when they are in an audience. Taking a vote, rank the attributes in order of importance. Then discuss why the top two attributes are more important than the others.
2. To practice impromptu speaking, members of a group should take turns playing the role of candidate in a job interview, while the rest of the group act as interviewers. Make the interview as realistic as possible, with serious questions and answers. After each candidate is interviewed, the group should give a brief critique of his or her verbal and nonverbal responses.

Building Internet Skills

www.mhhe.com/gregory7

1. On the Internet, you can find photos and video clips of people making gestures. Find a photo of a gesture that would be effective in a speech, print it, and write a one-paragraph summary of why you think the gesture seems to be effective.

Possible Strategy: Go to Lycos (www.multimedia.lycos.com), choose "Pictures" and search with the keyword "gesture."

2. Some speeches or performances are marred by cell phones ringing or people having cell phone conversations. Search the Internet to find three appropriate responses that speakers and performers have made in these situations.

Possible Strategy: Go to Google (www.google.com) and use these keywords: "cell phone rude audience."

Using PowerWeb

www.mhhe.com/gregory7

In "Do You Speak Body Language?" business executive Anne Warfield cites many instances of a person saying one thing with words while conveying the opposite nonverbally. Describe one such scenario. To find this article, visit www.mhhe.com/gregory7, click on STUDENT EDITION and then POWERWEB: CONTENTS.

Dr. Donna Brown, a psychiatrist in Little Rock, Arkansas, gives a presentation to educate the public about severe depression and suicide prevention. Dr. Brown believes that informative speaking is a vital part of her role in serving her community.

15

Speaking to Inform

Outline

Objectives

After studying this chapter, you should be able to:

1. Prepare an informative speech.
2. Identify four types of informative speeches.
3. Explain how to make information interesting and understandable.

One of the greatest heartbreaks for firefighters occurs when they fail to rescue a child from a burning building because the child—frightened by smoke and noise—hides under a bed or in a closet and is later found dead.

Saddest of all, sometimes children catch a glimpse of the masked firefighter but hide because they think they have seen a monster.

To prevent such tragedies, firefighter Eric Velez gives talks to children in his community, explaining why they should never hide during a fire. He displays firefighters' equipment, including the oxygen mask, which he encourages his listeners to play with and put on. "If you see us," Velez tells them, "don't hide. We are not monsters. We have come to rescue you."

Velez gives his presentations in English and Spanish. (Growing up in San Francisco, he learned Spanish from his immigrant parents: His mother is from Nicaragua, his father from Puerto Rico.)

Velez—and other firefighters throughout North America who give similar presentations—will never know how many lives they save through their talks, but it is a fact that informative speaking saves lives. For example, several months after his public speaking class, Pete Gentry of Swannanoa, North Carolina, rescued his

Left: When small children mistake a firefighter for a Darth Vader monster, a terrible tragedy can occur.
Below: During informative presentations, firefighter Eric Velez encourages children to play with and try on "scary" oxygen masks.

brother, who was choking on food, by using the Heimlich maneuver, which he had learned by listening to an informative speech delivered by student speaker Julie Parris.

In addition to saving lives, informative speakers help people learn new skills, solve problems, and acquire fascinating facts about the exciting world in which they live.

Your goals in informative speaking are to convey knowledge, create understanding, and help listeners remember important points. Your task is to be a teacher—not an advocate. To give facts—not opinions.

In this chapter we will look at four types of informative speeches and then discuss guidelines to help you create informative speeches that are clear, interesting, and memorable.

Types of Informative Speeches

SpeechMate CD-ROM

For samples, view Speech 2, 5, 6, or 7 on Disk 1 of the CD.

Informative speeches can be categorized in many different ways, but in this chapter we will concentrate on four of the most popular types: definition, description, process, and expository.

Definition Speech

Do you know what *synesthesia* is? Most people don't, so let me give you a dictionary definition: "a condition in which one type of stimulation evokes the sensation of another."

Still not sure what I'm talking about? Here are some elaborations.[1]

- Neurologist Richard Cytowič says that two people out of every million experience a mingling of senses so that they may taste a shape, hear a color, or see a sound. "Music, for example, is not just a sound and a melody, but it's like a visual fireworks that they see in front of them . . . rather than in the mind's eye."
- A woman named Kristen tastes words, and often the spelling affects the flavor. "Lori," for example, tastes like a pencil eraser, while "Laurie" tastes lemony.
- Persons who experience synesthesia, says Cytowič, are not crazy, but as children they often fear that they are, and they hide their sensitivity. Carol Steen, a New York artist, recalls, "When I was about 7, I was walking back from elementary school with a classmate, and we must have been learning how to write. I said that the letter 'A' was a wonderful shade of pink, and she was quiet, and then she looked at me and said, 'You're weird.' And I didn't say another word until I was 20."

extended definition a rich, full explanation of the meaning of a term

definition speech an oral presentation that gives an extended explanation of a concept

These examples and quotations constitute an **extended definition,** one that is richer and more meaningful than a dictionary explanation. That is what a **definition speech** is all about—giving an extended definition of a concept so that the listeners get a full, richly detailed picture of its meaning. While a dictionary definition would settle lightly on the listeners' brains and probably vanish overnight, an extended definition is likely to stick firmly. Here are some sample specific purpose statements for definition speeches:

- To define for my listeners the term *Luddite,* contrasting its 19th century origin with today's usage
- To explain to my audience the African-American spiritual holiday known as Kwanzaa
- To define for my listeners the spoils system in American politics
- To explain AI (artificial intelligence) to my audience

SpeechMate CD-ROM
For hundreds of sample topics, see the Topic Helper on Disk 1 of the CD.

Any of the support materials that we discussed in Chapter 8 (such as narratives, examples, vivid images, and statistics) can be applied to defining a topic. In a speech on iatrogenic injuries, Rosharna Hazel of Morgan State University in Maryland defined the term as "any injury caused by medical treatment" and then elaborated by giving two examples and some troubling statistics from a prestigious source.[2]

- Willie King of Baltimore was scheduled to have his right leg amputated below the knee, but during surgery, the surgeon incorrectly amputated his left leg instead.
- A woman named Martha entered a New York hospital to receive one of her last chemotherapy treatments in an apparently successful battle against cancer. She was given the wrong drug, however, and died a few days later.
- According to a study at Harvard University School of Public Health, "1.3 million Americans may suffer unexpected, disabling injuries in hospitals each year, and 198,000 may die as a result."

Sometimes the best way to define a topic is to compare or contrast it with a similar item. If you were trying to define what constitutes child abuse, for example, it would be helpful to contrast abuse with firm but loving discipline.

Description Speech

description speech an oral presentation that describes a person, place, object, or event

A **description speech** paints a vivid picture of a person, place, object, or event. As with all speeches, a description speech should make a point—and not be merely a list of facts or observations. Here are some specific purpose statements for description speeches:

- To describe to the audience the lift-off of a spaceship
- To describe to my listeners a typical FBI sting operation
- To inform my audience about working conditions in the emergency room of a major hospital
- To describe to my audience the highlights of the life of civil rights leader Rosa Parks

If you were describing an object or place, you might want to use the *spatial* pattern of organization. Here is an example of the spatial pattern as used in an outline describing New Zealand. The speaker travels from south to north.

Specific Purpose: To describe to my listeners the geographical variety of New Zealand

Central Idea: The two-island nation of New Zealand has more scenic variety than any other country on earth.

Main Points:

I. The South Island—colder because it is closer to the South Pole—reminds visitors of Norway.

- A. The Southern Alps, with snowcapped peaks over 10,000 feet, extend the entire length of the island.
- B. Fjords, streams, and lakes are unspoiled and breath takingly beautiful.

II. The North Island is like a compact version of the best of Europe and Asia.

- A. The cities suggest the elegance of Italy.
- B. The mountains and vineyards remind one of France.
- C. Active volcanoes look like those found in the Philippines.
- D. In the northernmost parts, the beaches and lush, tropical forests seem like Hawaii.

SpeechMate CD-ROM

For help in outlining your material, use the computerized Outline Tutor on Disk 1 of the CD.

Describing a person, living or dead, can make a fascinating speech. You might want to use the *chronological* pattern; in a speech on United Farm Workers co-founder Dolores Huerta, for example, you could discuss the major events of her life in the order in which they occurred. Or you might prefer to use the *topical* pattern, emphasizing three major features of Huerta's career:

Specific Purpose: To describe to my audience the life and accomplishments of Dolores Huerta

Central Idea: Dolores Huerta is one of the most influential labor leaders in United States history.

Main Points:

I. As co-founder of the United Farm Workers union, Huerta struggled to improve working conditions for migrant farm workers.

II. She is credited with introducing to the United States the idea of boycotting as a nonviolent tactic.

III. Though Huerta practiced nonviolence, she endured much suffering.

- A. She was arrested more than 20 times.
- B. In 1988 she was nearly killed by baton-swinging police officers who smashed two ribs and ruptured her spleen.

Process Speech

process speech
an oral presentation that analyzes how to do something or how something works

In a **process speech,** you are concerned with explaining the steps or stages by which something is done or made. There are two kinds of process speeches. In the first kind, you show the listeners how to *perform* a process so that they can actually use the skills later (this is sometimes called a *demonstration* speech). Here are some examples of specific purpose statements for this kind of speech:

- To teach my listeners how to remove a stain from clothing
- To demonstrate to my audience how to jump-start a car
- To show my audience how to stock and maintain a seawater aquarium
- To demonstrate to my listeners how to treat a bee sting

SpeechMate CD-ROM
For a sample demonstration speech, view Speech 5 ("How to Hide Valuables") on Disk 1 of the CD.

In the second kind of process speech, you provide information on "how something is done" or "how something works." Your goal is to *explain* a process so that the listeners understand the process, not necessarily so that they can perform it themselves. For example, let's say that you outline the steps by which counterfeiters print bogus money. You are showing these steps to satisfy the listeners' intellectual curiosity and also to teach them how to spot a counterfeit bill, not so that they can perform the job themselves. Here are some samples of specific purpose statements for this kind of speech:

- To explain to my audience how seeing-eye (or guide) dogs are trained
- To explain to my listeners how surgeons perform bloodless operations with laser beams
- To explain to my listeners how the ancient sculptors of Easter Island created their gigantic statues
- To explain to my listeners how astronomers discover unknown planets

Here are some guidelines for preparing a process speech.

1. Be sure to include all steps, even obvious ones. A lawyer bought a huge aquarium for his new office and then went out and spent hundreds of dollars at a pet shop for an assortment of exotic tropical fish. He returned to his office, filled the aquarium with water, and dumped the fish in. When all the fish died, he called the pet shop and found out why. The directions for the aquarium had neglected to mention that tap water must sit 24 hours before fish are added so that all the chlorine can evaporate. Otherwise, the fish will die of chlorine poisoning. Whoever wrote the directions for the aquarium probably assumed that any fish lover would know this fact, but that assumption was a mistake.

Don't omit obvious information that you assume "everyone knows." Give *all* steps, even ones that are simple and self-evident. What seems obvious to you may not be obvious to some listeners.

2. Use visual aids whenever possible. Because processes are often complicated, use visual aids, if at all possible, to help listeners understand and retain your points. One of the most effective visual aids is the demonstration, wherein you actually perform the process while talking about it. For example, if you wanted to teach cardiopulmonary resuscitation (CPR), you could demonstrate the steps on a dummy while you go through your explanations.

Use videotape for steps that are impossible to illustrate in the room where you are speaking. In a talk on making pottery, one speaker demonstrated as many steps as she could, and then used video to show the rest of the steps—firing an object in a kiln, applying glaze, and so on.

3. Involve the audience in physical activity whenever possible. If you involve the audience in a physical activity, you capitalize on more than just the listeners' sense of hearing and seeing; you also bring in touch and movement. There is an ancient Chinese proverb that says:

- I hear—and I forget.
- I see—and I remember.
- I do—and I understand.

The wisdom of this saying has been confirmed by psychologists, who have found that of the three main channels for learning new information, the auditory is weakest, the visual is stronger, and physical action is strongest of all. The best approach is to bring all three together. For example, if you were explaining how to do stretching exercises, you could explain the techniques (auditory) as you give a demonstration (visual); then you could have each listener stand and perform the exercises (physical action). Some audience involvement can be accomplished while the listeners remain in their chairs; for example, if you are speaking on sign language, you could have the listeners practice the hand signals as you teach them.

Note of caution: Get your instructor's approval before you incorporate any physical activity into a classroom speech. When you give a talk in the community beyond the college campus, use your best judgment. Make sure that you don't ask listeners to do something that would be embarrassing or awkward for some of them. If, for example, there were people with disabilities in the audience, would they be able to perform the task?

4. Proceed slowly. Always bear in mind that much of what you say may be new to the listeners. If you are giving instruction about how to make leather belts, for example, you might be describing activities that are so easy for you that you could perform them blindfolded, but they may be completely foreign to some members of the audience. That's why you should talk slowly and repeat key ideas if necessary. Give listeners ample time to absorb your points and form mental images.

5. Give warning of difficult steps. When you are ready to discuss especially difficult steps, use transitions to give the listeners a warning. For example, "The next step is a little tricky." Or: "This next step is the hardest one of all." This alerts the listeners that they need to pay extra special attention.

Sample Process Speech

Student speaker Marcus Brown presented a process speech on how to identify a poisonous plant.[3] As Brown explained his steps, he pointed to a PowerPoint slide (Figure 15.1).

How to Identify Poison Ivy

A few summers ago, I was on a backpacking trip in the mountains. At the end of our first day, we stopped to set up camp for the night, and I gathered firewood for our campfire. I must have brushed against poison ivy because the next morning my arms erupted with a horrible

Figure 15.1
This PowerPoint slide shows a poison ivy cluster, with its three leaflets always displayed in a distinctive pattern.

rash and blisters. My skin was burning and itching. It took me four weeks to get over the misery.

Poison ivy is the single most common cause of allergic reactions in the United States, according to the expert I consulted for this speech: Nina Gillespie, a botanist with the U.S. Department of Agriculture. Do you know how to identify poison ivy? Dr. Gillespie says that you can't identify it with a quick glance because it looks like many other plants, and its leaflets can have variations in shape, color, and texture. For example, they can be either shiny or dull, and they can be either dark green or light green.

Is there any hope, then, of identifying the villain? Yes, there are three steps that you can follow in order to be sure that you're looking at poison ivy.

First, see if the plant has clusters of leaves, with each cluster having just three leaflets. Poison ivy always comes in three-part "packages." As the old folk rhyme says, "Leaves of three/Let them be."

Second, see if there is just one leaflet at the very end of each cluster's stalk. We'll call this the end leaflet. It is always on a stalk that is longer than the stalks of the two lower leaflets. If you don't see a single leaflet at the end of the stalk, you're not looking at poison ivy.

Now, for the third step: Look below the end leaflet and see if there are two leaflets that are opposite each other. See if they have very short stalks. All poison ivy plants have the two lower leaflets. They are always opposite and they always have short stalks.

If the plant in front of you meets all of these conditions, there is no doubt about it: You are looking smack-dab at poison ivy. Let's review the steps: First, see if the cluster has just three leaflets. Second, see if the end leaflet is by itself at the end of a long stalk. Third, see if the two lower leaflets are opposite each other on short stalks.

If you verify that you are looking at poison ivy, I hope you know the next thing you should do: Back away and don't go near the stuff. I can tell you for a fact: If you give it a chance, it will eat you alive.

Expository Speech

expository speech
an oral report that explains a concept or situation

An **expository speech** (also called an oral report or lecture) involves explaining a concept or situation to the audience. For this speech, your instructor may want you to choose a topic with which you are not thoroughly familiar and then conduct research to gain command of the subject.

The expository speech may contain many features of the definition, descriptive, or process speeches. For example, if you chose to speak on how the bail system works, you would be explaining a process. What makes the expository speech different from the other types is that you must conduct in-depth research, using books, articles, and interviews, rather than relying on your own experiences.

Here are examples of specific purpose statements for expository speeches:

- To explain to my listeners recent findings about the intelligence of dolphins
- To inform my audience of the nature and scope of drug testing in the workplace
- To explain to my listeners how a consumer can use small claims court
- To report to the audience on the causes and impact of the internment of Japanese Americans during World War II
- To inform my audience on how DNA evidence is used in the courtroom today

SpeechMate CD-ROM
To see an informative speech in a career setting, view Anne M. Mulcahy's speech on Disk 2 of the CD.

Expository speeches are often organized in the *topical* pattern. As we saw in Chapter 10, you use the topical pattern to subdivide a central idea into main points, using logic and common sense as your guides. Here is an outline for an expository speech that uses the topical pattern:

Specific Purpose: To inform my audience about the dangers of quicksand

Central Idea: Found in almost every state of the United States, quicksand is a terrifying natural trap from which people can extricate themselves if they follow the correct steps.

Main Points:

I. Quicksand is as treacherous as the movies depict it.
   A. It has swallowed people.
   B. It has swallowed cars and trucks.

II. Quicksand is deceptive.
   A. The surface can appear as solid as the surrounding terrain.
   B. Underneath the surface is a sandy brew that is formed by water flowing upward from hidden springs.

III. If you step into quicksand, you can follow four easy steps that will save your life.
   A. Get rid of extra weight such as a backpack or coat.

B. Throw yourself flat on your back and "float."
C. Press your arms out onto the surface of the quicksand.
D. Moving with snail-like slowness, roll your way to firm ground.

Notice that this outline contains elements of description (point I), definition (point II), and process (point III).

Another pattern is the *fallacy–fact* pattern, which can also be called *myth–reality*. In this pattern, the speaker cites popular fallacies and then presents facts that refute them. Student speaker Bob Metzger used this pattern to refute three popular misconceptions about nutrition:

Specific Purpose: To give my audience accurate information to overcome three common misconceptions about nutrition

Central Idea: Eggs, spicy foods, and frozen vegetables do not deserve their bad nutritional reputation.

Main Points:

(Fallacy) I. "Eggs are bad for you" is a fallacy.
(Facts) A. Eggs get a "bad rap" because they are high in cholesterol, but what's important is the level of cholesterol in the blood, not in the food.
B. Saturated fat is what causes high cholesterol levels in the blood.
C. Eggs are low in saturated fat, so they do not make a significant contribution to high cholesterol levels in the blood.

(Fallacy) II. "Spicy food is bad for the stomach" is a fallacy.
(Facts) A. Medical studies of healthy persons who eat spice-rich Mexican and Indian foods found no damage or irritation in the protective lining of the stomach.
B. In a medical experiment in India, the stomach ulcers of patients who were fed spicy foods healed at the same rate as those of patients who were fed a bland diet.

(Fallacy) III. "Frozen vegetables are not as nutritious as fresh" is a fallacy.
(Facts) A. Quick freezing preserves all nutrients.
B. In fact, if fresh vegetables have been sitting on the produce aisle for too long, frozen vegetables are better.

Guidelines for Informative Speaking

In informative speaking, strive to make your message clear, interesting, and memorable. You can achieve this goal by applying the principles that we have covered so far in this book, plus the guidelines below.

Relate the Speech to the Listeners' Self-Interest

SpeechMate CD-ROM

To see a speaker relate a speech to the listeners' self-interest, view video clip 15.1 on Disk 1 of the CD.

Many listeners approach a speech with an attitude of: "Why should I care? Why should I pay attention? What's in it for me?" The best motivator in a speech, therefore, is something that has an impact on their lives.[4]

Let's say you are planning to give a process speech showing listeners how to clean their computers. How do you think your listeners will react when they discover what your topic is?

"B-o-r-ing!" they will probably say to themselves. "Why should I pay attention to this stuff?"

Your best strategy, therefore, is to appeal to their self-interest:

> Imagine you sit at your computer all weekend working on a big research paper. You are almost through when suddenly your computer fails. Not only does it fail, but it deletes your entire report. To make matters worse, the technician who repairs your computer charges you $250.
>
> This could happen to you if you don't clean and maintain your computer. Today I'd like to show you some easy steps you can take to safe guard your computer files and avoid repair bills.

Now your listeners see that your information can have an impact on their own lives. They should perk up and listen carefully.

Make Information Interesting

The most important element in an effective speech, says nationally known TV and radio reporter Nina Totenberg, is "interesting information."[5]

Many speeches are boring because the speakers deal primarily with *generalities,* which tend to be dull and vague. To make a speech lively, use generalities sparingly, and each time a generality is offered, follow it with lots of *specifics,* such as examples and ancedotes. Here is an example of a generalized statement, given by student speaker Carol Chen:

> Referees and umpires are being subjected to an increasing amount of violence during and after sports events.

To make this fact interesting to the audience, Chen gave verbal "snapshots" of typical incidents throughout the United States:

- Last January, after Referee Bob West disqualified a high school wrestler in Spokane, Washington, for an illegal mount, the 17-year-old athlete head-butted West so hard that the official was knocked unconscious.
- Last summer a group of teenage baseball players in Loveland, Texas, who had just been ejected from a recreation league game, attacked the umpire on the field; he suffered bruised ribs and needed four stitches to close the gash in his mouth.
- And in Philadelphia, a 6′4″ high school basketball star punched a 5′7″ referee who had just ejected him from a game.

Tips for your CAREER

Tip 15.1 For Long Presentations, Plan a Variety of Activities

Your boss asks you to conduct a three-hour workshop, scheduled for a Friday afternoon, to explain important procedures to a group of new employees. What do you do? Do you spend the entire three hours talking? No, not unless you want to put the group to sleep.

For long presentations, provide a variety of activities to keep your audience awake and attentive. Here are some suggested activities:

1. Invite audience participation.

At various intervals, or even throughout the entire presentation, encourage listeners to ask questions or make comments. By letting them take an active role, instead of sitting passively for three hours, you invigorate them and prevent them from daydreaming.

2. Use visual aids whenever possible.

Visuals provide variety and sparkle, and they can clarify and reinforce key points.

3. Give coffee or "stretch" breaks at various intervals.

A good rule of thumb for marathon sessions is to give a 15-minute break after every 45-minute period, even if the audience does not seem tired. In other words, don't wait until fatigue sets in. If you wait until the audience is nodding, you might lose their interest for the rest of the day. When you give a break, always announce the time for reassembly; when that time arrives, politely but firmly remind any stragglers that it is time to return to their seats. If you don't remind them, you will find that a 15-minute coffee break can stretch to 30 minutes.

4. Call on people at random.

If your presentation is in the form of a lecture, you can use the teachers' technique of calling on people at random to answer questions. This causes every listener to perk up because he or she is thinking, "I'd better pay attention because my name might be called next, and I don't want to be caught daydreaming." Call the person's name *after* you ask the question. (If you call the name before the question, everyone in the audience except the designated person might breathe a sigh of relief and fail to pay close attention to the question.)

5. Encourage listeners to take notes.

Some speakers pass out complimentary pens and pads at the beginning of their presentations in the hope that the listeners will use them to write down key points. There is, of course, a side benefit: Taking notes helps the listeners to stay alert and listen intelligently.

After hearing these examples, the audience would want to know why the assaults had become so frequent, so Chen explained:

> *The New York Times* speculates that young athletes see incidents on TV in which highly paid professional athletes verbally or physically abuse an official. What happens to them? They get only a mild reprimand or a minor fine. This encourages kids to imitate their heroes.

Note of caution: Give details, but not too many. You don't want to bore your audience with a tedious overload. "The secret of being tiresome," the French philosopher Voltaire said, "is in telling everything." Edit your material: Instead of giving all 14 examples that you have compiled for a point, cite just two or three.

Assess the Knowledge of Listeners

Analyze your listeners thoroughly before a speech (as discussed in Chapter 4) to find out what they know and what they don't know. This will keep you from committing two common mistakes.

1. Don't present information that the audience already knows. "One of the biggest time wasters in my life," says bank executive Ruth Johnson-Boggs, "is going to presentations and not hearing one single thing that I and everybody else in the room didn't already know."

To avoid making this mistake when she is a speaker, Johnson-Boggs says, she interviews several people who will be in the audience to make sure she is meeting their needs. "I always ask, 'What can I cover that will help you and not be a waste of your time?'"[6]

2. Don't talk over listeners' heads. Avoid using words, concepts, and allusions that the audience doesn't understand. It is easy to commit this mistake if you assume that your listeners possess a common body of information.[7] Recent polls have shown that many Americans lack the "common knowledge" that earlier generations possessed. Here are some examples:

- One in seven adult Americans can't find the United States on a world map.[8]
- Americans in the 18 to 29 age bracket were asked by the Gallup Poll to identify the nationality of famous historical figures. Surprisingly, 66 percent could not link Winston Churchill with England (or Great Britain), 49 percent failed to identify Napoleon Bonaparte with France, 37 percent were unable to tie Indira Gandhi to India, and 21 percent could not match Adolf Hitler to Germany.[9]
- The National Science Foundation found that 25 percent of adult Americans did not know that light travels faster than sound.[10]
- One-third of adults did not know which countries the United States fought in World War II.[11]

If you find out in advance what your audience doesn't know, you can define words or explain concepts whenever necessary. You can give background information and examples.

What should you do when your audience is mixed—that is, some know certain concepts already and some don't? How can you give explanations in a way that does not insult the intelligence of the listeners who already know the material? In some cases, you can give information in a casual, unobtrusive way. For example, let's say you are planning in your speech to cite a quotation by Adolf Hitler. Most college students know who Hitler was, but some do not. To inform the latter without insulting the intelligence of the former, you can say something like this: "In the 1920s, long before Adolf Hitler rose to power in Germany and long before he launched the German nation into World War II, he made the following prophetic statement . . ." An indirect approach like this permits you to sneak in a lot of background information.

In other cases, you may need to be straightforward in giving definitions or explanations. For example, if you need to define *recession* for a speech on economic cycles, do so directly and clearly. Knowledgeable listeners will not be offended by a quick definition as long as most of your speech supplies them with new material; in fact, they probably will welcome a chance to confirm the accuracy of their own understanding of the term.

Use the Familiar to Explain the Unfamiliar

When an Israeli leader toured the United States to drum up support for increased military aid to Israel, Dorothy Sarnoff, an American consultant, was hired to help him prepare his speeches. She gave him the following advice:

> If you describe Israel at its narrowest point by saying, "Israel is so narrow that we can be [easily] attacked," the Americans won't get it . . . Instead say, "Israel is so narrow that if you were driving on a[n] [American-style] highway, it would take you only twenty minutes to get from one side of Israel to the other."[12]

Sarnoff's advice was sound. When you want to explain or describe something that is unfamiliar to your audience, relate it to something that is familiar. Use comparisons, contrasts, and analogies. If, for example, you point out that divers in Acapulco, Mexico, astound tourists by diving into water from rocks 118 feet high, that statistic does not have much impact, unless you point out that a 118-foot plunge is equal to a dive from the roof of an 11-story building.

Similarly, to give listeners a mental picture of what the inside of a tornado is like, Dale Higgins said: "A tornado's funnel is like the vortex you see when you let water go down a drain." Since everyone has seen the swirling action of water going down a drain, the comparison helped the audience visualize a tornado's vortex.

Sample Informative Speech

Student speaker Julia Weber prepared and delivered a speech on getting a dream job. The outline is presented first, followed by a transcript of the actual speech.[13]

The Outline with Commentary

Commentary	**Finding Your Dream Job**
	General Purpose: To inform
	Specific Purpose To inform my listeners about what they need to consider in looking for a dream job
	Central Idea: To find your dream job, you should explore your passions, ask for help, and be realistic.
	INTRODUCTION
Weber grabs listeners' attention by describing one man's dream job.	**I.** Attention Material A. My cousin Michael has a dream job—car-swapper. 1. He works for a Ford dealership in the St. Louis area.

2. Suppose a customer wants a Thunderbird with certain features.
3. If it's not on the lot, the salespeople will call other cities until they find a dealer who has it and is willing to swap.
4. Michael will drive a new car to, say, Tulsa, Oklahoma, and return with the Thunderbird that the customer in St. Louis wants.

B. For Michael, this is a dream job.

The speaker doesn't just assume that the audience will know why the job is considered a dream job. She explains Michael's motivations.

1. He loves new cars.
2. He loves to travel.
3. "I can't believe I get paid for having so much fun."

II. Orienting Material

A. I, too, would like a dream job, so I investigated how to succeed in finding one.

She reveals why she chose her topic.

B. I found three key pieces of advice: You should explore your passions, ask for help, and be realistic.

Weber's central idea gives the audience a preview of the three main points in the body of the speech.

(*Transition:* Let's look at the details.)

BODY

I. Explore your passions. (Show first bullet on slide.) [See Figure 15.2.]

The speaker uses the build technique, showing bullet points, one at a time, until all the points fill the screen.

A. "Follow up on your enthusiasms," says Lisa Sugimoto of San Francisco, who has her dream job—chef.

The speaker gains credibility by citing the advice of a chef who has already found a dream job.

1. If you love to explore medical mysteries, consider a job in a medical laboratory. (Show photo.) [See Figure 15.3]
2. If you love to travel, consider being a tour guide. (Show photo.) [See Figure 15.4]
3. If you love growing food, consider a job in agriculture. (Show photo.) [See Figure 15.5]

B. Make a list of all your fantasies about future jobs. (Sugimoto)

On her outline, Weber puts the name of her source in parentheses at the end of a sentence. In the actual speech, she will weave the source name into the fabric of her remarks.

C. Don't forget hobbies—they can lead to good jobs. (Sugimoto)

1. One man performed magic tricks for his friends when he was a teenager.
2. He made money as a part-time magician in college.

Examples are effective ways to illustrate a point.

3. After graduation, he became a full-time magician, performing for birthday parties and other events.

D. Don't aim for the best-paying job, but one that you love. (Wall Street Journal)

1. Stockbroker Tim Barnes disliked his work and wanted to be a teacher.
2. He left Wall Street to teach social studies and English at New York's Academy of Environmental Science in Harlem.
3. Motivating seventh graders, he says, is more rewarding than being a stockbroker, even if the pay is less.

Note that throughout her speech, Weber mentions a variety of fields, thereby showing that her ideas are not limited to a few narrow professions.

(*Transition:* Let's turn to the second piece of advice.)

II. Ask for help. (Show second bullet on slide.) [See Figure 15.2.]

A. It's hard to analyze yourself.

1. Ask relatives and friends what they think you have a knack for.
2. Sometimes they can see possibilities that you would never think of.

B. One young woman liked to attend the weddings of friends and relatives. (Tonya Edwards, a career counselor)

1. She was also skilled at planning events.
2. When she helped organize a friend's wedding, an older woman said, "You know, you ought to think about becoming a wedding planner."
3. She had never considered it, but suddenly it seemed like the obvious career choice.
4. Now she is a successful wedding planner and she adores her job.

For each piece of advice that she reports, Weber gives an example or a story so that the audience will have a full understanding.

C. When you decide the kind of job you want, ask friends, relatives, classmates, and former co-workers to keep an eye out for you.

1. Accountant Tracy Patton loved bookkeeping, but couldn't work outside her home because she had to care for her disabled husband. (Wall Street Journal)
2. She asked friends to let her know if they heard of any accounting jobs that could be done at home.
3. One friend was at a dinner party and chatted with a man who happened to need a bookkeeper for his landscaping business.
4. Patton was alerted and she got the job, which permitted her to use her computer at home for the bookkeeping.

Weber wrote this outline in complete sentences and then used the outline to create brief notes. When she delivered the actual speech, she used only her notes. If you look at the transcript of her speech (immediately following the outline), you will see that she followed the basic ideas of her outline, but she used more words and sometimes slightly different phrasing. As explained in earlier chapters, this is an effective approach because it enables you to organize your material intelligently, while avoiding the mistake of reading a script.

D. On the Internet, join discussion groups in your fields of interest.

1. This way, you can communicate with people who already have the kind of job you want.
2. Ask about the good points and bad points of the job.
3. Ask for information about how you can break into the field.

(*Transition:* Now let's examine the third piece of advice.)

III. Be realistic. (Show third bullet on slide.) [See Figure 15.2.]

Instead of sugarcoating her subject matter, Weber gives candid warnings about the downside of job fantasies. This approach shows her honesty and her respect for her audience.

A. You should be realistic about your talents. (Wall Street Journal)

1. Don't fantasize about being a drummer in a rock band if you have no musical aptitude.
2. You need to look for a job that matches who you really are.

B. You should be realistic about your personality. (Wall Street Journal)

For this speech, The Wall Street Journal is a good source to cite because most people know that it is highly respected and considered trustworthy in the business world.

1. You fantasize about being an investigative TV reporter, but does the job fit your personality?
   a. If you are shy and introverted, you don't have the right temperament.
   b. A TV reporter must be brash and aggressive.
2. If you like to work alone, a computer job might be right for you.
3. If you need to constantly interact with other people, you might like to work as a teacher, health professional, or salesperson.

C. Be realistic about the negatives of a dream job.

1. No job is thrilling and rewarding all the time.
2. Even my cousin Michael, the car-swapper, admits a downside: he is tired of eating at fast-food restaurants along the highways.

Weber points out that even the subject of her glowing opener has at least one complaint about his job.

(*Transition:* Let me summarize)

CONCLUSION

I. Summary

A. In finding your dream job, explore your passions and make a list of what you have a knack for.

The speaker gives a brief summary of the key information of the speech.

B. Ask other people to help you spot good jobs that you are likely to enjoy.

C. Chase your dreams, but at the same time be realistic about whether a potential job matches your talents and personality.

II. Clincher

A. I hope that all of us can someday find the job of our dreams.

Weber closes with a delightful illustration, which she relates with a light touch.

B. Perhaps we can be as lucky as Arnold Carbone, who works for Ben & Jerry's as an ice-cream taster.

C. He tastes and evaluates more than 100 ideas for new ice-cream flavors every year.

D. Now that's a dream job!

BIBLIOGRAPHY

These entries use the MLA style, one of two styles shown in Table 6.4 in Chapter 6.

Edwards, Tonya, career counselor. Personal interview. 5 Aug. 2003.

Lee, Tony. "Strategies for Making Your Dream Job a Reality." Wall Street Journal Online. Retrieved 5 Sept. 2003 <http://www.careerjournal.com>.

Schiff, Nancy Rica. Odd Jobs: Portraits of Unusual Occupations. Berkeley, CA: Ten Speed Press, 2002.

Sugimoto, Lisa, chef in San Francisco. E-mail interview. 6 Aug. 2003.

Weber, Michael, car-swapper. Personal interview. 18 Aug. 2003.

E-mail is a convenient way to interview knowledgeable people in all parts of the world.

VISUAL AIDS

The visual aids are shown in Figures 15.2, 15.3, 15.4, and 15.5.

PowerPoint slide showing three main points

Three PowerPoint slides containing photos of various jobs

The Speech as Delivered

Here is a transcript of the speech as it was delivered by Julia Weber.

Finding Your Dream Job

My cousin Michael has what he considers a dream job. He's a car-swapper. Do you know what that means? Let me explain.

Michael works for one of the biggest Ford dealerships in the St. Louis area. Let's say a woman comes in and wants a red Thunderbird with certain interior features. The salespeople don't have it on the lot, so they call around the country until they find a dealer who does have it. Then they arrange a swap. For example, Michael may drive a new car to Tulsa, Oklahoma, and return with the Thunderbird that the woman in St. Louis wants.

This is Michael's dream job because he loves new cars and he loves to travel. He says, "I can't believe I get paid for having so much fun."

I would like to be like Michael and someday find my own dream job. So I investigated how to go about finding one. This morning I want to share the key advice that I discovered: First, explore your passions; second, ask for help; and third, be realistic. Let me give you more details.

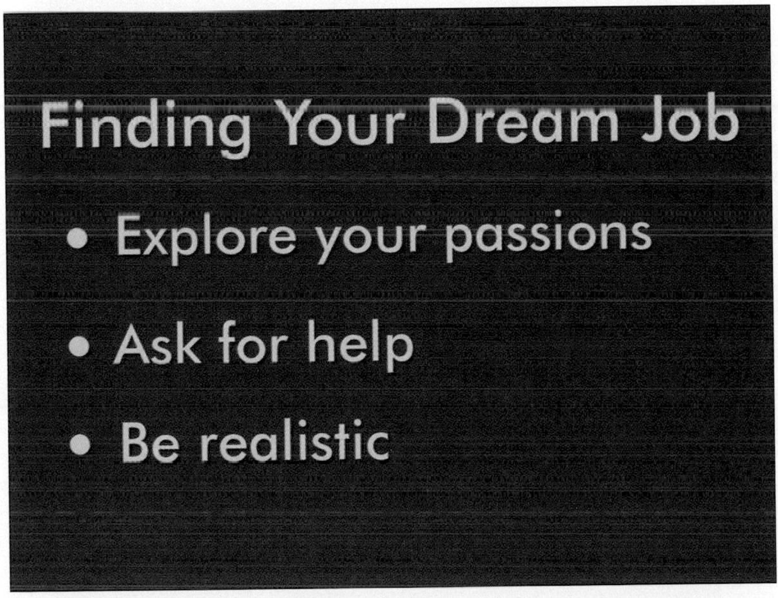

Figure 15.2
In her speech on dream jobs, Julia Weber used the build technique in PowerPoint, showing the first bullet and discussing it, and then adding the other bullets as she progressed through her speech.

The first piece of advice is to explore your passions. *[The speaker shows the first bullet on her PowerPoint slide in Figure 15.2.]* Lisa Sugimoto, who has her dream job as a chef in an upscale San Francisco restaurant, says you should follow up on your enthusiasms. Do you love to explore medical mysteries? Consider a job working in a medical laboratory. [Speaker shows Figure 15.3.] Do you love to travel? Consider a job as a tour guide. [Speaker shows Figure 15.4.] Do you love growing food? Consider a job in agriculture. [Speaker shows Figure 15.5.]

Figure 15.3
The speaker says, "Do you love to explore medical mysteries? Consider a job working in a medical laboratory."

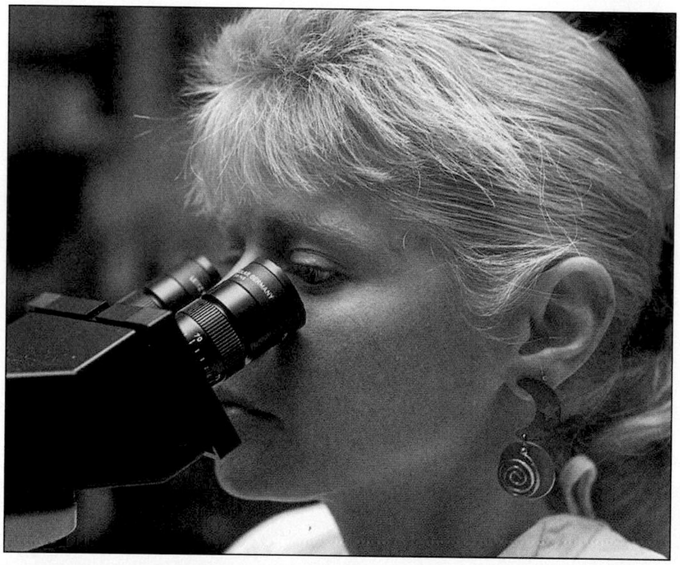

Figure 15.4
The speaker says, "Do you love to travel? Consider a job as a tour guide."

Figure 15.5
The speaker says, "Do you love growing food? Consider a job in agriculture."

She recommends that you make a list of all your fantasies about what kind of work you like to do. Don't overlook your hobbies because sometimes they can lead to good jobs. She mentions a man whose hobby as a teenager was performing magic tricks for his friends. In college, he earned some money part-time as a magician, and after he graduated, he became a full-time magician for social events such as children's birthday parties.

Try to find a job that you love, not necessarily the best-paying job. An article in *The Wall Street Journal* tells about Tim Barnes, who was a stockbroker but wasn't happy with his work. What he really wanted to do was be a teacher. Finally he left Wall Street, and he now teaches social studies and English at New York's Academy of Environmental Science in Harlem. He says motivating seventh graders is much more rewarding than his old job, even if he makes less money.

Now let's look at the second piece of advice that I found: Ask for help. *[The speaker shows the second bullet on her PowerPoint slide in Figure 15.2.]* It's hard to analyze yourself, so ask your relatives and friends what they think you have a knack for. Sometimes they can see potential jobs that you would never think about.

Tonya Edwards, a career counselor, tells the story of a young woman who enjoyed attending the weddings of friends and relatives. She was also good at planning events. Once she helped organize a friend's wedding, and an older woman told her, "You know, you ought to think about becoming a wedding planner." She had never thought about it, but suddenly it all made perfect sense to her. A few years later, she became a wedding planner, and today she is very successful, having all the business she can handle. Most important of all, she loves the job.

Once you have decided what kind of job you want, put the word out. Ask friends, relatives, classmates, and former coworkers to keep an eye out for you. An article in *The Wall Street Journal* tells about Tracy Patton, who was trained as an accountant and loved bookkeeping. The problem was, she couldn't work outside her home because she had to provide around-the-clock care for her disabled husband. She asked friends to alert her if they heard of any accounting jobs that she could do at home. At a dinner party, one of her friends was chatting with the owner of a landscaping business who just happened to need a bookkeeper. That conversation led to Patton getting the job and being allowed to do the bookkeeping on her computer at home.

One way to get help is to join Internet discussion groups in your fields of interest. This will permit you to communicate with people who are already doing what you want to do. Ask them about the pros and the cons. Ask them for ideas about how you can break into the field.

Finally, let's look at the third piece of advice that I found: Be realistic. *[The speaker shows the third bullet on her PowerPoint slide in Figure 15.2] The Wall Street Journal* says you should be realistic about your talents. Don't fantasize about being a drummer in a rock band if you have no musical aptitude. You need to look for a job that matches who you really are.

The *Journal* says you should also be realistic about your personality. Maybe you fantasize about being an investigative TV reporter. That's a glamorous and exciting job, but does it really fit with your personality? Let's say you are a shy, introverted person. You just don't have the right temperament to be a TV reporter. A TV reporter needs to be brash and aggressive.

Are you the kind of person who likes to work alone? A computer job might be right for you. On the other hand, are you the kind of person who needs to constantly interact with other people? You might enjoy working as a teacher or a health professional or a salesperson.

Be realistic about the potential downside of a dream job. You have to realize that no job is filled with thrills and rewards all the time. Even my cousin Michael, the car-swapper, admits that he gets tired of eating at fast-food restaurants along the highways.

Now I would like to summarize. To discover your dream job, you should look at your passions and make a list of what you have a knack for. Ask your friends, relatives, and associates to keep a lookout for jobs that you would probably enjoy. And be realistic about whether a particular job matches your talents and personality.

I hope that in the future you and I can find the job of our dreams. Maybe we can get lucky like a man I read about, Arnold Carbone, who works as an ice-cream taster for Ben & Jerry's. His job is to taste and evaluate more than 100 ideas for potential new ice-cream flavors every year.

Now that's my idea of a dream job!

For other informative speeches, see Appendix and CD Disk 1.

Resources for Review and Skill Building

www.mhhe.com/gregory7

This book's Online Learning Center Website and SpeechMate CD-ROM provide meaningful resources and tools for study and review, such as practice tests, key-term flashcards, and sample speech videos.

SpeechMate CD-ROM

Summary

The goals of informative speaking are to convey knowledge, create understanding, and help listeners remember important points. Four types of informative speeches were discussed in this chapter:

- *Definition* speeches give an extended definition of a concept so that listeners get a full, richly detailed picture of its meaning.
- *Description* speeches paint a vivid picture of a person, place, object, or event.
- *Process* speeches explain the steps or stages by which something is done or made.
- *Expository* speeches involve explaining a concept or situation to the audience. In-depth research should be conducted.

In developing an informative speech, keep these guidelines in mind: (1) Relate the speech to the listeners' self-interest, if at all possible. Show them explicitly the connection between your material and their personal lives. (2) Make the information interesting by going beyond generalities to give lots of specifics, such as examples and anecdotes. (3) Assess the knowledge of your listeners. Don't give them information they already know, and don't talk over their heads. (4) When you want to explain or describe something that is unfamiliar to your audience, relate it to something that is familiar.

Key Terms

definition speech, *350*
description speech, *350*
expository speech, *355*
extended definition, *350*
process speech, *351*

Review Questions

1. What is an extended definition? Why is it preferable in a speech to a dictionary definition?
2. Which two organizational patterns would be most appropriate for a speech on the life and achievements of astronaut Sally Ride?
3. What are the two kinds of process speeches?
4. In a process speech, why is it important to include all steps, even obvious ones?
5. In a process speech, at what point should you give listeners a warning?
6. Which organizational pattern would be most appropriate for a speech aimed at dispelling misconceptions about wolves?
7. Why is it important to relate a speech, if possible, to the listeners' self-interest?
8. Why is the issue of generalities versus specifics an important matter in informative speaking?
9. What should you do if some members of an audience know the meaning of a term but others do not?
10. A speaker says, "The lungs of a heavy smoker look like charred meat." What principle of informative speaking is the speaker using?

Building Critical-Thinking Skills

1. A student who wanted to teach his classmates how to perform CPR (cardiopulmonary resuscitation) began his speech by asking, "How many of you know CPR?" Everyone raised a hand. What error did the speaker make?
2. A handout from a dog-obedience class says, "Training a well-behaved dog takes time and practice. The more repetitions you do on a regular basis, the quicker your dog will understand. However, do not bore him. Keep your training sessions fun and interesting." Do you think this advice would apply to training humans? Justify your answer.

Building Teamwork Skills

1. If improperly developed, the topics below can be boring. In a group, brainstorm ways that each topic could be made interesting.
   a. Teaching methods
   b. Citizenship
   c. Transportation
2. The text advises that you relate a topic to listeners' self-interest. In a group, brainstorm how the following topics can be presented in a way that would satisfy a listener's attitude of "What's in it for me?"
   a. Social Security
   b. Rain forest destruction
   c. Secret video surveillance of employees
   d. Solar energy
   e. Homeless people

Building Internet Skills

www.mhhe.com/gregory7

1. Find and print an article that gives an extended definition of the term *cybercrime.*

Possible Strategy: Go to Yahoo's Full Coverage archive of articles (story.news.yahoo.com/fc) and enter the keyword "cybercrime."

2. In this chapter, you are advised to relate a speech to the listeners' self-interest. Find and print an article that shows how humans are impacted by mercury poisoning in fish.

Possible Strategy: Go to a search engine such as Google (www.google.com) and use these keywords: fish, mercury, and poisoning.

Using PowerWeb

www.mhhe.com/gregory7

One of the principles of this chapter is "Make information interesting." Read a speech entitled "Diversity, America's Treasure Chest," by Frank J. Belatti, chairman and CEO of AFC Enterprises. Find his analysis of the disparity between the wages of blacks and whites in the United States, and discuss whether he succeeds in making statistical information interesting. To find a transcript of this speech, visit www.mhhe.com/gregory7, click on STUDENT EDITION and then POWERWEB: CONTENTS

Peru's First Lady, Eliane Karp, speaks in rural Peru in her campaign to persuade the nation to pay women the same wages as men. "The woman works just as hard as the man in the house and the fields and is paid less," she says. "That should change." (Youths dressed in traditional Indian attire are seen in the background.)

16

Speaking to Persuade

Outline

Objectives

After studying this chapter, you should be able to:

1. Prepare a persuasive speech.
2. Identify two major types of persuasive speeches.
3. Identify four patterns for organizing a persuasive speech.

If you have ever organized a campus event, you know that it sometimes is hard to persuade students to attend. They are busy with a host of academic and social matters. Sadly, some events draw only two or three people.

At Western Carolina University, three students—Brandie Huffman, Alex Mize, and Britt Billings—led a publicity campaign aimed at persuading their classmates to participate in a Walk for Women, a march across campus designed to focus attention on Women's History Month and to raise funds for a new sexual assault awareness program at the university.[1]

In the weeks leading up to the event, the trio went around the campus speaking to classes and to campus organizations. In each speech, they distributed a commitment sheet, which listeners were asked to sign. The sheet said, "By placing your name on this sheet, you are committing to participate in the Walk for Women."[2]

The day of the march turned out to be bitterly cold, with temperatures in the low 20s. Although organizers feared that only a handful of people would show up, hundreds of students appeared. Many of them undoubtedly braved the cold and participated because they wanted to honor their commitment.

Huffman, Mize, and Billings demonstrated the usefulness of a sign-up sheet (a technique discussed in this chapter) and they also demonstrated the power of

Student speaker Alex Mize, flanked by Brandie Huffman (left) and Britt Billings, uses a commitment sheet as a persuasion technique at Western Carolina University.

persuasion—influencing, changing, or reinforcing what people think, believe, or do. Throughout your life, you face many tasks that require persuasion, ranging from one-to-one situations (such as convincing a bank executive to give you a loan for a new car), to small groups (persuading your fellow employees to join with you in presenting a grievance about working conditions), to large audiences (talking your club into holding its annual picnic at a particular site). In this chapter we will examine types of persuasive speeches and patterns of organization. In the next chapter we will look at techniques for developing persuasive speeches.

persuasion
the process of influencing, changing, or reinforcing listeners' ideas, attitudes, beliefs, or behaviors

Types of Persuasive Speeches

Persuasive speeches can be categorized in a variety of ways. One handy scheme labels them according to two objectives: (1) to influence thinking and (2) to motivate action. Sometimes these categories overlap (for example, you often have to influence thinking before you can motivate action).

Speech to Influence Thinking

The **speech to influence thinking** is an effort to convince people to adopt your position on a particular subject. (If some listeners agree with your ideas even before you speak, your job is to reinforce what they already think.) In some cases, you may want to implant ideas that are completely new to a particular audience; for example, you argue that within a few decades medical science will extend the average human lifespan to 140 years. In other cases, you may want to cast new light on an old issue; for example, you argue that the United States could have won independence from Great Britain without going to war.

speech to influence thinking
an oral presentation aimed at winning intellectual assent for a concept or proposition

Here are some sample specific purpose statements for this kind of speech:

- To convince my audience that, in most jobs, workers can put in shorter hours and still get the necessary work accomplished
- To convince my listeners that tribal healers in the Amazon rain forest have many skills and insights that can be useful to mainstream medicine
- To convince my listeners that immigrants continue to enrich American society and business life
- To convince my audience that panic attacks are caused by physiological, rather than psychological, factors

A subcategory of the speech to influence thinking is the **speech of refutation,** in which your main goal is to knock down arguments or ideas that you believe are false. You may want to attack what another speaker has said, or you might want to refute popularly held ideas or beliefs that you think are false. One student, for example, tried to explode the myth that mentally retarded people can contribute little to the workforce.

speech of refutation
an oral counterargument against a concept or proposition put forth by others

Here are some sample specific purpose statements for speeches of refutation:

- To convince my listeners to reject the view that alcoholism is a moral weakness instead of a disease
- To persuade my audience to reject the false picture of pigs as dirty, stupid animals
- To convince my audience that contrary to popular belief, solar power is a viable, inexpensive source of energy
- To persuade my audience to disbelieve claims by so-called psychics that they are able to predict future events

SpeechMate CD-ROM

To see sample persuasive speeches, view Speeches 4, 8, and 9 on Disk 1 and Robert Ingram's speech on Disk 2.

Refuting an argument is easier when you are dealing with facts than when you are dealing with deeply held beliefs. Suppose, for example, that you want to demolish the idea that brown sugar is more natural and therefore healthier than white sugar. You can refute this idea by citing nutrition experts who say that brown sugar offers no nutritional advantages because it is simply white sugar with small amounts of molasses or burnt sugar added for coloring. Since this assertion involves verifiable chemical facts, your persuasive task is easy. But suppose that you wanted to persuade an audience to reject the belief that children should be reared by their parents; instead, you argue, children should be reared by communes like the kibbutzim in Israel. Though you may win some respect for the value of your idea, you are highly unlikely to demolish the deeply held belief that children should grow up under the wings of their parents. Such core beliefs are extremely difficult to change.

Speech to Motivate Action

speech to motivate action
an oral presentation that tries to impel listeners to take action

Like the speech to influence thinking, the **speech to motivate action** tries to win people over to your way of thinking, but it also attempts one of the most challenging tasks of persuasion: getting people to take action. Your goal is to get listeners to respond in one or more of these ways: *start* a behavior (start taking first aid lessons, start investing in the stock market, start performing regular car maintenance), *continue* a behavior (continue donating blood, continue supporting a political party, continue eating low-fat foods), or *stop* a behavior (stop smoking, stop tailgating, stop overspending on a credit card account).

Here are some sample specific purpose statements for speeches to motivate action:

- To persuade my listeners to sign a petition aimed at requiring drivers over 75 to be retested each year for their driver's license
- To persuade my audience to eat fish as their chief source of protein
- To persuade my audience to try whitewater rafting
- To persuade my audience to treat AIDS patients with dignity and respect
- To persuade my listeners to demand the right to see the computer files that have been compiled on them by credit-rating companies and government agencies

Sometimes you want prompt action from your listeners ("Please vote for my candidate in today's election"); at other times, you simply want them to respond at any appropriate point in the future ("Whenever you see a child riding a bike, please slow down and drive very cautiously").

Here are some suggestions for getting action:

SpeechMate CD-ROM

For hundreds of sample topics, see Topic Helper on Disk 1.

Instead of hinting or implying, ask for the precise action that you want. You can't just "give the facts" and assume that your listeners will deduce what action should be taken; you must tell them *exactly* what you want them to do.

If you are speaking to an audience consisting of couples, and your subject is the shortage of foster parents for children without parents, don't be content to merely extol the virtues of foster parenting and hope some of the listeners will volunteer someday. Ask your listeners to become foster parents (and tell them how and where to sign up).

Late in his life, Henry Ford, founder of the Ford Motor Company, was chatting with an insurance agent whom he had known for many years. The agent, puzzled and hurt by the fact that Ford had never given him any business, finally asked, "Why didn't you ever buy insurance from me?"

Ford replied, "You never asked me."[3]

An old English proverb says, "Many things are lost for want of asking." Countless speakers, says Dr. Jerry Tarver of the University of Richmond, "are reluctant to 'ask for the sale.' They appear to have a naive faith that if audiences are given some pertinent facts and a few exhortations, all will be well. These speakers fail to realize that when conditions are right, conviction can be turned into action."[4]

Whenever possible, get a response—even if it's a small, token action—before listeners leave the room. Here is what happens in a typical speech aimed at motivating action:

> Imagine that you give a stirring speech on the destruction of elephant herds by greedy poachers and ivory traders. At the end you urge all listeners to go home and write a letter to the Secretary General of the United Nations calling for concerted international effort to save the elephants. And you ask them to telephone their friends to encourage them to do likewise. The listeners leave your speech highly motivated, vowing to themselves to write that letter and make those phone calls. But, unfortunately, very few ever do so. Everyone has good intentions, but life is busy and there are urgent personal matters to be taken care of. After a couple of weeks, the vows are forgotten.

I'm not suggesting that you refrain from asking listeners to make a response in the future. It's always a good idea to encourage people to take action tomorrow and next week and next year. But also try to get them to do something immediately—before they leave the room, before their commitment cools. You could say, "On your way out, please sign the petition on the table at the rear of the room." Even better, if time permits, is to circulate the petition for them to sign before they stand up to leave.

Striking while the iron is hot often brings you an important reward. Researchers have verified that if you persuade a person to take a positive step, even if it's a small one like signing a petition, you increase that person's commitment to your cause.[5] He or she now has made an investment of time and energy. If opponents try to persuade the person to believe the opposite of what you have espoused, he or she will be highly resistant to change (unless, of course, there is some compelling counterargument). Why? Because human beings feel a strong need to be consistent.[6] Going over to the other side would be inconsistent with an action like signing your petition.

Let's examine some on-the-spot responses that can help strengthen your listeners' support of your position.

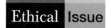

SpeechMate CD-ROM

For help in outlining your material, use the computerized Outline Tutor on the CD.

- **Petition.** Some people frown on this idea because they feel that petitions have become a cliché, and besides, public officials just dump them in the trash. I disagree. I think petitions sometimes are effective in bringing about a policy change. If a U.S. senator gets petitions with 500 signatures from the folks back home, he or she sits up and pays attention—these are 500 potential voters. Lawmakers and officeholders often switch their positions after receiving a big stack of petitions. Even if officials don't respond as you wish, getting signatures on a petition is never a futile gesture because you have increased the listeners' commitment to your idea.
- **Show of hands.** "Studies show that something as simple as having people raise their hands is more likely to get long-range results than depending, as too many speakers do, on mere mental assent," says Dr. Jerry Tarver.[7] Ask for a show of hands only when you're sure that most listeners will be eager and unembarrassed to make a public commitment.
- **Sign-up sheet.** For some future activity such as volunteer work, you can ask people to write down their names and phone numbers. This strategy can be effective because even if their ardor cools somewhat, most people will honor their promise to help when called upon later.
- **Written assignment.** Some speakers pass out paper and pens, and ask listeners to write down what action they intend to take as a result of the speech. It is hoped, of course, that the listeners will view the paper as a promise to themselves, and take it to their offices or homes and eventually act upon it. (While this technique may sound weak, the act of crystallizing one's thoughts and writing them on paper strengthens a person's resolve.)

Ethical Issue

Don't pressure listeners. Despite the desirability of getting audience action, don't browbeat, intimidate, manipulate, or beg. Don't single out and embarrass those listeners who decline to take action. Listeners who feel pressured might become so resentful that they will decline to support your cause simply out of spite.

Patterns of Organization

Organizing a speech effectively can enhance your persuasiveness. While any of the organizational patterns we studied in Chapter 10 can be used, four patterns below are especially strong in persuasive speeches: the motivated sequence, the problem–solution pattern, the statement-of-reasons pattern, and the comparative-advantages pattern.

Motivated Sequence

The **motivated sequence** is a commonsense approach to persuasion that was developed by Professor Alan H. Monroe.[8] The pattern is especially useful when you want to sell a product or service, or when you want to mobilize listeners to take a specific action (vote for your candidate, pick up litter). It has the virtue of being suitable for any type of audience—unaware, hostile, apathetic, neutral, or favorable. There are five steps in this pattern:

motivated sequence
a series of steps designed to propel a listener toward accepting the speaker's proposition

1. Attention. Grab the audience's attention at the beginning of your introduction, as discussed in Chapter 11.
2. Need. Show your audience that there is a serious problem that needs action.
3. Satisfaction. Satisfy the need by presenting a solution, and show how your solution works.
4. Visualization. Paint a picture of results. Your scenario can be *positive:* Help listeners visualize the good things that will happen when your solution is put into effect. Or it can be *negative:* show them the bad results if your solution is rejected.
5. Action. Request action from the listeners. Be specific: "Sign this petition" or "Write your legislators today—here are their addresses" or "You can volunteer in Room 211 this afternoon."

www.mhhe.com/gregory7
To review the steps of the motivated sequence, do the interactive exercise in Chapter 16 on this book's Website.

The following example is a condensed version of a speaker's outline. It has been scaled down so that we can focus on the steps in the motivated sequence:

INTRODUCTION

I. In Florida, a man who posed as a doctor gave anesthesia improperly during surgery, causing the patient to lapse into a coma and become brain dead. — *Attention*

II. Let's examine how many phony physicians there are in the United States and what we can do about them.

BODY

I. A U.S. House of Representatives subcommittee investigation revealed that as many as 10,000 physicians in the United States have degrees from fraudulent diploma mills (medical schools in name only) in foreign countries. — *Need*

II. Congress should set up a national clearinghouse. — *Satisfaction*

  A. The clearinghouse would investigate and list which medical schools in the world are legitimate and which are bogus.

  B. Using the clearinghouse's computerized list, hospitals and state medical boards could verify the credentials of all doctors.

III. You could be assured that the physician treating you and your loved ones is not a fake M.D. — *Visualization*

CONCLUSION

Action

I. By establishing a clearinghouse, Congress can protect patients from phony doctors.

II. Please sign my petition that will be sent to lawmakers urging them to set up a national clearinghouse as quickly as possible.

For another speech that uses the motivated sequence, see the sample outline and transcript at the end of this chapter.

Problem–Solution Pattern

problem–solution pattern
an arrangement of material that explores a problem and then offers a solution

For many audiences, the most persuasive approach is the **problem–solution pattern.** You show that a problem exists, and then you present the solution. This pattern is especially effective when listeners either don't know that a particular problem exists or don't know how serious it is. Here is the partial outline of a student speech by Adam Cohen on a dangerous national problem:

Specific Purpose: To convince my audience to support tougher enforcement of child-labor laws

Central Idea: Stronger enforcement of child-labor laws would reduce the number of deaths and injuries involving children and teenagers.

Main Points:

(Problem) I. Many children and teenagers are killed or maimed because they are illegally working at jobs that are supposed to be filled by adults.

- A. One child or teenager is killed on the job every five days in the United States.
- B. About 210,000 are injured annually, with 70,000 hurt badly enough to need emergency-room treatment.
- C. Some employers use underage workers for dangerous jobs such as roofing, mining, logging, meat slicing, and construction.

(Solution) II. The federal government should enforce the child-labor laws that already exist.

- A. Unlike the present situation, in which no one ever goes to jail for breaking child-labor laws, federal prosecuters should seek criminal indictments in cases involving serious danger.
- B. Unlike the present situation, in which the government routinely waives fines for violations, the government should assess a maximum fine of $40,000 for each violation.

In the speech itself, under the first main point, Cohen related news accounts of child-labor tragedies to show the audience that the problem was

Tips for your CAREER

Tip 16.1 Use Role Play to Change Behavior

If you own a restaurant and you want to persuade your servers to respond in a friendly manner towards cantankerous customers, you can give them examples of how to treat diners, you can urge them to be friendly, you can show training films. But none of these techniques will be as effective as having your employees engage in role play. In other words, you can stage mock situations: One person plays the role of the crabby complainer ("There's too much dressing on this salad!") while a server acts out the correct response (saying, with a smile, "I am so sorry—let me bring you another salad"). After each server's performance, give a critique and, if anything is wrong, ask him or her to try again.

Research studies have verified the power of role play to modify behavior. In one case, drug-abuse educators used role play with students at more than 400 middle and junior-high schools in Indiana, Kansas, and Missouri to help the students learn how to resist peer pressure. The students learned, for example, that if a friend says, "If you don't try this cocaine, you're a chicken," they can say, "If I said yes just to impress you, I'd really be a chicken." Five-year follow-up studies showed that students who had participated in role play were 20 to 40 percent less likely than other students to have tried drugs.

When you participate in role play, consider videotaping the session. You and your trainer can view the videotape together and discuss both strong and weak points in your simulation.

more serious than most people realized. Under the second main point, he gave specific examples of how enforcement should be carried out.

For the transcript of an entire speech that uses the problem–solution pattern, see the sample speech at the end of Chapter 8.

Statement-of-Reasons Pattern

statement-of-reasons pattern
an organizational scheme that lists reasons for a proposition

The **statement-of-reasons pattern,** a variation of the topical pattern (which we discussed in Chapter 10), gives reasons for the speaker's argument. It can be used for any persuasive speech, but it is especially useful when the audience leans toward your position but needs some justification for that leaning. In one community speech, Glenda O'Neill, an emergency-medicine physician, knew (from a questionnaire) that her listeners were suspicious of pharmaceutical drugs sold on the Internet by overseas companies, but they were unaware of the full extent of the dangers. So her task was to give them reasons for avoiding the drugs in case Internet advertisers ever tried to entice them. Here is the essence of her outline:

Specific Purpose: To persuade my listeners to spurn unregulated medications sold on the Internet by overseas companies

Central Idea: Unregulated medications that can be ordered on the Internet from overseas companies are often ineffective and dangerous.

Main Points:

(1st Reason) I. Some Internet medications contain little or none of the advertised active ingredients.

(2nd Reason) II. Some Internet medications may create adverse interaction with other drugs.

Tips for your CAREER

Tip 16.2 View Persuasion as a Long-Term Process

Persuasion in your career often requires a long time—weeks, months, or even years. Many successful persuaders treat their task as an ongoing process aimed at influencing people and nudging them toward a goal, rather than a one-shot event aimed at a quick decision.

At first glance, this tip may seem to contradict what was discussed earlier in the chapter: the need to be forthright in asking an audience to take action. But there really is no contradiction. Asking the audience to take prompt action is appropriate in many situations, such as urging an audience to vote for your political candidate. In other situations, however, you may be interacting with people over a span of time, and a one-time appeal might be less effective than long-term efforts that gradually move people toward a desired decision. For example, let's say you take a new job, and you want to convince your superiors to let you do most of your work in your home office. If you make a blunt request for this accommodation, you might get turned down. Using a gradual approach, however, you could occasionally do some projects in your home office as a way of demonstrating that you are capable of working productively at home. A year later, your superiors might be so impressed with your performance that they grant your request.

Successful long-term persuaders in the business world are good listeners who learn all they can about their clients, and then work in friendly collaboration. Imagine that a real estate agent meets a young couple who are in the market for a new house. Instead of pressing for a quick sale of any available house, the agent would be wise to get to know the couple and truly listen to their needs. She should show many different houses, making notes on which features the couple likes and dislikes. After a long process, the agent should be able to match the couple with a house that truly satisfies their needs. This approach is not only ethical, but it reaps a long-term benefit: The couple will tell their friends about the wonderful agent who is not pushy but takes time to really listen and is patient in finding the right home for her clients.

Whether you succeed or fail in persuasion often comes down to one key question: Are you trustworthy? Before people will buy your ideas, products, or services, they want to know whether they can trust you to guide them in the right direction. Proving your reliability may take time—another reason why long-term influence is often more effective than short-term argument.

(3rd Reason) III. Some Internet medications may worsen a patient's condition, even causing death.

In her speech, O'Neill developed each reason with examples and statistics.

Comparative-Advantages Pattern

comparative-advantages pattern
an organizational scheme that shows the superiority of one concept or approach over another

When listeners already agree with you that a problem exists but aren't sure which solution is best, you can use the **comparative-advantages pattern** to show that your recommended solution is superior to others. Let's say that your listeners agree with you that criminals must be punished, but they don't know whether prison is the best choice or whether some alternative sentence (such as probation, home confinement, or community service) would be better. If you feel that the latter is the preferred option, you can use the comparative-advantages pattern:

Specific Purpose: To persuade my audience that nonviolent offenders should be given alternative sentences instead of being sent to prison

Central Idea: An alternative sentence for nonviolent offenders is more beneficial to society and the offenders themselves than a prison sentence would be.

Special Techniques

How to Use Leave-Behinds

In a career setting, when you complete a presentation and sit down, don't make the mistake of thinking that your persuasive task is finished.

"No matter how impressed and convinced the people in that room are when you're through," says computer consultant Jim Seymour of Austin, Texas, "your message hasn't finally clicked until they've taken it back to their staff, superiors, engineers, sales forces, or other constituencies. If you expect them to be even half as persuasive as you were—and to get it right when they retell your story for you!—you need to arm them with the tools they need to make your case persuasively."

These tools can be contained in "leave-behinds"—materials that are distributed at the end of your question-and-answer period (and not before). Make sure that each listener receives a set.

Figure 16-A shows a sheet that was part of the leave-behinds used by student speaker Daniel O'Brien in a speech on driving while sleepy.

Leave-behinds might include the following:

1. *Summary.* A condensation of your key information will help listeners recall your points later, and it will provide a good abstract for those who didn't attend (the "constituencies" to which Seymour refers). The summary *must not exceed one page* because a busy person is likely to ignore or discard a lengthy abstract. If you have a packet of handouts, the summary should be the top sheet.
2. *Graphics.* Copies of key charts, diagrams, and tables can provide visual support.
3. *New points.* If you feel frustrated because you are allotted only 5 minutes for a speech but you need 20 minutes to cover all your points, you can focus on just a few points in the speech and cover the others on a leave-behind. Thus, if listeners hunger for more information, they have easy access to it.
4. *Bibliography of sources.* In your presentation, you might say, "I don't have time to name all the books and articles from which I got my information, but I have a bibliography that I'll give you after I finish." Not only is such a list helpful to listeners who want to pursue your subject further, but it also suggests to the audience that you are a careful researcher who strives for accuracy.
5. *File folders.* For paper handouts, consider providing labeled file folders so that listeners will have a simple way to store the leave-behinds in a file drawer. (Sometimes people toss handouts simply because they have no idea where to store them.)
6. *Samples and multimedia.* A sample product is a tangible reminder of your message. CD-ROMs and videotapes are also useful if they contain valuable information, but omit them if they are nothing more than high-tech "fluff."

For all important presentations, use leave-behinds. Like a rock tossed into a pond, they can create a ripple effect, causing your message to travel beyond the meeting room to influence many people.

Main Points:

(1st Advantage)	I.	An alternative sentence costs taxpayers about $19,000 less per offender each year than a prison term.
(2nd Advantage)	II.	Alternative sentences prevent offenders from learning criminal skills in prison and coming out embittered against society.
(3rd Advantage)	III.	Alternative sentences make it easier for offenders to get jobs because they don't carry the stigma of being an ex-con.

Each main point shows the superiority of alternative sentences over prison sentences.

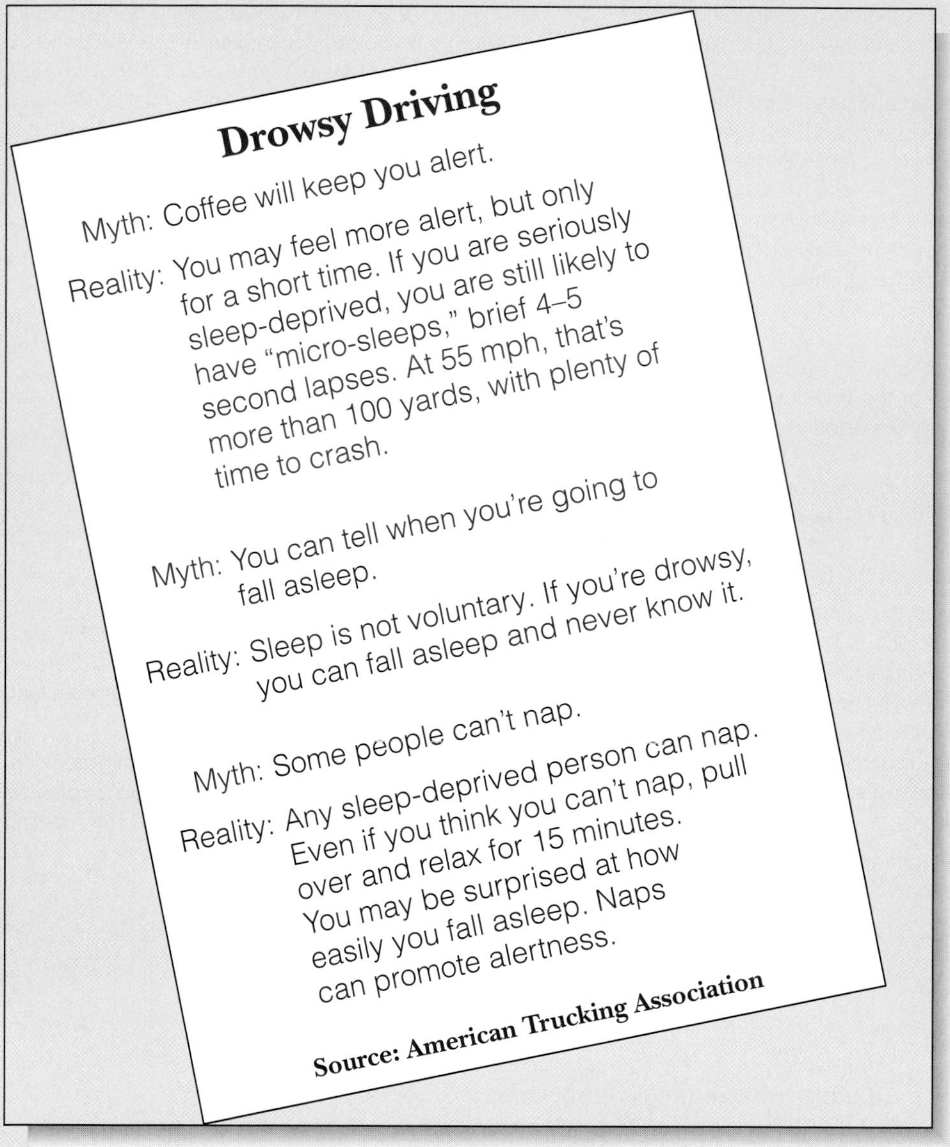

Drowsy Driving

Myth: Coffee will keep you alert.

Reality: You may feel more alert, but only for a short time. If you are seriously sleep-deprived, you are still likely to have "micro-sleeps," brief 4–5 second lapses. At 55 mph, that's more than 100 yards, with plenty of time to crash.

Myth: You can tell when you're going to fall asleep.

Reality: Sleep is not voluntary. If you're drowsy, you can fall asleep and never know it.

Myth: Some people can't nap.

Reality: Any sleep-deprived person can nap. Even if you think you can't nap, pull over and relax for 15 minutes. You may be surprised at how easily you fall asleep. Naps can promote alertness.

Source: American Trucking Association

Figure 16-A
At the end of a speech on driving while sleepy, student speaker Daniel O'Brien gave listeners some leave-behinds to take with them. The page shown here makes points that O'Brien did not have time to cover in the speech itself.

Sample Persuasive Speech

In a speech to motivate action, Naresh Chopra argues for mandatory E-911 service. His outline is presented first, with a commentary in the margin.[9] Note the discussion of the five steps of the motivated sequence.

The Outline with Commentary

E-911 Will Save Lives

General Purpose: To persuade

Specific Purpose: To persuade my audience to support mandatory E-911 service in every state in the United States

Central Idea: Emergency dispatchers in all states in the U.S. should be able to determine the precise location of anyone using a phone to call for help.

INTRODUCTION

I. Attention Material

- A. In Chicago, a 33-year-old executive was working late one night on the 21st floor of a high-rise office building. (Security magazine)
- B. A fire broke out, and she was not able to escape.
- C. She called 911 and gave the name of her office building.
- D. Firefighters came as quickly as possible, but they had trouble finding her because they didn't know exactly where she was on the 21st floor.
- E. In about an hour, they found her, but she was dead.

II. Orienting Material

- A. This shouldn't happen in a nation with advanced technology.
- B. Emergency dispatchers anywhere in the U.S. should be able to pinpoint the exact location of any phone.
- C. I will show you how this can be done.

(*Transition:* Let's start by examining the problem.)

BODY

I. We have the necessary technology, but it has been installed in only a few places.

- A. The technology is called E-911—short for Enhanced 911.
  1. Imagine you're lost on a camping trip.
  2. You call 911 on your cell phone.
  3. If you're in an area that has E-911, your exact location shows instantly on the dispatcher's screen.

Commentary

*For the **attention** step of the motivated sequence, Chopra uses a captivating story.*

Chopra gives his central idea and a preview of the body of the speech.

*For the **need** step, the speaker devotes the first main point to showing the full dimensions of the problem.*

Chopra wrote this outline in complete sentences, and then used brief notes on index cards for the actual delivery of the speech. If you examine the transcript of the speech (immediately following the outline), you will see that he followed the basic ideas of his outline, but used more words and somewhat different phrasing. This is an effective approach because it enabled him to organize his material intelligently, while avoiding the mistake of reading a script.

4. It is automatic—you don't even have to say a word.
5. E-911 uses GPS (Global Positioning System) to show your latitude and longitude.
6. Rescue workers carry GPS devices and can go straight to your location. (Security magazine)

B. Unfortunately, the technology hasn't been installed in most areas of the U.S.

1. Most states have not funded E-911 because they are in desperate need of money.
2. The few E-911 areas include the state of Rhode Island, the city of Houston, and some counties in Virginia, Illinois, and Indiana. (ABC News)
3. Since most Americans don't have access to E-911, what happens to us if we have an emergency and we can't tell 911 exactly where we are?

On his outline, the speaker puts the name of a source in parentheses at the end of a sentence. In the actual speech, he will weave the source name into the fabric of his remarks.

(*Transition:* Is there a solution?)

*In the **satisfaction** step, Chopra presents a solution and shows how it can work.*

II. States can impose a surcharge on cell phone bills, and then use the money to pay for E-911.

A. The first part is already happening.

1. Many states have been imposing a surcharge for the past few years.
2. The term surcharge means "additional tax."

B. The second part is not happening.

1. Most states have grabbed the E-911 funds and used them for other purposes.
2. Last year, California diverted $53 million and New York diverted $162 million. (USA Today)
3. Tom Wheeler, president of CTIA (Cellular Telecommunications and Internet Association), says, "Dozens of states have taken a hammer to their E-911 piggy banks and run off with these vital taxpayer funds, earmarked for public safety." (Wireless Week)

When an expert paints a vivid image, it is a good idea to quote directly rather than paraphrase.

C. There is a way that we can put a halt to this diversion of funds.

1. A bill now in Congress—H.R. 2898—would block states from siphoning off the E-911 surcharge. (U.S. House of Representatives)
2. States would be forced to spend the money for its intended purpose—establishment of E-911 service.

3. We need for the U.S. Congress to fund E-911 technology for every state.

(*Transition:* In the places that already have E-911, what is happening?)

III. Places that have E-911 say they are experiencing good results.

*In the **visualization** step, Chopra gives two stories that paint a positive picture of what happens when E-911 is adopted.*

A. One area includes some counties in Illinois.

1. An elderly couple were driving through southwestern Illinois last fall. (New York Times)
2. Their car caught fire, and they called 911.
3. They had no idea where they were.
4. Lucky for them, they were in St. Clair County, the first county in the nation to install E-911.
5. When they called 911, the dispatchers knew instantly their precise location.
6. In just a few minutes, rescuers arrived.
7. The couple escaped without injuries.

B. Another area includes some counties in Indiana.

Chopra's narratives, in which he uses lots of specific details, give a powerful boost to his argument.

1. On Nov. 17, 2001, the sheriff's office in Lake County, Indiana, received a desperate 911 call from a man on a boat. (CNN)
2. The man said he was lost in the fog on Lake Michigan.
3. Fortunately, the county had installed E-911 just a month before.
4. The dispatchers immediately knew the boat's longitude and latitude.
5. They alerted the Coast Guard, which sent out a vessel and rescued the man.

C. The rest of us deserve to have E-911 in our communities.

*In the **action** step, the speaker urges his listeners to sign a petition.*

1. I urge you to sign a petition at the end of class today.
2. It asks our federal legislators to support H.R. 2898 so that all Americans can have access to E-911.
3. I will send the petition to Washington tomorrow.

(*Transition:* I would like to summarize.)

CONCLUSION

I. Summary

A. E-911 can pinpoint the precise location of anyone who calls 911.

The speaker sums up the key information of the speech.

B. Sadly, E-911 is unavailable in most parts of the U.S. because many states have failed to pay to install the system.

C. States should use the surcharge that already exists and use the money as it was intended—to finance E-911.

D. We must pressure Congress to pass H.R. 2898 so that states will be forced to provide E-911 to everyone.

II. Clincher

A. In my introduction, I told of the executive who was trapped on the 21st floor of an office building.

B. Imagine that you are the one who is trapped.

C. Now pick up your cell phone and call 911.

D. If dispatchers have E-911, they will know exactly where you are, and they will send help in just a few seconds.

A poster with an upbeat message makes a graceful finale, as Chopra makes one final call for action.

E. (Show poster.) [Figure 16.1] E-911 will save lives, and maybe it will be your life that is saved.

F. Please sign the petition.

BIBLIOGRAPHY

See Chapter 6 for details on how to prepare bibliographies.

Brewin, Bob. "E-911 Services Successful Despite Limited Access." CNN.com. 2003. Retrieved 8 Sept. 2003 <http://cnn.com>.

Davidson, Paul. "Enhanced 911 Calls Still Far from Wide Coverage." USA Today 25 Oct. 2002: 1B.

"E-911 Implementation Act of 2003 (House Resolution 2898)." U.S. House of Representatives. 2003. Retrieved 7 Sept. 2003 <http://thomas.loc.gov>.

"Help on the Way?" ABC News. 2003. Retrieved 7 Sept. 2003 <abcnews.com>.

Louderback, Jim. "A Wireless 911 System Finds Those in Need." New York Times 18 July 2002: G7.

Maier, Anthony. "E-911 in the Office." Security Aug. 2003: 42.

Rockwell, Mark. "Rural Carriers Feel Pinch of E-911 Bill." Wireless Week 15 Aug. 2003: 14.

VISUAL AIDS

Poster as part of clincher

Figure 16.1
The speaker uses a poster in the conclusion of his speech. Note that he avoids the mistake of putting an excessive number of words on the visual.

The Speech as Delivered

Here is the transcript of Chopra's speech. Notice that the speaker uses the ideas of the outline without using the exact wording. In an extemporaneous speech, a speaker does not read or memorize a speech, but speaks from brief notes.

E-911 Will Save Lives

Although it was late at night and everyone else had gone home, a 33-year-old businesswoman was working on the 21st floor of a high-rise office building in Chicago. *Security* magazine says that a fire broke out on her floor, and she was unable to get out. Frantically she called 911 and told them the name of the office building. Firefighters were dispatched, but they couldn't find her immediately because they didn't know her exact location on the 21st floor. After an hour of searching, they finally found her, but by then, it was too late. She was dead.

With our advanced technology, we can do better than this. I believe that emergency dispatchers anywhere in the United States should be able to determine the precise location of any phone—including cell phones. In this speech, I will show you how this can be accomplished.

Let's begin by understanding the nature of the problem. We have the technology that we need, but it's been installed in just a few places. The technology is known as E-911. The "E" stands for enhanced. According to *Security* magazine, here's how it works: let's say you are on a camping trip and you become lost. You use your cell phone to call 911 for help. If you are located in an area that has E-911, your precise location is instantly flashed on the dispatcher's screen, even if you don't say a word. Thanks to GPS (Global Positioning System), your latitude and longitude are pinpointed, and rescue workers—who carry GPS devices—can go to the exact location.

This technology is wonderful, but it isn't available in most parts of the United States. The reason is that states are starved for cash, so they have not funded E-911. There are a few exceptions, according to *ABC News:* the state of Rhode Island, the city of Houston, and some counties in Virginia, Illinois, and Indiana. Most of us don't live in the areas that are blessed with E-911. What if we have an emergency and can't give the 911 dispatcher a precise location?

Is there a solution? Yes, a very simple one. States can place a surcharge on cell phone bills, and then use the revenues to pay for installation of E-911. Actually, the first part of this is already being done: For several years, many states have been imposing a surcharge. By the way, "surcharge" is really just a fancy word for additional tax. But what about the second part? Instead of using the revenues for E-911, most states have raided the E-911 funds and used them for other purposes. For example, *USA Today* says that last year, California diverted 53 million dollars and New York diverted 162 million dollars.

Wireless Week magazine quotes Tom Wheeler, president of CTIA (Cellular Telecommunications and Internet Association), as saying, "Dozens of states have taken a hammer to their E-911 piggy banks and run off with these vital taxpayer funds, earmarked for public safety."

Can we stop this outrageous diversion of funds? Yes, there is a bill currently being considered by Congress—H.R. 2898—that would block states from siphoning off the E-911 surcharge. In other words, states would be forced to spend the money for its intended purpose—establishment of E-911 service. We need for the U.S. Congress to fund E-911 technology for every state.

You may wonder, what is happening in the areas that already have E-911? The few areas that already have E-911 report good results. According to the *New York Times,* an elderly couple were driving in a remote area of southwestern Illinois last fall when their car suddenly caught fire. They called 911, but they had no idea where they were. Fortunately, they were in St. Clair County, the first county in the nation to install E-911. When the couple called 911, the dispatchers pinpointed exactly where they were, and rescuers arrived in just a few minutes. The couple escaped unharmed.

CNN reports that on Nov. 17, 2001, the Lake County, Indiana, sheriff's office got a 911 call from a desperate boater who was lost in the fog on Lake Michigan. The E-911 system that had been installed a month earlier pinpointed the boat's longitude and latitude instantly. The Coast Guard was alerted, and it sent out a vessel and rescued the boater.

I am happy with the results that are being seen in Illinois and Indiana, but the rest of the country also deserves to have E-911. All of us can take action. I have a petition that I would like to urge you to sign before you leave class today. This petition asks our lawmakers in the U.S. House and Senate to support H.R. 2898. As I have told you, this bill will guarantee that all Americans have access to E-911. Please sign the petition, and I promise you I will send it to Washington tomorrow morning.

Let's sum up. A wonderful technology—E-911—exists to pinpoint the exact location of a person who calls 911 for help. Unfortunately,

E-911 is not available in most parts of the country because many states have failed to finance installation of the system. All they have to do is use the surcharge that is already in place and is supposed to go toward E-911. To force the states to do the right thing, Congress should pass H.R. 2898. If the bill is passed, states will be obliged to offer E-911 service to everyone.

I began by telling you about the woman who was trapped on the 21st floor of an office building. Imagine that you are trapped in a similar situation. Then imagine that you pull out your cell phone and call 911. If the dispatchers have E-911, they won't even ask you, "Where are you?" because they will already know. And help will be on the way in a matter of seconds. [Speaker displays his poster. See Figure 16.1] E-911 *will* save lives. And one of those lives could be yours.

Please sign my petition at the end of class. Thank you.

For other sample persuasion speeches, see the sample speeches in Chapters 10 and 11, the outline and transcript in Chapter 12, and a persuasion speech in the Appendix. SpeechMate Disk 1 contains videos of several persuasive speeches.

Resources for Review and Skill Building

www.mhhe.com/gregory7

This book's Online Learning Center Website and SpeechMate CD-ROM provide meaningful resources and tools for study and review, such as practice tests, key-term flashcards, and sample speech videos.

SpeechMate CD-ROM

Summary

Persuasion—getting people to think or act in a certain way—is one of the most frequent tasks of the public speaker. Two major types of persuasive speeches are the speech to influence thinking and the speech to motivate action.

In the speech to influence thinking, your primary goal is to convince people to adopt your position. A subcategory of this kind of speech is the speech of refutation, in which your aim is to knock down arguments or ideas that you believe are false.

In the speech to motivate action, you should tell the listeners exactly what action you want them to take. Whenever possible, encourage them to take some action—even if it's a small, token action—immediately.

Of the many patterns that can be used for the persuasive speech, four are especially effective: the motivated sequence, problem–solution pattern, statement-of-reasons pattern, and comparative-advantages pattern.

Key Terms

comparative-advantages pattern, *382*
motivated sequence, *379*
persuasion, *374*
problem–solution pattern, *380*
speech of refutation, *375*
speech to influence thinking, *375*
speech to motivate action, *376*
statement-of-reasons pattern, *381*

Review Questions

1. What is the goal of the speech of refutation?
2. In a speech to motivate action, why should you try to get listeners to take action immediately?
3. Give three examples of immediate, on-the-spot audience action.
4. What is the goal of the *need* step of the motivated sequence?
5. What is the goal of the *satisfaction* step of the motivated sequence?
6. What is the goal of the *visualization* step of the motivated sequence?
7. What is the goal of the *action* step of the motivated sequence?
8. Which organizational pattern is useful when listeners don't know how serious a problem is?
9. When is the statement-of-reasons pattern especially effective?
10. When is the comparative-advantages pattern most effective?

Building Critical-Thinking Skills

1. Charities often give instructions like these to their fund-raisers: "If people decline to contribute, ask them to give just a token amount, such as a quarter or one dollar." These instructions are sometimes effective in building support for an organization because they follow one of the successful persuasive techniques discussed in this chapter. What is the technique?
2. Which organizational pattern is used in this partial outline (which shows the two main points of a speech)?

   I. Car thefts have risen in frequency throughout the United States.

   II. The number of thefts can be dramatically reduced if owners make their cars less vulnerable.

Building Teamwork Skills

1. Working in a group, create a brief synopsis for a television commercial that uses the motivated sequence. Some possible topics:
   a. Buying a certain brand of toothpaste
   b. Exercising at a spa or gym
   c. Donating blood to the Red Cross
   d. Buying a cellular telephone
2. The text discusses the effectiveness of role play. In a group, brainstorm a list of distracting or disruptive behaviors that audience members sometimes exhibit. Then let each person take turns playing the role of a speaker, while the rest of the group members in sequence act out the bad behaviors. The speaker's job is to respond to each undesired behavior in a firm but friendly manner. After each speaker finishes responding to the disrupters, the group should discuss how the speaker fared both verbally and nonverbally.

Building Internet Skills

www.mhhe.com/gregory7

1. When researching current issues, you often can find good information in magazine and newspaper articles. On the Internet, find a magazine or newspaper article that deals with the question, "Are organic foods better nutritionally than other foods?"

Possible Strategy: Go to one of the Internet sites listed under "Collections of Full-Text Articles" in Table 6.1 in Chapter 6.

2. The Internet is a rich source for bonus material that can be given to the audience as leave-behinds. Find and print a graphic showing how the concept of "lift" makes air flight possible.

Possible Strategy: Visit Websites listed in Table 9.1, "Free Multimedia Materials on the Internet," in Chapter 9. For searching, use these keywords: +airplane +lift +wing.

Using PowerWeb

www.mhhe.com/gregory7

In "Persuading Powerfully," Philip Vassallo advises you to "anticipate objections." What does this mean and what are the advantages, according to Vassallo? To find this article, visit www.mhhe.com/gregory7, click on STUDENT EDITION and then POWERWEB: CONTENTS.

Actress Julia Louis-Dreyfus gives speeches urging Americans to conserve energy in their homes as a way of saving money and reducing reliance on foreign oil. In order to persuade an audience, speakers often must demonstrate that they "practice what they preach." In her case, Louis-Dreyfus tells about the renovations that she and her husband made when they bought an old house. By adding insulation and solar panels, they cut their annual energy bill in half.

17

Persuasive Strategies

Outline

Knowing Your Audience
Analyze Listeners
Use a Persuasion Scale
Plan Strategy

Building Credibility
Explain Your Competence
Be Accurate
Show Your Open-Mindedness
Show Common Ground with Your Audience

Providing Evidence

Using Sound Reasoning
Deduction
Induction
Fallacies in Reasoning

Appealing to Motivations
Some Common Motivations
How to Motivate an Audience

Arousing Emotions

Objectives

After studying this chapter, you should be able to:

1. Describe how to analyze listeners, using a persuasion scale.
2. Explain how to build credibility with an audience in a persuasive speech.
3. Explain how to marshal convincing evidence in a persuasive speech.
4. Distinguish between deduction and induction as tools of reasoning in a persuasive speech.
5. Identify eight fallacies in reasoning.
6. Select motivational appeals for a persuasive speech.
7. Explain how to arouse emotions in a persuasive speech.

About one-third of teenagers in the United States choose not to wear seat belts when they travel in cars. They believe, according to a survey by car maker Volkswagen, that seat belt use is "uncool." Unfortunately, the price some of these teenagers pay for being cool is tragic. Of the 5,341 teens killed in motor vehicle crashes in 2002, experts estimate that 3,205 would have survived if they had been wearing seat belts.

Imagine that you are preparing a speech to persuade an audience of high school students to wear seat belts. Your primary target is the resistant one-third who decline to buckle up. Consider the two options shown in Figure 17.1 and decide which one would be more persuasive.

Figure 17.1

For a speech aimed at persuading teenagers to buckle their seat belts, which option would be more persuasive?

Option A

A speaker relates the story of Mary Reinhart, 17, of Deerfield, Wisconsin, who is shown visiting the roadside marker where her longtime boyfriend and two other friends were killed in a car crash. Reinhart was in the car, too, but she survived with just a few bruises. She was the only one wearing a seat belt. Police said that if the others had been wearing seat belts, they would not have been thrown from the car, and they probably would have survived with only minor injuries.

Option B

In some states, police can give tickets to a driver who is not wearing a seat belt. Imagine that a speaker in one of those states says to teenagers, "The police in our area are out in force, giving tickets to any driver who isn't buckled up. If you get a ticket, you must pay a fine, you risk having your car insurance premium raised, and you have to explain the matter to your parents."

The answer seems easy. Isn't Option A far more likely to scare teenagers into buckling up? Believe it or not, research indicates that Option B is more effective.

How could this be true? How could the threat of a traffic ticket be scarier than the threat of death? Researchers have found that for the resistant group of teenagers, Option A is unpersuasive. These kids consider themselves immortal. Death is a remote abstraction—something that happens to other people. On the other hand, getting a ticket and having to confront your parents—that's a different matter. A teen might reason, "With all those cops buzzing around, I could get a ticket. My old man would kill me. I guess I'd better buckle up."

For decades, educators and safety officials used variations of Option A, with little or no success in changing the behavior of the resistant group. By trial and error, they discovered that Option B seems to be the only approach that has any amount of success in changing behavior. (Of course, we are talking about relative success—some teenagers are not persuaded by either option.) The effectiveness of Option B can be seen when one compares those states that are "tough" (giving lots of tickets for failure to wear seat belts) and those states that are "soft" (having little or no enforcement). Random checks of seat belt usage show that the "tough" states have a much higher percentage of buckled-up teenagers than the "soft" states. And—no surprise—the "tough" states have a lower rate of teenage car-crash fatalities.[1]

The seat belt paradox demonstrates that a persuasive speech involves more than putting together a presentation that seems—to you—to be logical and effective. To get people to think or act a certain way, you must know how to reach them. This does not mean—as some students think—that you are being advised to manipulate your listeners. It means discovering who they are and how to meet their needs and interests.

In this chapter we will examine some practical techniques for reaching the audience in a persuasive speech. Here are six key questions that can guide you in your preparation of this kind of speech:

- Who are my listeners?
- How can I make myself and my ideas believable?
- What evidence would most likely convince these listeners?
- What form of reasoning would be most compelling?
- How can I appeal to the listeners' motivations?
- How can I arouse their emotions?

Let us examine each of these questions in greater detail.

Knowing Your Audience

As our seat belt scenario above demonstrates, the first step in persuasion is understanding your listeners. To truly understand them, you must find out where they are standing, then go over to that spot, stand in their shoes, and see the world as they see it. Only after you have seen the world from their perspective will you have any chance of leading them to where you want them to stand.

Here are some strategies for understanding your audience:

Analyze Listeners

www.mhhe.com/gregory7
Use Survey Tutor to prepare audience questionnaires.

How can you find out where listeners stand? Using the techniques discussed in Chapter 4, gather information about your audience. Interview some of the listeners to determine how much they know on your subject and what their beliefs and attitudes are. A questionnaire can be used to poll all members of the audience.

Use a Persuasion Scale

For analyzing an audience, consider using the persuasion scale in Table 17.1.[2] On the scale, mark where the listeners are in relation to your specific purpose *before* you speak. Then mark where you hope they will be *after* you speak. Knowing a starting point and an ideal finishing point will prevent you from giving a speech that fails to connect with your audience.

If you are wanting to persuade your audience to take steps to prevent theft of their bags at airports, it might be a mistake to assume that the audience is at Stage 6 (ready to take action by doing such things as disguising valuables). Perhaps they are really at Stage 1 (unaware of how frequently and easily bags are stolen). In that case, you should start at Stage 1 and move toward Stage 6.

Set a realistic goal. Don't feel that you are a failure if your listeners fall short of Stage 6. With some listeners, helping them go from Stage 1 to Stage 5 is a fine accomplishment. With other listeners, persuading them to move from Stage 2 to Stage 4 is a great triumph.

Plan Strategy

While some entire audiences may fit neatly into one category or another, many audiences are segmented—that is, you may find 16 listeners opposed to your view, 15 apathetic, 8 already convinced, and so on. (For the scale in Table 17.1, you can use color pens for each segment—for example, mark red for the start-

Table 17.1
Persuasion Scale

1	2	3	4	5	6
Unaware of the issue	Aware of the issue but opposed to your view	Aware of the issue but apathetic	Informed and interested but neutral on your view	Convinced of your view	Ready to take action

Tips for your CAREER

Tip 17.1 Don't Expect Universal Success

One of the greatest orations in American history—the Gettysburg Address—was a failure, in the opinion of some of Abraham Lincoln's contemporaries. An editorial in the *Chicago Times* on the day after his speech said, "The cheek of every American must tingle with shame as he reads the silly, flat and dishwatery utterances of the man who has to be pointed out to intelligent foreigners as the President of the United States."

Career Track, a company that sponsors business speeches and seminars throughout the United States, asks listeners to evaluate each of its speakers. No speaker has ever received 100 percent satisfaction. No matter who the speaker, no matter what the subject matter, at least 2 percent of listeners are dissatisfied. Even popular spellbinders can please no more than 98 percent.

In your career, do your best, try to meet the needs of all listeners, but remember that you can give an oration equal in greatness to the Gettysburg Address and still fail to please that intractable 2 percent.

ing point and finishing point for listeners who oppose your position, blue for neutral listeners, and black for favorable listeners.)

When you have several different segments, to which group should you devote your energies? An easy answer is: Try to meet the needs of everyone. While this is an admirable goal, it cannot always be achieved. Often there are priorities and variables beyond your control. Let's say that for a speech on a highly technical subject, you ascertain that 3 listeners are totally uninformed on your topic while the remaining 19 are well-informed. If you have been allotted only 10 minutes, you would be foolish to spend most of your time giving basic information to the 3 uninformed listeners. If the situation is reversed, with 19 uninformed and 3 well-informed, you should focus, of course, on the majority.

The best approach: Try to meet the needs of all listeners, but when this is impossible, choose the group that is most important. If, for example, you are trying to persuade a group of homeowners to buy mortgage insurance from your company, aim your remarks at those listeners who are predisposed to buying insurance but haven't yet chosen a company to buy from. Don't devote all your time and energy trying to win over those stubborn members of the audience who swear they will never buy insurance under any circumstances.

Despite the difficulty of meeting the needs of several different segments, there are some strategies you can employ. Using our persuasion scale, let's examine how to reach listeners with *starting* points at each of the six stages. As we proceed, study Table 17.2, which shows an example of how to apply our strategies.

1. **Unaware of the issue.** For people in the dark on your topic, start by explaining the situation and showing why your ideas are important. Later in the speech, try to convince them to adopt your view.
2. **Aware of the issue but opposed to your view.** Find out the listeners' reasons for opposing your view and then aim at refuting them. When listeners are strongly skeptical or hostile to an idea, a smart plan often is to delay divulging your central idea until the end of your speech (this idea will be discussed later in this chapter under inductive reasoning).

Table 17.2 Using the Persuasion Scale

Situation: A speech aimed at persuading listeners to support curtailment of theft from hotel and motel rooms.		
Position on Scale	**Strategy**	**Example**
1. Unaware of the issue	Explain the problem.	"Thefts from hotels and motels amount to more than $100 million each year. Items stolen are not just towels, but irons and ironing boards, hair dryers, bedspreads, blankets, pillows, wall-mounted telephones, coffee makers, lamps, mirrors, paintings, and TV remote controls."
2. Aware of the issue but opposed to your view	Refute opposing arguments or schemes.	"You may think that the solution is to seek police action, but this is not practical. The police don't have time to investigate and prosecute what they consider minor crimes."
3. Aware of the issue but apathetic	Show that the issue can impact listeners' lives.	"This kind of theft may seem inconsequential, but the American Hotel & Motel Association estimates that to make up for the thefts, hotels and motels have to price their rooms at 10 percent higher than they would otherwise. In other words, you and I must pay extra because of all this stealing."
4. Informed and interested but neutral on your view	Show that your proposal offers the best solution to the problem.	"I propose that hotels and motels require a $100 deposit when a person checks in. Then, when he or she is ready to check out, the room is quickly inspected and if nothing is missing, the $100 deposit is returned."
5. Convinced of your view	Reinforce existing beliefs and give new reasons for supporting your view.	"My proposal should not be an inconvenience for the honest person, and it can ensure that when we check into a room, we won't have to call the front desk and request a coffee maker to replace the one that the previous occupant of the room must have swiped."
6. Ready to take action	Show how, when, and where to take action.	"As you leave today, please sign the petition that details my proposal. I will make photocopies and send them to the headquarters of all the major hotel and motel chains."

Always show respect for opponents and their views. *Never* insult or belittle those who disagree; sarcastic or belligerent remarks make people defensive and all the more committed to their opinion. Try to persuade these people, but if that fails, be content if you can move them a few inches closer to your side. Sometimes the best you can hope for is to plant some seeds of doubt about their position that might someday sprout into full-blown conversion to your side.

3. Aware of the issue but apathetic. "Who cares?" is the attitude of listeners in this category. To break through their crust of apathy, show that the issue has an impact on their own lives.

4. Informed and interested but neutral on your view. People at this stage need little background information; you can plunge directly into convincing them that your position is correct or superior to other views.
5. Convinced of your view. For listeners who agree with you, try to reinforce their belief and, if possible, give them new reasons for supporting your position. Although they agree with your view, some listeners may not have considered or endorsed a plan of action; with them, your task is to demonstrate that your plan offers the best course of action.
6. Ready to take action. For speeches aimed at motivating action, this is the stage you want all listeners to reach (although you may not be able to bring every listener this far). Show listeners how, when, and where to take action.

As we noted above, it is often difficult (and sometimes impossible) to meet the needs of all listeners when their starting points are at different stages on our scale. But sometimes you can do so. All the examples in Table 17.2 could be integrated into one speech, permitting you to meet the needs of listeners at all six stages.

Building Credibility

At four-year colleges, should students be permitted to gain their degree in just three years?

If you had asked this question a decade ago, the answer would have been "no" at almost all schools, but today, an increasing number of colleges are saying "yes."

What happened to change policy so dramatically?

A decade ago, the presidents of two of the nation's top schools—Gerhard Casper of Stanford University and S. Frederick Starr of Oberlin College—announced their belief that American colleges should offer the three-year option. "There are some beautifully prepared people," said Starr, "who are quite capable of completing the material required for the B.A. in three years."[3]

Before these men spoke, most U.S. educators viewed the three-year degree as an absurd notion that would weaken students' preparation and competence. After the presidents spoke, many (but not all) educators changed their minds. Their reaction was probably something like this: "If the presidents of Stanford and Oberlin say that three-year degrees are not absurd and hurtful, then we should consider the idea."

This remarkable turnaround was due to the high credibility enjoyed by the two presidents. Because of their personal reputations and the prestige of their schools, they were deemed knowledegable and trustworthy.

This episode illustrates the power of **credibility**—a major source of persuasiveness in all human communication. Before listeners can accept your ideas, they want to know whether you are reliable, competent, and trustworthy.

credibility
degree to which a speaker is perceived to be believable, trustworthy, and competent

In your career, when you want to persuade people who know you well, your credibility boils down to how they assess your character. If you are a person who is known for honesty, fairness, and competence, you enter the speech with a powerful asset. If you are known for dishonesty, unfairness, or incompetence, you enter with a heavy liability.

Ethical Issue

In the speech itself, credibility is enhanced if your delivery is enthusiastic and if your speech is clear, well-organized, and well-reasoned.[4] In addition, you can build credibility by following these guidelines:

Explain Your Competence

If you have special expertise, be sure to let your audience know about it—modestly, of course. Don't boast; just give the facts. Describing your special competence enhances your credibility because it shows that you are speaking from personal experience. It says, "I've been there—I know what I'm talking about." Here is how student speaker Lauren Shriver bolstered her credibility during a speech:

> Deep-sea diving is not dangerous—if you follow all the safety rules. I've made over 50 dives myself, and I feel very safe because I'm very careful each time. I never allow myself to get slack and overconfident.

Shriver's information about her diving experience was necessary to give credibility to her remarks. Notice how she inserted her personal background in a modest way.

If you lack personal knowledge of a subject and therefore must rely on the authority of others, you can enhance your own credibility by showing that you have chosen competent sources. For example, in arguing that computers in the future will be capable of humanlike thinking, Don Stafford knew that his ideas might sound farfetched coming from a student, so he said:

> My information comes from the work of Dr. Patrick Winston, who for the past 10 years has been director of the Artificial Intelligence Laboratory at Massachusetts Institute of Technology. Let me explain an experiment that Dr. Winston carried out . . .

By quoting from an eminent authority, Stafford was able to give his speech instant credibility.

Be Accurate

Sloppiness with facts and figures can make your whole speech less believable. In a speech on child abuse, one student said that 55 percent of American parents abused their children—a statistic that listeners scoffed at during the question-and-answer period. (A few days later, the student sheepishly admitted to the instructor that the original source estimated 5.5 percent rather than 55—the overlooked decimal point made a huge difference.) When listeners believe you are wrong on a point, even when it's a small matter, they tend to distrust everything else you say.

Another destroyer of credibility is oversimplification. One student, who gave a talk on the desirability of eating whole-wheat bread, made this comment: "In the 1700s, rich people ate white refined bread, which caused them to grow sickly and weak. Meanwhile the poor people ate whole-wheat bread, which caused them to grow strong. Eventually the poor people overthrew the rich people in the revolutions at the end of the century." While diet may have played a part in health and disease during the 1700s, it is an oversimplification to say that white bread was the main factor in the revolutions that rocked the world in that century. Many complex social and economic factors were involved. When you oversimplify in this way, listeners view you as unreliable.

Show Your Open-Mindedness

"If you would convince others," Lord Chesterfield once said, "seem open to conviction yourself."[5] In other words, show that you are a reasonable person who is open-minded and receptive, and quite capable of being wrong. This approach is not only an ethical one, but it is also highly effective in building credibility. Audiences distrust fanatical know-it-alls who never admit that they might be mistaken.

In a community speech, Patricia Caldwell argued for the right of parents to teach their children at home instead of sending them to school. After citing cases of home-taught children excelling in college, she showed her open-mindedness by conceding that some parents are bad teachers:

> In one well-publicized case in Chicago a few months ago, the authorities brought legal action against a husband and wife for not sending their children to school. Their idea of a home school was to make the children—ages 7, 9, and 10—work all day instead of teaching them to read and write.[6]

Was it stupid for the speaker to relate an incident that seemed to negate her central idea (that some parents can do a better job of teaching than the public schools)? No, because she went on to say that bad parent-teachers are rare, and that periodic state inspections can weed them out. Rather than damaging her case, her concession strengthened it, for she showed herself to the audience as a fair minded individual who could be trusted. If you were a listener, wouldn't you trust her more than someone who asserted that *all* parents are good teachers?

It is especially important to be reasonable and open-minded during the question-and-answer period. I have seen some speakers do a good job in their speech, but when they are asked questions by listeners, they become rigid and defensive. They refuse to admit error or to concede that a listener has a good point. These speakers severely damage their own credibility and undo much of the persuasiveness of the speech itself.

Show Common Ground with Your Audience

When you are introduced to someone at a party, you try to find things that you have in common. You ask each other questions ("What is your major?" "Where are you from?") until you hit upon some interest that you share. Often a person introducing you will try to help you find common ground ("Rick, I'd like you to meet Michelle. She loves soccer as much as you do."). We try to find common ground because it not only helps us to make conversation but also helps us to feel comfortable with another person.

In a speech, listeners respect and trust a speaker who is similar to themselves, so your job is to show that to some degree you are like your listeners. This does not mean compromising your beliefs; it means highlighting those

Tips for your CAREER

Tip 17.2 In a Debate, Be Reasonable and Fair

Your boss knows that you strongly oppose a proposed policy, and she asks you to debate the issue with a colleague at the next staff meeting. What is your best approach? Should you demolish your foe with a slashing, take-no-prisoners assault, ripping him apart with sarcasm and scorn, while upholding your own view with an air of righteous indignation? No, this approach may sound effective, but it is actually counterproductive.

"Victory is not won by bluster," says Professor Douglas Hunt. "Inexperienced arguers tend to enter the arena like gladiators ready for combat . . . They often allow their commitment to one side of an argument to blind them to the virtues of the other. They argue so aggressively that the audience dismisses them as cranks." Effective arguers, in contrast, "are usually cautious, courteous, and reasonable . . . They understand, anticipate, and even sympathize with the arguments of their opponents . . . They give the impression of being reasonable people whose judgment can be trusted."

Avoid cheap shots—that is, unfair and unwarranted abuse or ridicule aimed at a person. For example, a speaker at a public forum on air pollution ridiculed environmentalists as "mushroom pickers who weep at the thought of a butterfly dying." If you throw such poisoned barbs, listeners who agree with you may laugh and applaud your cleverness, but listeners who are neutral or opposed to your position (the very people you want to win over) may discount everything you say. In fact, your unfairness may elicit sympathy for the other side.

characteristics you share with the audience. This is especially important if some of the listeners are hostile to your ideas. Say, for example, that you are speaking on gun control, and you know that half the listeners are already against your position. Here's what you can say:

> I'm talking on gun control today. I know that a lot of you are opposed to the position I'm going to take. I ask only that you hear me out and see if my arguments have any merit whatsoever. Though we may disagree on this subject, you and I have at least one thing in common: We want to see a reduction in the number of violent, gun-related crimes in our society.

With this kind of statement, you not only pinpoint common ground (opposition to crime) but also appeal to the audience's sense of fair play.

One of the best ways to build credibility is to show listeners that you identify with them—that you share (or have shared) their experiences or feelings. In recent years, Sarah Ferguson, the Duchess of York, has worked with the U.S. Surgeon General, NBC News, and Weight Watchers International to educate people on the dangers of obesity. "I know what it's like to be humiliated," she tells her audiences. Once weighing over 200 pounds, she was derided by British newspapers as "the Duchess of Pork."[7] In her presentations, Ferguson demonstrates that she has endured the same frustrations that many of her listeners have experienced:

> I think I've been on every single diet you could possibly think of. Hard-boiled eggs for a week. Grapes for a week. Every quick-fix diet, I've tried it. You can lose an awful lot of weight that way, but then, a week later—oh oh, the jeans are tight again.[8]

When listeners see the common ground they share with Ferguson, they are more inclined to trust her argument that obesity can be avoided through careful diet and daily exercise.

Sarah Ferguson, the Duchess of York, once weighed over 200 pounds and was derided by the British press as "the Duchess of Pork." How does this experience affect her credibility in her campaign against obesity? See text for details.

Providing Evidence

When you make an assertion in a speech, it is not enough to say, "Trust me on this" or "I know I'm right." The audience wants **evidence,** or proof. Evidence can be presented in the forms we discussed in Chapter 8: narratives, statistics, examples, testimony, and so on. For each main point in your speech, choose the evidence that is most likely to prove your point with a particular audience. Ask yourself these questions:

evidence
the facts, examples, statistics, testimony, and other information that support an assertion

1. Is the evidence *accurate*? Erroneous information would obviously undermine the credibility of your entire speech.
2. Is the evidence *up-to-date*? A research study conducted in the field of medicine in 1936 is almost certain to be outdated.
3. Is the evidence *typical*? An athlete may attribute his success to consuming five banana milkshakes a day, but is his diet common among athletes or is he probably the only one in the world with such a diet?

SpeechMate CD-ROM
To see a speaker who provides strong evidence, view Speech 4 ("Bicycle Helmets") on Disk 1.

Here are some tips on using evidence:

Choose evidence from reliable, reputable sources. While watching TV news one night, I was astounded by this story:

> A New York doctor reports that a patient experienced epileptic seizures whenever she heard the voice of Mary Hart, co-host of the TV show *Entertainment Tonight*. The seizures ceased when she stopped watching the show.

My immediate reaction was total disbelief. What nonsense! Hearing a person's voice cannot cause a seizure. But then the news anchor added:

> The woman was the subject of an article in the *New England Journal of Medicine* by Dr. Venkat Ramani, professor of neurology at Albany Medical College in New York.

Just as suddenly as I had disbelieved the story, I now believed it. Why? Because the *New England Journal of Medicine* is one of the mostly highly respected medical journals in the world and would not publish an article unless its editors considered it to be sound and reliable.

Evidence—especially the hard-to-believe variety—becomes much more convincing to the audience if you cite a reliable source. Be sure to give full details; instead of saying, "a judge," give her name and title: "Sharon Brown, Chief Justice of our state's Supreme Court."

Provide a variety of evidence. In some cases a single example or statistic may be sufficient to bolster an argument, but in most persuasive situations, multiple support is needed.

Use a vivid personal narrative whenever possible. Imagine that you are planning a speech on drunk driving. If you want to convince your listeners that they stand a chance of being victimized by a drunk driver, which of the following would be the more persuasive piece of evidence?

www.mhhe.com/gregory7
To test your knowledge of evidence, do the interactive exercise in Chapter 17 on this book's Website.

1. You relate the sad, shocking details of an automobile accident in which a drunk driver hit your car and killed one of your passengers.
2. You cite the fact that 25,000 people are killed in America each year in alcohol-related car accidents.

Though you would need to use both of these items in your speech, item 1 would be more persuasive for most listeners. But, you might ask, how can one solitary case be more persuasive than a statistic encompassing 25,000 people? Psychologists have conducted scores of experiments that indicate that one vivid narrative, told from the speaker's personal experience, is much more persuasive than its statistical status would imply.[9] "All other things being equal," writes social psychologist Elliot Aronson, "most people are more deeply influenced by one clear, vivid personal example than by an abundance of statistical data."[10]

While using a variety of evidence in your persuasive speeches, remember that your most powerful evidence may be found in your own pool of personal experiences.[11]

Using Sound Reasoning

reasoning
using logic to draw conclusions from evidence

Reasoning, the act of reaching conclusions on the basis of logical thinking, is a part of everyday life. If you take an umbrella with you on a walk because you notice heavy clouds massing in the sky, you are using reasoning to prevent yourself from getting soaked by the rain that will soon fall. While it is true that people are not always logical and rational, it is also true that they frequently can be persuaded by a message that appeals to their powers of reasoning.[12]

Let's look at two popular types of reasoning and then examine some common fallacies of reasoning.

Deduction

Imagine that you are driving a car on a highway at a speed that exceeds the speed limit by 15 miles per hour. Suddenly you see a police car parked behind a billboard; as you whiz past, you notice that a radar device is protruding from the police car. You slow down, but you know it is too late: you are certain to be stopped. Sure enough, you glance in your rearview mirror and see a second police car with lights flashing; the officer motions you to pull over.

How did you know that you were going to be stopped? By using **deduction**—a chain of reasoning that carries you from (1) a generalization to (2) a specific instance (of the generalization) to (3) a conclusion. In formal logic, this chain of reasoning is expressed in a form of argument known as a **syllogism:**

deduction
reasoning from a generalization to a specific conclusion

syllogism
a deductive scheme consisting of a major premise, a minor premise, and a conclusion

Major premise (generalization):	Motorists who are speeding when they pass a radar point are stopped by police.
Minor premise (specific instance):	I was speeding when I passed a radar point.
Conclusion:	Therefore, I will be stopped.

The Power of a Syllogism

Deductive reasoning with a syllogism is one of the most powerful tools of persuasion that a speaker can use. If you can convince your listeners to accept the major and minor premises, the conclusion is inescapable. The listeners are compelled by logic to accept it.

SpeechMate CD-ROM
To see a sample of deductive reasoning, view Video Clip 17.1.

Until her death in 1906, Susan B. Anthony was one of the foremost fighters for the right of women to vote—a right that was not fully secured until 1920, when the Nineteenth Amendment to the Constitution granted nationwide suffrage to women. In speeches delivered throughout the United States, Anthony used deductive logic as her persuasive strategy.[13] If we put the essence of her speeches in the form of a syllogism, it would look like this:

Major premise (generalization):	The Constitution guarantees all U.S. citizens the right to vote.
Minor premise (specific instance):	Women are U.S. citizens.
Conclusion:	Therefore, women have the right to vote.

To us today, this syllogism looks simple and obvious: How could Anthony have failed to persuade every listener? But bear in mind that in the 19th century many people viewed women as less than full-fledged citizens. In her speeches, Anthony had to devote her energies to convincing her audience of both the major premise and the minor premise. Those listeners whom she won over were then obliged by force of logic to accept her conclusion.

In a speech, deductive reasoning is convincing *only if both premises are true and are accepted by the audience as true.*[14] Would an audience be likely to accept the following chain of reasoning?

Major premise:	Cardiovascular exercise improves eyesight.
Minor premise:	Jogging is a form of cardiovascular exercise.
Conclusion:	Therefore, jogging improves eyesight.

The minor premise is true, but the major premise is false, so the entire syllogism is flawed. An audience would reject the conclusion.

How to Use a Syllogism

Of what value is a syllogism to you? In preparing a persuasive speech, you can use the power of deductive logic in two ways:

1. Putting your audience's reasoning into a syllogism helps you plan your persuasive strategy. Let's suppose that you are preparing a speech aimed at persuading your classmates to use on-line auctions to buy and sell products. From your interviews with them, you know that most are reluctant to use on-line auctions. On paper, you translate their reasoning into the form of a syllogism:

Major premise:	Financial transactions that permit the possibility of fraud should be avoided.
Minor premise:	On-line auctions are financial transactions that permit the possibility of fraud.
Conclusion:	Therefore, on-line auctions should be avoided.

When you analyze this syllogism, you see that your best point of attack is against the listeners' minor premise. Your main counterargument will be: On-line auctions have many safeguards to prevent fraud; for example, potential buyers can investigate the seller's reputation by reading a file of comments from previous buyers.

By looking at the architecture of your listeners' thoughts, you have enhanced your chances of tearing down what you consider a wall of error.

2. Putting your own thoughts into a syllogism helps you create a persuasive structure. Not every speech can be fashioned into a syllogism, but sometimes a syllogism gives you a handy framework for the task of persuasion. To continue with our auction example, you could create the following syllogism:

Major premise:	Auctions that are honest and reliable offer good bargains for consumers.
Minor premise:	On-line auctions are honest and reliable.
Conclusion:	Therefore, on-line auctions offer good bargains for consumers.

If you can convince listeners of the truth of both the major premise and the minor premise, force of logic will lead them to accept the conclusion.

Induction

induction
reasoning from specific evidence to a general conclusion

While deduction moves from the general to the specific, **induction** proceeds from the specific to the general. Imagine that you are a pediatrician seeing patients one January morning in your office:

- The first patient, age 9, complains of a runny nose, sore throat, headache, and muscle aches. You discover that she has a fever of 103°.
- The second patient, 7, has similar complaints and a fever of 102°.
- Third patient—same symptoms, plus a fever of 101.5°.
- Fourth patient—similar complaints and a fever of 102.5°.
- Fifth patient—similar symptoms and a fever of 103°.

You know from your medical training that these complaints are classic symptoms of influenza (or flu). You know that influenza is an epidemic disease, striking many people in a community, usually in winter. On the basis of what you have seen, you reason inductively that your community is experiencing an influenza epidemic. You use *specific* evidence (or isolated observations) to reach a *general* conclusion. In reaching this conclusion, however, you must take an *inductive leap.* You cannot prove that there is a flu epidemic simply because of your five patients. You are probably right, but your conclusion has to remain tentative (until further evidence is gathered, and the county health department declares an epidemic) because there is always the chance that some other explanation can account for your five patients' illness. Perhaps they have nasty colds or suffer from some new virus; perhaps no other patients with those symptoms will show up at your office during the remainder of the week. The chances are overwhelming that an influenza epidemic *is* the explanation, of course; but the point is that induction, unlike deduction, never leads to a certain conclusion, only a *very likely* one.

SpeechMate CD-ROM
To see a sample of inductive reasoning, view Video Clip 17.2.

The Usefulness of Induction

The inductive method is used frequently by scientists. They make isolated observations and then form a hypothesis. They may note, for instance, that the average temperature is rising each year in Sydney, Tokyo, Cairo, Rome, Copenhagen, Montreal, Lima, Mexico City, and Los Angeles. Therefore—now they take an inductive leap—the entire globe is warming up.

The inductive method has often led to useful discoveries. In World War II, British fighter planes had cockpit covers made of plastic. During combat a cover would sometimes shatter, causing pieces of plastic to become lodged in the pilots' eyes. In pilot after pilot, a British physician observed that the eyes were not damaged or infected by the plastic fragments. This observation led to the use of plastic to make artificial lenses, including contact lenses, for people's eyes.

How to Construct an Inductive Argument

Some public speakers construct their inductive arguments by following three steps: (1) ask a question, (2) answer the question by collecting as much specific evidence as possible, and (3) reach a conclusion based on the evidence. Here is an example:

Question: Do smoke detectors save lives?

Evidence:

Item 1: Five members of the Payne family in Cincinnati, Ohio, escaped unharmed from their burning home thanks to the alarm set off by a smoke detector.

Item 2: In a fire that destroyed a nursing home in Oakland, California, smoke detectors were credited with saving the lives of all 49 residents.

Item 3: A mother and two small children in Dearborn, Michigan, were rescued from a third-floor apartment where they had been trapped by fire; a smoke detector had awakened the mother and enabled her to call 911 promptly.

Conclusion: Smoke detectors save lives.

Is this all you need for evidence? No. Although the inductive reasoning up to this point is powerful, you would need to show that your examples are not isolated flukes. You could, for example, cite statistical studies:

- In a study of 392 home fires occurring during the night, 78 percent of the homeowners said they might have died if their smoke detectors had not alerted them.
- Of the 5,000 Americans who die each year in home fires, the National Safety Council estimates that 84 percent died because their homes either had no smoke detectors or had inoperative smoke detectors (containing dead batteries).

When you use inductive reasoning, you will convince an audience only if your evidence is strong. If you have weak evidence, your conclusion will be weak. In the preceding example, if you had used vague statements like "The manufacturers of smoke detectors assure us that their products will save lives," your evidence would have been too flimsy to support the conclusion.

When to Use Inductive Reasoning

While inductive reasoning can be used for all or part of any kind of persuasive speech, there are two situations in which it is especially effective:

1. Consider using inductive reasoning when your audience is likely to react to your central idea with skepticism or hostility. Earlier in this book, you were advised to state your central idea in the introduction of your speech; there is, however, an important exception to this guideline. If listeners are likely to have a negative reaction to your central idea, a wise strategy is to lead them through an inductive chain, saving the central idea for the latter part of the speech.

Student speaker Sherry Ferguson wanted to convince her public speaking class to buy anti-virus software, but she suspected that her classmates would be skeptical about spending money on what many people consider to be an unnecessary product. So she used an inductive process, saving her central idea for late in the speech.

> I have used a computer since I was 12. Until recently I never worried about computer viruses. I figured that my chances of getting hit by a virus were as remote as getting hit by a meteor while driving on the interstate.
>
> But two months ago, my luck ran out. I opened a cartoon in an e-mail attachment that a friend sent me, and the next day a virus wiped out everything on my hard drive. I had not backed up my files, and I lost all my notes and research information.
>
> I have a friend who opened the same cartoon, but his computer spotted the virus and eliminated it before it could do any damage. You see, my friend had spent $35 on anti-virus software.

Then Ferguson told of other people who had experienced similar outcomes—the ones without anti-virus software suffered harm, while the ones with the protection escaped unscathed. Finally, she was ready to present her central idea: "You should buy anti-virus software in order to protect your computer data."

Her inductive chain of examples must have been successful because most of the classmates—on their evaluation sheets—reported that they had been persuaded to buy the software.

An inductive line of reasoning helps listeners keep an open mind. When they watch you build your case block by block, they are more respectful and appreciative of the central idea when it is finally presented to them. This doesn't mean they will always agree with you, of course, but it does mean that those who are opposed to your ideas will probably see more merit to your case than they would if you announced your central idea in the introduction.

2. Use inductive reasoning when you wish to show the drama of discovery. Taking listeners down an inductive path can be fun and exciting. When representatives of Doumar Products Inc. appear at trade shows to sell Un-du, a product that neutralizes adhesives, they begin by demonstrating the product's ability to remove anything sticky—labels, price tags, masking tape, bumper stickers, and gum—without making a mess. In one amazing demonstration, they use Un-du to separate duct tape from single-ply toilet paper without damaging either, and then they show that after a few seconds of evaporation, the tape is once again sticky. After dazzling the audience with these discoveries, the presenters are ready to give their central idea—"Un-du is the best adhesive neutralizer on the market"—and ask listeners to buy the product. By now, making a sale is easy because "everyone's awed," according to the *New York Times.*[15]

Quick tip: If you have trouble remembering the difference between deduction and induction, keep in mind that they travel in opposite directions. Deduction (think of the word *deduct* in the sense of taking *away*) leads *away* from a generalization; it goes from general to specific, applying a general principle to a specific case. Induction (think of the first two letters *in*) leads *into,* or toward, a generalization; it goes from specific to general, accumulating specific instances that point toward a general idea.

Fallacies in Reasoning

A **fallacy** is an error in reasoning that renders an argument false or unreliable. You should become adept at recognizing fallacies so that (1) you can avoid using them in your own speeches—an ethical speaker would never knowingly mislead an audience—and (2) you can prevent yourself from being influenced by them when you listen to the speeches of others. Here are some common fallacies:

fallacy
an argument based on a false inference

Ethical Issue

Hasty Generalization

A **hasty generalization** is a conclusion that is reached on the basis of insufficient evidence. For example, "The two students who murdered classmates at Columbine High School in Colorado habitually wore all-black clothes. This shows that kids who wear all-black are potentially dangerous." The fact that two black-clad youths committed murder does not prove that all young people in black are a menace to society, although in the aftermath of the Columbine massacre, some news commentators made such an argument, and some school districts banned black clothing.[16]

hasty generalization
a conclusion that is based on inadequate evidence and is too broad to be fair

The hasty generalization is sometimes called "sweeping generalization" because it is so broad and so categorical that it ends up being unfair and inaccurate. It often includes words like *always, never, all,* and *none.* In a speech on the neglect of older Americans, one student said, "America is the only country in the world that has no regard for its elderly family members. All other countries have great respect for the age and wisdom of the elderly."

The speaker had a good point to make—that we need to take better care of our elderly—but he damaged his credibility by indulging in such an outrageously unfair generalization. Is it true that *all* Americans have *no* regard for the elderly? Don't some Americans have high regard for old people? Even if his accusation were true, how can he say that America is the *only* country exhibiting such neglect? Has he researched the situation in such nations as Zaire, Luxembourg, and Sri Lanka?

To make his argument reasonable and accurate, the speaker would need to modify the generalization to say: "Some Americans don't give their elderly family members the honor and attention that they deserve." Now the generalization would be acceptable to most listeners.

Red Herring

In seventeenth century England, according to legend, if criminals were being pursued by bloodhounds, they would drag a red herring (smoked fish) across the trail, confusing the dogs and making them veer off into a new direction.

red herring
diverting listeners from the real issue to an irrelevant matter

A **red herring** argument distracts listeners from the real issue and leads them toward an irrelevant issue. This trick is frequently used in political debates. One legislator, for example, may argue for laws protecting the California condor, and then an opponent counters, "How can we even think about birds when our most pressing problems deal with humans? Let's work on taking care of homeless people before we get all hot and bothered about animals."

The fallacy is also used in courtroom battles. If, say, a tobacco company is being sued by the government for endangering the health of citizens, a tobacco-company lawyer might try to divert the jury to a different subject: "Ladies and gentlemen of the jury, the government tells you that tobacco is poisonous, but they say nothing about alcohol. They say nothing about the 20,000 people killed each year by drunk drivers. I don't see the government suing whisky makers." Lawyers who employ this trick sometimes win their cases, but ethical speakers should never use it.

Attack on a Person

Some speakers try to win an argument by attacking a person rather than the person's ideas. For example: "Fitzroy has lived in upper-class luxury all his life, so how can we believe anything he says about government assistance for the poor? He obviously knows nothing about poverty." This **attack on a person,** sometimes known as *argumentum ad hominem* (argument against the man), is unfair and unethical. Fitzroy's arguments should be judged on how sound his ideas are, not on any aspect of his personal life.

attack on a person
criticizing an opponent rather than the opponent's argument

Attacks on a person are often used in the courtroom to discredit a witness ("Ladies and gentlemen of the jury, this witness admits that he's an atheist, so how can we trust him to tell us the truth?") and in politics to discredit a foe

("My opponent has gambled in Las Vegas at least five times. Do you want such a person to manage your tax dollars?"). Though this tactic may sometimes be effective, the ethical speaker never uses it, not only because it is dishonest and unfair but also because it can backfire and cause careful listeners to lose respect for the speaker.

False Cause

Beware of the fallacy of **false cause**—assuming that because events occur close together in time, they are necessarily related as cause and effect. A president takes office and four months later the unemployment rate goes up 1 percent. Can we say that the president's policies caused the rise in unemployment? It is possible that they did, but other factors may have caused the problem—for example, the economic policies of the previous administration.

false cause
assuming that because two events are related in time, the first caused the second

The fallacy of false cause also can occur when a speaker oversimplifies the causes of complex problems. Take, for example, a speaker who says that *the* cause of cancer is negative thinking. That explanation is simple and understandable—and wrong. While negative thinking may be implicated someday as a contributing factor in cancer, medical researchers say that no one thing has been isolated as *the* cause of cancer. The disease is probably caused by an interaction of several factors, including genetic predisposition, susceptibility of the immune system, the presence of a carcinogenic virus, and environmental irritants. Cancer is too complex to be explained by a single cause.

Building on an Unproven Assumption

Some speakers act as if an assertion has been proved when in fact it has not. Suppose that a speaker tells an audience: "Since distance learning with a computer is more effective than traditional classroom education, all of you should take your college courses on your home computers." The speaker is acting as if the superiority of distance learning is an established fact, when in reality many people disagree. An ethical speaker would first try to prove the merits of distance learning and then urge the audience to support it.

The fallacy of **building on an unproven assumption** (which is also called "begging the question") causes careful listeners to become resentful. They feel as if they are being tricked into giving assent to a proposition that they don't believe.

building on an unproven assumption
treating an opinion that is open to question as if it were already proved

False Analogy

When speakers use a **false analogy,** they make the mistake of assuming that because two things are alike in minor ways, they are also alike in major ways. For example, some people who want to stop illegal immigration from Mexico into the United States talk of "an invasion" by "an army of aliens" who overwhelm a "thin line of defenders."[17] While it is true that a large number of people cross the border, as would be the case in a military invasion, the analogy to war is erroneous. Mexican immigrants are not soldiers trying to conquer, but civilians looking for work. The "defenders" are border patrol officers whose job is not defense of the country but enforcement of immigration laws.

false analogy
creating a comparison that is exaggerated or erroneous

Here is another false analogy: "We can communicate effectively via satellite with people on the other side of the planet, so it should be easy for parents and children to communicate effectively within the intimate environment of their own homes." Upon close examination, this analogy falls apart. Satellite communication between nations is a purely technical matter of transmitting radio and television signals, whereas communication among family members is far more complex, involving psychological subtleties that are beyond the reach of technology.

Either-Or Reasoning

either-or fallacy
presenting only two alternatives when in fact more exist

The **either-or fallacy** occurs when a speaker offers only two alternatives, when in fact there are many. For example: "Either we halt the world's population growth, or we face widespread starvation." Aren't there other options, such as improving agriculture and slowing down the rate of population increase?

Stating an argument in stark, either-or terms makes a speaker appear unreasonable and dogmatic. Most problems should be seen as a complex mosaic of many colors—not a simple choice between pure red and pure green.

Straw Man

straw man
a weak opponent or dubious argument set up so that it can be easily defeated

To win arguments, some people create a **straw man,** a ridiculous caricature of what their opponents believe, and then beat it down with great ease. For example, the president of a company that sends spam (junk e-mail) argued that opponents who want to outlaw spam are anti-freedom. "These people want to curb free speech on the Internet. They want to deprive us of our right to communicate to the public."[18]

Did the speaker paint an accurate picture of anti-spammers? Of course not. Most anti-spam people advocate free speech on the Internet. They just don't want unsolicited garbage dumped daily into their electronic mailbox. A speaker like this spammer creates a straw man in order to look like a victor. Careful listeners, however, will spot the deception and lose confidence in the speaker.

Appealing to Motivations

motivations
the impulses and needs that stimulate a person to act in a certain way

Motivations are the needs, desires, or drives that impel a person toward a goal or away from some negative situation. People have hundreds of motivations, including love, happiness, health, social acceptance, financial security, adventure, and creativity.[19] If you show your listeners how your ideas can help them satisfy such needs and desires, you increase your chances of persuading them to adopt your point of view.[20] Here are some examples of how student speakers appealed to the motivations of their audiences:

SpeechMate CD-ROM
To see a speaker who appeals to motivations, view Video Clip 17.3.

- To raise money to buy food for starving people in Africa, LeeAnne Washington appealed to the motivation that most Americans have to help those less fortunate than themselves.
- To try to persuade listeners to use seat belts at all times in a car, Jason Bradley appealed to the strong drive that people have to protect themselves from harm.
- To try to convince listeners to invest in real estate, Glenda Jorgensen tapped the public's desire for financial security and wealth.

Some Common Motivations

Let's examine some of the more common motivations that audiences have. (This is a partial list—there are dozens of other motivations.)

- **Love and esteem.** People want to love and to be loved, to have good friends, to be esteemed at work and at home.
- **Health.** Your listeners want to avoid sickness, maintain their fitness and their health, and live a long time.
- **Safety.** People want to be protected from crime, and they want to use products that will not injure or kill them.
- **Success.** Most men and women wish for success of some sort, depending upon their individual definition of the term; for one person, success means making a million dollars, while for another, it is becoming the best violinist in an orchestra.
- **Financial security.** Most men and women desire a degree of financial security, though they would disagree on just how much money they need to achieve it.
- **Self-improvement.** Most people want to improve themselves, whether by learning a new skill or learning more effective ways of coping with life's problems.
- **Recreational pleasure.** People of all ages love to get away from the stress and toil of work by taking vacations, going to movies, eating at fine restaurants, and so on.
- **Altruism.** Many people have a sincere desire to help others, whether through donating blood in their communities or through sending food to starving children in a faraway land.

How to Motivate an Audience

Here are some tips for motivating an audience:

Focus on listeners' needs, rather than on your own. Imagine the following scenario:

> At a large metropolitan newspaper, Smithers is sports editor and Parks is business editor, and they have the same problem in their departments: being shorthanded. This means that they and their staffs are overworked and stressed-out. So each editor appears before the senior management council to request the hiring of a new reporter.
>
> In her plea, Smithers tells the managers that she and her staff are constantly frazzled because of long hours and a crushing workload.
>
> Taking a different approach, Parks says that if a new reporter is hired for her department, news coverage can be expanded and this, in turn, can help entice more people to subscribe to the newspaper.

Which editor is more likely to win her case? Parks—because she appeals to the needs of the managers (the need to provide good coverage and the need to sell more newspapers). Smithers' case is weakened by focusing on her own needs.

Table 17.3 Motivations and Appeals

Motivation	Appeal
Feeling good	Bicycling works out tension and makes you feel energetic and happy.
Looking good	Bicycling burns lots of calories, so it's ideal for weight control. It also tones up leg muscles.
Long-term health	Bicycling is excellent exercise for heart and lungs, thus helping prevent cardiovascular disease.
Friendship	Being on a bicycle is an instant passport to the world of cyclists. It's easy to strike up conversations with other riders, and you can often make new friends. Cycling also provides an enjoyable activity to share with old friends.
Adventure	With a bicycle you can explore out-of-the-way places, travel long distances in a single day, and experience the thrill of flying down a steep mountain road.
Competition	If you enjoy competing, there are bike races in almost every city or town.

Appeal to more than one motivation. Whenever possible, appeal to several motivations at the same time. Listeners who are not reached by one appeal may be influenced by another. Suppose, for example, that you were trying to persuade your listeners to take up bicycling. Table 17.3 shows some of the motivations that you could identify, coupled with appropriate appeals.

By appealing to more than one motivation, you increase your chances of persuading the audience. For example, the listener who is already in superb health may not be reached by any of the first three items, but might be swayed by one of the last three.

Determine the strongest motivational appeals. As part of your audience analysis, ask yourself, "What are the *strongest* motivational appeals that I can make to this particular audience?" Then decide how you can work those appeals into your persuasive strategy.

Martha Ramsey, a representative for a cellular-telephone company, learned to use many motivational appeals in trying to gain new customers; for instance, she would point out the convenience of having a phone in your car. But the most powerful motivational factor, she determined, was safety. Therefore, she would emphasize safety in her sales talks: "I tell them, 'If you or members of your family are stranded in a dangerous or isolated area, or if someone threatens harm, a cellular phone can save your life. Think of your monthly cellular phone bill as a payment on an insurance policy.'"[21]

Anticipate conflicting needs. In analyzing the motivations of your listeners, ask yourself, "Will any need that I plan to emphasize conflict with some of their strongest desires and needs?" If so, confront the problem explicitly in your speech (in other words, don't pretend that the problem doesn't exist). Let's say that you urge your audience to invest in the stock market. From your audience analysis, you know that some listeners have a strong motivation to make money quickly and easily, but at the same time they have an equally strong desire not to "gamble" with their savings. To win over such listeners, you must acknowledge their ambivalence and work to overcome it (perhaps by saying, "I know many of you are worried that investing in the stock market is a gamble—a high-risk roll of the dice—but are you aware that you can choose a low-risk investment such as a mutual fund?").

Arousing Emotions

Emotions are "stirred up" feelings that can be either positive (amusement, love, joy) or negative (fear, anger, sadness). You can use emotional appeals to stimulate listeners and rouse them to action.

How can emotions be evoked? By using support materials (such as provocative narratives) or powerful language (such as vivid metaphors).

As an example of how emotions can be used effectively, here is an excerpt from a speech by student speaker Ralph Barnes on how persons with disabilities are sometimes victimized:

> Theresa Delzatto, 35, of Hartford, Connecticut, is paralyzed from the neck down. She survives on a Social Security check and lives in public housing. Just before Christmas last year, she went to Wal-Mart in her wheelchair to do some Christmas shopping. She went to the courtesy desk and explained that she could not use her arms, and she asked for assistance. An 18-year-old clerk was assigned to take items from the shelves and put them in her cart. When she was ready to pay, the clerk helped out by taking Delzatto's debit card from her purse and handing it to the cashier. But then—believe it or not—the clerk never returned the card! Instead she and a 17-year-old cousin went on a shopping spree with the card and racked up more than $400 worth of purchases. They were later arrested and charged with larceny, but the money was long gone. The theft wiped out all of Delzatto's money. She told the *Hartford Courant,* "I'm at the point where I'm just ready to give in. It destroyed most of my independence." Can you believe that anyone could be so mean—especially at Christmas?[22]

This story was effective in eliciting anger—an appropriate emotion for listeners to experience as they learned of the outrages that are sometimes committed against people with disabilities.

Here are some tips on arousing emotions:

Always combine emotional appeals with rational appeals. If you appeal only to emotions, you play a risky game because you give the audience only one underpinning for a belief. Here's an example:

> Two speakers were debating the morality of the death penalty for convicted murderers. The first speaker, who was opposed to the penalty, concentrated on the ghastly horrors of electrocution, showing grisly photographs and giving lurid descriptions of charred flesh and prolonged suffering. The second speaker quickly conceded that electrocution was barbaric and argued instead for the death penalty by means of lethal injection, which he described as more humane. He gave philosophical and moral justifications for the death penalty, and then he aroused emotions in the listeners by describing the terrible

> ordeal of victims of crime and their families. From comments made by listeners at the end, it was clear that the second speaker had convinced previously neutral listeners to adopt his position.

Regardless of how you feel about this controversial issue, I hope you can see that because the first speaker dealt only with emotions, he let himself be outmaneuvered. There are many sound arguments that can be made against the death penalty; if he had used some of them—in addition to his emotional appeal—he might have won over some listeners to his view.

While people can be swayed by emotional appeals, they also need to think of themselves as rational. They need to have reasons for the feelings and passions they embrace in their hearts. If you use logic and emotion together, you have a more powerful speech than if you use either one alone.[23]

Know how to use fear. Over the years communicators have wondered how much fear one should evoke in trying to persuade people. For example, if you want to convince an audience to avoid tailgating on the highway, would you be more successful with some low-fear visual aids, such as a chart on traffic fatalities, or with some high-fear graphics, such as a gory, full-color videotape of victims of a terrible car wreck? Research favors the latter. "The overwhelming weight of experimental data," writes psychologist Elliot Aronson, "suggests that . . . the more frightened a person is by a communication, the more likely he or she is to take positive preventive action."[24] Research also indicates that high-fear messages are most effective when they are coupled with specific instructions on how to take action. For example, a high-fear message on rabies would be more persuasive if it included instructions on how to avoid the disease than if it left out such instructions.[25] (The information above applies to adults—not to the bravado teenagers discussed at the beginning of this chapter.)

Ethical Issue

Use emotional appeals ethically. Any emotion can be exploited in the wrong way. Fear and loathing, desirable when targeted at an infectious disease, are undesirable when aimed at a minority group. Unfortunately, some politicians have demonstrated that creating or exploiting fears and hatreds can win elections. If you are an ethical speaker, however, you will never let short-term gain entice you into using such tactics. If, for example, you are trying to mobilize public opinion to save an endangered species of bird, you will not demonize homebuilders who want to build on the bird's natural habitat; you will not foment hatred by falsely portraying them as merciless killers. Instead you will channel emotional appeals in appropriate ways—by generating sadness over the possible disappearance of the bird or by appealing to the happiness listeners might feel over saving endangered creatures.

To determine whether you are acting ethically, identify each emotion you want to arouse and then answer the following questions.

- Is the emotion worthy of compassionate, trustworthy people in the context of your topic? (If some politicians candidly answered this question and acted ethically, they would cease creating scapegoats to vilify in election campaigns.)
- Does the emotion reinforce, rather than replace, solid evidence and sound logic? (If not, is it because your case is unsupportable and illogical?)

- In arousing this emotion, are you treating the issue and the opposing side with fairness? (Put yourself in the shoes of an opponent and see if your treatment looks fair from that perspective.)

If you cannot answer yes to all three, your ethical footing is shaky. You should omit the emotional appeal or alter the speech.

Develop the emotional appeals inherent in some pieces of evidence. Often you don't need to hunt for emotional appeals to add to your accumulation of evidence. All you need to do is develop the evidence already collected so that it moves the listeners. Let's say that while preparing a speech on the appalling murder rate, you found this statistic: About 25,000 homicides occurred in the United States last year. You can state that figure in your speech and then develop it for emotional impact: "That means that every 22 minutes, another American is shot . . . stabbed . . . beaten . . . or strangled to death." By expressing a fact in this dramatic way, you help your listeners feel the magnitude of the problem. Note that vivid language ("stabbed," "beaten," and so on) enhances the emotional impact.

Resources for Review and Skill Building

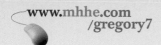

www.mhhe.com/gregory7

This book's Online Learning Center Website and SpeechMate CD-ROM provide meaningful resources and tools for study and review, such as practice tests, key-term flashcards, and sample speech videos.

SpeechMate CD-ROM

Summary

To be effective in persuasion, you must have a thorough *knowledge of the audience.* Find out exactly where your listeners stand concerning your view. Are they opposed, apathetic, neutral, or already convinced? Then plan a strategy to move them toward your position.

During a persuasive speech, enhance *credibility* with the audience by explaining your competence, by being honest and careful with speech material, by remaining open-minded, and by showing common ground with listeners.

Build your case by using strong *evidence* (such as statistics, examples, and testimony) that is accurate, up-to-date, and typical. Try to use a variety of sources, all of them reliable and reputable.

Use sound *reasoning* as a powerful tool of persuasion. Two popular forms are deductive reasoning, in which you take a generalization or principle and apply it to a specific case, and inductive reasoning, in which you observe specific instances and then form a generalization. In using logic, avoid these fallacies: hasty generalization, red herring, attack on a person, false cause, building on an unproven assumption, false analogy, either-or reasoning, or straw man attacks.

Whenever possible, appeal to listeners' *motivations* —their needs, desires, and drives that impel them toward a goal or away from some negative situation. Focus on the listeners' needs, not your own. If possible, appeal to more than one motivation, and anticipate conflicting needs.

Finally, try to arouse the listeners' *emotions,* making sure that you always combine emotional appeals with rational appeals, and that you always use emotions ethically.

Key Terms

attack on a person, *412*
building on an unproven assumption, *413*
credibility, *401*
deduction, *407*
either-or fallacy, *414*
evidence, *405*
fallacy, *411*
false analogy, *413*
false cause, *413*
hasty generalization, *411*
induction, *408*
motivations, *414*
reasoning, *406*
red herring, *412*
straw man, *414*
syllogism, *407*

Review Questions

1. Why are sarcastic remarks inappropriate when directed toward listeners who are hostile to your view?
2. Why is it a good idea in many cases to tell the audience why you are competent to speak on your particular subject?
3. How is an audience likely to react if you are careless with your facts and ideas?
4. Which is more persuasive with the typical audience: one vivid personal narrative or a series of statistical data?
5. What is the difference between deduction and induction?
6. Why should a speaker never use the logical fallacy called "attack on a person"?
7. What is the "straw man" fallacy?
8. What is a "red herring" argument?
9. List at least five motivations that all listeners have.
10. Why should emotional appeals always be accompanied by rational appeals?

Building Critical-Thinking Skills

1. One of the most influential books in American history, *Silent Spring*, was published in 1962 as a warning against the health hazards of pesticides. Its author, Rachel Carson, was attacked by a scientist who questioned her concern for future generations because she was an unmarried woman with no children. What fallacy of reasoning was the scientist using? Why was the criticism invalid?

2. Sherlock Holmes, the famous fictional detective, solved crimes by using reasoning like this:
   - Watchdogs bark at strangers.
   - When Jenkins was murdered, the dogs did not bark.
   - Jenkins was not killed by a stranger.

   Which form of reasoning did Holmes use? Which form of reasoning would a typical modern detective use in solving a murder case?

Building Teamwork Skills

1. In a survey reported by *Health* magazine, 89 percent of adults said they know they should exercise three times a week for good health, but only 27 percent actually do. In a group, compile a list of excuses that people might use for not exercising. Then, for each excuse, brainstorm strategies that a speaker could use to discourage it.

2. Working in a group, list the motivations that students in a typical high school class are likely to have. Then brainstorm how an Army recruiter could appeal to each motivation in a speech aimed at persuading the students to join the military.

Building Internet Skills

www.mhhe.com/gregory7

1. On a controversial issue, find and print two articles—one on each side of the issue.

Possible Strategy: Go to Yahoo! (www.yahoo.com) and click on "News and Media" and select a subcategory. Choose a topic that interests you and examine the news articles.

2. Consult a search engine for documents that contain both of these keywords: *credibility* and *speaker*. Browse through several documents and write down a sentence that states at least one thing that can help or hurt credibility.

Possible Strategy: Go to a search engine such as Google (www.google.com) or AltaVista (www.altavista.com) and type your query (+credibility +speaker) in the search box.

Using PowerWeb

www.mhhe.com/gregory7

In a speech entitled "Closing the Digital Divide," William B. Harrison Jr., CEO of J.P. Morgan Chase & Co., tells about a fascinating experiment that his company financed at a school in Brooklyn, New York. What evidence does he provide to support his argument that the experiment was a success? To find a transcript of this speech, visit www.mhhe.com/gregory7, click on STUDENT EDITION and then POWERWEB: CONTENTS.

In a special ceremony a few weeks after the September 11 terrorist attacks, ABC TV reporter Emily Lopez of New York City pays tribute to the victims and heroes of that day. Speeches of tribute are one of the types of special occasion speeches discussed in this chapter.

18

Special Types of Speeches

Outline

Objectives

After studying this chapter, you should be able to:

1. Prepare an entertaining speech.
2. Prepare a speech of introduction.
3. Prepare a speech of presentation.
4. Prepare a speech of acceptance.
5. Prepare a speech of tribute.
6. Prepare an inspirational speech.
7. Identify potential pitfalls in using humor in a speech.

"Humor to heal the body and inspiration to feed the soul." That's the speechmaking formula used by Eathan O'Bryant, a player and goodwill ambassador for the Harlem Globetrotters basketball team who frequently gives talks at children's hospitals. He entertains his listeners with tricks such as spinning a basketball on a fingertip, and he inspires them by learning each child's name and offering individualized words of encouragement. "My goal is to give hope," he says. "If you have hope, you have life."

His presentations have a powerful impact. "He brightens the entire hospital," said one administrator. "Kids who haven't smiled in weeks have faces filled with glee." At the end of a speech, children rush forward to touch him, get his autograph, and have their picture taken with him.

O'Bryant, who was a basketball star at a Houston, Texas, high school and at the University of Nevada, says that his visits to hospitals are more important than playing on the court. "My definition of a hero," he says, "is someone who puts others' needs in front of his or her own."[1]

O'Bryant's talks are a blend of entertainment and inspiration—special types of speechmaking that will be discussed in this chapter. Though most of the speeches that you will give in your lifetime will probably be informative or persuasive, there are occasions when you may be called upon to give other kinds—an entertaining

Basketball player Eathan O'Bryant spins a basketball as he poses for a photo with one of his teenage listeners at a children's hospital. O'Bryant gives talks that are both entertaining and inspirational.

speech at a banquet, a brief speech introducing the main speaker at a convention, a few words announcing the presentation of an award, a eulogy at a funeral to honor a close friend, an acceptance speech to thank an organization for giving you an award, or an inspirational speech to lift the morale of your subordinates or fellow employees.

Entertaining (or After-Dinner) Speech

An **entertaining speech** provides amusement or diversion for the audience. It should be light and enjoyable, and easy to listen to. It can be given at any hour in any setting—boardroom, school, church, hotel banquet room, convention hall. It is frequently referred to as an "after-dinner speech" because it is often given after a luncheon or dinner at an organizational meeting, convention, or banquet. People who have just eaten a big meal want to sit back, relax, and enjoy a talk. They don't want to work hard mentally; they don't want to hear anything negative and gloomy.

entertaining speech
an oral address designed to amuse or engage listeners

An entertaining speech can be similar to an informative or persuasive speech, but it has this important difference: The primary goal is not to inform or persuade, but to create an interesting diversion—an enjoyable experience—for the audience. In other words, while you may include a few elements of persuasion and information, you should weave them unobtrusively and gracefully into the cloth of entertainment.

Techniques for Entertaining

To entertain, do you have to tell jokes that elicit belly laughs, shrieks of glee, or deep chuckles? Not necessarily. Joke-telling is just one option among many (see the Special Techniques feature "How to Use Humor" in this chapter). Here are some devices you can use to entertain an audience.

Anecdotes, Examples, and Quotations

Using a single theme, some speakers string together anecdotes, examples, or quotations as if creating a string of pearls—one bright jewel after another. In a speech on the crackpot predictions that so-called experts have made over the centuries, Sarah Caldwell-Evans gave her audience one astonishing quotation after another. Here's an instance:

> When women began to enter all-male professions at the beginning of the 20th century, many prominent men warned that such work would be disastrous for women. Here's what a professor at Berlin University, Hans Friedenthal, said in 1904: "Brain work will cause the 'new woman' to become bald, while increasing masculinity and contempt for beauty will induce the growth of hair on the face. In the future, therefore, women will be bald and will wear long mustaches and patriarchal beards."

Narratives

An interesting journey, exciting adventure, or comical sequence of events can make an enjoyable speech. For example:

- A speaker related her encounter with a grizzly bear while backpacking in the Rocky Mountains.
- A police officer gave an hour-by-hour account of the extraordinary security measures taken by the Secret Service when a presidential candidate made a campaign stop in one city.
- One speaker told of the mishaps and misunderstandings that caused her to arrive late and frazzled at her wedding.

Descriptions

You can entertain with vivid descriptions of fascinating places, interesting persons, or intriguing objects. For example:

- In order to give her audience an impression of the bright colors and exotic varieties of birds in the Amazonian rain forest, one speaker showed color slides she had taken of birds in a Brazilian zoo.
- Recalling a visit to a hermit, who had lived alone in a remote mountain cabin for over 50 years, a speaker described the hermit and his spartan dwelling.
- At the meeting of a culinary club, the chef of a gourmet restaurant gave an after-dinner talk in which he described various French pastries. As the chef discussed each type of pastry, a sample was served to each listener.

An entertaining speech does not need to be as elaborately structured as an informative or persuasive speech, but it should have a unifying theme—in other words, all your material should tie together—and it should have the standard three parts of a speech: (1) an introduction to gain the attention and interest of the audience, (2) a body that develops the theme in satisfying detail, and (3) a conclusion that provides a graceful finale.

Choose a topic that you find enjoyable, and as you deliver your speech, try to convey your enjoyment to the audience. Be light and good-natured. Have fun along with your listeners.

Sample Entertaining Speech

Below is a sample entertaining speech, delivered by student speaker Anthony Rossi, who is able to find humor in a subject that usually has no humor—crime.[2]

Incompetent Criminals

There is nothing funny about crime, but sometimes criminals are so bumbling and incompetent, you can't keep from smiling and shaking your head in disbelief.

Take Denise and Jeffrey Lagrimas of Oroville, California, who volunteered to be hosts at a "neighborhood watch" meeting. This is a meeting for residents to discuss ways to fight crime in the neighborhood. Mr. and Mrs. Lagrimas were perfect hosts—they served refreshments in their home while two police officers told residents about a rash of local burglaries and how they could safeguard their homes.

When the meeting was over, one of the residents, Nancy Miller, waited outside and told the officers that she had seen her TV set and Christmas stockings inside the Lagrimas's home. Furthermore, Mrs. Lagrimas was wearing Miller's dress! The officers got a search warrant and revisited the Lagrimas's home. They found $9,000 worth of stolen property.

This story is just one of many news stories collected from America's newspapers by Chuck Shepherd, a former Washington, D.C., criminal-defense attorney, in a book called *America's Least Competent Criminals.* Most of my stories come from this book.

Why do criminals make such incredible blunders? Some psychiatrists theorize that many criminals have an unconscious desire to be caught. This theory could be a possible explanation for the behavior of Mr. and Mrs. Lagrimas.

It might also explain the actions of Shelbie Arabie, who escaped from a prison in Angola, Louisiana. As he traveled across the South, he sent a series of taunting postcards to prison officials. The basic message was: "Having a wonderful time—catch me if you can." You guessed it: The postmarks on his cards left a paper trail that ended in his capture—in Florida.

But in some cases maybe it's not a desire to be caught. Maybe it's just carelessness. A Louisville, Kentucky, man named Kharl Fulton was on the lam in Los Angeles after being charged with drug offenses. He volunteered to become a contestant on the TV show *The Price Is Right* and was spotted by a former co-worker, who tipped off the police. Mistake number one was appearing on national TV. Mistake number two was using his real name. When officers contacted the TV show's producers, they got Fulton's address from the application he had filed to appear on the show. Giving his real address was mistake number three.

Maybe the stupid behavior of some criminals is due to—well, just plain stupidity. A 34-year-old prisoner in Cranston, Rhode Island, had served 89 days of a 90-day sentence. He chose to escape with only one day to go, and of course he was captured. Now he had to face another jail term for escaping. Not very smart.

If you think I'm being unkind in using the word "stupid," let me ask you how else you would describe the behavior of Bruce Damon, who held up the Mutual Federal Savings Bank near Brockton, Massachusetts. Using a gun, Damon demanded $40 million. When the teller explained that the bank kept only $40,000 on the premises, he said, "Okay, $40,000." Now get this: He demanded not cash, but a check! You can imagine the ending. He was arrested a short time later when he tried to deposit the check into his account in another bank. Not very smart.

I wish I could say that all criminals are bumbling and incompetent. Unfortunately, many are clever and successful. But it is a pleasure to

How to Use Humor

> "My mother," stand-up comedian Judy Tenuta says, "used to tell me, 'You won't amount to anything because you procrastinate!'"
>
> I said, "Just wait."

Humor used effectively is a good way to keep an audience interested in your speech. It creates a bond of friendship between you and the listeners, and it puts them into a receptive, trusting mood. Here are some guidelines.

1. Use humor only when it is appropriate.
A speech about a solemn subject such as euthanasia would not lend itself to an injection of humor.

2. Tell jokes at your own risk.
A popular kind of humor is the joke—a funny story that depends on a punch line for its success. If you are an accomplished humorist, you may be able to use jokes effectively, but I don't recommend that any novice speaker use them, for these reasons: (1) jokes usually don't tie in smoothly with the rest of the speech, (2) few speakers (whether experienced or inexperienced) can tell jokes well, (3) a joke that is successful with your friends might bomb with a large audience, (4) the audience may have heard the joke already, and (5) the audience may not be in a receptive mood.

I have seen speakers tell a joke that no one laughed at—not one single soul. Maybe the audience had heard the joke before, or maybe it was too early in the morning or too late in the evening. Whatever the reason, a joke that fizzles can be devastating to the speaker's morale. "But it looks so easy on TV," some students say. It looks easy and *is* easy because TV joketellers have advantages that most speakers lack: They have studio audiences that are predisposed to laugh at virtually any joke the comedians tell (your audiences will probably not be poised for laughter in this way). They have a supporting cast of gag writers who test the jokes out before they are used. Most important of all, they have years of joke-telling experience before they appear on national TV.

3. Use low-key humor.
You can use other kinds of humor besides jokes. A mildly amusing story, quotation, or observation can be as effective as a side-splitting joke. The best thing about low-key humor is that it's safe. While the success of a joke depends on the audience laughing immediately after the punch line, the success of a light story or witty observation does not depend on laughter—or even smiles. Sometimes the only audience response is an inner delight. In a speech urging her listeners to invest in the stock market, student speaker Jacqueline Wallace said:

> If you invest in blue chip stocks, you will have the satisfaction of getting a dividend check every three months from each of your investments. As the writer Dorothy Parker once said, "The two most beautiful words in the English language are 'check enclosed.'"

Notice that the Dorothy Parker quotation was the kind of wry humor that does not depend on belly laughs; also notice that Wallace tied the humor in with the purpose of her speech. This is an example of how you can sneak humor in, so that the audience sees it as part of your speech, not as a "joke." If they laugh or smile, fine; if they don't, no harm has been done. It's still enjoyable and relevant.

4. Humor must always relate to the subject matter.
Never tell an amusing story about a farmer unless your speech is about farming and the story ties in with the rest of the speech.

5. Never use humor that might be offensive to any person in the audience.
Avoid humor that is obscene or that ridicules members of any group in society (racial, ethnic, religious, political, gender, and so on). Even if the audience contains no members of a particular group, you are unwise to ridicule that group because you risk alienating listeners who dislike such humor.

6. Never let your face show that you expect laughter or smiles.
Let's say that you cleverly inject a delicious note of ironic humor into your introduction. After you make your humorous remark, don't stand with an expectant grin on your face. If no one smiles back or laughs, you will feel very foolish. By the way, failure to get any smiles or laughs doesn't necessarily mean that the listeners did not appreciate your humor. As I mentioned above, some kinds of humor elicit only an inner delight.

7. If listeners are spread apart, move them together.
If you have 15 people scattered about in a large hall, it will be easier to make contact with them if you first have them move to seats at the front and center. Nightclub comedians are very sensitive to seating arrangements; they make sure tables are pushed close together because they know that patrons are more likely to laugh if they are jammed together in warm coziness. Some comedians would never tell jokes to an audience widely scattered in a large room; people feel isolated, and they are afraid that if they laugh,

they will be conspicuous. (Have you ever noticed that funny movies are funnier if you see them in a packed theater than if you see them in a sparsely attended theater?)

8. Consider using self-deprecating humor in some situations.

Benjamin Franklin was a speaker who was willing to poke fun at himself in a speech. For example, he liked to tell audiences about an incident that occurred in Paris while he was attending a public gathering that featured many speeches. He spoke French, but he had trouble understanding the formal, rhetorical language of French orators. Wishing to appear polite, he decided that he would applaud whenever he noticed a distinguished woman, Mme. de Boufflers, express satisfaction. After the meeting, his grandson said to him, "But Grandpapa, you always applauded, and louder than anybody else, when they were praising you."

Many good speakers tell humorous anecdotes at their own expense because it's an effective way to build rapport with the audience—to create a bond of warmth, trust, and acceptance. Franklin's listeners must have been delighted to learn that the Great Man was capable of committing a faux pas, just like everyone else, and they loved him all the more.

Self-deprecating humor brings you an immediate reward. When your listeners smile or laugh, your nervous tension eases up considerably. You become lighter and more comfortable with your audience. You banish the burden of having to be a flawless speaker giving a flawless speech. You can relax and be yourself: a human being with foibles and faults just like anybody else.

Poke fun at any aspect of yourself except your nervousness (in Chapter 2 we discussed why you should never call attention to your jitters), and tie your humor to the speech or the occasion. At the beginning of a speech on attention deficit/hyperactivity disorder (ADHD), Henry Bortell, a psychologist, wanted to show his audience that he wasn't a smug know-it-all who thought he was superior to people with ADHD. So he told the story of "the only time I ever missed a speaking engagement. I simply forgot about it, until I got an angry phone call the next day from the organization that had invited me. What hurts the most is that my topic was supposed to be—I kid you not—'How to Improve Your Memory.'"

The listeners laughed, and they probably felt warmth for a speaker who was not afraid to reveal that he had faults.

Don't use self-deprecating humor if you have not yet established your expertise or authority. For example, if you are a new employee who is making a presentation to the board of directors of a corporation, self-effacing humor could weaken your credibility. By contrast, if you are a manager whose confidence and power are well-known to your audience of subordinates, laughing at yourself can build rapport.

come across a criminal like Raymond Baker, who tried to rob a bank in Detroit. He wrote a long, rambling stick-up note explaining the personal misfortunes that had caused him to turn to crime. The note was so hard to decipher that it took a teller several minutes to read it—enough time for a hidden alarm to summon police to capture Baker.

Wouldn't it be wonderful if all criminals were as incompetent as the ones I've described to you today?

speech of introduction
a brief talk that introduces a speaker to an audience

Speech of Introduction

The **speech of introduction** is designed for one speaker to introduce another to an audience. For example:

- At a meeting of her civic club, Paula Moreno spoke briefly on why she was supporting a particular candidate for Congress and then turned the lectern over to the candidate.
- Theodore Lansing, a university librarian, stood up in front of 1,500 delegates at a national librarians' convention and introduced the keynote speaker, a renowned writer of science fiction.

When you introduce one friend to another, you want them to get interested in each other and to like each other: When you introduce a speaker to an audience, you want to achieve the same goal. You want speaker and audience to be interested in each other and to feel warmth and friendliness.

An introduction should mention the speaker's name several times (so that everyone can catch it), and it should give background information to enhance the speaker's credibility with the audience. Your tone of voice and facial expression should convey enthusiasm for the speech to come.

Here are some guidelines for speeches of introduction.

Ask the speaker ahead of time what kind of introduction he or she would like. Some speakers will write out their introduction and send it to you in advance. While you should not actually read the document (because this would be boring to the audience), you should use it as the basis for your remarks. If the speaker provides you with a lengthy résumé or list of accomplishments, select those items that would be most appropriate for the audience and the occasion. The speaker also may want you to establish ground rules about questions; for example, "Mayor Brown will take questions at the end of her speech."

Be sure to pronounce the speaker's name correctly. If you have any doubt about how to pronounce the speaker's name, verify the pronunciation beforehand. If the name is difficult to pronounce, practice saying it in advance so that you don't stumble during your introduction.

Use the name the speaker prefers. If you are scheduled to introduce Dr. Elizabeth Wilson, find out beforehand what she wants to be called. Don't assume that she prefers to be called "Dr. Wilson." It could be that for this particular audience she prefers the informality of "Elizabeth" or even her nickname, "Liz."

Set the proper tone. When you introduce someone, you help set the tone for the speech to follow. Be careful to set the right tone—a humorous tone for a humorous speech, a serious tone for a serious speech. Consult with the speaker in advance to ensure that you understand the tone he or she wants you to set.

Avoid long introductions. A good rule of thumb is to keep an introduction under three minutes. After all, an audience wants to hear the speaker, not the introducer:

Avoid exaggeration. If you exaggerate the speaker's abilities or credentials, you build up unrealistic expectations in the audience. Consider this kind of introduction: "Our speaker tonight is a funny person who will have you laughing so hard you'll have to clutch your sides." Or: "The speaker will give us insights that are wise and brilliant." Such statements raise expectations that are very difficult for the speaker to meet. If the listeners are expecting one of the world's funniest speakers, or one of the wisest, they may be disappointed. Also, excessive praise can make speakers overly anxious because they feel enormous pressure to live up to their billing.

Find out whether the speaker wants you to discuss the topic. Some speakers will want you to discuss the significance of their topic (to help prepare the audience for the speech); other speakers prefer to save all discussion of the topic until *they* step to the lectern.

Never steal the speaker's material. Imagine this scenario: You are about to deliver a speech to an audience of 1,000 people, and suddenly you realize that the person introducing you is telling the very anecdote that you had carefully planned as the opener of your speech. How in the world are you going to begin your talk? Such nightmares actually happen, say professional speakers. The introducer uses a joke, anecdote, key statistic, or quotation that the speaker had planned to include. Or the introducer summarizes the subject matter in a way that duplicates or contradicts the subsequent speech. When you are an introducer, stay away from the speaker's material unless you and the speaker have worked out an agreement on exactly what you may cover. Your job is to set the stage, not steal it.

The following introduction of Joseph Conte was delivered at a meeting of a genealogical society; the introducer had consulted with Conte in advance to make sure that he did not steal any of the speaker's speech.

SpeechMate
CD-ROM

For sample speeches of introduction, see the Mulcahy and Ingram speeches on Disk 2.

> Our speaker tonight, Joseph Conte, will talk to us about how to set up a computerized ancestry record. Mr. Conte brings a lot of personal experience to this subject. The great-grandson of immigrants from Italy, he has traced his own family roots back to Florence. He has put all of his genealogical records onto a computer, using a program that was created by a Mormon group in Salt Lake City. Mr. Conte has a background of expertise in scholarly detective work: For the past decade he has been a researcher for the National Archives in Washington, D.C., specializing in 19th and 20th century immigration. Mr. Conte, welcome to our society and thank you for taking the time to share your knowledge with us.

Speech of Presentation

Awards or honors are often bestowed upon individuals for their service to business, institution, community, church, or club. It is customary for a brief speech to be made before the award is presented.

The **speech of presentation** should include the following elements: (1) any background information that would help the audience understand the purpose or circumstances of the award, (2) the criteria used for selecting the recipient, and (3) the achievements of the recipient. In many cases, it is customary to withhold the name of the recipient until the very end of the speech, as a way of building suspense.

speech of presentation
an address designed to formally present an award or honor

If humor is used, it should be handled very carefully. If you try to make a joke about the recipient, you may seem to be belittling him or her. At one company banquet, a department head gave an award for 10 years of service to a subordinate and used the occasion to tease him with a mock insult: "The only reason we keep him on the payroll is because his father worked here for 40 years." The "humor" was similar to the kind of bantering that the boss and the subordinate engaged in during a typical workday, but at the awards banquet, with his family present, the subordinate felt humiliated.

Here is a model speech of presentation delivered by Meredith Brody at the annual meeting of a community theater:

> The John Cleese Award is given each year to the top actor or actress in our theater. As most of you know, the award is given in honor of the British actor John Cleese of *Monty Python* and *Fawlty Towers* fame. The winner is selected by ballots circulated to all our members. Our winner this year is a seasoned veteran of our stage, a person who always performs with intelligence, audacity, and élan. I am pleased to announce that the winner of the third annual John Cleese Award is . . . James Colton!

Speech of Acceptance

speech of acceptance
oral remarks made by the recipient of an award or honor

If you are ever given an award, a promotion, or some other sort of public recognition, you may be called upon to "say a few words." Giving a **speech of acceptance** is difficult because you want to sound appreciative without being syrupy, and you want to sound deserving without being egotistical. Here are some guidelines to follow.

Thank those who played a part in your achieving the honor. If a few individuals made your recognition possible, mention them by name; if a lot of people did, mention the most important contributors to your success and say something like this, "There are many others but they are too numerous to name. Nevertheless, I am grateful to all of them."

Thank the organization giving you the award and recognize the work it is doing. If, for example, you are cited by the United Way as top fund-raiser of the year, spend a few moments extolling the great work that United Way does in helping the unfortunate and needy.

Don't exaggerate your gratitude. If you receive an award for perfect attendance at your club's meetings, don't say, "This is the greatest honor I've ever received or ever hope to receive," unless, of course, you mean it. Exaggeration makes you seem insincere.

Be brief. I have seen some ceremonies marred because an award recipient viewed the acceptance speech as a chance to expound on his or her pet ideas. If you deliver a lengthy oration, the people who are giving you the honor may regret their choice. Make a few sincere remarks—and then sit down.

Here is a sample acceptance speech, given by Rita Goldberg, who was honored by a chapter of the Lions Club for her work with disabled persons:

> I want to thank you for choosing me to receive your Distinguished Service Award. In the past year I couldn't have accomplished half of what I did without the help of Henry and Judith Fletcher. I am grateful to them for their valuable assistance. And I am grateful to you Lions for setting up programs for the visually impaired. Because of your compassion and your work, you have made it easy for volunteers like me to help the disabled. Again, thank you for this honor.

Tips for your CAREER

Tip 18.1 Offer Toasts That Are Sincere and Warm

You may be called upon someday to offer a toast, especially at a wedding reception. The hallmarks of a good toast are sincerity and warmth. A lengthy "speech" is not required; in fact, some of the best toasts are short and simple, such as (at a wedding), "Here's to Maggie and Zack. May your future be filled with much happiness." (By the way, traditional etiquette requires that the word "congratulations" be offered only to the groom—never to the bride.)

Some persons offering toasts tell of their admiration for the honorees and relate some personal anecdotes. This is fine as long as the remarks are sincere and appropriate for the occasion. Avoid clever barbs, risqué comments, and all forms of teasing.

Try to express the best sentiments of the entire audience. "Recently, at a wedding," says Mary Farrell, a New York City editor, "the best man focused his remarks *only* on the personal relationship he had with the groom—he didn't even mention the bride! In contrast, when the maid of honor toasted the *couple,* she tried to phrase her remarks to reflect the sentiments of everyone present. I felt as though I was giving the toast—along with the entire gathering."

Speech of Tribute

A **speech of tribute** praises or celebrates a person, a group, an institution, or an event. It conveys gratitude, respect, or admiration. For example, the leader of a veterans' organization might pay tribute on Memorial Day to comrades who had died on the field of battle. At a retirement banquet, you might give a brief talk lauding the work of a colleague who is stepping down after 25 years with your organization.

speech of tribute
an oration in praise of someone or something

A speech of tribute should be completely positive. It is not appropriate to point out faults or dredge up old disputes. Concentrate all remarks on the praiseworthy and noble.

Sample Speech of Tribute

SpeechMate CD-ROM
To see a sample speech of tribute, view Speech 10 ("Three Celebrity Heroes").

In the U.S. House of Representatives, Rep. Loretta Sanchez of California delivered the following speech of tribute. (In keeping with tradition, she addressed her remarks to the Speaker of the House, though she was actually speaking to the entire body.)

Tribute to Working Wardrobes

Mr. Speaker, today I rise to pay tribute to one of Orange County's outstanding community service groups, Working Wardrobes, which is dedicated to assisting survivors of domestic violence to achieve self-sufficiency in their lives.

Working Wardrobes began in 1990 when six Orange County business women decided to initiate a program which would help victims of domestic violence regain their dignity, integrity and self-respect. Over 60,000 women in Orange County are severely beaten each year as a result of domestic violence. This cycle of domestic violence also affects children who are 1,000 times more likely to become abusers themselves.

Through programs such as Career/Life Skills Workshops and annual "Days of Self-Esteem," survivors are given the extra edge they need to be successful in their search for a career and the confidence needed to make changes in their lives.

Colleagues, please join with me today in recognizing Working Wardrobes for excellence in providing victims of domestic violence with educational programs that have given them a new beginning in life.[3]

The Eulogy

eulogy
a laudatory oration in honor of someone who has died

One kind of tribute speech that you are likely to make is a **eulogy**—a speech of praise for a friend, relative, or colleague who has died. A eulogy should be dignified, without exaggerated sentimentality. (Though humor is usually out of place in a eulogy, it is sometimes appropriate: One student described the funeral of an uncle who had been a "colorful character" well known for his storytelling abilities; in one of the eulogies for this uncle, the speaker recited some of the humorous tales, and everyone smiled in warm remembrance of the yarn-spinning uncle.)

A eulogy should focus on the *significance* of the person's life and deeds, rather than on a mere recital of biographical facts. In other words, how did this man or woman enrich our lives? What inspiration or lessons can we draw from this person's life?

www.mhhe.com/gregory7
To review a key point about eulogies, do the interactive exercise in Chapter 17 on this book's Website.

Inspirational Speech

inspirational speech
an address that tries to stimulate listeners to a high level of feeling or activity

The goal of the **inspirational speech** is to stir positive emotions—to cause people to feel excited, uplifted, encouraged. You may need to give inspirational speeches at various times in your life. Let's say, for example, that you are manager of an office or department, and you give your staff an upbeat, "you-can-do-it" speech to motivate them to do their best work. Or you coach a children's softball team and you give the boys and girls a "pep talk" before a game to encourage them to play well.

The inspirational speech is similar to the persuasive speech, with the two purposes often overlapping. The main difference is that in the inspirational speech, you devote yourself almost solely to stirring emotions, while in the persuasive speech, you use emotional appeals as just one of many techniques.

Delivery is an important dimension of inspirational speaking. To inspire other people, *you* must be inspired. Your facial expression, your posture, your tone of voice—everything about you must convey zest and enthusiasm.

An inspirational speech should tap the emotional power of vivid language. An example of effective use of language can be found in a speech delivered by Dan Crenshaw to a support group of parents of mentally ill children. Here is a section from the speech:

> We must learn to live fully and joyfully in the here and now, setting aside all our pain from the past and all our worries about the future. Fulton Oursler said, "We crucify ourselves between two thieves: regret for yesterday and fear of tomorrow."

If we live in the past or in the future, we miss what today has to offer.
We miss the glistening beauty of a puddle of water.
We miss the soothing melody of a love song.
We miss the glint of wonder in a child's eyes.
We miss the lingering aroma of fresh-baked cinnamon rolls.
We miss the beautiful arrangement of clouds in the sky.
We miss the satisfaction of rubbing a dog's fur.

The past is over. Think of it as a bullet. Once it's fired, it's finished. The future is not yet here, and may never come for us. Today is all we have. Treasure *today,* celebrate *today,* live *today.*[4]

Crenshaw made effective use of the techniques of *repetition* and *parallel structure* (which we discussed in Chapter 13).

SpeechMate CD-ROM

To see an example of inspirational speaking, view Dr. Richard F. Corlin's speech on Disk 2 of the CD.

Resources for Review and Skill Building

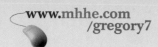

www.mhhe.com/gregory7

This book's Online Learning Center Website and SpeechMate CD-ROM provide meaningful resources and tools for study and review, such as practice tests, key-term flashcards, and sample speech videos.

SpeechMate CD-ROM

Summary

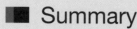

While informative and persuasive speeches are the most frequent types, there are occasions when a speech must serve other purposes. When you need to entertain an audience, as in an after-dinner talk, your remarks should be light and diverting; any elements of information or persuasion should be gracefully woven into the fabric of entertainment. One device for an entertaining speech is to string together anecdotes, examples, or quotations on a single theme. Extended narratives or descriptions also can be entertaining.

Using humor in a speech is an effective way to create a bond of warmth and friendliness with an audience. Be cautious in telling jokes because they can be risky, and listeners may have heard the joke already. A safer type is low-key humor, such as a mildly amusing story, quotation, or observation. Whatever humor you use should relate to the topic and not be offensive to any person in the audience.

When you are asked to introduce a speaker, convey enthusiasm for the speaker and the topic, and give whatever background information is necessary to enhance the speaker's credibility.

When you make a speech of presentation, focus your remarks on the award and the recipient. When you are called upon to "say a few words" in acceptance of an award or promotion, thank the people who gave you the honor and acknowledge the help of those who made your success possible.

When you give a speech of tribute, praise the person, group, institution, or event being honored, avoiding any negativity.

When you speak to inspire an audience, devote yourself to stirring emotions, using a dynamic delivery to convey your zest and enthusiasm.

Key Terms

entertaining speech, *425*
eulogy, *434*
inspirational speech, *434*
speech of acceptance, *432*
speech of introduction, *429*
speech of presentation, *431*
speech of tribute, *433*

Review Questions

1. Why would an informative speech on a difficult, highly technical subject usually be inappropriate for an after-dinner audience?
2. In what situation is self-deprecating humor inadvisable?
3. List four guidelines for the speech of acceptance.
4. What is the function of the speech of tribute?
5. What are the risks that a speaker takes when telling a joke?
6. If you are asked to introduce a speaker, why should you coordinate your remarks beforehand with those of the speaker?
7. When introducing a speaker, some introducers use the speaker's first name, others use the last name. What advice does the text give on this issue?
8. In which kind of special occasions speech does the speaker often withhold an honoree's name until the last sentence?
9. What should be the focus of a eulogy?
10. What is the main difference between an inspirational speech and a persuasive speech?

Building Critical-Thinking Skills

1. One speaker told his audience, "Before I left for this speech, my wife gave me some advice: 'Don't try to be charming, witty, or intellectual. Just be yourself.'" What kind of humor is the speaker using?
2. "Our speaker tonight," says the master of ceremonies, "will outline the five key steps in rescuing a person who is in danger of drowning. Let me give you a quick preview of these steps." What mistake is the master of ceremonies making?

Building Teamwork Skills

1. Working in a group, decide on a topic and then prepare and deliver an entertaining talk, with each member of the group speaking in turn. Some possible topics:
   a. An embarrassing moment
   b. Good vacation spots
   c. The weird behavior of pets
2. In a group, choose a person (living or dead) whom everyone admires. Create a speech of tribute to that person.

Building Internet Skills

www.mhhe.com /gregory7

1. For speeches of tribute to famous persons, you can find many biographies on the Internet. Find and print biographical information about a person you admire.

Possible Strategy: Go to Yahoo! (www.yahoo.com) and click on "Society & Culture" and then "People." Visit one of the biography sites listed.

2. Find an inspirational speech by one of America's great orators (such as Martin Luther King Jr., Frederick Douglass, Abraham Lincoln, Jane Addams, or Chief Joseph). Write down at least one sentence that shows the use of stirring, emotional language.

Possible Strategy: Go to a speech archives site, where you can read or hear great speeches from the past. Some options: Douglass: Archives of American Public Address (douglassarchives.org), Historic Audio Archives (www.webcorp.com/sounds/index.htm), and the History Channel (www.historychannel.com/speeches/index.html).

Using PowerWeb

www.mhhe.com /gregory7

Dr. Donald J. Palmisano, professor of surgery at Tulane University School of Medicine, gave an inspirational speech entitled "Medicine a Noble Professor." Read the speech, choose what you consider the most moving passage, and explain why you think the excerpt was powerful. To find a transcript of this speech, visit www.mhhe.com/gregory7, click on STUDENT EDITION and then POWERWEB: CONTENTS.

Teams and committees are vital parts of most organizations, but their work can be sabotaged by poor communication. To operate efficiently, small groups must have a leader who is firm but not dictatorial and participants who are committed to a fair, honest exchange of ideas.

19

Speaking in Groups

Outline

Responsibilities of Leaders

Responsibilities of Participants

The Reflective-Thinking Method

Team Presentations
Symposium
Panel Discussion

Objectives

After studying this chapter, you should be able to:

1. Serve as a leader or a participant in a small group meeting.
2. Describe the responsibilities of both leaders and participants in small groups.
3. Identify and explain the seven steps of the reflective-thinking method.
4. Serve as moderator or panelist in a panel discussion.

Randy Theis, an employee of the Des Moines (Iowa) Water Works, became ill with cancer a few years ago, and a series of operations forced him to use up all his sick leave. With a family of five children, Theis faced financial ruin. He asked the company to extend the number of sick days that he could take, but management declined, citing skyrocketing health insurance costs.

At this point, a group of fellow employees got together to try to find a solution to the problem. After a brainstorming session, the group came up with an ingenious plan: It would ask the company to allow employees to donate their own sick leave days to Theis.

The group approached management, which approved the idea and changed its regulations to allow sick leave transfers. Twenty-five workers signed up immediately to give Theis some of their sick leave.[1]

This creative solution to a human problem illustrates the value of small groups. Members of small groups can pool their resources, ideas, and labor; they can catch and correct errors that might slip past an individual. "Group IQ"—a term used by Yale psychologist Robert Sternberg—is often higher than individual IQs (or intelligence level). "A close-knit team, drawing on the particular strengths and skills of each member of the group, may be smarter and more effective than any individual member of the group," says Sternberg.[2]

While the superiority of small groups over individuals is obvious, small groups also have advantages over large conglomerations of people: They act with greater

In their company's snack room, these engineers work together on a project as a team. For problem solving, "group IQ" is believed to be higher than individual IQs.

quickness, flexibility, and resourcefulness. Large corporations such as Federal Express, Motorola, Xerox, and Wal-Mart have learned that putting employees into small task forces is the most effective way to compete successfully in today's global economy. When General Motors set up a new car division—Saturn—it gave its teams of workers an extraordinary amount of power to make decisions about production and sales. Saturn soon became GM's most profitable division.[3]

In this chapter, we will focus on meetings—the means by which small groups do their collective work. If carried out properly, meetings give group members a chance to discuss ideas, solve problems, reach decisions, and resolve differences. Meetings provide close eye-to-eye contact with lively interaction between participants.

To perform well in meetings, groups should (1) have a purpose, (2) secure the cooperation of all members, and (3) have effective leadership.

Let us take a closer look at the roles of the leader and the participants.

Responsibilities of Leaders

Some people think that because they aren't striving to become a high-level manager, they don't need to learn how to lead a meeting. This is a mistake. Employees at all levels are frequently called upon to lead small groups. You might be asked to chair a committee to plan a staff holiday party, or you might head a task force to make recommendations for improving employee morale.

When you are the leader of a small group, here are some guidelines for planning and conducting a meeting:

Establish an agenda. An **agenda** is a list of items that need to be covered in a meeting. When there is no agenda, groups often spend all their time and energy on minor items and never get around to the major issues. As leader, decide in advance what issues should be discussed (be sure to consult the participants on what topics they want to include). Then write out an agenda, ranking items from most important to least important. Be sure that group members receive the agenda well before the meeting so that they can be prepared. At the beginning of the meeting, ask the participants if they want to alter the agenda. If circumstances prevent you from preparing an agenda in advance, take a few moments at the beginning of the meeting to establish the agenda: Ask group members for their suggestions and then rank-order the items on a chalkboard for everyone to see. If your group is working against a deadline, you may need to establish a timetable—for example, allotting 10 minutes for discussion of Item A, 15 minutes for Item B, and so on. (A special kind of agenda, using the reflective-thinking method, will be discussed later in this chapter.)

agenda
document listing what is to be accomplished during a meeting

www.mhhe.com/gregory7

To test your knowledge of agendas, do the interactive exercise in Chapter 19 on this book's Website. Also see a template for agendas under Business Documents Templates.

Start the meeting on time. If some group members fail to arrive at the designated time, you may be tempted to delay the start of the meeting in the hope that they will soon appear. This is a mistake for two reasons: (1) You are being discourteous to those who were punctual; their time is valuable and should not be wasted. (2) You are setting a bad precedent for future meetings. If the people who arrived on time see you wait for latecomers, they will perceive you as a leader who starts meetings late, so they also will probably arrive late for the next meeting. If the same thing happens each time, some group members will arrive later and later for meetings.

Set a friendly tone. Start off with a friendly, upbeat welcome. If some of the participants don't know each other, introduce all the members of the group, one at a time, or let them introduce themselves.

Make sure that minutes are kept. If the group is not a formal committee with a previously designated recorder, appoint someone to take notes and later prepare **minutes** of the meeting. Minutes are a record of what was discussed and accomplished during a meeting. They should be circulated to group members as soon after the meeting as possible. While minutes are obviously valuable for absentees, they are also important for people who were present—to remind them of their responsibilities for the next meeting. Minutes should consist of five elements: (1) agenda item, (2) decision reached, (3) action required, (4) person(s) responsible for taking action, and (5) target date for completion of action.[4] At each meeting, the minutes of the previous session should be briefly reviewed to make sure that tasks have been completed.

minutes
written record of what occurred at a meeting

Make sure all participants know the purpose of the meeting and the scope of the group's power. Even if you have circulated an agenda in advance, you still should review the purpose of the meeting. Some participants may not have read the agenda carefully or correctly, while others may have forgotten what it contained. Refresh their memories; make sure everyone knows the task that the group faces. Also review the scope of the group's power, so that participants don't labor under false ideas of what the group can or cannot do. Group members need to know the following: Does the group have the power to make a decision, or is it being asked simply to recommend a decision? Will the group reach a decision and then carry it out, or will someone else actually carry out the decision? Is the group's decision subject to change by a higher authority?

Encourage participation. In some groups, especially ones led by a boss, the leader does all the talking. Such meetings are really a waste of time. When you are a leader, guide the discussion, but don't dominate it. Encourage the free flow of ideas from all members of the group. This is more than a matter of politeness: Group-created decisions are usually better than leader-dictated decisions because people tend to support what they have helped create. If, for example, you are the manager of five employees and you call them together and dictate a policy, the employees may grumble behind your back and even sabotage the policy. But if you call your people together and spend a few hours letting *them* hammer out the same policy, they will feel a strong commitment to it—now it is *their* idea, *their* policy.

Guide the discussion. As leader, you should move the discussion along from point to point on the agenda. If participants go off on tangents, diplomatically pull them back to the task at hand. (You can say something like, "That's an interesting point, but let's stick to our agenda; if we have any time left over, we can come back to your idea.") If a participant talks too much, not giving others a chance to speak, gently but firmly intervene. (You can say, for example, "Good point; if I may interrupt, I would like to hear how the others are reacting to what you just said.") If a participant is shy or unusually quiet, you can try to elicit comments. Rather than a "yes or no" question (such as "Do you have anything you would like to say?"), ask open-ended questions (such as, "How do you think we can solve this problem?"). If the person says, "I don't know," press no further—there is no need to badger or embarrass the person. It may be that he or she truly has no particular contribution to make on the issue. If participants become hostile toward one another, try to mediate by finding common ground and by helping them concentrate on issues instead of resorting to personal attacks.

Discourage side conversations. Meetings can be marred if two or more people break off from the group's activities and hold a private discussion. This, of course, is rude to the other group members, and it prevents the group from staying together as a team. As leader, you should gently shepherd the wayward members back into the fold. If two members are carrying on a private conversation, you can say, "It looks as if you've come up with something interesting. Could you share it with the group?" This technique usually has one of two results: The offenders share their comments with the group, or (if they have been chatting about unrelated matters) they grin sheepishly, decline to reveal the content of their discussion, and return to participation with the group.

Summarize periodically. Since you are playing the role of guide, you should occasionally let the participants know where they are located on their journey toward the group's goal. Summarize what has been accomplished, and indicate work that still needs to be done. For example: "Let's see where we stand. We have decided that Item A and Item B should be recommended to the board of directors. But we still need to tackle Problem C . . . " Keep your summaries brief; just say enough to help the participants gain their bearings.

Keep meetings short. Probably because of high school and college, where classes are often 50 minutes long, many people act as if 50 minutes is the *required* length of a meeting, and they are reluctant to end a meeting sooner. This is nonsense: Some groups can complete all required work in much less time.

Never exceed one hour without a break. Most small-group meetings should last no longer than one hour. Anything longer will cause fatigue and a dropoff in the group's effectiveness. If one hour is not enough time to handle the group's work, a series of one-hour meetings should be set up. If, for some reason, the group is obliged to conduct all of its business in one day or during an afternoon, one-hour sessions should be interspersed with coffee or "stretch" breaks.

End the meeting. At the end of a meeting, summarize what the group has accomplished, set the time and place for the next meeting, make sure that all participants know their assignments for the next meeting, and express appreciation for the work that the group has done.

Follow up. After the meeting, make sure that minutes are written and distributed to each participant and that all participants carry out their assignments.

Responsibilities of Participants

While leadership of a small group is important, the participants themselves play a vital role. In one community, a committee was formed to plan and finance the construction of a new swimming pool for a YMCA. The committee included a cross-section of community talent—for example, a financier who was experienced at fund-raising, an engineer who was knowledgeable about pool construction, and a swimming instructor who knew what kind of pool the public wanted. When the committee met, it was effective in overseeing the design and construction of an excellent pool because the participants were able to share their ideas and expertise.

When you are a participant in a small group, here are some guidelines to keep in mind.

Prepare for every meeting. Find out in advance what is going to be discussed at the meeting and then decide what contributions you can make. Jot down items that you think need to be discussed. Do whatever research, background reading, and interviewing that might be necessary to make you well-informed or to bolster your position on an issue. If documentation is likely to be requested for some of your data, bring notes to the meeting so that you can cite your sources.

Arrive on time. Meetings cannot work effectively if some participants straggle in late. Make sure that you arrive at the appointed time. Even better, arrive a bit early; this will give you a chance to chat informally with the other participants and create a mood of friendliness.

Participate in group discussion. Don't sit back and let others do the work of the group. Join the discussion and contribute your ideas and opinions. This does not necessarily mean giving a brief speech or saying something brilliant. You can enter the discussion by asking questions, especially when points need to be clarified; by expressing support for ideas that you like; and by paraphrasing other members' ideas to determine if you are understanding them correctly.

If possible, speak up early in the meeting. If you have the opportunity to make a contribution to the group, do so at the earliest possible time. This serves as an "icebreaker," causing you to draw closer (psychologically) to the other members of the group and making you more attentive to the discussion. The longer you wait to speak, the harder it becomes to enter the discussion. This does not mean that you should blurt out the first thing that pops into your head; never speak impulsively or aimlessly. But when a chance to make a genuine contribution arises, take advantage of it.

Exhibit positive nonverbal behavior. Nonverbal cues, such as clothes, facial expression, posture, and eye contact, speak as powerfully as words. In a meeting, avoid slumping in your chair because that conveys boredom, negativity, or lack of confidence. Instead, sit in an alert but relaxed posture that shows you are both comfortable and confident. Whether you are playing the role of speaker or listener, look people in the eye. Your facial expression should convey openness and friendliness.

Don't treat your own ideas as beyond criticism. Some group members act as if criticism of their ideas is an attack upon themselves, so they fight ferociously to defend their position. What they are really defending is not their ideas, but their ego. Unfortunately, when people are busy defending their ego, they refuse to listen to what their critics are saying, they refuse to budge an inch from their position, and they sometimes prevent a group from making progress. When you present your ideas to a group, recognize that no human is perfect and that a wise and mature person readily admits the possibility of being in error.

Don't monopolize the meeting. Give others a fair chance to state their views.

Stick to the point. A common problem in meetings is for participants to stray off the subject and get bogged down in irrelevant matters. Before speaking, ask yourself if what you plan to say is truly related to the purpose of the meeting.

Treat all group members fairly. All too often, some group members form coalitions with people who already agree with them, and then they freeze out the rest of the group (by not listening carefully to what they say, by not giving them sufficient eye contact, by not soliciting and respecting their ideas). Aside from being rude, this cold-shoulder treatment cripples the effectiveness of the group; members who feel frozen-out tend to contribute little. Treat each person in the group with dignity and respect.

Express dissenting views. Some group members never raise objections or express views contrary to the majority. There are a number of reasons for this timidity: fear of being ridiculed, fear of antagonizing others, or fear of displeasing the leader (especially if he or she is the boss). When you disagree with an idea being discussed by the group, it is a mistake to remain silent. Group decisions that are made in a mood of pseudounanimity are often poor decisions.

Avoid personal attacks. Conflict—a clash of ideas or opinions—is healthy in group discussion. It exposes weaknesses in plans; it separates the workable from the unworkable. While conflict is desirable, it should always be centered on *issues,* not on personalities. In other words, disagree without being disagreeable.

Whenever possible, express objections in the form of a question. While you should certainly speak up when you think an idea is poor, there is a diplomatic way to offer criticism. If you blurt out, "Oh no, that will never work," you might deflate the person who suggested the idea, and even provoke hostility. A better approach is to ask a question such as: "How could we make this work?" As the group members try to answer the question, they often come to the conclusion you hoped they would reach—that the idea *is* unworkable—without hostility or bad feelings.

hidden agenda
an ulterior motive

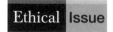

Ethical Issue

Don't work from a hidden agenda. A group's work can be sabotaged if some members pretend to be committed to the goals of the group, but in reality have **hidden agendas**—that is, unannounced private goals that conflict with the group's goals. One frequent hidden agenda is the desire to curry favor with a superior. One or more members of a committee will agree with the chairperson—the boss—even though they feel strongly that the boss's ideas are flawed. They would rather see the committee's efforts fail than go on record as disagreeing with their superior.

Don't carry on private conversations. A whispered conversation by two or three participants is rude and insulting to the speaker; it is also damaging to the work of the group since it cuts off teamwork and undermines cooperation.

The Reflective-Thinking Method

For every human problem, the American essayist H. L. Mencken said, "there is always an easy solution—neat, plausible, and wrong." Unfortunately, many business and professional groups leap at easy, but wrong solutions. In the 1980s, when Coca-Cola began to lose market share in its battle with Pepsi, the "neat, plausible" solution was to change the Coca-Cola formula and make it as sweet as Pepsi—an easy solution that turned out to be a huge blunder. Sales plummeted because millions of Coca-Cola lovers disliked the new Coke. Soon the embarrassed company resumed making the original formula (which was sold as Coca-Cola Classic).

A more effective technique for solving problems is the **reflective-thinking method,** a step-by-step procedure derived from the writings of the American philosopher John Dewey.[5] These steps should be taken in the order given below.

reflective-thinking method
a structured system for solving problems

Define the Problem

Defining a problem clearly and precisely can save time and (in the business world) money. Here are some tips.

Phrase the problem in the form of a question. Instead of "We have traffic jams on our campus," say, "How can we eliminate the traffic jams that occur on our campus every afternoon?" The question format helps create a probing, problem-solving atmosphere. Make sure the question is open-ended (that is, not one that can be answered by a simple yes or no).

Avoid wording that suggests a solution. If you say "How can we finance the hiring of more security officers to eliminate traffic jams on campus?" you are stating that you already know the best solution. You risk cutting off discussion that might lead to a different solution—one that is even better than hiring more security officers.

Avoid vagueness. Be as specific as possible. Instead of "How can we improve our campus?" say, "How can we discourage people from littering the campus with trash?"

Analyze the Problem

A problem-solving group should scrutinize the problem in order to learn as much as it can. Key questions that should be asked are

- What are the causes of the problem?
- What are the effects of the problem? (How severe is it? Are many people affected or just a few?)

In the Coca-Cola fiasco, corporate planners should have tried harder to determine the real cause of Coke's loss of market share to Pepsi. Was it the taste of Coke? Did people prefer a sweeter drink without the traditional Coca-Cola zing? Coca-Cola's management thought so, and their blunder flowed from this faulty analysis.

If you own a restaurant, and some of your customers have complained about slow service, your problem-solving team should focus on causes. Is slow service caused by the servers? If so, is it because they are lazy or inefficient, or is it because each of them is assigned too many tables? Or can the slow service be blamed solely on the cooks? If so, is it because they are lazy or inefficient? Or are they understaffed?

You need to get a clear picture of the cause of a problem before the problem-solving process can continue.

Establish Criteria for Evaluating Solutions

Imagine you are on a task force assigned to solve this problem: Many students can't find an available computer on your campus when they need one for their assignments. After hours of study and discussion, your group recommends that the college open a new computer lab in the library and stock it with 50 new computers. Total cost: $200,000. But the idea is quickly shot down by administrators. It's four times what the college can afford. Now it's back to the drawing board for you and your task force. Your group could have saved itself much time and effort if it had known that it could recommend spending no more than $50,000.

This scenario shows why a group should write down the criteria—the standards or conditions—by which to judge a solution. To establish criteria, a group should ask these key questions:

- What must a proposed solution do?
- What must it avoid?
- What restrictions of time, money, and space must be considered?

Criteria should be rank-ordered in terms of importance. For the computer problem, the task force might end up with these criteria: (1) A computer lab must not cost more than $50,000. (2) It must contain computers that are compatible with those used in engineering and business classes. (3) It must be accessible to students from 8 A.M. until midnight.

Suggest Possible Solutions

When a group takes its next step—suggesting possible solutions—it must show patience and avoid leaping at the first idea that comes along. Putting a wide variety of possible solutions on the table can enhance the chances of making a sound decision.

brainstorming
generating many ideas quickly and uncritically

One of the best techniques for generating potential solutions is **brainstorming:** Participants rapidly, and at random, volunteer ideas while the group leader (or designated person) writes them on a board or pad. Many of the ingenious products that we use daily were invented or improved as a result of brainstorming. For example, Post-it® notes, those popular slips of stick-on paper, were invented by the 3M Corporation as a result of a small-group brainstorming session.[6]

For brainstorming to work effectively, there must be an atmosphere of total acceptance—no one analyzes, judges, ridicules, or rejects any of the ideas as they are being generated. Nothing is too wild or crazy to be jotted down.

Total acceptance is vital because (1) it encourages the flow of creative thinking and (2) an idea that seems far-fetched and impractical at first glance might eventually prove to be a good idea. In New York City, the Gaia Institute wanted to develop a prototype of a rooftop garden, so that someday gardens can be built throughout Manhattan to help clean the air, cool the city, and provide fresh vegetables. But there was a major problem: How can you have soil rich enough to grow plants, yet light enough so that the roof doesn't cave in? One idea sounded strange when it was introduced, but it proved to be fruitful when it was tried: Mix soil, which is heavy, with shredded polystyrene, which is light. The resulting compost worked; the soil was rich enough to grow vegetables, but not so heavy as to cause the roof to collapse. If the prototype is copied elsewhere, there will be a bonus: The gardens can help solve the ecological problem of how to dispose of polystyrene found in thrown-away styrofoam cups.[7]

Choose the Best Solution

After the brainstorming session, a group should analyze, weigh, and discuss its ideas in order to come up with the best solution. The solution chosen must meet the following standards:

- The solution must satisfy the criteria previously established.
- The group must have the authority to put the solution into effect (or recommend that it be put into effect).
- The solution must not solve one problem but create another.

Decide How to Implement the Solution

A solution may sound fine, but can it be realistically implemented? The next step is to decide how to put the solution into action.

Suppose a campus task force decides that the solution to a shortage of computers is for the college to buy laptop computers and rent them to students for the school year. How will this be carried out? Who will be in charge of the rentals? What will happen if some computers are lost or stolen? Is there money available for repairs?

Decide How to Test the Solution

Many groups hammer out a solution to a problem but never follow up to determine whether their solution really solved the problem. The last task of the problem-solving group is to decide how to find out if the solution really works.

If a group recommends hiring more security officers to solve traffic jams on campus, it could design a follow-up study to test its solution. If student motorists now require about 15 minutes to exit the campus in the afternoon, the group can set up a test like this: If the hiring of more officers results in an average exit time of 9 or more minutes, the solution has failed to alleviate the problem. But if the average exit time is less than 9 minutes, the solution is effective.

Team Presentations

While most group work is done in private, there are some occasions when a team makes a presentation to an audience. Two popular forms of team presentations are the symposium and the panel discussion.

Symposium

A **symposium** is a series of brief speeches on a common topic, each usually discussing a different aspect of the topic. In some cases, the speakers might be members of a problem-solving group who present their ideas and conclusions to a larger group. A symposium usually features a question-and-answer period after the speeches, and sometimes includes a panel discussion.

symposium
a meeting featuring short addresses by different people on the same topic

When you prepare and deliver a speech as part of a symposium, use the same skills and techniques as those of solo speechmaking, but work in advance with other members of your team to avoid duplication of material.

Panel Discussion

In a **panel discussion,** a team converses on a topic in front of an audience. A panel is usually made up of three to eight team members and is led by a moderator. Though there are many different methods of conducting a panel discussion, a common pattern is for panelists to give a brief opening statement and then discuss the subject among themselves, with the moderator serving as referee. At the end of the discussion, the audience is usually invited to ask questions.

panel discussion
consideration of a topic by a small group in the presence of an audience

Because of the variety of viewpoints and the liveliness of informed conversation, audiences enjoy a good panel discussion.

Guidelines for the Moderator

Much of the success (or failure) of a panel discussion is determined by the moderator. He or she must keep the discussion moving along smoothly, restrain the long-winded or domineering panelist from hogging the show, draw out the reticent panelist, and field questions from the audience. Here are some guidelines to follow when you are a moderator.

Arrange the setting. You and the panelists can be seated at a table facing the audience. Or, even better, you can be seated in a semicircle so that all members of the panel can see one another, while still remaining visible to the audience. A large name card should be placed in front of each panelist so that the audience will know the participants' names.

Brief panel members in advance. Well before the meeting, give panel members clear instructions on exactly what they are expected to cover in their opening remarks. Are they supposed to argue the "pro" or "con" position? Are they supposed to speak on only one aspect of the topic? (For information-giving discussions, you may want to assign each panel member a subtopic, according to his or her area of expertise, so that there is not much overlap among speakers.) Instruct the panelists not to bring and read written statements because this would kill the spontaneity that is desired in a panel discussion, but tell them that they are free to bring notes.

Before the meeting, prepare a list of items that you think should be discussed. This ensures that no important issues are inadvertently omitted. If the discussion begins to lag or go off into irrelevancies, you will have material from which to derive questions.

Prepare and deliver an introduction. At the beginning of the program, introduce the topic and the speakers, and explain the ground rules for the discussion; be sure to let listeners know if and when they will be permitted to ask questions.

Moderate the discussion. Give each panelist a chance to make an opening statement (within the time constraints previously announced) and then encourage the panelists to question one another or comment upon each other's remarks. Be neutral in the discussion but be prepared to ask questions if there is an awkward lull or if a panelist says something confusing or leaves out important information. Listen carefully to what each panelist says so that you don't embarrass yourself by asking questions on subjects that have already been discussed.

Maintain friendly, but firm, control. Don't let a panelist lead everyone off on a tangent that is far afield of the speech topic. During the question-and-answer session, don't let a member of the audience make a long-winded speech; interrupt kindly but firmly and say, "We need to give other people a chance to ask questions." If a panelist exceeds the time limit for opening remarks or monopolizes the discussion time, gently break in and say, "I'm sorry to interrupt, but let's hear from other members of the panel on their ideas concerning . . . " If a reticent panelist says very little, draw him or her out with specific, pertinent questions.

Be respectful of all panelists, including those with whom you disagree. Think of yourself not as a district attorney who must interrogate and skewer criminal defendants, but as a gracious host or hostess who stimulates guests to engage in lively conversation.

Ask open-ended questions rather than questions that elicit a simple yes or no. For example, ask "How can we make sure our homes are safe from burglars?" rather than "Is burglary on the increase in our community?"

End the program at the agreed-upon time. Wrap up the proceedings on time and in a prearranged way, perhaps by letting each panelist summarize briefly his or her position. You may want to summarize the key points made during the discussion (to do this, you would need to take notes throughout the program). Thank the panelists and the audience for their participation. If some members of the audience are still interested in continuing the discussion, you may want to invite them to talk to the panelists individually after the program is over.

Guidelines for Panelists

If you are a member of a panel, here are some guidelines to keep in mind.

Prepare for the discussion in the same way you prepare for a speech. Find out all that you can about the audience and the occasion: On what particular aspect of the topic are you expected to speak? Who are the other panelists and what will they cover? Will there be questions from the audience? What are the time constraints?

Prepare notes for the panel, but not a written statement. If you write out your remarks, you may be tempted to read them and thereby spoil the spontaneity that is desired in a panel discussion. In addition to notes, you may want to bring supporting data (such as bibliographical sources or statistics) from which to draw in case you are asked to document a point.

Respect the time limits set by the moderator. If, for example, you are asked to keep your opening remarks under two minutes, be careful to do so.

In the give-and-take of the discussion, be brief. If the other panelists or listeners want to hear more from you, they will ask.

Stay on the subject. Resist the temptation to ramble off into extraneous matters.

Be respectful and considerate of your fellow panelists. Don't squelch them with sarcasm, ridicule, or an overbearing attitude. Don't upstage them by trying to be the one to answer all the questions from the audience.

Tips for your CAREER

Tip 19.1 Strive to Improve Communication Skills

As you give speeches during your career, I hope that you will try to become better and better as a communicator. Here are three suggestions:

1. Seek opportunities for speaking.

The best way to improve your skills is to actually give speeches, so look for opportunities in your career and in your community. An excellent place to practice is in a Toastmasters club, where your speaking skills will be critiqued in a friendly, supportive atmosphere. For the name and phone number of the club nearest you, visit the Toastmasters' Website (www.toastmasters.org) or write Toastmasters International, P.O. Box 9052, Mission Viejo, California 92690.

2. Seek feedback.

See the guidelines in Tip 1.1 in Chapter 1.

3. Be a lifetime student of public speaking.

You can improve your own speaking skills by studying the speechmaking of others. Whenever you listen to a speech, make notes on what works and what doesn't work. Which delivery techniques were effective? Which were ineffective? What speech material seemed to please the listeners? What seemed to bore them? Keep your notes in a file for future reference, so that you can profit from both the successes and the failures of others.

Listen carefully to the comments of other panelists and members of the audience. If some people disagree with you, try to understand and appreciate their position instead of hastily launching a counterattack. Then be prepared to follow the next guideline.

Be willing to alter your position. If you listen with an open mind, you may see merit in others' views, and you may decide that you need to modify your original position. Though such a shift may seem like an embarrassing loss of face, it actually causes the audience to have greater respect for you. It shows you are a person who possesses intellectual courage, flexibility, and integrity.

Resources for Review and Skill Building

www.mhhe.com/gregory7

This book's Online Learning Center Website and SpeechMate CD-ROM provide meaningful resources and tools for study and review, such as practice tests, key-term flashcards, and sample speech videos.

SpeechMate CD-ROM

Summary

Small groups are important elements in business and professional life, and much of the work of small groups is done in meetings. To lead a meeting, establish an agenda and make sure that it is followed; encourage all members to participate in group discussions; and guide the discussion to make sure that it stays on the subject. When you are a participant in a small group meeting, enter the discussion with a positive attitude and an open mind.

One of the most effective agendas for problem solving is known as the reflective-thinking method. It involves seven steps: defining the problem; analyzing it; establishing criteria for evaluating solutions; suggesting possible solutions; choosing the best solution; deciding how to implement the solution; and deciding how to test the solution.

Sometimes groups appear in public to discuss or debate an issue. Two popular formats for team presentations are the symposium (a series of brief speeches on a common topic) and the panel discussion (an informal presentation involving a moderator and panelists).

Key Terms

agenda, *441*
brainstorming, *448*
hidden agenda, *446*
minutes, *442*
panel discussion, *449*
reflective-thinking method, *446*
symposium, *449*

Review Questions

1. Why is an agenda necessary for a meeting?
2. Why should a participant speak up, if possible, early in a meeting?
3. If you disagree with what everyone else in the group is saying, what should you do?
4. What is the best way to express objections to an idea?
5. If a meeting must last more than an hour, what should the leader do?
6. What is a hidden agenda?
7. What are the seven steps of the reflective-thinking method?
8. What should a group leader do after a meeting?
9. What are the duties of the moderator in a panel discussion?
10. What are the duties of panelists in a panel discussion?

Building Critical-Thinking Skills

1. A football huddle is a type of group meeting. Fran Tarkenton, former star quarterback for the Minnesota Vikings, says, "Many of my best plays were the result of input by other team members. For example, outside receivers often told me that they could run a specific pattern against the defense, and we adjusted to run those plays. I would guess that 50 percent of my touchdowns came about by my receivers suggesting pass patterns." How could Tarkenton's insights be applied to business meetings?

2. Some communication experts say that group meetings lose a great deal of their effectiveness when group members number more than 12. Assuming that this statement is true, what would account for a decline in effectiveness?

Building Teamwork Skills

1. In a group, use the steps of the reflective-thinking method (as shown in this chapter) to discuss how to solve a problem on your campus or in your community. Choose a leader to guide the discussion.

2. Using guidelines from your instructor, conduct either a symposium or panel discussion to present the findings from the problem-solving assignment above.

Building Internet Skills

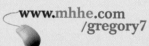

www.mhhe.com/gregory7

1. Many groups, such as the governing boards of colleges, conduct their meetings under the rules of parliamentary procedure, a formalized system for ensuring that meetings run smoothly and fairly. Find a Website devoted to these rules and print a page that explains how motions are handled.

Possible Strategy: Go to Yahoo! (www.yahoo.com), choose "Reference," and then "Parliamentary Procedure." Visit several of the sites listed.

2. On the Internet, thousands of organizations post their agendas for meetings (as well as their minutes). Find and print an agenda that is highly structured and gives a timetable for segments of a meeting.

Possible Strategy: Go to a search engine such as Google (www.google.com) and type a query (+ agenda + meeting) in the search box. Examine sites until you find the kind of agenda specified.

Using PowerWeb

www.mhhe.com/gregory7

An article entitled "Cheat Wave" tells of a high school teacher who flunked students for plagiarizing. Read the article and imagine that you are on a problem-solving committee at Piper High School assigned to find a solution to the problem of cheating in the school. Using the reflective-thinking method discussed in this chapter, how would you define the problem? To find this article, visit www.mhhe.com/gregory7, click on STUDENT EDITION and then POWERWEB: CONTENTS.

Appendix

Sample Speeches

Self-Introduction Speech

In 1990, when Mutodi Neshehe (Figure A.1) was 15, his parents in South Africa sent him abroad in order to save his life. At the time, South Africa was torn by violence because the ruling white minority of the population denied freedom to the black majority under a system of racial segregation known as apartheid. (In 1994, apartheid was abolished and a nonracial democracy was established, based on majority rule.) While most college students don't have a life story as dramatic as this one, Neshehe's self-introduction speech is a good model to follow because he uses specific details and anecdotes to give a full, interesting picture of who he is. The speech was given in a public speaking class at Asheville-Buncombe Technical Community College.

Figure A.1
Mutodi Neshehe speaks in front of the flag of his native country, South Africa, during his self-introduction speech.

My Love for Learning

Mutodi Neshehe

1 My name is Mutodi Neshehe. I was born and raised in Soweto, a township near Johannesburg, South Africa. I am the youngest of three sons, so of course everybody called me "Baby." By the age of 12, I was already involved in the political unrest caused by apartheid. My parents were dissatisfied with the direction that black youths in South Africa were taking. After observing my involvement in the riots and boycotts, my parents decided—when I was 15—to take all the money they had and send me to the United States.

2 My life in the U.S. started in January 1990 when my parents enrolled me at a private all-boys boarding school in Arden, North Carolina, called Christ School. Needless to say, I didn't like being there because I was alone and amongst strangers who had the luxury of going home during holidays. I called home crying every night, begging my parents to let me come back home. One night, my father responded with a series of questions, "What are you going to do when you get home?" and "Do you want to end up like your friends—in prison or dead?" That was the last night I cried about wanting to come home.

3 Due to the bold, sincere questions that my father asked, my attitude changed for the better. I started making the honor roll frequently and I excelled on the athletic field. I played soccer and basketball and ran track for three years until I graduated in 1993. That fall, I began college at Montreat College, where I was surprised to find out that

my tuition was financed through grants, donations, work-study, and a soccer scholarship. I won the race for class president my freshman year, and I was the "international student spokesman" for a few years. I enjoyed the mountains and the people of Montreat, and I also enjoyed playing soccer for the school all four years I was there.

I moved to Asheville in the fall of 1997 and started working in some of downtown's famous restaurants. I'm an outdoors person, and I worked from Thursday to Saturday and then hiked and camped from Sunday to Thursday and had to be at work Thursday evening. I had a lot of time on my hands, and I started working with a friend of mine as a lumberjack. We never worked in the winter, so I found myself camping and reading a lot. Then I realized that I could continue reading and learning—and get credit for it, so I enrolled in A-B Tech in search of a management degree. I have always been interested in the business world, and I ran for the vice presidency of the North Carolina chapter of Phi Beta Lambda, which is an academic competition organization for business students, and I won. 4

I love to learn and I love to see places, and that's why I recommend traveling and experience as educational tools for everybody. I've seen a lot, but yet I impatiently want to see more. I stay busy because I cannot stand wasting time. I have two good jobs as an assistant operator of the Chalet Club, a resort in Lake Lure, and as a "model scout" for Worldwide Modeling Group in Atlanta. I am going to graduate in the summer of 2001, but I am still going to keep learning whether it means taking classes somewhere or just through hands-on experience. 5

Informative Speech

For her informative speech, student speaker Wendy Wong carried out extensive research and created an interesting, well-organized report on her findings.

The *Titanic:* Two Erroneous Beliefs

Wendy Wong

When the *Titanic* was launched in 1912, it was the biggest ship in the world. It was as long as three football fields, it was 25 stories high, and it weighed 45,000 tons. It was also a luxurious hotel, and some of the world's wealthiest people were on board for its maiden voyage from Southampton, England, to New York City. Just four days into its voyage—at about 11:40 on the night of April 14, 1912—it struck ice in the North Atlantic, and sank in just two and a half hours. *[Speaker displays PowerPoint slide shown in Figure A.2.]* Tragically, out of 2,207 people on board, only 705 survived. The other 1,502 died because there were not enough lifeboats. *[Speaker displays PowerPoint slide shown in Figure A.3.]* 1

I have been fascinated by the *Titanic* ever since I saw the movie starring Leonardo DiCaprio and Kate Winslet. You might say I'm obsessed. I've read seven books and many Internet articles. There's a lot of disagreement among experts over what actually happened that night. I've decided that the most reliable experts are two sea captains who have written about the sinking. One of them is Joseph Conrad, a novelist and former sea captain who wrote an article about the *Titanic* a few months after it sank. The other is David G. Brown, author of a new book, *The Last Log of the Titanic.* Brown has served as a ship's captain and he teaches U.S. Coast Guard safety courses. I find these two the most trustworthy because they write from many years of experience in handling large ships. 2

Figure A.2
The speaker uses a PowerPoint slide to show an artist's imaginative rendition of the sinking of the *Titanic* in the icy waters of the North Atlantic.

3 Based on what these sea captains say, I want to show you that the *Titanic* disaster happened because of two beliefs that were tragically erroneous.

4 Let's look at the first of these beliefs: The captain of the *Titanic*—Edward John Smith—believed that ice was just a nuisance, an inconvenience—not a great danger. In the past, some ships in the North Atlantic had hit icebergs or underwater ice shelves, and a few of these encounters had caused sinkings and death. But Captain Smith thought that ice was no match for the mighty *Titanic,* with its massive size and strength. On that fateful night, he ran the ship at full speed—22.5 knots, which is the same as 26 miles per hour. That may not sound fast, but it is actually very fast for a gigantic ship at sea, especially when you consider the momentum it throws against anything it collides with.

5 Captain Smith received several warnings from other ships during the day. Icebergs and scattered clumps of ice in the area were so bad that one ship even stopped to wait out the night. But Captain Smith ignored the warnings because he didn't think they were relevant for his ship, which was so much larger than the other ships. If the *Titanic* encountered an iceberg, it could swerve in time. If it hit underwater ice, it would resist damage because of its strong steel plates.

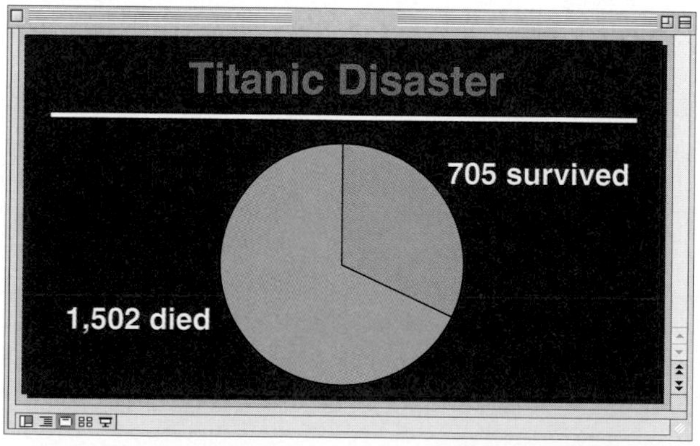

Figure A.3
A pie graph on a PowerPoint slide dramatizes the staggering number of deaths—all of which could have been prevented if the *Titanic* had carried enough lifeboats.

As Captain Smith looked out at the blobs of ice he was knifing through, he must have felt invincible. Captain Brown says, "Any danger from the sea seemed so trivial when one stood 60 feet off the water, surrounded by tons of steel." 6

Events proved that Captain Smith was wrong, of course. When an iceberg suddenly loomed ahead, the ship swerved to go around it, but contact was made. Captain Brown says that the *Titanic* did not actually collide with the iceberg, but instead scraped over a submerged ice shelf, ripping holes in the bottom of the ship and letting water flood in. 7

If the *Titanic* had been moving slowly, the ice would have caused little or no damage. It was Captain Smith's erroneous belief in his technological superiority over ice that caused the fatal damage. 8

While one erroneous belief doomed the ship, another erroneous belief doomed the passengers: The builders and owners of the ship believed that in a worst-case accident, the *Titanic* would sink very slowly. 9

The builders of the *Titanic* never believed that the ship was unsinkable. The word "unsinkable" was used by the news media, and it became part of the mythology surrounding the disaster. The builders knew that any ship could sink, especially if it collided with another vessel in fog. Fog—not ice—was what mariners feared most. 10

The *Titanic's* designers tried to make the ship as safe as possible. They created 16 watertight compartments in the lower section of the ship. Because of these compartments, they believed that the ship could sustain a moderate collision and not be crippled. They also believed that even if the ship was badly damaged by a very severe collision, it would sink slowly and stay afloat for several days. It would probably be able to limp into the nearest port. This belief is why the *Titanic* failed to carry enough lifeboats for everyone on board. The owners—White Star Line—believed that even in a worst-case accident, a relatively small number of lifeboats would be sufficient because they would be used only to ferry passengers from the sinking ship to a rescue ship. Rescue ships could be counted on because the North Atlantic shipping lanes were filled with many ships. These ships could be alerted by means of "wireless" (or radio) transmissions, which had recently been invented. There would be ample time to ferry all the passengers to safety. 11

The *Titanic* disaster, of course, showed the folly of the builders and owners. It demonstrated that even a supposedly well-designed ship can sink rapidly, and that a sufficient number of lifeboats are needed. Shortly after the sinking, international rules were adopted, requiring that every ship have lifeboat space for each person on board. 12

To summarize, the *Titanic* disaster took many lives because of two erroneous beliefs: Captain Smith's belief that ice was merely an inconvenience and the *Titanic* builders' and owners' belief that in the worst of accidents, the ship would sink very slowly and stay afloat for a few days. 13

Today, we can avoid making blunders like these if we remember the great lesson of the *Titanic:* Human beings are foolish if they have blind, unquestioning faith in technology. 14

Persuasive Speech (Motivated Sequence)

In this persuasive speech, student speaker Daniel O'Brien uses the five-step motivated sequence to organize his material. For more information about the motivated sequence, see Chapter 16.

A Wake-Up Call for Drowsy Drivers

Daniel O'Brien

1 Last October, an 18-year-old student at Texas A&M, Brandon Kallmeyer, was driving his pick-up truck along a highway in College Station, Texas, when he fell asleep at the wheel. His truck left the road and struck six students who were walking along the highway on their way to a party. All six were killed. Police said Kallmeyer, who was uninjured, had not been drinking.

2 Accidents caused by drowsy drivers can never be completely eliminated, but there is one thing we can do right now to bring the number down. All we have to do is install one simple safety feature on our roadways. I got most of my information from the Website of the National Highway Traffic Safety Administration and from an e-mail interview with an expert on highway safety: Per Garder, who is a professor of Civil and Environmental Engineering at the University of Maine in Orono.

3 Before we go into the details of a solution, let's examine just how serious the problem is. Drowsy driving is a major killer on our roadways. Statistics compiled by the federal government show that driver fatigue is the primary cause of at least 150,000 police-reported crashes in the United States each year. These crashes result in more than 10,000 deaths and 96,000 injuries.

4 We Americans simply don't get enough sleep. The National Sleep Foundation says the average American gets only six hours of sleep each night. This is not enough for full alertness. The Foundation did a survey of 1,000 adults. More than half said that during the past year, they had driven while drowsy. Researchers at the University of South Australia tested the reflexes and alertness of drowsy persons, and they concluded that "driving while drowsy" is as dangerous as "driving while drunk"—depending, of course, on the level of drowsiness and the level of drunkenness.

5 There are many myths about drowsy driving. One of them is that younger drivers are more alert than the rest of the driving population. This is just not true. Studies show that males under 25 are the segment of the population that is most likely to fall asleep at the wheel. Another myth is that winding roads are the most dangerous. In reality, the worst situation is a straight highway, because of the hypnotic effect. *[Speaker shows PowerPoint slide in Figure A.4.]* Unfortunately, I don't have time to cover all of the other myths, but I have listed them on some handouts that you can pick up at the end of class. *[See Figure 16-A in Chapter 16.]*

6 The obvious solution for drowsy driving is for everyone to get more sleep, but this is easier said than done. While we're waiting for everyone to wise up and get lots of sleep, what can we do about the problem? We can reduce the number of accidents by installing rumble strips on all highways. Experts say that most crashes involving drowsy drivers are known as "run-off-road" accidents. This means that the car strays off the road and flips over or hits an object on the side of the road. Rumble strips are patterns in the pavement—either raised or grooved—and they discourage running off the road. When a driver strays, the car runs over the strips, causing a loud rumbling sound and a vibration in the steering wheel. The sound and vibration can wake up a sleeping driver and give him or her enough time to regain control of the car. Here is a picture of rumble strips on Interstate 80 in Nebraska. *[Speaker shows PowerPoint slide in Figure A.5]* Notice the series of grooved depressions. Some states prefer to use raised thermoplastic strips, which not only make noise when a car runs over them, but also reflect light at night and in wet weather.

7 Unfortunately, rumble strips are not used everywhere. Currently 34 states have them on portions of interstate highways, but only a handful of states use them on secondary roads. The National Highway Traffic Safety Administration estimates that

Figure A.4 (left)
A straight highway creates a hypnotic effect that is especially dangerous for drowsy drivers.

Figure A.5 (right)
Seeing a rumble strip on a Nebraska interstate helps the audience to visualize the system.

rumble strips placed on all major roads could cut the rate of run-off-road crashes by 50 percent. That means that each year we might save 5,000 lives and prevent 48,000 injuries.

Rumble strips can be installed inexpensively and quickly. Consider the Pennsylvania Turnpike. When it installed rumble strips, the cost was only 30 cents per foot. And it took only six hours to install strips on both shoulders of one mile of highway. 8

Now that we've seen how little money and time is involved, let's look at the big benefit we will receive. A couple of states have installed many long stretches of rumble strips. These states have reported a significant decline in run-off-road crashes. The Pennsylvania Turnpike reported a 70 percent drop in run-off-road crashes after rumble strips were installed. Yes, you heard me right: 70 percent! The New York State Thruway had a 34 percent drop. 9

I envision the day when all states will install rumble strips on every single mile of interstate highway and every single mile of secondary roads. And let's begin with our own state. I have a petition asking our state legislators to take this action now. I urge you to sign it, and I will mail it off right away. 10

To summarize, we cannot completely eliminate accidents caused by drowsy driving, but we can bring the number down by installing rumble strips on all roadways. Please sign my petition. 11

In the words of a federal highway official, Kathryn Harrington-Hughes, rumble strips are "a wake-up call for drowsy drivers." Now it's time to give our legislators a wake-up call. 12

End Notes

Preface

1. Norman Cousins, Quotations home page, www.geocities.com/~spanoudi/quote.html (accessed November 14, 2002).

Chapter 1

1. Mary Ignatius, e-mail interview, January 8, 2003.
2. Ibid.
3. In author's e-mail survey (February–March 2000) of 742 business and professional speakers, 487 said that in college they had taken either a public speaking course or a communication course with a public speaking component; of the 487 who had received training, 91 percent rated the course as "highly valuable."
4. "Communication Skills Course Aids Diagnosis of Depressed Patients," *Geriatrics,* March 2000, p. 22; Christine Kemp-Longmore, "Conflict Resolution in the Workplace," *Black Collegian,* February 2000, p. 131.
5. Ann L. Darling and Deanna P. Dannels, "Practicing Engineers Talk About the Importance of Talk: A Report on Oral Communication in the Workplace," *Communication Education,* January 2003, pp. 1–16; "Oral Communication Skills Rank First Among Employers," results of survey of Fortune 500 companies by National Association of Colleges and Employers, www.naceweb.org (accessed May 8, 2000).
6. Marilyn Mackes, executive director, National Association of Colleges and Employers, e-mail interview, May 8, 2000.
7. Cristina Silva, human resources manager, Camillus Enterprises, Los Angeles, in "The Manager's Tutorial," www.managercoaching.org (accessed August 23, 2000).
8. Karen Walker was a student in the author's public speaking class.
9. John Locke, seventeenth century English philosopher, "Essay Concerning Human Understanding," electronic text posted by Oregon State University, www.orst.edu/instruct/phl302/texts/locke/locke1/Book3a.html (accessed December 4, 2000).
10. Thanks to Jenny Stubbs of Business Designs, Inc., for relating this anecdote about a colleague.
11. Slogan used in an advertisement by Hitachi, Ltd., Tokyo, Japan, included in a stereo system package (undated).
12. David W. Richardson, management consultant, Westport, Connecticut, e-mail interview, May 9, 2000.
13. Jack Brilhart et al., "Ethics in Public Speaking," supplementary materials for COM115 at Southwest Missouri State University, commedia.smsu.edu/basiccourseset.html (accessed December 4, 2000).
14. *Aesop's Fables— Online Collection,* www.pacificnet.net/~johnr/aesop (accessed May 10, 2000).
15. This story was related to the author by an official of the company on the condition that the company's name not be used.
16. Will Rogers, quoted at *Quotation World,* s-2000.com/quoteworld (accessed May 18, 2000).
17. "Better Off Brunette," *Health* magazine, www.healthmag.com (accessed September 6, 2000).
18. "Platinium Blondes Are Labelled as Dumb," British Broadcasting Corporation, news.bbc.co.uk (accessed September 6, 2000).
19. American Civil Liberties Union, "Driving While Black or Brown," www.aclu.org (accessed May 17, 2000).
20. Nido R. Qubein, *Communicate Like a Pro* (Englewood Cliffs, NJ: Prentice Hall, 1983), p. 67.
21. James ("Doc") Blakely, professional speaker, Wharton, Texas, e-mail interview, May 4, 2000.

Chapter 2

1. Tom Beer, "Leonardo DiCaprio: Back in the Game," *Biography Magazine,* January 2003, p. 53; "Profile: Leonardo DiCaprio," AllMoviePortal.com, www.allmovieportal.com/c/leonardodicaprio.html, (accessed April 11, 2003); "Young Lion," Gallery 21, www.members.tripod.com/treggy88/younglionpg1.html (accessed April 13, 2003); "Leonardo's Stage Fright," The Completely Unofficial Leonardo DiCaprio Home Page, www.dicaprio.com (accessed April 13, 2003).
2. The term *stage fright* originated in the world of theater, but it is used today to designate the nervousness or fear experienced by a person before or during an appearance in front of any kind of audience. Other terms that are sometimes used to describe this condition are *speech fright, speech anxiety,* and *communication apprehension.*
3. Lynn Snowden, "Speak Easy," *Impress,* Winter 2000, p. 40.
4. Jim Seymour, *Jim Seymour's PC Productivity Bible* (New York: Brady, 1991), p. 119.
5. Reggie Jackson, interview during an ABC sports telecast, October 2, 1984.
6. John Farmer, Wolfe & Farmer Law Firm, Norton, Virginia, as quoted by his sister, Dr. Betty Farmer, Western Carolina University, e-mail correspondence, January 19, 2000.
7. *Elayne Snyder, Speak for Yourself—with Confidence* (New York: New American Library, 1983), p. 113.
8. I. A. R. Wylie, quoted in *Shyness and Speech Anxiety,* www.berea.edu/cec/h/shy.html (accessed April 6, 2003).
9. Kent E. Menzel and Lori J. Carrell, "The Relationship between Preparation and Performance in Public Speaking," *Communication Education,* January 1994, p. 17.
10. Joel Weldon, professional speaker, Scottsdale, Arizona, e-mail interview, December 4, 2000.
11. Ibid.
12. Ali MacGraw, quoted in James Link, "Dealing with Stage Fright," *Cosmopolitan,* October 1982, p. 112.

13. "In the Spotlight: Kristin Kreuk," *Biography Magazine,* June 2003, p. 14; Donna Freydkin, "Halle Berry," *People Profiles,* people.aol.com/people (accessed April 5, 2003); Dotson Rader, "He Turns Shy into Funny," *Parade,* May 9, 1993, pp. 4–5; Philip Zimbardo, *Psychology and Life,* 11th ed. (Glenview, IL: Scott, Foresman, 1985), p. 448; and miscellaneous other sources.

14. Joe W. Boyd, professional speaker, Bellingham, Washington, e-mail interview, December 4, 2000.

15. Carlos Jimenez, member of Toastmasters International, quoted in Toastmasters District 39 (Northern California) online newsletter, www.district39.org (accessed June 13, 2000).

16. Joe Ayres, "Using Visual Aids to Reduce Speech Anxiety," *Communication Research Reports,* June–December 1991, pp. 73–79.

17. Henry Heimlich, M.D., Cincinnati, Ohio, telephone interview, January 8, 2000.

18. Danielle Kennedy, professional speaker, Sun Valley, Idaho, e-mail interview, June 8, 2000.

19. Michael T. Motley, "Taking the Terror out of Talk," *Psychology Today,* January 1988, p. 49.

20. Ronald M. Rapee and Lina Lim, "Discrepancy between Self- and Observer Ratings of Performance in Social Phobics," *Journal of Abnormal Psychology,* November 1992, pp. 728–31.

21. Dick Cavett, quoted in "Talk Shows: Dick Cavett," www.talkshows.about.com/tvradio/talkshows/msubcavett.htm (accessed May 26, 2000).

22. David Segal, "Verdict: The Defense Can't Rest Too Often," *Washington Post On-Line,* www.washingtonpost.com (accessed May 2, 2000).

23. Earl Nightingale, *Communicate What You Think* (Chicago: Nightingale-Conant Corp., 1976), Audiocassette #11.

24. Maggie Paley, "Modern Image Signal: Voice," *Vogue,* August 1984, p. 412.

25. Motley, "Taking the Terror out of Talk," p. 49.

Chapter 3

1. Joanna Meyer, M.D., Atlanta, Georgia, personal interview, February 6, 2000. Dr. Meyer was a physician in the emergency department in Grady Hospital in Atlanta at the time of the incident.

2. Keith Davis, quoted in "How to Be a Better Listener," The Small Business Knowledge Base, www.bizmove.com (accessed June 25, 2000).

3. Lyman K. Steil, "Your Personal Listening Profile," booklet published by Sperry Corporation, undated, p. 5.

4. Scot Ober, *Contemporary Business Communication,* 2nd ed. (Boston: Houghton Mifflin, 1995), p. 509.

5. Lyman K. Steil, interview in *U.S. News & World Report,* May 26, 1980, p. 65.

6. Andrew D. Wolvin and Carolyn Gwynn Coakley, "A Survey of the Status of Listening Training in Some Fortune 500 Corporations," *Communication Education,* April 1991, pp. 152–64.

7. Thomas D. Zweifel, "Be Still and Hear," Swiss Consulting Group, www.swissconsultinggroup.com (accessed June 23, 2000).

8. Ralph G. Nichols, "Listening Is a 10-Part Skill," in *Efficient Reading,* ed. James I. Brown (Boston: D.C. Heath, 1962), p. 101.

9. Enid S. Waldhart and Robert N. Bostrom, "Notetaking, Listening, and Modes of Retention," paper presented to the International Listening Association, Washington, D.C., 1981; Francis J. Divesta and G. Susan Gray, "Listening and Note Taking II: Immediate and Delayed Recall as Functions of Variations in Thematic Continuity, Note Taking, and Length of Listening Review Intervals," *Journal of Educational Psychology* 64 (1973), pp. 278–87.

10. Nichols, "Listening Is a 10-Part Skill," pp. 101–102.

11. Margaret Lane, "Are You Really Listening?" *Reader's Digest World,* www.readersdigest.com (accessed June 13, 2000).

12. Julie Hill, "Confronting the Ring of Rudeness," *Presentations,* March 2000, p. 13.

13. Ibid.

14. Abby Ellin, "The Laptop Ate My Attention Span," *New York Times,* April 16, 2000, p. BU-15.

15. Jodi Wilgoren, "A Revolution in Education Clicks into Place," *New York Times,* March 26, 2000, p. 1.

16. This incident occurred at Northwestern University. It was related to me by David Collins of Indianapolis, Indiana, one of the students involved in the experiment and now a retired psychology professor. Similar experiments have been tried, with varying degrees of success, at other colleges. Some reports of these experiments seem to have been exaggerated, and are sometimes included in collections of "urban legends."

17. Anonymous speaker quoted by Ronald B. Adler, *Communicating at Work,* 2nd ed. (New York: Random House, 1986), p. 88.

Chapter 4

1. Joan Higginbotham, NASA astronaut, e-mail interview, June 19, 2000; "Biographical Data: Joan E. Higginbotham," Lyndon B. Johnson Space Center, www.jsc.nasa.gov (accessed June 13, 2000).

2. "Astronaut Wows Student Audience," *News-Times On-Line Edition,* Fairfield, Connecticut, January 8, 2000, www.newstimes.com (accessed June 14, 2000).

3. The "drowning while thirsting" analogy has been attributed to several different writers. At "Resources for IT Professionals," www.technosphere.net (accessed June 5, 2001), I found it attributed to Hugh Arscott.

4. Maria Silveira, e-mail interview, June 9, 2003. Silveira is a volunteer for the Wheelchair Foundation, www.wheelchairfoundation.org.

5. Greg Anrig Jr., "Taxpayers' Revenge," in *How to Manage Your Taxes,* a booklet published by *Money* magazine, undated, pp. 2–3.

6. Ibid.

7. "American Businesswomen Face Obstacles Abroad," *The Wall Street Journal On-Line,* March 1, 2000, interactive.wsj.com (accessed June 19, 2000).

8. "Cultural Diversity and Racial Sensitivity," Texas Commission on Law Enforcement Officer Standards and Education,

www.utexas.edu/cee/dec/tcleose/cultdiv/chp2.html (accessed August 5, 2000); "Non-Verbal Commuication Modes," article posted for Intercultural Business Relations course at Andrews University, www2.andrews.edu/~tidwell/bsad560/NonVerbal.html (accessed August 5, 2000).

9. Mary Ellen Guffey, *Business Communication: Process & Product,* 2nd ed. (Cincinnati, OH: South-Western Publishing, 1997), p. 50.
10. Ibid., p. 56.
11. LaTresa Pearson, "Think Globally, Present Locally," *Presentations,* April 1996, p. 22.
12. Ibid., p. 27.
13. Scott H. Lewis, "Toastmasters of Disability," *Toastmaster,* February 1993, p. 5.
14. Unattributed advice was featured on an Easter Seals calendar, published by Easter Seals, an organization devoted to people with disabilities.
15. Deborah L. Harmon, *Serving Students with Disabilities* (Asheville, NC: Asheville-Buncombe Technical Community College, 1994), pp. 7–9.
16. Ibid., p. 9.
17. Ibid.
18. Helen Sloss Luey et al., "Hard-of-Hearing or Deaf," *Social Work,* March 1995, p. 177.
19. Harmon, *Serving Students with Disabilities,* p. 9.
20. Sharon Lynn Campbell, "Helping the Toastmaster of Disability," *Toastmaster,* February 1993, p. 15.
21. Kitty O. Locker, *Business and Administrative Communication,* 5th ed. (New York: McGraw-Hill, 2000), p. 45.
22. Fred Ebel, "Know Your Audience," *Toastmaster,* June 1985, p. 20.
23. Thomas Leech, San Diego, California, consultant, "Tips and Articles," Winning Presentations, www.winning-presentations.com (accessed December 2, 2000).
24. John Naber, professional speaker, Pasadena, California, telephone interview, November 12, 2000.

Chapter 5

1. Anne C. Paine, "Oberlin's First Volcanologist Seeks Answers to Eruptive Questions," Oberlin College, www.oberlin.edu/colrelat/ats/story/castro.html (accessed April 11, 2003).
2. Adapted from an advertisement by United Technologies Corporation in *The Wall Street Journal,* date unavailable.

Chapter 6

1. Dr. Lindsay Bridges, family physician, speech presented at Clear Air Rally, Asheville (North Carolina) City-County Plaza, April 5, 2000.
2. "Going to Great Lengths for a Good Parking Space," *Chronicle of Higher Education,* February 4, 2000, p. A14.

Chapter 7

1. Dan Milea, M.D., et al., "Blindness in a Strict Vegan," *New England Journal of Medicine,* March 23, 2000, p. 897.
2. Student speaker Raven Sanders gave the author permission to relate events leading up to her speech.
3. Robert T. Carroll, "Full Moon and Lunar Effects," The Skeptic's Dictionary, www.skepdic.com (accessed September 25, 2000).
4. Dr. John Palmer, professor of physiology at the University of Massachusetts in Amherst, who studies lunar rhythms in marine organisms, quoted in "Are People More Active During a Full Moon?" *Boston Globe Online,* www.boston.com (accessed September 25, 2000); "Lunar Influence," Association for Rational Thought, www.cincinnatiskeptics.org (accessed September 25, 2000).
5. S. Ong et al., "Labour Ward Activity and the Lunar Cycle," *Journal of Obstetrics and Gynecology,* www.ccspublishing.com/J_obg.htm (accessed September 25, 2000).
6. Keith Logan, "Warts—What to Do About Them," *Pediatrics for Parents,* www.momsrefuge.com/pediatrics (accessed September 22, 2000).
7. Frederic Golden, "Now a Word from Our Doctors," *Time Magazine Online,* www.time.com (accessed September 22, 2000).
8. "Vox Pop," *Time,* November 28, 1994, p. 20.
9. Kenneth L. Woodward, "The Rites of Americans," *Newsweek,* November 29, 1993, p. 80.
10. Ibid.
11. Cullen Murphy, "Scapegroup," *Atlantic,* April 1995, p. 24.
12. Kathi Ames, "Lying with Polls," *Poll Watchers,* www.pollwatchers.com (accessed September 25, 2000).
13. Nicholas Wade, "Scientists Map Ulcer Bacterium's Genetic Code," *New York Times,* CyberTimes on the Internet, August 7, 1997, www.nytimes.com (accessed September 23, 2000); Charlene Laino, "Proving Ulcers' Bacterial Guts," MSNBC, www.msnbc.com (accessed September 23, 2000).
14. Arthur Butz, biography at Institute for Historical Review, ihr.org/bios/butz.htm (accessed September 23, 2000).
15. Michele Pullia Turk, "Ephedrine's Deadly Edge," *U.S.News Online,* www.usnews.com (accessed September 24, 2000).
16. Laura Bird, "Corporate Critics Complain Companies Hide Behind 'Grass-Roots' Campaigns," *The Wall Street Journal Online,* interactive.wsj.com (accessed September 24, 2000).
17. Ibid.
18. Sheldon Rampton and John Stauber, *Trust Us, We're Experts!* (New York: Jeremy P. Tacher/Putnam, 2001), pp. 16–17.
19. "Current Net Hoaxes," About.com, www.about.com (accessed September 24, 2000).
20. "Flash Your Headlights and Die!" About.com, www.about.com (accessed September 24, 2000).
21. Bunko Squad, "Quackery," Wellness Web, www.wellweb.com/ALTERN/bunko/bunko.htm (accessed September 24, 2000).
22. "Purple Grape Juice May Help Prevent Heart Attacks," Reuters news report, March 18, 1997, at Electric Library, www.elibrary.com (accessed September 22, 2000).
23. Tom Kirby, "117 Ideas for Better Business Presentations," pamphlet distributed by Tom Kirby Associates, St. Petersburg, Florida.

24. U.S. Copyright Act, at Legal Information Institute, Cornell University, www.law.cornell.edu:80/topics/copyright.html (accessed September 26, 2000).
25. "When Works Pass into the Public Domain," University of North Carolina Library, www.unc.edu/~unclng/public-d.htm (accessed September 26, 2000).
26. *The Chicago Manual of Style,* 14th ed. (Chicago: University of Chicago Press, 1993), p. 146.
27. The Trustees of California State University, "Fair Use: Overview and Meaning for Higher Education," Consortium for Educational Technology in University System, www.cetus.org (accessed September 25, 2000).
28. William Rodarmor, "Rights of Passage," *New Media,* (September 1993), pp. 49–56.
29. Steven Blaize, "Who Owns Rita Hayworth? Multimedia Rights: Yours and Theirs," *Digital Video,* November 1994, p. 63.

Chapter 8

1. Student speaker Rob Russo derived his information from these sources: Oliver P. Kreyden, "Botulinum Toxin: From Poison to Pharmaceutical," in Oliver P. Kreyden et al, *Hyperhidrosis and Botulinum Toxin in Dermatology* (Basel, Switzerland: Karger, 2002), pp. 94–100; Sheldon H. Gottlieb, "Vipers, Venom, and Life-Saving Snakes," *Diabetes Forecast,* November 2001, p. 48; Arlene Weintraub et al, "Medicine's Wild Kingdom," *Business Week,* February 3, 2003, p. 70; "Feed a Cold, Starve a Fever, Poison a Headache," *Harvard Health Letter,* February 2000, p. 7.
2. Nancy Li derived her material from Howard Topoff, "Slave-Making Queens," *Scientific American,* www.sciam.com (accessed September 4, 2000).
3. Examples derived from Jessica Speart, "The New Drug Mules," *New York Times,* June 11, 1995, pp. 44–45.
4. "Black North Carolina Student Receives Kidney from His White Science Teacher," *Jet,* May 8, 2000, p. 31; Paula Chin and Michaele Ballard, "Lesson in Generosity," *People,* May 8, 2000, p. 213.
5. Katrina Benjamin was interviewed by student speaker Diane Woolsey.
6. Steven Greenhouse, "I.B.M. Explores Shift of Some Jobs Overseas," *New York Times,* July 22, 2003, p. C1.
7. Joshua Quittner, "Cracks in the Net," *Time,* February 27, 1995, p. 34.
8. Arnold Barnett, professor, Massachusetts Institute of Technology, "How Numbers Are Tricking You," Technology Review, www.techreview.com (accessed September 12, 2000).
9. Karen Miyamoto gave permission for her classroom speech to be printed.

Chapter 9

1. Kelly M. O'Donnell, Ph.D., visiting professor of biology, Universidade de São Paulo, e-mail interview, August 5, 2003.
2. Shu-Ling Lai, "Influence of Audio-Visual Presentations on Learning Abstract Concepts," *International Journal of Instructional Media* 27 (2000), pp. 199–206.
3. Experiment conducted by the author using two groups, each comprised of 40 students; see also Michael E. Patterson, Donald F. Dansereau, and Dianna Newbern, "Effects of Communication Aids and Strategies on Cooperative Teaching," *Journal of Educational Psychology,* December 1992, pp. 453–61.
4. ABC *Primetime Live,* televised report on faked disabilities, May 12, 1994.
5. "The Effects of the Use of Overhead Transparencies on Business Meetings," Wharton Applied Research Center, University of Pennsylvania, September 1981; see also Ruth Ann Smith, "The Effects of Visual and Verbal Advertising Information on Consumers' Inferences," *Journal of Advertising,* December 1991, pp. 13–23; and J. B. Carroll, *Human Cognitive Abilities: A Survey of Factor-Analaytic Studies* (Cambridge, England: Cambridge University Press, 1993).
6. Hower J. Hsia, "On Channel Effectiveness," *AV Communication Review,* Fall 1968, pp. 248–50.
7. Miyuki Sugimori, candy sculptor, telephone interview, January 18, 2000.
8. Kirsten Schabacker, "A Short, Snappy Guide to Meaningful Meetings," *Working Woman,* June 1991, p. 73.

Chapter 10

1. "Anti-Tobacco Lobby," Cancer Patients Aid Association, www.cpaaindia.org (accessed July 14, 2000).
2. Ruby Bhatia, host of the *Kinetic Mega Show* on Indian television, e-mail interview, July 17, 2000.
3. Wesley J. Smith, "Inside Small-Claims Court," *Home Office Computing,* September 1994, p. 32.
4. Experiment, conducted by the author, replicates numerous psychologists' studies, which reach the same conclusion.
5. Harry Sharp Jr. and Thomas McClung, "Effect of Organization on the Speaker's Ethos," *Speech Monographs* 33 (1966), pp. 182–84.
6. Information in this section was derived from research notes of student speaker Bob Bates, who relied primarily on Daniel Goleman, "How Stress Erodes Health," *International Herald Tribune,* December 17, 1992, p. 8; and "Marital Tiffs Spark Immune Swoon," *Science News,* September 4, 1993, p. 153.
7. Used with permission from student Amber Wright.
8. Marcia Yudkin, "Eschew Podium Odium," *Toastmaster,* February 1992, p. 18.

Chapter 11

1. Mike McCurley and Diana S. Friedman, attorneys, Dallas, Texas, in "The Art of Persuasion," American Academy of Matrimonial Lawyers, www.aaml.org/artof.htm (accessed October 17, 2000).
2. Michelle Roberts, Washington, D.C., attorney, telephone interview, May 19, 2000; David Segal, "Verdict: The Defense Can't Rest Too Often," *Washington Post On-Line,* www.washingtonpost.com (accessed May 2, 2000).
3. Myrna Marofsky, quoted in *Speaker's Idea File* (September 1993), p. 18.
4. Cynthia Wray, Western Carolina University, gave permission for this excerpt to be used.

5. Sullivan derived her material from R. C. Lewontin, "The Confusion over Cloning," *New York Review of Books,* October 23, 1997, p. 18.

6. Don Aslett, *Is There a Speech Inside You?* (Cincinnati: Writer's Digest Books, 1989), p. 30.

7. Joel Weldon, professional speaker, Scottsdale, Arizona, e-mail interview, December 4, 2000.

8. John E. Baird, "The Effects of Speech Summaries upon Audience Comprehension of Expository Speeches of Varying Quality and Complexity," *Central States Speech Journal* 25 (1974), pp. 124–25.

9. Adapted from Edward L. Friedman, *The Speechmaker's Complete Handbook* (New York: Harper & Row, 1955), p. 16.

10. Adapted from Tari Lynn Porter, "By Hook or by Look," *Toastmaster,* July 1987, p. 5.

11. Introduction and conclusion printed with the permission of Amber Wright.

Chapter 12

1. "John Woo: Biography," *Internet Movie Database Inc.,* http://www.imdb.com (accessed July 9, 2003).

2. Ronald T. Kellogg, "Effectiveness of Prewriting Strategies as a Function of Task Demands," *American Journal of Psychology,* Fall 1990, pp. 327–42.

3. Outline, notes, and speech by Anthony Silva used with his permission.

4. Mike Edelhart and Carol Ellison, "Build Images with Words at the Core," *PC/Publishing,* April 1990, p. 75.

Chapter 13

1. Montel Williams, quotations regarding multiple sclerosis, www.montelshow.com (accessed September 1, 2003).

2. J. Alexander Tanford, Indiana University School of Law, *The Trial Process: Law, Tactics, and Ethics,* 3rd ed. (Newark, NJ: LexisNexis, 2002), p. 47.

3. Anthony Pratkanis and Elliot Aronson, *Age of Propaganda: The Everyday Use and Abuse of Persuasion* (New York: W.H. Freeman & Co., 1992), p. 25.

4. Ibid., p. 44.

5. C. J. Ducasse, quoted by Jerome Agel and Walter D. Glanze in *Pearls of Wisdom* (New York: Harper & Row, 1987), p. 1.

6. "Change Your Name and Reap," *Communication Briefings,* April 1993, p. 4.

7. Steve May, *The Story File: 1,001 Contemporary Illustrations for Speakers, Writers and Preachers* (Peabody, MA: Hendrickson Publishers, 2000), p. 5.

8. Janet Elliott, "That's No Lady, That's My Wife," *Toastmaster,* August 1986, p. 15.

9. Frederick Crews, *The Random House Handbook,* 6th ed. (New York: McGraw-Hill, 1992), p. 347.

10. "Wishful Thinking," *Vitality,* April 1997, p. 7.

11. Dennis Kessinger, "The Agents of Imagery," *Toastmaster,* March 1993, p. 5.

12. Technically, the term *wetland* can cover marshes and bogs as well as swamps, but in popular usage, wetland is a synonym for swamp.

13. Don Bagin, "Here's a Frightful Implication," *Communication Briefings,* December 1989, p. 3.

14. Quoted in "Academia," *Quarterly Review of Doublespeak,* October 1994, p. 11.

15. Courtland L. Bovée and John V. Thill, *Business Communication Today,* 5th ed. (Upper Saddle River, NJ: Prentice Hall, 1998), p. 179.

16. Edward T. Thompson, "How to Write Clearly," reprint of advertisement by International Paper Company, undated.

17. William Zinsser, *On Writing Well,* 3rd ed. (New York: Harper & Row, 1985), p. 110.

18. Doublespeak is a hybrid word based on "doublethink" and "newspeak" from George Orwell's novel *1984.*

19. *Quarterly Review of Doublespeak* is no longer published in print form, but is available free on-line from the National Council of Teachers of English, www.ncte.org.

20. William Lutz, *Doublespeak* (New York: Harper, 1989), pp. 1–7.

21. Sheldon Rampton and John Stauber, *Trust Us, We're Experts!* (New York: Jeremy P. Tacher/Putnam, 2001), p. 292.

22. Lutz, *Doublespeak,* pp. 2–3.

23. "Doublespeak," in *The Oxford Companion to the English Language* (Oxford: Oxford University Press, 1992). p. 320.

24. "Animals," *Quarterly Review of Doublespeak,* July 1997, p. 11.

25. "UN: Countries Urged to Cooperate in Delivering War Criminals to Tribunal on Former Yugoslavia," M2PressWIRE, November 5, 1997, www.elibrary.com (accessed January 2, 1998).

26. Lutz, *Doublespeak,* p. 6.

27. Doublespeak exercise, University Writing Center, Bloomsburg University, departments.bloomu.edu/english/111doublespeak.htm (accessed September 1, 2003).

28. Lutz, *Doublespeak,* p. 6.

29. Reported in *Editor's Workshop,* May 1990, p. 16.

30. "Doublespeak Here and There," *Quarterly Review of Doublespeak,* April 1991, p. 1.

31. Adapted from Gary Jennings, *World of Words* (New York: Atheneum, 1984), pp. 123–24.

32. Unidentified biologist, quoted by William D. Lutz, "Jargon," in *The Oxford Companion to the English Language* (Oxford: Oxford University Press, 1992). p. 544.

33. Ibid.

34. Lutz, "Jargon," p. 544.

35. Quoted in John Daintith and Amanda Isaacs, *Medical Quotes* (Oxford: Facts on File, 1989), p. 106.

36. Information comes from the Hope Heart Institute in Seattle, as reported in "Jargon, Literacy, and Health," *Healthy Bites,* December 1997, p. 1.

37. Adapted from Toby Fulwiler and Alan R. Hayakawa, *The Blair Handbook* (Englewood Cliffs, NJ: Prentice Hall, 1994), p. 451.

38. Bergen Evans and Cornelia Evans, *A Dictionary of Contemporary American Usage* (New York: Random House, 1957), p. 258.

39. Lynn Quitman Troyka, *Simon & Schuster Handbook for Writers,* 3rd ed. (Englewood Cliffs, NJ: Prentice Hall, 1993), p. 425.
40. Quoted by Carol Richardson, "Words to the Wise", *Toastmaster,* December 1990, p. 22.
41. Theodore Solotaroff, quoted in Frederick Crews, *The Random House Handbook,* 6th ed. (New York: McGraw-Hill, 1992), p. 276.
42. Statistics courtesy of student speaker Frank Harrison.
43. Winston Churchill, as quoted in William Safire and Leonard Safir, *Good Advice* (New York: Times Books, 1982), p. 253.
44. Ibid., p. 294.
45. Leon G. Schiffman and Leslie Lazar Kanuk, *Consumer Behavior,* 5th ed. (Englewood Cliffs, NJ: Prentice Hall, 1994), p. 205.
46. This example is adapted from a discussion of Shakespeare in the "Muse of Fire" episode of the PBS television series *The Story of English,* narrated by Robert MacNeil.

Chapter 14

1. Patricia Pena, telephone interview, July 20, 2000; miscellaneous articles by Advocates for Cell Phone Safety, www.geocities.com/morganleepena; Julie Deardorff, "Bereaved Mother Declares War on Use of Car Phones," *Chicago Tribune,* www.chicagotribune.com (accessed June 24, 2000); Tom Rybarczyk, "Pennsylvania Lawmaker Proposes Cell Phone Ban for Drivers," *Philadelphia Inquirer,* July 17, 2003, p. 1.
2. R. T. Kingman, quoted by Thomas Leech, San Diego, California, consultant, in "Tips and Articles," Winning Presentations, www.winning-presentations.com (accessed December 2, 2000).
3. Elayne Snyder, *Speak for Yourself—With Confidence* (New York: New American Library, 1983), p. 69.
4. Ibid.
5. Waldo W. Braden, "Abraham Lincoln," in *American Orators Before 1900,* ed. Bernard K. Duffy and Halford R. Ryan (New York: Greenwood Press, 1987), p. 207.
6. Steve Allen, *How to Make a Speech* (New York: McGraw-Hill, 1986), p. 12.
7. Arnold "Nick" Carter, professional speaker, Niles, Illinois, e-mail interview, January 13, 2000.
8. John V. Thill and Courtland L. Bovée, *Excellence in Business Communication* (New York: McGraw-Hill, 1993), p. 455; Dr. Frederick Gilbert, Redwood City, California, quoted in "Speaking to Diverse Groups," *Communication Briefings,* January 1995, p. 3.
9. Most items in the table are adapted from Jeffrey C. Hahner et al, *Speaking Clearly: Improving Voice and Diction,* 5th ed. (New York: McGraw Hill, 1997).
10. Yvette Ortiz, Ph.D., telephone interview, January 21, 2000.
11. Roger Ailes, *You Are the Message* (Homewood, IL: Dow Jones-Irwin, 1988), p. 20.
12. Ibid., p. 30.
13. Ibid.; Robert Rosenthal and Bella M. DePaulo, "Expectations, Discrepancies, and Courtesies in Nonverbal Communication," *Western Journal of Speech Communication* 43 (Spring 1979), pp. 76–95.
14. Janet Stone and Jane Bachner, *Speaking Up* (New York: Carroll and Graf, 1994), p. 62.
15. Dawn E. Waldrop, "What You Wear Is Almost as Important as What You Say," *Presentations,* July 2000, p. 74.
16. Jack Valenti, *Speak Up with Confidence* (New York: William Morrow, 1982), pp. 74–75.
17. Danny Cox, professional speaker, Tustin, California, e-mail interview, February 15, 2000.
18. Dorothy Sarnoff, *Never Be Nervous Again* (New York: Crown, 1987), p. 43.
19. Cristina Stuart, *How to Be an Effective Speaker* (Lincolnwood, IL: NTC Business Books, 1989), p. 67.
20. Robert Garmston and Bruce Wellman, "Answering Questions," *Educational Leadership,* February 1994, p. 88.
21. Tom Kirby, "117 Ideas for Better Business Presentations," pamphlet distributed by Tom Kirby Associates, St. Petersburg, Florida.
22. "Practice ideas, not words" is a popular saying in Toastmasters clubs.

Chapter 15

1. "Synaesthesia," National Central University (Taiwan), www.ncu.edu.tw/~daysa/synesthesia.htm (accessed December 6, 2000).
2. From "Our Bodies Are Like Machines," a speech delivered by Rosharna Hazel, Morgan State University, Maryland, in the 1995 Contest of the Interstate Oratorical Association, reprinted from *Winning Orations of the Interstate Oratorical Association,* 1995, pp. 45–47.
3. Speech used with permission of student speaker Marcus Brown.
4. H. B. Reed, "Meaning as a Factor in Learning," *Journal of Educational Psychology,* December 1992, p. 395.
5. Suzanne Frey, "Nina Totenberg," *Toastmaster,* December 1993, p. 27.
6. Ruth Johnson-Boggs, First Union National Bank, personal interview, May 17, 1997.
7. Adapted from Reid Buckley, *Speaking in Public,* (New York: Harper, 1988), pp. 37–38, and William Zinsser, *On Writing Well,* 3rd ed. (New York: Harper & Row, 1985), p. 134.
8. "One in Seven Adult Americans Can't Find the U.S. on a World Map," *National Geographic,* June 2000, p. A-33.
9. "Prime Numbers," *Chronicle of Higher Education,* July 7, 2000, p. A10.
10. Associated Press, "Americans Fare Poorly on Basic Science Survey," *Asheville Citizen-Times,* May 24, 1996, p. 1.
11. Anne Cronin, "America's Grade on 20th Century European Wars," *New York Times,* December 3, 1995, p. E-5.
12. Dorothy Sarnoff, *Make the Most of Your Best* (New York: Doubleday, 1981), p. 51.
13. Outline and speech used by permission of Julia Weber.

Chapter 16

1. Betty Farmer, Ph.D., Department Head, Communication and Theatre Arts, Western Carolina University, personal interview, March 4, 2002.
2. Brandie Huffman, Alex Mize, and Britt Billings, students at Western Carolina University, personal interview, March 4, 2002.
3. Carol Doniek Wydra, M.S., and Thomas P. Sattler, Ed.D., "Success in Sales," *Fitness World,* www.fitnessworld.com/library/marketing/mgtmemo0699.html (accessed February 5, 2000).
4. Dr. Jerry Tarver in "Writing for Results," *Speechwriter's Newsletter* archives, Lawrence Ragan Communications, www.ragan.com (accessed February 24, 2000).
5. Erwin P. Bettinghaus, *Persuasive Communication,* 3rd ed. (New York: Holt, Rinehart and Winston, 1980), pp. 32–33.
6. Elliot Aronson, *The Social Animal,* 6th ed. (New York: W.H. Freeman & Co., 1992), pp. 115–69.
7. Tarver, "Writing for Results."
8. The late Alan H. Monroe, a speech professor, was the author of *Monroe's Principles and Types of Speech,* first published in 1935 by Scott, Foresman.
9. Outline and speech used with permission of Naresh Chopra.

Chapter 17

1. Martha Irvine, "Young Americans Still Shunning Seat Belts," Associated Press/Yahoo! News, news.yahoo.com/news, August 3, 2003 (accessed September 8, 2003); Matthew L. Wald, "Urging Young to Buckle Up, Officials Try Switch in Tactics," *New York Times,* May 20, 2003, p. A18.
2. Scale adapted from one developed by Sandy Linver, president of Speakeasy, Inc., a consulting firm with offices in Atlanta and San Francisco. See www.speakeasyinc.com.
3. "Three-Year Degrees," Stamats Communications, Inc., www.stamats.com (accessed February 14, 2000).
4. Judee K. Burgoon, Thomas Birk, and Michael Pfau, "Nonverbal Behaviors, Persuasion, and Credibility," *Human Communication Research,* Fall 1990, pp. 140–69.
5. Lord Chesterfield, quoted by William Safire and Leonard Safir, *Good Advice* (New York: Times Books, 1982), p. 60.
6. Used with permission from Patricia Caldwell.
7. Sarah Ferguson, Duchess of York, e-mail interview, February 2, 2000.
8. "A Conversation with Sarah, Duchess of York, on Losing Weight," Weight Watchers International, www.weightwatchers.com (accessed February 1, 2000).
9. Elliot Aronson, *The Social Animal,* 6th ed. (New York: W.H. Freeman & Co., 1992), p. 90.
10. Ibid., p. 91.
11. Dean C. Kazoleas of West Virginia University found that both quantitative (statistical) and qualitative (narrative) evidence can be persuasive, but that attitude change produced by the latter seems to be longer lasting. Dean C. Kazoleas, "A Comparison of the Persuasive Effectiveness of Qualitative versus Quantitative Evidence: A Test of Explanatory Hypotheses," *Communication Quarterly,* Winter 1993, pp. 40–50.
12. Jeanne Fahnestock and Marie Secor, "Teaching Argument: A Theory of Types," *College Composition and Communication* 34 (February 1983), pp. 20–30.
13. For this example I am indebted to Thomas Montalbo, *The Power of Eloquence* (Englewood Cliffs, NJ: Prentice Hall, 1984), p. 64.
14. Aristotle, Analytica Posteriora, Book I, in *Introduction to Aristotle* (New York: Modern Library, 1947), pp. 9–34.
15. Barnaby J. Feder, "Good Product. Sound Plans. No Sure Thing," *New York Times on the Web,* www.nytimes.com (accessed January 7, 2000).
16. Several Internet sites (such as www.theroc.org/updates/blanc.htm and metalab.unc.edu/stayfree/13/banned_text.html) discuss bans on black clothing by school districts.
17. War analogies are used by anti-immigrant groups such as Alien Nation (www.newnation.org) and have even been used by CBS Evening News: "CBS Sees Immigrants as an 'Army of Invaders,'" *EXTRA!/Update,* April 2000, p. 3.
18. Unidentified corporate executive quoted by an antispam website, www.pdi.net/~eristic/junkmail (accessed February 14, 2000).
19. Rudy Schrocer, "Maslow's Hierarchy of Needs as a Framework for Identifying Emotional Triggers," *Marketing Review,* February 1991, pp. 26–28; Abraham H. Maslow, *Motivation and Personality* (New York: Harper & Row, 1970).
20. Ann Bainbridge Frymier and Gary M. Shulman, "'What's in It for Me?': Increasing Content Relevance to Enhance Students' Motivation," *Communication Education,* January 1995, pp. 40–50.
21. Martha Ramsey, U.S. Cellular Co., personal interview, July 23, 1994.
22. The speaker derived this story from Christine Dempsey, "Shopper Says Employee Helped, Then Took Card," *Hartford Courant,* www.ctnow.com (accessed February 16, 2000).
23. See essay entitled "Introduction to Argumentation and Persuasion" and other links posted by Professor Laurie Walczak of Illinois State University, lilt.ilstu.edu/llwalcz.
24. Aronson, *The Social Animal,* p. 85.
25. Ken Chapman, "Fear Appeal Research: Perspective and Application," *Proceedings of the American Marketing Association,* Summer 1992, pp. 1–9.

Chapter 18

1. Eathan O'Bryant, player and goodwill ambassador for Harlem Globetrotters basketball team, personal interview, March 30, 2000.
2. Speech used with permission of Anthony Rossi.
3. Hon. Loretta Sanchez, "Tribute to Working Wardrobes," *Congressional Record,* October 17, 2000, p. E1806.
4. Remarks courtesy of Dan Crenshaw, mental-health counselor.

Chapter 19

1. Daniel Goleman, Paul Kaufman, and Michael Ray, *The Creative Spirit* (New York: Dutton, 1992), p. 139.
2. Ibid., p. 121.
3. David Holzman, "When Workers Run the Show," *Working Woman,* August 1993, p. 38.
4. Adapted from Harold Tyler, as quoted in *Decker Communications Report,* March 1984, p. 1.
5. John Dewey, *How We Think* (Boston: Heath, 1933), pp. 106–15.
6. Jay Cocks, "Let's Get Crazy!" *Time,* June 11, 1990, p. 41.
7. Goleman, Kaufman, and Ray, *The Creative Spirit,* p. 167.

Tips for Your Career

Tip 1.2 Therese Myers, quoted in Bronwyn Fryer, "Pointers for Public Speaking," *PC World,* November 1991, p. 238; Arnold "Nick" Carter, professional speaker, Niles, Illinois, e-mail interview, January 13, 2000.

Tip 3.1 William McWhirter, "Major Overhaul," *Time,* December 30, 1991, p. 57

Tip 5.1 Jane Tompkins, "Teach by the Values You Preach," *Harper's,* September 1991, p. 30.

Tip 7.1 John Leo, "The Answer Is 45 Cents," *U.S. News and World Report Online,* www.usnews.com (accessed September 22, 2000). The program on "ear candling" was seen on an NBC affiliate, August 4, 2000. Dangers of ear candling: Janice M. Horowitz, "Ear Candling," *Time,* June 19, 2000, p. 24; Lisa M. L. Dryer, medical student at the University of Minnesota–Duluth Medical School, "Ear Candling," Quackwatch, www.quackwatch.com (accessed September 23, 2000).

Tip 7.2 Linda King, wildlife biologist with the Florida Fish and Wildlife Conservation Commission, West Palm Beach, Florida, personal interview, July 10, 2002.

Tip 9.1 Preston Bradley, vice president, Graystone Corporation, personal correspondence with the author.

Tip 9.2 Ellen Neuborne, "Top Four PowerPoint Gaffes," *Sales & Marketing Management,* June 2003, p. 22; Lance Secretan, "Inspirational Teaching," *Industry Week,* May 21, 2001, p. 19; Carl Zucker, CEO, Willowbrook Enterprises, personal interview, January 8, 2003.

Tip 12.1 "Employee Video," *Videomaker,* May 1994, p. 13; "American Preaching: A Dying Art?" *Time,* December 31, 1979, p. 64.

Tip 13.1 Ron Hoff, *"I Can See You Naked": A Fearless Guide to Making Great Presentations,* rev. ed. (Kansas City: Andres and McMeel, 1992), pp. 224–25.

Tip 14.1 Cristina Stuart, *How to Be an Effective Speaker* (Lincolnwood, IL: NTC Business Books, 1989), p. 69.

Tip 14.2 Rosita Perez, professional speaker, Brandon, Florida, in response to author's survey, November 1984; Sandy Linver, *Speak Easy* (New York: Summit Books, 1978), p. 121; Steve Allen, *How to Make a Speech* (New York: McGraw-Hill, 1986), p. 120.

Tip 16.1 Richard Lacayo, "What Would It Take to Get America off Drugs?" *Time,* November 9, 1992), p. 41.

Tip 17.1 Lincoln critic quoted by Clifton Fadiman, ed., *The American Treasury, 1455–1955* (New York: Harper & Brothers, 1955), p. 152; Lilly Walters, *Secrets of Successful Speakers* (New York: McGraw-Hill, 1993), p. 37.

Tip 17.2 Douglas Hunt, *The Riverside Guide to Writing* (Boston: Houghton Mifflin, 1991), p. 158.

Special Techniques

How to Use Leave-Behinds: Jim Seymour, "The Importance of Leave-Behinds," ZD Net, www.zdnet.com (accessed December 3, 2000)

How to Use Humor: Judy Tenuta, quoted at Quotation Ring, publish.uwo.ca/~dpicard/frame.htm (accessed December 18, 2000); Marc G. Weinberger and Charles S. Gulas, "The Impact of Humor in Advertising," *Journal of Advertising,* December 1992, pp. 35–39; Carl Van Doren, *Benjamin Franklin* (New York: Viking, 1938), p. 650; Edmund Fuller, ed., *Thesaurus of Anecdotes* (New York: Avenel, 1990), p. 21; Laurie Schloff and Marcia Yudkin, *Smart Speaking* (New York: Henry Holt, 1991), p. 121.

Photo Credits

All photos are by Hamilton Gregory except:

p. 2: AP/Wide World Photos; p. 4: © Rachel Epstein/Photo Edit, p. 9: © PhotoDisc/Getty Images; p. 28: © Reuters; p. 32: AP/Wide World Photos; p. 39: © Corbis/Royalty Free; p. 41: © Michael Newman/Photo Edit; p. 46: © William Thomas Cain/Getty Images; p. 48: Royalty-Free Division/© Comstock Images, p. 54: AP/Wide World Photos; p. 57: © Arthur Tilley/FPG/PictureQuest; p. 64: AP/Wide World Photos; p. 66L: NASA; p. 66R: © PhotoDisc/Getty Images; p. 74: Scott Manchester © The Press Democrat, Santa Rosa, CA; p. 87: AP/Wide World Photos; p. 95: Courtesy of Oberlin College. Photo: Al Fuchs, Oberlin College; p. 146: © PhotoDisc/Getty Images; p. 166: AP/Wide World Photos; p. 168: © Reuters; p. 172: © Keri Pickett/Time Pix; p. 180L/R: AP/Wide World Photos; p. 179: © Reuters; p. 100: AP/Wide World Photos; p. 205: AP/Wide World Photos; p. 252: © Robert Nickelsberg/Time Pix; p. 254: AP/Wide World Photos; p. 274: © David Young-Wolff/Photo Edit; p. 276: © Reuters; p. 288T: © Bill Varie/CORBIS; p. 288B: © Photo Disc/Getty Images; p. 298: AP/Wide World Photos; p. 300: AP/Wide World Photos; p. 309: © Frederick M. Brown/Getty Images; p. 318: AP/Wide World Photos; p. 331: AP/Wide World Photos; p. 336: © Bill Wippert/Buffalo News; p: 397: AP/Wide World Photos; p. 346: AP/Wide World Photos; p. 372: AP/Wide World Photos; p. 394: © Chris Weeks/Getty Images; p. 396T: AP/Wide World Photos; p. 396B: ©LWA-Dann Tardif/CORBIS; 405: © Mark Godfrey, courtesy of Weight Watchers International; p. 438: © Cindy Charles/Photo Edit; p. 440: © Photo Disc/Getty Images; p. 461L: © Photo Disc/Getty Images; p. 461R: AP/Wide World Photos; p. 464: © Corbis

Index